INTERNATIONAL HANDBOOK OF PSYCHOLOGY

EDITED BY

Albert R. Gilgen

AND

Carol K. Gilgen

Greenwood Press

NEW YORK • WESTPORT, CONNECTICUT

Library of Congress Cataloging-in-Publication Data

International handbook of psychology.

Bibliography: p.
Includes indexes.
1. Psychology—History—20th century.
2. Psychologists—History—20th century. I. Gilgen,
Albert R., 1930–   . II. Gilgen, Carol K.
BF105.I57 1987   150'.9'04   86-29457
ISBN 0-313-23832-4 (lib. bdg. : alk. paper)

Copyright © 1987 by Albert R. Gilgen and Carol K. Gilgen

All rights reserved. No portion of this book may be
reproduced, by any process or technique, without the
express written consent of the publisher.

Library of Congress Catalog Card Number: 86-29457
ISBN: 0-313-23832-4

First published in 1987

Greenwood Press, Inc.
88 Post Road West, Westport, Connecticut 06881

Printed in the United States of America

The paper used in this book complies with the
Permanent Paper Standard issued by the National
Information Standards Organization (Z39.48-1984).

10 9 8 7 6 5 4 3 2 1

International
Handbook
of
Psychology

To our grandsons,
Christopher and Jamie,
with the hope that
international scientific
exchange may contribute
to peace in their time

Contents

TABLES   xi

FIGURES   xv

PREFACE   xvii

Introduction   1
  Albert R. Gilgen and Carol K. Gilgen

Black Africa   24
  M. O. A. Durojaiye

Australia   37
  Mary Creighton Nixon

Austria   67
  Giselher Guttmann

Brazil   79
  Angela M. B. Biaggio

Canada   97
  Terrence P. Hogan and Timothy V. Hogan

People's Republic of China   109
  Zhang Hou-can

Colombia   125
  Ruben Ardila

Cuba   137
  Gerardo Marín

Czechoslovakia   145
    Josef Linhart and Miloslav Kodým

Denmark   161
    Simo Køppe

Egypt   172
    Safwat Ernest Farag

France   184
    Alain Trognon (Coordinator), Jacqueline Carroy,
    Marie-Ange Chabert, Matty Chiva, Yvette Hatwell,
    Patrick Mendelsohn, Alexandre Dorna,
    Jacques-Marie Jakobi, Benjamin Matalon,
    Liliane Salhani, Jacques Leplat, Michel Hurtig,
    Evelyne Cauzinille-Marmeche, and Annick Weil-Barais

Federal Republic of Germany   208
    Carl F. Graumann and Alexandre Métraux

German Democratic Republic   222
    Hans-Dieter Schmidt

India   239
    Durganand Sinha

Israel   258
    Esther Halpern

Japan   274
    Takayoshi Kaneko

Mexico   297
    Rolando Diaz-Loving and Adrian Medina-Liberty

The Netherlands   324
    Pieter J. van Strien, Charles J. de Wolff, and
    Roelf J. Takens

Norway   347
    Holger Ursin

Poland   368
    Lidia Grzesiuk

Contents

South Africa   392
    I. van W. Raubenheimer

Soviet Union   418
    Boris F. Lomov

Spain   440
    Mariano Yela

Sweden   461
    Kenneth Hugdahl and Arne Öhman

Turkey   484
    Gündüz Y. H. Vassaf

United Kingdom   502
    Ian J. Donald and David Canter

United States   534
    Albert R. Gilgen

Venezuela   557
    José Miguel Salazar and Ligia M. Sánchez

Yugoslavia   574
    Vid Pečjak

NAME INDEX   587
SUBJECT INDEX   607
CONTRIBUTORS   619

Tables

Australia

1. College and University Psychology Department Teaching Programs   43

2. Enrollments in College and University Departments of Psychology, Shown as Percentages at Each Level   44

3. Estimated Employment of Graduates and Diplomates, 1982   48

4. Research Reported by College and University Departments of Psychology   50

5. Australian Publications in Twenty-One Journals, 1974–1982   54

6. Sources of Research Funds for College and University Departments of Psychology, 1983   56

7. Sources of Degrees Held by Professors in University Psychology Departments, 1928–1982   57

Brazil

1. Number and Percentage of Psychologists Associated with Each Regional Council of Psychology, 1983   89

2. Numbers and Percentages of Journal Articles in Three General Areas   90

Canada

1. Canadian Universities Providing Doctoral-Level Training in Psychology   101

2. Canadian Universities with Doctoral-Level Programs in Clinical Psychology   102

3. Recipients of Awards for Distinguished Contributions to   104
   Canadian Psychology

Colombia

1. Psychology Programs in Colombia   128
2. Presidents of the Colombian Federation of Psychology   132

Denmark

1. Employment Situations for Psychologists, 1982   165

France

1. Employment Settings of Work Psychologists   202

German Democratic Republic

1. Curriculum at GDR Psychology Departments   227

India

1. Post-1950 Publications in Different Areas of Psychology   249

Japan

1. Distribution of JPA Members According to Work Settings: 280
   1958, 1970, 1982
2. Governmental Funding Trends: Kaken-Hi Fund Grants for   282
   Psychological Research Projects Every Fifth Year from 1957
3. Demographic Trends of the Annual Conventions of the   286
   Japanese Psychological Association after World War II
4. Approximate Number of JPA Members in Five Research   287
   Divisions for 1970 and 1980 and the Percentages of Articles
   in *JJP* and *JPR* during the 1975–1979 Period Published by
   the Members of These Divisions
5. Trends in Research Interests According to Number of Papers   288
   Read in Respective Research Divisions at JPA Conventions
6. Number of Papers Read at the Conventions of the Japanese   291
   Society of Social Psychology for the 1967–1972 and 1973–
   1978 Periods Classified by Research Area

Mexico

1. Students Registered in Each Specialty   302

2. Departments of Psychology in Mexico   303

3. Research Articles by Area   310

The Netherlands

1. Major Subjects Covered by Psychology Departments   329

2. Volume of Research in the Social Sciences in Terms of   337
   Man-Year Equivalents, Differentiated According to
   Disciplines and Noting the Sources of Funding at the
   Universities and the Research Centers Allied to the
   Universities in 1981

3. Newly Enrolled Psychology Students and Students   344
   Completing Their Drs. Degrees (Differentiated by Sex)

Norway

1. Most Frequently Cited Norwegian Authors in Psychology,   353
   1975–1982

South Africa

1. Institute Memberships, 1985   395

2. Funding of Research and Development in the Human   409
   Sciences in South Africa

United Kingdom

1. Topic Areas of British University Examinations in   513
   Psychology

Yugoslavia

1. Psychological Publications   582

Figures

Australia

1. Mean Relative Emphases for Colleges and Universities   49

People's Republic of China

1. Structure of the Chinese Psychological Society   113

German Democratic Republic

1. Relationships among Psychological Organizations   224

The Netherlands

1. Unemployed Psychologists   343

Yugoslavia

1. Papers Delivered at Congresses   580
2. Congress Papers by Major Area   581

Preface

This volume presents a collection of endogenous perspectives on psychology in twenty-nine countries and Black Africa. The focus is on the nature and scope of contemporary psychology and major developments since World War II. Work on the project commenced in 1982; most of the chapters were completed in 1984 and 1985.

A general outline was offered to the contributors and nearly all of the reviews follow a similar format. Nevertheless, there is considerable variation relative to those matters emphasized. This was expected and adds to the interest of the book. Some chapters may seem polemic for a handbook, but we believe they reflect the dynamic and controversial nature of the field, particularly in certain countries, and, therefore, are appropriate for a work that attempts to depict candidly the discipline worldwide.

In addition to providing information about psychology in other nations and parts of the globe, the reviews allow readers to identify the main factors that bear on the characteristics of the discipline in different countries. This is perhaps the major contribution of the book. Clearly, in order to understand the development and nature of national psychologies or to make meaningful comparative analyses, many variables must be considered. Factors which we found to be of greatest significance are listed and explored in the Introduction.

While a majority of the chapters concern psychology in European and North American countries, psychology in South America, Africa, Asia and Australia are also represented. Included are highly industrialized Eastern and Western bloc nations, a variety of Third World countries, nations with long histories and some new since the end of World War II, countries where one language and culture predominate and others which are made up of two or more major linguistic and cultural populations. Because of the international prominence attained by Piaget, we had hoped to offer a review of psychology in Switzerland; however, it did not materialize. Fortunately, Piaget's work is mentioned in the chapter on France and frequently discussed elsewhere.

A principal challenge was finding qualified psychologists who had the interest and time to contribute a chapter to this book. Complementing a literature search to identify individuals who had already written about developments in their countries, we contacted psychologists who, because of their connections or expertise in international psychology, were in a position to suggest potential contributors. Especially helpful in this regard were Steven B. Kennedy (International Affairs Office, APA), Virginia S. Sexton, Henryk Misiak, Karl H. Pribram, Josef Brozek, Harry C. Triandis, Melvin H. Marx, Wayne H. Holtzman, John A. Popplestone, Joseph R. Royce, Ann Frodi, C. C. Ching (Jing Qicheng), Gerardo Marín, Durganand Sinha, Boris Lomov, and Claude Levy-Leboyer.

Others who deserve recognition are Vera Sullivan, Ann Thill, Ethelyn Snyder, Patricia Murphy, and Coleen Wagner, who typed and proofread the manuscripts. Our daughter, Beth Gerken, provided further assistance with some of the proofreading. We appreciate, too, the one-semester leave of absence granted to Albert R. Gilgen by the University of Northern Iowa for the purpose of preparing a review of psychology in the United States and the financial support from John Downey, dean of the Graduate College, for telephone calls, photocopying, and other essential services. Our thanks extend also to Cynthia Harris, Mary Sive, and Todd Adkins, our editors at Greenwood Press, whose assistance helped ease considerably a very demanding task.

Introduction

Albert R. Gilgen and Carol K. Gilgen

THE INTERNATIONAL PERSPECTIVE IN PSYCHOLOGY:
A HISTORICAL OVERVIEW

Psychologists from different countries have been interested in exchanging information ever since psychology emerged as a separate discipline of study in Europe and the United States in the 1880s. The First International Congress took place in 1889 in Paris under the leadership of J. M. Charcot and T. Ribot. Prior to World War I, five more congresses convened in London (1892), Munich (1896), Paris (1900), Rome (1905), and Geneva (1909). Between the two world wars five such meetings occurred, four in Europe and one, the 1929 congress in New Haven, Connecticut, in the United States. Following World War II, international congresses have convened every three years.

It is interesting to note that much of the early initiative for the international meetings came from French or other French-speaking psychologists. Not only were Charcot and Ribot instrumental in bringing psychologists together but Henri Piéron was, apparently, present at every congress from 1900 to 1957 (Misiak & Sexton, 1966, p. 472). In addition, French-Swiss psychologist Edouard Claparéde was secretary for many years of the International Committee of Congresses, the body which organized the meetings.

Claparéde also played a key role in the founding of the International Association of Applied Psychology in 1920. The First International Congress of Applied Psychology took place the same year in Geneva. By 1986 membership had grown to about 3,000. One wonders whether or not French-speaking psychologists were the early leaders in internationalizing psychology, even though psychology as a separate discipline emerged in Germany, because French was the foremost language of scholarship and science in the nineteenth century.

The fact that students from so many different countries studied with Wilhelm Wundt in Leipzig also brought an international dimension to the discipline even as it was in the process of coming into being, primarily in Europe and North America.

The *Psychological Index*, an annual bibliography of publications in psychology and cognate fields, first appeared in 1895. Forty-two volumes covering the period from 1894 through 1935 were published. Originally edited by J. Mark Baldwin (Princeton University) and J. McKeen Cattell (Columbia University), the first edition was actually compiled by Howard C. Warren (Princeton) and Livingston Farrand (Columbia). Cooperating editors were American psychologists, with the exception of Alfred Binet, Carl Stumpf, and James Sully. Many of the works listed, however, were by European scholars.

The *Psychological Abstracts*, first published in 1927 and edited by Walter S. Hunter and Raymond R. Willoughby, both at Clark University, was clearly an international venture since publications from many countries were abstracted and prominent foreign psychologists served as consultants. Among them were F. C. Bartlett (Cambridge University), V. M. Bekhterev (Leningrad), E. Claparéde (University of Geneva), A. Michotte (University of Louvain), and H. Piéron (Sorbonne).

Also important in fostering psychology as an international discipline was the publication in 1929 of the *Psychological register*, edited by Carl Murchison (Clark University) in cooperation with Bartlett, Pieron, Karl Bühler (University of Vienna), Stefan Blachowski (University of Poznan), Sante De Sanctis (University of Rome), Thorleiffe G. Hegge (University of Oslo), Matataro Matsumoto (Tokyo Imperial University), and A. L. Schniermann (Bekhterev Reflexological Institute). Z. Y. Kuo and E. Shen provided the names of the Chinese psychologists included. Murchison believed that the most serious omissions in the book involved psychologists in Holland and Latin America.

Murchison edited a second edition of the *Psychological register* published in 1932. Upon publication of this work, the 1929 edition was called volume two and the 1932 edition, volume three. Volume one was to include "psychologists who died previous to the initiation of this series" (p. ix). However, to our knowledge, the series ended with the 1932 edition. The 1929 *Register* listed psychologists from twenty-nine countries, and the 1932 volume psychologists from forty nations.

It was not until 1958 that another international listing of psychologists, the *International directory of psychologists* was published, followed in 1966 and 1980 by second and third editions. These directories exclude psychologists in the United States because they can be found in the APA (American Psychological Association) directories.

During the mid- to late 1940s, a number of developments indicate that there was a renewal of interest in internationalizing psychology. To some degree all were related to the aftermath of World War II. The APA's Committee on International Relations, for example, was established in 1944 to help rehabilitate psychological facilities in war-torn Europe. This committee also made plans for resuming international congresses which had been suspended since 1937. The first post–World War II Congress took place in Edinburgh, Scotland, in 1948.

In 1946, what had originally been the National Council of Women Psychologists (founded in 1941) was renamed the International Council of Women Psychologists. In 1959 membership was opened to both men and women and the organization became the International Council of Psychologists (ICP). The ICP has played a significant role during the last twenty-five years or so in encouraging psychologists to become less provincial in their outlooks by holding meetings and publishing a newsletter.

Certain agencies of the United Nations such as the World Health Organization (WHO) and the United Nations Educational, Scientific and Cultural Organization (UNESCO) played important roles in funding cross-national and cross-cultural studies. WHO, for instance, supported the work of John Bowlby which led to his book *Maternal care and mental health* (1951). The World Federation for Mental Health was a consultative body to the UN.

In the years immediately following World War II, the U.S. Office of Naval Research (ONR) initiated a liaison scientist program. By 1985, twenty-one psychologists had taken part (Sinaiko, 1985). During the same period, the Fulbright-Hays program which has played such an important role in the exchange of scholars, including psychologists, was established. The importance of this program in revitalizing psychology in certain European countries, in helping the discipline get started in other nations, and in enriching American psychology cannot be overestimated.

In the decade of the 1950s, four particularly important developments relative to the internationalizing of psychology took place: the first volume of the *Annual Review of Psychology*, a series which seeks to promote collaboration among scholars of all nations, appeared in 1950 (see Gilgen & Hultman, 1979, for a listing of the most-referred-to psychologists during the 1950–1975 period); the International Union of Scientific Psychology which later became the International Union of Psychological Science (IUPsyS), an organization of national psychological associations rather than individuals, was established in 1951 (by 1986 there were forty-five members); the Interamerican Society of Psychology, which seeks to foster communication among psychologists in North and South America was also founded in 1951 (by 1986 the membership of this organization was about 1,500); and the first edition of the above-mentioned *International directory of psychologists* was published in 1958 (while H. S. Langfeld and E. G. Boring played leadership roles in arranging for this publication, Eugene Jacobson at the University of Michigan and H. C. J. Duijker at the University of Amsterdam were the editors).

During the 1950s other events of consequence were the founding of the French-Language Association of Scientific Psychology in 1952 (there are now 600 members); the publication of Otto Klineberg's *Social psychology* (Klineberg has throughout his career contributed to and advocated cross-cultural psychology); the establishment in Zurich in 1955 of the International Association for Analytical Psychology which promotes Jungian psychology; the exploration by Roger W. Russell, APA's secretary at that time, of how "psychology might contribute to national policy" since the discipline appeared to play no important role in government (APA Committee on Psychology in National and International Affairs, 1962); publication of B. Simon's *Psychology in the Soviet Union* (1957); A. Mintz's two reviews of Soviet psychology which appeared respectively in the 1958 and 1959 *Annual Review of Psychology*; Gregory Razran's studies of Soviet psychology starting in 1958 which by 1964 had resulted in fourteen reports, many in *Science* and three in the *American Psychologist* (see Razran, 1964); an APA symposium on "Reciprocal Influences in International Psychology" (among the participants were Gordon Allport, Henry P. David, and Nevitt Sanford); and, finally, the initiation by APA of a program on national and international affairs, first as a working group under the direction of Roger W. Russell and then, starting in the fall of 1960, as a standing committee directed by Charles E. Osgood (APA Committee on Psychology in National and International Affairs, 1962). International Congresses of Psychology took place in 1951 (Stockholm), 1954 (Montreal), and 1957 (Brussels).

Taking a look at the 1960s, a joint meeting of the IUPsyS and APA in France in 1962 resulted in a volume entitled *International opportunities for advanced training and research in psychology* which, according to Roger W. Russell (1984), "proved historically to be an important step in the internationalization of the discipline." Also in 1962 the aforementioned report by APA's Committee on National and International Affairs, chaired by Charles Osgood, focused on ways psychology could help work toward and maintain peace. The concern over psychology's potential contribution to world peace was further exemplified by Osgood's article "The psychologist in international affairs" (1964) and the second report of the Committee on Psychology in National and International Affairs (Solomon, 1964).

Additionally, during the 1960s, the *Annual Review of Psychology* published two more reviews of Soviet psychology (Brozek, 1962, 1964) and one on Japanese psychology (Tanaka, 1966). In 1966, the second edition of the *International directory of psychologists*, edited as was the first edition by Jacobson and Duijker, was completed. An edited volume on Russian psychology also appeared (O'Connor, 1966). Of particular importance was the publication in 1963 of *Systems and theories in psychology* by Melvin H. Marx and William A. Hillix, which included in an appendix reviews of European psychology (James Drever), Soviet psychology (Josef Brozek), and Oriental psychology (Shinkuro Iwahara). This was the first widely used American textbook to remind instructors and students that important developments were taking place in psychology in other parts of the world. Similarly, the book *Influence of culture on visual perception* (Segall, Campbell, & Herskovits, 1966) demonstrated the importance of cross-cultural research, as did an article in volume one of the *International Journal of Psychology* by N. Frijda and G. Jahoda (1966), and a chapter by J. Whiting (1968) in volume two of the *Handbook of social psychology* edited by G. Lindzey and E. Aronson. Harry Triandis, who has over the years made important contributions to cross-cultural and international psychology, also began publishing significant articles. Another book, the importance of which will become increasingly apparent, we believe, is *Psychological research in Communist China: 1949–1966* by Robert and Ai-li S. Chin published in 1969. To our knowledge, this is the only book-length analysis of Chinese psychology written in English just as the Cultural Revolution was getting under way. The founding by John Popplestone of the Cheiron Society (International Society for the History of the Behavioral and Social Sciences) is further evidence that the benefits of internationalizing psychology and related disciplines were well recognized by the late 1960s, at least by a small cadre of psychologists. Facilitating the broadcasting of information about published scholarship and research in psychology was the commencement of publication in 1969 of *Current contents: Social & behavioral sciences* which by 1983 annually reproduced the tables of contents of over 1,300 journals in the social and behavioral sciences around the world.

During the early 1970s, the work in cross-cultural psychology by pioneers such as Otto Klineberg, as well as H. Triandis, G. Jahoda, M. Segall, D. T. Campbell, M. Herskovits, R. Brislin, and others whose contributions accelerated in the 1960s, was beginning to have more of an impact on the discipline. The *Journal of Cross-Cultural Psychology* was established in 1970 under the editorship of W. J. Lonner; the International Association of Cross-Cultural Psychology came into being in 1972 through the initiative of John Dawson at the University of Hong Kong, and the *Annual Review of Psychology* published "Psychology and culture" by Triandis, Malpass, and Davidson in 1973.

Another review of Japanese psychology also appeared in 1972 (Tanaka & England). Leah G. Fein wrote a short book on women in national and international psychology (1974) published by the International Council of Psychologists. Gardner Murphy and Joseph K. Kovach in their history of psychology decried the provincialism of American psychology (1972).

The first psychologist to attempt an analysis of contemporary psychology from an international perspective was, to our knowledge, American-trained Colombian psychologist Ruben Ardila whose book *La psicologia contemporanea, panorama internacional* [Contemporary psychology: An international overview] was published in Argentina in 1972. He has since made many contributions to international psychology (see, for example, his chapter on Colombian psychology in this book).

The *Social Sciences Citation Index* commenced publication in the early 1970s. While the first year covered is 1969, the earliest publication date is apparently 1974. These volumes have been an important indicator of the information exchange taking place internationally within psychology. During the early 1970s, on-line computer information retrieval systems became commercially available. Since then interactive retrieval systems accessing more and expanded data bases have been installed in libraries in many countries. While most of the information is in English, some is in French, German, Italian, Norwegian, and other languages.

Though the opening of the People's Republic of China (PRC) did not begin in earnest until the late 1970s, it is interesting to note that Harold W. Stevenson (University of Michigan) and William Kessen (Yale University) visited the PRC in 1973 as members of a delegation on early childhood development. In 1975, W. Kessen published *Childhood in China*, which was an account of this visit. Australian psychologists were also among the first Western psychologists to be invited to the PRC in the 1970s.

In the late 1970s, the most significant publication relative to the internationalizing of psychology was *Psychology around the world*, edited by Virginia S. Sexton and Henryk Misiak (1976). This book is the first extensive collection of perspectives on psychology in many different countries compiled by North American psychologists. Unfortunately, this fine work is now out of print.

Other books of note published during the 1975–1979 period include *Psychology in Australia* (Nixon & Taft, 1977), *Soviet and Western perspectives in social psychology* (Strickland, 1979), and *International directory of psychology: A guide to people, places and policies* (Wolman, 1979). Important *American Psychologist* efforts include the "international issue" (1977, *32*, 11), an article by Roy Malpass entitled "Theory and method in cross-cultural psychology" (1977), an article by Giorgis and Helms on training international students from developing nations as psychologists (1978), and Hsiao's short analysis of psychology in China (1977).

By the late 1970s, increasing numbers of international associations had been founded. In 1975, for instance, the International Federation of Psychological-Medical Organizations was established, while in 1977 and 1978, respectively, the French-Speaking Neuropsychological Society and the International Society for Political Psychology were created.

The most dramatic development of the late 1970s was, undoubtedly, the opening of the People's Republic of China. In 1979, C. C. Ching (Jing Qi-cheng), then deputy-director, Institute of Psychology, Chinese Academy of Sciences, attended the APA convention, and further exchanges were arranged. He is now president of the Chinese Psychological Association. Exchanges between Chinese psychologists and psychologists in other countries have increased during the 1980s.

If the number of international meetings having to do with some aspect of the psychological domain which now take place is an index of interest on the part of psychologists in sharing information and perspectives with colleagues in other countries, then one would have to conclude that such an interest is indeed widespread. Every issue of the *American Psychologist* now lists twenty to fifty such meetings. With adequate time and money one could spend almost every day of the year at an international conference.

Among the most significant publications of the early 1980s are the *Handbook of cross-cultural psychology* Vol. 1–6 (Triandis, Lambert, Berry, Lonner, Heron, Brislin, & Draguns, 1980–81); the third edition of the *International directory of psychologists*, edited by Jacobson and the late Gunther Reinert (University of Trier), who died during the project (1980); more books and papers on psychology in particular countries and regions including articles on the Third World; several significant analyses of international psychology; and APA study entitled

The undergraduate psychology curriculum from an intercultural perspective: Selected courses (Scheirer & Rogers, 1983); six important articles on international education in psychology in the September 1984 issue of the *American Psychologist* (the articles were written by Steven Kennedy, James Scheirer and Anne Rogers; Michael Cole; Harry Triandis and Richard Brislin; Roger Russell; Virginia Sexton and Henryk Misiak; and Judith Torney-Purta); and the *Encyclopedia of psychology* (1984), an impressive four-volume work edited by Raymond J. Corsini with many foreign contributors.

Publications concerned with particular countries or regions include C. C. Ching's "Psychology in the Peoples' Republic of China" (1980); Hans-Dieter Schmidt's "Psychology in the German Democratic Republic" in the 1980 *Annual Review of Psychology*; L. B. Brown's *Psychology in contemporary China* (1981); Harold W. Stevenson's article on child development in the Peoples' Republic of China (1981) coauthored with S. Y. Lee and J. Stigler; Mary M. Wright and C. Roger Myers' *History of academic psychology in Canada* (1982); Ruben Ardila's "Psychology in Latin America" which appeared in the 1982 *Annual Review of Psychology*; Albert R. Gilgen's *American psychology since World War II: A profile of the discipline* (1982); Boris Lomov's review of Soviet psychology in the *American Psychologist* (1982); *Issues in cognition: Proceedings of a joint conference in psychology* (APA, 1984), which included papers by American and Chinese psychologists who took part in the Wingspread Conference (August-September 1983) cosponsored by the National Academy of Sciences and the Chinese Academy of Sciences; W. Lauterbach's *Soviet psychotherapy* (1984); Rogelio Diaz-Guerrero's "Contemporary psychology in Mexico" in the 1984 *Annual Review of Psychology*; *Psychology in a Third World country: The Indian experience* (Sinha, 1985); Alex Kozulin's social history of Soviet psychology (1984); the entire April 1984 issue of the *International Journal of Psychology* entitled "The impact of psychology on Third World development," edited by Durganand Sinha and Wayne H. Holtzman with contributions by Wolfgang Schwendler (UNESCO), Durganand Sinha (India), Alfredo Lagmay (Philippines), Hiroshi Azuma (Japan), C. C. Ching (People's Republic of China), Levon H. Melikian (Qatar), Harry C. Triandis (USA), Albert Cherns (UK), José Miguel Salazar (Venezuela), Rogelio Diaz-Guerrero (Mexico), M. O. A. Durojaiye (Nigeria), Cigdem Kagitgibasi (Turkey), Amir H. Mehryar (Iran), J. B. P. Sinha (India), and Robert Serpell (Zambia); and Alex Kozulin's 1986 article in the *American Psychologist* on the concept of activity in Soviet psychology.

Moreover, the following six articles comprising the "Psychology in the public forum" section of the March 1986 issue of the *American Psychologist* deserve mention: "Psychology and policy around the world: Widening psychology's sphere of influence" (Kennedy & David), "Child development research and the Third World: A future of mutual interest?" (Wagner), "The professional psychologist in Europe" (McPherson), "Professional psychology and private health services: Developing trends in the Federal Republic of Germany" (Brengelmann and Wittchen), "Population development and reproductive behavior: Perspectives for population and health psychology'' (David), and "Clinical psychologists in the primary health care system in the Netherlands" (Derksen).

Other publications appearing in the 1980s concerned with enough countries to make them truly international in scope include a book by David Levinson and Martin J. Malone entitled *Toward explaining human culture: A critical review of the findings of world-wide cross-cultural research* (1980); *Educational psychology in a changing world* (Siann & Ugwuegbu, 1980); a listing of psychology journals in various countries and regions (Smith, 1980); an article by M. M. Fichter and H.-U. Wittchen, "Clinical psychology and psychotherapy: A survey of the present state of professionalization in 23 countries" (1980); Otto Klineberg's article on international educational exchanges (1981); Mark R. Rosenzweig's paper "Trends in development and status of psychology: An international perspective" (1982); Ruben Ardila's analysis of international psychology published in the *American Psychologist* (1982a); *Current issues in European social psychology: Vol. 1. European studies in social psychology* (1983), edited by Willem Doise and Serge Moscovici; and Rosenzweig's *American Psychologist* article "U.S. psychology and world psychology" (1984).

Besides the increasing number of publications on national, regional, and international psychology since the mid–1970s, more international organizations such as the French-Language Association of Work Psychology (1980), the International Organization of Psychophysiology (1982), and the International Society for Theoretical Psychology (1985) were founded. One of the most significant developments, however, was the admission of the International Union of Psychological Science (IUPsyS) to the International Council of Scientific Unions (ICSU). Membership of the IUPsyS in the ICSU is clear evidence that psychology has achieved considerable maturity and respect as a science and profession internationally.

Further augmenting information retrieval during the early 1980s was the inauguration by APA of the PsycINFO data base ("psychology's most comprehensive information source"), PsycSCAN (a series of subject-oriented quarterlies of abstracts), and PsycALERT (a data base of publications which have at any particular time not yet become part of PsycINFO). In addition, PSYNDEX, published in Germany, includes psychological literature from German-language countries.

THE POST–WORLD WAR II PERIOD: POLITICO-ECONOMIC CHANGES

Work on this project has made us keenly aware of the fact that the nature, scope, and development of psychology worldwide during the last forty years in many ways reflects major political or economic conditions and events. There is no question, for example, that the characteristics and transformations of the discipline internationally throughout the post–World War II period have been a function to some degree of the wartime devastation of much of urban Europe and Asia; the emergence of the United States as the dominant nation in the world economically, scientifically, technologically, and for a while culturally; the tensions and dynamics induced by the Cold War; the impending nuclear presence; the revitalization of Western Europe aided by the Marshall Plan; the rebuilding and consolidation of the Soviet Union and Eastern bloc nations; decolonization, particularly in Africa and India; the establishment of the state of Israel amid continuing turmoil and strife in the Middle East; open hostilities elsewhere, especially in Korea, Vietnam, Afghanistan, and Central America; an increasing sense of the needs and strengths of Third World countries; the Communist takeover of China and the spread of Marxist-Leninist ideology to a number of other places; population growth; the economic fortunes of individual countries; the rise and fall of oil prices; the tremendous development of Japan's industrial might; the electronics revolution bringing with it television and computers; the information explosion; the growth of commercial air travel; and the acceptance of English as the major scholarly and scientific language.

FACTORS BEARING ON THE NATURE, SCOPE, AND COURSE OF NATIONAL PSYCHOLOGIES

It is clear both from the reviews of national psychologies in this book and previous studies of international psychology (Sexton & Misiak, 1976; Rosenzweig, 1982, 1984; Ardila, 1982a; Russell, 1984; Sinha & Holtzman, 1984) that many factors play a role in determining the characteristics and course of psychology in any specific country. Among the most apparent are the following:

General economic conditions

Resources available for higher education and educational research, mental health, science and technology, libraries, and psychology itself

The degree to which research and curricula are planned by central governmental agencies

Job opportunities for psychologists

Insurance coverage for services provided by psychologists in private practice (if private practice is an option)

The period of time psychology as a separate discipline has been in existence

The degree to which the field is viewed as a useful profession relative to societal needs and goals

The extent to which psychology is perceived as contributing, along with other areas of study, to the production of a more enlightened or educated citizenry

The relative importance of academic research and applied specialties comprising the discipline

The degree to which psychology has been imported from other countries

The particular countries from which most of the literature, theories, findings, methodologies, and psychometric instruments have been imported

The niche psychology is able to fill or establish relative to other disciplines, especially education, psychometrics, psychiatry, physiology, and perhaps ethology

The number of well-trained psychologists and the orientations of those assuming leadership roles

The universities from which psychologists received their advanced degrees

The level of training deemed adequate to be considered a psychologist

The degree to which psychologists are defined and protected by legislation

The extent to which the public is protected against psychological incompetence and quackery by formal guidelines and legislation

The number and types of psychological organizations and the relationships among them

The perception of the field by the general public

The degree to which psychology must conform to a particular ideology or set of societal values and assumptions

The extent to which dogma decrees that research, theory, and practice must be integrated

The influence of North American psychology

The influence of Soviet psychology

The influence of psychoanalysis

The influence of Piaget

The strength of regional and shared cultural influences

Language and culture are vital forces that can hardly be overemphasized. Psychologists in English-speaking countries and those in other countries who know English have an advantage since most of the psychological literature is in English. Those also able to read German, French, and/or Russian as well are even better off. Whether a nation has one primary language and culture, such as Denmark, two like Canada, or more, as in Yugoslavia, is as significant as whether or not a country is part of a bloc of nations or a bridge or buffer state between regions with different cultures or ideologies.

Another determinant relates to publication. The extent to which the prestige and status of psychologists is a function of their publishing in major (usually Western) journals and the scope of the publishing industry in the country are each powerful influences. As Mary Nixon observes in her chapter on Australia, a country with a smaller-scale publishing industry will naturally be prone to importing textbooks, for example, but materials prepared in another culture may not be ideally suited to that country's needs.

THE MOST IMPORTANT DEVELOPMENTS IN PSYCHOLOGY

In the context of the factors listed, let us now consider what we view as among the most important characteristics of, and developments in, psychology worldwide during the post–World War II period. These center around the profound influence of U.S. psychology; the postwar recovery of psychology in Europe and Asia; the influence of Marxism-Leninism; psychological developments in the Third World; the particularly vigorous expansion of applied fields; the influence of psychoanalysis, behavioral approaches, and Piaget; and a reaffirmation of the complexity of human psychological functioning.

The U.S. Influence

The U.S. influence on psychology internationally was unquestionably dominant during the 1946–1986 period. Contributing to the midcentury shift of the geographic center of the discipline from Europe to North America were the move to the United States to escape Nazi oppression of most European psychoanalysts, the major Gestalt psychologists, and a variety of other prominent psychologists during the 1930s and early 1940s (a fair number of European psychologists also fled to Turkey and South America); a large U.S. publishing industry and increasingly efficient ways to produce, store, and retrieve information which ensured that English would be the primary language of scholarship, science, psychometrics, and technology; well-funded aid and exchange programs, at least until the early 1970s; the development by American psychologists like B. F. Skinner, Fred Keller, and Albert Bandura of practical ways to modify human behavior in educational, industrial, penal, and psychotherapeutic settings; and the emphasis on short-run experimental research which is easy to export and import even though the approach may in many instances produce trivial or irrelevant findings.

However, it should be noted that, despite the enormous impact of U.S. psychology, few American psychologists have made important theoretical contributions. Furthermore, the conceptual fragmentation of American psychology has, we think, inhibited to some extent the U.S. impression on the discipline internationally as a scholarly field of study. For some perspectives on this matter see Koch (1971), Staats (1981, 1983), Staats & Mos (in press), and Gilgen (1970, in press).

The Revitalization of Europe, the Soviet Union, and Asia

It is apparent from reading the chapters by contributors in Europe, the Soviet Union, and Japan that psychology has rebounded very well in those nations devastated by World War II as well as neutral countries such as Sweden. However, the period of vigorous growth in most places ended by the late 1970s; since then there has been some stagnation and even retrenchment. Though U.S. psychology still predominates in terms of sheer numbers of psychologists, facilities, publications, and general resources, productive research programs and well-established applied subfields can now be found in all countries that have achieved significant industrial recovery and economic growth during the last forty years, along with psychologists whose work has achieved regional and international recognition. In many cases, of course, recognition is still restricted to particular specialties or subfields. Worthy of note here is the strong interest that Spanish psychologists have had in the history of psychology. It is hoped that in the not too distant future general textbooks of psychology, whether published in the United States, the Netherlands, West or East Germany, France, the Soviet Union, or some place else, will mention important work regardless of where it was done.

The development of strong disciplines of psychology throughout the world has brought with it a more critical stance toward American psychology, emanating not only from psychologists with different ideologies but also from psychologists in Western countries who question the fruitfulness of some of the research methodologies and applied orientations favored by mainstream American psychologists (see, for example, the chapter on psychology in the United Kingdom). As the international exchange of information has accelerated in recent years, all the major approaches including those tied to Marxist-Leninist assumptions and Piaget's theory and methodologies have undergone more critical appraisals. This is a sign of progress and should lead to exciting new advances.

The Marxist-Leninist Influence

One of the most consequential developments since World War II has been the influence on psychology of Marxist-Leninist thinking. Naturally this impact has been most all-encompassing in the Eastern Bloc nations and, until the early 1960s, in the People's Republic of China; but many Third World psychologists as well as some psychologists in every country where the field has taken root have been influenced by the perspectives of Marx and Lenin on things psychological.

It is not possible to make a detailed analysis of Marxist-Leninist psychologies on the basis of the relevant reviews in this book. Nevertheless, it appears that all strongly emphasize research and applications planned by the central government and focused on building a socialist society; the integration of theory, research, and practice; and a dialectical-materialist view concerning the nature of the universe. Moreover, consciousness is viewed as a quality of the human brain, reflecting accurately the complex world of each person interacting in a purposeful way with his or her surround. Communication, social interaction, the cultural context, and psychological development are also stressed.

A special challenge for Marxist-Leninist psychologists is motivation of the work force in societies which deemphasize competition. And their intriguing explanation for the large numbers of psychologists in Western countries, particularly the United States, is that capitalism with its emphasis on competition places tremendous psychological stress on the populace (see the chapter on the German Democratic Republic).

Of the psychologies reviewed in this book, the Soviet, Czechoslovak, East German, and Cuban appear to be most formally structured by Marxist-Leninist principles and assumptions; the Polish and Yugoslav psychologies seem more eclectic. Regulation theory is apparently a contribution primarily of Polish psychologists.

Among the most interesting dynamics to observe during the next decade or two should be those generated by the interplay between highly structured Marxist-Leninist conceptions of the field and the loosely organized Western psychologies. If the avenues of communication remain open, this process should be mutually beneficial. Carl Graumann and Alexandre Métraux (Federal Republic of Germany) note that Western and Eastern European psychologists have already joined together to form the European Association of Experimental Social Psychology.

Psychology in the Third World

The "Third World" refers to the so-called developing countries in Latin America, Africa, and Asia. The assumption is that once these countries achieve a reasonable level of urbanization and industrialization, they will be considered developed. It is important to realize at the outset that while poverty, starvation, and lack of health care are conditions everyone wants to avoid, using urban, industrial nations as standards against which to judge the development of other countries is being increasingly questioned.

Be that as it may, there is no question that Third World countries share characteristics and problems insofar as psychology as a discipline is concerned. There is usually inadequate funding for educational programs, research facilities and equipment, books and journals, and professional organizations. Consequently, there are too few well-trained psychologists and there is far too much dependence on affluent countries for financial assistance, publications, the training of psychologists, tests, research findings, theoretical orientations, and standards and formats for conducting research or doing applied work. Particularly troublesome is the fact that imported psychometric instruments, psychological information, theoretical assumptions, and techniques for engaging in psychological inquiry and practice are sometimes of only limited relevance in different cultural settings. What is most distressing is that psychologists and other professional users of tests in some countries use instruments developed in the United States and elsewhere instead of developing and standardizing their own (see, for example, the chapter on Turkey).

As the field has become better established in Third World countries, and the inappropriateness of large segments of imported psychology has been recognized, there has emerged a tendency to criticize the work of the exporter (usually the United States or another Western country). Much of this criticism is misplaced since it is up to the psychologists in each nation and/or culture to determine the appropriateness of research findings, assumptions, models, theories, and methodologies whether imported or endogenous. What may inhibit this process, however, is the personal conflict in some of the most well-trained and talented psychologists between the desire to gain prominence by publishing in Western journals, which usually requires that they do Western-style experimental research, and the desire or perhaps the duty to conduct studies relevant and useful to their own countries (see the chapter on India). In spite of the many limitations associated with importing psychology from other countries, one wonders how psychology as a separate field of study could establish itself in some Third World countries without such an initial stage of development, even though endogenization gradually follows (Azuma, 1984).

Another problem faced by many Third World psychologists is a function of most of the psychological literature being in English. (That which is not in English is primarily in French, German, or Russian.) This means that the preponderance of psychologists in developing nations must minimally learn English and have access to libraries reasonably well stocked with major journals and books as well as offering computerized information-retrieval capabilities.

While all countries with limited resources which import psychology from other nations have characteristics in common, there are also interesting differences. We shall touch on some of the major ones in the ensuing review of psychology in the principal developing areas of the world.

Latin America

In many Latin American countries, psychology has been established for a long time. Therefore, although the impact of important European and North American developments such as psychoanalysis, behavioral orientations, Piaget's work, social psychological theory and research, and experimental methodologies has been considerable, these developments have usually been assimilated in a selective and reasoned fashion. As José Miguel Salazar and Ligia M. Sanchez, authors of the chapter on psychology in Venezuela, write, "Psychologists who emphasize the experimental analysis of behavior tend to laud the virtues of North American psychology; those who look to Western Europe (particularly the Piagetian School) are in the developmental field; and interest in creating a Latin-American psychology is most frequently found among social psychologists."

Other interesting aspects of psychology in Latin America include the improving status of women in the field (see Colombia), the extraordinary growth of the discipline in Brazil, the vigor of research as well as applied areas in Mexico, the Marxist-Leninist orientation in Cuba, the relatively modest interchange between Spanish and Latin American psychologists, and the increasing importance of the Interamerican Society of Psychology, in addition to more questioning of the relevance of imported research findings and methodologies and intervention strategies for Latin American countries.

Africa

The situation in Africa is complex. In North Africa, Egyptian psychology has had a strong influence within the Arab world, and the status of the discipline in nations that produce oil is closely tied to the level of prosperity financed by its sale. This has been particularly the case in the Arab Gulf states.

In sub-Saharan Africa, made up of countries newly independent since the end of World War II, psychology is still very much in the formative state. Modern helping professionals such as psychologists and psychiatrists are in many places viewed with mistrust; the people prefer to seek assistance from witch doctors, herbalists, and other traditional healers. Where psychology has progressed, it is closely tied to education.

One of the most unfortunate aspects of psychology in Black Africa is the fact that the exchange of information among psychologists in the various countries is inhibited not only by the multiplicity of endogenous languages but because in some countries the scholarly and scientific language is English while in others it is French or Portuguese. Among the European colonizers of Africa, France has apparently provided the most support to professionals in former African colonies for regional conferences and so forth.

South Africa is, of course, unique among African nations. Highly industrialized and affluent yet beset with serious problems, psychology is a vigorous and well-established field. There appears to be a robust interest in industrial psychology, which may in part be a reflection of Dutch influence there, as industrial psychology is also a strong applied area in the Netherlands. Despite the policy of apartheid, South African psychology has had some influence on the field in such Black African countries as Zambia and Zimbabwe.

Asia

In the region called the Middle East, the development of psychology in Israel is unique in the sense that both European and North American psychologists contributed to the establishment of the field. Psychoanalysis was strongly represented from the beginning although the relevance of this orientation for the country as it was developing was questioned from the outset. During the forty years since World War II, a productive discipline with a strong research tradition and well-developed applied subfields has emerged. Of special interest is the fact that the kibbutzim have afforded a natural laboratory for studying nontraditional, communal child-rearing practices.

The chapter on Turkey focuses on the consequences of countries importing their psychologies from other countries and the state of dependency this creates. The misuse of imported psychometric instruments is a very serious problem according to the chapter's author, Gündüz Vassaf. Disturbing, too, is his contention that criticism of some of the questionable practices going on within the field is suppressed because it is felt that such criticism will give the profession a bad name.

The other Asian countries represented in this book are Japan, the People's Republic of China, and India. Japan is distinctive in being a non-Western country which industrialized quickly (Azuma, 1984). Japanese psychology is a mature field, mostly in the Western tradition. As in China, a unique research opportunity has been created by the fact that the written language is expressed in both pictographic and Latin-letter formats. This has generated some fruitful studies.

The history of psychology in China is a fascinating, sometimes tragic, story. Strongly influenced by American psychology prior to the founding of the People's Republic of China in 1949, Chinese psychology came under the Soviet influence during the 1950s. In the early 1960s, there was increasing interest in developing a more endogenous discipline and Maoism was embraced. During the Cultural Revolution (1966–1976) psychology was virtually discontinued. Afterward, the People's Republic of China, much interested in modernization, opened its doors to foreign scholars and sent its own professionals abroad. Psychology seems to be regaining its momentum, particularly in those subfields having to do with education, child development, and worker productivity.

India is unusual among Third World Asian countries because, while a high percentage of its population has an extremely low standard of living and it is beset by serious regional differences, it has a highly developed scientific and technological enterprise. As Eugene Garfield has concluded on the basis of his survey of the number of articles published in the natural sciences, "India is clearly the research 'superpower' of the Third World" (Garfield, 1983, p. 10).

Although the natural sciences are quite handsomely supported in India, psychology fares less well and there are serious deficiencies in terms of funds for education, research, and applied work. Inhibiting progress is a fragmented national psychological organization, competing organizations, journals which accept articles of poor quality, and the divided loyalties of psychologists who are torn between doing experimental studies publishable in Western journals and conducting the field research that is better suited to the needs of Indian society.

The Vigorous Expansion of Applied Fields

Perhaps the most universal development in psychology worldwide has been the more rapid growth of applied rather than academic/research subfields. While one finds distinguished researchers in all countries which can afford the necessary facilities, equipment, libraries, and so forth, psychology as a discipline is supported by societies (particularly when funding is meager) only if psychologists are perceived as being able to play constructive roles in the areas of education, the production of goods and services, mental health, and, in some instances, sports. This is true whatever the politics or ideology of a country.

Judgments of how psychology can contribute to the betterment of societies nonetheless vary. In affluent Western countries psychology is viewed as a way to help produce an educated citizenry as well as provide professional services that are primarily oriented toward individual health and enrichment. In Marxist-Leninist countries, research, theory, and practical applications are seen as integrated and directed, via plans developed by the central government, toward outcomes which will contribute to the development of socialist societies. And in Third World countries, most of which by definition have very limited resources, there is frequently an idealized view of psychology as a tool for bettering the lot of the people (see Mehryar, 1984).

Whatever the country, however, it seems clear that support for academic/research psychology is largely dependent on how successful psychologists are at demonstrating their usefulness to society. Certainly, the dramatic growth of post–World War II psychology in the United States was directly linked to the very rapid expansion of its applied specialties, principally clinical psychology, counseling psychology, and educational psychology (Gilgen, 1982).

The Influence of Psychoanalysis

Giselher Guttmann begins his chapter on Austrian psychology by stating, "The first question asked of an Austrian psychologist abroad almost always deals with Sigmund Freud or psychoanalysis. Vienna, being the cradle of depth psychology, will of course remain identified with this field of study." He goes on to point out that Austrian psychology, however, was little influenced by Freud and that the discipline in his country has emphasized an empirical, mathematical, natural science approach.

Though a comprehensive determination of the psychoanalytic influence on psychology worldwide cannot be predicated merely from the chapters in this book, some general observations may be made. First, psychoanalysis has had its most significant impact in the United States (see Gilgen, 1982). Second, Marxist-Leninist psychologies have completely rejected psychoanalysis because of its emphasis on unconscious motivation. Third, in the United Kingdom, Freud apparently exerted only a minimal influence on psychology although he spent his last days there, and the country's other social sciences have been more noticeably affected by psychoanalytic perspectives (see the chapter by Ian Donald and David Canter). Fourth, the psychoanalytic influence (particularly the orientation of Melanie Klein) has been considerable in some Latin American countries. And, finally, psychoanalytic thinking has played a role in the psychologies of most other countries with well-established disciplines. Developments in Norway during the 1930s surrounding the career of Wilhelm Reich in that country after he left Germany and before he came to the United States are particularly intriguing.

The Influence of Behavior Therapy and Behavior Modification

"Behavior Therapy" originally referred to procedures devised by psychologists such as Joseph Wolpe and Hans Eysenck based primarily on the principles and methodologies associated with classical (Pavlovian) conditioning. Behavior modification, on the other hand, derives from the work of B. F. Skinner and involves operant conditioning. During the post–World War II period, behavioral approaches, including contemporary cognitive-behavioral and social-behavioral orientations, have had a profound influence on clinical and educational psychology, especially in the United States.

Interestingly, while Skinner is not often mentioned in the chapters by psychologists outside of North America, behavioral applied psychology is represented in most non-Communist countries. Although the overly simple views concerning the control of human behavior which characterized early behavioral therapies and educational techniques have been rejected by most psychologists (even in the United States), there is still a tendency to stereotype American psychology as founded on simplistic conceptions of human nature. This criticism comes not only from Marxist-Leninist but also from some hermeneutical, cross-cultural, humanistic, and existential psychologists regardless of their nationalities.

The Influence of Piaget

Swiss psychologist Jean Piaget is the most frequently mentioned psychologist worldwide. His influence has been international not only because of the power of his theory, which acknowledges genetic as well as environmental factors, and the usefulness of his research techniques but because his work is relevant for education, child development, and understanding the cognitive processes. These are areas of concern in all societies whether capitalist, Marxist-Leninist, affluent, or developing. Furthermore, in contrast with early behavioral outlooks such as Skinner's, the Piagetian orientation recognizes the complexity of human psychological functioning. In that sense Piaget both contributed to, and was part of, a general movement on the part of psychologists everywhere toward acknowledging the intricacies of the psychological domain.

A Reaffirmation of the Complexity of Human Psychological Functioning

Many developments have contributed to a general reaffirmation of the complexity of human psychological functioning. In the United States, the limitations of simplistic S-R (stimulus-response) theories, the influence of such modern structuralists as Piaget and Noam Chomsky, advances in the neurosciences and computer simulation, and the growth of applied fields led to the cognitive revolution by the late 1970s (see Gilgen, 1982). In Marxist-Leninist psychologies, with their emphasis on the interrelationships among activity, consciousness, thinking, affective processes, communication, and personality, there has always been an acknowledgment of the dynamic complexities of the psychological domain. Now cross-cultural and Third World psychologists have made it clear that in order to understand the thought processes, feelings, and actions of any particular person, one must first understand that individual's culture.

CONCLUDING THOUGHTS

Fast and relatively inexpensive travel and sophisticated information production, storage, and retrieval systems should in the not-too-distant future make scholarly, scientific, and applied fields truly international. The potential benefits of such a development are obvious.

For conceptually fragmented fields such as psychology, however, the availability of more and more information may be a mixed blessing. Even today, psychologists in the United States and other countries with access to the major literature find it difficult to keep up with all the published findings and ideas which might have some relevance for their work. Additional information will, most certainly, compound the problem.

The need for more psychologists concerned with conceptual fragmentation who are trained to unravel and explicate the structure of the psychological domain is apparent. More specifically, what needs to be done internationally is to develop a field of theoretical psychology analogous to theoretical physics, devoted to the epistemology of psychology. Marxist-Leninist psychologists already recognize the problem and are working to organize systematically the field. It is time for psychologists in the United States and other major producers of psychological information to take up the challenge (see Staats, 1983).

An optimistic outlook is in order because, while the availability of more information may not in and of itself lead to progress in psychology, increasing contacts among psychologists from different countries are laying the groundwork of professional debate for a productive future.

REFERENCES

American Psychological Association. (1962). Committee on Psychology in National and International Affairs. *American Psychologist, 17*, 50–52.

American Psychological Association. (1984). *Issues in cognition: Proceedings of a joint conference in psychology.* Proceedings of a joint conference sponsored by the U.S. National Academy of Sciences and the Chinese Academy of Sciences, held in Racine, Wisconsin, August-September 1983.

Ardila, R. (1972). *La psicologia contemporanea, panorama internacional* [Contemporary psychology: An international overview]. Buenos Aires: Paidos.

Ardila, R. (1982). International psychology. *American Psychologist, 37*, 323–329. (a)

Ardila, R. (1982). Psychology in Latin America. *Annual Review of Psychology, 33*, 103–122. (b)

Azuma, H. (1984). Psychology in a non-Western country. *International Journal of Psychology, 19*, 45–55.

Baldwin, J. M., & Cattell, J. M. (Eds.). (1895). *Psychological Index*. Princeton: Psychological Review Co.

Bowlby, J. (1951). *Maternal care and mental health.* New York: Schocken Books.

Brown, L. B. (1981). *Psychology in contemporary China.* New York: Pergamon Press.

Brozek, J. (1962). Current status of psychology in the U.S.S.R. *Annual Review of Psychology, 13*, 515–566.

Brozek, J. (1964). Recent developments in Soviet psychology. *Annual Review of Psychology, 15*, 493–594.

Chin, R., & Chin, Ai-li S. (1969). *Psychological research in Communist China: 1949–1966.* Cambridge, MA: MIT Press.

Ching, C. C. (Jing Qicheng). (1980). Psychology in the People's Republic of China. *American Psychologist, 35,* 1084–1089.

Cole, M. (1984). The world beyond our borders: What might our students need to know about it? *American Psychologist, 39,* 998–1005.

Corsini, R. J. (Ed.). (1984). *Encyclopedia of psychology* (4 vol.). New York: Wiley.

Diaz-Guerrero, R. (1984). Contemporary psychology in Mexico. *Annual Review of Psychology, 35,* 83–112.

Doise, W., & Moscovici, S. (Eds.). (1983). *Current issues in European social psychology: Vol. 1. European studies in social psychology.* Cambridge, England: Cambridge University Press.

Fein, L. G. (1974). *International understanding: Cultural differences in the development of cognitive processes: Women in national and international psychology.* New York: International Council of Psychologists.

Fichter, M. M., & Wittchen, H.-U. (1980). Clinical psychology and psychotherapy: A survey of the present state of professionalization in 23 countries. *American Psychologist, 35,* 16–25.

Frijda, N., & Jahoda, G. (1966). On the scope and methods of cross-cultural research. *International Journal of Psychology, 1,* 109–127.

Garfield, E. (1983). Third World research: Part 1. Where it is published, and how often it is cited. *Current Contents, 33,* 5–15.

Gilgen, A. R. (Ed.). (1970). *Contemporary scientific psychology.* New York: Academic Press.

Gilgen, A. R. (1982). *American psychology since World War II: A profile of the discipline.* Westport, CT: Greenwood Press.

Gilgen, A. R. (in press). The psychological level of organization in nature and the interdependencies among major psychological concepts. In A. W. Staats & L. P. Mos (Eds.), *Annals of theoretical psychology* (Vol. 5). New York: Plenum.

Gilgen, A. R., & Hultman, S. K. (1979). Authorities and subject matter areas emphasized in the *Annual Review of Psychology, 1950–1974. Psychological Reports, 44,* 1255–1262.

Giorgis, T. W., & Helms, J. E. (1978). Training international students from developing nations as psychologists: A challenge for American psychology. *American Psychologist, 33,* 945–950.

Hsiao, S. (1977). Psychology in China. *American Psychologist, 32,* 374–376.

Hunter, W. S., & Willoughby, R. R. (Eds.). (1927). *Psychological Abstracts.* Washington, D.C.: American Psychological Association.

Jacobson, E. H., & Duijker, H. C. J. (Eds.). (1958). *International directory of psychologists, exclusive of the U.S.A.* Assen, the Netherlands: Royal Van Gorcum. [A second edition also edited by Jacobson and Duijker was published in 1966 by the same publisher; the third edition was edited by Jacobson and Gunther Reinert and published in 1980 by North-Holland.]

Kennedy, S., & David, H. P. (1986). Psychology and policy around the world: Widening psychology's sphere of influence (Introduction to five articles). *American Psychologist, 41,* 296–314.

Kennedy, S., Scheirer, J., & Rogers, A. (1984). The price of success: Our monocultural science. *American Psychologist, 39,* 966–967.

Kessen, W. (1975). *Childhood in China.* New Haven, CT: Yale University Press.

Klineberg, O. (1954). *Social psychology.* New York: Holt, Rinehart, & Winston.

Klineberg, O. (1981). International educational exchange: The problem of evaluation. *American Psychologist*, *36*, 192–199.

Koch, S. (1971). Reflections on the state of psychology. *Social Research*, *38*, 669–709.

Kozulin, A. (1984). *Psychology in Utopia: Toward a social history of Soviet psychology.* Cambridge, MA: MIT Press.

Kozulin, A. (1986). The concept of activity in Soviet psychology: Vigotsky, his disciples and critics. *American Psychologist*, *41*, 264–274.

Lauterbach, W. (1984). *Soviet psychotherapy.* New York: Pergamon Press. (Original work published 1978 in German.)

Levinson, D., & Malone, M. J. (1980). *Toward explaining human culture: A critical review of the findings of world-wide cross-cultural research.* New Haven, CT: HRAF Press.

Lomov, B. (1982). Soviet psychology: Its historical origins and contemporary status. *American Psychologist*, *37*, 580–586.

Malpass, R. S. (1977). Theory and method in cross-cultural psychology. *American Psychologist*, *32*, 1069–1079.

Marx, M. H., & Hillix, W. A. (1963). *Systems and theories in psychology.* New York: McGraw-Hill.

Mehryar, A. H. (1984). The role of psychology in national development: Wishful thinking and reality. *International Journal of Psychology*, *19*, 159–167.

Mintz, A. (1958). Recent developments in psychology in the U.S.S.R. *Annual Review of Psychology*, *9*, 453–504.

Mintz, A. (1959). Further developments in psychology in the U.S.S.R. *Annual Review of Psychology*, *10*, 455–487.

Misiak, H., & Sexton, V. S. (1966). *History of psychology: An overview.* New York: Grune & Stratton.

Murchison, C. (Ed.). (1929). *The Psychological register.* Worcester, MA: Clark University Press. [Another edition was published in 1932.]

Murphy, G., & Kovach, J. K. (1972). *Historical introduction to modern psychology.* New York: Harcourt Brace Jovanovich.

Nixon, M., & Taft, R. (Eds.). (1977). *Psychology in Australia.* New York: Pergamon Press.

O'Connor, N. (Ed.). (1966). *Present-day Russian psychology.* New York: Pergamon Press.

Osgood, C. E. (1964). The psychologist in international affairs. *American Psychologist*, *19*, 111–118.

Pallak, M. S., & Cole, M. (1977). The international issue of the *American Psychologist*. *American Psychologist*, *32*, 11.

Razran, G. (1964). Growth, scope, and direction of current Soviet psychology: The 1963 All-Union Congress. *American Psychologist*, *19*, 342–349.

Rosenzweig, M. R. (1982). Trends in development and status of psychology: An international perspective. *International Journal of Psychology*, *17*, 117–140.

Rosenzweig, M. R. (1984). U.S. psychology and world psychology. *American Psychologist*, *39*, 877–884.

Russell, R. W. (1984). Psychology in its world context. *American Psychologist*, *39*, 1017–1025.

Scheirer, C. J., & Rogers, A. M. (1983). *The undergraduate curriculum from an inter-*

cultural perspective: Selected courses. Washington, DC: American Psychological Association.

Schmidt, H.-D. (1980). Psychology in the German Democratic Republic. *Annual Review of Psychology, 31*, 195–209.

Segall, M., Campbell, D. T., & Herskovits, M. J. (1966). *Influence of culture on visual perception*. Indianapolis: Bobbs-Merrill.

Sexton, V. S., & Misiak, H. (Eds.). (1976). *Psychology around the world*. Monterey, CA: Brooks/Cole.

Sexton, V. S., & Misiak, H. (1984). American psychologists and psychology abroad. *American Psychologist, 39*, 1026–1031.

Siann, G., & Ugwuegbu, D. C. E. (1980). *Educational psychology in a changing world*. London: Allen & Unwin.

Simon, B. (1957). *Psychology in the Soviet Union*. Stanford, CA: Stanford University Press.

Sinaiko, H. W. (1985). European psychology and the Office of Naval Research. *American Psychologist, 40*, 861–862.

Sinha, D. (1985). *Psychology in a Third World country: The Indian experience*. Beverly Hills, CA: Sage.

Sinha, D., & Holtzman, W. H. (Eds.). (1984). The impact of psychology on Third World development. *International Journal of Psychology, 19* (entire issue).

Smith, N. W. (1980). Psychology journals throughout the world listed by (1) country or (2) region. *Catalog of Selected Documents in Psychology, 10*, Ms. 2151.

Solomon, L. N. (1964). The Committee on Psychology in National and International Affairs. *American Psychologist, 19*, 105–110.

Staats, A. W. (1981). Social behaviorism, unified theory, unified theory construction methods, and the Zeitgeist of separatism. *American Psychologist, 36*, 239–256.

Staats, A. W. (1983). *Psychology's crisis of disunity*. New York: Praeger.

Staats, A. W., & Mos, L. P. (Eds.). (in press). *Annals of theoretical psychology* (Vol. 5). New York: Plenum.

Stevenson, H. W., Lee, S. Y., & Stigler, J. (1981, Summer). The reemergence of child development in the People's Republic of China. *Newsletter, Society for Research in Child Development*, 1–6.

Strickland, L. H. (Ed.). (1979). *Soviet and Western perspectives in social psychology*. New York: Pergamon Press.

Tanaka, Y. (1966). Status of Japanese experimental psychology. *Annual Review of Psychology, 17*, 233–272.

Tanaka, Y., & England, G. W. (1972). Psychology in Japan. *Annual Review of Psychology, 23*, 695–732.

Torney-Purta, J. (1984). Annotated bibliography of materials for adding an international dimension to undergraduate courses in developmental and social psychology. *American Psychologist, 39*, 1032–1042.

Triandis, H. C., & Brislin, R. W. (1984). Cross-cultural psychology. *American Psychologist, 39*, 1006–1016.

Triandis, H. C., Lambert, W., Berry, J., Lonner, W., Heron, A., Brislin, R., & Draguns, J. (Eds.). (1980–1981). *Handbook of cross-cultural psychology* (Vols. 1–6). Boston: Allyn and Bacon.

Triandis, H. C., Malpass, R. S., & Davidson, A. R. (1973). Psychology and culture. *Annual Review of Psychology, 24*, 355–378.

Wagner, D. A. (1986). Child development research and the Third World: A future of mutual interest? *American Psychologist, 41*, 298–301.

Whiting, J. (1968). Methods and problems in cross-cultural research. In G. Lindzey & E. Aronson (Eds.), *Handbook of social psychology* (Vol. 2, pp. 693–728). Reading, MA: Addison-Wesley.

Wolman, B. B. (Ed.). (1979). *International directory of psychology: A guide to people, places, and policies.* New York: Plenum.

Wright, M. J., & Myers, C. R. (Eds.). (1982). *History of academic psychology in Canada.* Toronto: Hogrefe.

Black Africa

M. O. A. Durojaiye

Psychology as an academic and a professional discipline is a newcomer to Black Africa. The history of psychology in many of the countries south of the Sahara and north of the Limpopo River may be regarded as a history of gradual cultural interchange. In these countries psychology was always taught as part of the training of teachers. Teacher education took place in normal schools, in seminaries, and later in colleges for student teachers. The dictum "to teach John Latin, you must know John and you must know Latin" was almost a motto of teacher-training establishments no matter how undistinguished they were. So it came about that child study has been the first aspect of psychology known in many African countries since 1920 when it became accepted that those who teach pupils the three "R"'s (reading, writing, and 'rithmetic) must have some training beyond being able to read, write, and count.

CHILD STUDY: FIRST AMONG AFRICAN PSYCHOLOGICAL RESEARCH AREAS

Teacher training was, until twenty years ago, the concern mainly of Christian missionaries in all African countries. It still is in some. Child study took the form of understanding children as physical and spiritual beings. While in Europe and America psychology was an offspring of philosophy, in Africa a proper appreciation of the origins of psychology requires us to recognize that the field issued out of missionary education wherein theological ideas concerning the spiritual importance of human beings were an important focus.

Usually every teacher-trainee was encouraged to study a particular child, to recount the child's development, to observe his younger siblings, and to monitor progress during the practical teaching exercises which were integral to teacher training. Everything was naturally rudimentary. The teacher-trainee would have only an elementary education lasting from six to ten years, depending on how quickly he could earn promotion from one class to the next. School fees had to be paid; thus, in planting and harvesting seasons, parents thought nothing of keeping their boys on the farm even during promotion examinations. Children would frequently repeat classes but at least they had full stomachs. The education of girls was rare until recently.

The student teacher was never told he or she was being taught psychology. Perhaps it was too big and difficult a word for someone with just an elementary education. More likely, however, the tutor did not know the term either. Be that as it may, the teacher-trainee was taught to remember that some pupils learn with difficulty and some with ease. In addition, the everlasting principles of learning imprinted on all teacher-trainees were that (a) each child is different from every other child; (b) learning is easier when you proceed from known material to the unknown and from the simple to the difficult; (c) practice makes learning stick; and (d) praise and blame, punishment and reward can be used to aid learning.

MAGIC, WITCHCRAFT, TRADITIONAL BELIEFS, AND AFRICAN PSYCHOLOGY

The ability to predict or forecast events, to speculate on causality, and to make certain things happen was an indication of the supernatural powers possessed by traditional healers, witchcraft practitioners, diviners, and priests and priestesses who were the custodians of the different gods Africans traditionally worshipped. There were gods of thunder, rivers, the sun, rain, and iron, to mention but a few. People believed that some individuals could predict rain, eclipses, floods, and bumper harvests. Some individuals were known to be capable of saving or taking lives, of curing or causing illnesses, and endowing people with wealth or bringing about abject poverty.

Within this context, psychology as the study of human behavior was generally frowned upon. The field's most grievous offenses were that it claimed to predict human behavior, account for human phenomena, explain causality, and trace human failures to human weakness. In other words, psychologists were criticized for trying to preempt the supernatural powers of those who traditionally claimed these powers as their own.

It was therefore not an accident that when I applied in 1961 to study psychology, after over a decade of work in education, I was seriously and lovingly advised by the chairman of the African scholarship board not to pursue such a course. He said, "My son, we are helping the missionaries to eradicate Black witchcraft which made people predict different human problems and we think we are winning; why should we now allow you to go and study psychology which will help *you* predict human behavior? Do you want to replace Black witchcraft with White witchcraft?" I failed to convince him and had to work my way, without support, through my university training and early career in psychology. Fortunately, the situation has changed dramatically. Psychology is now known not to be witchcraft. It is respected as a serious discipline, a good career choice, and a field that may contribute to national development. Nonetheless the discipline is clearly in its infancy.

EARLY PSYCHOLOGICAL RESEARCH IN AFRICA

The "midwife" role played by teacher education for psychology in Africa holds for all Black African countries known to me. These include former British colonies (Botswana, Gambia, Ghana, Kenya, Lesotho, Nigeria, Sierra Leone, Sudan, Swaziland, Tanzania, Zambia, and Zimbabwe); former French colonies (Benin, Burundi, Chad, Gabon, Guinea, Ivory Coast, Mali, Niger, Ruanda, Senegal, Togo, and Zaire); the former joint British and French colony of Cameroon; former Portuguese colonies (Angola, Guinea Bissau, and Mozambique); and the never colonized, though strongly Western-influenced, nations of Ethiopia (invaded by Italy in 1935 but freed in 1941) and Liberia. The precolonial belief systems of all these countries were sufficiently similar for the sociocultural background of psychology in Black Africa to have been essentially uniform throughout the countries enumerated.

The development of psychology in various countries, however, does reflect the colonizing countries' attitudes, areas of expertise, and interests. Apart from travelers' tales by Verney Lovat Cameron (1877), among the earliest reported psychological investigations in Africa were those by a German, E. Franke (1915), and a Frenchman, A. L. Cureau (1915). These studies were carried out in the Congo and Tanzania. More anthropological than psychological in nature, they were followed by the work of eminent anthropologist and Africanist Ruth Benedict (1934). However, it is the research of the great British psychologist F. C. Bartlett, entitled "Psychological methods for the study of 'hard' and 'soft' features of a culture" (1946), that I see as setting the standard for psychological inquiry in Africa. That standard was vigorously pursued and advanced by a series of studies done by A. Ombredane in the Congo from 1951 through 1958 and by G. Jahoda in Ghana since 1954.

Early publications by Africans on psychology in Africa were by psychiatrists S. Falade in Senegal (1955) and T. A. Lambo in Nigeria (1959). It may be said, therefore, that psychological curiosity, inquiry, and investigations predated formal psychological education in Black Africa. There was, of course, research going on in South Africa, the results of which allegedly showed that the white race was superior to the black. Concerning Arab African countries, on the other hand, I know little about any psychological research apart from that done by El Kousi in educational psychology. This may be due to my lack of proficiency in Arabic.

With the advent of university education in African countries and much later the establishment of psychology departments, psychological research by African psychologists increased.

TRAINING OPPORTUNITIES IN PSYCHOLOGY IN BLACK AFRICA

History speaks of the great, but now extinct, ancient University of Sankore which existed in West Africa in the fourteenth century. Old, but less ancient, universities still exist in Egypt. Modern African universities have more recent origins and better prospects for continuance than Sankore even though intermittent economic strains do not allow for steady growth. The oldest modern university in Black Africa is in Freetown, Sierra Leone. Fourah Bay College was founded in the nineteenth century, but it is not known for its psychology department. In Uganda, Makerere, originally established as a technical college in 1922, became the University of East Africa in 1950 and Makerere University in 1970. It had a department of educational psychology for ten years (1963–1973) and a subdepartment of social psychology from 1967 to 1973 before a department of psychology was instituted in 1973.

The first department of psychology in Black Africa was created at the University of Nigeria in Nsukka in 1960, the year the university was founded. Four years later a department was set up at the University of Lagos, just two years after that institution was established. Universities that formerly taught psychology within sociology departments (such as Legon in Ghana, the University of Ife in Nigeria, and Ibadan, the premier university of Nigeria) now have separate departments of psychology. The much newer University of Jos in Nigeria also has a department of psychology. Liberia has always looked to the United States for its model of psychology. Elsewhere in West Africa, however, the main thrust of psychological training has been within teacher education. The French West African countries of Benin, Togo, Ivory Coast, and Senegal, for example, offer psychology courses, but all within teacher education programs rather than in separate psychology departments.

In East and Southern Africa, Nairobi (Kenya) has followed the example of Makerere. Tanzanian psychological studies continue to take place within teacher education and sociology programs. Zambia and Zimbabwe, two of the three formerly federated countries of Central Africa, both have departments of psychology. In Zambia, productive research took place at the Human Development Research Unit from 1961 until 1981; that unit is now a department of psychology. Zimbabwe has had a department for over ten years. In Malawi, psychology is still emerging. It is probably accurate to say that the recognition of psychology as a discipline and profession is far more developed in Zambia and Zimbabwe than in any other Black African nations.

This is not to say that Zaire, Gabon, Ruanda, Burundi, Malawi, and other such countries have no arrangements for teaching psychology. While the main vehicle for such teaching is through educational programs, some universities do have departments of psychology. Zaire and Cameroon, like all French-speaking African countries, are each known to have a strong *Ecole Normale Supérieure* where psychology is an important subject for all teachers being trained to work in senior and junior high schools.

THE CONTENT OF PSYCHOLOGY COURSES

The psychology taught in African universities is, in my opinion, best described as humanistic. Humanistic psychology is of necessity a meaningful, though not yet fully articulated, approach to the psychological sciences in Africa. This approach arises from the need to meet the pressing and urgent problems of daily living in the African environment. As a consequence of the struggle involved in the transition from traditional to modern societies, African countries are looking, rather tacitly at present, to psychology and sociology for answers to problems associated with essential attitude changes.

Another challenge is the rather elusive entity known as "the African personality," said to be easy-going; sociable; eager to please; longing for mutual understanding, mutual respect, and mutual cooperation; and sociocentric in behavior. The African psychology teacher and psychology student are both naturally inclined to studies and branches of psychology that deal with these traits. Thus, favorite research concerns and areas are social psychology; human growth and development; human learning; clinical psychology; psychological aspects of psychiatry, guidance, and counseling; personality theories; and applied topics which focus on attitude change, national development through the enhancement of human resources, and educational and organizational psychology.

Also playing an important role in determining what African psychologists study is the fact that many Black African countries are forced by their traditional life styles, their historical roots, their links with ancestral considerations, and the beliefs of their people in such apparently supernatural powers as witchcraft, sorcery, the evil eye, divination, oracles, and incantations to seek meaning, understanding, and explanations for these phenomena. This will not be accomplished by anthropologists, but by African psychologists employing psychological techniques.

A further determinant of what African psychologists are able to do is the high cost of psychological facilities, apparatus, and gadgets—for example, animal laboratories and computers, commonplace in psychology departments in Europe and the United States. African university departments of psychology are forced by economic factors to emphasize those branches of psychology where costs are low and to avoid areas such as psychophysics, psychopharmacology, and physiological psychology where lack of funds becomes a prohibitive factor.

Only time will tell if psychology in Africa will enrich psychological knowledge through replicable advances in humanistic psychology. It is hoped that psychology in Africa will not be impoverished because of its inability, in the foreseeable future, to establish experimental laboratories and engage in highly sophisticated research.

Fortunately, cross-cultural psychology and research on acculturation have fostered communication and collaboration between Western and non-Western psychologists. However, the exchange of psychological knowledge between African and non-African psychology is not yet an entirely two-way process. African psychologists continue to receive more than they give as far as contributions to knowledge are concerned. Euro-American psychologists generally take away more than they leave behind when cross-cultural field studies are undertaken. Participation as equal partners in the design, execution, and publication of research is a desirable goal which many serious African and non-African psychologists working in Africa are anxious to achieve. Perhaps someday African psychologists will design cross-cultural projects to study the resilience of humanistic psychological traits in technologically advanced societies.

Courses in English-speaking African universities usually lead to a degree in psychology based on the English university model. Entry qualifications are either (a) at least two advanced-level passes and three ordinary-level passes in attaining the General Certificate of Education (an alternative not now available in England also exists); or (b) a minimum of five ordinary-level passes in attaining the General Certificate of Education. In both cases competency in mathematics and a scientific subject is generally required for entry. Students who enroll with a minimum of two advanced-level subjects are usually at least eighteen years old and pursue the degree for three years or more. Those with ordinary-level entry qualifications are normally sixteen years old and take four years to complete the degree program. Successful candidates earn the B.Sc. Social Science (Psychology), the B.Sc. (Psychology), or the B.A. (Psychology) degree, depending on whether the psychology program in which they are involved is offered by a faculty of social science, science, or arts and humanities.

In French-speaking universities the curriculum and requirements follow the French model. Entry to a degree program usually requires the baccalaureate. This is not a bachelor's degree but an entry credential. International schools throughout Africa now accept both the baccalaureate and passes in advanced- and ordinary-level examinations as admission requirements, in part to widen the choice of universities for students.

Most of the teachers in psychology departments are at present Africans. The change from predominately American, British, or French to African staffs began in the 1960s. At that time roughly half of the university psychology instructors were whites and half were Black Africans. Today the overall ratio is 20 percent whites and 80 percent Black Africans. Senior African staff members, however, were trained in the United Kingdom, France, or the United States.

RECENT RESEARCH AND PUBLICATIONS IN AFRICAN PSYCHOLOGY

As mentioned earlier, psychological studies in Africa at the beginning of the twentieth century were anthropological in design. During the ensuing decades, though, a great deal has been published about psychology in Africa. Reviews of psychology in Africa, for example, have been written by Levine (1961), Crijns (1962), Doob (1965), Wickert (1967), Munroe, Munroe, and Levine (1972), Armer (1974), Hoorweg (1976), Wober (1975), and Durojaiye (1984).

According to Marais and Hoorweg (1971), published psychological research in Africa has shown steady growth since the 1920s with the years from 1954 to 1961 representing the period of most vigorous output. Although only two psychological studies by Black Africans had been published by 1961, publications by Black African psychologists have increased significantly from 1971 until the present. With the psychologists trained by African psychology departments engaging in psychological research, the number of publications by Black Africans has, in fact, increased tenfold during the last decade. Even so, far more investigations are reported in mimeographed papers for departmental seminars and discussions than are published in professional journals. The major reason is lack of funds. Books and journals are expensive and paying subscribers scarce, so few African journals of psychology exist. The exceptions are the *Nigerian Journal of Psychology* (which does not always appear regularly), the *African Journal of Psychology* (published only once to my knowledge), and the *Journal of Psychology in Africa* (published by French-speaking psychologists). Despite intermittent appearance, these journals provide a stimulating forum for those doing research in education and psychology.

THE USE OF PSYCHOLOGY IN AFRICAN COUNTRIES

Without doubt education is the major consumer of psychological knowledge in Africa. All teacher-training colleges, no matter how short the duration of their courses, no matter how low the qualifications of their entrants, and no matter what level of teaching their students are being trained for, teach educational psychology. Not surprisingly then, the largest employer of psychologists in Africa is the educational enterprise. Psychologists work as teachers at various levels and are employed by examination councils, ministries of education, test development agencies, curriculum-development sections of educational administrations, special schools, psycho-educational services, and guidance and counseling agencies. Fifty percent of all psychologists, in fact, work in educational settings.

Psychologists are also found in industries, administrative positions, social service agencies, and hospitals; but employment opportunities in areas where psychology could be of the utmost value have yet to be created. Psychologists could, for example, make important contributions relative to personnel practices, production rates in industry, job satisfaction, administrative practices, and the operation of social service agencies and hospitals. Furthermore, there are few clinical and community psychologists employed in psychiatric and general hospitals.

When African countries realize that psychologists can assist with the problems intrinsic to attitude change and attitude formation as well as efforts directed toward improving the quality of life of their people, psychology will become a useful profession. Governmental officials and employers must appreciate and understand what it is that well-trained psychologists can offer them. Finally, psychologists will have to do more to enhance their discipline's image.

ACHIEVEMENTS OF PSYCHOLOGY IN AFRICA

Psychology used teacher education to gain a foothold in Africa as a discipline and profession. It is gratifying that teacher education is the greatest beneficiary of psychological knowledge in Africa today. Teaching has, for instance, benefited from theories of learning, and motivational findings have been used to encourage students to learn. The effects of practice, punishment, incentives, and inhibitory and facilitative processes have all contributed to our understanding of how children learn. Studies of human development in the African setting and what can be done to encourage such development have been applied to teaching situations, as have the findings on the importance of continuous assessment. A recent UNESCO publication illustrated succinctly the contributions of psychology to education and teaching in Africa (Durojaiye, 1979).

Public health is beginning to benefit from psychology, too. A number of clinical psychologists now work throughout the length and breadth of the African continent cooperating with psychiatrists and other medical practitioners in the amelioration of psychological problems. Psychologists also help to make hospitalization less painful. Moreover, the use of psychological knowledge and skills in the administration of primary health care and in promoting maternal and child health has become significant.

Since African countries are still aspiring to become technological societies, the utilization of psychology in industrial and organizational settings has not been as widespread as one might wish. The few psychologists employed in industry and commerce function as personnel managers and as advertising and promotion specialists. This area of service is expected to grow with the increasing industrialization of many African countries.

In the area of personnel selection psychologists provide expertise with regard to tests and measurements. Evaluation is the main focus here. Usually the work has to do with educational selection or employment. Tests are available from Nigeria's Test Development and Research Office (TEDRO) in Lagos, established in 1970, and the Educational and Occupational Assessment Services (EOAS) of Zambia, an agency created in 1964 along with the Psychological Assessment Service (PAS). In East Africa, the Makerere Institute of Social Research (MISR), founded in the early 1960s, has provided a facility for the design, construction, and testing of various educational selection tests. Other testing activities have been carried out for personnel selection purposes in Ghana (1960) and in many of the French-speaking countries (see Durojaiye, 1984; Machungwa, Kathuria, & Westenholz-Bless, 1984).

PROFESSIONAL RECOGNITION AND A CODE OF ETHICS
FOR PRACTICING PSYCHOLOGISTS

Of all Black African countries, Zimbabwe has the most explicitly stated regulations for the professional practice of psychologists. Psychology degree programs in that country prepare successful candidates for employment as psychologists. Graduate training is usually required for specific areas such as clinical, industrial, or educational psychology. The would-be practitioner must apply for a license and adhere to a written code of ethics.

Zambia also has a relatively comprehensive policy concerning the employment of psychologists. The mining industry is a major employer, and, as has been indicated before, educational systems employ many psychologists, especially for their testing programs. The influence of South African psychology on the development of the field as a profession in both of these countries, especially Zimbabwe, has been considerable.

Elsewhere in Africa there are no coherent policies governing psychological practice, primarily because most psychologists are employed by university departments of education, psychology, sociology, and business administration and faculties of medicine. Not many are in private practice.

In Francophone countries, psychology is still practiced mainly within government ministries. Few French expatriates set up private practices. Again, many psychologists are employed as instructors by universities and the *Ecole Normale Supérieure*.

In Algeria, Morocco, and Tunisia, psychological practices established by French expatriates are now largely continued by men and women native to these countries. Some high-level administrators in the ministries of labor, social services, education, health, and commerce are psychologists. In these countries the role of psychology in many spheres of life is clearly recognized.

It is hoped that, in the near future, many Black African countries that have training programs for psychologists will also provide employment opportunities for psychology graduates. This will be accomplished when the leadership realizes that psychologists can contribute to the improvement of the quality of life of the people through changing some of their basic attitudes. Nigeria now graduates over 100 psychologists every year from five universities. As already mentioned, a large percentage of them are in civil service posts, in industries, and in universities and teachers colleges. Private practice is not yet a lucrative enterprise though the services private practitioners could render are numerous. They could, for example, provide guidance and counseling services to children and young adults seeking help with educational, personal, or vocational problems. More specifically, many parents are worried about their children's bedwetting, petty stealing, drug use, lethargy, minor neuroses, truancy, and sexual misbehavior. Certainly, psychologists could offer useful advice to these parents and their offspring.

In my opinion, there are three reasons why the private practice of psychology has been unprofitable in African countries. First, there is a deep-rooted confusion, even in the minds of highly educated Nigerians, concerning the nature of, and differences between, psychiatry and psychology. Psychiatrists are viewed as a necessary evil to help mad people. Madness is a source of deep shame and abject despair for the families of psychotic patients. To be seen in a psychiatrist's office is to earn the pity of neighbors who tend to avoid such people and assume that madness runs in families. This is why psychiatrists are not in private practice in Nigeria. The psychiatric hospitals where they work are in remote and secluded parts of cities or in rural areas. Since the distinctions between psychologists and psychiatrists are not clear to most people, both are viewed as specialists to whom only the mad are sent.

Because psychology is such a new field, a great deal of public relations work and promotion will have to be done before the African public sees psychology as relevant for normal people, useful for avoiding the distresses that can lead to psychotic tendencies, and a service that can help people develop coping devices for the exigences of normally hectic, everyday life. This is the second reason why private practice is unprofitable in Africa.

The third reason is the continuing existence of traditional counselors, native healers, herbalists, practitioners of witchcraft, religious leaders of new Christian orders such as the Celestial Church of Christ, and faith healers. Although their methods and claims have doubtful validity, spontaneous remission works for them just as it does for psychiatrists and psychologists. These practitioners, however, have an important advantage: their adherents believe in them. The complete trust and faith that they engender are more than any psychologist can elicit at this time.

ASSOCIATIONS, CONFERENCES, AND THE NEED FOR A NETWORK OF AFRICAN PSYCHOLOGISTS

Among Black African countries, Nigeria has the most psychologists with degrees and at least three years of experience. A degree and such experience are the requisites for membership in the Nigerian Psychological Association (NPA) which now numbers over 200 members. Those belonging to the organization have degrees from the United States, the United Kingdom, other European countries, and, since 1965, Nigeria. The NPA holds annual conferences and shows promise of continuing growth. Poor communication and meager finances, however, represent formidable problems. Many Nigerian psychologists find it difficult to pay subscription and registration fees even though these charges are low.

Journals, newsletters, and bulletins appear sporadically and are frequently of poor quality. As a result, a great deal of good research, relevant to the problems encountered in the Nigerian environment, goes unreported. Furthermore, Nigeria has not been able to join the International Union of Psychological Science because it cannot find the foreign exchange facility with which to pay its dues regularly.

There is in the country no shortage of ideas or personnel, and no lack of good will, yet Nigerian psychologists have yet to contribute much to the field.

Of the psychological organizations in Black Africa, only the Zimbabwe Psychological Association (ZPA) is a member of the International Union of Psychological Science, and it is the only African psychological association included in the *International Directory of Psychologists* (Pawlik, 1985). This is quite an accomplishment since the membership of the ZPA is not large. Many other African nations have no psychological associations to speak of, primarily because there are few qualified psychologists in these countries.

One response to the need for contact among psychologists was the establishment of the Association of African Psychologists in French-speaking Africa. Psychologists in all the former French African colonies participate. The French government, through one of its agencies, supports annual meetings of the association, which met in Yaounde, Cameroon, in 1975 and in Dakar, Senegal, in 1980. Meetings have also been held in other French-speaking countries. The language of these conferences is of course French, a fact that has made it impossible for English-speaking African psychologists to participate. I did attend the 1975 conference in Cameroon under the auspices of the International Union of Psychological Science as both English and French are spoken in that country.

Attempts at that meeting to extend membership to English-speaking psychologists, though welcomed enthusiastically, did not materialize because of the language barrier and limited funds. While the French government agency provided monies for the participation of psychologists from French-speaking countries, no such provision was made for psychologists from English-speaking nations.

In 1972 and 1976, the African chapter of the International Association for Cross-Cultural Psychology met at Ibadan and Nairobi, respectively. Participation of African psychologists was again inhibited by the language barrier and limited financial support. Only English-speaking African psychologists attended these meetings, joined by a few from abroad who could pay for their fares and lodgings or who were sponsored by their universities or foundations in Europe and the United States. Efforts to hold conferences in Lagos, Nigeria, in 1980, in Harare, Zimbabwe, in 1982, and in Algiers, Algeria, in 1984 were unsuccessful. Money is still the major problem. So it is that psychology in Africa remains parochial within each African country, stunted by poor communication, and lacking regular journals, newsletters, or bulletins or a professional network. A task I have set for myself is to establish a meaningful forum for the cross-fertilization of psychological ideas among psychologists in both English- and French-speaking countries within a few years.

CURRENT RESEARCH TRENDS

Current psychological investigations in Africa are chiefly designed to investigate African behavioral characteristics and patterns of human growth and development in African settings. There is a serious effort to make psychology an indigenous discipline useful to national development. At the same time, some African psychologists do research in the traditional areas of the field such as perception, learning, thinking, creativity, child-rearing practices, and behavior analysis (both normal and deviant).

PROSPECTS FOR PSYCHOLOGY IN AFRICA

Psychology will become increasingly accepted and appreciated in Black African countries as the number of qualified African psychologists grows and contributions to educational, clinical, and social services and national development become more evident. Nearly all psychologists and psychological associations in Africa have as their principal goal involvement in the solution of societal problems. The more that goal is realized, the brighter the future of psychology will be.

The pool of qualified psychologists in Africa is expanding. In Nigeria, the number has grown from less than twenty in 1970 to over 200 in 1985. This tenfold increase over a period of fifteen years is the norm in most Black African countries. In Arab African nations the same trend is apparent. In Egypt, for example, the membership of the Egyptian Association of Psychological Studies is now approximately 300. When the Egyptian Association for Psychologists, as it was then called, was formed in 1964, there were far fewer members.

In conclusion, the change from colonialism to nationalism in Africa brought with it changes in psychology relative to the personnel involved, the focus of research, research orientations, and training opportunities. The course of development has, of course, not been smooth. Hampered by language differences and limited funds, both face-to-face interchanges of ideas and the broadcasting of information through publication have been much too infrequent. Nevertheless, the prospects that psychology can contribute to national development and be a factor in the solution of societal problems are good.

REFERENCES

Armer, J. M. (1974). *African social psychology: A review and annotated bibliography*. New York: Africana Press.

Bartlett, F. C. (1946). Psychological methods for the study of ''hard'' and ''soft'' features of a culture. *Africa, 16*, 145–155.

Benedict, R. (1934). *Patterns of culture*. Boston: Houghton Mifflin.

Cameron, V. L. (1877). *Across Africa*. London: Dalby, Ishister.

Crijns, A. G. J. (1962). African intelligence: A critical survey of cross-cultural research in Africa south of the Sahara. *Journal of Social Psychology, 57*, 283–301.

Cureau, A. L. (1915). *Savage man in Central Africa: A study of primitive races in the French Congo* (E. Andrews, Trans.). London: Allen & Unwin.

Doob, L. W. (1965). Psychology. In R. Lystad (Ed.), *The African world*. London: Pall Mall Press.

Durojaiye, M. O. A. (1979). African universities' contribution to studies on child development in Africa and the reform of education in Africa. A study prepared for the International Educational Reporting Services. International Bureau of Education, Experiments and Innovations in Education. Paris: UNESCO.

Durojaiye, M. O. A. (1984). The impact of psychological testing on educational and personnel selection in Africa. *International Journal of Psychology, 19*, 135–144.

Falade, S. (1955). *Le développement psychomoteur du jeune Africain originaire du Sénégal au cours de la première année* [The psychomotor development of a young African originally from Senegal during his first year]. Paris: Foulon.

Franke, E. (1915). *The mental development of Negro children*. Leipzig: Voigtlander.

Hoorweg, J. C. (1976). Africa (South of the Sahara). In V. S. Sexton & H. Misiak (Eds.), *Psychology around the world*. Monterey, CA: Brooks/Cole.

Jahoda, G. (1954). A note on Ashanti names and their relationship to personality. *British Journal of Psychology, 45*, 192–195.

Lambo, T. A. (1959). Mental health in Nigeria. *World Mental Health, 11*, 131–138.

Levine, R. A. (1961). Africa. In F. L. K. Hsu (Ed.), *Psychological anthropology*. Homewood, IL: Dorsey.

Machungwa, P. D., Kathuria, R., & Westenholz-Bless, C. (1984, February). Occupational testing in Zambia. *Reports of the Psychological Department. University of Zambia*, No. 4 (34).

Marais, H. C., & Hoorweg, J. C. (1971). Psychology in Africa: A bibliographical survey. *International Journal of Psychology, 6*, 329–355.

Munroe, R. L., Munroe, R. H., & Levine, R. A. (1972). Africa. In F. L. K. Hsu (Ed.), *Psychological anthropology* (2nd ed.). Cambridge, MA: Schenkman.

Ombredane, A. (1951). Principes pour une étude psychologique des Noirs du Congo Belge [Principles for a psychological study of Blacks in the Belgian Congo]. *L'Année Psychologique, 30*, 521–547.

Pawlik, K. (1985). *International directory of psychologists*. Amsterdam: North Holland.

Wickert, F. R. (1967). *Readings in African psychology from French language sources*. East Lansing: African Studies Center, Michigan State University.

Wober, M. J. (1975). *Psychology in Africa*. London: International Institute of African Studies.

Australia

Mary Creighton Nixon

Australia is sometimes described as the largest island or the smallest continent on the planet. Measuring over 4,000 kilometers (2,500 miles) from east to west and over 3,700 kilometers (2,300 miles) from north to south, it consists of one large landmass and a number of islands, the largest of which constitutes the state of Tasmania. Australia's closest neighbors are Papua New Guinea and Indonesia to the north and New Zealand to the southeast. Although Australia has nearly the same area as the mainland of the United States, its population is approximately 15,400,000, about 6.5 percent of that of the United States.

European settlement in Australia began in 1788, and until 1900 the country consisted of indigenous tribes and a number of British colonies. Australia became an independent nation in 1901 and remains a member of the British Commonwealth.

PSYCHOLOGY IN AUSTRALIA

At the end of World War II, Australia had three departments of psychology, one each in the universities of Sydney and Western Australia, and one in Sydney University's subsidiary, the College of New England, in the provincial city of Armidale. This college later became the University of New England. By 1983 seventeen universities had departments of psychology, and three university schools of education and ten tertiary colleges and institutes taught psychology programs accredited by the Australian Psychological Society for purposes of membership. In just under forty years, psychology in Australia had expanded remarkably.

DEFINITIONS

In this chapter, psychology refers not only to the teaching and research carried out in university and college departments of psychology but to all the work of those people who identify themselves as psychologists on the basis of training and experience. Psychology overlaps with other disciplines and professions.

Teaching and research in psychology is done to varying extents in schools of biological science and medicine, social work, economics, education and elsewhere.

Australian psychology has always been highly empirical, a legacy from its pioneers in the universities of Sydney and Western Australia. There are still signs that those pioneers regarded the advancement and dissemination of knowledge as only marginally more important than its application in practical service, especially in education and industry (O'Neil, 1977). Most Australian psychologists view human action as being explicable in terms that are independently verifiable and universally applicable.

Psychological practice defies definition. Yet in acts of parliament drawn up to register psychologists, some attempt has been made to state what it is that psychologists can do that other people cannot do (or cannot do as well). Five of the six state governments have introduced legislation that requires psychologists to register in order to practice. Not all the acts attempt to define psychology or psychological practice; difficulties in legal enforcement arise both for the states that attempt to define psychological practice and for those that do not. It is almost impossible to state practices that are unique to psychologists. One act (South Australia, *Psychological Act 1973*) reduces the practices that are uniquely psychological to the administration and interpretation of individual tests of intelligence and personality. Another act includes tests and testing along with other practices:

"Psychological practice" or the "practice of psychology" means—

   (a) the evaluation of behavior or cognitive processes or personality or adjustment in individuals or in groups through the interpretation of tests for assessing mental abilities, aptitudes, interests, attitudes, emotions, motivation, or personality characteristics;
   (b) the use of any method or practice calculated to assist persons or groups with adjustment or emotional or behavior problems in the areas of work, family, school, or personal relationships; or
   (c) the administration of any prescribed test or the use of any prescribed technique device or instrument for assessing mental abilities, aptitudes, interests, attitudes, emotions, motivation, or personality characteristics—

but does not include the interpretation of tests or the use of any method or practice by a teacher in the ordinary course of teaching or research in a university, State school, registered school or other prescribed educational institution; and to "practice psychology" has a corresponding meaning.

                                 (Victoria, *Psychological Practices Act 1965*, 2 [1])

Psychology's edges are blurred and much psychological knowledge is not exclusive to the discipline. The uniqueness of being a psychologist resides in training and knowledge which permits a systematic, rather than intuitive, approach to the study of behavior.

ORGANIZATIONAL STRUCTURES

Research and teaching in psychology are carried out principally in the universities and other tertiary institutes and colleges. Those institutions whose programs of training have been accredited by the Australian Psychological Society for purposes of membership are listed in Appendix 1, along with other bodies associated with psychological research and practice: the Australian Psychological Society, the Australian Academy of Social Sciences, and the Australian Council for Educational Research. A number of tertiary institutions other than those specified in Appendix 1 teach psychology, and increasing numbers of secondary schools include some psychology in their curricula.

The Australian Psychological Society is the national association for psychologists. It grew out of, and replaced, the Australian Branch of the British Psychological Society, which provided a focus for Australian psychologists from 1945 until 1966. The Australian Psychological Society had over 4,000 members in 1983, made up of honorary fellows, fellows, members, and associate members, all of whom can vote. Students of psychology may become student subscribers of the society and people whose qualifications in psychology are less than sufficient for membership may be admitted as affiliates (given certain conditions).

Since 1972, the Australian Psychological Society has operated as an accrediting body for courses of training. The society's Course Development and Accreditation Committee assumes that persons who become psychologists should be knowledgeable about the social and biological bases and concomitants of behavior, research design and statistics, and have some practical training. The committee expects course work in cognition, comparative and physiological psychology, developmental psychology, learning, memory and perception, social and organizational psychology, personality and motivation, individual differences, clinical and abnormal psychology. Through its accreditation processes the society exerts a considerable influence upon the teaching of psychology, which, in turn, reinforces the standards the Membership Committee uses to assess membership applications.

The Australian Psychological Society's concern with promoting high standards of psychological practice is expressed in a *Code of professional conduct and advice to members* (1970). A revised *Code of professional conduct* was accepted at the society's 1986 annual general meeting.

The society publishes two journals and a bulletin. The *Australian Journal of Psychology* has appeared since 1949 and accepts theoretical and empirical papers bearing on psychology as a scientific discipline. The *Australian Psychologist* began publication in 1966 and features professionally oriented research reports and comment. The *Bulletin of the Australian Psychological Society* first appeared in 1979; it includes comments, news, and information for members and is published six times a year (Gray, 1984).

The society incorporates two divisions, the Division of Scientific Affairs (DSA) and the Division of Professional Affairs (DPA), and several special interest boards which are subordinate to the divisions. In a sample of 285 members drawn for the purposes of this chapter, 62 percent did not belong to a board. As for the remainder, 18 percent belonged to the Clinical Psychology Board, 11 percent to each of the Counseling and Occupational Psychology Boards, 4 percent to the Educational and Developmental Psychology Board, and 2 percent to the Forensic Psychology Board. A number of people were associated with more than one board, but, considering the large percentage who do not belong to a board, it seems unlikely that the society's structure accurately reflects the functions of psychologists. An unknown, but considerable, number of psychologists are not members of the society, some from choice, but more, probably, because their qualifications do not meet the society's current standards for membership. A few attempts have been made to establish other associations but these have usually been short-lived.

Psychology in Australia reflects the country's male ethos. In a sample of 285 members of the Australian Psychological Society, 62 percent were male and 38 percent were female. Only one woman (Jacqueline Goodnow) has been appointed to a chair in psychology, and only one woman (Mary Nixon) has been president of the Australian Psychological Society. Between 1975 and 1977 women held fewer than one in six positions at the rank of lecturer or above in Australian university psychology departments, although the women's academic qualifications were higher than the men's (Over & Moore, 1980). The proportion of women in the Australian Psychological Society has increased slightly over time: in 1970 it was 31 percent (Mears, 1975); in 1975, 37 percent (Over & Moore, 1980); and in 1983, 38 percent (excluding associate members). If American trends (Over & Moore, 1980) are repeated in Australia, an increasing number of women will pursue higher studies in psychology. Ironically, as women become better qualified, the growth rate of the profession has been slowed by economic factors, and positions which women might have filled have disappeared.

The Australian Council for Educational Research, established in 1930 with funds from the Carnegie Corporation (Connell, 1980), has also played a significant role in the development of Australian psychology. It has sponsored important psychological work, particularly in the fields of ability and intelligence testing, educational attainments, and educational practice. Many of the country's senior psychologists have worked or collaborated with this organization. The council develops psychological and educational tests and is the principal Australian agent for tests produced abroad. In recent years its psychological work has decreased while its educational functions have increased, but its test services remain important for psychology.

CURRICULUM MODELS

Major programs and laboratories are located in the universities. In a study of Australian research in psychology, Day (1977) established the following categories: assessment of human ability and personality, experimental psychology with human subjects, social psychology and personality, abnormal and clinical psychology, educational and applied psychology, comparative and physiological psychology, psychological theory, research methodology, experimental design and statistics, and history of psychology. These categories were adopted for the purposes of this chapter, and in the last quarter of 1983 I undertook a survey of research, publication, and teaching. In this study the name of the first category was changed to individual differences in personality and human abilities and their assessment. Experimental psychology with human subjects was divided into adult (age not a major variable), developmental, and special field—for example, cognition and behavior modification. One new category, cross-cultural psychology, was added.

The universities and colleges that teach accredited psychology programs were invited to indicate how these categories featured in their curricula at both undergraduate and graduate levels. Seventeen university departments (fourteen psychology departments, three education departments) and nine college departments responded.

In order to understand the results reported in some of the tables that follow, it is necessary to know something about the structure of Australian bachelor's degrees. In the universities an undergraduate pass degree in psychology includes a three-year major sequence of courses in psychology and other subjects. The psychology component is at least one-third of the total three years of study. An honors degree takes four years, and the fourth (honors) year is devoted entirely to psychology; at least half of the work over four years toward an honors degree is focused on the study of psychology. The structure of the degree varies somewhat from university to university, but the proportion of study centered on psychology is similar. An Australian bachelor's degree is based on more psychological subject matter than a North American bachelor's degree and somewhat less than a British bachelor's (O'Neil & Walker, 1958; Lovibond, 1977). Honors degrees are awarded as first, second, or third class, with first-class honors being the most meritorious.

Some colleges and institutes, like universities, award degrees at the end of three years of study. Colleges that were originally teacher-training institutions still train teachers and award degrees after four years of study. None of the colleges provides honors programs. The psychology studied for a college degree approximates that required to earn a university pass degree. Four-year college courses that include teacher training were classified for the purposes of this chapter as three-year psychology programs. A fourth year of study in psychology may be taken as a one-year graduate diploma or course work master's program. Some two-year course work master's programs admit students who hold only a three-year pass degree with a major sequence in psychology, but most master's programs require students to complete a four-year sequence. That is, students entering a master's program will in most cases have previously earned either an honors degree or a pass degree plus a graduate diploma.

Entry to doctoral programs requires at least a good honors degree or its equivalent. Some students earn a master's degree before proceeding to doctoral studies.

The major work for a research degree at either the master's or doctoral level is a thesis. Research students engage in less course work than their North American counterparts but typically do more course work than British students (Keats, 1977).

Table 1 shows the mean percentage of the major subject-matter areas in teaching programs. Colleges and universities reported very similar content, save that universities place more emphasis on experimental psychology with human subjects (36 percent compared with the colleges' 24 percent) and colleges emphasize research methodology, experimental design, and statistics more (22 percent compared with the universities' 12 percent). The latter difference may indicate that colleges require students to learn more about computing techniques than that required by most universities.

Experimental psychology with human subjects, as taught in the major sequence, broke down similarly for the colleges and universities. In the university honors stream it accounts for 34 percent of the requirements, about a third of that devoted to work with adults and less than a third given to developmental psychology. The proportions are similar to those for the major sequence. Graduate programs show somewhat greater diversity, with more time given to abnormal and clinical psychology and to educational and applied psychology, although experimental psychology with human subjects still contributes the highest percentage. When experimental psychology at the graduate level was broken down into components, it became apparent that developmental psychology plays a larger part in college than university programs. Some college graduate diplomas concentrate on developmental and educational psychology with a heavy emphasis on developmental work. Undergraduate programs include substantial laboratory experience but requirements vary a great deal among institutions especially at the fourth-year level; for instance, an honors research program is usually planned individually for each student and its components depend upon a person's needs.

Enrollments in psychology have fallen slightly from 1978 to 1983, an increase in college enrollments offset by a larger fall in university enrollments. Table 2 makes it abundantly clear that most students take a pass degree after three years and do not pursue either honors or graduate studies in psychology departments. The two education schools that offer accredited fourth-year pass programs (Monash and La Trobe universities) take a relatively small number of students for training in educational psychology with an applied orientation. From 1978 to 1983 college enrollments in graduate studies (mainly fourth year) increased very slightly, from 7 percent to 9 percent, but university admissions to graduate studies increased from 18 percent to 29 percent of the total. The increase in the university psychology departments was mainly at the graduate level. About half the students who enroll in Year One go on to Year Three. Psychology provides service courses for many students whose major studies are in other disciplines.

TEXTBOOKS

Most of the universities and colleges contacted provided lists of textbooks and reference books, although it was not always easy to decide whether a given title

Table 1

College and University Psychology Department Teaching Programs

Subject Matter Taught	Mean Percentages				
	Years 1, 2, 3		Honors (University only)	Graduate studies	
	College	University		College	University
A. Individual differences and their assessment	11	8	7	10	11
B. Experimental psychology with human subjects	21	38	34	25	27
Adult	(25)*	(34)*	(34)*	(7)*	(30)*
Developmental	(29)*	(26)*	(27)*	(50)*	(26)*
Other special fields	(46)*	(40)*	(39)*	(43)*	(44)*
C. Social psychology and personality	13	10	11	2	9
D. Cross cultural	2	3	3	0	1
E. Abnormal and clinical	6	9	9	17	17
F. Educational and applied	4	3	9	21	15
G. Comparative and physiological	9	9	6	2	4
H. Psychological theory	11	4	7	9	5
I. Research methods, experimental design, statistics	21	12	12	14	10
J. History of psychology	2	4	3	0	1

*Percentage within this category.

Table 2
Enrollments in College (n = 9) and University (n = 10) Departments of Psychology, Shown as Percentages at Each Level

	Year 1	Year 2	Year 3	Year 4 Honors	Year 4 Graduate Diploma	Masters Course Work	Masters Research	Ph.D.
1978								
Colleges	43	29	20	0	6	.3	.6	0
Universities	37	25	20	3	2	6	3	4
1983								
Colleges	39	28	23	0	8	.4	1	0
Universities	33	22	18	4	2	11	4	6

Total enrollments reported:

1978	Colleges	1582
	Universities	5782
1983	Colleges	2071
	Universities	4576

Estimated enrollments for all psychology departments:

1983	Colleges (n=10)	2301
	Universities (n=17)	8088
	Total	10389

was intended as a text or as a reference for extended reading. The total number of titles was very large. A few appeared more than once within the teaching programs of a single institution and frequently across institutions. While tallying proved difficult and may be unreliable because of conflicting information, the most frequently reported texts appeared to be (*published in Australia): Anastasi, A. *Psychological testing*; Atkinson, R. L., Atkinson, R. C., & Hilgard, E. R. *Introduction to psychology*; Atrens, D. M., & Curthoys, I. S. *The neurosciences and behaviour*;* Davison, G. C., & Neale, J. M. *Abnormal psychology: An experimental clinical approach*; Gardner, G., Innes, J. M., Forgas, J. P., O'Driscoll, M., Pearce, P. L., & Newton, J. W. *Social psychology*;* Ivey, A. E., & Simek-Downing, L. *Counselling and psychotherapy: Skills, theory and practice*; and Nie, N. H., Hull, C. H., Jenkins, J. C., Steinbrenner, K., & Bent, D. H. *Statistical package for the social sciences*.

Textbooks obviously influence the development of the discipline. Notably, only two of the seven most frequently cited texts were Australian publications. The dominant influence is from United States publications, for both college and university teaching (about 74 to 80 percent are U.S. books, 13 to 15 percent are from the United Kingdom, and 6 to 11 percent are Australian). This is not surprising, if only because of differences in the scale of publishing in Australia and the United States. But the extensive use of American texts shapes students' conceptions and may inhibit development of distinctively Australian views of psychology. Moreover, real-world psychological issues and relevant methods for dealing with them often call for local knowledge and methods of analysis. Textbooks prepared in a different culture provide poor training for these needs. Lovibond (1977) noted dissatisfaction with American introductory textbooks and pointed out that fortunately Australian teaching programs range well beyond them. This is true even during the first year of training.

ABSTRACTS AND INDEXES

Since no Australian index of psychological publications exists, Australian psychologists use other, mainly English-language, sources. Abstracts and indexes are readily available in college and university libraries, in state libraries in the capital cities, and in the National Library in Canberra. Until recently, access to these resources was limited to people living in the capital cities and to students and staff of colleges and universities. Now, more and more regional and specialized libraries can call upon the holdings of large, relatively well-equipped libraries by means of electronic technology. Libraries, however, are hard pressed to respond promptly to the needs of readers outside of urban centers and find it very difficult to service readers who are hundreds or even thousands of miles away.

Psychologists in the big cities can keep up with their area of study through library research and journal subscriptions, although the libraries have more readers than they can comfortably accommodate. Psychologists in provincial towns and smaller towns are likely to find access to up-to-date material, other than that in the journals they buy, very difficult.

RELATIONSHIPS WITH OTHER DISCIPLINES

Three disciplines with which Australian psychology associates closely are education, medicine, and law. Psychologists work in state education departments as counselors and guidance officers; the term "school psychologist" is not much used. Most college and university schools of education have psychologists on their staffs. Three university education schools offer psychology programs accredited by the Australian Psychological Society: Deakin (a four-year undergraduate program), La Trobe (a graduate Bachelor of Education in counseling), and Monash (a graduate Diploma in Educational Psychology). A good deal of research and research training in educational psychology at the master's and doctoral levels is done in schools of education; this is reflected in the data on publications (Table 5).

Psychologists work in university departments of psychiatry, psychological medicine and neurology associated with hospitals and psychiatric clinics, and in state government health services. All acts to register psychologists are under the jurisdiction of ministers of health, a cause for simmering resentment in some quarters (Smith, 1984).

In recent years psychology has developed mutually beneficial relationships with the legal profession. The Australian Law Reform Commission has sought submissions on evidence law from psychologists (Kirby, 1978, 1984; Thomson, 1984) and on other matters where psychological research can cast new light on legal processes. The Australian Family Court employs psychologists as court counselors to lessen personal trauma, reduce litigation, and increase opportunities for reconciliation or at least for agreement in cases of family breakdown (Moloney, 1984). Extremely useful perspectives on confidentiality in psychological and social work practice have come from a lawyer (Fox, 1968, 1984). A lawyer and a psychologist have debated issues concerning psychological evidence, particularly the presentation of expert testimony in court (Cattermole, 1984; Wardlaw, 1984a, 1984b).

The employment of psychologists provides a clue as to psychology's relationships with other disciplines. In 1971, Kidd surveyed the employment of psychologists in Australia and estimated that 2,154 persons were employed full-time as psychologists. According to his figures, 20 percent were university teachers (in psychology, psychiatry, education, and other departments), 13 percent were college teachers, and 16 percent were employed in clinical psychology, 27 percent in counseling services, 9 percent in personnel psychology, 8 percent in vocational and social psychology, and 6 percent in market research, marketing, and mass media psychology. Kidd found psychologists in all sorts of occupations, with about 17 percent of those majoring in psychology obtaining jobs with the label "psychologist." He also discovered that employers looked upon psychology as a "strong discipline," but were more impressed by the statistical emphasis of the field than by its psychological content.

In 1981, Over in a follow-up study to Kidd's work examined employment prospects for psychology graduates. By that time the growth of psychology departments had greatly increased the number of graduates and raised the level of training. Over concluded that many more students were entering courses beyond their third year of study. However, economic restrictions reduced job prospectives relative to the situation a decade before.

A look at Table 3 shows that the percentage going into tertiary teaching at the end of 1982 was much lower than in 1971 when Kidd did his study, and the percentages going into clinical psychology were higher, which was a cause for concern since there is reason to question the methodological strengths of clinical graduate programs (see Tables 4 and 5). The majority of Kidd's counseling psychologists worked in schools; the 1982 percentages for educational psychology are similar. Data from the three university education schools are not shown in Table 3. Deakin, which offers a full undergraduate program and research graduate studies, expected 20 percent of its graduates to enter tertiary teaching and research and 40 percent to continue their studies. The other two education schools offer an accredited fourth year of study in psychology, and research programs at the master's and doctoral levels. They differed sharply in what they expected their graduates and diplomates to do. One expected 75 percent of them to enter clinical and counseling work; the other expected 80 percent to engage in secondary school teaching. None of the three education schools thought a sizeable percentage would become educational psychologists. By contrast, the colleges estimate that about a third of their graduates and diplomates will work in educational psychology.

Psychology interacts with other disciplines at many levels and in many settings. This began a long time ago (O'Neil, 1977; Bucklow, 1977) and has apparently continued.

THEORETICAL ORIENTATIONS AND ASSUMPTIONS

Psychology in Australian universities, as indicated by the data obtained in our survey, is highly experimental, heavily engaged in the study of human behavior, and fairly balanced between the social and biological components of behavior. In the colleges, psychology is somewhat less experimental, very heavily engaged in the study of human behavior, and much concerned with social factors and dimensions. Figure 1 shows that these trends are consistent across the undergraduate years and in research, and that the college and university mean ratings remain distinct. A given department may differ somewhat from the picture given in Figure 1, but the trends were consistent.

The universities reported over five times as much research activity as the colleges. When allowance was made for the number of institutions in each category, the universities are still producing more than three times as much

Table 3

Estimated Employment of Graduates and Diplomates, 1982

				Mean Percentages			
	Tertiary teaching/ Research	Industrial psychology	Clinical psychology	Educational psychology	Further study	Primary/ secondary teaching	Other/ not known
University psychology departments (n=6)	12	9	33	16	15	0	16
Colleges (n=8)	4	17	6	29	10	16	17

Figure 1
Mean Relative Emphases for Colleges (•) (n = 9) and Universities (○) (n = 10)

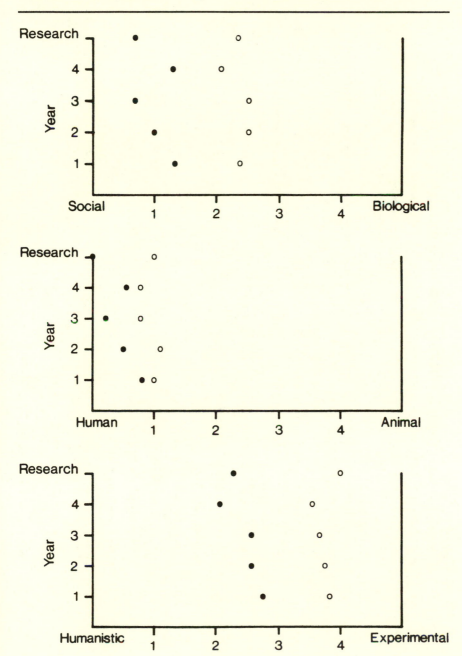

Table 4
Research Reported by College and University Departments of Psychology

Categories	Mean percentages	
	Colleges (n=9)	Universities (n=14)
A. Individual differences and their assessment	13	4
B. Experimental psychology with human subjects	20	31
Adult	(9)*	(42)*
Developmental	(45)*	(16)*
Other special fields	(46)*	(42)*
C. Social psychology and personality	18	10
D. Cross cultural	6	5
E. Abnormal and clinical	6	10
F. Educational and applied	31	15
G. Comparative and physiological	2	11
H. Psychological theory	0	5
I. Research methods, experimental design, statistics	6	4
J. History of psychology	0	4

*Percentages within this category.

research as the colleges. These disparities make comparisons based on Table 4 very dubious. The colleges were established as teaching institutions; they are not expected to engage extensively in research. Universities, on the other hand, are expected to do so. Table 4 indicates that experimental and human studies are highly emphasized, particularly in the universities, and shows that the main contribution from college research has been to educational and applied psychology.

Some interesting discrepancies appeared when teaching programs (Table 1) were compared with reported research (Table 4). Institutions reported offering courses in research methodology, research design, and statistics, yet precious little research in those areas appears to be going on. One frequently cited textbook was Nie, Hull, Jenkins, Steinbrenner, and Bent's *Statistical package for the social sciences* (1975); if students are merely being trained to use existing techniques, then this is cause for some alarm, especially at a time when electronic data-processing techniques change continuously. It is true that 13 percent of Australian publications were, according to our study, in these areas (Table 5), and that fact may indicate sufficient concern for the research competence of young psychologists.

Abnormal and clinical psychology occupies a proportion of graduate training (Table 1) greater than seems warranted by reported research (Table 4) or publications (Table 5). A field so bound up with service to clients requires vigorous on-going research programs that are not seen in the data presented here. Work may be published in journals other than those scanned, but the number of clinical studies reported is not impressive. In 1977, Williams looked forward optimistically to increasing investigatory endeavors in clinical and counseling psychology; his forecast does not appear to have been borne out.

Tables 1, 4, and 5 do show substantial agreement. Research, publication, and teaching on the whole go hand in hand, a positive sign for the discipline.

DEMOGRAPHIC AND ORGANIZATIONAL INFLUENCES

Organizations

At the end of World War II there were only six universities in Australia, in the capital cities, with university colleges in Canberra and Armidale. There were only three psychology departments. Two new universities were established during the 1940s: the Australian National University in Canberra in 1946 and the New South Wales University of Technology (soon renamed the University of New South Wales) in Sydney in 1949.

An expanding population, increased demand for an educated work force, and higher educational aspirations put severe strains on the universities. In 1957 the Australian government set up a committee of inquiry into university resources. The committee recommended major changes, including the establishment of new universities, increased funding, and systematic support for both students and research. By the early 1960s the universities were better funded and better staffed than they had been, but their earlier plight is well evidenced by figures from the University of Sydney Psychology Department: between 1945 and 1958 the staff increased by 27 percent and between 1945 and 1963 by 173 percent, but the number of undergraduates went up respectively by 83 percent and 317 percent (O'Neil, personal communication, October 25, 1983). From 1953 to 1963 students increased from 607 to 2,569. With faculty heavily engaged in teaching, and very few resources, it is not surprising that research output was meager (Day, 1977). Yet during the years just after World War II Australian psychologists established a national society, held lively annual conferences, and founded a learned journal.

During the 1960s and 1970s, the university colleges became autonomous universities, and several new universities came into existence. At the same time, great changes occurred in teachers' colleges, agricultural colleges, technical colleges, and institutes of technology. Many of these had been organized and run by state government departments for the purpose of training people for employment in those departments. Some existing colleges were amalgamated and additional ones established. The new institutions were funded separately from government departments, becoming autonomous multipurpose tertiary colleges. The ten colleges that run psychology programs accredited by the Australian Psychological Society are among these institutions.

By the end of the 1970s, the period of economic prosperity and expanding employment which made possible the expansion of tertiary education was over. The 1980s are not only characterized by funding reductions and enrollment decreases, but also by aging staffs and fewer opportunities for employment for young graduates, even those with high qualifications and great promise. Research, teaching, and applied work in psychology have been cut back along with the activities of other disciplines. While psychology is less likely to be seen as an essential service than medicine, engineering, or law it should certainly be perceived as being as valuable to society as social work. But in Australia social work would probably rank ahead of psychology in this regard. Subsequently, psychology's share of resources may be cut back even more.

Membership Trends

At its founding in 1945 the Australian Branch of the British Psychological Society had fewer than 200 members. The Australian Psychological Society was formed in 1966 with 941 members and membership had grown to over 4,000 by 1982 (Gray, 1984), an increase of about 9 percent annually. Gray also showed that the percentage of members in academic positions dropped from 38 percent in 1970 to 30 percent in 1980. Another change may have been in proportion of men to women (now about 60:40), already noted.

The number of psychologists registered under state registration acts gives another indication of the size of the psychological community. Approximately

2,300 psychologists were registered in 1983 (Smith, 1984). Since New South Wales, the most populous state, and the one with the largest number of psychologists, has not enacted legislation to register psychologists, this is obviously an underestimation. Furthermore, registration acts exempt teachers of psychology from registration; hence, few academics are registered.

Publications

For this chapter twenty-one journals were scanned and articles by Australian psychologists were allocated to the categories used previously to analyze research and the content of teaching programs (with some expansion under experimental psychology). Appendix 2 lists these journals. Results were checked against the rank ordering found by Rushton and Roediger (1978) from the 1975 *Science Citation Index Journal Citation Reports* and the listing given by Smith and Caulley (1981) for journals of educational psychology. Table 5 shows the number and percentage of articles in each category for the nine-year period. In 1977, Day carried out a similar study based on a smaller number of journals but including higher degree theses and Australian Psychological Society conference abstracts in addition to published articles. Table 5 shows that experimental psychology with human subjects accounted for a substantial amount of published research (21 percent) in conformance with Day's findings. In contrast with Day's results, however, educational and applied psychology contributed significantly to the 1983 total (22 percent), as did research methodology, experimental design, and statistics. Work in social psychology and personality was substantial in both 1977 and the present study. Over the period from 1945 to 1972, Day found that research output increased by a multiple of twelve. The present study found an annual publication rate slightly less than that indicated by Day's figures, but since he included unpublished theses and conference abstracts, it seems fair to conclude that the research output has been well maintained since 1977.

FUNDING OF THE DISCIPLINE

Australian colleges and universities depend very heavily upon government funding and few of them are well endowed. The funding of research and teaching in psychology reflects the country's economic conditions and the policies and priorities of the government.

A sizeable majority of psychologists are in government service. A smaller number work in industry and commerce, and fewer still are self-employed as consulting psychologists. While Australian psychology has developed rapidly since 1945, neither the Australian Psychological Society nor groups of researchers or practitioners have generated financial resources sufficient to support independent research institutes or provide scholarships for deserving students.

Funding of colleges and universities increased during the 1960s in the wake of the 1957 Australian government study. From the late 1970s, however, poor

Table 5
Australian Publications in Twenty-One Journals, 1974–1982

Categories	n	%
A. Individual differences and their assessment	43	6
B. Experimental psychology with human subjects	149	21
Adult	(37)*	(25)*
Developmental	(47)*	(32)*
Cognition	(19)*	(13)*
Behavior modification	(14)*	(9)*
Other special fields	(32)*	(21)*
C. Social psychology and personality	104	15
D. Cross cultural	34	5
E. Abnormal and clinical	39	6
F. Educational and applied	157	22
G. Comparative and physiological	43	6
H. Psychological theory	30	4
I. Research methods, experimental design, statistics	94	13
J. History of psychology	7	1
Total	700	

*Number/percentage within this category.

economic conditions worldwide have operated to the detriment of higher education, including psychology.

During the period of prosperity, two Australian government instrumentalities came into being: the Australian Research Grants Committee (subsequently "Committee" was changed to "Scheme"; ARGS) and the Educational Research and Development Committee (ERDC). Both allocated public funds for research, including psychological studies. The Educational Research and Development Committee fell victim to government cutbacks in the late 1970s and the Australian Research Grants Scheme survived with a reduced budget. The latter, in conjunction with the National Health and Medical Research Council (NHMRC), provides major support for psychological research. Table 6 shows the sources of research funds reported by the departments surveyed for this chapter (some departments did not report sources of research funds). First, very little funding comes to psychological research from either industry and commerce or private benefactors. More than half of the universities' research monies comes from governmental grant-giving bodies while about a third comes from their own budgets. The colleges receive meager external support and do very little research.

SOCIETAL INFLUENCES

As shown by Table 7, between 1928 and 1982, forty-nine people were appointed professors of psychology in Australian universities. Three of these have held professorial appointments in two different universities (Hammer, Over, and Scott) and their degrees were tallied for both appointments. Of all degrees held by professors, 49 percent were awarded by Australian universities, 23 percent by the University of Sydney. Clearly, Australia has been to a large extent self-supporting in psychological leadership, with the University of Sydney exerting the predominant influence. Since only one professorial appointment in psychology existed before 1945 (Henry Tasman Lovell, M.A. [Sydney], dr.phil. [Jenal]), this influence is largely due to post–World War II developments under William Matthew O'Neil, who headed the Sydney department from 1945 to 1965. Only the British universities are the source of more degrees held by psychology professors than the University of Sydney.

During World War II, psychologists in the Australian armed services proved themselves competent in personnel assessment, selection, training, management, and welfare. The armed forces still maintain psychological services for these purposes, notably the Australian Army Psychology Corps, the only such military unit in the English-speaking world (Owens, 1977). Together with colleagues in the Australian Department of Labour and National Service (since reorganized as the Department of Employment and Youth Affairs), psychologists employed by the military developed effective procedures for occupational psychology (Bucklow, 1977). Indeed a number of them, after demobilization, made careers in government or industrial institutions or as management consultants. A new generation of occupational psychologists now finds that in addition to employ-

Table 6

Sources of Research Funds for College and University Departments of Psychology, 1983

		Mean Percentages			
	University/ College budget	ARGS, NHMRC, or similar bodies abroad	Goverment Departments	Industry/ Commerce	Other
Colleges (n=9)	71	10	13	4	2
Universities (n=12)	30	54	11	2	3

Table 7
**Sources of Degrees Held by Professors in University Psychology Departments,
1928–1982**

Institutions	Number of Degrees	%
Australian universities		
Sydney	26	23
Melbourne	10	9
Adelaide	7	6
Western Australia	5	4
Queensland	4	4
Other	3	3
British universities	31	27
United States universities	22	20
European universities	2	2
New Zealand universities	2	2
South African universities	1	1
Total	113	

Source: O'Neil, 1983

57

ment counseling they must tackle the psychological problems associated with unemployment, retirement, and frequent job changes (Gurney & Taylor, 1981; Taylor & Gurney, 1984).

In the wake of the 1957 study of the universities, a substantial number of government scholarships became available for both undergraduate and graduate study. Psychology proved a popular subject. The scholarship schemes brought to tertiary study increasing numbers of young people whose parents did not have a college or university education. Among the new generations of students were children of families who had fled Europe before the war or who came to Australia as migrants during the postwar years. Many came to find a better life for their children than appeared possible in Europe (Steinkalk, 1982; Taft, 1966).

Other scholarship and aid schemes brought to Australia large numbers of students from Asia, particularly from the Southeast Asian countries. Some studied psychology and took back what they learned to their own countries. One small Asian psychological association even sought and obtained permission to adopt the Australian Psychological Society's *Code of professional conduct* (1970).

Major influences on Australian psychology have come through the exchange of college and university staff, especially with Britain and North America. Many Australian psychologists completed graduate or postdoctoral studies abroad before returning to positions in Australia. Others took positions overseas, especially in Canada, Britain, and Southeast Asia. Generous leave policies permit Australian academics to spend time in colleges and universities in other countries for research purposes, and universities encourage their personnel to attend international conferences and seminars. Australian psychologists take advantage of these opportunities and have involved themselves in conferences and in such organizations as the Assembly of the International Union of Psychological Science out of proportion to their numbers (Russell, 1977). Their efforts led to the 1988 Congress of the International Union of Psychological Science being scheduled in Sydney, the first time the congress will convene in the Southern Hemisphere.

The first act to register psychologists was passed in 1965 (*Psychological Practices Act 1965*), and the practice of psychology has changed in response to statutory regulation. At first many psychologists opposed this form of regulation, but most now recognize that the discipline benefits from this control.

Australian psychologists are part of worldwide psychology and keep abreast of developments in other countries. They can certainly take pride in their discipline's standing in the international psychological community.

NOTABLE PSYCHOLOGISTS

The Academy of the Social Sciences in Australia has elected twenty-four psychologists as fellows (Appendix 1, Academies) in recognition of scholarly and other contributions. Fifteen of these fellows are, or were until retirement, professors in psychology departments; five are, or were, professors in education departments. One (N. L. Munn) chose to retire in Australia, where he spent his early years, after a notable career in the United States. One (W. M. O'Neil) was professor of psychology and then deputy vice-chancellor of the University of Sydney until he retired. One (R. W. Russell) was vice-chancellor of Flinders University until his recent retirement. One (A. Richardson) is a reader in psychology. There is only one woman among the fellows: Jacqueline Goodnow.

Eminence is often assessed through examination of publication rates and citations in the *Social Science Citation Index* (for example, Over & Moore, 1979; White & White, 1978). For the period 1970–1975, White and White found that for a sample of 299 Australian academic psychologists, 10 percent of the sample was responsible for 36 percent of the publications, and 60 percent of the citations referred to 10 percent of the sample. Over and Moore examined citation rates for 1975, 1976, and 1977 for a total of 271 academic psychologists. They concluded that although Australian psychology departments had a relatively high publication rate, citation rates were not generally high by international standards. Those individuals who did rate highly according to international norms were: N. T. Feather, A. J. Yates, W. A. Scott, A. T. Welford, P. W. Sheehan, R. H. Day, S. H. Lovibond, R. F. Over, J. J. Goodnow and L. Mann. All of these held professorial appointments at that time, and all but two are fellows of the Academy of the Social Sciences.

MAJOR NEEDS

As the momentum generated by expansion during the 1960s and 1970s slowed in the 1980s, Australian psychologists have taken stock of their achievements and needs. Based on data and publications gathered for this chapter and other work (Nixon, 1984; Nixon & Taft, 1977), it is clear that Australia has psychological research achievements and teaching institutions of which it can be proud. Psychologists make contributions in educational, health, welfare, and industrial settings. Their services have been recognized in five of the six states by acts of parliament for the registration of psychologists. However, the development of research and teaching programs on the one hand and the demands of practical service on the other have since the 1940s and 1950s weakened the links between those who are engaged in extending and disseminating knowledge and those whose task it is to transform that knowledge into service. The Australian Psychological Society has not been very successful in maintaining those links, but efforts are under way to try to strengthen them. The society adopted a new organizational structure in 1981 (Gray, 1984) in an attempt to meet psychologists' needs more effectively. One object was to increase collaboration among teachers, researchers, and providers of psychological services, so that the work of each group informs and strengthens that of the others.

Most psychologists in practice in Australia hold three- or four-year degree qualifications. The degree programs provide a good introduction to the discipline of psychology; they do not provide training in practical service. Graduate training programs in specialist areas are badly needed, programs which unite research and practice streams and provide intern experience for young graduates.

Psychologists required to provide practical help to clients seek methods from whatever sources are available, sometimes without exploring adequately the resources of their own discipline, sometimes falling prey to purveyors of spurious beliefs and procedures. Sometimes they are obliged, by institutional demands, to adopt the methodologies of other professions or to act as the handmaidens of other professions (medicine or education, for instance); they thereby dilute the contribution that psychological knowledge and skills could make (Noble, 1984). Registration of psychologists may help to ensure that those who offer psychological services are adequately trained in both the knowledge base and the practical skills of the discipline. But registration depends on support in the form of professional commitment to scientific advancement and high ethical standards, if it is to serve psychology effectively. The discipline needs more people with such a commitment.

NOTE

For assistance and advice during preparation of this chapter I offer my thanks to the following: Monash University Faculty of Education for financial and clerical assistance; the college and university departments that responded to my request for information; Josephine Monaco, research assistant; and Ross Day, Sally Kent, William O'Neil, Ronald Taft, and Alison Turtle, who reviewed the first draft.

REFERENCES

Anastasi, A. (1982). *Psychological testing* (5th ed.). New York: Macmillan.

Atkinson, R. L., Atkinson, R. C., & Hilgard, E. R. (1983). *Introduction to psychology* (7th ed.). New York: Harcourt Brace Jovanovich.

Atrens, D. M., & Curthoys, I. S. (1982). *The neurosciences and behaviour: An introduction*. Sydney: Academic Press.

Australian Psychological Society. (1970). *Code of professional conduct and advice to members*. Melbourne: Author.

Bucklow, M. (1977). Applied psychology in Australia: The history. In M. C. Nixon & R. Taft (Eds.), *Psychology in Australia: Achievements and prospects* (pp. 23–34). Sydney: Pergamon Press.

Cattermole, G. A. (1984). The psychologist as an expert witness. In M. C. Nixon (Ed.), *Issues in psychological practice* (pp. 121–132). Melbourne: Longman Cheshire.

Connell, W. F. (1980). *The Australian Council for Educational Research 1930–80*. Melbourne: Australian Council for Educational Research.

Davison, G. C., & Neale, J. M. (1982). *Abnormal psychology: An experimental clinical approach* (3rd ed.). New York: Wiley.

Day, R. H. (1977). Psychological research in universities and colleges. In M. C. Nixon & R. Taft (Eds.), *Psychology in Australia: Achievements and prospects* (pp. 54–68). Sydney: Pergamon Press.

Fox, R. G. (1968). Legal aspects of confidentiality. *Australian Psychologist, 3*, 53–75.

Fox, R. G. (1984). Ethical and legal principles of confidentiality for psychologists and social workers. In M. C. Nixon (Ed.), *Issues in psychological practice* (pp. 147–187). Melbourne: Longman Cheshire.

Gardner, G., Innes, J. M., Forgas, J. P., O'Driscoll, M., Pearce, P. L., & Newton, J. W. (1980). *Social psychology*. Sydney: Prentice-Hall.

Gray, K. C. (1984). The Australian Psychological Society. In M. C. Nixon (Ed.), *Issues in psychological practice* (pp. 1–25). Melbourne: Longman Cheshire.

Gurney, R. M., & Taylor, K. F. (1981). Research on unemployment: Defects, neglect and prospects. *Bulletin of the British Psychological Society, 34*, 349–352.

Ivey, A. E., & Simek-Downing, L. (1980). *Counselling and psycho-therapy: Skills, theory and practice*. Englewood Cliffs, NJ: Prentice-Hall.

Keats, J. A. (1977). Graduate education in psychology in Australia. In M. C. Nixon & R. Taft (Eds.), *Psychology in Australia: Achievements and prospects* (pp. 118–127). Sydney: Pergamon Press.

Kidd, G. A. (1971). *The employment of psychologists in Australia*. Sydney University Appointments Board.

Kirby, M. D. (1978). Psychology and the law: A minuet. *Australian Psychologist, 13*, 339–356.

Kirby, M. D. (1984). Psychology and evidence law reform. In M. C. Nixon (Ed.), *Issues in psychological practice* (pp. 93–106). Melbourne: Longman Cheshire.

Lovibond, S. H. (1977). Undergraduate teaching in psychology in Australian universities. In M. C. Nixon & R. Taft (Eds.), *Psychology in Australia: Achievements and prospects* (pp. 100–117). Sydney: Pergamon Press.

Mears, J. (1975). Women in Australian psychology: Identity. *Australian Psychologist, 10*, 293–297.

Moloney, L. (1984). Psychological reports and child disposition: Experiences in the Family Court of Australia. In M. C. Nixon (Ed.), *Issues in psychological practice* (pp. 227–233). Melbourne: Longman Cheshire.

Nie, N. H., Hull, C. H., Jenkins, J. C., Steinbrenner, K., & Bent, D. H. (1975). *Statistical package for the social sciences* (2nd ed.). New York: McGraw-Hill.

Nixon, M. C. (Ed.). (1984). *Issues in psychological practice*. Melbourne: Longman Cheshire.

Nixon, M. C., & Taft, R. (Eds.). (1977). *Psychology in Australia: Achievements and prospects*. Sydney: Pergamon Press.

Noble, W. (1984). *Ethics, psychologists' practices, and psychology theory*. In M. C. Nixon (Ed.), *Issues in psychological practice* (pp. 50–80). Melbourne: Longman Cheshire.

O'Neil, W. M. (1977). Teaching and practice of psychology in the first phases. In M. C. Nixon & R. Taft (Eds.), *Psychology in Australia: Achievements and prospects* (pp. 2–22). Sydney: Pergamon Press.

O'Neil, W. M. (1983). One hundred years of psychology in Australia: 1881–1980. *Bulletin of the Australian Psychological Society, 5* (6), 8–20, 36.

O'Neil, W. M., & Walker, K. F. (1958). Psychology in the universities. *Australian Journal of Psychology, 10*, 7–18.

Over, R. (1981). Employment prospects for psychology graduates in Australia. *Australian Psychologist, 16*, 335–345.

Over, R., & Moore, D. (1979). Citation statistics for psychologists in Australian universities: 1975–1977. *Australian Psychologist, 14*, 319–327.

Over, R., & Moore, D. (1980). Research productivity and impact of men and women in psychology departments of Australian universities, 1975–1977. *Australian Psychologist, 15,* 413–418.

Owens, A. G. (1977). Psychology in the armed services. In M. C. Nixon & R. Taft (Eds.), *Psychology in Australia: Achievements and prospects* (pp. 202–213). Sydney: Pergamon Press.

Rushton, J. P., & Roediger, H. L. (1978). An evaluation of 80 psychology journals based on the *Science Citation Index. American Psychologist, 33,* 520–523.

Russell, R. W. (1977). Australian psychologists in the world context. In M. C. Nixon and R. Taft (Eds.), *Psychology in Australia: Achievements and prospects* (pp. 286–298). Sydney: Pergamon Press.

Smith, N. L., & Caulley, D. N. (1981). The evaluation of educational journals through the study of citations. *Educational Researcher, 10* (5), 11–12, 22–24.

Smith, R. L. (1984). Registration of psychologists: Issues and implications. In M. C. Nixon (Ed.), *Issues in psychological practice* (pp. 234–251). Melbourne: Longman Cheshire.

South Australia. *Psychological Act 1973.*

Steinkalk, E. (1982). *The adaptation of Soviet Jews in Victoria: A study of adolescent immigrants and their parents.* Unpublished Ph.D. thesis, Monash University, Clayton, 3168.

Taft, R. (1966). *From stranger to citizen.* London: Tavistock.

Taylor, K. F., & Gurney, R. M. (1984). So you're thinking of studying unemployment? In M. C. Nixon (Ed.), *Issues in psychological practice* (pp. 285–299). Melbourne: Longman Cheshire.

Thomson, D. M. (1984). Towards a more efficient judicial system: Observations of an experimental psychologist. In M. C. Nixon (Ed.), *Issues in psychological practice* (pp. 107–119). Melbourne: Longman Cheshire.

Victoria. *Psychological Practices Act 1965.*

Wardlaw, G. (1984). Confidentiality, the courts and psychologists. In M. C. Nixon (Ed.), *Issues in psychological practice* (pp. 195–204). Melbourne: Longman Cheshire. (a)

Wardlaw, G. (1984). The psychologist in court: Some guidelines on the presentation of psychological evidence. In M. C. Nixon (Ed.), *Issues in psychological practice* (pp. 133–143). Melbourne: Longman Cheshire. (b)

White, K. G., & White, M. J. (1978). On the relation between productivity and impact. *Australian Psychologist, 13,* 369–374.

Williams, C. (1977). Research in clinical and counselling psychology. In M. C. Nixon & R. Taft (Eds.), *Psychology in Australia: Achievements and prospects* (pp. 69–91). Sydney: Pergamon Press.

APPENDIX 1

Academies

Academy of the Social Sciences in Australia, founded 1952 (name changed from Social Sciences Research Council of Australia in 1971). *Psychologists who are Fellows (*Retired):* Champion, R. A., University of Sydney; Day, R. H., Monash University; Dunn,

S. S.,* Monash University; Feather, N. T., Flinders University of South Australia; Gibb, C. A.,* Australian National University; Glow, P. H., University of Adelaide; Goodnow, J., Macquarie University; Keats, J. A., University of Newcastle; Lovibond, S. H.,* University of New South Wales; McDonald, R., Macquarie University; Mann, L., Flinders University of South Australia; Munn, N. L.,* University of Adelaide; O'Neil, W. M.,* University of Sydney; Over, R., La Trobe University; Richardson, A., University of Western Australia; Ross, J., University of Western Australia; Russell, R. W.,* Flinders University of South Australia; Scott, W. A., Australian National University; Sheehan, P. W., University of Queensland; Singer, G., La Trobe University; Spearritt, D., University of Sydney; Sutclifffe, J. P., University of Sydney; Taft, R.,* Monash University; and Wallace, I., Deakin University.

Learned Societies

Australian Branch of the British Psychological Society, established 1945; and Australian Psychological Society, 191 Royal Parade, Parkville, Victoria, 3052, founded 1966.

Research and Service Institutions

Australian Council for Educational Research, Radford House, Frederick Street, Hawthorn, Victoria, 3122, established 1930.

Australian Universities with Psychology Departments Offering APS Accredited Psychology Courses

Australian National University, Canberra, Australian Capital Territory, 2600, founded 1946; psychology department established between 1950 and 1959. Foundation Professor of Psychology appointed in 1956 (Cecil Austin Gibb, OBE); research and teaching staff—27.

Flinders University of South Australia, Bedford Park, South Australia, 5042, founded 1966 (formerly the University of Adelaide at Bedford Park, established 1963); psychology department established between 1960 and 1969. Foundation Professor of Psychology appointed in 1968 (Norman Thomas Feather); research and teaching staff—17.

James Cook University of North Queensland, Townsville, Queensland, 4811, founded 1970; psychology department (Department of Behavioural Sciences) established between 1970 and 1977. Foundation Professor of Psychology appointed in 1974 (William Abbott Scott); research and teaching staff—13; students enrolled in 1983—170.

La Trobe University, Bundoora, Victoria, 3083, founded 1964; psychology department established between 1970 and 1977. Foundation Professor of Psychology appointed in 1971 (George Singer); research and teaching staff—23.

Macquarie University, North Ryde, New South Wales, 2113, founded 1964 (opened 1967); School of Behavioural Sciences established between 1960 and 1969. Foundation Professor of Psychology appointed in 1966 (Ian Kellie Waterhouse); research and teaching staff—39; students enrolled in psychology in 1983—607. (Note: Some coursework masters' programs are taught in conjunction with the School of Education.)

Monash University, Wellington Road, Clayton, Victoria, 3168, founded 1958 (opened 1961); psychology department established between 1960 and 1969. Foundation Professor of Psychology appointed in 1964 (Ross Henry Day); research and teaching staff—14; students enrolled in psychology in 1983—235.

Murdoch University, Murdoch, Western Australia, 6150, founded 1973; postgraduate teaching began 1974; undergraduate teaching began 1975; psychology department established between 1970 and 1979. Foundation Professor of Psychology appointed in 1975 (Robert Douglass Savage); research and teaching staff—10.

University of Adelaide, GPO Box 498, Adelaide, South Australia 5001, founded 1874 (opened 1876); psychology department established between 1950 and 1959; first head of department: Arthur W. Meadows. Foundation Professor of Psychology appointed in 1959 (Malcolm Alexander Jeeves); research and teaching staff—14; students enrolled in psychology in 1983—623.

University of Melbourne, Parkville, Victoria, 3052, founded 1853; teaching began 1855; psychology department established between 1940 and 1949. Foundation Professor of Psychology appointed in 1946 (Oscar Adolph Oeser); research and teaching staff—29; students enrolled in psychology in 1983—537.

University of New England, Armidale, New South Wales, 2351, founded 1954 (formerly New England University College of the University of Sydney); psychology department established between 1930 and 1939. Foundation Professor of Psychology appointed in 1954 (Duncan Howie); research and teaching staff—36; students enrolled in psychology in 1983—894.

University of New South Wales, P.O. Box 1, Kensington, New South Wales, 2033, founded 1948 (formerly the New South Wales University of Technology); School of Psychology established between 1950 and 1959. Foundation Professor of Psychology appointed in 1953 (John Faithfull Clark); research and teaching staff—31.

University of Newcastle, Newcastle, New South Wales, 2308, founded 1965 (formerly Newcastle University College of the University of New South Wales); psychology department established between 1950 and 1959; first head of department: Donald Martin. Foundation Professor of Psychology appointed in 1965 (John Augustus Keats); research and teaching staff—22; students enrolled in psychology in 1983—218.

University of Queensland, St. Lucia, Queensland, 4067, founded 1909; psychology department established between 1950 and 1959. Foundation Professor of Psychology appointed in 1955 (Donald William McElwain); research and teaching staff—47.

University of Sydney, Sydney, New South Wales, 2006, founded 1850; Psychology department established in 1928. Foundation Professor of Psychology appointed in 1928 (Henry Tasman Lovell); research and teaching staff—74; students enrolled in psychology in 1983—1,586.

University of Tasmania, GPO Box 252C, Hobart, Tasmania, 7000, founded 1890; psychology department established in 1951. Foundation Professor of Psychology appointed in 1965 (James Alexander Cardno); research and teaching staff—13; students enrolled in psychology in 1983—132.

University of Western Australia, Nedlands, Western Australia, 6009, founded 1911; psychology department established in 1930; first head of department: Hugh L. Fowler. Foundation Professor of Psychology appointed in 1952 (Kenneth Frederick Walker); research and teaching staff—28; students enrolled in psychology in 1983—441.

University of Wollongong, P.O. Box 1144, Wollongong, New South Wales, 2500, founded 1975 (formerly the Wollongong University College of the University of New South Wales); psychology department established between 1960 and 1969. Foundation

Professor of Psychology appointed in 1973 (Alexander Marshall Clarke); research and teaching staff—14; students enrolled in psychology in 1983—185.

Australian Universities with Education Departments Offering APS Accredited Psychology Courses

Deakin University, Waurn Ponds, Victoria, 3217, founded 1974; School of Education—Education Studies Centre; psychology research and teaching staff—13; students enrolled in psychology in 1983—214.

La Trobe University, Bundoora, Victoria, 3083, founded 1964; School of Education: Centre for the Study of Teaching and Human Interaction; psychology research and teaching staff—13; students enrolled in psychology in 1983—28 (year 4 B.Ed., and research degree students).

Monash University, Wellington Road, Clayton, Victoria, 3168, founded 1958, opened 1961; Education Faculty founded in 1964; psychology research and teaching staff—9; students enrolled in psychology in 1983—45 (year 4 graduate diploma and research degree students).

Australian Institutes and Colleges Offering APS Accredited Psychology Courses

Canberra College of Advanced Education, P.O. Box 1, Belconnen, Australian Capital Territory, 2616, founded 1967; School of Education; psychology research and teaching staff—9; students enrolled in psychology in 1983—16 (master's by coursework and master's by research only).

Chisholm Institute of Technology, Caulfield East, Victoria, 3145, founded 1982 (formerly the Caulfield Institute of Technology, established 1968); Department of Applied Psychology; research and teaching staff—13; students enrolled in psychology in 1983—335.

Darling Downs Institute of Advanced Education, P.O. Darling Heights, Queensland, 4350, founded 1967. Department of Behavioural Sciences.

Gippsland Institute of Advanced Education, P.O. Box 42, Churchill, Victoria, 3842, founded 1970; Psychology Department; research and teaching staff—6; students enrolled in psychology in 1983—710.

Melbourne College of Advanced Education, Carlton, Victoria, 3052, founded 1983 (formerly Melbourne State College, established 1973; formerly Melbourne Teachers' College); Psychology Department; teaching staff—11; students enrolled in psychology in 1983—55.

Mitchell College of Advanced Education, Bathurst, New South Wales, 2795, founded 1970 (formerly Bathurst Teachers' College); School of Social Sciences and Welfare Studies (psychology is taught within this school); research and teaching staff—18; students enrolled in psychology in 1983—180.

Phillip Institute of Technology, Plenty Road, Bundoora, Victoria, 3083, founded 1982 (formerly Preston Institute of Technology, founded 1968); Psychology Department; research and teaching staff—10; students enrolled in psychology in 1983—16 (graduate diploma and research master's).

Royal Melbourne Institute of Technology, Swanston Street, Carlton, Victoria, 3052, founded 1882; classes commenced 1887; Department of Social Sciences; psychology research and teaching staff—24; students enrolled in psychology in 1983—27 (graduate diploma and research master's only).

Swinburne Institute of Technology, John Street, Hawthorn, Victoria, 3122, founded 1913 (formerly Eastern Suburbs Technical College, founded 1908); Psychology Department; research and teaching staff—7; students enrolled in psychology in 1983—519.

Western Australian Institute of Technology, Hayman Road, South Bentley, Western Australia, 6012, founded 1967; Psychology Department; research and teaching staff—12; students enrolled in psychology in 1983—213.

APPENDIX 2

Journals searched for Australian publications, 1974–1982: *American Educational Research Journal, Australian Journal of Psychology, Australian Psychologist, Behaviour Research and Therapy, British Journal of Educational Psychology, British Journal of Psychology, Child Development, Cognitive Psychology, Educational and Psychological Measurement, Journal of Abnormal Psychology, Journal of Comparative and Physiological Psychology, Journal of Cross-Cultural Psychology, Journal of Experimental Child Psychology, Journal of Experimental Psychology (Animal Behaviour Processes, General, Human Learning and Memory, Human Perception and Performance), Journal of Personality and Social Psychology, Journal of Verbal Learning and Verbal Behaviour, Learning and Motivation,* and *Psychological Review.*

Austria

Giselher Guttmann

THE NATURE AND SCOPE OF THE DISCIPLINE

The first question asked of an Austrian psychologist abroad almost always deals with Sigmund Freud or psychoanalysis. Vienna, being the cradle of depth psychology, will remain identified with this field of study. Nevertheless, the answer, today as in the past, will undoubtedly be that the psychologist's interests and research lie elsewhere, namely in empirical methods, the natural sciences, and a psychology emphasizing mathematical approaches, closely tied to biology.

It is no coincidence that Freud and the leading Viennese psychologists of the day were more or less strangers, even antagonists. Karl Bühler, head of the first Institute of Psychology at the University of Vienna, never met Freud, although the latter lived only a few blocks away from this institute. Charlotte Bühler noted in her autobiography that her husband's relations to psychoanalysis "were predominantly negative, the causes being diverse, one of the most compelling being that Karl's main interest lay in the field of Experimental Psychology" (1972, p. 29).

Karl Bühler's successor, Hubert Rohracher, head of the Viennese Institute from 1943 to 1972, concurred when he wrote, "I never heard his [Freud's] name mentioned in psychologists' circles; he was considered purely a physician with whose ideas one did not need to deal" (1972, p. 266).

This is the crux of the matter: Freud was a physician and held his lectures at the School of Medicine. It just would not have occurred to the early psychologists, the founders of the Viennese School, to view him as one of their own.

In the meantime, this perspective has been greatly modified and the contacts between the members of the Institute for Depth Psychology, whose head is Hans Strotzka, and experimental psychologists have become quite close at both the personal and the scientific level, although the Institute for Depth Psychology is still an integral part of the medical school. The situation concerning the other well-known Austrian psychotherapeutic schools such as Alfred Adler's individual psychology and Viktor Frankl's logotherapy is similar.

In defining Austrian psychology within the context of its history, the Viennese approach is seen as representative of Austrian psychology in general. Alexius Meinong (1853–1920), of the University of Graz, was best known for his "theory of objects." It is not evident from his philosophical stance that Meinong was also avidly interested in experimental psychology. He founded a privately funded research laboratory which was exceedingly well equipped according to the standards of the day. In 1886–1887, he held the first lectures on experimental psychology in Austria. Likewise Theodor Erismann in Innsbruck, during the early days of psychology, not only fostered his philosophical tendencies but demonstrated remarkable creativity as a researcher in experimental psychology. He invented the "reversal goggles" in his attempt to study the learning processes involved in visual perception.

Perhaps this tenacious penchant for empirical-experimental research is an expression of the fact that psychology at the Viennese university, founded by the Habsburg Rudolf IV in 1365 as the second German-language institution of its kind in Europe, was essentially a handmaiden to theology (*ancilla theologiae*) for centuries. Not until 1848 was this state of affairs altered, by the Thun-Hohenstein Reform. As a consequence, a critical, scientific, intellectual approach blossomed with Ernst Mach, Ludwig Boltzmann, and Moritz Schlick at its vanguard. Schlick was the leader of a small group whose purpose was to reform philosophy. Known as the Vienna Circle, and involving Hans Hahn, Viktor Kraft, Herbert Feigl, Otto Neurath, and Rudolf Carnap, the group was to found logical empiricism. Although they never attended a meeting of the Vienna Circle, Karl Popper and Ludwig Wittgenstein did have close personal contacts with its members. (Sir Karl Popper has referred to himself in personal communication as a "student of Karl Bühler.")

The most important scientific organization for Austrian psychologists, namely the Deutsche Gesellschaft für Psychologie (German Association of Psychology), is shared with psychologists from West Germany and Switzerland. This is an incorporated society established exclusively for those psychologists who are involved in research and higher education. Its headquarters are in Göttingen, Germany (FRG).

The interests of psychologists in professional practice in Austria are represented by the Berufsverband Österreichischer Psychologen, BÖP (Austrian Federation of Professional Psychologists). This group seeks legal recognition of the activities of academically educated psychologists and works to protect the public from self-proclaimed, untrained would-be psychologists.

Major Programs and Laboratories

Scientific research is primarily carried on at the following university institutes of psychology:

Department of Educational Psychology at the Institute of Education—University Graz, Hans-Sachs-Gasse 3/2, A–8010 Graz. *Fields of emphasis*: applications of learning theory to clinical practice, and behavior therapy.

Institute of Medical Psychology and Psychotherapy—University Graz, Auenbrugger-platz 22, A–8036 Graz.

Institute of Psychology—Karl-Franzens-University Graz, Schubertstrasse 6a/II, 1–8010 Graz. *Fields of emphasis*: learning processes in the context of various areas of psychology; learning-theoretical approaches to the explanation of psychophysiological regularities; and psychometrics and information theory.

Institute for Psychology—University Innsbruck, Peter-Mayr-Strasse 1a and Sonnen-burgstrasse 16, A–6020 Innsbruck. *Fields of emphasis*: traffic psychology and psycho-pharmacological problems.

Institute of Psychology—University for Educational Sciences, Klagenfurt, Universi-tätsstrasse 65–67, A–9010 Klagenfurt.

Institute for Education and Psychology—Johannes Kepler-University, Linz, A–4040 Linz/Donau, Auhof.

Institute for Psychology—University Salzburg, Akademiestrasse 22 and 26, A–5020 Salzburg. *Fields of emphasis*: clinical psychology, the psychology of music, theories of intelligence and personality, and the psychological significance of brainwave phenomena.

Institute for Psychology—University of Vienna, Liebiggasse 5, A–1010 Vienna. Includes the following four departments:

—Department of Applied and Clinical Psychology—University of Vienna. *Research areas emphasized*: autism, verbal comprehension, and interactional analyses.

—Department of Developmental and Educational Psychology—University of Vienna. *Research areas emphasized*: learning theories, the interdependence of intelligence and success in school, the observation of preschool behaviors.

—Department of General and Experimental Psychology. *Research areas emphasized*: brainwave phenomena, event-related potentials, DC potentials and behavioral capabilities, Brain-Trigger-Design (regulation of a performance situation by the examined person's own brain), regulation of behavior through biofeedback, and other self-control techniques.

—Department of Methodology and Differential Psychology—University of Vienna. *Research areas emphasized*: psychometrics, development of probabilistic models for measuring psychological phenomena, and methods of optimizing parameter estimation.

Austria's most exclusive and highest-ranking body committed to intellectual pursuit is the Austrian Academy of Sciences. Membership is on a purely elective basis and limited to a select intellectual elite. The field of psychology is represented by one member, Dr. Giselher Guttmann, professor, University of Vienna. The following institutions under the patronage of the academy are engaged in psychologically oriented research:

The Research Station for Ethnology—The Konrad Lorenz Institute, Adolf Lorenz-Gasse 2, A–3422 Greifenstein-Altenberg.

Institute for Brain Research, Neurological Institute of the University of Vienna Schwarz-spanierstrasse 17, A–1090 Vienna.

Institute for Comparative Behavioral Research, Savoyenstrasse la, A–1160 Vienna.

Other institutions not associated with universities also engage in research and offer a wide variety of psychological services. These include:

Institute for Traffic Psychology, Austrian Board of Traffic Safety, Ötzeltgasse 3, A–1031 Vienna.

Ludwig Boltzmann Institute for Learning Research, Ettenreichgasse 45a, A–1100 Vienna.

Psychological Service of the National Army (Bundesministerium für Landesverteidigung), Maria-Theresien-Kaserne, Am Fasangarten 2, A–1300 Vienna.

Psychological Services for the Elementary and Secondary Schools, Federal Ministry of Education, the Arts and Sports (Bundesministerium für Unterricht, Kunst, und Sport), for Austria in general: Minoritenplatz 5, A–1010 Vienna; for Vienna specifically: Burggasse 14–16, A–1070 Vienna.

Psychological Services in the Penal Institutions, Federal Ministry of Justice (Bundesministerium für Justiz), Museumsstrasse 7, (Palais Trautson), A–1070 Vienna.

Rehabilitation Center of the General Accident Insurance Co. (Meidling), Adalbert-Stifter-Strasse 65–67, A–1200 Vienna.

Student Counseling Service, Federal Ministry of Science and Research (Bundesministerium für Wissenschaft und Forschung) Türkenstrasse 4, A–1090 Vienna.

This is just a small sample of the many Austrian institutes providing psychological services. The ones listed are those with a scientific emphasis.

Primary Functions of Psychologists

Approximately 42 percent of all professionally active Austrian psychologists live in Greater Vienna. About 85 percent of this group consider their psychological specialty their main source of income. However, almost 40 percent of those working in this metropolitan area also have other occupations, albeit in fields related to their practice, because of the need to supplement their incomes. These complementary activities include writing, providing therapy, lecturing and teaching, testing, and counseling. More than half (52.6 percent) of the professional psychologists are employed by government agencies, not quite a fourth (23 percent) are self-employed, about 15 percent are engaged by private firms, and almost 10 percent work for an association that is supported by public funds. Because of the concentration of the population, most job opportunities are found in and around Vienna.

Funding of the Discipline

The university institutes are federally financed but their research budgets are modest. For extensive projects, the following institutions provide funds for those who have stated their cases most convincingly: Fonds zur Förderung der wissenschaftlichen Forschung (Funds for the Encouragement of Scientific Research), Forschungsförderungsfonds für die gewerbliche Wirtschaft (Funds from the Association of Industry and Trade), Ludwig Boltzmann Society, the Austrian National Bank, and the Jubiläumsfonds (Anniversary Funds).

Curriculum Models

College-preparatory high-school students are introduced to psychology by means of a survey course which is mandatory for all for students in the eleventh year of schooling. The university curriculum, enacted by parliament in 1973, is uniform for all of Austria. The academic degree of *Magister*, approximately the equivalent of a master's degree, can be attained after a minimum of ten semesters of study. The highest degree awarded is the Doctor of Philosophy.

The first stage of study (duration: four to six semesters) serves to present fundamental concepts and methods. This phase involves a total of eighty units (hours/week) in the form of lectures, practical studies, and proseminars. The emphasis is on general psychology, neuropsychology, psychometrics, developmental psychology, and differential psychology.

The second and concluding stage provides more basic knowledge of fundamentals in addition to specific training in the various fields open to professional psychologists. During this period, the curriculum is more heavily weighted toward the fields of applied, social, and clinical psychology as well as diagnostics, therapeutic methods, and the like, but it also provides for continued and intensified study in the areas offered during the first stage. Altogether eighty-four units (hours/week) are prescribed for this part of the study program which culminates in the *Diplomarbeit*, the master's thesis.

Major Journals

The only Austrian psychological journal is *Psychologie in Österreich* (Psychology in Austria), edited by the Austrian Association of Professional Psychologists (BÖP), Liebiggasse 5, A–1010 Vienna. Much Austrian psychological research work is published in the following German professional reviews: *Archiv für Psychologie* (Archive for Psychology), *Zeitschrift für Klinische Psychologie* (Journal of Clinical Psychology), *Zeitschrift für Differentielle und Diagnostische Psychologie* (Journal for Differential and Diagnostic Psychology), *Zeitschrift für Experimentelle und Angewandte Psychologie* (Journal of Experimental and Applied Psychology), *Psychologische Rundschau* (Psychological Review), and *The German Journal of Psychology—A Quarterly of Abstracts and Review Articles*.

Most Widely Used Introductory Textbooks

The following books are representative of the material presented in introductory courses at Austrian universities. The double asterisk (**) indicates books written by Austrian psychologists occupying chairs in psychology. The single asterisk (*) identifies authors who have received the doctoral degree at, or are employed by, an Austrian university. We are pleased that many of the books used in Austrian psychology are by Austrian psychologists and that some have been translated for use in other countries.

Angermaier, W. F., & Peters, M. (1973). *Bedingte Reaktionen* [Conditioned reactions]. Berlin: Springer-Verlag.

Blöschl, L. (1974). *Grundlagen und Methoden der Verhaltenstherapie* [Principles and methods of behavior therapy]. Bern: Hans Huber.**

Boerner, K. (1980). *Das psychologische Gutachten* [Psychological expertise]. Weinheim-Basel: Beltz Verlag.

Brenner, C. (1972). *Grundzüge der Psychoanalyse* [An elementary textbook of psychoanalysis]. Frankfurt am Main: Fischer Verlag.

Clauss, G., & Ebner, H. (1978). *Grundlagen der Statistik* [Fundamentals of statistics]. Berlin: Volk und Wissen–Volkseigener Verlag.

Davison, G. C., & Neale, J. M. (1982). *Klinische Psychologie* [Clinical psychology]. Munich: Urban & Schwarzenberg.

Faller, A. (1976). *Der Körper des Menschen* [The human body]. Stuttgart: DTB-Georg Thieme Verlag.

Fischer, G. (1974). *Einführung in die Theorie psychologischer Tests* [Introduction to the theory of psychological tests]. Bern: Hans Huber.**

Gage, N. L., & Berliner, D. C. (1979). *Pädagogische Psychologie* [Educational psychology] (Vols. 1, 2). Munich: Urban & Schwarzenberg.

Guttmann, G. (1972). *Einführung in die Neuropsychologie* [Introduction to neuropsychology]. Bern: Hans Huber.**

Guttmann, G. (1983). *Lehrbuch der Neuropsychologie* [Textbook of neuropsychology]. Bern: Hans Huber.**

Herkner, W. (1981). *Einführung in die Sozialpsychologie* [Introduction to social psychology]. Bern: Hans Huber.*

Hilgard, E. R., & Bower, G. H. (1966). *Theorien des Lernens* [Theories of learning]. Stuttgart: Ernst Klett Verlag.

Hofstätter, P. R. (1977). *Persönlichkeitsforschung* [Researching personality]. Stuttgart: Alfred Kröner Verlag.

Innerhofer, P. (1981). *Beratung und Begutachtung im Bereich der verhaltensgestörten Pädagogik* [Counseling and diagnosing in the pedagogy of the behaviorally disturbed]. Kurseinheit 2: *Verhaltensbeobachtung und Verhaltensanalyse* [Observance and analysis of behavior]. Fernuniversität, Gesamthochschule Hagen.**

Krech, D., & Crutchfield, R. S. (1976). *Grundlagen der Psychologie* [Elements of psychology]. Weinheim-Basel: Beltz Verlag.

Lindsay, P. H., & Norman, D. A. (1977). *Human information processing: An introduction to psychology*. New York: Academic Press.

Meili, R., & Rohracher, H. (1972). *Lehrbuch der experimentellen Psychologie* [Textbook of experimental psychology]. Bern: Hans Huber.**

Mittenecker, E., & Raab, E. (1973). *Informationstheorien für Psychologen* [Information theory for psychologists]. Göttingen: Hogrefe.**

Mussen, P. H., Conger, J. J., & Kagan, J. (1976). *Lehrbuch der Kinderpsychologie* [Child development and personality]. Stuttgart: Ernst Klett Verlag.

Pauli, R., & Arnold, W. (1972). *Experimentelles Praktikum* [Experimental practicum] (Vol. 1); *Diagnostisches Praktikum* [Diagnostic practicum] (Vol. 2). Stuttgart: Gustav Fischer Verlag.

Pawlik, K. (1971). *Dimensionen des Verhaltens* [The dimensions of behaviour]. Bern: Hans Huber.*

Rohracher, H. (1976). *Einführung in die Psychologie* [Introduction to psychology]. Munich: Urban & Schwarzenberg.**

Roth, E., Oswald, W. D., & Daumenlang, K. (1980). *Intelligenz* [Intelligence]. Stuttgart: Kohlhammer.

Schadé, J. P. (1977). *Die Funktion des Nervensystems* [The function of the nervous system]. Stuttgart: Gustav Fischer Verlag.

Strotzka, H. (Ed.). (1978). *Fallstudien zur Psychotherapie* [Case studies in psychotherapy]. Munich: Urban & Schwarzenberg.**

Strotzka, H. (Ed.). (1979). *Psychotherapie: Grundlagen, Verfahren, Indikationen* [Psychotherapy: Bases, methods, indications]. Munich: Urban & Schwarzenberg.**

Strotzka, H. (Ed.). (1980). *Der Psychotherapeut im Spannungsfeld der Institutionen* [The psychotherapist and the often charged dealings with institutions]. Munich: Urban & Schwarzenberg.**

Weinert, F. E., Graumann, C. F., Heckhausen, H., Hofer, M., et al. (Eds.). (1974). *Pädagogische Psychologie* (Vols. 1, 2) [Educational psychology]. Frankfurt am Main: Funk-Kolleg, Fischer Taschenbuch Verlag.

Zimbardo, P. G. (1979). *Essentials of psychology and life.* Palo Alto, CA: Scott, Foresman.

Availability of *Psychological Abstracts* and Citation Indexes

The *Psychological Abstracts* as well as the most important periodicals are available at the libraries of the institutes and at the main library facilities of the universities. The great majority are American publications; but many are Austrian, English, and German, and several are French, Hungarian, Scandinavian, Swiss, or other, some dating back to the turn of the century.

The main library of the University of Vienna is connected to the international data bank "Psyndex." Via the German Institute for Medical Documentation and Information, where Psyndex is implemented, the Austrian universities connect to the data base "Psycinfo," which is compatible with Psyndex.

Major Needs

The lack of a legal definition of the title, responsibilities, and rights of academically trained psychologists in Austria overshadows any other problem. The title "psychologist" is not protected by law in Austria; therefore, any fly-by-night can proclaim him- or herself a "psychologist," regardless of his or her training, and set up practice. Partly for this reason, the psychologist also has no legal mandate to offer therapy, an activity reserved for physicians, and according to present law he or she is relegated to a subordinate role in this process and assigned the title of counselor. The age-old separation of psychology from medicine, as indicated at the beginning of this chapter, continues and has become a bane to professional psychologists as well as to the ever-growing public seeking help from qualified practitioners. For thirty years the Federation of Professional Psychologists, abetted by an increasing number of over-burdened psychiatrists, has been urging parliament to adopt laws that reflect the public reality as well as the rightful needs of academically trained psychologists, all to no avail.

Relationships with Other Disciplines

In the post–World War II period, the fellows of the various psychological institutes have developed surprisingly harmonious and congenial relationships, particularly with the medical profession which they had hitherto persistently neglected and which had neglected them. These now lively interdisciplinary contacts are manifested in shared research and frequent collaboration in applying findings to the needs of the public. Such is the case especially in the fields of psychotherapy, psychiatry, pathology, psychopharmacology, neurology, neurosurgery, neurophysiology, and neurobiochemistry. Certainly the fact that Hubert Rohracher's successor, G. Guttmann, as long-term former head of the Viennese Institute, has had extensive academic training as a biologist has been significant in bringing about this merging of efforts and interests.

Additional collaborative work takes place regularly involving developmental psychologists and their colleagues at the Institutes for Education. This is a natural continuation of time-tested cooperation, since educational psychology in Austria began in those institutes.

Unique to Austria, as far as I know, is a common organization for all psychotherapeutic associations. After having spent years in preparing for its inception, Hans Strotzka (head of the Institute for Depth Psychology) in 1982 was able to bring about an organization representing the interests common to all of the various member groups and to stimulate and make possible communication among them. This was no mean task, for the associations are themselves in many cases quite heterogeneous. But now psychoanalysts, psychologists, client-centered therapists, Adlerians, behavior therapists, members of the clergy, social workers, and other helping professionals have a forum as well as a common identification which enables them to organize their services in a rational way.

MAJOR TRENDS AND INFLUENCES
SINCE WORLD WAR II

In Austria, the field of psychology did not really blossom prior to World War II. All of the previously mentioned organizations were founded in the postwar period. Very few students majored in psychology before the end of the war, but following the conflict, enrollments increased and growth has continued. This resulted in a significant increase in the membership of the Association of Professional Psychologists.

The most important institution supporting scientific research, the Forschungsfonds, was established in 1967 by parliamentary act and its existence is ensured by federal law. The initial endowment for its first fiscal year was a relatively modest 31 million Austrian schillings, but in the meantime it has grown considerably to about 200 million schillings per annum. Another major contributor to the funding of scientific research, the Ludwig Boltzmann Society, constituted in 1960, now awards about 55 million Austrian schillings annually.

Every graduate of an Austrian secondary school with a college-preparatory background has free access to the universities. There are no restrictions, quotas, or mandatory GPAs (grade point averages); and entrance examinations are not administered. Following the international trend, more and more entrants to the universities choose psychology as their major. In spite of excessive enrollments in psychology, no plans are under way to restrict native Austrians from majoring in psychology. Only small numbers of foreign students, however, are admitted.

Research and Theory

Psychology is experimental in emphasis at all Austrian universities and research centers. The psychometric aspects of the field, though, vary according to the needs of the different regions. The program of study nationwide is determined by federal law, a fact which guarantees a relatively homogeneous scientific instructional orientation best characterized as theoretical/experimental/methodological.

The Viennese School has always been devoted to investigating the biological bases of psychic phenomena and continues to uphold this tradition. Increasingly, emphasis has shifted from inquiries of a purely theoretical nature to the application of findings for practical purposes. For quite some time we have been studying brainwave parameters of performance. The cortical DC potential has proven to be a remarkably sensitive indicator of on-going cerebral activity. The possibility of improving performance has even been successfully demonstrated in the classroom. For four years now, pupils in elementary and secondary schools have been learning to usher in the decisive "teachable moment" concomitant with specific, crucial phases of instruction by virtue of techniques of self-control. Consolidation is then assured by carrying out particular learning strategies, involving repetition for optimal results. This model, developed by Guttmann and his coworkers, exemplifies the combination of theory and practice typical of the work being done in Vienna.

G. Fischer and his staff have made widely acclaimed contributions to the field of mathematical psychology, concentrating their efforts on the development of probabilistic models applicable to the measurement of change.

Worldwide Influence

Subsequent to 1945, the experimental tradition of the Viennese School of psychology, initiated by Karl Bühler, was carried on by Hubert Rohracher, one of the central figures in experimental psychology in the German-speaking countries. He was instrumental in creating the Austrian's role of providing a bridge or link between East and West and kept close professional, as well as personal, contacts with many colleagues in Eastern Europe. Another influential Austrian psychological researcher (now professor emeritus) is Ivo Kohler, whose studies on perception (reversal goggles) were widely acclaimed.

Although Konrad Lorenz, Nobel Prize laureate (medicine) of 1973, did not study psychology formally, he developed close scientific and personal friendships with psychologists all over the world. His long-standing affiliation with the Department of Experimental Psychology at the University of Vienna has resulted in many enriching exchanges.

It would serve little purpose to list those scientists presently active at the Austrian universities, all of whom have close contacts with the international community. Instead, mention will be made of some of those who have left Austria and are working abroad in the spirit of our traditions. Representative of this large group three deserve special mention: Lienert, Pawlik, and Toman.

Gustav Lienert studied psychology and medicine in Vienna and graduated with degrees in both fields. He left for Marburg, West Germany, and is now professor in Nürnberg and honorary professor in Vienna, having been at several universities (Hamburg, Düsseldorf) in the interim. He has gained considerable reknown in the area of psychological research methodology and written pioneering textbooks on statistical techniques, while at the same time continuing research in the field of psychopharmacology.

Kurt Pawlik graduated from the University of Vienna, where he continued his academic career to become dozent (associate professor). He then spent a sabbatical in the United States with Cattell. He returned to Europe, assuming a chair in psychology at the University of Hamburg and is still active there. The union of methodological and biological interests best characterizes his research. He has contributed extensively to the field of psychometrics, particularly in relation to factor analysis, and to biological psychology in the areas of brainwave phenomena and the biochemistry of learning.

Walter Toman, named assistant professor under Rohracher, completed psychoanalytic training but chose to do experimental research. After spending several years in the United States, he was summoned to Germany (Erlangen, Nürnberg) where he achieved the designation of professor.

Future Directions

In the context of Austrian traditions, the most fruitful approaches in the future should involve more cooperation with mathematical statistics and biology. It is also essential that no division be drawn between theoretical research and applications of research findings. It is in fact paramount that the results of systematic investigations be readily available for application to everyday problems. We in Austria have met with notable success in our endeavor to achieve this goal.

Austria's role as a neutral zone between East and West should also continue to be emphasized; in this sense, we hope for a continuation of the close contacts Austrian scientific psychologists have with members of the scientific communities of other countries.

NOTE

Thanks are due to Susan Etlinger for her advice and help and for translating this manuscript into English.

REFERENCES

Bühler, C. (1972). Charlotte Bühler. In L. J. Pongratz, W. Traxel, & E. G. Wehner (Eds.), *Psychologie in Selbstdarstellung* [Psychology in self-portrayal] (Chap. 1). Bern: Hans Huber.

Rohracher, H. (1972). Hubert Rohracher. In L. J. Pongratz, W. Traxel, & E. G. Wehner (Eds.), *Psychologie in Selbstdarstellung* [Psychology in self-portrayal] (Chap. 9). Bern: Hans Huber.

SUGGESTED READINGS

Eschbach, A. (1985). Karl Bühler. Bericht über sein Wirken an der Universität Wien von 1922–1938 [Karl Bühler. Report on his activity at the University of Vienna from 1922 to 1938]. In D. Albert (Ed.), *Bericht über den 34. Kongress der Deutschen Gesellschaft für Psychologie in Wien 1984, Bd.I: Grundlagenforschung.* Göttingen: Hogrefe.

Fischer, G. H. (1985). Geschichte des Wiener Instituts für Psychologie—Einleitende Worte zur Vortragsreihe [The history of the Viennese Institute for Psychology: Introductory words to the lecture series]. In D. Albert (Ed.), *Bericht über den 34. Kongress der Deutschen Gesellschaft für Psychologie in Wien 1984, Bd.I: Grundlagenforschung.* Göttingen: Hogrefe.

Fischer, K. R. (1985). Aus dem Wiener Kreis—Egon Brunswiks Psychologie als Einheitswissenschaft [From the Vienna Circle—Egon Brunswik's psychology as unified science]. In D. Albert (Ed.), *Bericht über den 34. Kongress der Deutschen Gesellschaft für Psychologie in Wien 1984, Bd.I: Grundlagenforschung.* Göttingen: Hogrefe.

Huber, H. P. (1985). Erlebnispsychologie auf biologischer Grundlage: Das Lebenswerk von Hubert Rohracher [The biological basis of experimental psychology: Hubert Rohracher's lifework]. In D. Albert (Ed.), *Bericht über den 34. Kongress der Deutschen Gesellschaft für Psychologie in Wien 1984, Bd.I: Grundlagenforschung.* Göttingen: Hogrefe.

Mittenecker, E. (1985). Egon Brunswiks Beiträge zur Theorie und Methodologie der

Psychologie [Egon Brunswik's contributions to the theory and methodology of psychology]. In D. Albert (Ed.), *Bericht über den 34. Kongress der Deutschen Gesellschaft für Psychologie in Wien 1984, Bd.I: Grundlagenforschung*. Göttingen: Hogrefe.

Neurath, P. (1985). Paul F. Lazarsfeld (1901–1976). Vom Wiener Psychologen zum amerikanischen Soziologen [Paul F. Lazarsfeld (1901–1976): From Viennese psychologist to American sociologist]. In D. Albert (Ed.), *Bericht über den 34. Kongress der Deutschen Gesellschaft für Psychologie in Wien 1984, Bd.I: Grundlagenforschung*. Göttingen: Hogrefe.

Pawlik, K. (1985). Das Wiener Psychologische Institut: Historische und persönliche Reflexionen zur "Wiener Schule" [The Viennese Institute for Psychology: Historical and personal reflections on the "Viennese School"]. In D. Albert (Ed.), *Bericht über den 34. Kongress der Deutschen Gesellschaft für Psychologie in Wien 1984, Bd.I: Grundlagenforschung*. Göttingen: Hogrefe.

Rohracher, H. (1976). Austria. In V. S. Sexton and H. Misiak (Eds.), *Psychology around the world*. Monterey, CA: Brooks/Cole.

Schenk-Danzinger, L. (1985). Werk und Bedeutung von Charlotte Bühler [The work and significance of Charlotte Bühler]. In D. Albert (Ed.), *Bericht über den 34. Kongress der Deutschen Gesellschaft für Psychologie in Wien 1984, Bd.I: Grundlagenforschung*. Göttingen: Hogrefe.

Schultz, D. (1975). *A history of modern psychology*. New York: Academic Press. (See Chapter 13—"Psychoanalysis: The beginnings"—and Chapter 14—"Psychoanalysis: After the founding"—for a review of a field that has not been considered a mainstay of academic psychology in Austria.)

Zusne, L. (1984). *Biographical dictionary of psychology*. Westport, CT: Greenwood Press. (Refer to Appendix C, "Austria" (pp. 513–514), and then to each psychologist of interest listed alphabetically.)

Brazil

Angela M. B. Biaggio

INTRODUCTION: HISTORICAL OVERVIEW

Psychology in Brazil sprang out of philosophy, education, and the medical sciences. An analysis of these influences as well as more recent social, political, and economic factors is essential to understanding how psychology developed in this country during the post–World War II period (1946–1983).

Brazilian psychology originated within philosophy. Pfromm Netto (1981), citing Martins (1950, 1956, 1969, 1972, 1975), Amora (1948), and others, traces psychology's development in Brazil from philosophy and religion, linking it to Western thought via the Portuguese, who controlled the country from the time of discovery (1500) until independence (1822) and continued to have a strong bearing on Brazilian culture long after.

The second influence on psychology in Brazil came from the field of education. Prior to 1934, there were no Brazilian universities although the country did have some independent faculties or schools, mainly in the fields of law, philosophy, engineering, and the medical sciences. The first psychological laboratories in Brazil were established at normal schools for teachers. Many contributions to what is now known as educational psychology were made in these centers. M. B. Lourenço Filho, Noemy da Silveira Rudolfer, and Helena Antipoff were the major figures in this area.

Lourenço Filho, among his many distinguished accomplishments, founded Instituto Nacional de Estudos e Pesquisas (INEP) [National Institute for Pedagogical Studies] and is the author of a reading-readiness test widely employed in Brazil and known as the "ABC" test in several other countries. Noemy Rudolfer was the head of the psychology laboratory at the Normal School in São Paulo, later called the Laboratory of Educational Psychology of the Institute of Education, and still later the Laboratory of the Chair of Educational Psychology of the Faculty of Philosophy, Sciences, and Letters of the University of São Paulo. Helena Antipoff (1892–1974), a former assistant to Claparède, established the Pestalozzi Society of Brazil and became the leader of an important group of psychologists and educators concerned with the problems of exceptional children. Her influence spread from Belo Horizonte, Minas Gerais, to other parts of Brazil.

Important works of foreign psychologists written during the first half of the century were translated into Portuguese. These included publications by French psychologists Piéron, Claparède, Binet and Simon, Wallon, Guillaumé, and Decroly and such Americans as Dewey and Thorndike. According to Cabral (1950), the "normalist" era preceded the university era in Brazilian psychology. (As a personal note, when I did my doctoral work in the United States in the mid–1960s, some of my professors were surprised to find that my mother had studied Piaget in a normal school in Brazil in the 1930s.)

The external influences on Brazilian psychology in its early years came primarily from Europe and were mainly French. They did not become predominantly American until the 1960s (Biaggio & Benkö, 1975).

The third influence on psychology derived from the medical sciences, especially psychoneurology and social medicine (Lourenço Filho, 1955). Many valuable contributions were made by Brazilian medical doctors in these fields. When the first university courses in psychology were established in the late 1950s, and at least during the two decades that followed, most professors were medical doctors, especially psychiatrists and psychoanalysts. This led to an overemphasis on clinical psychology and psychotherapy as the ultimate goal of psychologists. (Biaggio, 1982). As Eliza Velloso (1970, p. 12) pointed out:

In countries where Psychology has reached greater maturity, the psychologist's noble task is undoubtedly research; this is the scientific attribution for which the psychologist is better prepared than his collaborators in the field of mental health and which confers upon him a high status. Among us, however, research is rejected by many and the practice of clinical psychology, more precisely, psychotherapy, is idealized.

In the same vein Velloso, in 1979, noted:

Among psychologists in Rio, interest in psychoanalysis has come to prevail overwhelmingly in the last fifteen years, reaching the proportions of a fad, which can eventually even harm the essential seriousness of psychotherapeutic work of any kind; there has developed a serious, non-scientific prejudice against any technique that is not psychoanalytic, and there exists radical, vehement partisanism among Freudian, Kleinian, culturalist, and other orientations.

Another landmark of Brazilian psychology in the applied field was the establishment of the Institute for Personnel Selection and Guidance (ISOP) of the Foundation Getulio Vargas (FGV) in 1947, in Rio de Janeiro, directed during its first seventeen years by Emilio Mira y Lopez (1896–1964). Its activities range from personnel selection and vocational guidance to applied research activities, publishing the most important national psychology journal, and offering graduate programs, including the only doctoral program in Rio de Janeiro (one of the three now available in the country).

University-level psychology courses in Brazil were first offered during the 1950s at the Catholic University (PUC) of Rio de Janeiro in 1953 under the leadership of Hans L. Lippmann and Antonius Benkö, and at the University of São Paulo (USP) in 1958. These courses were regulated and given formal status with psychology recognized as a profession in 1962 (Law 4119). Graduate training in psychology began in 1966.

NATURE AND SCOPE OF THE DISCIPLINE

Definition of Psychology/Psychological

Conceptions of psychology in Brazil vary. To those psychologists close to the philosophical influence, psychology is the study of the soul, spiritual things, and judgmental processes. To those connected with education, psychology is intertwined with pedagogy. And to those identified with psychiatry, psychology is equated with the treatment of the emotionally disturbed. The third position is perhaps the most common currently, and the psychoanalytic perspective is considered by many students, laymen, and even some professionals as the most appropriate view of the human psychological state. At the same time, since a large percentage of psychology books in Brazil are translations of European or North American works, the definition of psychology as the science of behavior is known though not necessarily accepted by most students. At a formal level, Law 4119 defines the attributes of clinical, educational, and industrial-organizational psychologists; therefore, many people assume that all psychologists must fit into one of these categories.

Organizational Structure

There are basically three types of psychological organizations in Brazil, all of them started rather recently since the law acknowledging psychology as a profession and as a university degree program dates back only to 1962.

First, there is the Federal Council of Psychology and eight Regional Councils of Psychology. These councils were created by Law 5766 in 1971; they are administratively and financially autonomous. The functions of the councils include determining the orientation of the field, serving a disciplinary role, monitoring the professional practice of psychology, and promulgating ethical principles.

The Federal Council of Psychology controls the Regional Councils. The latter have their members elected by psychologists whereas the members of the Federal Council are elected by delegates of the Regional Councils. The main responsibilities of the Federal Council are issuing the resolutions and instructions necessary for the enforcement of relevant laws and defining the competency requirements of psychologists. The Federal Council also functions as a court of professional ethics and acts as a consultative agency in matters relating to psychology.

The Regional Councils have analogous functions. In order to work, all applied psychologists must register and pay annual dues. University professors and researchers do not need to register unless they teach practical subjects or supervise students in applied settings. The states, regions, and territories associated with the Federal Council and the eight Regional Councils are:

1st Region: Federal District, States of Acre, Amazonas, Goiás, Pará, Rondônia, and federal territories of Amapá and Roraima

2nd Region: Alagoas, Ceará, Maranhão, Paraíba, Pernambuco, Piauí, Rio Grande do Norte, and Federal Territory of Fernando de Noronha

3rd Region: Bahia and Sergipe

4th Region: Minas Gerais and Espírito Santo

5th Region: Rio de Janeiro

6th Region: São Paulo, Mato Grosso, and Mato Grosso do Sul

7th Region: Rio Grande de Sul and Santa Catarina

8th Region: Paraná

The second type of organization includes various associations or societies. These are more academic in nature with their general goal being to promote psychological knowledge and ensure contact among psychologists. Some of them, such as the Associação Brasileira de Psicologia Aplicada (ABPA) of Rio de Janeiro, publish journals and promote congresses, conferences, and seminars. There is no national association equivalent to the American Psychological Association, but participation in some of the regional associations is high. The Associação Brasileira de Psicologia (ABP) of São Paulo represents the country in the International Union of Psychological Science (IUPsyS). The names and addresses of the three major associations follow:

Associação Brasileira de Psicologia, Cx. Postal, 11454—Cidade Universitária—Butantã, 05508—São Paulo, SP.

Associação Brasileira de Psicologia Aplicada, Rua da Candelária, 6–3ọ. andar, 20091—Rio de Janeiro, RJ.

Sociedade de Psicologia de Ribeirão Preto, Caixa Postal, 1006, 14100—Ribeirão Preto, SP.

The newest organization, the National Association of Graduate Study in Psychology, coordinates the activities of the graduate programs and research centers in psychology. This association was founded in 1983 and its first board was elected during the annual meeting of the Brazilian Society for the Advancement of Science (SBPC) in Belém, Pará. The objectives of this association are to stimulate research in psychology by fostering scientific training, publishing scientific papers, financing research, and encouraging cooperation among researchers and institutions. Members of this association are not individuals but institutions.

The third category of psychological organization consists of the *Sindicatos* or "unions," which have only recently come into being. These try to protect the rights of psychologists and promote better salaries and other benefits. They include:

Sindicato dos Psicólogos do Estado do Paraná, Rua Angelo Sampaio, 1344, 80000— Curitiba, PR.

Sindicato dos Psicólogos do Estado do Rio de Janeiro, Rua do Catete, 142—3ọ. andar, 22220—Rio de Janeiro, RJ.

Sindicato dos Psicólogos do Estado de São Paulo, Av. Brig. Faria Lima, 1084—2ọ. andar, 01452—São Paulo, SP.

Sindicato dos Psicólogos do Rio Grande do Sul, Rua Vigário José Inácio, 371 S/1904, Galeria do Rosário, 90000—Porto Alegre, RS.

Major Programs

The degree of psychologist, which entitles one to engage in professional practice, involves a five-year undergraduate program. There are over 100 undergraduate programs in Brazil, although many of them offer only the first four years and lead to the equivalent of a bachelor's degree. This degree entitles one to teach psychology at the secondary level but not to practice professionally.

In 1966 the first programs leading to masters' degrees were created and a few years later (1974) the first doctoral programs opened up. It was, however, possible to obtain a doctorate in psychology in Brazil even prior to the university reform of 1966 by writing a doctoral dissertation.

The following departments have graduate programs in psychology:

Universidade de Brasília, Departamento de Psicologia, Brasília, DF.

Pontifícia Universidade Católica de Campinas, Departamento de Psicologia, Campinas, SP.

Universidade Federal da Paraíba, Departamento de Psicologia, João Pessoa, Paraíba.

Universidade Federal de Pernambuco, Departamento de Psicologia, Recife— Pernambuco.

Pontifícia Universidade Católica do Rio Grande do Sul, Instituto de Psicologia, Porto Alegre, RS.

Universidade Federal do Rio Grande do Sul, Pós-Graduação em Educação, Porto Alegre, RS.

Universidade Católica do Rio de Janeiro, Departamento de Psicologia, Rio de Janeiro, RJ.

Universidade Federal do Rio de Janeiro, Instituto de Psicologia, Rio de Janeiro, RJ.

Universidade Gama Filho, Departamento de Psicologia, Rio de Janeiro, RJ.

Fundação Getúlio Vargas, Centro de Pós-Graduação em Psicologia Aplicada, Pr. de Botafogo, Rio de Janeiro, RJ.

Instituto Metodista de Ensino Superior, Departamento de Psicologia, São Paulo, SP.

Pontifícia Universidade Católica de São Paulo, Departamênto de Psicologia, São Paulo, SP.

Universidade de São Paulo, Instituto de Psicologia, São Paulo, SP.

In addition, Ribeirão Preto is an excellent research center though it has no degree programs, and the graduate program in education of the Federal University of Rio Grande do Sul, a facility where much research in educational psychology is conducted, offers both master's degrees and doctorates.

Primary Functions of Psychologists

According to Law 4119 (1962), individuals who hold a psychologist diploma are entitled to teach psychology courses that are part of psychology curricula and engage in private practice. It is the function of psychologists to utilize their professional skills for (a) psychological diagnosis, (b) guidance and personnel selection, (c) psycho-educational orientation, and (d) finding solutions for problems of adjustment.

In 1974, the Federal Council of Psychologists issued a resolution adopting the following definition of psychologist from the International Labor Organization (OIT), published in 1968, as the basic description of the profession, translated by the author from the Portuguese (Oficina Intl. del Trabajo, *Classificación Internacional uniforme de occupaciones*, revised edition, 1982, Genebra, OIT, 1970):

A psychologist: a) studies the behavior and mental mechanisms of human beings, conducts research about psychological problems that are relevant to the field of medical sciences, education, and industry, and recommends adequate treatment; b) plans and performs experiments and studies on human beings, in order to determine mental and physical characteristics; c) analyzes the influence of hereditary, environment, and other factors on the mental structure and the behavior of individuals; d) performs diagnoses, treatment, and the prevention of emotional and personality disturbances, as well as of problems associated with adjusting to the social and work milieu; e) constructs and administers psychological tests in order to determine intelligence, personality, aptitudes, attitudes, and other characteristics and interprets the data collected and makes pertinent recommendations.

A psychologist may specialize in one of the particular applications of psychology such as the diagnosis and treatment of mental disorders, the psychological problems of children, and psychological problems of a professional nature such as those related to the selection, training, and orientation of workers. (p. 102)

Because of recurrent problems associated with professional overlap among psychology, psychiatry, and school counseling, the Federal Council of Psychology issued Resolution #008182 in 1982, defining key terms (psychological methods, psychological diagnosis, professional orientation, professional selection, psychopedagogical orientation, and solutions to problems of adjustment) mentioned in Law 4119 which established the functions of psychologists.

Funding of the Discipline

Funds for the discipline are scarce. Support of graduate programs comes primarily from Brazilian government sources such as the Coordination of Improvement of Higher Teaching (CAPES) and the National Research Council (CNPq). In educational psychology, some money is provided by the National Institute for Pedagogical Studies (INEP), while in clinical psychology, support, mostly for applied activities, derives from the Ministry of Health and the Ministry of Social Security (INAMPS).

Curriculum Models

The Federal Council of Education issued Resolution #403, which established the minimum curriculum for psychology programs in the spirit of Law 4119. The following subjects are required for the bachelor's degree: physiology, statistics, general and experimental psychology, personality, social psychology, and psychopathology.

For the degree of psychologist, a course in the techniques of psychological examination and counseling as well as professional ethics is also required. In addition, students must take one of the following courses: psychology of the exceptional person, group dynamics and human relations, therapeutic pedagogy, school psychology and learning problems, theories and techniques of psychotherapy, personnel selection and guidance, or industrial psychology. Also mandated are 500 hours of supervised practicum.

Each program usually involves about 200 credits distributed over approximately five years and may demand subjects beyond those stipulated by the Federal Council on Education. Some religious universities, for example, require several semesters of theology. Others specify mathematics, developmental psychology, and so forth.

The Federal Council of Education also regulates graduate programs. An important landmark for graduate work was Resolution #977/65 (Rapporteur: Newton Sucupira). Graduate work is now based on the American tradition with a two-stage program (master's and Ph.D.) following undergraduate education. The need for the development of scholars to teach and carry out research is recognized. Thus, the function of the university is to create new knowledge as well as disseminate information.

There are two meanings of the term "graduate work" in Brazil: *sensu stricto* and *sensu lato*. The first refers to academic programs that lead to a master's or doctoral degree. The second refers to courses of specialization that are more specific in scope and are geared toward professional and technical competence rather than the training of scientists.

The Federal Council of Education defines graduate work but only has jurisdiction over courses that lead to a professional degree. It is also important to note that the council may accredit courses though not interfere with their organization and content.

As indicated in Resolution #977/65, the master's program must take at least one year, and doctoral programs involve a minimum of two years. Both programs include regular courses, seminars, and a thesis. For the doctoral degree, an "original contribution to knowledge" is required; whereas the master's degree thesis must show mastery of a particular topic. Knowledge of a foreign language, usually English or French, is required. The master's degree is not a prerequisite for doctoral work but is generally attained. An undergraduate degree in the field of intended graduate study is not necessary but work should be in a related field. Graduate programs are required to include both a major and a minor field.

Major Journals

The most widely recognized psychology journal in Brazil is *Arquivos Brasileiros de Psicologia* [Brazilian Archives of Psychology] published by ISOP/FGV and issued regularly since 1948. Other journals include *Boletim de Psicologia* [Psychological Bulletin] (Sociedade de Psicologia de São Paulo); *Boletim* [Bulletin] (Rio de Janeiro); *Boletim* [Bulletin] (Society of Psychology of Rio Grande do Sul); *Revista de Psicologia normal e patológica* [Review of Normal and Abnormal Psychology] (São Paulo); *Psicologia: Teoria e Pesquisa* [Psychology: Theories of Practice] (University of Brasília); *Alter* (Brasília); and *Psico* [Psyche] (Catholic University of Rio Grande do Sul). A few of these publications, however, have been discontinued, others are published infrequently, and some do not have a wide audience.

In 1983, the Federal Council of Psychology started publication of *Psicologia, Ciência e Profissão* [Psychology: Science and Profession]. *Psicologia Atual* [Current Psychology] is a new journal in the style of *Psychology Today* devised for lay people and students. Nevertheless, the journal is of high quality and timely. *Cadernos de Pesquisa* [Research Notebooks] (Fundação Carlos Chagas) is an educational journal that publishes much psychological material.

The Most Widely Used Textbooks

Textbooks are seldom used in psychology and the social sciences in Brazil. Both faculty and students feel that textbooks standardize information and inhibit individual interests, library usage, and creativity. Rather, students are given a list of approximately twenty sources from which to choose for each subject they take. Some books, however, are recommended most frequently. In my experience, the following authors and books are popular:

Translations of foreign authors: Hall and Lindzey's *Theories of Personality*; Hilgard's *Theories of Learning*; all the works of Freud and Piaget; and many of the publications by Helen Bee, Mussen, Conger and Kagan, Anne Anastasi (*Psychological Testing*), Carl Rogers, Skinner, Keller and Schoenfeld, Foucault, and Lacan.

Brazilian authors: Aroldo Rodrigues, *Psicologia Social* [Social Psychology]; Angela Biaggio, *Psicologia do Desenvolvimento* [Developmental Psychology]; Maria Helena Novaes, *Psicologia Escolar* [School Psychology]; and Odette Lourenço van Kolck, *Testes Psicológicos* [Psychological Tests].

Availability of Abstracts

The only available general abstracts are those issued by CAPES, with summaries of master's and doctoral theses approved by Brazilian programs. The periodical *Arquivios Brasileiros de Psicologia* is abstracted by APA's *Psychological Abstracts*.

Major Needs

It is difficult to identify the major needs of psychology in a country where the field has only recently become a science because there are so many deficiencies, all related to the social, political, and economic context. Let us focus on three issues: the professional nature of our university tradition; the democratization of university education beginning in the early 1970s and the consequent proliferation of psychology courses without sufficiently prepared faculty; and the lack of financial resources for libraries, research, and adequate salaries for faculty.

Paim (1983) criticizes the deeply rooted Brazilian tradition that universities exist solely to prepare people for professions. There is little conception of the university as a place where research is conducted and where knowledge is pursued for the sake of knowledge. "Our tragedy," says Paim, "is the reduction of knowledge to a handful of professions." This outlook manifests itself both in the spirit of Law 4119 which defined the profession of psychology and in the "minimum curriculum" required by the Federal Council of Education. Most of the faculty who train the new generation of psychologists are in applied fields and work only part-time at the universities. Except in the graduate programs, little research is conducted and, even there, for many the master's thesis is the only research ever conducted. In this context, there is a major need for the stimulation of interest in research, theorizing, and basic knowledge. A great contradiction exists in the attitude of many Brazilian psychologists because they are very critical of importing foreign theories and models but want an overemphasis on application and relevance. However, if everyone in Brazil wants to do applied work, theories and basic knowledge will certainly continue to be imported.

While this problem has its roots in our oldest traditions, the second issue, the democratization of the university and consequent proliferation of psychology programs, is closely related to the recent political, social and economic history of the country. The government which came to power in 1964 inaugurated an era that became known as the "Brazilian economic miracle." Huge loans from banks in the United States and Europe allowed industry to develop. More money was allocated to education. University degrees, which previously were the privilege of an elite comprising less than 1 percent of the population, became more common. In a penetrating analysis of the state of psychology in Brazil, Angelini (1975) pointed out that in São Paulo, by the early 1970s, there were already twenty-eight psychology programs. Angelini also discussed resulting problems such as the ensuing surplus of psychologists, the difficulties involved in maintaining quality teaching, and the need for specialization. The preference of Brazilian psychologists for private clinical practice poses a particularly serious problem since this is an area of psychology that should require graduate training and a period of close supervision. In addition, the overemphasis of private clinical practice restricts the services of psychologists to a socioeconomic elite. Recently, however, community psychology, preventive programs, and a serious concern with problems of the lower classes have emerged in Brazil. Students and younger psychologists are very conscious of the need for more flexible curricula and programs appropriate to the country's needs.

Relationships with Other Disciplines

As mentioned before, Brazilian psychology had its origins in philosophy, education, and psychiatry; and relationships with these areas remain close. Recently, pressing social problems have fostered interdisciplinary work, especially with sociology, political science, and anthropology. Observations in natural settings, case studies, and participant observer techniques are, as a consequence, becoming very popular. This development has, to some degree, inhibited rigorous training in formal research design and statistics just when these approaches were increasingly being taught in graduate programs.

Finally, there are some conflicts between psychologists and school counselors and between psychologists and psychiatrists concerning professional territoriality.

MAJOR TRENDS AND INFLUENCES SINCE WORLD WAR II

Demographic and Organizational Indexes

Since psychology is such a new field in Brazil, much of what has already been presented indicates what has occurred since World War II. Membership in the Regional Councils of Psychology, as of 1983, is shown in Table 1 and gives some idea of the scope of the discipline.

Concerning publication trends, Seminério and Figueiredo (1973) published an analysis covering 610 articles from six journals over a ten-year period (1962–1971). Table 2 presents the percentages of theoretical-experimental, applied, and psychometric articles published each year.

Table 1
Number and Percentage of Psychologists Associated with Each Regional Council of Psychology, 1983

Region	Number	Percentage
1. States in the north central and northwestern part of the country	2,076	5.53
2. States in the northeastern area	3,025	8.05
3. States in the east (Bahia and Sergipe)	648	1.72
4. States in the central and eastern areas (Minas Gerais and Espírito Santo)	3,532	9.40
5. The state of Rio de Janeiro	7,201	19.16
6. The states of São Paulo, Mato Grosso and Mato Grosso do Sul	17,438	46.40
7. The states of Rio Grande do Sul and Santa Catarina	2,134	5.68
8. The state of Paraná	1,526	4.06
TOTAL..	37,580	100.00

More current publication trend studies are not available, but an examination of recent issues of *Arquivos Brasileiros de Psicologia* (1975–1983) shows a tendency toward a higher percentage of empirical studies in social, developmental, clinical, organizational, community, and educational areas. This trend may be a result of graduate programs which have encouraged research.

Research and Theory

Major Orientations and Assumptions

Psychoanalytic theory is the most influential theoretical formulation in Brazilian psychology. The medical model is also widely adopted and it is assumed

Table 2
Numbers and Percentages of Journal Articles in Three General Areas

Year	Theoretical – Experimental		Applied		Psychometrics		Total
	No.	Percentage	No.	Percentage	No.	Percentage	No.
1962	8	32	12	48	5	20	25
63	17	34	19	38	14	28	50
64	20	43	19	40	8	17	47
65	18	39	15	33	13	28	46
66	16	32	24	48	10	20	50
67	20	21	43	46	30	33	93
68	24	26	43	46	28	28	95
69	19	23	40	48	24	29	83
70	21	40	19	36	12	24	52
71	25	36	31	45	13	19	69

Source: Adapted from Seminério and Figueiredo, 1973.

that for every symptom there is an underlying cause. The viewpoints of Freud and Melanie Klein predominate in the more traditional circles such as exist in Porto Alegre. In other centers a variety of psychoanalytic revisionists such as Jung, the culturalists, W. Reich, and, more recently, Lacan and Foucault are also popular as is Argentinian A. Aberastury.

The psychoanalytic perspective is most pronounced in the areas of clinical and personality psychology. Piaget, however, is the most influential psychologist in the social, educational, and developmental fields. The current elementary school curriculum in Brazil is, in fact, largely based on Piagetian theory. Argentinian psychologist Antonio Battro has been responsible for the inception of Piagetian study centers in Rio Grande do Sul and São Paulo. In Rio de Janeiro, Lauro de Oliveira Lima has promoted two international Piagetian congresses and has established an experimental Piagetian school. Zelia Chiarottino and Lino de Macedo in São Paulo; Lea Fagundes in Rio Grande do Sul; Analucia Schliemann, David Carraher, and Terezinha Carraher in Pernambuco; and Cleonice Camino in Paraíba are among Brazil's most prominent Piagetian researchers.

The behaviorist model was a tardy arrival in Brazil. It was only in the late 1960s that the Brazilian government, by providing scholarships, started encouraging graduate students to get their training in the United States. This occurred because the university reform of 1965 started requiring master's degrees of university professors. Around that time Brazilian education shifted from the European to the American model; however, philosophical and humanistic traditions remained firmly ingrained in the attitudes of psychologists. This, together with political resentment toward the United States, may have led to a rejection of the behavioristic model. Nevertheless, through the efforts of psychologists such as Fred Keller, Robert Berryman, and Carolina M. Bori, the work of Skinner became better known, especially in Brasília and São Paulo. Gradually Brazilian psychologists became familiar with the work of Bandura, and behavior modification gained moderate acceptance, but it certainly does not constitute the mainstream of Brazilian psychology. In organizational psychology, Maslow and Herzberg are popular theorists.

Questions of Most Concern

There is a great preoccupation among Brazilian psychologists with social problems, especially the poverty that besets the majority of the population. Consequently, there are doubts about the relevance and usefulness of theoretical models, constructs, and problems originating in developed countries as well as laboratory experimentation. There is also a rejection of quantitative, scientifically rigorous methods, accompanied by a search for qualitative methods better suited to the solution of Brazil's problems.

Major Contributions

The contributions of several psychologists who played an important role in the historical development of psychology in Brazil have already been mentioned in earlier sections. These include Lourenço Filho, Noemy da Silveira Rudolfer, Helena Antipoff, and Mira y Lopez. Others deserve special recognition for their scientific contributions, their dedication to the teaching of psychology and organization of degree programs, and their work in the establishment of the discipline. Among these are Antonius Benkö, at the Catholic University of Rio de Janeiro; Arrigo Angelini, Carolina M. Bori, and Dante M. Leite at the University of São Paulo; American psychologists Fred Keller and Robert Berryman at the University of Brasília; Nilton Campos and Antonio Gomes Penna at the University of Brazil, now known as Federal University of Rio de Janeiro; Franco Seminério from ISOP, Foundation Getúlio Vargas, in Rio de Janeiro; and Pedro Parafita Bessa and Pierre Weil at Belo Horizonte.

Currently, the psychologists who have achieved considerable international recognition are Aroldo Rodrigues, Arrigo Angelini, and João Claudio Todorov. Rodrigues (Ph.D. in social psychology from U.C.L.A.; fellow of the Division of Personality and Social Psychology of the American Psychological Association) has published several books and research articles, mainly on balance theory. He was president of the Interamerican Society of Psychology from 1979 to 1981. Angelini, who has published approximately sixty articles in educational, personality, and counseling psychology, worked with Atkinson and McClelland on achievement motivation. He was also president of the Interamerican Society of Psychology from 1971 to 1973 and president of the first Federal Council of Psychology (1973–1978). He received the Interamerican Award from the Interamerican Society of Psychology in 1979. Todorov has published internationally in the area of experimental analysis of behavior.

Psychologists who stand out because of their scientific productivity and leadership activities in graduate programs and research centers include Leoncio Camino (first coordinator of the graduate program in psychology at the Federal University of Paraíba); Maria Alice M. D'Amorim (whose work catalyzed the growth of community psychology), also at Paraíba; Thereza Mettell (ethological studies of children) at the University of Brasília; Samuel Pfromm Netto (communications and educational technology) and Nelson Rosamilha (anxiety and learning) at the University of São Paulo; Maria Helena Novaes Mira (school psychology) in Rio de Janeiro; Juracy Marques (educational psychology) at the Federal University of Rio Grande do Sul; and Maria Clotilde Rossetti Ferreira (developmental psychology) at the University of São Paulo at Ribeirão Preto.

The following are psychologists with a strong interest in the history of psychology:

Arrigo Angelini, Universidade de São Paulo, Instituto de Psicologia, São Paulo, SP.

Angela Biaggio, Universidade Federal do Rio Grande do Sul, Pós-Graduação em Educação, Porto Alegre, RS.

Antonio Gomes Penna, Universidade Federal do Rio de Janeiro, Instituto de Psicologia, Rio de Janeiro, RJ.

Samuel Pfromm Netto, Universidade de São Paulo, Instituto de Psicologia, São Paulo, SP.

Aroldo Rodrigues, Universidade Gama Filho, Departamento de Psicologia, Rio de Janeiro, RJ.

Applied Areas

Because Brazilian psychology has a predominantly applied nature, it is not surprising that much has been done in clinical, school, and industrial psychology. Clinical psychology has profited from the contributions of medical doctors, usually psychoanalysts, such as Durval Marcondes, Angelo Gaiarsa, and Decio de Souza, in addition to those of psychologists Eliza Velloso and Terezinha Lins de Albuquerque at the Center for Youth Guidance (COJ) of the Ministry of Health.

In school psychology the experimental work developed at the Guatemala School by Terezinha Lins de Albuquerque and Maria Helena Novaes Mira is noteworthy. In industrial psychology (including personnel selection, guidance, and organizational psychology), the first institutions to conduct psychological research were the railway services and the Senai and Senac (National Services for Industrial and Commercial Learning).

The Institute for Personnel Selection and Guidance (ISOP) of the Foundation Getulio Vargas in Rio de Janeiro was one of the earliest centers for applied psychological work and remains an important psychological facility. In the Department of Psychology of Ribeirão Preto, original research on visual perception with applications for traffic problems is being conducted by Rainier Rosenstraten and his group.

Contributions to Other Disciplines and Society

In the field of education, Angelini, by the early 1970s, urged the cooperation of psychologists in confronting the problems posed by a fast-growing population in a developing country. At that time, the emphasis was on solving problems of illiteracy, mainly adult illiteracy, which is still approximately 30 percent. MOBRAL (Movement for Adult Literacy), a Ministry of Education program, involved many psychologists. Additional opportunities for psychology to address the huge task of educating so many young people in such a large country came through work on educational television and education through other mass communications media. Pfromm Netto is one of the psychologists who has been a leader in this field. More recently, preschool children from economically deprived homes and abandoned children have become a prominent concern of educators and psychologists.

In clinical psychology, there is growing interest in helping both the urban middle and upper classes who present all sorts of problems typical of industrialized countries, as well as the huge masses of poor who live on the outskirts of major cities or in rural areas. The latter present a challenge not only in terms of relevant theories and methods but also in regard to adequate financial support. Psychologists have assisted the judiciary services, too, through psychodiagnostic work and counseling with prisoners. The focus of industrial psychologists has been on personnel selection, group dynamics, and traditional applications of psychology to the problems of industry.

PERSPECTIVES ON PSYCHOLOGY IN OTHER COUNTRIES

In my experience, Brazilians have many stereotypes about psychology in other countries. Some idealize the work done in Europe, seeing it as profound and humanistic. American psychology is viewed by many as too quantitative, mechanistic, deterministic, and materialistic. Psychology in the Soviet Union is believed to be entirely based on classical conditioning, although there are enlightened persons who have heard of the work of Luria and Vygotsky. What is being done in Eastern Europe and China has ignited interest and some mistrust, and the little information available about Cuba's mental health programs arouses curiosity.

FUTURE DIRECTIONS

There is increasing interest among Brazilian psychologists in clinical psychology; community psychology; Piagetian cognitive psychology; qualitative, alternative methodologies; socially relevant work; and action research. Furthermore, all the social sciences in Brazil are converging toward the aim of ameliorating the social and economic problems of the population within a democratic framework.

NOTE

The author wishes to acknowledge the cooperation of the following Brazilian colleagues: Arrigo L. Angelini, Samuel Pfromm Netto, and Nelson Rosamilha, from the University of São Paulo; Athayde Ribeiro da Silva, from Instituto de Seleção e Orientação Profissional (ISOP) of the Fundação Getúlio Vargas (Rio de Janeiro); and Jairo Eduardo Borges Andrade, vice-president of the Federal Council of Psychology, all of whom contributed informative materials and publications.

REFERENCES

Amora, A. S. (1948). El-Rei Dom Duarte e o Leal Conselheiro [King Dom Duarte and the loyal counselor]. *Boletim da Faculdade de Filosofia, Ciencias e Letras da Universidade de São Paulo, 93.*

Angelini, A. L. (1975). Aspectos atuais da profissão de psicólogo no Brasil [Current aspects of the profession of psychologist in Brazil]. *Cadernos de Psicologia*

Aplicada, Centro de Orientação e Seleção Psicotécnica, Porto Alegre, Universidade Federal do Rio Grande do Sul, *3* (1).

Biaggio, A. (1982). Note: Historical aspects of clinical psychology in Brazil. *Interdisciplinaria* (Buenos Aires), *3*, 207–213.

Biaggio, A., & Benkö, A. (1975). *American and European influences on Brazilian psychology*. Paper presented at the annual meeting of the American Psychological Association, Chicago.

Cabral, A. C. M. (1950). A psicologia no Brasil [Psychology in Brazil]. *Boletim da Faculdade de Filosofia, Ciencias e Letras da Universidade de São Paulo, 119*, 11–51.

Lourenço Filho, M. B. (1955). *A psicologia no Brasil* [Psychology in Brazil]. In F. Azevedo (Ed.), *As ciencias no Brasil* [Sciences in Brazil] (Vol. 2, pp. 263–296). São Paulo: Mellioramentos.

Martins, M. (1950). *Correntes da filosofia religiosa em Braga, nos séculos IV a VII* [Trends in religious philosophy in Braga, from the fourth to the seventh century]. Porto: Tavares Martins.

Martins, M. (1956). *Estudos de literatura medieval* [Studies in medieval literature]. Braga: Cruz.

Martins, M. (1969). *Estudos de cultura medieval* [Studies in medieval culture]. Lisbon: Verbo.

Martins, M. (1972). *Estudos de cultura medieval* [Studies in medieval culture] (Vol. 2). Braga: Magnificat.

Martins, M. (1975). *Alegorias, símbolos e exemplos morais da literatura medieval portuguesa* [Allegories, symbols, and moral examples from Portuguese medieval literature]. Lisbon: Brotéria.

Paim, A. (1983, December 18). Criar uma tradição humanista [To create a humanistic tradition]. *Journal do Brasil*.

Pfromm Netto, S. (1981). A psicologia no Brasil [Psychology in Brazil]. In M. G. Ferri & S. Motoyamma (Eds.), *Historia das ciências no Brasil* (Vol. 3, pp. 235–276). São Paulo: Editora Pedagógica Universitária/CNPq.

Seminério, F. L. P., & Figueiredo, J. C. (1973). A psicologia no Brasil [Psychology in Brazil]. *Arquivos Brasileiros de Psicologia Aplicada, 25*, 147–162.

Velloso, E. D. (1970). Evolução da psicologia clínica no Brasil [The development of clinical psychology in Brazil]. *Arquivos Brasileiros de Psicologia Aplicada, 22*, 9–14.

Velloso, E. D. (1979). *Psicologia clínica no Brasil* [Clinical psychology in Brazil]. Lecture read at the Second Seminar on the History of Different Areas of Psychology, Institute of Psychology, University of São Paulo.

SUGGESTED READINGS

Angelini, A. L. (1966). Psychology in Brazil. In *International opportunities for advanced training and research in psychology*. Washington, DC: American Psychological Association.

Angelini, A. L. (1973). Applied psychology and problems of Brazil as a developing country. *Interamerican Journal of Psychology, 7*, 65–75.

Angelini, A. L. (1978). Analisis de la formación en psicologia en Brasil en los ultimos años [Analysis of the teaching of psychology in Brazil]. *Boletim de la Sociedad de Psicologia del Uruguay, 47*, 33–38.

Angelini, A. L. (1978). Las estructuras legales y la profesión de psicologo en el Brasil [Legal structures and the profession of psychologist in Brazil]. In R. Ardila (Ed.), *La profesión de psicologo*. Mexico: Trillas.

Bertin, M. A. (1974). *An overview of psychology in Latin America*. Arlington, VA: Department of the Navy Office of Naval Research.

Biaggio, A. (1980). *Psychology in Brazil*. Paper presented at the annual meeting of the American Psychological Association, Montreal.

Biaggio, A. (1982). *Graduate study in psychology in Brazil*. Paper presented at the annual meeting of the American Psychological Association, Washington, DC.

Lourenço Filho, M. B. (1970). A psicologia no Brasil nos últimos 25 años [Psychology in Brazil in the last five years]. *Arquivos Brasileiros de Psicologia Aplicada, 23* (3), 143–151.

Martins, M. (1969). *Introdução histórica à vivência do tempo e da morte* [Historical introduction to the experience of time and death] (Vol. 1–2). Braga: Cruz.

Rodrigues, A. (1982). *Evaluation of graduate programs in psychology in Brazil*. Paper presented at the annual meeting of the American Psychological Association, Washington, DC.

Canada

Terrence P. Hogan and Timothy V. Hogan

The first course in psychology in Canada, which was distinctly philosophical in emphasis, was taught as early as 1838 at Dalhousie University in the city now known as Halifax, Nova Scotia. As was the case in other parts of North America and Europe, instruction in psychology on a regular basis was being offered by the late 1800s at the University of Toronto, McGill University, Dalhousie, and what is today the University of Ottawa. Experimental psychology in the modern sense was introduced at Toronto and McGill around the turn of the century. Applied psychology was taught during the 1920s at both Toronto and McGill, and psychologists began affiliating with hospitals, schools, and industry at that time.

Since the early 1900s pyschology has generally been defined as the science of human behavior by Canadian psychologists, mirroring in most ways developments and definitions characteristic of U.S. psychology. While differences exist, particularly in applied areas, between psychology in Canada and the United States due to different legal traditions, the bilingual nature of Canada, and disparate governmental structures, these differences are few when compared to the many similarities.

In 1939, the Canadian Psychological Association was formed, primarily in response to the outbreak of World War II. There were then only fifty psychologists teaching in Canadian colleges and universities. The years following the war were characterized by considerable growth and consolidation. The Canadian Psychological Association began holding annual conventions and published its first journal, the *Canadian Journal of Psychology*. Both enhanced scholarly and professional communication. Increasingly, psychologists delivered psychological services in applied settings and in the process complemented the efforts being made to establish psychology as a respected discipline within Canadian universities.

During the late 1950s, provincial associations of psychologists came into being which attempted to bring about legislation governing the practice of psychology. The period of greatest expansion, however, was the 1960s. These were years of unprecedented growth for psychology in both university and applied settings. By the mid–1970s, psychology was taught in all Canadian universities and psychologists were working in communities across the nation in hospitals, schools, prisons, community agencies for the disabled, counseling centers and clinics, and a host of other governmental and nongovernmental social agencies. Moreover, psychology had begun to take hold in business and industry.

Today there are an estimated 7,500 psychologists in Canada trained at the master's and doctoral levels. They do psychological assessment, engage in a variety of counseling and therapeutic activities, provide consultation to many segments of society, conduct research, and are involved in sundry educational tasks.

ORGANIZATIONAL STRUCTURE

Canadian Psychological Association (CPA)

The Canadian Psychological Association is a voluntary organization comprised of about 3,500 psychologists. The association fosters unity, coherence, and a sense of shared identity among the various elements of Canadian psychology. The usual diversity of interests among psychologists is made more complex in Canada by the immense geography, differing language groups, and the multicultural nature of Canada as a nation of immigrants. The association maintains a strong and balanced commitment to psychology both as a science and as a profession.

The CPA publishes three quarterly journals in psychology and a quarterly newsletter. In addition to its annual conventions, the association sponsors a number of special instructional institutes. It also represents psychology to groups such as federal government ministries, in particular those dealing with health and social issues; the Social Sciences and Humanities Research Council of Canada; the Natural Science and Engineering Research Council of Canada; the Medical Research Council of Canada; the National Research Council; other learned and scientific societies and associations; the Social Science Federation of Canada; the International Union of Psychological Science; and other international scientific bodies.

The CPA has its permanent secretariat in Ottawa, Ontario, the capital of Canada. (The central office is located at 558 King Edward Avenue, Ottawa, Ontario K1N 7N6, Canada. Its telephone number is (613) 238–4409.) The association assists the various ministries of the federal government and other organizations concerned with education, health, research, the administration of justice, and industry. While representing the needs of psychologists, it also takes part in seeking answers to the nation's social problems. Finally, it helps other professional groups develop national standards, ethical principles, and guidelines for research.

Provincial Associations

The organization of psychology at the provincial level varies across the country since, under the Canadian constitution, the regulation of professions is a provincial rather than a federal responsibility. Psychology is formally organized in all ten provinces and two territories of Canada. Four provinces (Manitoba, Nova Scotia, Ontario, and Saskatchewan) have two associations. In each case one is a fraternal, voluntary group which represents the professional, scientific, and social interests of psychologists whereas the other is a regulatory body which psychologists must join if they want to be practicing psychologists. Four provinces (British Columbia, Quebec, New Brunswick, and Alberta) along with the Northwest Territories combine the fraternal and regulatory functions into one organization. Two provinces (Prince Edward Island and Newfoundland) do not as yet have regulatory bodies governing psychology, although each has a fraternal association, and the Yukon has a statute governing the practice of psychology, but no voluntary association.

Other Psychological Associations in Canada

In addition to the Canadian Psychological Association and the various provincial associations, the following three psychological groups should be noted:

Council of Provincial Associations of Psychology (CPAP). Founded in 1968, this organization is comprised of representatives of all of the provincial associations and the CPA. As an umbrella group it meets twice yearly to share information concerning developments within the profession. It also tries to represent the concerns of provincial psychological associations at the national level, particularly in regard to the policies and actions of the federal government.

Canadian Registry of Health Service Providers in Psychology. This organization, founded in 1984, was established to form a register of psychologists who meet standards relating to the provision of health services. The registry is intended to be used by various health-service organizations to identify competent professional psychologists working in the health area.

Accreditation Panel. In 1984, the CPA approved the formation of the Accreditation Panel for Psychology Programs and Internships. This panel oversees the national accreditation process for clinical psychology training in Canadian universities and applied service settings.

Although these organizations have diverse relationships with the CPA, they all use the central office facilities and the address of the national organization.

FUNCTIONS OF PSYCHOLOGISTS

The major functions of Canadian psychologists are research, teaching, and the practice of psychology in public and private settings. Most instruction in psychology takes place at the postsecondary level, principally in universities, with some introductory courses being offered by community colleges. Psychology departments exist in all of the fifty major universities in Canada. Thirty-five university programs include graduate training in psychology; twenty-six universities offer doctoral programs. There are separate departments of educational psychology at five universities, all of which have graduate programs and three of which train students at the doctoral level. One university has a distinct counseling psychology program. Table 1 lists all of the universities with doctoral programs.

Clinical psychology has become a major focus of psychological education in Canada. Currently there are twenty-eight clinical psychology training programs. Twenty-four have doctoral programs (see Table 2). While several Canadian universities have clinical programs accredited by the American Psychological Association, the Canadian Psychological Association has recently established its own accreditation procedures.

The structure and curriculum of both undergraduate and graduate programs in Canada reflect the historical amalgam of American and British traditions intrinsic to Canadian higher education. At the undergraduate level, psychology programs are typically offered within both general degree programs and honors degree programs. By tradition, students intending to pursue graduate study in psychology enroll in honors programs which tend to be more intensive and longer than general programs. However, an increasing number of graduate students are being admitted from general degree programs. The nature of the curriculum at the undergraduate level is eclectic with required courses in general psychology, research methods, and statistics being augmented by a wide variety of optional offerings in the various substantive areas of the discipline. Graduate programs are, by and large, research-oriented; distinct master's programs and Ph.D. programs are available. In all programs, students have to take courses, pass a variety of examinations, and do independent research. In both clinical and other applied programs, lengthy periods of supervised experience are further required.

FUNCTIONS OF APPLIED PSYCHOLOGISTS IN CANADA

In 1984, a survey was undertaken by the CPA of persons involved in the delivery of psychological services. Over 1,100 psychologists responded. Concerning the respondents, the findings indicated that:

Over 73 percent were between 25 and 45 years of age

62 percent were males, 32 percent were females, and 6 percent did not identify themselves as to sex

73 percent stated that English was their first language and 27 percent indicated that French was their first language

Table 1
Canadian Universities Providing Doctoral-Level Training in Psychology (From East to West)

Memorial University of Newfoundland	St. John's, Newfoundland
Dalhousie University	Halifax, Nova Scotia
University of New Brunswick	Fredericton, N.B.
Université Laval	Quebec, Quebec
Université de Montreal	Montreal, Quebec
Concordia University	Montreal, Quebec
Carleton University	Ottawa, Ontario
Ottawa University	Ottawa, Ontario
Queen's University	Kingston, Ontario
Ontario Institute for Studies in Education	Toronto, Ontario
University of Toronto	Toronto, Ontario
York University	Toronto, Ontario
McMaster University	Hamilton, Ontario
Guelph University	Guelph, Ontario
University of Waterloo	Kitchener, Ontario
The University of Western Ontario*	London, Ontario
University of Windsor	Windsor, Ontario
The University of Manitoba	Winnipeg, Manitoba
The University of Regina	Regina, Saskatchewan
University of Saskatchewan*	Saskatoon, Saskatchewan
The University of Calgary*	Calgary, Alberta
The University of Alberta*	Edmonton, Alberta
The University of British Columbia*+	Vancouver, B.C.
Simon Fraser University	Burnaby, B.C.
University of Victoria	Victoria, B.C.

*Department of Psychology and Educational Psychology
†Department of Counseling

Table 2
Canadian Universities with Doctoral-Level Programs in Clinical Psychology
(From East to West)

Memorial University of Newfoundland	St. John's, Newfoundland
Université Laval	Quebec, Quebec
Université de Montreal	Montreal, Quebec
McGill University	Montreal, Quebec
Concordia University	Montreal, Quebec
Ottawa University	Ottawa, Ontario
Queen's University	Kingston, Ontario
Ontario Institute for Studies in Education	Toronto, Ontario
York University	Toronto, Ontario
McMaster University	Hamilton, Ontario
University of Waterloo	Kitchener, Ontario
The University of Western Ontario*	London, Ontario
University of Windsor	Windsor, Ontario
The University of Manitoba	Winnipeg, Manitoba
The University of Regina	Regina, Saskatchewan
University of Saskatchewan*	Saskatoon, Saskatchewan
The University of Calgary*	Calgary, Alberta
The University of Alberta*	Edmonton, Alberta
The University of British Columbia*	Vancouver, B.C.
Simon Fraser University	Burnaby, B.C.
University of Victoria	Victoria, B.C.

*Department of Psychology and Educational Psychology
Acadia University, Lakehead University, Université de Moncton, and St. Mary's University also provide clinical programs at the master's level.

89 percent were Canadian citizens with the remainder being permanent residents or on work permits

52 percent were from central Canada (Ontario and Quebec) and 80 percent were from the most populous provinces in the country (Ontario, Quebec, British Columbia, and Alberta)

60 percent held a doctoral degree and 40 percent a master's degree

39 percent provided health services

9 percent were in private practice

58 percent did psychotherapy

48 percent engaged in psychological evaluation

39 percent were involved in consulting.

While only 5 percent of the respondents indicated that neuropsychology was their field of practice, over 42 percent thought that this would be an important area in which to specialize in the future. Forty-two percent of the respondents also thought that learning and educational assessment would be among their prime professional concerns in the future. Finally, a large majority of respondents believed that "normals" with ordinary but significant life problems would eventually be the type of clients psychologists primarily worked with.

The survey also showed that psychologists in Canada are not much involved in industrial-organizational psychology or in other nonclinical or noncounseling fields. This is probably a function of the nature of applied psychological training here.

RESEARCH AND THEORY

Psychology in Canada is part of the mainstream of modern psychology. Canadian psychologists include representatives of most major orientations and no school of thought appears to predominate. Research covers a variety of areas with empirical and experimental methodologies being the norm.

A number of Canadian psychologists are, or have been, recognized internationally for their work. The CPA initiated two major awards in 1979 to reflect the contributions of Canadian psychologists. One recognizes distinguished contributions to Canadian psychology "as a science," the other distinguished contributions to Canadian psychology "as a profession." Table 3 lists the recipients of these awards and the major area of their contributions.

D. O. Hebb, the first recipient of the CPA Award for Distinguished Contributions to Canadian Psychology as a Science was Canada's most influential psychologist in recent times. Hebb's work in the neurosciences, perception, learning, motivation, and thinking are known and respected throughout the world. His influence on the development of psychology in Canada was similarly great.

Table 3
Recipients of Awards for Distinguished Contributions to Canadian Psychology

For Contributions to the Science of Psychology

1980	Donald Hebb	Neuropsychology
1981	Brenda Milner	Neuropsychology
1982	Allan Paivio	Cognition
1983	Endel Tulving	Memory
1984	Wallace Lambert	Bilingualism
1985	Doreen Kimura	Neuropsychology

For Contributions to the Profession of Psychology

1980	Virginia Douglas	Clinical Psychology
1981	Park Davidson	Clinical/Community Psychology
1982	Edward Webster	Industrial/Organizational
1983	Terrence Hogan	Professional Practice
1984	C. Roger Myers	Organization of Canadian Psychology
1985	David Belanger	Development of Psychology (Especially in French Canada)

PSYCHOLOGISTS WITH A STRONG INTEREST IN THE HISTORY OF PSYCHOLOGY

The work of Mary Wright and the late Roger Myers, which resulted in the book *History of academic psychology in Canada* (1982), covers much of the history of psychology in this country. Wright continues to work in this area. In addition, James Inglis, professor of psychology at Queen's University in Kingston, and David Belanger, professor of psychology at the Université de Montréal in Montreal, are actively involved in studying the history of psychology.

MAJOR PSYCHOLOGICAL JOURNALS

The CPA publishes three major journals, *Canadian Psychologist*, the *Canadian Journal of Psychology*, and the *Canadian Journal of Behavioral Science*. A fourth important journal, *Canada's Mental Health*, is published by the Health Protection Branch of the Ministry of Health and Welfare. Furthermore, the CPA distributes a bimonthly newsletter, *Highlights*, to all members, informing them of current activities, employment opportunities, meetings, and so forth, and sends the quarterly *Applied Division Newsletter of the Canadian Psychological Association* to the approximately 1,000 psychologists in Canada who are members of the Applied Division. Articles in the three major CPA publications are abstracted in *Psychological Abstracts* and included in relevant citation indexes. Subscriptions and submissions relative to the four primary journals have increased steadily in recent years.

The *Canadian Psychologist* (formerly the *Canadian Psychological Review*) is the official journal of the CPA. The publication features articles of general interest to the membership, placing special emphasis on issues concerned with the development of the discipline within Canadian society. Also published are book reviews, the association's official reports, and news and notes about the organization.

The *Canadian Journal of Psychology*, a quarterly, is the major journal publishing research and theoretical articles in experimental and general psychology. Most of the substantive areas of the field are covered; the National Research Council of Canada pays for some of the publication costs.

The *Canadian Journal of Behavioral Science*, also a quarterly, publishes articles about work in the applied areas of psychology. Research and theoretical articles in social, personality, abnormal, educational, developmental, and child psychology are included. The journal receives financial support from the Social Sciences and Humanities Research Council of Canada.

MAJOR TRENDS AND INFLUENCES

As should be evident, psychology in Canada has grown and matured significantly since World War II. Membership in the national and provincial associations has increased steadily as large numbers of psychologists were trained and entered the field. At the same time the number of publications has increased and the quality of published work improved.

The development of psychology in Canada, as mentioned earlier, has been influenced by both the social structure and geography of the nation. The country is multicultural and the population concentrated witihin a region only 150 kilometers wide extending from the Atlantic to the Pacific oceans.

The effect on psychology of Canada's having two founding nations is particularly apparent. While Canadian psychology belongs to the mainstream of North American psychology, the field has been affected by developments unique to the anglophone and francophone parts of Canada. The academic and professional traditions associated with the English and French cultures, for example, are reflected in the structures of the universities and professions in the English and French regions of Canada. The somewhat strained cohabitation of these two cultures has also generated interest in research on the learning of second languages and the impact on educational and health-care systems of bilingualism. Also affecting the milieu of the country is the encouragement given immigrant groups to preserve their own cultures and traditions. This has resulted in a "mosaic" rather than a "melting pot" society. In this sense Canada is quite different from the United States.

The fact that Canada is the world's second largest country in area with its relatively small population (about 23 million) spread across 10,000 kilometers in a narrow band along the northern border of the United States resulting in widely spaced population centers has had, in conjunction with the Canadian form of government which gives the ten provinces a variety of rights and responsibilities not shared with the federal government, a significant influence on Canadian psychology. There is no question that the different approaches to health care and education which one finds in Canada, for instance, are in large measure an outcome of this particular combination of factors. This diversity has naturally had a bearing on what psychologists in different parts of the country are expected and trained to do.

Another influence on Canadian psychology was the institution in 1966 of a Medicare system in Canada that provides fees for the services of physicians and a number of other health-care professionals but excludes psychologists. Psychologists are actively promoting the inclusion of their services under provincial Medicare schemes across the country, but in the meantime most psychological practitioners function as salaried professionals in hospitals, social agencies, and government facilities.

Since education is also a provincial responsibility, the funding of universities has been heavily influenced by provincial commitments to higher education. While the federal government has made financial grants to provinces for the support of higher education (and health services as well), the way these funds have been used has varied from province to province. There is a continuing debate between the federal government and provincial governments on the financing of postsecondary education. Universities are, in fact, much concerned at this time about the stability of their financial resources. It should also be noted that private university education as it is known elsewhere in the world, particularly in the United States, does not exist in Canada where virtually all universities are supported by the public purse.

Research funding has traditionally been a federal responsibility in Canada although provinces are increasingly beginning to provide some monies for research. Psychologists in Canada, depending upon their specialty, are eligible for support from three major granting councils, as follows:

The *Medical Research Council (MRC) of Canada* supports health-related research in a variety of areas, including psychology. While all university researchers doing health-related work are eligible for support from the MRC, most of its dollars go for research done in faculties of medicine. Its budget in 1984–1985 totaled 153.2 million Canadian dollars.

The *Natural Sciences and Engineering Research Council (NSERC) of Canada* supports research in the physical and biological sciences and engineering. Some experimental psychological studies are covered by its mandate. For example, research in physiological psychology and on sensation, perception, and cognitive processes is supported. NSERC currently funds only those researchers associated with universities. Its budget in 1984–1985 was 311.5 million Canadian dollars.

The *Social Sciences and Humanities Research Council of Canada* provides funds for research in the humanities and social sciences. In psychology, it supports a broad range of subfields including social psychology, developmental psychology, and personality, to name but a few. Its budget in 1984–1985 was 62.8 million Canadian dollars.

In addition to the three councils granting federal funds for extramural research, the federal government supports the National Research Council (NRC) which is the chief intramural research body in the country. The NRC supports principal laboratories across the country with most of its efforts devoted to the natural sciences and engineering. The NRC supports relatively little work in psychology. Finally, two federal bodies have responsibility in the area of science policy. One is the Ministry of Science and Technology which is a major ministry of the Canadian government. The second is the Science Council of Canada which advises the federal government on the development of science and research in the country.

In summary, Canadian psychology is a vigorous discipline. The field is not only established in all of the academic centers in the country and active in research, but it is among the most popular areas of study. Psychology is also one of the foremost professions in Canada, particularly among those providing services in health and social agencies. While the gains made by the discipline and the profession have been substantial during the past twenty-five years, the future promises further significant developments.

REFERENCE

Wright, M. J., & Myers, C. R. (Eds.). (1982). *History of academic psychology in Canada*. Toronto: Hogrefe.

SUGGESTED READINGS

Appley, M. A., & Richwood, J. (1967). *La psychologie au Canada*. Etude spéciale 3, Secrétariat des Sciences, Ottawa: Conseil privé.

Berry, H. W. (1974). Canadian psychology: Some social and applied emphases. *Canadian Psychologist, 15*, 132–139.

Endler, N. S., Rushton, J. P., Roediger, H. L. (1978). Productivity and scholarly impact (citations) of British, Canadian, and U.S. departments of psychology (1975). *American Psychologist, 33*, 1064–1082.

Harris, R. S. (1976). *A history of higher education in Canada, 1663–1960*. Toronto: University of Toronto Press.

Wright, M. J. (1969). Canadian psychology comes of age. *Canadian Psychologist, 10*, 229–253.

People's Republic of China

Zhang Hou-can

A BRIEF HISTORY OF CHINESE PSYCHOLOGY

Chinese psychological thought can be traced back to antiquity. During the past 2,500 years, China has produced many eminent thinkers and scholars such as Confucius (551–479 B.C.), Mencius (372–289 B.C.), Xun Kuang (298–238 B.C.), and Wang Chong (A.D. 27–97), all of whom discussed basic issues in psychology such as human nature, the psyche, mind-body relations, and the essence of dreams. But it was not until the mid-nineteenth century that Chinese scholars had contact with Western psychology. Rong Hung (1828–1912), who studied psychology, physiology, and philosophy in the United States in 1847, was one of the first Chinese scholars to travel abroad to learn the new sciences in the West. In 1889, Yan Yong-jing translated Joseph Haven's *Mental philosophy* into Chinese. This was the first book dealing specifically with psychology published in China.

With a new pedagogical system established and modern Western sciences introduced into China early in the twentieth century, psychology became an independent branch of science. Soon psychology courses were offered in some teacher-training schools, colleges, and universities. In 1927, the first laboratory of psychology was set up in Beijing University. The Chinese Psychological Society was founded in 1921. These events represent the early beginnings of modern Chinese psychology.

The history of modern Chinese psychology can be divided into two main phases. The first extends from the 1920s to 1949, when the People's Republic of China was founded; the second extends from 1949 to the present. During the first stage, Chinese psychologists made some contributions, but achievements were modest. In 1921, the Chinese Psychological Society (CPS) was founded in Nanjing, and Professor Zhang Yao-xiang was chosen as president. One year later, the first Chinese journal of psychology, entitled *Psychology*, came into existence, and in 1928 the Institute of Psychology of the Academia Sinica was set up in Nanjing. Many young psychologists went to America and European countries to study Western psychology. By the end of the 1920s, approximately ten departments of psychology had been established at various colleges and universities. After 1931, the Chinese Testing Society and the Chinese Psychoanalytic Society were founded. Several psychology journals and about 400 books were published, 40 percent of which were translations. At that time the members of CPS totaled nearly 300, and among them were the late professors Chen Daqi, Lu Zhi-wei, and Sun Kuo-hua; professors Tang Yue and Zhou Xian-geng (who are still at Beijing University); Pan Shuh (now the honorary director of the Institute of Psychology of the Chinese Academy of Sciences and honorary president of CPS); Chen Li (former president of Hangzhou University); and Gao Jue-fu (professor at Nanjing Normal University). These veteran psychologists have made great contributions to Chinese psychology.

During the Anti-Japanese War, some psychology departments and research institutes closed down, and others moved to southwestern China. All activities of the CPS stopped. In spite of extreme difficulties, some psychologists continued teaching and research. It was not until China won the war, however, that research and teaching in psychology fully revived.

In short, during the first period of Chinese psychology, Chinese psychologists learned mainly from Western psychology. Chinese psychology had no distinctive and unique characteristics.

The founding of the People's Republic of China marks the beginning of the second phase of modern Chinese psychology. Under the leadership of the People's Government, psychology, like other sciences, advanced rapidly though with difficulty. Excluding developments in Taiwan Province, the second phase of development can be subdivided into the periods from 1949 to 1956, from 1956 to 1966, from 1966 to 1976, and from 1977 until the present.

The 1949–1956 Period

In 1950, the CPS resumed its activity after thirteen years of suspension, while the Chinese Academy of Sciences prepared to set up a laboratory of psychology. In 1956, the new Institute of Psychology, which became the biggest and most advanced center for research in psychology, was established. But educational reform in China had either discontinued the psychology departments or incorporated them into philosophy or education departments at the normal universities and teachers' colleges. During this period Chinese psychologists studied Marxism, Leninism, and Mao's thoughts as guiding principles to be applied to the service of the socialist reconstruction of society. Some Soviet psychologists were invited to give lectures in China and Chinese psychologists took the psychology of the Soviet Union as a model, advocating the study of Pavlovian conditioned reflexes and using Soviet psychological textbooks. Western psychology was abandoned during this period.

In 1955, the First Chinese Psychology Congress was held in Beijing and fundamental problems in psychology were discussed. At this time Chinese psychology was represented by three periodicals: *Acta Psychologica Sinica* (1956–1966), *Psychological Information* (1953–1954), and *Psychological Translations* (1956–1958).

The 1956–1966 Period

During the ten years of the socialist construction (1956–1965), Chinese psychologists did their best to follow Marxism, Leninism, and Mao's thought by combining theory and practice to do research for the economic and cultural building of a socialist society. Among the topics studied were the neural and biochemical bases of learning and memory, the cognitive development of children, and children's abilities to solve mathematical problems. Applied research in the fields of education, industry, and medicine was particularly fruitful. A group psychotherapy called "short-term synthetic therapy for neurasthenia" was quite successful. Engineering psychologists designed a color system for use in railway light signals and helped in the specification of illumination standards for factories and schools.

Unfortunately, along with the vigorous development of Chinese psychology, a Leftist movement criticizing the bourgeois direction of psychology started in 1958, first at Beijing Normal University and then all over the country. Teaching and research in psychology stopped. One year later, although a lesson was drawn from the 1958 movement and a new policy set by Chairman Mao of "letting a hundred flowers blossom and a hundred schools of thought extend," Chinese psychologists were still somewhat confused as to the nature of scientific psychology. The impact of the 1958 movement was so persistent that its influence was again manifested during the Cultural Revolution when Chinese psychology was almost abandoned.

In 1960 the Second Congress of the CPS convened, during which the objects, functions, methods, and nature of scientific psychology were discussed and a three-year research plan formulated. Research and the teaching of psychology revived. There were more students specializing or majoring in psychology at Beijing University, Beijing Normal University, East-China Normal University, and Nanking Teachers' Institute than before. In order to meet the demands of teaching psychology at the university level, Cao Ri-chang, Pan Shuh, and Zhu Zhi-xian took the responsibility for editing and publishing *General Psychology, Educational Psychology*, and *Child Psychology*, respectively, as textbooks to be used in China. At that time the membership of the CPS totaled about 700.

The 1966–1976 Period

During the ten years (1966–1976) of the Cultural Revolution, psychology was once more negatively infuenced by Leftist philosophy. With psychology considered a pseudoscience and a bourgeois ideology, it was abolished completely; psychologists were mistreated and obliged to give up their research and teaching.

Some psychologists were sent to remote areas to do physical labor on farms. Psychology entered a dark age.

From 1977 Until the Present

After the Cultural Revolution, psychology was rehabilitated. Teaching and research in psychology resumed, and independent departments of psychology were again established in major Chinese universities, such as Beijing University, Beijing Normal University, and Hangzhou University. At present there are four departments with 500 university students majoring in psychology. The students of normal universities, teachers' colleges, educational institutes, medical institutes, and athletic institutes are required to take psychology as basic courses. In 1978, the psychology departments at the universities and the Institute of Psychology of the Chinese Academy of Sciences began to enroll graduate students. Now more than 100 graduate students are working for their master's or doctoral degrees. The opportunity to achieve these degrees in China had been suspended since 1950. Even more important was the admission of the CPS to the International Union of Psychological Science (IUPsyS) in 1980, marking a new period which opened up relationships between the psychologists of China and those of other countries.

In 1984, there were 2,000 members in the Chinese Psychological Society. The CPS is sponsored and funded by the Chinese Association of Science and Technology. The aim of the CPS is to unite psychologists throughout the country in order to facilitate the development of academic activities as well as promote research and faculty exchanges. Qualifications for membership are a level of competence equivalent to the M.A. or M.S. degree, graduation from a department of psychology, and more than three years of professional work in psychology, or an equivalent background. The structure of the CPS is depicted in Figure 1.

At the end of 1984, the Fourth Chinese Psychology Congress was held. Professor Pan Shuh, who had been president of the CPS since 1950, was elected honorary president. Professor Jing Qicheng (C. C. Ching) of the Institute of Psychology of the Chinese Academy of Sciences was elected president of CPS, Professor Chen Li of Hang-zhou University and Professor Zhang Hou-can of Beijing Normal University were elected vice-presidents, and Professor Xu Liancang of the Institute of Psychology of the Chinese Academy of Sciences was elected secretary-general. The two major publications of the CPS are *Acta Psychologica Sinica* and *Information on Psychology*.

RECENT ADVANCES IN PSYCHOLOGICAL RESEARCH

As previously indicated, Chinese psychology was not revived until after the Cultural Revolution. However, with the support of the government and the efforts of Chinese psychologists, teaching and research in psychology developed rapidly. Research in psychology is conducted mainly in the Institute of Psychology and

Figure 1
Structure of the Chinese Psychological Society

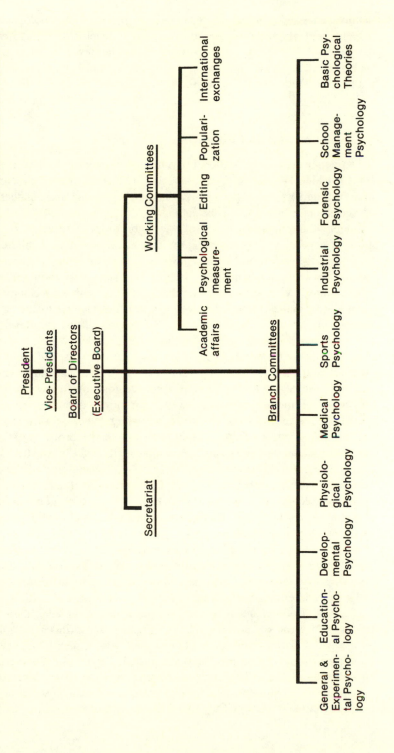

in universities and colleges. There are three main areas of psychological research, namely, general and experimental psychology, developmental and educational psychology, and physiological and medical psychology. Psychological research is also developing in the fields of sports, industrial management, law, economics, philosophy, literature, and other social sciences.

Developmental and Educational Psychology

Developmental and educational psychology has always been a lively field of study in China. About two-thirds of the 2,000 Chinese psychologists are working in normal universities or pedagogical institutes, teaching and conducting developmental and educational investigations.

Cognitive development is one of the major topics of study. J. H. Liu and a group of psychologists (Liu, Wang, & Zhang, 1984) analyzed children's ability to solve mathematical problems. They considered part-whole connections as the basis of mastering mathematical concepts, and the understanding of part-whole relationships is viewed as reflecting the level of cognitive development of children. These studies provided new principles for teaching mathematics in the schools. F. Liu and his group (Liu, 1981) summarized the development of numerical concepts in children. At the age of three a child begins to form number concepts and counts numbers up to ten. Four- to five-year-old children, on the other hand, are able to count up to forty objects. Between six and eight, children can use numerals as tools and form three- to four-digit numbers. Only when children reach the age of nine to twelve can they master numbers higher than 10,000. Moreover, they are able to reason with numbers, forms, integers, decimals, and fractions. Recently, studies were done on the formation of the concepts of volume, serial numbers, and intersection set (Shen, Liu, et al., 1984; Liu & Zhao, 1983). It was found that a period of rapid development of the concept of ''volume'' takes place between the ages of twelve and fifteen. The development of the intersection set conception goes from a direct cognition (sensory-motor) stage to a representation inferential stage (age 9–10) and finally reaches a stage of abstract logical reasoning (age 11–15).

In 1978, R. Z. Shao and her coworkers (Shao & Lee, 1980) studied primary-school children's ability to reason by analogy relative to six relational conceptions involving tools and their uses, part-whole, opposition, juxtaposition, species, and cause and effect. Liu and his group (Zhao & Liu, 1982; Li & Liu, 1982) studied the development of the knowledge of natural objects, their spatial relations, and speed of movement in kindergarten and primary-school children. At the age of six to seven, the child can master more than two elements at the same time but not know how they are related. Later, relations are discovered and integrations of elements achieved which represent a higher level of cognitive development. Z. X. Zhu and his group (Zhu, 1982) made a series of studies on children's thinking ability. They found that classification is an important process in thinking. The nature of the material, cultural background, and educational conditions all influence the quality of the classification process.

The development in children of the Chinese language, a pictographic communication medium with a unique writing and structural system, has attracted much research attention. According to T. M. Wu and Z. Y. Xu (Wu & Xu, 1979), the language development of Chinese children is divided into six stages: simple pronunciation (0–3 months), the production of successive syllables (4–8 months), commencement of speech (8–12 months), the production of word sequences (12 months–1.5 years), the utterance of simple sentences (1.5–2 years), and the use of complex sentences (2–3 years). Progress from utilizing words to mastering parts of speech implies a transition from the concrete to the abstract. M. S. Zhu, J. Z. Wu, and X. C. Miao (1980) stressed that the development of simple declarative sentence structure during the two- to six-year-old period proceeds from chaos to a gradual differentiation, from looseness to tightness, and from stereotypes to extensiveness and flexibility. The three- to four-year-old Chinese child can master more than 1,200 words. Research on sentence comprehension disclosed that a two- to three-year-old child can only master simple sentences but by five to six years of age he or she is able to understand complex sentences. Studies have also been done on the frequency and length of various forms of speech at different age levels.

B. S. Li and his group (Cen & Li, 1982) conducted a five-year study involving a survey in eighteen districts of China to study the development of moral judgment and the concept of justice in five- to eleven-year-old children. He pointed out that the concept of "public" as opposed to "private" evolves through the following stages: the child first describes things in terms of his or her own pleasure and pain, obtains next a general distinction between "private" and "public," then develops a collective consciousness, and finally arrives at a level of making moral judgments according to a principle of abstract collectivism. Z. X. Zhu and his group (Zhu, et al., 1982) made a survey of students' motivation, interests, and ideals in ten provinces and cities. Some investigators have studied attribution and locus of control. They discovered that students tend to attribute their success in school to superior abilities and their failure to lack of diligence. This is different from the traditional Chinese belief that success and failure are related to diligence and degree of hard work.

Using psychological principles to improve the teaching of school subjects is an important objective of Chinese psychology. Z. L. Feng (1976) suggested reformation in arithmetic teaching by combining written, mental, and abacus calculations. C. D. Lin (1983) stressed training ways of thinking to improve the learning process. Since 1963, Z. H. Lu (1984) has conducted experiments on self-teaching techniques, for example, instruction in which middle-school students learn mathematics on their own. He identified nine psychological principles according to which textbooks were written. Results of the experimental class showed that those studying independently had far better achievement scores, learning ability, and scope of knowledge than the control group taught by traditional teaching methods. The new learning method is being tried out in 100 classes in thirty-two provinces and cities.

In 1983, China's new educational policy asserted that education should serve modernization, cater to the needs of the world, and fit in with the future. This has initiated a new area of research. Computer courses are being taught in 230 middle schools. A national computer-teaching center has been established. Although this effort is a modest one as yet, it is a pioneer endeavor which may have long-term prospects. Some psychological investigations are being conducted in this area. For example, research has been done on the cognitive requirements for learning computer programming and the relationships between learning science courses and learning how to program. Some studies showed that a variety of abilities are related to the ability to do computer programming; spatial ability, in particular, appears to be highly correlated with this talent.

In recent years, psychologists have become aware of the importance of psychological testing, particularly in the assessment of mental diseases. Various Western tests, such as the Stanford-Binet, WISC-R, WAIS, and MMPI have been revised and adapted for Chinese use. Also the CPI, Bender-Gestalt, Draw-a-Man Test, and Embedded Figure Test are being tried out. Some of these have been used as psychodiagnostic tools. H. C. Zhang (Zhang, Meng, et al., 1981), using the embedded figures to study the cognitive styles of students, obtained data on the development of field dependence and field independence and the relationship of this dimension to learning achievement, interest, personality characteristics, and leadership qualities. Chinese psychologists are now aware that revising Western tests is not enough; it is necessary to construct tests that are specifically suited to Chinese culture. Progress is under way to design new tests for young children; a new personality inventory appropriate for university students is also being developed. In addition, Zhang and her group analyzed national college entrance examinations in order to help improve the Chinese higher-education admission system.

General and Experimental Psychology

The main center for research in general and experimental psychology is the Institute of Psychology of the Chinese Academy of Sciences. Much research has been conducted for national standardization purposes. Q. C. Jing and his collaborators (Jing, Yu, Jiao, & Chen, 1979) conducted studies on the visual functioning of Chinese subjects under different levels of illumination. B. Y. He and his group (1979) confirmed the spectral luminous efficiency function curves of the CIE standard observer.

There have been about a dozen papers published on color vision. They fall into three categories: color-matching experiments, preference of Chinese facial color studies, and color after-effects research. Jing and others conducted color-matching experiments. Lin and others (Lin, Sun, Ji, & Peng, 1981) made flesh-color measurements of 600 women subjects from different Chinese geographic districts; these matched colors were compared with the preferred flesh color to improve the quality of television broadcasting. In another experiment Lin found that the ability to match colors seemed to improve markedly at two-and-a-half years of age. S. L. Jiao and her colleagues (Jiao, Ji, & Zhang, 1982) used psychophysical methods to study monocular and binocular contingent after-effects. They discovered that after the eyes are adapted separately to an expanding spiral and binocularly to a contracting spiral, the stationary test spiral subse-quently appeared to be contracting when viewed monocularly but expanding when seen binocularly. In the case of the McCollough effect, test gratings appeared different in color when viewed with one eye than when viewed with both eyes after monocular and binocular preadaptation to complementary color-tilt combinations. This can be interpreted as evidence that there are unique monocular and binocular aspects of visual function.

Recently, a number of studies were made on the learning of and memory for Chinese characters relative to hemispheratic lateralization. X. C. Zeng (1983), for example, compared the relative difficulty of children learning Chinese char-acters and Latin alphabetical characters (Pinyin) and found that first graders made more errors in writing Pinyin than in writing Chinese characters. It indicated that Chinese characters were easier to learn, memorize, and write than the Pinyin system based on Latin letters. The errors commonly observed in the Pinyin mode involved mirror-image letters such as b–d, p–q, and letters of velar and alveolar nasal sounds. D. L. Peng and associates found that in free association tasks there was some degree of correspondence between information retrieval from semantic memory and semantic distance (Peng, Guo, & Zhang, 1985). The inference model proposed by Collins and Quillian has been verified. The morphological effect of Chinese characters is not an important factor in retrieval time. J. B. Yang made use of psychological principles in standardizing the structural factors of Chinese characters, which is very important for encoding the information conveyed by the Chinese language.

The asymmetry of hemispheric functions in recognition of Chinese characters has been studied. The results showed that without the interference of noise there was no marked difference between the left and right visual fields in the recognition of Chinese characters. But when the difficulty of recognition reaches a fairly high level, the dominance of the right visual field becomes obvious.

D. L. Peng (Peng, Guo, & Zhang, 1985) studied judgments of Chinese char-acters using words of similar phonetic, graphic, and semantic characteristics. The results showed that graphic discrimination resulted in the shortest reaction time. It seems that phonetic coding is not a necessary link in the retrieval of the meaning of a word or character. Another study also showed that concrete words more easily give rise to representations than abstract words.

B. L. Yu, Q. C. Jing, R. X. Peng, and H. A. Simon (1984) collaborated in a study of short-term memory (STM) capacity for Chinese words and phrases under simultaneous presentations. The findings support the hypothesis that STM is capable of storing a fixed number of familiar chunks whatever the material but is strongly affected by frequency and complexity. Subvocal oral articulation is also indispensable for the retention of Chinese characters in STM.

In 1984 W. T. Zhang collaborated with Peng, Jing, and Simon in designing another experiment to determine how may chunks one can memorize in the Chinese language. Using one-syllable words, two-syllable words, and four-character idioms as test materials, they ran some immediate-recall experiments and some rote-learning experiments. The results showed that the findings of Chinese-language experiments closely resemble those of Western-language experiments. In both cases, the STM span measured in chunks more closely approaches constancy than the span measured in other units; it also shows a tendency to decrease gradually with increase in chunk complexity. In terms of chunk units, relative constancy was further observed in the time required for rote learning of stimuli, and time-dimension appeared to be little dependent on chunk complexity. The positive effect of visual character form for STM storage is obvious, especially for low-familiarty materials.

The results of a series of experiments by J. T. Zhang and Z. Fang (1984) show that the perception of Chinese colloquial sounds is mainly influenced by three factors: acoustic characteristics, speech production activity, and statistical frequency. Among these, acoustic characteristics play a basic role. With undistorted phonetic signals, acoustic characteristics are most significant. When speech sounds are somewhat distorted, the perception of signals and decoding activities start to conflict with each other, and the effect of speech production activity is more significant. When speech sounds are severely distorted, the perceiving process is influenced by a statistical decision process. The four tones in a syllable, as a component part of the phoneme system, add more information to the perception of syllables.

The experiments on laterality and the perception of speech sounds indicate that the right ear is dominant in the perception of Chinese initial consonants and words. In addition, S. Wang (1981) has investigated haptic sensation; J. Z. Li, R. J. Guo, and Y. M. Chen (1982) have studied artificial intelligence and learning by computer; M. L. Zuo and coworkers (1984) and S. F. Zhang (1984) carried out a series of cross-cultural studies on the cognitive development of children from different minorities in Yunnan province; and M. C. Ma and Z. Q. Cao (1983) proposed a fuzzy-set model for categorical judgment and designed a new scale called the multistage evaluation method.

Physiological and Medical Psychology

In recent years, physiological and medical psychologists have focused mostly on the neural and biochemical bases of memory and learning, the structure and function of the hippocampus, and related topics. S. X. Liu and P. Z. Kuang (1982) investigated the effect of the rehabilitation of the brain on the learning processes of rats. X. S. Xiao and R. Q. Wan and their associates (1983) worked on the effect of vasopressin on the processes of memory consolidation, their results suggesting that gamma amino butyric acid (GABA) might be involved in memory consolidation facilitated by arginine-8-vasopressin (AVP). G. D. Sun and L. C. Guan (1984) investigated the effects of LSD on behavior and the activity of neurons in the dorsal hippocampus nucleus in rabbits. K. L. Yan (1983) worked on memory and learning using rats with ventral or dorsal parts of the hippocampus damaged.

C. M. Tang, L. H. Sun, and W. J. Lin (1984) conducted some experiments on animal behavior under stress, which indicated that socialization is important in determining animal and human behavior. Another study by the same authors, "Inhibition of catecholamine biosynthesis and learning ability in socially isolated rats," showed that alpha methyl tyrosine and diethyldithiocarbamate have no effect on learning and memory of the isolated animal, and the observed decline of their learning ability may be caused by a decrease in the amount of noradrenalin (NA) and dopamine related with the decrease of NA in the cortex (Tang, Sun, & Lin, 1984). As to the electrophysiological features of the cerebral cortex and certain nuclei, Z. H. Xue and J. Shao (1983) published a paper about the inhibiting function of electrical stimulation on the subcortical brain, and Q. E. Wu (1984) studied the electrical activity of the hippocampus of rabbits.

Chinese psychologists have also conducted research on clinical problems such as primary depression, minimal brain damage, and congenital insensitivity to pain. W. J. Lin and C. M. Tang (1984) discovered that 1.73% of primary-school children were hyperactive and that the socioeconomic status and educational level of the parents play important roles in the incidence of hyperactivity. B. Y. Zhang and Z. G. Chen (1983) investigated patients with cardiovascular disease and found that those with coronary heart disease who were overaroused by successive electrical stimulation tended to habituate more slowly to the stimulation in terms of electrodermal response amplitude. S. L. Xu and her group (Xu, Wu, & Sun, 1984) suggested that there may be two types of people with congenital insensitivity to pain: those evidencing pain reactions without the sensation of pain and those experiencing neither pain sensations nor pain reactions. It is possible, in other words, for someone to have "pain" responses without feeling pain. The results verified the two-component theory of pain.

In the early 1950s, Chinese medical psychologists made psychodiagnoses, did counseling, and provided treatment in hospitals, but such work was later discontinued. After that, psychologists collaborated with medical workers in the treatment of neurasthenia using what were called "comprehensive short-term methods" including group psychotherapy. Stress was relieved by inducing the correct understanding by the patient of the nature of the illness and helping the person overcome the problem using his or her own initiative. This kind of treatment was then widely used for ulcers, hypertension, and schizophrenia with notable results. Since the 1960s research on analgesia based on acupuncture has also produced good results.

Since the end of the 1970s, psychologists have again been engaged in psychological diagnosis, testing, treatment, and neuropsychology. Recently, X. T.

Li (Li & Zhu, 1984) published a treatise about speech disorders of people suffering from damaged blood vessels in the brain, and C. Q. Hu (Hu, Zhu, et al., 1983) studied language disorders of invalids with vascular brain problems. By observing the change in the thought processes of split-brain patients, it was suggested that the excision of the corpus callosum not only checks the spread of epilepsy but also helps sustain the intelligence of sufferers. Counseling is now done both in hospitals and public institutions.

Other Branches of Psychology

Engineering psychology is less well developed than other branches of psychology in the People's Republic of China because of the country's low level of industrialization. In the 1960s and 1970s, those studies which were done concentrated on lighting standards, the design of signal systems, visual displays, and noise control. Results obtained were used to establish a variety of national standards. Recently, due to increasing industrial progress, some research has concerned the study of the dynamic conditions and multiple factors involved in the integrated evaluation of systems and mental workload.

Since the 1980s, L. C. Xu and his group (1984), in coping with the new economic reforms of China, have initiated research on leadership in enterprises and factories and ways to improve the effectiveness of management. This work is of much interest to the Chinese government. At Hangzhou University managerial psychology is flourishing. A special section of organizational psychology was established in the department of psychology to train personnel in this special field.

In recent years sports psychology, although limited to a small number of psychologists, has made significant contributions to the training of national athletes who have done well in international competitions. In 1949, social psychology was forbidden and considered a pseudoscience contradictory to Marxist historical materialism. Only after the Cultural Revolution were Chinese psychologists able to do research work in this field. Some achievements have also been made in the study of juvenile delinquency and forensic psychology.

Meanwhile, much work has been done on the basic theories of psychology and new ideological viewpoints put forth relative to a series of basic problems relating to the nature of psychology, its tasks, its objectives, and its methods. Because Chinese psychology has been almost eradicated several times in its short history, basic theoretical research based on Marxism needs to be strengthened and erroneous Leftist influences guarded against.

At the present time, psychology is viewed as a branch of science standing between the natural and social sciences. The human mind has both natural and social features; these social and natural aspects are mutually dependent, not separated from each other. Nevertheless, as far as the specific objectives of research in psychology are concerned, people can choose from a variety of research topics and areas. Much attention has been paid to psychological methodology. Professor Pan Shuh, for example, proposed that there be a special dialectical materialistic psychological methodology that could promote China's construction. Besides establishing a Marxist Chinese psychology, Chinese theoreticians are both introducing contemporary foreign psychological orientations into China and collecting and editing the brilliant psychological ideas found in Chinese history. A textbook, entitled *History of chinese psychology*, describing Chinese psychology from the Chin period (221–207 B.C.) to modern times, edited by Gao Jue-fu and other psychologists, was scheduled for publication in 1986.

EPILOGUE

Chinese psychology has undergone a long and complicated history. As the Chinese people strive to achieve economic reform and realize the Four Modernizations, involving industry, agriculture, science and technology, and national defense, Chinese psychology is gaining in importance. It can assist in the modernization process and play a role, too, in everyday life, helping to promote the moral development of the people. Psychology in China has recently become more popular and is attracting more people, especially young people. Chinese psychology has regained international recognition in the 1980s following the CPS admission into the IUPsyS, with Jing Qicheng being a member of its executive committee in 1984. Chinese psychology clearly has a bright and promising future.

REFERENCES

Cen, H. Z., & Li, B. S. (1982). The effects of training of moral judgements among children. *Acta Psychologica Sinica, 14*, 4.

Feng, Z. L. (1976). Reform of the method of written calculation by combining written, mental and abacus calculations. *Journal of Beijing Normal University*, no. 3.

He, B. Y., et al. (1979). A systematic study of relative spectral luminosity among Chinese people. *Acta Psychologica Sinica, 1*.

Hu, C. Q., Zhu, Y. L., et al. (1983). The supportive effect of spoken language on written language: A neurolinguistic analysis based on cases of brain damage. *Acta Psychologica Sinica, 15*, 3.

Jiao, S. L., Ji, G. P., & Zhang, W. T. (1982). The decay process of the opposite monocular and binocular McCollough Effects and of the Tilt After-effect. *Acta Psychologica Sinica, 14*, 1.

Jing, Q. C. (C. C. Ching), Jiao, S. L., Yu, B. L., & Hu, W. S. (1979). *Colorimetry*. Beijing: Science Press.

Jing, Q. C. (C. C. Ching), Yu, B. L., Jiao, S. L., & Chen, Y. M. (1979). Effects of change of illumination on visual discrimination. *Acta Psychologica Sinica, 3*.

Li, J. Z., Guo, R. J., & Chen, Y. M. (1981). A Chinese language understanding system. *Acta Psychologica Sinica, 14*, 1.

Li, J. Z., Guo, R. J., & Chen, Y. M. (1982). A Chinese language understanding system—CLUS I. *Acta Psychologica Sinica, 14*, 1.

Li, W. F., & Liu, F. (1982). An experimental study of the development of 5–11 year olds' cognition of two spatial relationships. *Acta Psychologica Sinica, 14*, 2.

Li, X. T., & Zhu, Y. L. (1984). Language disorders of patients suffering from blood-vessel brain damage. *Proceedings of the Fifth Academic Conference of CPS.*

Lin, C. D. (1983). The development and fostering of primary school pupils' ideology in mathematical operations. *Educational Research*, 10.

Lin, W. J., & Tang, C. M. (1984). Hyperactive children and their home environment. *Proceedings of the Fifth Academic Conference of CPS.*

Lin, Z. X., Sun, X. R., Ji, G. P., & Peng, R. X. (1981). Measurement of skin colors of Chinese children and adolescents. *Acta Psychologica Sinica, 13*, 1.

Liu, F. (1981). Current developmental psychology in China. *Acta Psychologica Sinica, 13*, 2.

Liu, F., & Zhao, S. W. (1983). A study of the development of 8–15 year olds' concept of intersection set and their ability in resolving intersection problem studies relative to the development of children's cognitive structure. *Acta Psychologica Sinica, 15*, 2.

Liu, J. H., Wang, X. T., & Zhang, M. L. (1984). Development of children's cognition of the part-whole relationship concerning numbers and arithmetic. *Issues in Cognition: Proceedings of a Joint Conference in Psychology*, NAS/CAS.

Liu, S. X., & Kuang, P. Z. (1982). Effects of hippocampus damage on learning and memory in rats. *Acta Psychologica Sinica, 14*, 1.

Lu, Z. H. (1984). A study of the psychology of learning in increasing the effectiveness of self-study. *Acta Psychologica Sinica, 16*, 4.

Ma, M. C., & Cao, Z. Q. (1983). A Fuzzy-Set Model for category judgment and the Multistage Evaluation Method. *Acta Psychologica Sinica, 15*, 2.

Peng, D. L., Guo, D. J., & Zhang, S. L. (1985). The retrieval of information of Chinese characters in making similarity judgments. *Acta Psychologica Sinica, 17*.

Shao, R. Z., & Lee, D.(1980). The characteristics of children's analogical reasoning. *Proceedings of the Second National Symposium in Developmental Psychology.* Beijing: People's Press.

Shen, J. X., Liu, F., et al. (1984). Research on the development of the ''volume'' concept of 5 to 17 year-old children and youth. *Acta Psychologica Sinica, 16*, 2.

Sun, G. D., Guan, L. C., et al. (1984). The effects of LSD on the behavior and activity of neurons in the dorsal hippocampus nucleus in rabbits. *Acta Psychologica Sinica, 16*, 3.

Tang, C. M., Sun, L. H., & Lin, W. J. (1984). Inhibition of catecholamine biosynthesis and learning ability in socially isolated rats. *Acta Psychologica Sinica, 16*, 3.

Tang, C. M., Sun, L. H., et al. (1984). Effects of social isolation on the behavior of grown-up rats during social stress. *Acta Psychologica Sinica, 16*, 4.

Wang, S. (1981). A comparison of two modes of haptic length perception. *Acta Psychologica Sinica, 13*, 1.

Wu, Q. E. (1984). The electrical activity of hippocampus during learning in rabbits. *Proceedings of the Third National Symposium in Physiological Psycology of CPS.*

Wu, T. M., & Xu, Z. Y. (1979). A preliminary analysis of language development in children during the first three years. *Acta Psychologica Sinica, 11*, 2.

Xiao, X. S., Wan, R. Q., et al. (1983). The effect of vasopressin on the processes of memory consolidation. *Acta Psychologica Sinica, 15*, 1.

Xu, L. C., Xue, A. Y., Wang, D., & Chen, L. (1984). Assessment of the behavior of leadership in enterprises. *Proceedings of the Fifth Academic Conference of CPS*.

Xu, S. L., Wu, Z. Y., & Sun, C. H. (1984). The psychological and physiological characteristics of two patients with congenital insensitivity to pain. *Acta Psychologica Sinica, 16*, 3.

Xue, Z. H., & Shao, J. (1983). Inhibitory effects of subcortical brain stimulation. *Acta Psychologica Sinica, 15*, 4.

Yan, K. L. (1983). Effects of damage of the ventral or dorsal parts of hippocampus on memory and learning of rats. *Proceedings of the Second Congress of Physiological Psychology*.

Yu, B. L., Jing, Q. C., Peng, R. X., & Simon, H. A. (1984). STM capacity for Chinese words and phrases under simultaneous presentations. *Issues in Cognition: Proceedings of a Joint Conference in Psychology*, NAS/CAS.

Zeng, X. C. (1983). Chinese characters are easy to learn and easy to use. *Educational Research*, no. 2.

Zhang, B. Y., & Chen, Z. G. (1983). Psychological reactions in cardiovascular disease: I. Preliminary research on the arousal level and habituation of coronary heart disease. *Acta Psychologica Sinica, 15*, 2.

Zhang, H. C., Meng, Q. M., et al. (1981). Studies of cognitive style. *Acta Psychologica Sinica, 13*, 3.

Zhang, H. C., et al. (1983). (Testing study group of B.N.U.) A study of College Entrance Examination papers in recent years. *Educational Research*, no. 6.

Zhang, J. T., & Fang, Z. (1984). Research findings on the perception of Chinese speech sounds. *Issues in Cognition: Proceedings of a Joint Conference in Psychology*, NAS/CAS.

Zhang, S. F. (1984). Research on the development of adolescent morality among Lahu and Hani nationalities in Xishuang Banna in Yunan Province. *Acta Psychologica Sinica, 16*, 4.

Zhang, W. T., Peng, R. X., Jing, Q. C., & Simon, H. A. (1984). STM capacity for Chinese words and idioms with visual and auditory presentations. *Issues in Cognition: Proceedings of a Joint Conference in Psychology*, NAS/CAS.

Zhao, S. W., & Liu, F. (1982). An experimental study on 6–10 yr. olds' development of cognition of some common natural things. *Acta Psychologica Sinica, 14*, 4.

Zhu, M. S., Wu, J. Z., & Miao, X. C. (1980). A survey of the development of oral language in young children. *Proceedings of the Second National Symposium in Developmental Psychology*, CPS.

Zhu, Z. X. (1982). *Issues in the psychology of child development* (pp. 255–294). Beijing: Beijing Normal University Press.

Zhu, Z. X., et al. (1982). The study of ideals, motives, and interests of adolescents in schools in ten provinces and cities. *Acta Psychologica Sinica, 14*, 2.

Zuo, M. L., Liu, J. Z., et al. (1984). A study of the comparison of the development of the concept of number series in 5 to 11 year-old children in five districts in China. *Acta Psychologica Sinica, 16*, 2.

SUGGESTED READINGS

Ching, C. C. (Jing Qicheng). (1980). Psychology in the People's Republic of China. *American Psychologist, 35*, 1084–1089.

Ching, C. C. (Jing Qicheng) (1984). Psychology in China. In R. J. Corsini (Ed.), *Encyclopedia of psychology* (Vol. 3, pp. 120–122). New York: John Wiley.

Ching, C. C. (Jing Qicheng), & Jiao, S. L. (1981). Sensory and perceptual studies in the People's Republic of China. *Psychologia, 24*, 133–145.

Colombia

Ruben Ardila

The development of psychology in Colombia has been both rich and varied. The country has the second oldest psychology training program in Latin America and a strong research tradition. Psychology is a profession recognized by the Colombian government, and many important events have shaped the discipline.

The situation is very different from that in other Latin American countries, as I have indicated in previous publications. Although Mexico and Brazil have a higher level of development in psychology, Colombia has been very receptive to the science and the profession of psychology. I anticipate that this positive trend will continue.

NATURE AND SCOPE OF THE DISCIPLINE

Definition of Psychology

Most contemporary psychologists in Colombia probably define psychology as the science of behavior. Previously it was defined as the science of mind, and originally as the study of the soul. These changes of definition imply progress in the sense of moving toward more objectivity.

Among the "primitive" people who inhabited what we today call Latin America, many psychological concepts and ideas are found. Rather than being "imported" from Europe with the arrival of the Spaniards, psychology was implicit in many of the philosophical conceptualizations of the Mayas, the Aztecs, the Incas, and the Chibchas. The last group lived in what is now Colombia. The philosophical conceptions of the Chibchas included views toward the soul, man's purpose in the world, relations between the sexes, happiness, the meaning of existence, and other matters that in a broad sense are considered psychological. More advanced concepts can be found among the Mayas and other groups; in any case, psychology was not an imported discipline but a natural development in this part of South America.

The Spaniards, on the other hand, brought to Latin America perspectives on the soul that were part of the philosophy of Aristotle and St. Thomas. These formed the mainstream of philosophical psychology in Latin America for 400 years, particularly in the countries with a more developed philosophical tradition, such as Mexico, Peru, and Argentina. In Colombia a number of universities were founded (the Universidad Tomasina, the Universidad Javeriana, the Universidad del Rosario), all with a philosophical orientation based on scholasticism. The Universidad Tomasina (today Universidad Santo Tomás) is the oldest in Colombia and the third oldest in Latin America.

Besides philosophy, another source from which psychology sprang is medicine. A number of medical theses were written in the nineteenth century on psychological topics, such as hypnosis, the causes of mental illness, hysteria, psychosomatic diseases, alcoholism, mental retardation, and the psychoses.

Education is the third root of psychology in Colombia. For many years this country has been very concerned with educational problems, helping to eliminate illiteracy, new methods of training large groups of students, special education, and so forth. Before 1948, the year in which the first psychology training program was founded in Colombia, psychology was a subject area studied by educators, physicians, and philosophers. The Colombians have always had a strong interest in literary "culture" within which psychology fits very well. Psychology courses were taught in the schools of medicine and philosophy; the typical audience consisted of students of medicine, philosophy, and education.

Organizational Structure

The situation changed with the arrival in Colombia of Mercedes Rodrigo, a Spanish psychologist who left Spain because of the Spanish Civil War and was invited to the National University of Colombia to organize the selection of students for the faculty of medicine. She was an expert in psychometrics and well aware of international developments in the discipline, particularly in Switzerland and the United States. She stayed in Colombia from 1939 to 1950.

The psychometric work that Rodrigo and her collaborators had to perform at the National University of Colombia was very demanding, and she decided that it was necessary to train psychologists to help her in this enterprise. In 1948 the first psychology program in the country and in South America was opened at the National University of Colombia, becoming only the second program started in Latin America (the earliest was in Guatemala, at the University of St. Carlos). The American Psychological Association invited Rodrigo to tour the main psychology departments of the United States before opening this program.

A group of Colombian psychologists graduated in 1952, but Rodrigo had been forced to leave the country in 1950 for political reasons and settled down in Puerto Rico. The Institute of Applied Psychology of the National University of Colombia became the Faculty of Psychology and later the Department of Psychology. It has continued training psychologists without interruption since then.

Another important development was the founding of the Colombian Federation of Psychology, the professional association of psychologists in the country. It began as the student association of the Institute of Applied Psychology of the National University of Colombia, in 1955. Three years later it developed fully into a professional association which has continued to represent Colombian psychologists. In 1969 the federation was accepted as a member of the International Union of Psychological Science.

The Colombian Society of Psychology was founded in 1978; it performs professional and scientific duties. There are other associations, among them the Foundation for the Advancement of Psychology that publishes the *Revista Latinoamericana de Psicología* [Latin American Journal of Psychology] and *Avances en Psicología Clínica Latinoamericana* [Advances in Latin American Clinical Psychology]; the Colombian Association for Behavior Analysis and Behavior Therapy, founded in 1982, that publishes the *Revista de Análisis del Comportamiento* [Journal of Behavior Analysis]; the Colombian Association of Psychology and Educational Technology; the Society of Industrial and Organizational Psychologists; and others. The majority of these societies were founded in the 1980s.

Alamoc (the Latin American Association for the Analysis and Modification of Behavior) was established in Colombia in 1975. It has members from throughout Latin America, the United States, and Spain. One of its congresses, the second, was organized in Bogotá in June 1979. Although not exclusively a Colombian psychological association, it has been very active in the country. The scope of Alamoc is international, but its origin is Colombian.

Major Programs

Colombia has thirteen psychology programs at the undergraduate level and one graduate program (see Table 1). The only graduate program, located at the University of St. Thomas, is in clinical psychology.

However, psychology in Colombia follows a professional model, as is the case in the rest of Latin America. There is a five-year curriculum involving all the areas of psychology and related disciplines (mathematics, statistics, biology, physiology, sociology, anthropology, and neuroanatomy). At the end of the training period, the student must submit a thesis, usually of an experimental nature, and do practical work under the supervision of a psychologist. The degree "psychologist" allows him or her to work in any area of the discipline. No graduate study is required. The training program is similar to those in other professions such as engineering and law.

Primary Functions of Psychologists

The profession of psychology has been recognized and regulated by law since 1983. The proposal for legal recognition and regulation was presented to the Colombian government in 1972, as part of the five-year plan (1970–1975) to

Table 1
Psychology Programs in Colombia

National University of Colombia (Bogotá)

Javeriana University (Bogotá)

University of the Andes (Bogotá)

Incca University of Colombia (Bogotá)

University of St. Thomas (Bogotá), undergraduate and graduate programs

Catholic University of Colombia (Bogotá)

K. Lorenz Institute of Science and Technology (Bogotá)

University of San Buenaventura (Medellín)

University of Antioquia (Medellín)

University of the North (Barranquilla)

Metropolitana University (Barranquilla)

University of Valle (Cali)

Cooperative University (Manizales)

develop psychology in the country, but not approved until December 28, 1983 (Law 58). In spite of the high level of development of the profession in the country, attaining legal status took longer in Colombia than in some other Latin American countries.

By the terms of this regulation, the primary functions of psychologists are utilization of psychological methods and techniques for basic and applied research; teaching; psychological diagnosis; psychotherapy; guidance, vocational and professional selection and orientation; analysis and modification of behavior in individuals and groups; and psychological prophylaxis (Article 11, Law 58 of 1983). Guidelines are also provided concerning ethics, the training of psychologists, relations with other disciplines, the social function of psychology, and so forth.

The main areas of applied work are clinical psychology, educational psychology, industrial and organizational psychology, and social psychology. The field with the best occupational opportunities is industrial psychology. The area in which most psychologists are interested is clinical psychology.

Funding of the Discipline

As a professionally oriented discipline, psychology in Colombia tends to emphasize institutional work and private practice. Many psychologists are employed in governmental offices (24 percent) and by industries, hospitals, universities, prisons, schools, and other agencies. A relatively small proportion (6 percent) are engaged in private practice, which includes those working in clinical, industrial, and educational areas.

There are several funding institutions in the country. The main one is the Colombian Fund for the Support of Science (Colciencias), which supports basic research in all areas of science, including psychology. Another is Icfes, the governmental agency that is in charge of the quality of higher education in the country; psychology research projects have been funded by Icfes. Private foundations also devote money for psychological research.

At present, a relevant and well-designed research project in psychology usually finds an agency to support it financially. Because of the great emphasis in the country on education, psychology has been given a high priority.

Curriculum Models

Colombia's five-year professional program in psychology includes training in all areas of the field and is terminal, meaning that no graduate work is required. Nevertheless, a number of Colombian psychologists have studied for advanced degrees (M.A., M.S., Ph.D., or Doctor of Psychology). Some of them (approximately 120) received their graduate training at the University of St. Thomas in Bogotá. Others obtained their degrees in the United States, France, Belgium, and even in Poland and the Soviet Union.

In 1974, I organized a meeting of Latin American chairpersons of psychology departments in Bogotá with the financial assistance of UNESCO and the support of the International Union of Psychological Science. As a result of that meeting, a Latin American training model was developed (see Ardila, 1978) which is the general curriculum followed by Colombian training programs and by the majority of the countries in Latin America.

Major Journals

The first journal of psychology published in Colombia was *Revista de Psicología* [Journal of Psychology], begun in 1956 at the National University of Colombia. A pioneer publication, it was issued regularly until the 1970s and now appears irregularly.

Revista Latinoamericana de Psicología [Latin American Journal of Psychology] is considered the leading psychological journal in the Spanish language. It was founded in January 1969 and has been published regularly since then. Special issues have come out on topics such as behavior therapy, Latin American experimental psychology, sexual behavior, industrial and organizational psychology, clinical psychology, early experiences, biofeedback, educational psychology, social psychology, and gerontological psychology.

Informe Colombiano de Psicología [Colombian Bulletin of Psychology] began publication in 1981 and is devoted to all areas of psychology, with special emphasis on topics of social relevance.

Avances en Psicología Clínica Latinoamericana [Advances in Latin American Clinical Psychology] has been published since 1982 by the Foundation for the Advancement of Psychology. It is devoted to clinical psychology from a Latin American perspective.

Revista de Psicología Ocupacional [Journal of Occupational Psychology] contains articles on work psychology, industrial and organizational psychology, and related fields. The first issue appeared in 1982.

Revista de la Federación Colombiana de Psicología [Journal of the Colombian Federation of Psychology] is devoted mainly to professional issues. It was established in 1982.

Cuadernos de Psicología [Psychology Notebooks] comes out of the Department of Psychology of the University of Valle, in Cali. It began in 1978.

Revista de Análisis del Comportamiento [Journal of Behavior Analysis] is the official publication of the Colombian Association for Behavior Analysis and Behavior Therapy. The journal originally appeared in 1983.

Probably the majority of Colombian psychologists read one or more of these journals. However, the *Revista Latinoamericana de Psicología* has the greatest circulation throughout the world.

The Most Widely Used Introductory Textbooks

Many things can be learned about psychology in a country if we know the books from which students receive their first exposure to psychology. Twenty years ago, psychology instructors were proud of *not* using any textbook for their classes. They used to say that North American textbooks were "too mechanistic" and German textbooks "too philosophical." At the present time the situation is different, and textbooks are used in all the psychology training programs in Colombia.

Editorial Trillas, of Mexico, is the foremost publisher of psychology books in Latin America. Fontanella (of Barcelona) and Paidós (of Buenos Aires) are also important. Many other publishing houses offer large collections of psychology books.

Whittaker's *Introduction to psychology* (translated into Spanish as *Psicología*) is the most widely used textbook for an introduction to psychology. Other books used are Morgan's *Introduction to psychology* (*Introducción a la psicología*), Ruch's and Zimbardo's *Psychology and life* (*Psicología y vida*), and Landauer's *Psychology: A brief overview* (in Spanish it is entitled *Psicología*).

Psychological Abstracts

When psychology students in Colombia write their theses, they use the Pasar (PsyInfo) system. All the major universities subscribe to *Psychological Abstracts* and *PsycScan*, and these are frequently consulted by students and professors of psychology.

Major Needs

Several years ago I published an article (Ardila, 1971) concerning the professional problems of psychology in Latin America. By now the majority of the problems have been solved, at least partially, or at least by some countries (Mexico, Brazil, Colombia).

Psychology in Colombia needs better-equipped laboratories and libraries, more communication with the rest of the world, and increased research activity. The need for the "internationalization" of psychology remains salient.

Relationships with Other Disciplines

Psychology has had difficult relationships with psychiatry, psychoanalysis, and psychopedagogics (school psychology). The problem between psychology and psychiatry centered on the issue of psychotherapy, which was solved when well-trained clinical psychologists began to cooperate on equal terms with psychiatrists. At the present time psychologists do psychotherapy in institutions and in private practice, without the supervision of psychiatrists or of any other professionals.

The controversies with psychoanalysis were more conceptual and philosophical. Issues concerned the medical model versus the sociopsychological model of mental disorders, general problems associated with mental health, the reality of psychoanalytical constructs, the length of therapy, and so forth.

In Colombia, school psychologists are called "psychopedagogs." Their training is shorter than that of psychologists (four years instead of five), is less practical, and does not include clinical work. The majority of Colombian psychologists feel that psychopedagogs should not be allowed to use the title of "psychologist." The debate continues.

With other disciplines the relationships are better, for instance between industrial psychologists and industrial engineers and administrators. Sociologists and psychologists also amicably share much professional territory within the social sciences.

TRENDS SINCE WORLD WAR II

The profession of psychology grew significantly in Colombia after World War II. The Institute of Applied Psychology of the National University of Colombia was opened in 1948; most of the training programs began in the 1970s.

Table 2
Presidents of the Colombian Federation of Psychology

---

1.   José Rodriguez-Valderrama (1958-1969)

2.   Alvaro Jimenez-Cadena (1969-1970)

3.   Rubén Ardila (1970-1974)

4.   Orlando Urdaneta (1974-1976)

5.   José A. Sanchez (1976-1978)

6.   Floralba C. de Becerra (1979-1981)

7.   Blanca V. de Angarita (1981-1983)

8.   Orlando Urdaneta (1983-1985)

I have already mentioned the main psychological organizations. The list of presidents of the Colombian Federation of Psychology is given in Table 2.

At the present time there are approximately 2,500 psychologists in Colombia, and 5,500 psychology students. These numbers are much lower than the numbers in other Latin American countries such as Argentina, Mexico, and Brazil. Strict regulation of the number of psychologists has helped the profession to attain a high standing and to keep its growth at a manageable level. Unemployment is rare among Colombian psychologists in spite of the new training programs that have been opened in the last few years.

Research is done in many areas, among them social psychology and the experimental analysis of behavior, as well as physiological psychology and developmental psychology. The first two are the main areas of research in Latin America.

The thesis that a psychology student has to write to get his or her degree at the end of the five-year training program is usually of an experimental nature (theoretical theses are very rare, but correlational research is relatively frequent). This thesis is in many cases the only research effort that a Colombian psychologist undertakes during his or her life. Few psychologists work mainly in research; those who do are usually associated with universities, research institutions, or foundations.

As is the case in other Latin countries, there are more women than men in psychology in Colombia. This is very different from the situation in the United States. Although in the past discrimination existed against women in important positions, such discrimination has practically disappeared. The field of psychology in Colombia is made up of approximately 60 percent women and 40 percent men. Important roles assumed by women psychologists include serving as chairpersons of psychology departments (currently four out of thirteen psychology departments are chaired by women) and presidents of the Colombian Federation of Psychology (of the seven past presidents of the federation, two have been women).

Societal influences on the study of psychology are very clear. One of them is the great importance given to education in the country. Colombia has a long humanistic and literary, but not a scientific, tradition. Furthermore, social problems are very grave and there is serious concern about them. Because psychology is considered a "human" science that deals with social problems, it has attracted large numbers of students. Entrance examinations exist in all Colombian universities, and in the majority of them only 10 percent of the applicants are admitted to psychology programs (medicine accepts 8 percent of applicants). The training is scientifically oriented, with an emphasis on mathematics, physiology, experimental psychology, psychology of learning, and experimental design. The student acquires research skills and practical training that become the tools for future work.

In 1970 a five-year plan was implemented to raise the level of Colombian psychology (see Ardila, 1975). In the plan it was considered necessary to do more research; to improve the practical training of psychologists; to diminish considerably the influence of psychiatrists and other medical doctors; to obtain legal recognition for psychologists, particularly in the area of psychotherapy; to write more psychology books in Spanish; and to organize national and international congresses. This period from 1970 to 1975 had a decisive influence on the development and strengthening of Colombian psychology. The Colombian Federation of Psychology, at that time the only psychological association of the country, and the departments of psychology worked energetically to implement the goals of the plan. The present status of the discipline in Colombia is a consequence in part of this five-year plan.

Future directions should follow current trends with continued improvement of some aspects and development of new areas of research and application. It is probable that Colombian psychology will remain an important science and profession, internally strong and outwardly concerned with relevant social problems.

ADDRESSES

Addresses are given for associations of psychologists, psychology journals, and training programs (departments of psychology). In each category, alphabetical order is used. Names are given in the Spanish original and in English.

Associations

Asociación Colombiana de Análisis y Terapia del Comportamiento (Colombian Association for Behavior Analysis and Behavior Therapy), Apartado 15346, Bogotá, Colombia.

Asociación Colombiana de Psicología y Tecnología Educativa (Colombian Association of Psychology and Educational Technology), Attn. Margarita Guzmán, Calle 88 No. 49–23, Entre Ríos, Bogotá, Colombia.

Asociación de Psicólogos Industriales y Organizacionales (Association of Industrial and Organizational Psychologists), Calle 30 A No. 6–22, Oficina 1903, Bogotá, Colombia.

Asociación Latinoamericana de Análisis y Modificación del Comportamiento (Latin American Association for Behavior Analysis and Modification), Apartado 52127, Bogotá, Colombia.

Federación Colombiana de Psicología (Colombian Federation of Psychology), Apartado 5253, Bogotá, Colombia.

Fundación para el Avance de la Psicología (Foundation for the Advancement of Psychology), Apartado 52366, Bogotá, Colombia.

Sociedad Colombiana de Psicología (Colombian Society of Psychology), Apartado 11673, Bogotá, Colombia.

Journals

Avances en Psicología Clínica Latinoamericana (Advances in Latin American Clinical Psychology), Apartado 52127, Bogotá, Colombia.

Cuadernos de Psicología (Psychology Notebooks), Departamento de Psicología, Universidad del Valle, Cali, Colombia.

Informe Colombiano de Psicología (Colombian Bulletin of Psychology), Carrera 13 No. 35–27, Oficina 203, Bogotá, Colombia.

Revista de Análisis del Comportamiento (Journal of Behavior Analysis), Apartado 15346, Bogotá, Colombia.

Revista de la Federación Colombiana de Psicología (Journal of the Colombian Federation of Psychology), Apartado 5253, Bogotá, Colombia.

Revista de Psicología (Journal of Psychology), Departamento de Psicología, Universidad Nacional de Colombia, Ciudad Universitaria, Bogotá, Colombia.

Revista de Psicología Ocupacional (Journal of Occupational Psychology), Apartado 2402, Medellín, Colombia.

Revista Latinoamericana de Psicología (Latin American Journal of Psychology), Apartado 52127, Bogotá, Colombia.

Psychology Training Programs

Instituto K. Lorenz de Ciencia y Tecnología (K. Lorenz Institute of Science and Technology), Calle 76, Carreras 7 y 8, Bogotá, Colombia.

Universidad Católica de Colombia (Catholic University of Colombia), Facultad de Psicología, Diagonal 47 No. 15–50, Bogotá, Colombia.

Universidad Cooperativa (Cooperative University), Apartado 868, Manizales, Colombia.

Universidad de Antioquia (University of Antioquia), Departamento de Psicología, Ciudad Universitaria, Medellín, Colombia.

Universidad de los Andes (University of the Andes), Departamento de Psicología, Carrera 1, Calle 18, Bogotá, Colombia.

Universidad de San Buenaventura (University of San Buenaventura), Facultad de Psicología, Calle 56 C No. 51–46, Medellín, Colombia.

Universidad del Norte (University of the North), División de Psicología, Apartado 1569, Barranquilla, Colombia.

Universidad del Valle (University of Valle), Departamento de Psicología, Apartado 2188, Cali, Colombia.

Universidad Incca de Colombia (Inca University of Colombia), Escuela de Psicología, Carrera 13 No. 24–15, Bogotá, Colombia.

Universidad Javeriana (Javeriana University), Facultad de Psicología, Carrera 7 No. 41–00, Bogotá, Colombia.

Universidad Metropolitana (Metropolitan University), Facultad de Psicología, Apartado 50576, Barranquilla, Colombia.

Universidad Nacional de Colombia (National University of Colombia), Departamento de Psicología, Ciudad Universitaria, Bogotá, Colombia.

Universidad Santo Tomás (St. Thomas University), Carrera 9 No. 5123, Bogotá, Colombia.

REFERENCES

Ardila, R. (1971). Professional problems of psychology in Latin America. *Revista Interamericana de Psicología*, *5*, 53–58.
Ardila, R. (1975). La historia de la psicología colombiana y el plan quinquenal 1970–1975 [The history of psychology and the plan for 1970–1975]. *Revista Latinoamericana de Psicología, 7*, 435–446.
Ardila, R. (Ed.). (1978). *La profesión del psicólogo* [The profession of psychology]. México: Trillas.

SUGGESTED READINGS

Ardila, R. (1973). *La psicología en Colombia, desarrollo histórico* [Psychology in Colombia: A historical perspective]. México: Trillas.
Ardila, R. (1980). Historiography of Latin American psychology. In J. Brozek & L. J. Pongratz (Eds.), *Historiography of modern psychology* (pp. 111–118). Toronto: Hogrefe.
Ardila, R. (1982). International psychology. *American Psychologist, 37*, 323–329.
Ardila, R. (1982). Psychology in Latin America today. *Annual Review of Psychology, 33*, 103–122.
Ardila, R. (1986). *La psicología en América Latina: pasado, presente y futuro* [Psychology in Latin America: Past, present and future]. México: Siglo XXI.
Ardila, R., & Castro, L. (1973). The role of applied psychology in the national development programmes in Colombia. *International Review of Applied Psychology, 22*, 65–75.

Ardila, R., & Pereira, F. (1975). Psychotherapy in Colombia. *Revista Interamericana de Psicología*, *9*, 149–163.

Cuba

Gerardo Marín

Psychology in Cuba since World War II must be viewed in the context of two dramatically different periods, the first covering the time before the socialist revolution of 1959, the other extending from 1959 to the present. The period before the revolution has been characterized by various authors (for example, Bernal, 1985) as one in which Cuban psychologists were influenced by psychology in the United States. The postrevolutionary period has been marked by substantial and rapid growth of the profession and the shaping of psychological knowledge within a Marxist conception of humanity which considers social relations basic to understanding human behavior (De La Torre Molina, 1983). Since the latter period encompasses contemporary Cuban psychology, the information provided in this chapter concerns developments during the past twenty-five years.

DEFINITION OF PSYCHOLOGY AND PSYCHOLOGICAL ACTIVITIES

In a recent article on the social role of psychologists in Cuba, Mitjans Martínez and Febles Elejalde (1983) define the philosophical orientation of Cuban psychology as based on a Marxist philosophy that provides psychology with a framework for perceiving human beings as historical/social in nature. A direct implication of this philosophical orientation is the emphasis placed on "activity" as a mediating concept between stimulus and response (S–Activity–R). In this sense, "activity is understood not as a reaction but as a system that has its own structure and development and that does not exist outside of social relationships" (Mitjans Martínez & Febles Elejalde, 1983, p. 10).

At the crux of this framework, the dialectic/materialistic conception of psychology is presented as an open system, that is, a conceptual system in the process of being developed. It therefore requires an analysis of previous psychological knowledge and theories.

One of the key areas of application of psychology in Cuba is in the promotion and care of physical health. Both in terms of the numbers of psychologists working within the Ministry of Health as well as innovativeness, health psychology occupies an important role in Cuban psychology. This field is defined by García Averasturi (1980) as "the promotion of those psychological aspects, cognitive, emotional and behavioral, that favor health and the development of individual potentialities, including the family, school, and place of employment" (p. 4).

ORGANIZATIONAL STRUCTURE

Several organizations are of importance in understanding postrevolutionary Cuban psychology. At one level are those composed of psychologists working for the central government's ministries such as health and education. At another level there are professional organizations that promote the development of the discipline.

The largest number of psychologists working under one given organizational structure are found within the Ministerio de Salud Publica (MINSAP) [Ministry of Public Health]. Here the National Group in Psychology (Grupo Nacional de Psicología) was established in 1968 in order to coordinate and direct the activities of psychologists within the various health institutions in the country. In 1969 the first group of psychologists was sent to the polyclinics of Havana (the primary health-care institutions in the country which serve approximately 25,000 inhabitants). The National Group in Psychology is currently headed by a psychologist (Lourdes García Averasturi) in Havana. Other than coordinating the activities of psychologists who work for the Ministry of Health throughout the country, the association also decides on the type of professional activities that can be carried out by psychologists and helps the ministry's officials set priorities, develop new programs, and assist in any other concern or program that is related to psychology. The National Group communicates with the Provincial Groups in Psychology (there is one in each of the fifteen provinces that make up the country) in order to carry out the National Plans of Activities that are proposed by the ministry. At the lower levels in this pyramidal structure are the various polyclinics, hospitals, and other health-care institutions that employ psychologists and which carry out the day-to-day activities planned by the two organizational entities already mentioned (García Averasturi, 1980).

Currently there are two professional associations in psychology, neither of which is a member of the International Union of Psychological Science (IUPsyS). The oldest is the Cuban Society of Health Psychology (Sociedad Cubana de Psicología de la Salud) founded in 1974 and a member of the Council of Scientific Societies of the Ministry of Health. Lourdes García was its first president and Noemí Perez Valdés is currently the head of the society. Two national meetings have been sponsored by the society, and in 1980 it cosponsored with the Sociedad Interamericana de Psicología (SIP) [Interamerican Society of Psychology] an International Seminar on Psychology in the Community with over 300 participants from abroad. An International Seminar on Health Psychology was held in December 1984, also with the cosponsorship of the Interamerican Society of Psychology.

The newest professional association is the Society of Cuban Psychologists (Sociedad de Psicólogos de Cuba), founded in 1981 and made up primarily of psychologists outside the Ministry of Health. Fernando Gonzalez, from the University of Havana, is its current president.

PRIMARY FUNCTIONS OF PSYCHOLOGISTS

A number of authors have recently written on the professional functions carried out by Cuban psychologists since the 1959 revolution (for example, Bernal, 1985; De La Torre Molina, 1983; García Averasturi, 1980, 1983, 1985; Mitjans Martínez & Febles Elejalde, 1983; and Perez Valdés & Calvo Montalvo, 1985). In general, the activities of Cuban psychologists take place within the following areas: developmental and pedagogical psychology, psychology of work, social psychology, clinical psychology, and health psychology.

Cuban psychologists working in education perceive their primary concern as "forming and developing [an individual's] personality within the process of installing socialism in Cuba" (Mitjans Martínez & Febles Elejalde, 1983, p. 12). In this sense, psychologists in developmental and pedagogical psychology are concerned with the psychological development of individuals and implications of human development for the education of children and young adults. Among the concerns of these psychologists are children's perceptions of the world, value orientations, social relations and life styles; personality development; political and attitudinal development; self-esteem; motivation; and moral development. They are also interested in issues more directly concerned with schooling, such as preschool education, sensory and perceptual development, games and the development of thinking, and vocational orientation (Mitjans Martínez & Febles Elejalde, 1983). These psychologists not only do basic research but are involved in the education and orientation of children, their parents, and all of the other professionals that make up an educational institution.

Clinical work is usually carried out at the various health service delivery institutions, given that private practice is practically nonexistent. Those psychologists assigned to polyclinics by the Ministry of Public Health have as one of their responsibilities providing clinical services to the people served by each facility. Other psychologists are assigned to psychiatric hospitals where their main work is to offer clinical services in a more traditional setting (about twenty-two psychologists are employed by the Psychiatric Hospital of Havana). Clinical services provided to chronic patients at psychiatric hospitals are based primarily on occupational therapy where the goal is to reinstate the patient in the community as soon as possible through a variety of physical activities (for example, paid work, physical exercise, sports, and art). Clinical psychologists work in interdisciplinary teams at large psychiatric hospitals such as the one in Havana with treatment plans designed by a team of psychologists, psychiatrists, nurses, and other health professionals (Perez Valdés & Calvo Montalvo, 1985). Finally, a number of clinical psychologists use a community approach to promote educational activities for the population-at-large; for example, they provide orientation sessions for various community groups and their leaders, including the Committees for the Defense of the Revolution, (CDR) and the Federation of Cuban Women (FMC).

The psychologists at the Ministry of Public Health not only carry on psychological counseling and related clinical activities but are involved in the education of the population in health practices; training health personnel; serving as consultants for physicians, nurses, and dentists; and research. Specific examples of the professional work of these psychologists include training expectant parents; planning and carrying out educational activities for the population in areas such as exercise, smoking cessation, and the control of obesity; treating individuals with psychosomatic and chronic illnesses (hypertension, ulcers, asthma, physical disabilities); advising health personnel on service-delivery strategies; and consulting at schools and factories on the physical and mental health implications of their activities as well as identifying difficulties experienced by their personnel. A key role of Cuban health psychologists has to do with those activities associated with the birth of children. These include caring for expectant mothers, providing psychological support for expectant parents, training mothers for the birth experience, attending to individuals unable to conceive or who habitually abort, helping those who experience sexual dysfunctions, and promoting birth control measures. Health psychologists together with physicians, dentists, and nurses also help analyze and improve the health services (García Averasturi, 1980, 1983, 1985).

A number of psychologists are employed in areas related to the work place. They do research and consult about problems associated with the organization of work teams; the improvement of the work environment; evaluating, training, orienting, and selecting employees; worker motivation; and job development.

Social psychologists occupy an important role in Cuban society, contributing their knowledge to areas such as the structure, functioning, and development of community groups; the formation and change of attitudes and social values; market research; public opinion; and the identification of the psychologically relevant characteristics of the various institutions in the country (Mitjans Martínenz & Febles Elejalde, 1983).

Cuban psychologists are also involved in the training and preparation of athletes (sports psychology), university teaching, and conducting basic research at the various specialized institutes maintained by some of the ministries (health, work, education, and so forth).

Psychometricians, too, make important contributions to the services being provided by psychologists within the Ministry of Health. Psychometricians (*psicometristas*) are individuals who have three years of postsecondary education at a technical institute and whose primary role includes administering and scoring psychological tests, leading discussion groups, and collecting data for research and evaluative studies. Psychometricians were first trained in 1971 and are found at most Ministry of Health institutions.

TRAINING AND CURRICULUM MODELS

Previous to the 1959 revolution, two private institutions, Universidad de Santo Tomás de Villanueva and the Universidad Masonica de Jose Martí, and the state institutions of higher learning provided training in psychology. At the two private universities, psychology was a separate professional career track, while at the state institutions, training in psychology was part of the philosophy curriculum (Bernal, 1985). Before the 1959 socialist revolution, a substantial number of Cuban professionals also received their training abroad.

The private universities that offered psychological training were closed after the revolution, and in 1961 the first school of psychology was created at the Universidad de Las Villas. In 1962, a second school of psychology (Facultad de Psicología) was established at the University of Havana; in 1976 it became autonomous, that is, independent of the natural sciences with which it had been associated in the past (Bernal, 1985). The first group of students from the University of Havana graduated in 1966 and included those psychologists who are now the leaders of Cuban psychology.

Both universities follow a similar curriculum model that is being developed largely by the faculty at the University of Havana. The overall emphasis in training (like that of most Latin American nations) is to produce general psychologists who can function in a number of professional roles within hospitals, schools, factories, research institutes, and so forth. Primary attention is given to practical matters so that psychology students are able to apply psychological knowledge appropriately wherever they work. Training usually takes five years and involves a short research project (*tesina*) at the end of the course requirements. The first three years include basic training in psychology with emphasis placed on the country's problems and the works of Cuban psychologists. During this period students are also expected to read original works of well-known theorists. The last two years are spent looking in greater detail at the various applied areas (for example, educational, clinical, and social). Students obtain the degree of *Licenciado en Psicología* at the end of five years of training which is roughly equivalent to a professional master's degree in the United States. In 1983, the School of Psychology at the University of Havana had forty-three full-time professors of whom thirteen had a doctoral-level degree (usually obtained in the Soviet Union or in the German Democratic Republic).

Guiding principles in the professional training of psychologists at the University of Havana are the understanding of personality and communication as central areas of psychological inquiry. Emphasis is also placed on the theoretical and empirical integration of psychological knowledge produced in Socialist and non-Socialist countries in order to understand human beings as a whole. Research methods are perceived as ways of interpreting reality and not as representing a philosophical outlook. Training is based on materialistic and dialectic perspectives.

MAJOR JOURNALS

Two major journals publish original articles on psychology: the *Revista del Hospital Psiquiátrico de La Habana* [Journal of Hospital Psychiatry in Havana] and the *Boletín de Psicología* [Psychological Bulletin]. The journal *Psicología y Educación* [Psychology of Education] was briefly published in the 1970s by the Ministry of Education.

The *Revista del Hospital Psiquiátrico de La Habana* published its twenty-fifth volume in 1984, each volume usually consisting of four issues. Edited by Edmundo Gutierrez Agramonte, this journal mostly features psychiatric articles, although in recent years it has included a substantial number of psychological research reports (for a review, see Marín, 1985). It is published by the Psychiatric Hospital of Havana (Avenida de la Independencia No. 26520, Mazorra, Habana, Cuba). Subscriptions can be obtained from Ediciones Cubanas, Apartado 605, Ciudad de La Habana, Cuba.

The *Boletín de Psicología* is published irregularly by the Department of Psychology of the Psychiatric Hospital of Havana. It contains articles by psychologists from Cuba and abroad and also includes Spanish translations of the works of prominent foreign psychologists (recent issues have carried articles by Piaget and Zeigarnik). The *Boletín* is edited by Noemí Perez Valdés; subscriptions can be obtained from the same source mentioned above for the *Revista del Hospital Psiquiátrico de La Habana*.

The National Group in Psychology publishes on a sporadic basis the journal *Actualidades en Psicología* [Current Developments in Psychology] with Spanish translations of research articles of interest to psychologists working in the health field. This publication is edited by Lourdes García Averasturi (Grupo Nacional de Psicología, Ministerio de Salud Pública, La Habana, Cuba).

The School of Psychology of the University of Havana has plans to publish the *Revista Cubana de Psicología* [Journal of Cuban Psychology]. For further information contact: Facultad de Psicología, Universidad de La Habana, La Habana, Cuba.

MAJOR DEVELOPMENTS

Demographic Indexes

It is difficult to estimate the number of psychologists in Cuba before the 1959 revolution, but it is certain that some left the country during the early 1960s. Around 1966 the first group of psychologists trained by the new School of Psychology of the University of Havana took jobs at the Ministry of Public

Health, and by 1980 the agency employed 310 psychologists and 350 psycho-metricians (García Averasturi, 1980). By 1984 the number of psychologists had increased to 500.

There are approximately 300 students of psychology now at the University of Havana and a similar number at the University of Las Villas. Interest in psychology has clearly been increasing since the early 1960s. It is important to note that the growth of the profession is a reflection or product of central planning, as is the case in most Socialist nations. The growing number of psychologists can be perceived, then, as a sign that the important role of psychologists in postrevolutionary Cuba is being recognized.

Research

Mention has been made of the research carried out by psychologists in their various professional roles. Important research is also being done at the two schools of psychology. For example, at the School of Psychology of the University of Havana research on the following topics took place during 1983: the personalities of young adults; student failure in educational settings; utilization of computers in psychology; characteristics of psychology in Latin America; sexual therapy and education; deviations in social behavior; accidents at work; cognitive processes in education; moral development; and social problems. A wealth of psychological inquiry is also found at other research institutions. This is exemplified by the increasing number of publications beginning to appear (for example, Gonzalez Rey, 1983; Calvino Valdes-Fauly, 1983; Gonzales Pacheco, 1983; or see review by Marín, 1985).

Relationships with Other Disciplines

Of particular importance are the partnerships that psychologists experience with other health professionals, particularly psychiatrists and physicians. This is noteworthy when the professional status of psychlogists in Cuba is compared with that of other Latin American nations. Thanks to the responsible work of the early Cuban psychologists during the first years of the revolution, psychologists now enjoy a collegial relationship with other professionals. Because of their professional training and experience, the advice of psychologists is sought after and respected with regard to matters as diverse as clinical diagnosis, psychopathology, mass educational campaigns, the training of professionals, the implementation of social change, the delivery of health services, and the design of school curricula. The respect experienced by psychologists will most likely be further enhanced because of the support provided by institutional coordinating groups such as the National Group in Psychology at the Ministry of Public Health and the solid training being offered at the universities.

NOTE

The author wishes to thank Drs. Guillermo Bernal and Barbara VanOss Marín for providing him with a prepublication copy of the special issue of the *Journal of Community Psychology*, dedicated to Cuban community psychology. Special thanks are also expressed to the various Cuban colleagues who at one time or another provided information crucial to this chapter; among them Lourdes García Averasturi, Noemí Perez Valdéz, and Fernando Gonzalez deserve special mention.

REFERENCES

Bernal, G. (1985). A history of psychology in Cuba. *Journal of Community Psychology*, *13*, 222–235.

Calvino Valdes-Fauly, M.A. (1983). Estudio diagnóstico experimental de la estructura semántica de la conciencia [Experimental diagnostic study of the semantic structure of consciousness]. *Revista del Hospital Psiquiátrico de La Habana, 24*, 59–73.

De La Torre Molina, C. (1983). Influencia de la psicología norteamericana en el dessarollo y crisis actual de la psicología clinica en America Latina [Influence of North American psychology on the development of the present crisis of clinical psychology in Latin America]. *Revista del Hospital Psiquiátrico de La Habana, 24*, 21–34.

García Averasturi, L. (1980). La psicología de la salud en Cuba: Situación actual y perspectivas [Health psychology in Cuba: Present situation and perspectives]. *Areito, 6*, 16–19.

García Averasturi, L. (1983). *Aspectos psicosociales influyentes en el logro de salud para todos* [Psychological factors influencing the attainment of health for everyone]. Paper presented during the Health for All Conference, Havana, Cuba, July.

García Averasturi, L. (1985). Community health psychology in Cuba. *Journal of Community Psychology, 13*, 117–123.

Gonzalez Pacheco, O. (1983). La autorregulación moral del comportamiento [Moral self-regulation of behaviors]. *Revista del Hospital Psiquiátrico de La Habana, 24*, 87–120.

Gonzalez Rey, F. (1983). La communicación: Su importancia en el desarrollo de la personalidad [Communication: Its importance in personality development]. *Revista del Hospital Psiquiátrico de La Habana, 24*, 35–52.

Marín, B. V. (1985). Community psychology in Cuba: A literature review. *Journal of Community Psychology, 13*, 138–154.

Mitjans Martínez, A., & Febles Elejalde, M. (1983). La función social del psicologo en Cuba [The social function of the psychologist in Cuba]. *Revista del Hospital Psiquiátrico de La Habana, 24*, 5–20.

Perez Valdés, N., & Calvo Montalvo, N. (1985). Psychology in the rehabilitation of the chronic mental patient. *Journal of Community Psychology, 13*, 155–161.

Rodriguez Almeyda, L. (1980). La psicología de la communidad en Cuba [Psychology of the community in Cuba]. *Areito, 6*, 20–22.

Czechoslovakia

Josef Linhart and Miloslav Kodým

The origins of Czechoslovak psychology date back to the works of J. A. Komenský (1592–1670), better known to the rest of the world as Comenius. An intellectual leader of seventeenth-century Europe, this outstanding Czech educator and philosopher made important theoretical contributions to the development of both child and educational psychology that were far ahead of his time.

The materialist basis of Czechoslovak psychology was established in the eighteenth century by Jiří Procházka (1749–1820). His neurophysiological formulations led to a theory of reflexes well before the findings of Sechenov and Pavlov, the first Russian physiologists in this area, were published.

Experimental psychology in Czechoslovakia is rooted in the nineteenth-century work of Jan Evangelista Purkyně [Purkinje] (1787–1869), who was a physician, biologist, physiologist, and renowned professor at Charles University in Prague. Psychology as an independent discipline emerged at Charles University early in the twentieth century when František Krejčí (1858–1934) founded the first institute of psychology there.

Czechoslovak psychology did not begin to develop significantly, however, until the Republic of Czechoslovakia was formed in 1918. Courses in psychology were then offered by the philosophical faculties not only in Prague but also at the University of Brno. The discipline achieved a research base of its own in 1932 when the Czechoslovak Central Psychotechnical Institute opened in Prague, with a branch office in Bratislava. In addition to conducting research, the institute provided occupational counseling. Furthermore, educational psychology had its genesis within the department of education.

During this time, the theoretical framework of Czechoslovak psychology was strongly influenced by positivist philosophy although traces of a materialist tradition remained. There was particular interest in the psychological study of shape perception, psychotechnics, and German characterology.

The German Fascist occupation of Czechoslovakia commencing in the late 1930s led to the closing of the country's universities and temporarily slowed the progress of Czech psychology. A measure of continuity was nevertheless preserved through the work carried on at the Prague Institute of Human Labor which emerged from a reorganization of the Central Psychotechnical Institute.

OVERVIEW OF POST–WORLD WAR II PSYCHOLOGY

The end of World War II in 1945 brought with it fundamental changes within Czechoslovak society. These changes, in turn, provided guidelines for the planned development of Czechoslovak psychology. Following the inevitable clash between different conceptions of the discipline, progressive Marxist-Leninist theory gained an increasingly firm foothold in psychology because of the guidance provided by the Communist party of Czechoslovakia. Translations of Soviet scientific publications and textbooks were much relied on.

Psychology also developed as an applied science in liberated Czechoslovakia at the Institute of Human Labor. Psychological knowledge was utilized mainly in education, the nationalized industries, transportation, and clinical practice.

Czechoslovak psychology reached an important milestone when independent faculties of psychology were established first at Charles University in Prague in 1950 and later at the universities in Brno, Bratislava, Olomouc, and Košice. This was the start of a systematic program for Czechoslovak psychology that involved training more specialists at the universities, offering different types of advanced courses, and organizing a system of scientific education in keeping with the conditions of Socialist society, including the introduction of graduate assistantships and the degrees of candidate and doctor of psychological sciences. In addition, new agencies were set up in all the administrative regions of the country to conduct research and provide routine psychological services.

In 1957 the first psychological journal, *Československá Psychologie* [Czechoslovak Psychology], was founded, primarily to serve as a forum for Czechoslovak psychologists. A year later, the Czechoslovak Psychological Society, originally founded in 1927 but disbanded during the German occupation, was reorganized as part of the Czechoslovak Academy of Sciences (ČSAV).

Gradually, a number of central psychological institutes arose within the framework of the Czechoslovak Academy of Sciences. In 1954, first as part of the J. A. Komenský Pedagogical Institute, a department of psychology was created to become a nucleus for the subsequent establishment of an independent institute of psychology. In 1955, the Slovak Academy of Sciences in Bratislava inaugurated its first independent psychological facility, the Psychological Laboratory, which in 1963 became the present-day Slovak Academy of Sciences Institute of Experimental Psychology. In Prague, an independent Psychological Institute of ČSAV was established in 1967. At the same time, a branch unit was installed in Brno that became independent in 1970 and is now known as the ČSAV Psychological Laboratory.

In order to coordinate research and to ensure comprehensive control of the psychological and pedagogical disciplines, the Czechoslovak Academy of Sciences, in 1961, founded the ČSAV Scientific College for Pedagogics and Psychology. Thanks to the accomplishments of this institution and the support given by the Communist party of Czechoslovakia and other authoritative bodies in the country, significant research has taken place in both the theoretical and practical spheres of psychology.

There has also been a marked increase in the number of psychologists in Czechoslovakia. The Czechoslovak Psychological Society now has a membership of over 2,000 in contrast to the few dozen members comprising the organization at its reinstatement in 1958. Since 1958, ten psychological congresses, five Czechoslovak and five Slovak, have been organized by the society attesting to its vigor.

In addition, four international psychological conferences have been held in Prague. These meetings signify the increasing cooperation among psychologists worldwide which has greatly benefited Czechoslovak psychology not only because such cooperative efforts foster the exchange of scientific information and personnel but also because they promote certain research activities. Coordination of research was particularly encouraged by the conferences of psychologists from the Socialist countries held in Prague in 1973, 1974, and 1982.

The main purpose of the psychological sciences in Czechoslovakia is to share in the task of building an advanced Socialist society. Psychologists play an active role in the fulfillment of the State Plan of Basic Research designed to meet social needs.

In Czechoslovakia psychology is concerned with the laws of psychic processes and phenomena which are functions, or characteristics, of the brain and reflect objective reality. Psychology relates the origin and development of psychological processes and states, such as consciousness, to activity. This is the starting point for the historical and systemic approach of contemporary Marxist psychologists. The perspective encompasses developmental and social contexts, personality, and the biological and physiological dimensions of human functioning.

THE ORGANIZATIONAL STRUCTURE OF THE DISCIPLINE

The three independent psychological facilities of the Czechoslovak Academy of Sciences located in Prague, Brno, and Bratislava as well as the psychological unit of the ČSAV J. A. Komenský Pedagogical Institute in Prague are responsible for the initiation and coordination of psychological research in Czechoslovakia. The focus is on basic research and projects are assigned according to the State Plan of Basic Research. Personnel outside the ČSAV also take part in these projects as they progress through a three-stage cycle of basic research, applied research, and practice. Financial support is provided by government agencies and the ČSAV.

A major contribution to the development of the science comes from universities' schools of psychology, particularly those concerned with the training of psychologists. In the Czech section of the country these are the schools of psychology at Charles University in Prague, at J. E. Purkyně University in Brno, and at Palacký University in Olomouc. The oldest independent school of psychology, at Prague, consists of the departments of general and educational psychology, psychophysiology and clinical psychology, social psychology, and occupational and managerial psychology. In addition to their instructional activities, all of these departments conduct research, mainly within the guidelines of the State Plan of Basic Research. The problems investigated include those related to the planning and monitoring of activity, social communication and cooperation, work-team efficiency, and various neuropsychological processes. Applied research is carried out by departmental units working within the ministries of education, health care, psychiatry, industrial production, and trade.

We shall discuss first the research conducted at psychological facilities in the Czech section of the country and then that done at laboratories and departmental units located in the Slovak region. As will be apparent, most centers of psychological study are in the Czech part of the country.

The Organizational Structure of Czech Psychology

The Psychological Institute of the ČSAV[1] founded in 1967 when the department of psychology of the J. A. Komenský Pedagogical Institute became autonomous, plays a significant role in Czechoslovak psychology. The institute emphasizes research in general psychology, developmental psychology, the psychology of personality, social psychology, and comparative psychology. General psychology includes the study of learning, thinking, problem solving, and physiological processes. Social psychological investigations deal mainly with communication, motivation, and socialization.

Since 1970, research and theoretical work at the institute has centered on the thought processes. Particular emphasis has been placed on determining the relationships between activity and learning, activity and consciousness, and thought and learning, in addition to studying reflection as a basic psychological process. Examples of specific research projects include studies on paired-associate learning, verbal learning relative to major linguistic variables, and learning in different occupational settings. In collaboration with the department of social psychology, social factors related to activity and learning have been examined with a view to group management of the dynamics involved. More specifically, communication strategies, motivational variables, and factors having to do with personality and socialization have been investigated. Increasing methodological sophistication led, in 1976, to the establishment of the institute's mathematical and technical department.

The research done in the areas of general, developmental, comparative, social, and mathematical psychology is generated by societal needs. Psychologists have, for instance, been called upon to investigate basic cognitive processes, problems associated with managing people, and variables involved in education. The institute has gained prominence for its theoretical, methodological, and experimental work including field studies and longitudinal investigations. It is a center for advanced education and published the journal *Československá Psychologie*[2] [Czechoslovak Psychology] as well as a bulletin.

In coordinating projects assigned by the State Plan of Basic Research, the institute cooperates closely with psychologists at other facilities. It initiated and organized the four widely acclaimed international conferences focused on psychological development, learning, and the cognitive processes, held in Prague. The first of these took place in 1971 with subsequent meetings occurring every four years. The institute also plays a role in organizing a regular meeting of psychologists from the Danubian countries.

Significant contributions to Marxist-oriented psychology by the institute include a new approach to the psychology of learning and thought, the establishment of social psychology in Czechoslovakia, and a theory of reflection and active autoregulation of the human personality within a given sociohistorical context. This theory is relevant for general, developmental, and social psychology. Moreover, important published research has expanded our understanding of the volitional processes, human learning, the ethical development of children, group activities, and the key psychological problems associated with cognition and motivation. Finally, the institute has developed a number of psychometric techniques.

The ČSAV Psychological Laboratory in Brno specializes in research on personality structure and development, creativity, and values. Studies include broadly based longitudinal investigations of the psychological development of children and adolescents. The general approach is interdisciplinary and, recently, international. The laboratory cooperates with scientific institutions concerned with psychology and its practical applications in educational and other settings. This facility not only conducts scientific investigations but also critically analyzes and evaluates bourgeois psychological theories.

The Department of Pedagogical Psychology and Laboratory of Programmed Learning of the J. A. Komenský (Comenius) Pedagogical Institute of the Czechoslovak Academy of Sciences in Prague consists of eleven scientists divided into three research teams. One group examines problems associated with programmed learning, the second studies the motivation of students, and the third analyzes verbal abilities and the development of verbal skills in children. The primary functions of this department are to study how young people develop in a Socialist society and to devise educational techniques which will increase teacher effectiveness and improve student motivation. Research findings have been widely applied in the schools and in teacher-training programs.

In the fields of education, applied psychological research takes place in university departments of psychology and at pedagogical research institutions. Studies concern what teachers should teach, effective teaching techniques, mental hygiene in schools, and the relationships between personality factors and effective instruction. Much of the personality research is done at the Central Institute for Pedagogical Staff Education. Furthermore, the department of education maintains consulting centers in each of the country's administrative regions. These offer professional advice to schools and parents concerning problems children may be having in school. They also provide occupational counseling.

In the field of health care, psychological research and training occur in a number of institutions run by the Department of Health Care. These include the Institute for Advanced Medical and Pharmaceutical Studies; the Institute for Mother and Child Care, a unit of the Research Institute for Psychiatry; the Institute of Health Education; and the Institute of Hygiene and Epidemiology. All of these facilities are located in Prague. Additionally, psychological services are offered by the regional institutes of national health.

The Institute for Advanced Medical and Pharmaceutical Studies employs eight psychologists working in what is called the Cabinet of Psychology. This group is responsible primarily for training physicians, clinical psychologists, and other university graduates in clinical and medical psychology. Instruction focuses mainly on normal and pathological personality development, interpersonal relationships, and the use of psychological research methods in medicine.

Psychological studies at the Institute for Mother and Child Care involve both psychologists and medical specialists, who examine child behavior and development during early infancy and throughout the long-term follow-up care these professionals provide, especially for at-risk babies. The institute contributes importantly to both developmental psychology and the practical areas of child care and education.

The psychologists attached to the Research Institute for Psychiatry work on a wide range of clinical problems but tend to concentrate on the psychological aspects of stressful situations, ways to manage and reduce stress or anxiety, deviant behavior in the context of different experimental models, and alcoholism and its prevention. The findings of this group have had relevance for preventative medicine, research in occupational settings, and the training of cosmonauts.

The psychological investigations conducted by the Institute of Health Education mostly concern psychological factors involved in the development and prevention of cardiovascular diseases. Some of this work has achieved international prominence.

Also in the field of health care, psychologists serve as consultants at clinics specializing in marital counseling and provide psychological services for clinical departments and the regional institutes of national health. The department of mental hygiene and occupational psychology at the Institute of Hygiene and Epidemiology in Prague, where psychologists do research alongside medical specialists, offers methodological expertise to practicing psychologists and coordinates their projects.

In the industrial area, psychologists are employed by many government agencies. Those associated with the Institute of the Ministry of Industry, for example, provide advanced courses for executives, consult, and conduct research. Work has been done on increasing the social competency of supervisory workers, ways to improve training programs in the context of modern production facilities, and other problems which fall within the boundaries of occupational psychology. Psychologists are also attached to large enterprises such as the metallurgical and chemical industries and utilities. These psychologists help solve problems which arise in day-to-day plant operations.

Psychologists at the Transportation Research Institute in Prague and the Railway Research Institute in both Prague and Plzeň serve as diagnosticians, consultants, and researchers. Their expertise is particularly valuable in matters having to do with safety and the training of drivers, train engineers, airplane pilots, and traffic controllers. Psychologists also work at the Prague Research Institute of Trade. Here they cooperate with economists and sociologists in marketing studies having to do with consumer behavior, needs and purchasing habits, motivational factors involved in shopping, and consumer types. They also do human factors research and serve as consultants to specific companies and industries on issues having to do with trade and marketing.

The Organizational Structure of Slovak Psychology

Psychology in Slovakia began to acquire its own special character while developing within Czechoslovak psychology as a whole, in the context of such institutions as the J. A. Komenský (Comenius) University Philosophical Faculty, the Psychological Institute, and the Slovak Matica, a cultural-scientific association. Following World War II, Slovak psychology moved away from an eclectic-positivistic orientation in order to meet the needs of a new Socialist society. Contact between Czech and Slovak psychologists was resumed and they met at a 1957 conference in Smolenica to discuss their dedication to the goals of socialism. In 1949 the Bratislava Comenius University Philosophical Faculty had introduced an independent psychological teaching specialization and in 1957 a psychological institute was established. In 1965, a School of Pedagogical Psychology with a department of educational psychology was created. At present the School of Psychology of the Philosophical Faculty in Bratislava has departments of general psychology, medical psychology, and occupational psychology.

In 1952, a section of psychology was started at the Philosophical Institute of the Slovak Academy of Sciences (SAV). Its function was to work out principles for the restructuring of the psychological sciences based on Marxist-Leninist assumptions. In 1955, this section was instrumental in the creation of the psychological laboratory of the SAV, the first professional institute for basic psychological research in all of Czechoslovakia. In 1963, the laboratory was transformed into the present Institute of Experimental Psychology of the SAV in Bratislava.

This institute consists of departments of general psychology, engineering psychology, human psychophysiology, and personality supplemented by units designed to integrate the institute's activities—one for the modeling of psychological processes and statistics, the other for generating general theory and methodology.

There are other subdivisions which provide additional expertise with regard to technical and scientific matters.

Since 1965, the institute has published the journal *Studia Psychologica*.[3] Initially most of the articles included in this publication were in Slovak or in Czech. Since 1970, however, the journal has had an international editorial board consisting of representatives of the psychological sciences from the various Socialist countries. Research articles of interest to a more general audience are published in *News of the Institute of Experimental Psychology*. The institute also publishes the proceedings of the international conferences it has organized as well as monographs and textbooks.

The Psychological Institute of the Comenius University Philosophical Faculty in Bratislava[4] specializes in comparative and physiological psychology. In addition, it includes a teaching and service subdivision, a psychological consulting center that contributes to graduate education, and a laboratory which designs and builds psychological apparatus. Its staff of about seventy professionals plays an important role in training future specialists in psychology and in providing lectures on psychology at other facilities.

In 1964, the Ministry of Education of the Slovak Socialist Republic established what is now the Research Institute of Pediatric Psychology and Psychopathology in Bratislava.[5] Research units conduct studies on semantic and cognitive development, socialization, psychopathology, and methodological and organizational matters. This facility is now the country's largest psychological center.

During the immediate postwar years, there were not many psychologists in Czechoslovakia doing practical psychological work. However, the 1950s saw a systematic expansion of applied psychology. In the early 1960s, an increasing number of psychologists became engaged in projects associated with industrial production. A few relatively independent research centers were set up in the chemical, engineering, and construction industries. By the end of the 1960s, psychologists worked in a variety of other industrial fields. Psychological centers were also established in educational institutions, and state agencies started to employ psychologists.

In 1958, the psychological section of the Slovak Academy of Sciences organized a general assembly of the Slovak Psychological Society. At its founding, the Slovak Psychological Society had a membership of forty-nine; now there are 850 members, including 700 professional psychologists. The society holds conferences and congresses and helps organize the meetings of psychologists of the Danubian countries held in Smolenica. These meetings were, in fact, initiated by the Institute of Experimental Psychology of the SAV.

As a part of the State Plan of Basic Research, Slovak psychologists study the psychophysiological mechanisms associated with autoregulation, rational stress, short-term memory, and so forth. The human factors intrinsic to computer technology are examined at the Institute of Experimental Psychology of the SAV. Research at the Psychological Institute of the Comenius University Philosophical Faculty focuses on the regulation of motivational factors and successful action.

The Research Institute of Pediatric Psychology and Psychopathology conducts studies on normal and pathological cognitive functioning and personality. This research includes investigations into normal and retarded cognitive development, processes and problems underlying language development, and the effects of frustration in school settings on personality formation.

In the management area, Slovak psychologists have in recent years investigated problems connected with education, work, social security, and health care. University and other psychological research facilities have, for example, conducted studies on the role of teachers in the instructional process, the relationships between personality and the intellectual capabilities of teachers and teaching effectiveness, the factors involved in the adaptability of pupils to school settings, and ethical issues. The psychology department of the Czechoslovak Research Institute of Social Welfare in Bratislava investigates worker motivation in various occupations.

Since 1969, future psychologists have also been able to receive training at the other Slovak university, in Košice. Moreover, the faculty there has been engaged in a number of significant scientific studies.

MAIN RESEARCH OBJECTIVES OF CZECHOSLOVAK PSYCHOLOGY

While developing within the social sciences, psychology in Czechoslovakia is closely linked to biology, particularly those aspects of biology concerned with evolution, physiology, and cybernetics. At the same time, Czechoslovak psychology is based on Marxist-Leninist philosophy, especially dialectical materialism. Several conferences and numerous discussions produced a document called "The Development, Present State, and Objectives of the Social Sciences in the Czechoslovak Socialist Republic" issued by the Presidium of the Central Committee of the Communist party of Czechoslovakia. The plan detailed in this document was adopted in 1974 and has served as a guide for the further development of the social sciences including psychology. Stressed are the role of the human factor in social consciousness and science as a tool for building an advanced Socialist society. The main tasks for psychology are to complete the ideological rebirth of the discipline, to formulate long-range programs that meet the needs of Socialist society, to strengthen its educational and research base, and to foster cooperation with psychologists in other countries.

More specifically, Czechoslovak psychology is concerned with the following problems and issues:

(a) the basic methodological and theoretical problems of Marxist psychology and the critical reassessment of one-sided Western psychological schools of thought, particularly behaviorism, anthropological existentialism, Freudianism, and phenomenology

(b) the objective laws underlying the formation of both social and individual consciousness and, within this context, the study of the development of scientific world views in young people and adults

(c) the laws underlying human work and creativity in different walks of life within Socialist society (occupational psychology and the psychology of scientific and artistic work)

(d) the development of the psychological makeup and personality of Socialist man

(e) cognitive processes and their regulatory function in people's activities

(f) social factors in human psychological development such as those relating to the motivational aspects of achieving an active approach to life and work

(g) psychological variables associated with the organization of work, the relationships that develop between individuals in production teams, and the linkage between various social organizations and optimum productivity in different work settings and under various living conditions

(h) the psychological foundations of education and training, including the relationship between Communist education and career choices

(i) the psychological aspects of the health-care system with a view to evaluating methods of prevention, psychotherapy, and the general treatment of mental and somatic diseases

These areas of concern provide the basis for the assignments detailed in the State Plan of Basic Research. While psychological research is well organized within Czechoslovakia, efforts are being made to further coordinate Czechoslovak work with that of psychologists in the Soviet Union and the other Socialist countries.

Theoretical and Methodological Foundations

Theoretical psychology is not adequately developed in Czechoslovakia, nor are enough psychologists working in this area. The primary theoretical task is to derive the laws and concepts from dialectical materialism that relate to psychology and the social sciences in general. Involved is a systematically identified set of problems, the solution of which requires the joint efforts of both social and natural scientists.

Central to the theoretical work of psychologists is the psychological or mental development of the human being which involves human actions or activity, learning and thought processes, and personality. This complex set of interrelated processes is being examined within the context of a theory of reflection based on the Marxist views concerning cognition and practice. Czechoslovak psychologists have published a number of theory-oriented monographs which, in conjunction with work done by Soviet psychologists (S. L. Rubinstein, A. N. Leontiev, B. F. Lomov, and others), aim at a new synthesis of contemporary psychology worldwide.

Unlike pragmatically and existentially oriented Western psychology, which treats thought, goal-oriented behavior, initiative, attitudes toward work, and personal commitment as independent and isolated processes, psychologists in

Czechoslovakia strive for a comprehensive approach. Although stimulus-response models and the pragmatic conception of activity as mere adaptation to the surrounding environment have already been theoretically refuted, they continue to exercise considerable influence in capitalist countries, notably in the area of industrial management. Marxist psychology, in contrast, emphasizes the human capability to become creative and to control and direct action. The relationships among human action (activity), consciousness, and personality are especially salient. It has been well demonstrated by recent research, in the Soviet Union as well as in Czechoslovakia, that these aspects of the human condition must be studied as a unified whole. When viewed from this perspective, personality formation and structure are seen in a new light, partly as an intersection of social relationships, and partly as the stable product of psychological processes and actions generated by comprehensive autoregulatory processes which allow each person to interact with his or her environment. Of particular importance for the psychological theorizing and research being done in both the Slovak and Czech regions of the country is the conception of the psychological regulation of activity.

Within this new systematic perspective, Czech psychologists have derived a theory of learning that takes into account both phylogenetic and ontogenetic contexts. Learning is understood to be a process of constructing new components of behavior and activity and new characteristics of consciousness and personality (Linhart, 1970, 1982). When learning takes place, a person actively overcomes the discrepancies between an initial state of uncertainty and the results that must be achieved. This process is accompanied by the simultaneous development of individual human abilities. The fact that people learn throughout their entire lives is extremely important and is well recognized by Socialist societies. This theory of learning has applications in education, social control, and psychotherapy.

The developmental approach is intrinsic to Czechoslovak psychology. The psychological processes that arise in people as a reflection of objective reality are seen as basic to the existence of the mental realm. Developmental research, therefore, takes into account human cultural history in addition to phylogenetic and ontogenetic factors.

Now considered intrinsic to general psychology, these new theoretical viewpoints have influenced both experimental psychology and such applied fields as educational psychology, clinical psychology, abnormal psychology, consulting psychology, engineering psychology, and social psychology. Highly qualified psychologists are, in fact, working in all areas because, in Czechoslovakia, theory and practice are in dialectical unity. Theoretical progress has also played a role in generating interest and research in psychosemiotics, psycholinguistics, forensic psychology, and biodromal psychology.

Representative Research

The Institute of Experimental Psychology in Bratislava is noted for a psychobiological orientation which harmonizes the social and cognitive emphases characteristic of Slovak psychology. The introduction of various mathematical procedures and experimental methodologies assures that research is both precise and scientific and facilitative of interdisciplinary cooperation. The institute exercises considerable influence on all Slovak psychologists. It has fostered the development of innovative specialties such as engineering psychology and new research areas involving, for example, information theory and computer technology. The cooperation of psychologists with cyberneticists and scientists is also furthered by the institute.

Its specific accomplishments include over 230 experimental projects; the development of numerous statistical procedures, computer programs, and research methods and equipment; and critical analyses of behaviorism, structuralism, and humanistic psychology. Particularly noteworthy is the formulation of a view of perception as dependent on diverse intrapsychic and stochastic variables. There has also been intensive investigation of the different types and stages of short-term memory within a more general cognitive context and within the context of personality. Also in the cognitive area, psychologists in Bratislava have derived new ways of conceiving individual differences in thinking and the processes involved in rational representation.

In psychophysiology, investigators at the institute have helped to clarify the ways that the bioelectric reactivity of the skin serves as an indicator of psychological regulatory activities. Studied too have been the physiological correlates of cognitive functioning which are a function of personality differences.

In the field of engineering psychology, psychologists have developed new ways of measuring the physical and mental fatigue experienced by workers operating semiautomatic equipment and helped formulate relevant job specifications. Moreover, psychologists have participated in interdisciplinary research on stress.

Experimental studies of personality have been especially fruitful. Factor-analytic investigations have uncovered new relationships between creativity and age, occupational status, and specific abilities. Considerable progress has been made in identifying the optimal combination of variables in the regulation of personality-determined activity. The work of the institute in Bratislava has received considerable international attention. Numerous invitations to take part in collaborative research have been extended.

Turning our attention now to the work conducted at the Psychological Institute of the Czechoslovak Academy of Sciences in Prague, it is clear that psychologists at this institution have made substantive contributions to the field. They have, for example, helped clarify the nature of the psychological processes involved in creativity, decision making, problem solving, learning, and other aspects of human functioning. They have also explored the emergence of higher levels of psychological reflection associated with various types of activity and learning within the overall principles of development and reflection. In the process they have furthered our understanding of the still inadequately explored relationships intrinsic to the dialectical unity of human consciousness and actions.

Within this general research area, Linhart and his associates are investigating the conscious understanding of problem situations, language-mediated communication, and the semiological interpretation of sign structures. Also being systematically explored are the processes of concept formation as specific manifestations of the reflection of objective reality and the correspondence between problem solving and dynamic decision making.

Furthermore, psychologists at the institute in Prague study the ways that plans control or determine human activity. This research, involving the elucidation of the relationships and interfaces between planned and actual activity, is founded on the Marxist assumptions that external reality is objectively reflected in human consciousness and that human decisions are based on rational interpretations of life situations. Of particular interest are questions having to do with the roles that cognitive and motivational processes play in determining the human activity underlying work and learning. Research results have been applied to socioeconomic management.

Projects investigating the conditions supporting sound physical and psychological development represent an important area of concern for some staff members at the institute. This work is done by psychologists in cooperation with medical and sports specialists and is closely linked to evolutionary biological research. The information derived is of relevance to the formation and management of groups including teams. Findings pertain to such problems as raising the socioeconomic effectiveness of groups, identifying ways to instill a sense of group responsibility, increasing the effectiveness of group learning, and determining how to ensure that group members develop attitudes and relationships consonant with the social, technological, and scientific needs of society.

What is learned from these and other studies is applied at the institute to design further projects and improve research methodologies. In general, the approach involves a combination of experimental laboratory techniques and program-based modeling under natural conditions. This strategy has been particularly successful in the study of social learning, with many of the findings utilized to raise worker efficiency and develop correct ideological outlooks. The findings have, in fact, been found relevant to many of the problems identified by the Communist party congresses and the government.

In the area of creativity and personality, research at the institute has focused on the impact of increasing automation on worker morale and creative ability. Since many functions are increasingly taken over by machines, it is essential, as part of social planning, to assure that workers are not dehumanized and deprived of the sense of pride and satisfaction associated with challenging occupational activities.

Fundamental to understanding the relationships between creativity and personality is the study of the structure of intellectual abilities. In contrast with most previous investigations of intelligence, which are noncomprehensive and usually ignore social contexts and personality structure, research at the institute takes place within a systematic historical framework.

To conclude, the above is only a sampling of the psychological research being done in Czechoslovakia. Many other interesting studies have been done or are now in progress. The particular investigations discussed here, however, have been especially productive in terms of published results and international recognition.

TEXTBOOKS

While textbooks written by Czechoslovak psychologists are not available for all subfields, such texts do exist in general psychology, educational psychology, the psychology of physical education, the psychology of management, and medical psychology. Widely used books include:

In general psychology—Linhart, J., et al. (1981). *Essentials of general psychology.* Prague: State Pedagogical Publishing House (in Czech); Pardel, T., & Boroš, J. (1979). *Essentials of general psychology.* Bratislava: Slovak Pedagogical Publishing House (in Slovak); Linhart, J. (1982). *Essentials of the psychology of learning.* Prague: State Pedagogical Publishing House (in Czech).

In educational psychology—Ďurič, L. (1981). *Introduction to educational psychology.* Bratislava: Slovak Pedagogical Publishing House (in Slovak).

In the psychology of physical education—Vaněk, M., et al. (1980). *Psychology of sports.* Prague: State Pedagogical Publishing House (in Czech); Kodým, M., et al. (in press). *Psychology of physical education.* Prague: State Pedagogical Publishing House (in Czech).

In the psychology of management—Khol, J. (1982). *Psychology of management.* Prague: State Pedagogical Publishing House (in Czech).

In medical psychology—Kondáš, O. (1980). *Clinical psychology.* Bratislava: Osveta (in Slovak).

THE FUTURE DEVELOPMENT OF CZECHOSLOVAK PSYCHOLOGY

As the number of psychologists has increased, it has become necessary to identify new ways of utilizing the expertise of these professionals. Efforts have been under way recently to define the legal and administrative status of psychologists and to specify formally their competencies relative to theoretical and applied matters. At recent meetings of both Slovak and Czech psychologists, there was a general consensus that a serious effort should be made to provide for a more balanced development of the various branches of psychology.

The significance of Marxist psychology for the progress of Czechoslovak society is becoming increasingly apparent. Working with professionals from other disciplines, because an interdisciplinary approach is essential, psychologists will continue to study the interrelationships among consciousness formation, personality, and motivation in order to determine how these complex aspects of human functioning relate to human action. Underlying all planning for the discipline of psychology is the goal of improving the lives of the Czechoslovak people and strengthening their social awareness.

NOTES

1. Psychological Institute, ČSAV, Husova 4, 110 00 Prague 1.
2. *Československá Psychologie* is a journal of psychological theory and practice edited by Professor Dr. M. Kodým, CSc., Director—Psychological Institute of the ČSAV, Úvoz 24, 118 00 Prague 1.
3. *Studia Psychologica* is a journal for basic research in the psychological sciences edited by D. Kováč. DrSc., Director of the Institute of Experimental Psychology of the Slovak Academy of Sciences, Kocelova 15, 801 00 Bratislava, CSSR.
4. Psychological Institute, Comenius University Philosophical Faculty, Bratislava, Gondova 2, 806 01, Bratislava, CSSR.
5. Research Institute of Pediatric Psychology and Psychopathology, Legionárska 4, 801 00 Bratislava, CSSR.

REFERENCES

Linhart, J. (1970). *Process and structure of human learning.* Moscow: Progress (in Russian). [Prague: Academia, 1972 (in Czech). Warsaw: State Science Publishing House, 1972 (in Polish).]
Linhart, J. (1982). *Psychologie učení* [Psychology of learning]. Prague: SPN.

SUGGESTED READINGS

Bureš, Z. (1981). *Psychology of work and its uses.* Prague: Praće (in Czech).
Čáp, J. (1980). *Psychology for teachers.* Prague: State Pedagogical Publishing House (in Czech).
Chalupa, B. (1973). *Creativity in science and technology.* Brno: J. E. Purkyně University Philosophical Faculty Press (in Czech).
Helus, Z. (1982). *The conception of the pupil and personality prospects.* Prague: State Pedagogical Publishing House (in Czech).
Hlavsa, J., et al., (1981). *Psychological problems of education for creativity.* Prague: State Pedagogical Publishing House (in Czech).
Homola, M. (1977). *Motivation of human behavior.* Prague: State Pedagogical Publishing House (in Czech).
Jurovský, A. (1980). *Man's personality at work.* Bratislava: Práca (in Slovak).
Kodým, M. (1977). *Determinants of motor skills.* Prague: Czechoslovak Union of Physical Education (in Czech).
Kodým, M. (Ed.). (1984). Psychological development, learning and personality formation. *Proceedings of the 4th Prague International Psychological Conference.* Prague: Academia.
Kollárik, T. (1979). *Psychological aspects of work satisfaction.* Bratislava: Psychodiagnostic and Didactic Tests (in Slovak).
Kondáš, O. (1981). *Psychohygiene of the weekday.* Bratislava: Osvěta (in Slovak).

Konečný, B., and Bouchal, M. (1979). *Psychology in medicine*. Prague: Avicenum (in Czech).

Koščo, J., et al. (1980). *Theory and practice of psychological consulting services*. Bratislava: Slovak Pedagogical Publishing House (in Slovak).

Kováč. D. (1982). Psychology in Czechoslovakia: 1976–1980. *Československá psychologie, 2* (in Slovak).

Linhart, J. (1949). *American pragmatism*. Prague: Melantrich (in Czech). [Moscow: Foreign Languages Publishing House, (in Russian). Moscow: Foreign Languages Publishing House, 1954 (in Chinese).]

Linhart, J. (1976). *Activity and learning*. Prague: Academia (in Czech).

Linhart, J., and Novák, V. (1985). *The principle of reflection in biology and psychology*. Prague: Academia (in Czech).

Mikšík, O. (1979). *Topical problems of personality psychology*. Prague: Horizont (in Czech).

Pardel, T. (1978). *General psychology*. Bratislava: Slovak Pedagogical Publishing House (in Slovak).

Radil, T. (1978). *Sleep and wakefulness*. Prague: Academia (in Czech).

Růžička, J. (1979). *Psychology in work with people*. Prague: Svoboda (in Czech).

Sedlák, J. (1981). *Working fatigue*. Prague: Academia (in Czech).

Šípoš, I. (1978). *General psychology*. Bratislava: Slovak Pedagogical Publishing House (in Slovak).

Denmark

Simo Køppe

Denmark can claim one of the first psychological laboratories in the world. The facility was established in 1886 in Copenhagen by Alfred Lehman (1858–1921), an engineer who became interested in psychophysics and studied for some years with Wilhelm Wundt in Germany. Originally known as the Psychophysical Laboratory, it was renamed the Psychological Laboratory of the University of Copenhagen in 1924. Until the 1950s, this was the only place in Denmark where university-level psychological research was conducted.

Before 1918, there was no formal psychology curriculum in Denmark. Those interested in studying psychology had to enroll in programs leading to the Master of Arts degree in philosophy with an emphasis in psychology. In 1918, however, the Master of Arts degree in psychology, which is still offered today, was established. The program leading to this degree serves to train people for research and for academic positions; it does not prepare them to work in applied settings. During and following World War II, graduate studies in a wide variety of psychological specialties were implemented, first at the University of Copenhagen and later at the Royal Danish School of Educational Studies.

THE TRAINING OF PSYCHOLOGISTS

University Programs

At the University of Copenhagen, the training of psychologists takes place in two institutes, the Psychological Laboratory and the Institute of Clinical Psychology. The former has a full-time staff of forty-five: three professors, thirty associate and assistant professors, and twelve students with scholarships. The latter has a staff of one full professor, nineteen associate and assistant professors, and one scholarship holder. In addition, there are six postgraduates associated with the clinical program. Those being trained work under supervision in a clinic assisting with the treatment of both children and adults. In 1982, 323 clients were referred to this facility.

Students may also train to become psychologists at the University of Aarhus. Here programs are offered by the Psychological Institute staffed by five full professors, twenty-one associate and assistant professors, and six students with scholarships.

During each of the last two years, about 300 students were enrolled in the graduate programs in psychology at the two universities. Each institution offers two types of programs. In addition to the Master of Arts, the degree of Candidate of Psychology is conferred on students who have successfully prepared for a practical career.

The Candidate of Psychology degree, while designed as a five-and-one-half-year program, ususally takes more than eight years to complete. Students go through four levels of training. At the beginning level, they must complete a laboratory course designed to provide insights into the relationships between theory and real-world problems. In the process, students are made aware of the strengths and limitations of person-oriented, social-oriented, and organism-oriented research and conceptions. At the first level they also take courses in the philosophy of science, genetics, physiological psychology, and research methodology. In order to move to the second level students must pass a number of major examinations. They then concentrate on developmental and educational psychology along with psychiatry and criminology. While on the third level students must pass examinations in vocational psychology, clinical psychology, and educational psychology; become familiar with several psychological professions via a short practicum; work for four months in a psychological setting under supervision; and write a thesis of about eighty pages on a chosen subject. At the fourth level, the last phase of training, students take a course in the legal aspects of psychological practice and must pass tests in psychometrics, social psychology, and general psychology. In major subject-matter areas, students often write lengthy papers but may elect oral evaluations. For minor subjects, however, written examinations are generally required.

The program leading to a Master of Arts, the research degree, is more flexible. Although the first level of training is the same as for students enrolled in the candidate program, the rest of the curriculum (the next two levels) requires completing a large-scale experimental project, carrying out a significant theoretical study, and documenting knowledge of the major areas of psychology with a relevant list of completed readings. The degree is awarded upon delivery of a public lecture. Most students take about ten years to complete what is formally considered to be a six-year program. Only about ten people start this program each year.

As a brief historical note, until the early 1970s, all students at the University of Copenhagen had to pass a course in philosophy (*filosofikum*). The course was usually taken during the first year and paralleled the main program of study. From the 1880s on, much of the philosophy curriculum consisted of psychological theory, and because textbooks written in Danish were not available Danish philosophers wrote their own. For many years, the most widely read Danish psychology textbook both in Denmark and in other countries was *Psychology* by Harad Høffding (1843–1931). The book originally appeared in 1882 but several editions were published until the 1930s. It was translated into several languages. While Høffding was not a research scientist himself, he presented a clear review and synthesis of what had been done by others.

In 1945, the Danish philosopher Jørgen Jørgensen (1894–1969) published *Psykologi pa biologisk grundlag*, [The Biological foundations of psychology], a textbook which was widely used in Denmark. A prominent logical positivist, Jørgensen tried to integrate the behavioral, phenomenological, and physiological aspects of psychology. He also introduced behaviorism to Danish psychology. His text was, incidentally, the last to be written specifically for the *filosofikum*.

Programs at the Royal Danish School of Educational Studies

The Royal Danish School of Educational Studies offers higher-level instruction for teachers who have already completed teacher training. In 1965, the school was assigned the task of offering a program in school psychology. A few years later, programs were added in educational research methodologies for professionals associated with Danish schools, teacher-training colleges, and facilities concerned with the education of adults. Currently, the Institute for Educational Psychology at the school is staffed by seven full professors, twenty-six associate and assistant professors, and four people on scholarships.

Students who pass the teacher-college examinations and have had two years of teaching experience may enroll in the graduate program which leads to the Candidate in Educational Psychology degree. The three-year program covers a wide variety of material with emphasis on personality, developmental, and educational psychology. In the last few years, annual enrollment in the program has numbered approximately 500.

Programs Offered by University Centers

Because of the increasing utilization of psychological knowledge and procedures by society as a whole and because of the introduction of psychology courses in secondary schools, two-year programs in psychology were initiated for psychology teachers in the early 1970s at the two newly founded university centers in Roskilde and Aalborg. Those enrolled may work toward a graduate degree if they expand their studies to include the courses required in another major field. The focus of the curriculum is on theories of socialization, learning processes, developmental psychology, and societal needs. The university centers are each staffed by two professors and ten associate professors.

RESEARCH SETTINGS

Psychological research in Denmark takes place mostly at the University of Copenhagen, the University of Aarhus, and the Royal Danish School of Educational Studies but is also conducted at the Pedagogical Institute of Denmark, the Social Research Institute, the Technological Institute, the Military Psychological Service, and the Danish Directorate of Work. The latter establishments have no teaching function. In addition, psychological investigations are carried out in applied settings by clinical psychologists and school psychologists. Finally, the Danish Research Council for the Humanities solicits research proposals and supports projects that generally take no longer than one year. Funding is for travel, publications, translations, and other incidental expenses.

PROFESSIONAL ASSOCIATIONS

Most psychologists in Denmark are members of the Association of Danish Psychologists. Membership is open to those holding the Candidate of Psychology, Master of Arts, or Candidate of Pedagogical Psychology degree. Some psychologists with the Candidate of Pedagogical Psychology degree are also members of the National Association for School Psychologists while others with the Master of Arts degree belong to the Association of Danish Magisters. A few Danish psychologists are members of the Danish section of the International Psychoanalytic Association. The Association of Danish Psychologists, however, is the organization primarily responsible for the interests of psychologists in matters of law, ethics, and employment.

JOURNALS AND OTHER PUBLICATIONS

The Association of Danish Psychologists circulates a periodical called the *Danish Psychologist News* twice monthly. The association is also involved in the publication of the *Scandinavian Journal of Psychology*. Approximately every six months a group of psychologists at the two universities issues *Psyche and Logos* and *Udkast*. Danish psychologists also contribute to the *Scandinavian Review of Psychoanalysis*, and the Danish Psychological Press, an independent publishing firm, offers standardized test materials and other psychological publications. Both the Psychological Institute and the Institute of Clinical Psychology distribute series of reports, mostly monographs.

THE EMPLOYMENT OF DANISH PSYCHOLOGISTS

Ninety-six percent of employed Danish psychologists work for public institutions; the rest are in private practice. Unfortunately, 17 percent of all psychologists with graduate degrees are unemployed. Table 1 presents information concerning the numbers of psychologists in each major employment category.

Table 1
Employment Situations for Psychologists, 1982

Teaching and research	315
Clinical school psychologists	275
School psychologists	500
Social administration	242
Hospital psychologists	216
Special care and treatment institutions	78
Private enterprise	76
The state ministries	41
Vocational psychology	30
Prisons, libraries, and other facilities	18
Unemployed	310

Psychologists in Teaching and Research

Psychologists in teaching and research include psychologists who are instructors at teachers colleges as well as those with teaching and research positions at the universities and the Royal Danish School of Educational Studies. In 1984, the qualifications for various university positions were changed. In order to become a full-time associate professor, one must now first be awarded a candidate's scholarship for two-and-one-half years. This scholarship is a research post with few teaching obligations. Then one must attain a four-year assistant professorship requiring half-time teaching and half-time research. Only then can one apply for an associate professorship, which involves 50 percent teaching, 40 percent research, and 10 percent administrative duties. At the universities, it is also possible to be considered for a three-year senior scholar's position. The top position of full professor is the goal of academicians who have distinguished themselves as associate professors.

School Psychologists and Clinical School Psychologists

As can be seen from Table 1, more Danish psychologists are employed in the categories of school and clinical school psychologists than in any other. While most school psychologists hold the Candidate of Pedagogical Psychology degree, clinical school psychologists have earned the Candidate of Psychology degree. Both types of psychologists work mainly at centers that provide psychological services for elementary schools. They diagnose and treat children with social and psychological problems. Counseling and therapy frequently involve the entire family. School psychologists are also responsible for providing whatever special education is required.

Psychologists in Social Administration

Psychologists employed in social administration fulfill many different functions. They advise the state and various communes and engage in relevant research. They also cooperate in planning social programs and are engaged in the fight against drugs and criminality.

Hospital Psychologists

Hospital psychologists include clinical and clinical school psychologists who work at mental hospitals or in neurological, pediatric, and other departments at general hospitals. They are primarily engaged in psychological diagnosis but also take part in providing individual and group therapy. There is no formal authorization of clinical psychologists by the medical profession and only a few training opportunities for graduate students in hospital settings are available for clinicians. No government-approved training programs in psychotherapy for psychologists exist at the present time.

Psychologists in Private Practice

Psychologists in private practice are primarily engaged in psychotherapeutic work or management consulting.

Unemployed Psychologists

As noted, the number of unemployed Danish psychologists at this time is high, about 17 percent. While the total number of male and female psychologists in Denmark is about the same, two-thirds of the unemployed psychologists are women.

DEVELOPMENTS IN DANISH PSYCHOLOGY PRIOR TO 1960

Before discussing developments in theory and basic research, a few words about applied psychology are in order. Although there were still relatively few well-trained psychologists by the 1940s, applied psychology in Denmark had started to expand in the 1930s. The first school psychologists, for example, were appointed in 1934. As a consequence, applied research concerned mostly developmental aspects of the educational process and individual differences. Prominent researchers included H. Meyer, S. Rifbjerg, H. Tordrup, A. M. Nørvig, and T. Sigsgaard. Sigsgaard was later appointed professor at the Royal Danish School of Educational Studies.

Another rapidly expanding area in those days was occupational psychology or, more accurately, the field of psychotechnics. The most productive psychologist in this area was P. Bahnsen, who, along with his coworkers, developed training guides for those entering a variety of occupations. Clinical psychology was for many years dominated by psychiatrists. The few well-trained clinical psychologists who did exist tended to be psychoanalysts, for example, S. Naesgaard and A. Rattleff.

Until the end of the 1950s, most of the significant psychological research in Denmark took place at the Psychological Laboratory of the University of Copenhagen. As already mentioned, Alfred Lehmann founded this laboratory in 1886. He remained in charge of the facilty until 1922, when Edgar Rubin (1886–1951) succeeded him.

In contrast with Lehmann, who was first and foremost a psychophysicist, Rubin was more phenomenologically oriented. Between 1911 and 1913, while studying in Göttingen, Rubin performed his landmark perceptual experiments on the figure-ground relationship. These studies became the basis of his dissertation, "Visually experienced figures" (1915), which was later translated into German.

Rubin remained preoccupied throughout his professional career with the question of what it means to describe phenomena as precisely and scientifically as possible. While he disavowed classical associationism and believed that consciousness is characterized by irreducible entities, he also objected to what he considered to be uncritical use of the concept 'wholeness' by Gestalt psychologists. Rubin is best described as a scientific, but not a philosophical, phenomenologist. He was not much influenced by Husserl but did take everyday experiences as the starting point of his research (see Rubin, 1949).

A harsh critic, Rubin made strong demands on what he considered the scientific approach. His extreme stance was in fact counterproductive in that it apparently prevented other psychologists from publishing their research. It is no coincidence that during Rubin's tenure at the Psychological Laboratory, no psychological dissertations were published.

Following Rubin's death in 1951, two professors were appointed at the Psychological Laboratory: Edgar Tanekjaer Rasmussen, in 1953, and Frans From, in 1954. Both continued the phenomenological tradition. Rasmussen, originally a mathematician, was much interested in the cognitive aspects of conscious experience relative to the environment. In his two principal studies, conducted between 1956 and 1960, he attempted to construct a psychological system based on the proposition that all psychological experiences, including the motivational, can and must be described as phenomena in consciousness. Frans From, on the other hand, beginning with his doctoral thesis in 1953 (translated into English in 1971), was interested primarily in person perception. In his work he describes the various psychological and immaterial attributes one ascribes to all objects, including people.

The following list of dissertations published in Denmark between 1900 and 1960 provides a sense of the research interests of Danish psychologists during that period (the date, name of the psychologist, and title of the dissertation are given in each case):

1913—R. H. Pedersen, "On individual mental differences"

1915—Edgar Rubin, "Visually experienced figures"

1922—Sigurd Naesgaard, "On the structure of consciousness"

1953—Franz From, "Perception of other people"

1956—Kristian Holt-Hansen, "After-effects in the behavior of mice" (in English)

1958—Anker Rattleff, "Form, color, and emotions"

1959—K. B. Madsen, "Theories of motivation" (in English)

1959—Martin Johansen, "Voluminal figural phenomena."

DEVELOPMENTS IN DANISH PSYCHOLOGY SINCE 1960

Since the early 1960s, Danish psychology has diversified and grown dramatically. In 1960 three scientific professionals made up the staff of the Psychological Laboratory; by 1980, the number had risen to forty-five. Including the psychologists associated with the Psychological Institute in Aarhus founded in 1968 and those at the Institute for Clinical Psychology, 108 psychological professionals now work at the two universities.

Underlying this expansion of Danish psychology was an economic boom accompanied by an explosive increase in students. As happened in other Western countries, these developments led by the late 1960s to the so-called student rebellion. In psychology, many student interests were not represented by the traditionally oriented faculty members and courses of that time. Consequently, many of the new psychologists hired by the universities specialized in areas more in tune with student interests. While some feel that this trend went too far too quickly, it did produce psychology departments with much greater diversity. It should be mentioned that this development was augmented by the belief on the part of many of the younger psychologists that Danish psychology had been excessively preoccupied with the phenomenological orientation.

From today's perspective there is little doubt that the almost revolutionary changes which started about twenty years ago created a productive milieu for Danish psychology along with some confusion. Contemporary Danish psychologists are now involved in all major concerns of the field. It is clear that no common paradigm unites the discipline in Denmark. Because Danish psychology is diverse and fragmented, it is timely that the *Scandinavian Journal of Psychology* has initiated a series of surveys of work done mostly during the last fifteen years. The first survey concerns dialectical and hermeneutical psychology (Dreier and Kvale, 1984).

The diversity of interests in Danish psychology is exemplified by the following list of dissertations published since 1960:

1961—S. A. Tordrup, "Age and school level"

1961—Asger Langkjaer, "Contributions to a general normology or theory of purpose-setting" (in English)

1962—Lise Østergaard, "A psychological analysis of schizophrenic thought disturbances"

1962—Gerhard Nielsen, "Studies in self-confrontation" (in English)

1963—Kaj Spelling, "Intelligence and race"

1966—Helle Høpfner Nielsen, "A psychological study of children with cerebral palsy" (in English)

1967—Eggert Petersen, "Sanctions and satisfaction"

1969—I. K. Moustgaard, "Autokinesis"

1970—Iven Rewentlow, "Studies of complex psychobiological phenomena"

1970—Strange Ross, "On the relationship between neural excitation and sustained sinuscoidal acoustic stimulation" (in English)

1970—Rolf Villanger, "Intellectual impairment in different cerebral lesions" (in English)

1972—Jørgen Hviid, "Reactions of nonhandicapped toward handicapped individuals"

1972—Henrik Poulsen, "Cognitive structures and processes"

1974—Frede Knudsen, Stereokinesis

1974—Birthe Kyng, "Conditions of growth and development

1975—Wenja Rothe, "The Rorschach Test in developmental psychological perspective

1976—Maria Stenild, "Conceptual learning"

1977—Finn Rasborg, "Choice of today, condition of tomorrow"

1978—Torsten Ingemann Nielsen, "Acts"

1978—Helmuth Nyborg, "The Rod-and-Frame Test and the field dependence dimension" (in English)

1981—Nini Praetorius, "Subject and object"

1983—Per Schultz Jørgensen, "The social relationship"

1983—Jens Mammen, "The human sense"

SOURCES OF INFORMATION ABOUT DANISH PSYCHOLOGY

Significant collections of psychological publications can be found at the two university libraries, the Royal Library in Copenhagen, the Pedagogical Library of Denmark, and the State Library in Aarhus. (For further information on these collections, see B. Hjorland, *The Royal Library Professional Bibliographies*, 1981.)

Information about research done at the various institutions of higher learning can be obtained from annual reports. A particularly useful publication about Danish psychology during the period from 1947 to 1982 was published by the Association of Danish Psychologists in 1982. In addition, the employment information presented in Table 1 is derived from the *Danish Psychologist*, volume 37, 1983, and additional information about the employment settings of Danish psychologists appears in the December 1983 issue of *Danish Psychology News*.

To find out about the specific research reports published by Danish psychologists, the following references are useful: B. Hjorland and V. L. Knudsen, *Danish Psychological Bibliography 1948–1975*, Danish Library School of Copenhagen, 1976; and annual bibliographies of articles and books published in the Scandinavian countries offered by *Nordic Psychology*. Another valuable source is the quarterly list of journals relevant to psychology that *Nordic Psychology* publishes.

A recent search of *Psychological Abstracts* by PsycInfo indicates that many Danish psychological publications are not included in this widely used reference of psychological research. While articles and books having to do with neuropsychology, psychochemistry, biologically oriented psychiatry, and behavioristic research are well represented, those in other areas of the field are less likely to be noted. K. B. Madsen, a prominent professor at the Royal Danish School of Educational Studies, has since 1959 written twenty internationally recognized articles, many of them translated into several languages, but the search of the *Abstracts* retrieved only one. Of the seven research reports concerning experiments conducted by Professor Axel Larsen (Institute for Clinical Psychology) and Professor Claus Bundesen (Psychological Laboratory) during the past eight years on the perceptual transformation of figures, only two were brought to light by the information search. Finally, Professor Ole Dreier has written six important publications concerning psychology and dialectical materialism as well as the contributions of the Berlin School in West Germany. Not a single one of them were picked up by PsycInfo. While these are only examples, they clearly show that even the most extensive data bank of psychological literature now available is far from complete, at least in the international arena.

RELEVANT ADDRESSES

Aalborg University Center, Langagervej 2, DK–9000 Aalborg.

Association of Danish Magister, Lyngbyvej 32 F, DK–2100 Kbh. Ø.

Association of Danish Psychologists, Bjerregards Sidevej 4, DK–2500 Valby.

The Danish Directorat of Work, Købmagergade 19, DK–1150 Kbh. V.

The Danish Research Council for the Humanities, Holmens Kanal 7, DK–1060 Kbh. K.

Institute for Clinical Psychology, Copenhagen University, Njalsgade 94, DK–2300 Kbh. S.

The Military Psychological Service, Chr. Voldgade 8, DK–1424 Kbh. K.

The National Association for School Psychologists, Vejlemosevej 55, 2840 Holte.

The Pedagogical Institute of Denmark, Hermodsgade 29, DK–2200 Kbh. N.

Psychological Institute, Aarhus University, Asylvej 4, DK–8240 Risskov.

Psychological Laboratory, Copenhagen University, Njalsgade 94, DK–2300 Copenhagen S.

Roskilde University Center, Postbox 260, DK–4000 Roskilde.

The Royal Danish School of Educational Studies, Emdrupvej lol, DK–2400 Kbh. NV.

The Social Research Institute, Borgergade 28, DK–1300 Kbh. K.

Technological Institute, Gregersensvej, 2630 Tastrup.

REFERENCES

Dreier, O., & Kvale, S. (1984). Dialectical and hermeneutical psychology. *Scandinavian Journal of Psychology, 25*, 5–29.

From, F. (1971). *Perception of other people*. New York: Columbia University Press.

Høffding, H. (1912). *Psychology*. London.

Rubin, E. (1915). Synsoplevede figurer, studier i psykologisk analyse. [Observable visual figures: Studies in psychological analysis]. 1. del. København og Kristiania: Gyldendal, Nordisk forlag.

Rubin, E. (1921). Visuell wahrgenommene Figuren. Studien in psychologisher Analyse [Observable visual figures: Studies in psychological analysis]. København: Gyldendal.

Rubin, E. (1949). *Experimenta psychologica* [Experimental psychology]. København: Munksgaard.

SUGGESTED READINGS

From, F., Moustgaard, I. K., Frimuth Peterson, A., & Willanger, R. (1980). *Psykologi. Københavns Universitet, 1479–1979* [Psychology. The University of Copenhagen, 1479–1979] (Vol. 10). København: GAD.

Køppe, S. (1983). *Psykologiens udvikling og formidling i Danmark i perioden 1850–1980* [The development and influence of psychology in Denmark from 1850 to 1980]. København.

Madsen, K. B. (1976). Denmark. In V. S. Sexton & H. Misiak (Eds.), *Psychology around the world*. Monterey, CA: Brooks/Cole.

Nordenbo, S. E. (Ed.). (1976). Dansk filosofi og psykologi 1926–1976 [Danish philosophy and psychology from 1926 to 1976]. København: K. Købmagergade 50 Filosofisk Institut, Københavns Universitet: i samarbejde med Psykologisk Laboratorium, Københavns Universitet.

Egypt

Safwat Ernest Farag

Psychology is one of the well-established disciplines in the Egyptian universities, although the role of psychologists is still limited and ambiguous. To define this field, one must go back to its historical roots in modern Egypt.

It is still possible to find an Egyptian psychologist who identifies himself as a psychoanalyst, functionalist, Gestalt psychologist, or experimentalist (King, 1984). The controversy as to whether psychology is the science of behavior or the exploration, through insight, of the depths of man's mind has influenced the structure and trends of the various departments of psychology in Egypt's universities.

While this controversy continues, it is not openly expressed. Rather, it is implied in the works, interests, and writings of psychologists and displayed in their cooperation (or lack of it) and attitudes toward applied problems and the scientific community in general.

HISTORICAL BACKGROUND

Although the first modern university in Egypt was founded in 1908, the first Egyptian book in psychology was not published until 1920. Authored by an unknown physician, this book consisted of twenty-four pages and was entitled *The scientific method of measuring intelligence*. It dealt with the old Binet scale of intelligence. Simplifying the concept of intelligence and the techniques of measurement without, however, any mention of Alfred Binet, the book was clearly meant for the layman. Other psychologically relevant books had been published before 1920, but they were "about" psychology, not "in" psychology.

The first well-written and systematically organized Egyptian books on psychological topics were the secondary-school textbooks within the social sciences curriculum. Published during the late 1920s, they contained chapters devoted to instincts, motives, sensations, perception, and intelligence.

The period between the two world wars witnessed the beginnings of psychology in Egypt, but not its birth as a science.[1] The three men responsible for establishing the discipline in Egypt were Abel Aziz El Kousi, Youssef Mourad, and Mostafa Zewar.

El Kousi obtained his Ph.D. in psychology in 1934 from London University, was a student of Cyril Burt, and had direct contact with Charles Spearman. He returned from Britain to the Teachers' School (now the College of Education) in Cairo, an institute which is part of the Ministry of Education. There he established the first department of educational psychology and the first public psychological clinic, which still offers its services under the supervision of that college's Department of Mental Health. As a result of the influence of this man, who wrote more than ten books, the Teachers' School, although not then a university college, sent the largest number of graduates from Egypt to Britain and the United States to earn their doctorates.

His interests and background inspired research projects. After 1952, in his post of vice-minister of education, he changed the educational programs for primary schools to conform to Gestalt theories of perception and learning. Moreover, El Kousi's efforts extended to the Arab countries, not only as an educational expert working for the United Nations but also as a psychologist directing or participating in large projects in collaboration with Arab universities and research centers.

Youssef Mourad received his doctorate from the Sorbonne in Paris. His research topic was "La vie de l'intelligence." He began lecturing at Cairo University in 1940 in the context of the philosophy curriculum of the Faculty of Arts. Mourad established the first psychological laboratory in Egypt and served as an advisor for more than twenty M.A. and Ph.D. theses. He published the best-known introductory psychology textbook in Arabic, *Principles of psychology*, and served as editor of the *Journal of Psychology*, which appeared for more than eight years, being discontinued in 1953. Mourad supported and supervised the publication and translation into Arabic of a series of basic source materials in psychology under the title *Integrated psychology publications*.

Before he retired, Mourad had succeeded in establishing the first postgraduate diploma, the Diploma of Applied Psychology. This credential acknowledged the training of graduate psychology students through the philosophy curriculum, with strong emphasis on clinical psychology. Despite his theoretical training in France, Mourad encouraged empirical study and surrounded himself with a select group of students working in different areas of research. His open meetings on Friday mornings during the 1940s and 1950s were attended by many members of the local scientific community.

Mostafa Zewar, a colleague of Mourad, was also trained in France, in medicine and psychoanalysis. He was an orthodox Freudian who returned to Cairo two years after Mourad. Through his personal influence Zewar successfully established psychoanalysis and basic Freudian concepts in Egypt, and he collaborated with Mourad in editing the *Journal of Psychology*.

Zewar left Cairo University to establish psychology at the newly founded Alexandria University in the late 1940s, subsequently leaving that position to assume the position of professor and chairman of psychology at another new university in Cairo, Ain Shams. Although Zewar is a pure psychoanalyst, he is also a model scholar who provided space and laboratory facilities for all areas of experimental psychology. Physiology, biology, statistics, and psychometry were first offered to Egyptian students of psychology in Zewar's department. Within a few years the Ain Shams psychology staff became Egypt's largest, with highly qualified and active members, some of whose advanced degrees had been earned in Britain and the United States and some of whom were Zewar's own students who specialized in psychoanalysis.

RECENT STATUS

Psychology at both Cairo University and Alexandria University was originally part of the philosophy curriculum, whereas it belonged to the sociology curriculum at Ain Shams University. These were the three largest Egyptian universities until the end of the 1940s.[2]

By 1973, the discipline had gained formal academic recognition as a distinct field and more than five independent departments had been organized in various Egyptian universities. Nevertheless, because of the shortage of qualified staff, it became difficult to establish separate departments in other Egyptian universities. This shortage resulted from a severe "brain drain" in all areas of specialization, including psychology. Emigration to the United States and Canada in combination with much higher faculty salaries in the Gulf oil countries' universities decimated Egypt's psychology departments. The number of Egyptian staff members in the Arab oil countries' universities is now ten times that in Egyptian universities.[3]

Each Egyptian university permits its staff members to assume temporary positions in Arab universities under certain conditions, set by government policy. One of these conditions is that the number of persons involved should not exceed 25 percent of a university's faculty, while another is that any member hired should spend no more than four years outside his or her department.

Actually, the majority of the persons employed by Arab universities decides not to return after these four years; preferring their new jobs, they resign their Egyptian positions. As a consequence their productivity decreases; they rarely do empirical work in these new societies because of political and traditional prohibitions against investigating topics such a sexual behavior, attitude formation, and personality disorders. Even when the problem area is innocuous, gathering data can be difficult, especially for foreigners.

Departments of psychology are located in faculties of arts; however, educational psychology and mental health are distinct departments of colleges of education. The students of these colleges are trained to be schoolteachers rather than psychologists. Recently, these colleges have been reorganized as university colleges, separate from the Ministry of Education, but the nature of the training has not changed.

Within the faculty of arts, training in psychology for the B.A. degree includes biology, physiology, sociology, history of psychology, philosophy of science, statistics, and psychometrics in addition to courses in general psychology, genetic psychology, physiological psychology, social psychology, group dynamics, personality, experimental psychology and laboratory training, clinical psychology, learning, and mental deficiency.

Undergraduate curricula are similarly described in all Egyptian universities but differ in content and sources. A new student can immediately observe the diversity of approaches upon starting to read the materials assigned or recommended by the various departments.

Training in clinical psychology at Cairo University involves practice in public clinics and state mental hospitals. Students in the other universities, however, do not have the opportunity to work in applied settings.[4]

Only three universities offer postgraduate diplomas, a one-year applied psychology diploma, with strong emphasis on clinical psychology, at Cairo and Minia, and a two-year psychology service diploma at Ain Shams University. All the Egyptian universities award M.A. and Ph.D. degrees in psychology.

Four courses, usually two semesters each, are prerequisite for enrollment in master's degree research. These include advanced courses in psychological methodology, computer programming, contemporary approaches in psychology, and advanced techniques in psychometric statistics. Only students who have passed these four courses with high grades are permitted to continue the additional two to four years of empirical research required for the master's degree. The Ph.D. requires an additional three to four years. Master's and Ph.D. projects both demand research involving empirical tests and statistics.

REFERENCES AND TEXTBOOKS

Although Egyptian students study the English language for six years before enrolling in a university, most prefer materials written in Arabic and find real difficulty in reading English. This is the case despite the fact that they continue studying English at the university and have to pass a psychology examination in English during their first year at the university.

The major references and textbooks are in Arabic. Some are well-known, being extensively used throughout Egypt and the Arab world. These include Ezzat Rajeh, *The basis of psychology*; Abdel Aziz El Kousi, *Principles of mental health*; Foad El Bahie, *Statistics and the measurement of intellect*; Ramzia El Gharib, *Measurement in psychology and education* and *Theories of learning*; El Sayed Khayri, *Statistics in psychological, sociological and educational research*; Mostafa Souief, *Introduction to social psychology*; Louis K. Milika, *Clinical psychology*; Ahmed Abdel Khalek, *Basic personality dimensions* and *Personality questionnaires*; and two books by Safwat Farag, *Psychometry* and *Factor analysis for behavioral sciences*.

The number of psychology books issued in Egypt has exceeded 200 a year over the last five years, and this number is increasing. Because Cairo is the main publishing center of the Arab world, Egyptian publications find their way to all Arab universities. Current issues of major periodicals and journals are available in university libraries.

Translation of basic reference materials into Arabic is widespread. Egyptian law does not require permission from foreign authors or publishers for translation; foreign copyrights are not protected, since Egypt is not a member of the international copyright pact.[5]

Major works of well-known authors have been translated into Arabic; many of the classics in psychology have been translated numerous times by different people. The most current books in English are available through libraries, bookshops, and the Annual International Book Fair in Cairo. The international fair lasts for ten days every year, with publishers from more than fifty countries exhibiting and selling their publications.

PERIODICALS AND PUBLICATIONS

Since the spring of 1953, when Mourad published the last issue of his *Journal of Psychology* because of what he referred to as the prevailing "unsuitable" atmosphere,[6] Egypt has had no regular psychological journal, though several edited books have appeared instead.

The *Yearbook of psychology*, a publication of the Egyptian Society for Psychological Studies, has been issued four times during the last eight years and is oriented toward empirical and theoretical work, including dissertation abstracts. Its continued existence, however, is threatened by financial problems. Louis Milika has edited *Readings in social psychology in the Arab world*, an excellent source book with carefully chosen empirical selections from Egypt and all the Arab countries. With the fourth volume issued this year, it concerns a wide variety of research activities in social psychology. The papers are grouped by category, and a critical introduction by the editor accompanies each collection of papers. Ahmed Abdel Khalek edits *Research in behavior and personality* which is published at regular intervals. Volume four appeared recently. Despite the book's basic orientation toward personality research, it includes studies having to do with cognition, psychopathology, and attitudes.

Editors complain of a shortage of material, but this is frequently due to publication delays which sometimes fail to give an author the opportunity to publish findings within a reasonable time after his or her study has been completed. Also, publishers are little interested in edited books, preferring textbooks intended for the large population of students.

In addition to these books there are three periodicals not devoted exclusively to psychology that publish psychological research: the *National Social Review* and the *National Review of Criminology*, both issued by the National Center for Criminological and Sociological Research (NCCSR), and the *Egyptian Journal of Psychiatry*, published by the Egyptian Psychiatric Association. The first two journals are largely concerned with social psychological research, especially that having to do with attitudes and socialization, although they sometimes publish studies in testing or personality. The *Journal of Psychiatry* is concerned with clinical psychology and mental retardation; like the two national reviews, this journal appears in both Arabic and English. Many Egyptian psychologists write in English and publish in British and American journals.

RESEARCH ACTIVITIES

A survey of the articles and research reports published during the last five years shows that 75 percent were individually authored, with all costs of each project including typing, testing, and data processing paid for by the author. There is little collaborative research and that which is done is limited to funded projects. Ahmed Abdel Khalek in Alexandria carried out a long-term investigation in the area of personality; Kadri Hefni is studying aggression and conflict; and Nahed Ramzi has been working for more than fifteen years on the psychology of women, investigating everything from the image of women portrayed by the mass media to cognitive and personality characteristics of females. Other long-range projects include the Creativity Project at Cairo University, supervised by Mostafa Souief and conducted by the departmental staff, extending over a period of more than twenty years. Many of the Egyptian psychologists involved work jointly with British or American colleagues. Among them are Mostafa Souief, Kadri Hefni, Safwat Farag, and Ahmed Abdel Khalek.

No large grants are allocated for psychological studies, although very small research awards are offered to university staff members. The Academy of Scientific Research and the National Center for Criminological and Sociological Research provide some funding for projects that are in the public interest or focused on applied problems. Such grants cover all project costs including fees, wages, printing, field work, data processing and computer facilities, and publication of final reports.

Some of the major projects completed or in progress through the NCCSR grants to psychologists are a cannabis study directed by Mostafa Souief, with more than ten reports having been issued in both Arabic and English (this investigation is still under way but is now called "The Standing Program for Drug Research"); work on the standardization of the General Aptitude Test Battery (GATB) by Mahmoud Abdel Kader; a survey of the preschool mentally retarded children in Egypt by Emad Eldin Sultan; a study of nonrational thinking in myths by Roshdi Fam; "The national character," a study by Safwat Farag; "Psychological factors in enuresis," by Rashad Kafafi and Lila Abdel Gaw'wad; "Youth values," by Nahed Saleh; "Psychological needs of the Sinai people after the Israeli withdrawal in 1978," by Nahed Ramzi; and "The national image," by Nagib Iskandar. Expanding the Unit for psychological Research in the NCCSR, a new section, the Organization of Public Opinion Assessment, was added in 1976. Psychologists associated with this facility work in the field of attitude and public-opinion polling.

In addition to state funding, grants for some investigations have been received from American sources. Examples of projects supported by such monies include "Functional correlates of mild to moderate malnutrition" and "Comparative evaluation of the voluntary treatment of opium addicts."

To present a paper or research report in Egypt is a real problem, since the only Egyptian psychological conference took place in 1971. A conference was to be held every two years, but no serious effort has been made to achieve this goal. The Egyptian Association for Psychological Studies, however, did hold a conference in April 1985.

Egyptian psychologists are able to share their research findings at the International Conference for Statistics, Computer Sciences, Social Research, and Population Studies held in Cairo every year.[7] The papers presented at these meetings are published; nonetheless, many Egyptian psychologists prefer to present their works at European or American conferences.

TESTS

During the early 1950s an active test movement emerged in Egypt. Young scholars returning from Europe and the United States worked on tests and questionnaires. During this decade the Stanford-Binet, 1937 (Form L) was translated and modified by Mohamed Abdel Salam and Louis Milika to fit Egyptian culture, and the Wechsler-Bellvue and the Wechsler Intelligence Scale for Children (WISC) were appropriately adopted by Milika and Emad Eldin Ismail. The MMPI was also translated into Arabic and standardized to some degree using local norms. In addition, the Rorschach inkblot technique and the TAT have been used. Because of the lack of grants and the large costs involved, the standardization of psychometric instruments imported from Western countries was not appropriately carried out for many years.

The pioneers and leaders of the mid-1950s test movement were Louis Milika, Emad Ismail, and Mohamed Abdel Salam. Since then, dozens of popular tests and scales have been translated and adapted to the Egyptian environment; in some cases adequate norms have been determined.

Among the many tests of cognitive skills and personality currently being used in Egyptian society, some of the best known are the Thurstone Primary Mental Abilities (PMA), the General Aptitude Test Battery (GATB), the Guilford-Zimmerman Personality Inventory, the Guilford Tests of Creativity, the Eysenck Personality Inventory (EPI) and Personality Questionnaire (EPQ), the Fitts Tennessee Self-Concept Scale, The Vineland Social Maturity Scale, and the Adaptive Behavior Scale. Batteries of job preference and special abilities tests are also in use. Many of these scales have been translated and published by several individuals.

Egyptian psychologists have also been active in developing new tests and questionnaires. Khairi, for instance, has prepared a locally standardized test of intelligence consisting of two parts, the Preparatory School Intelligence Test and the Secondary School Intelligence Test. Several Egyptian psychologists have also proposed new conceptions relevant to testing in the areas of cognition and personality.

Useful reviews of tests in use in Egypt can be found in several sources (Milika, 1977; Alogazi (El Ogazi), 1979; Abdel Khalek, 1984). The Arabic forms of these tests and scales are currently employed in all Arabic-speaking countries, with minimal modifications in wording to conform to local dialects. Efforts are under way to gather appropriate reliability and validity data.

One of the major problems associated with psychometrics in Egypt is that the sale of tests is not regulated. Anyone can buy a test from a publisher without restrictions. This leads to unethical use of tests and threatens their validity. Unfortunately, the Egyptian Association for Psychological Studies is making no effort to remedy this problem, and no public or academic organization is taking responsibility for test regulation.

ROLES OF PSYCHOLOGISTS

Psychologists in Egyptian society serve many functions, though their contributions are not adequately recognized. In every industrial firm, there is at least one psychologist and perhaps a team working in a special department or section. Individuals so employed are engaged in three major tasks: selecting personnel on the basis of psychological tests of aptitudes, special abilities, and skills; recommending individuals for promotion; and providing testing services for those with psychological problems. These same tasks are performed in the Egyptian armed forces under the supervision of university staff members. Also, a few public schools have a psychologist working in cooperation with a sociologist or social worker.

Clinical psychologists, especially those who have earned a Cairo University applied diploma, work in state and private mental hospitals. Their main duties are testing psychotics, neurotics, and the mentally retarded. Testing is directed toward defining organicity and psychological dysfunctions in perception, memory, personality, and so forth. Psychologists work within a multidisciplinary structure that usually involves much cooperation and little conflict with psychiatrists. The latter, because they have received some training in psychoanalysis, view neurosis and psychosis from the Freudian perspective and are generally opposed to psychologists serving as psychotherapists.

Mental retardation is the problem to which psychologists devote their main efforts. They administer tests to evaluate intelligence and adaptive behavior, then work to develop skills and modify behavior in ways which enable the retarded to make maximum use of their capabilities.

Five state mental hospitals in Egypt are controlled by the Ministry of Health: three in Cairo; one in Alexandria; and one in Tanta, in the middle of the Nile delta. These hospitals, however, are poorly equipped, lack adequate facilities, and fail to provide good service.

Abbassiya Mental Hospital in Cairo is the biggest facility, with a large staff and about 2,000 beds, including 700 beds for females. There is a section for criminals as well as separate units for retarded children and adults. A department of clinical psychology offers diverse services including testing, diagnosis, and practica for university students studying clinical psychology.

The second largest institution is Khanka Mental Hospital, in a suburb east of Cairo. This is a spacious facility including large farms, where more than 2,000 patients are hospitalized. It includes a section for criminals and one for drug abusers. The staff is small and the psychological clinical resources are limited, but the institution is better organized and provides better services than Abbassiya.

Helwan Mental Health Hospital, southwest of Cairo, has only 300 beds and few facilities when compared with the other two hospitals. A well-trained team of clinical psychologists, though, covers the different aspects of clinical service. The remaining state hospitals, Tanta and Ma'amora (Alexandria), are even smaller, each equipped with approximately 100 beds, minimal staff including the nursing team, and a psychological clinic.

Private mental institutions are numerous. In Cairo alone there are five hospitals where psychotics and the retarded are hospitalized. These offer intensive care and have high standards compared to the state hospitals. Each has a clinical psychology staff, usually working under the direct supervision of a university staff member. Some of these hospitals offer psychotherapy, including behavior therapy to outpatients. Facilities for psychological research are also available, and many scientific meetings and small conferences are held yearly in these hospitals.

Because of limited opportunities for training in clinical psychology and the opposition by psychiatrists, Egyptian psychologists, even those with much experience, have little hope of doing psychotherapy, though they feel qualified to do so. Their role remains confined primarily to that of psychodiagnostician.

Psychotherapists are governed by legal regulations. In 1958, Law 198 restricted the practice of psychotherapy to the following five groups:

1. psychiatrists who obtain the neuropsychiatry diploma from one of the Egyptian universities

2. psychiatrists who obtain an equivalent diploma from a foreign university, with non-Egyptians required to pass an examination

3. university graduates who obtain advanced diplomas in psychotherapy from accredited Egyptian or foreign institutions

4. members of the psychotherapy associations, either in Egypt or abroad, who pass an examination before a standing committee of the Ministry of Health

5. graduates in psychology who specialize in psychotherapy for at least two years in any accredited institution and who pass the Ministry of Health's examination (Milika, 1977, pp. 23–24)

Psychiatrists are authorized to practice psychotherapy (by definition); university staff members in psychology departments, regardless of their specializations, are licensed as well to operate clinics. They have only to ask permission of the permanent committee of the Ministry of Health.

On account of the absence of any diploma of clinical psychology in the Egyptian universities, the lack of public interest, and ambiguity as to what it is that constitutes psychotherapy, there are only seven clinical psychologists with licenses and clinics in the country, all in Cairo. Two of them are psychoanalysts, the others are behavior therapists.

While the majority of students earning degrees in psychology find positions in a variety of fields, top graduates obtain preferred posts in institutions for juvenile delinquents, facilities for the mentally retarded, and state agencies with social and psychological functions such as the Birth Control Agency, the Ministry of Industry, the Production Efficiency Department, and the National Center for Criminological and Sociological Research. Every department of psychiatry, neurology, and phoniatrics[8] at Egyptian universities is attached to a psychological support unit. Most psychologists, however, are employed as schoolteachers or civil servants in the various state departments.

ORGANIZATIONS

The oldest and largest organization is the Egyptian Association for Psychological Studies.[9] An academically oriented group belonging to the Egyptian Scientific Union, it has about 300 members, all of whom are university staff members. No more than fifty persons are actively involved at any one time, however. Monthly lectures during the academic year, offered by members or guests, constitute the organization's major activity. Since 1978 the association has issued the *Yearbook of Psychology*, but because of lack of funds only four issues have been published. The association exerts no ethical or professional influence on its members or on society. It also has little contact with other national and international organizations.

A second professional organization was established in 1981, the Egyptian Psychological Association (EPA), with more than 200 academic and nonacademic members. The association concentrates on offering services to its members, such as establishing ethical standards for the profession, providing training programs in therapeutic techniques, and publishing valid tests. It also aims to supply members with the latest technical information and arrange for adequate facilities. The EPA[10] is still new and weak, with few resources; it needs much support from its members in order to fulfill its responsibilities.

Other organizations play a similar role to that of the Egyptian Association of Psychological Studies. Many Egyptian psychologists belong to one or more of the following associations: the Egyptian Psychiatric Association,[11] the Egyptian Society for Mental Health,[12] and the Egyptian Progressive Psychiatric Association.[13] All of these organizations, unfortunately, suffer from inadequate financial support.

FINAL COMMENT

There is a lack of sustained focus in the Egyptian scientific and professional community. This is particularly true with regard to psychology since many Egyptian psychologists have positions both at home and in other countries. A serious restructuring of science in Egypt will be necessary before a more stable scientific enterprise can be established.

A current project which may help Egyptian psychologists develop more sense of an indigenous field is a review of the history of psychology in Egypt based on original sources, conducted by Kadri Hefni, Abdel Halim Mahmoud, and Safwat Farag now in press. In addition, an extensive study funded by NCCSR and directed by Farag, documenting psychological literature from the beginning of the century until 1980, is in progress. More than 3,000 works have been collected, summarized, and cited. This study was published in two volumes in 1986.

Psychology in Egypt is similar to psychology in Western countries in its diversity of approaches, trends, research, and problems. Personnel are competent in both academic and professional areas, but resources and facilities are scarce. Personal contributions are frequently substantial; however, projects designed to improve societal conditions in some way and involving collaborative efforts generally fail to reach their goals.

The field still lacks the features of a productive scientific community. There is no strong organizational base ensuring regular conferences, periodicals, funds for applied research, and publishing facilities. When these deficiencies are remedied, most psychologists abroad may be motivated to return home.

NOTES

I wish to thank Mr. M. Budek for his critical reading of the manuscript.

1. Pioneers such as Ismail El Kabbani and Kamel El Nahhas had participated, from the late 1920s on, in teaching and writing about psychology. Through their ministerial posts, these leaders encouraged missions of Teachers' School graduates to European universities. El Kabbani developed and translated tests of intelligence, playing an important role in this and other areas of educational psychology.

2. There are presently more than twenty universities throughout the country.

3. By the end of 1984, the numbers of psychologists at Egyptian universities were as follows: Cairo University, 5; Ain Shams, 7; Alexandria, 4; Tanta, 2; and Minia, 2; whereas the Egyptian staffs in some Arab countries numbered in Saudi Arabia: King Saud University, 20; King Abdel Aziz, 18; and Imam Mohamed Ibn Saud, 14; in Kuwait: Kuwait University, 17; in United Arab Emirates: United Arab Emirate University, 15; in Qatar: Qatar University, 12; and more than 40 other staff members in colleges and small universities in the Arab countries.

4. No more than fifty students enroll in the Cairo University psychology department every academic year, whereas this number exceeds 800 in both Alexandria and Ain Shams universities. Large numbers also enroll in the regional and minor universities.

5. A by-product of this situation is that Egyptian publications are likewise not protected outside Egypt, and reprints of hundreds of Egyptian books have been issued in Beirut, Lebanon, and elsewhere without permission from either the author or the publisher.

6. A year after Nasser's coup d'état, in 1952, at a time when many of the university staff members had been fired in a political movement against so-called corruption.

7. The General Secretary is Professor A. A. Sarhan, Computer Center, Ain Shams University, Cairo, Egypt.

8. An alternative term referring to speech pathology and audiology.

9. Address: 1, Osiris St., Tager Building, 1st floor, Garden City, Cairo, Egypt.

10. Address: Hedaya El Kaddah, General Secretary, Psychological Clinic, Abbassiya Mental Hospital, Cairo, Egypt.

11. Address: Dr. A. M. Ashour, Department of Psychiatry, Faculty of Medicine, Ain Shams University, Cairo, Egypt.

12. Address: Dr. Gamal Aboel Azaim, 1 Orabi St., Downtown, Cairo, Egypt.

13. Address: Dr. Y. El Rakhawi, Department of Psychiatry, Faculty of Medicine, Cairo University, Egypt.

REFERENCES

Abdel Khalek, A. (1984). *Personality questionnaires* (2nd ed.). Alexandria: Dar El-maarefa Elgamyai (in Arabic).

Alogazi, M. Y. (1979). *Directory of Arabic psychological tests*. Cairo: Central Agency for University Books (in Arabic).

King, D. W. (1984). Psychology in the Arab Republic of Egypt. *International Psychologist, 25*, 3, 7–8.

Milika, L. K. (1977). *Clinical psychology* (1st ed.). Cairo: El Haya'a El Ama Lil Ketab (in Arabic).

France

Alain Trognon, Coordinator

BACKGROUND

Within the French Cartesian tradition the major issue was the relationship between mind and body. During the eighteenth century, J. de la Mettrie (1709–1751) offered a materialist answer to the problem while E. Condillac, opposing rationalism, emphasized a radical empiricist point of view affirming the unity of physiological and psychological phenomena and proposing that all mental processes derive from sensation. During the late 1700s and early 1800s the so-called ideologues sought to develop a "science of man." Among them the physician and philosopher P. Cabanis (1757–1808) contended that physical (that is, organic) factors and moral or psychological factors have a reciprocal influence on each other. His writings generated an important controversy concerning the relationships between the organic and psychological realms.

Until the 1870s there were three "psychologies" in France. Psychiatrists such as Esquirol and Morel developed observational and analytic techniques which they sometimes referred to as psychological. Their major work was *Annales médico-psychologiques*. "Magnetists" and hypnotists such as Puységur, Bertrand, and Liébeault, on the other hand, emphasized the effects of psychological states and processes on the physical and initiated what D. H. Tuke called psychotherapeutics. Finally, the thinking of philosophers such as Maine de Biran, Jouffroy, and Garnier embraced a spiritualist academic psychology. In general, the psychology of that time had to do with the philosophical study of the soul's faculties and was taught in both secondary schools and universities.

In 1870, Hippolyte Taine published *De l'intelligence* and Théodule Ribot, *La psychologie anglaise contemporaine*. Both works were manifestoes for a physiological psychology dissociated from spiritualist psychology. They promoted the viewpoints of Condillac and Cabanis as well as the orientations of German and British thinkers such as Wilhelm Wundt, Herbert Spencer, and James Stuart Mill. They also published works on psychopathology.

During the same period, physicians J. Charcot (1825–1893) and H. Bernheim

(1837–1919) rediscovered hypnotic phenomena. Although there are differences in their viewpoints, the two men were strong advocates of a medically oriented academic psychology. They rallied Ribot to their cause and the next generation of French psychologists, which included Pierre Janet and Georges Dumas, had degrees in both medicine and philosophy. The methodology taught was primarily "psychopathological."

Ribot founded the journal *La revue philosophique* in 1876 which included many psychological articles. In 1885, Charcot, Ribot, and Richet established the Society of Physiological Psychology and for some years published a brief psychological review. The first chair of experimental and comparative psychology was created for Ribot in 1887 at the prestigious Collège de France. In the process Ribot emerged as the "father" of French psychology.

In 1889, the government set up the first French psychological laboratory, a small facility first directed by H. Beaunis, a physiologist and hypnotist and a friend and colleague of Bernheim. In 1894, Alfred Binet succeeded Beaunis. At that time Binet, a pupil of Charcot and like Beaunis trained in physiology and hypnotism, had not yet constructed his famous intelligence test. Beaunis and Charcot founded *L'année psychologue*, the first prestigious French psychological journal. Because Binet was not trained in both medicine and philosophy, however, he was not eligible to succeed Ribot at the Collège de France and Janet received the appointment. As a consequence Binet had no students and subjects and spent little time in his laboratory. An opportunity came to work with primary-school students, however, and the rest is history.

In 1890, Charcot established a modest laboratory for Janet in his hospital (Salpétrière), and in 1901 Janet organized the Société Française de Psychologie (SFP). In 1904 Janet and Dumas founded the first French journal on psychopathology, *Le journal de psychologie normale et pathologique*. By 1900, French psychology, after going through a period beset by much controversy, emerged as a new discipline with research facilities, a prestigious chair, and respected journals.

But the real growth of French psychology started after World War II. Gradually, the discipline became more autonomous as universities offered specific diplomas in the field, employment opportunities increased, and several departments of psychology were created. Twenty-seven universities in France, including five in Paris, now offer instruction in psychology; over 35,000 students are enrolled in psychology programs.

In 1950 the SFP was a small and exclusive learned society with only fifty-six members. But in 1955, responding to the growth of the discipline, five specialized sections were constituted (clinical, industrial, child, experimental, and physiological). Local branches were organized as well. The number of members jumped to 1,128 by 1965, with the clinical and industrial sections experiencing the most growth. While membership in the society has continued to expand during the last twenty years, it has not fully reflected the large increase in the number of psychologists. In part this is due to the fact that there is no legal obligation for practitioners to belong to any society. However, the SFP has had the reputation of being a scholarly society not open to professionals. Lately, efforts have been made to change the old image of the society and the number of members has risen to 1,500, including 500 clinicians. The SFP is now truly representative of both research and applied psychology. Attracting university teachers, researchers, and applied psychologists, the SFP is the only group which can legitimately represent the profession in international organizations, in particular the IUPsyS (International Union of Psychological Science), an organization it helped create. In 1985, a law giving legal status to the title "psychologist" was passed. Psychology in France has clearly made great strides during the last several decades.

Jacqueline Carroy

CLINICAL PSYCHOLOGY

Training

In 1947, thanks to Daniel Lagache, a national diploma, the *licence de psychologie*, was instituted. At the time, clinical psychology was not a separate branch of psychology, but Lagache defined and advocated the clinical method in psychology, a method based on the extensive study of individuals through interviews, tests, and biographical studies. The method, in spite of its medical origin, is not limited to psychopathology; it can also be applied to the study of normal people and even small groups. When psychologists with the new *licence* started to work in mental health settings using the clinical method, they called themselves *clinical psychologists*, although medical doctors still insisted that the words "clinical" and "clinician" be restricted to the practice of medicine.

The appellation clinical psychologist was made official in 1955 upon the establishment of a Clinical Psychology Section by the SFP. In 1958, clinical psychology was officially recognized by the University of Paris when Juliette Favez-Boutonnier gave a series of lectures called "Clinical Psychology," a domain she wanted to differentiate from psychopathology and psychoanalysis. Clinical psychology, she argued, is concerned with "the individual in his actual situation, i.e., always involved in relationships with others." In 1959, in Paris, she created France's first laboratory of clinical psychology.

In 1967, curricular reforms took place at the University of Paris. The first *certificat de psychologie clinique* was introduced. And in 1968, the student movement fostered in psychology radical opposition to the prevailing psychometric and scientific orientation, especially in clinical psychology. Students and professionals wanted, instead, a client-centered approach based on direct relationships with those seeking help. These changes were strongly supported by psychologists with psychoanalytic training and, in the field of mental health, by those opposed to psychiatry. In 1969, a second important reform modified the structure of the University of Paris, and several new departments of psychology were opened.

Since 1967, training has included two years of general studies in psycshology leading to the *Diplôme d'études universitaires générales* (D.E.U.G.) which is equivalent to the B.A. degree, then one year leading to the *licence* degree and one year to earn the *maîtrise* (master's degree) when specialization begins. Afterward two different courses of study are offered: the *Diplôme d'études supérieures spécialisées* (D.E.S.S.), a very competitive program for those who want to pursue careers in applied psychology, and the *Diplôme d'études approfondies* (D.E.A.), oriented toward research and doctoral studies.

Recently, a unique intermediate doctorate has been offered which may be obtained after the successful completion of five or six years of research. Although the present curriculum gives more importance to practical training than the previous course of study, most young psychologists feel the need for further supervised work when they start their professional careers. Many pursue advanced theoretical studies and seek additional experience in projective testing and other diagnostic and therapeutic techniques. According to a 1968 nationwide statistical survey involving 663 French clinical psychologists, 87 percent pursued postuniversity training, mostly of a technical nature, and 17 percent were engaged in personal psychoanalysis. A more recent survey (1982) concerning 250 clinical psychologists from Brittany, found that 56 percent did postuniversity training, mostly in theoretical areas, and 15 percent were engaged in personal psychoanalysis.

There are also a few private institutes and schools of psychology. Their programs are quite similar to those offered by the universities.

The Profession of Clinical Psychology

The number of clinical psychologists has grown considerably since 1970. A national survey, conducted in 1968, estimated that some 1,000 clinical psychologists worked in the public sector. While exact current data are not available, the figure is now probably between 8,000 and 10,000. An increasing number of psychologists not only serve to alleviate mental disease and societal maladjustments but also work with babies in maternity hospitals and nurseries, old people, and judges engaged in divorce cases. Among other places, psychologists are found in police departments, helping with the selection and training of police personnel.

School psychology, vocational counseling, and marriage counseling are separate professions with their own training. New measures are being taken to standardize these professions and make them part of the discipline of psychology with the same training requirements.

Not many French psychologists are engaged in private practice. The French public welfare system (Sécurité Sociale) makes no provision for psychological consultation, and the French are not accustomed to paying for services they view as medical in nature.

Clinical psychologists work mostly in interdisciplinary teams. Their main functions are evaluation, psychotherapy, and institutional intervention, such as management of meetings and resolution of conflicts. Until the late 1960s, evaluation, particularly diagnostic testing, was the main function of clinical psychologists. Now more time is spent in psychotherapy. Even when psychologists perform diagnostic evaluations, they depend less on testing and more on simple interviews.

Some time ago the official medical association (Ordre National des Medécins) branded the practice of psychotherapy by psychologists as illegal. Now, although the legal situation has not changed, the psychotherapeutic skills of psychologists are more generally recognized and explicitly sought out by medical doctors.

Practicing psychologists do little research. Decisions concerning research are made by department heads. However, the government has recently offered support to psychologists to use some of their professional time for research and further training.

Research is still designed and conducted either by teams of practicing psychologists working in laboratories or research units associated with various health centers, especially at the Centre Hospitalo-Universitaire (CHU), or in university laboratories where doctoral studies are being done. These research units may work under contract to scientific government agencies and often include professional researchers.

There are also a few independent public and private research centers, where interdisciplinary teams work on specialized areas of research. Two good examples are the Centre de Recherches Interdisciplinaires de Vaucresson (CRIV) where sociologists, jurists, and psychologists study delinquency and the Centre de Gérontologie Claude Bernard where biologists, physiologists, and psychologists do research on aging.

Research Funding

Two highly centralized government agencies provide financial support for major projects: the Centre National de la Recherche Scientifique [National Center for Scientific Research] (CNRS) and the Institut National de la Santé et de la Recherche Médicale [National Institute for Health and Medical Research] (INSERM). They finance researchers and generally no large-scale studies can be undertaken and developed without them. The Ministry of Education also provides some funds to university laboratories, but the amounts are small. Research programs sponsored by government agencies have to do with matters of societal concern. Finally, private companies, especially the pharmaceutical firms, support some research projects.

In spite of all the difficulties involved in obtaining time and funds for research, clinical psychology has an undeniable vitality in France. National and international congresses and symposia involving clinical psychologists take place almost every week. While lacking a large psychological program, famous laboratory, and a clinical journal, France boasts a large number of small research centers publishing numerous papers in various psychological, psychiatric, and psychoanalytic publications.

The Most Productive Fields in French Clinical Psychological Research

The most important areas of research in French clinical psychology include early childhood, cognitive deficiencies and disorders, projective techniques, and small groups. Specific research interests of some of the clinical psychologists who achieved prominence during the period from 1945 to 1986 follow.

Early Childhood

Development scale for infants (Irène Lézine, 1951)

Attachment of infants to their environments (Irène Lézine, René Zazzo, Mira Stamback, 1960–1980)

Diseases and behavioral problems in early childhood (René Diatkine, Serge Lebovici and collaborators, Soulé and collaborators)

Somatic diseases of infants and infant-mother relationship problems (Rosine Debray, the Paris somatic school, Danièle Rapoport)

Importance of early physical contact for the development of a delineation between the self and the non-self leading to a new psychoanalytic concept, the "moi-peau" (skin-ego) (Didier Anzieu)

Nonverbal communication and social expression of emotions (Matty Chiva)

Character formation in the young child (Geneviève Boulanger-Balleyguier, Laboratoire de Psychologie Clinique, Tours)

The abandoned child (Nathalie Loutre)

Cognitive Deficiencies and Disorders

Description of the "dyspraxie" syndrorme (Julian de Ajuriaguerra, Jean Bergès, Mira Stamback, and collaborators at Hôpital Henri-Rousselle, 1 rue Cabanis, 75014 Paris)

Arithmetic disorders (Claire Meljac, Anne Lefèvre) and writing disorders (Julian de Ajuriaguerra, Marguerite Auzias at Hôpital Henri Rousselle)

Research on mental deficiency from two different orientations: the psychometric (René Zazzo, Matty Chiva and collaborators at Hôpital Henri Rousselle) and the psychodynamic and psychoanalytic (Roger Misès, Roger and Michèle Perron and collaborators, Fondation Vallée, 7 rue Bensérade, 94250 Gentilly, 1960–1970)

Abnormal development of mentally retarded and psychotic children viewed from both a psychometric and psychoanalytic approach (Roger Misès and collaborators at Fondation Vallée)

Construction of a scale for the measurement of logical abilities based on Piaget's orientation (Echelle de Pensée Logique, François Longeot)

Study of cognitive disharmony and description of the ROR syndrome (Retard d'Organisation du Raisonnement) in individuals with normal IQs (Bernard and Marie-Luce Gibello)

Factors involved in mental development according to Piaget and Freud (Monique Pinol-Douriez, Université de Provence, Aix-en-Provence)

Projective Techniques

Projective techniques are open to psychoanalytic interpretation but remain a typically clinical and psychological exploratory tool. Specific studies involving the Rorschach test concern the psychopathology of epilepsy (Françoise Minkovska, 1937–1950); norms for children (Cécile Beizman, 1961–1974); diagnosis of psychotic and prepsychotic children (Nina Rausch de Traubenberg, Marie-France Boizou, Hôpital de la Salpétrière, Paris); and psychoanalytic interpretations of the Rorschach (Catherine Chabert).

Research has also been done on psychoanalytic interpretations of the TAT (Vika Shentoub, Rosine Debray, Françoise Brelet) and the construction of new thematic tests such as the *Développement Personnel et Image* (Roger Perron, 1969) and *Patte noire* [Black Leg] (Louis Corman).

Small Groups

Fifteen years of small-group research have led to theoretical concepts based on both psychoanalytic and systemic theories that have influenced training and therapy. Psychoanalytic approaches to small groups have to do with psychic group dynamics and transactional analysis (Didier Anzieu; René Kaes, Université de Lyon 11; Claude Revault d'allonnes and collaborators, Laboratoire de Psychologie Clinique Individuelle et Sociale, Paris). They also have applications in family therapy (André Ruffiot, Grenoble).

Other Clinical Research Areas

Significant research has occurred as well in the areas of psychometrics, adolescence, gerontology, neuropsychology, and the psychological effects of disease. Specific topics of interest are listed below.

Psychometrics

Development of techniques for measuring motor, spatial, rhythmic, and social abilities in children (René Zazzo, Mira Stamback, Hilda Santucci, Roger Perron, Claire Meljac, 1955–1970, at Hôpital Henri Rousselle)

Development of psychometric techniques for adult mental patients (Pierre Pichot, Jacques Perse, Hôpital Sainte Anne, Paris, 1950–1970)

Adolescence

Human development and personal identity (Hector Tomé and collaborators, 41 rue Gay-Lussac, Paris; Pierre Tap and collaborators, at Laboratoire Personnalisation et Changement Sociaux, 5 allée Antonio Machado, 31058 Toulouse Cedex)

Research on anxiety and depression in normal adolescents: computerized analysis of nightmare reports (Hector Tomé)

Juvenile delinquency (Jacques Selosse, Université de Lille 3; Centre de Recherches Interdisciplinaires de Vaucresson, 54 rue de Garches, 92420 Vaucresson)

Social determinants of maladjustment (Claude Veil, Institut Georges Heuyer, 150 avenue Paul Vaillant-Couturier, 93330 Neuilly sur Marne)

Gerontology

New instruments for evaluating the mental abilities of people over eighty (Jean Poitrenaud and collaborators at Centre de Gérontologie Claude Bernard, 49 rue Mirabeau, 75016 Paris)

Research on factors determining interindividual variations of aging (Jean Poitrenaud and collaborators)

Psychosocial aspects of aging (Maximilienne Gautrat)

Neuropsychology

A wide variety of studies have been done at the Laboratoire de Neuro-psychologie et de Neuro-linguistique, Hôpital Sainte Anne and Hôpital La Salpétrière, Paris.

Psychological Effects of Disease

Psychological effects of physical illness and hospitalization on children (Ginette Raimbault and collaborators, Groupe de Recherche Psychanalyse et Sciences Sociales en Santé Publique, Hôpital Necker, 149 rue de Sèvres, 75015 Paris

Loss and restructuring of human identity in medical environments (Michèle Grosclaude and collaborators, Laboratoire de Psychologie Clinique, Strasbourg)

The Thinking of Clinical Psychologists

Studies by Monique de Bonis, Laboratoire de Psychologie Médicale, 102 rue de la Santé, Paris

Research on the reports of expert witnesses in forensic psychiatry by Loic Villerbu and collaborators (Université de Rennes, 6 avenue Gaston Berger, 35043 Rennes Cedex)

Marie-Ange Chabert and Matty Chiva

EXPERIMENTAL PSYCHOLOGY

Nature and Scope of the Discipline

Experimental psychology has developed rapidly since the end of World War II. As a result, in particular, of the efforts of P. Fraisse (Laboratoire de Psychologie Expérimentale et Comparée de la Sorbonne), who campaigned vigorously for the teaching of scientific psychology and trained several generations of researchers, numerous research centers in experimental psychology were established in Paris and in other French university towns. The recent history of scientific psychology is characterized by significant theoretical, thematic, and methodological developments.

From a theoretical point of view, the most significant development has been the resurgence of cognitive psychology. Experimental psychology can no longer do without a conceptual restructuring of the complex nonobservable processes intervening between variations in the environment and behavioral modifications. The psychology of behavior and of its basic functions has given way to a psychology of knowledge.

From the thematic point of view, one of the most notable changes in recent years has to do with the attention psychologists now pay to what we could call social demands or contexts. While socially relevant research requires much financial support, the availability of new computerized recording techniques and a policy of contracting for specific studies open up the possibility of fulfilling at least partially the new needs. In addition, experimental psychology may, with the declining influence of such unifying perspectives as behaviorism and Piaget's theory, abandon the aim of explaining human behavior in terms of mechanisms which are independent of essential contexts.

Methodologically, scientific psychology has been much influenced by computer science and the new means of recording, processing, and producing experimental data. The computer science model and the accompanying mode of thought have thoroughly infused psychology. Research on artificial intelligence, where the aim is to understand and describe human intelligence in order to simulate it, is a striking example of this infusion. Another development characterizes present-day research in France, namely, attempts to bring several approaches to bear on the same question. The work of M. Reuchlin (Laboratoire de Psychologie Différentielle, Paris) on the differential study of cognitive development illustrates this trend.

Major Research Areas

Research projects center on three main areas: (1) studies primarily concerned with the cognitive functioning of adults, (2) investigations of perceptuo-motor and intellectual development in children, and (3) methodological studies. The reader will note that in France there is a great deal of overlap and interaction between the first two lines of research.

Cognitive Functioning in Adults

Sensory and Motor Activities. The sensory systems and the means through which the human being transforms sensory data into perceptual experiences are generally considered to be intrinsic aspects of human cognitive functioning. This area of study, which lies at the interfaces of psychophysiology, neuropsychology, and cognitive psychology, has been strongly influenced by technological progress. Research necessitates a big investment in facilities and equipment and is therefore concentrated in the large laboratories.

A list of important research programs follows (only the head of each program is given):

Auditory and visual perception (Laboratoire de Psychologie Expérimentale, Paris V, C. Bonnet)

Visual perceptual exploration (Laboratoire de Psychologie Expérimentale, Paris V, Groupe "Regard," A. Levy-Schoen)

Vocal and gestural organization (Laboratoire de Psychologie Expérimentale, Paris V, B. de Boysson-Bardies)

Cognitive and perceptuo-motor spatial activities (Laboratoire de Psychologie Expérimentale, Grenoble, Y. Hatwell)

Cognition and movement (Cognition and Mouvement, CNRS, Marseille, J. Pailhous)

Neuropsychology of sensorimotor processes (Laboratoire de Neuropsychologie Humaine, Marseille, M. Brouchon)

Complex Cognitive Activities. Historically, research in this field in France was influenced by the work of Switzerland's J. Piaget (Université de Genève, Suisse) relative to the development of logical operations and by the studies of P. Oleron (Laboratoire de Psychologie Génétique) on higher intellectual activities and language. Today, all projects bearing on the intermediate processing stages between the input of information and the overt response are said to be concerned with complex cognitive activities. Research on learning, language and understanding, problem solving, judgment, and, more generally, everything concerning the representation of knowledge in memory are approached today from contemporary cognitive orientations.

Psycholinguistics. Psycholinguistics has as its goal the formulation of a speaker/ listener model which will account for both speech production and the construction of representations when compehension takes place. Research in France is being done concerning:

Perception and the comprehension of spoken language (Laboratoire de Psychologie Expérimentale, Paris V, J. Segui, M. F. Ehrlich)

Cognitive functioning of the speaker (Centre de Recherche en Psychologie Cognitive, Aix-en-Provence, J. Pynte)

Language, representation, and knowledge (Centre de Psychologie Cognitive, Paris-Sud, J. F. Le Ny)

Psychology of language comprehension and production (Laboratoire de Psychologie, Poitiers, J. P. Rossi, E. Esperet)

Acquisition and use of symbolic systems (Laboratoire de Psychologie, Dijon, M. Fayol)

Social and individual aspects of language; intercultural language interactions (Laboratoire de Recherches sur les Dimensions Sociales et les Incidences Subjectives du Langage, Strasbourg, A. Tabouret-Keller)

Aspects of Cognitive Functioning. The following is representative research:

Animal learning, computer simulation of animal learning (Département de Psychologie Animale, INP9, CNRS, H. Durup and P. Bovet)

Classical conditioning and automation (Laboratoire de Psychologie Différentielle, Paris, P. Perruchet)

Learning and animal behavior (Laboratoire de Psychologie Expérimentale, Montpellier, M. Blancheteau)

Representation and knowledge, images and cognitive representation, temporal characteristics of visual imagery (Centre de Psychologie Cognitive, Paris-Sud, M. Denis)

Context, memory, and cognition (Laboratoire de Psychologie Expérimentale, Grenoble, G. Tiberghien)

Psychology and computer science, knowledge representation in human and artificial systems, simulation of cognitive functioning by expert-systems (Laboratoire Psychologie et Informatique, Rouen, J. Mathieu)

Differential studies of information-processing modalities: intellectual activities, cognitive learning, cognitive aspects of personality (Laboratoire de Psychologie Différentielle, Paris, J. Bacher and M. Reuchlin; Laboratoire de Psychologie, Rouen, J. Caron; Laboratoire de Psychopathologie, Paris, Sainte Anne, M. de Bonis)

Chronobiology of cognition, cognitive processes, and psychopathology: role of sleeping in information processing; sleep, cognition, and psychopathology; and hemispheric asymmetry in cognitive functioning (Laboratoire de Psychologie, Lille, P. Leconte and P. Lecocq)

Neuropsychology (Groupe de Recherche de Neuropsychologie, Hôpital Pitié Salpétrière, Paris, M. F. Beauvois)

Hemispheric dissymetry, representation, and rehabilitation (Perception et Mouvement, Marseille, J. Blanc-Garin)

Hemispheric specialization (Laboratoire de Psychologie Expérimentale, Grenoble, Y. Hatwell)

Complex Goal-Directed Cognitive Activities. Research concerns include:

Judgmental processes (Centre de Recherche en Psychologie Cognitive, Aix-en-Provence, J. M. Fabre)

Cognitive activities in the elaboration and use of technical objects and languages: planning of activity, behavior microanalysis, temporal aspects of activity (Laboratoire de Psychologie du Travail, Paris, J. Leplat)

Cognition and graphing: transformation of the "drawing" professions, role of command languages (Centre de Recherche en Psychologie Cognitive, Aix-en-Provence, J. P. Poitou)

Acquisition mechanisms and problem solving (Laboratoire de Psychologie, Paris VIII, J. F. Richard)

Didactics and the acquisition of scientific knowledge (École des Hautes Études en Sciences Sociales, Paris, G. Vergnaud)

Psychology of art and cultural activities (Paris X, R. Frances, and M. Imberty)

Development: From Child to Adult

This field of development is one of the traditional pillars of research in France; it has developed under the impetus given by the EHESS (F. Bresson and P. Greco) and the Laboratoire de Psychologie Expérimentale de la Sorbonne (E. Vurpillot). In recent years, two main concerns have emerged in this field: the genesis of cognitive functioning in the individual and personality formation and the socialization of the child.

Research on young infants has been particularly fruitful, as has been the case in other countries, and has brought about a renewal of interest in the early stages of development (initial capabilities, motor programs, first communications, and so forth). In a more general sense, purely structuralist "stages" conceptions of development in childhood have given way to analyses of the relationships between structure and function, often expressed in terms of strategies.

Perceptuo-motor Activities.

Construction of spatial systems of reference and visual activities in infancy and childhood (Laboratoire de Psycho-Biologie de l'Enfant, Paris, H. Bloch and G. Pierault-Le Bonniec)

Visual activities and visual and haptic cross-modal transfer in infancy (Laboratoire de Psychologie Génétique, Paris, M. G. Pécheux)

Early development of interhemispheric specialization and communication (Laboratoire de Neurosciences Fonctionnelles, Marseille, CNRS, S. de Schonen)

Early links between perception and motor acts (Laboratoire de Psychologie Expérimentale, Paris V, B. de Boysson-Bardies)

Visual, proprioceptive, and haptic intermodal integration; and motor development (Laboratoire de Psychologie Expérimentale, Grenoble, Y. Hatwell)

Visuo-manual coordinations in childhood (INP, Marseille, L. Hay)

Regulatory mechanisms coordinating cognitive and sensorimotor processes in children: locomotor behavior (Cognition et Mouvement, CNRS, Marseille, J. Pailhous)

Complex Cognitive Activities.

Language perception in infancy (Centre d'Étude des Processus Cognitifs et du Langage, Paris, J. Mehler)

Language development and functioning in school interaction situations (Laboratoire de Psychologie Expérimentale, Poitiers, S. Ehrlich)

Cross-cultural language research on morphosyntactic constraints and the study of pragmatic dimensions of language (Laboratoire de Psychologie Expérimentale, Paris V, M. Kail)

Cognitive development: multiplicative class and additive relations groupings and additive number structure (Laboratoire de Psychologie, Paris VIII, A. Nguyen-Xuan)

Cognitive development of preoperational children (Centre de Recherche en Psychologie Cognitive, Aix-en-Provence, F. Orsini-Bouichou)

Logical problem-solving procedures in children four to ten years old: modeling of classificatory behavior in young children (Centre de Recherche en Psychologie Cognitive, Aix-en-provence, C. Bastien)

Classificatory and programming activities (Laboratoire de Psychologie Expérimentale, Grenoble, F. Longeot)

Structure and cognitive functioning (Laboratoire de Psychologie Différentielle, Paris, J. Lautrey; Laboratoire de Psychologie Génétique, Paris, J. Bideaud)

Memory and problem solving in childhood (Laboratoire de Psychologie Expérimentale et Comparée, Nice, C. Florès)

Socialization of the child (Laboratoire de Psychologie Génétique, Université de Paris V, J. Beaudichon; Centre de Recherche en Psychologie Cognitive, Aix-en-Provence, M. Gilly and J. P. Codol)

Methodological Research

Concurrently with their experimental work, many research centers do studies of research methodology, statistical techniques, and instrumentation. Specific issues investigated include:

Development of methodologies and applied techniques (Laboratoire de Psychologie du Travail, Paris, J. Leplat)

Learning models, methods for the study of problem-solving protocols, adaptive production systems (Laboratoire de Psychologie, Paris VIII, J. F. Richard, C. Georges)

Theoretical and methodological problems involved in the didactics of mathematics (EHESS, Paris, G. Vergnaud)

Factor analysis and hypothesis testing, psycho-socio-educative inquiry (Laboratoire de Psychologie Différentielle, Paris, F. Bacher)

Statistical inference and validation models (Groupe Mathématiques et Psychologie, Paris, B. Lecoutre, H. Rouanet)

Methodological research in experimental psychology (Laboratoire de Psychologie Expérimentale, Paris V, D. Lépine)

Addresses

Centre d'Étude des Processus Cognitifs et du Langage EHESS, 54 Bld Raspail F—75270 Paris Cedex 06.

Centre de Psychologie Cognitive—Centre Scientifique d'Orsay, Bâtiment 335—F—91405 Orsay Cedex.

Centre de Recherche en Psychologie Cognitive, Université de Provence, 29 avenue Robert Schuman F—13621 Aix-en-Provence Cedex.

Clinique des Maladies Mentales et de l'Encéphale, Centre Psychiatrique Sainte Anne, 100 rue de la Santé, F—75014 Paris.

Greco "Didactique"—EHESS, 54 Bld Raspail F—75270 Paris Cedex 06.

Groupe de Recherche de Neuropsychologie, Hôpital Pitié-Salpétrière, 47 Bld de l'Hôpital, F—75651 Paris Cedex 13.

Groupe "Mathématiques et Psychologie," UER de Mathématiques—Paris V, 12 rue Cujas F—75005 Paris.

Laboratoire de Neuropsychologie Humaine, 2 rue de la Charité—F—13002 Marseille.

Laboratoire de Neurosciences Fonctionnelles (CNRS) 13 Chemin Joseph Aiguier, F—13277 Marseille Cedex 9.

Laboratoire de Psycho-Biologie de l'Enfant, EPHE Illème Section, 41 rue Gay-Lussac, F—75005 Paris.

Laboratoire de Psychologie, Paris VIII—2 rue de la Liberte—F—93526 Saint-Denis Cedex 02.

Laboratoire de Psychologie, Université de Poitiers, 95 avenue du Recteur Pineau, F—86022 Poitiers Cedex.

Laboratoire de Psychologie Différentielle, INETOP, Arts et Métiers—41 rue Gay—Lussac, F—75005 Paris.

Laboratoire de Psychologie du Travail, INOP-EPHE—41 rue Gay-Lussac, F—75005 Paris.

Laboratoire de Psychologie Expérimentale, Université de Grenoble II, BP 47 X, F—38040 Grenoble Cedex.

Laboratoire de Psychologie Expérimentale, Université de Paris V, 28 rue Serpente, F—75006 Paris.

Laboratoire de Psychologie Expérimentale, Université Paul Valéry, BP 5043, F—34032 Montpellier Cedex.

Laboratoire de Psychologie Expérimentale et Comparée Université de Nice, 98 Bld Edouard Herriot, BP 257, F—06036 Nice Cedex.

Laboratoire de Psychologie Génétique, Paris V—Sorbonne—46 rue Saint-Jacques, F—75005 Paris.

Laboratoire de Recherches sur le Langage (LADISIS) 12 rue Goethe, F—6700 Strasbourg.

Laboratoire "Psychologie et Informatique," Université de Rouen, Bâtiment Faculté des Lettres, F—76130 Mont Saint Aignan.

Perception et Mouvement, IBHOP—5 rue des Géraniums, F—13014 Marseille.

Yvette Hatwell and Patrick Mendelsohn

SOCIAL PSYCHOLOGY

In France, social psychology may belong to either the psychology or sociology curriculum. It is also an autonomous research field and profession. There is a Section of Social Psychology in the Société Française de Psychologie.

Laboratories and research centers in social psychology are found in most university psychology departments, the École des Hautes Études en Sciences Sociales, the CNRS, and, in some research institutions such as INSERM and INRA. The most important university research groups are associated with the CNRS.

The Laboratoire de Psychologie Sociale (CNRS, associated with the University of Paris VII) conducts research on norms and emotions in social interactions; influence, conformity, dissimilation, and conversion; information processing in complex social systems (studies of beliefs and ideology); information processing and behavioral adaptation in socioecological fields; sociohistorical and socio-linguistic perspectives in the study of identity strategies; and theories of "em-prise" (influence or control) and psychosocial causality.

Common to all of these research topics is the study of people exchanging information with their environments (be it complex social fields, physical sur-rounds, or another individual) and the processing of this information through a "cognitive filter." The above research is mostly experimental but conducted either in the laboratory or in natural settings.

The Groupe de Recherches sur la Parole (Jeune Equipe CNRS, associated with the University of Paris VIII) is noted for its investigations of sign systems in communication, rules and principles which structure communication, the social influence in communication, and methodological issues associated with interview procedures and content analysis. Studies concerning sign systems have to do with the syntactic and semantic variables and processes involved in verbal com-munication, a new taxonomy relevant to nonverbal communication, and the proxemics of human interactions viewed as communication systems. Investi-gations of communication contracts take into account rules and principles which structure communication. Research on social influence examines communication in all types of situations; methodological investigations, as indicated before, focus on interview techniques and content analysis.

In general, the GRP is mainly interested in both interpersonal and media-produced communication. Consequently, a global "communication contract" theory is being developed and verified through studies of the interactions among verbal, nonverbal, and paraverbal sign systems, where meaning originates. Other research bears on such pragmatic issues as the validation and acceptance of communication contracts.

Also at the University of Paris VIII, the Groupe de Recherches sur l'Idéolo-logique et le Fonctionnement Socio-cognitif pursues experimental research on the epistemology of ordinary life experiences and their relationships with ideo-logical systems of representations. More specifically, research is focused on implicit theories of personality, particularly their recent historical evolution, and the ways people try to account for, and explain, disabilities associated with illness and aging.

The Laboratoire de Psychologie Sociale de l'Université Paris V carries out both fundamental research and descriptive field work. Research focuses on in-dividual cognition (person perception, causal attribution) and interactions in small groups (social influence, persuasive communication, negotiations). Field re-search has as its goal a systematic description of collective phenomena. Studies deal with attitudes and beliefs, socialization and identity, and cognitive repre-sentations based mostly on surveys, interviews, and content analyses of relevant documents. One team does environmental investigations of the effects of noise on human behavior.

The Laboratoire de Psychologie Sociale de l'École des Hautes Études en Sciences Sociales works mainly in two areas: the first has to do with representations of the social and physical environment, the second with social influences. At present, some research in the first area bears on the way an ideology such as Marxism is interpreted by the public at large; other studies pertain to representations of urban space and the role of genetic factors in the acquisition and moral judgment by children. The latter two research projects are being done in collaboration with British scientists.

Current research on social influence deals with the relationships between attitude change and social contexts. In addition, there are studies of the militants of the Front National, an extreme right-wing group. Finally, research is being done on psychology as a profession. Of special interest are the professionalization of American psychology at the turn of the century and contemporary views of psychologists as professionals.

Clinical social psychology is strongly represented in the Universities of Paris VII, X, and XIII. While a variety of theoretical orientations are invoked, research tends to be concerned with the concept of power. Major issues being investigated are modes of social intervention; relationships among body image, sexuality, procreation, and family dynamics; groups, organizations, and institutions; and social differentiation and ostracism.

The Laboratoire de Personnalisation et Changements Sociaux of the University of Toulouse le Mirail studies the processes through which personal changes and changes in social values and frameworks are linked. These dynamics are investigated in the context of education, work, life style, sociopolitical background, and family roles.

In Montpellier, the Laboratoire de Psychologie Sociale has been preoccupied of late with research on communication between groups, the creation and dissemination of scientific knowledge and technical information, the psychosociological analysis of work conditions, and the evaluation of professional roles.

The Centre de Recherche Psyschologie Cognitive of Aix-en-Provence has been engaged primarily in research on the cognitive aspects of social behavior and the perception of interindividual similarity. Presently the focus is on the evolution of cognitive functions during the *période préopératoire* (the emphasis is on pertinent socio-family functions), social and socioeducational regulation in individual cognitive constructions, and the structure and dynamics of cognitive systems in social interaction. It should also be noted that a network of social psychologists in southeastern France, centered in Grenoble, concentrates on the psychology of everyday experiences and ideology.

Not all laboratories and research teams are mentioned here. Considerable research, much of it original in nature, is also being conducted within university departments of education, and there are other investigations going on where the aims are not always specifically related to social psychology per se. For example, significant studies have been done, or are taking place, concerning catastrophes, environmental stress, social and cultural aspects of being handicapped, and accidents at work.

Students preparing to become social psychologists receive strong training in experimental, empirical, and clinical methodologies and theories. Social psychologists assume positions such as training directors or program coordinators in public or private institutions, marketing specialists, researchers, and consultants on transportation, urbanization, moral and political issues, communication, and social and cultural changes. Many social psychologists now orient themselves toward ergonomics and industrial psychology.

Alexandre Dorna, Jacques-Marie Jakobi,
Benjamin Matalon, and Liliane Salhani

WORK PSYCHOLOGY

Work psychology has to do with the psychological aspects of people at work. While this field is primarily an applied specialty in France, scientific and/or theoretical research also takes place. Work psychology forms a branch of the Société Française de Psychologie. In addition, the French Language Work Psychology Association (Association de Psychologie du Travail de Langue Française), which organizes a congress every other year, was founded in 1980. Many work psychologists are also members of the International Association of Applied Psychology and the French Language Society of Ergonomics (Société d'Ergonomie de Langue Française).

Research Facilities

Research is done primarily in university laboratories. The most important of these are:

Laboratoire de Psychologie du Travail de l'École Pratique des Hautes Études (3e Section), 41 rue Gay-Lussac—75005 Paris.

Laboratoire de Psychologie du Travail du Conservatoire National des Arts et Métiers (same address).

Laboratoire de Neurophysiologie du Travail—Ergonomie du Conservatoire National des Arts et Métiers (same address).

Laboratoire de Psychologie de l'Apprentissage—IBHOP 13014 Marseille.

Also important are research and teaching units associated with the following universities: Paris V, Paris X, Paris XIII, Aix-en-Provence, Toulouse le Mirail, and Toulouse Paul Sabatier.

Psychological research is also done at laboratories which are part of the Institut National de Recherche pour les Transports et leur Sécurité, Institut National de

Recherche et Sécurité, Institut National de Recherche en Informatique et Automatique, and other research institutes.

Publications

In France, articles about research in work psychology are published mainly in *Le Travail Humain* [Human Work]. Issue Number 1 (1984), published on the journal's fiftieth anniversary, presents a history of the field which, to a certain extent, corresponds to the history of the entire discipline. Articles about work are also found in *Revue de Psychologie Appliquée, Bulletin de Psychologie*, and *Le Journal des Psychologues*. The *Bulletin du CERP*, published from 1952 to 1976, specialized in work psychology, and the work psychology branch of the SFP publishes a bulletin entitled *Psychologie du Travail* [Work Psychology] for its own members.

In 1980, a special 360-page issue of *Bulletin de Psychologie* was dedicated to work psychology. It contains a survey of research in various fields as well as information about educational systems in France, associations to which some work psychologists belong, and the status of work psychologists in general.

Reference Books

The first four volumes of M. Reuchlin's treatise on applied psychology (published by PUF, Paris, 1970) contain chapters on work psychology. C. Lévy-Leboyer and J. C. Spérandio's analysis of work psychology is being printed by PUF (Paris). The following books are also worth mentioning: *An introduction to work psychology* (J. Leplat and X. Cuny, 1984, PUF, Paris), which includes a list of books specializing mainly in specific areas of work psychology; *Psychology in ergonomics* (J. C. Spérandio, 1980, PUF, Paris); and *The psychologist and the firm* (C. Lévy-Leboyer, 1980, Masson, Paris).

Curriculum Models

Work psychologists are trained at the University of Paris and at the Conservatoire National des Arts et Métiers. After graduating with a master's in psychology (or receiving any similar degree involving four years of postsecondary school study), they read for the Diplôme d'Études Supérieures Spécialisées (D.E.S.S.), an advanced and more specialized degree. A new degree program, representing a higher level of competency, is being planned. The most advanced degree in work psychology generally involves the publication of a thesis.

Professional Aspects of Work Psychology

The work psychology branch of the SFP has about 400 members. A 1982 study by Moulin appearing in *Psychologie du Travail*, No. 14, shows that the

Table 1
Employment Settings of Work Psychologists

	Numbers	
Agency or Enterprise	1979	1985
Association for Vocational Training of Adults (AFPA)	330	550
Post and Telecommunications (PTT)	54	50
French Railways (SNCF)	26	32
Renault	20	29
Paris Transport (RATP)	8	23
Other	44	48
TOTAL	482	732

median age of psychologists is forty-five. Two surveys, conducted in 1979 and 1982, show that more than half of work psychologists are involved in all aspects of vocational training, recruitment, and job placement. Others deal with administrative management; work organization; personnel management; relations with other firms, boards of directors, and so forth; and rehabilitation.

Men are engaged in a broader range of professional activities and tend to have higher-level jobs than women, but then they are, on the average, older. The activities of a work psychologist are related to his or her knowledge of psychology and various other fields such as engineering, management, economics, pedagogics, sociology, and medicine. About 42 percent of work psychologists are employed by government agencies or national corporations, 38 percent work for private companies, and 18 percent are in private practice.

Table 1 presents information about the number of work psychologists employed by major public agencies or enterprises (based on surveys done in 1979 and 1985). The increases occurring between 1979 and 1985 are to some degree a function of the fact that the criteria used to classify someone as a psychologist changed.

Developments

Developments in research and practice in French work psychology are similar to those witnessed in other countries. These trends are determined by two sets of factors which have to do with increasing employment opportunities and transformations of work. The latter result primarily from new technologies that significantly change the ways things are produced. New systems of production and data processing, as well as their implementation in organizations, raise problems that cannot be solved by rules of thumb. Psychologists' contributions to finding solutions can be considerable because of their knowledge of the ways work may be organized, working conditions improved, and so on. Technical changes frequently require retraining of workers, and work psychologists play a role in designing and implementing appropriate retraining programs. Social pressure for the improvement of working conditions also provides an incentive for people to study work psychology.

There has been increasing differentiation and specialization in French psychology as a whole and even within work psychology. Ergonomical psychology, the psychology of organizations, and training psychology, for example, have gained considerable autonomy. These branches, along with other specialties, have developed significantly in France.

There is also a strong interest in creating links between the findings and conceptions of work psychology and more general theoretical frameworks. Many work psychologists attend refresher courses to become knowledgeable about developments in other subfields of psychology. This tendency complements an interest on the part of researchers who are interested in studies and observations made in work settings. As a result of this cross-fertilization of knowledge and perspectives, French psychologists have, without question, made original contributions to the field by developing techniques for analyzing cognitive processes associated with work.

Jacques Leplat

CHILD PSYCHOLOGY

From the beginning, French child psychology has emphasized the study of the relationships between the development of the child and his or her environment. The field has been strongly influenced by the somewhat contradictory viewpoints of H. Wallon and J. Piaget. French child psychologists in general believe that meaningful research requires viewing the infant/child as a functional developing unit and taking into consideration what constitutes reality for the young person, integrating relevant biological and social factors and variables, and formulating investigations that take into account contexts such as family and school that surround the developing human being.

While the child is considered as a totality, separate psychological processes are of course studied. When, for example, cognitive development is investigated, however, the child as a whole is always the primary referent. Areas of research which have been central to French child psychology include play, drawing, and individual differences (particularly relative to mental retardation). Psychoanalysis has had little influence on the field in France.

Child Psychology as a Profession

Paradoxically, the long history and vigorous presence of child psychology as a scientific field in France have not been accompanied by the development of the area as an applied specialty or profession. On the other hand, school psychologists and some clinical psychologists are child specialists and depend, in part, on the research findings and theoretical perspectives of child psychologists.

Psychology was officially introduced into French state schools during the 1950s, largely as a result of Wallon's efforts. There are now several thousand school psychologists, the majority of whom work in elementary schools. These specialists have at least five years of teaching experience and two years of university courses in school psychology. Most have considerably more university training.

Originally, school psychologists were primarily employed to diagnose learning disabilities, through psychological testing, and to provide guidance with regard to the placement of children in special classes. More recently, the functions of school psychologists have expanded to include working as part of "psychopedagogical assistance groups" in normal elementary schools. Here they work with other specialists not only diagnosing and providing help to individual children but also working to improve the educational system.

Many of the six to eight thousand clinical psychologists in France work in hospitals, guidance centers, or other facilities which specialize in helping maladapted children and adolescents. A substantial number of the psychologists in private practice (a number that is increasing in France) also specialize in the treatment of children.

The basic task of clinical psychologists is to determine the underlying motivations and dynamics that may be at the root of problems a child is having at school or at home and to provide therapeutic services. There is little information as to the specific functions child clinical psychologists perform; however, there is evidence that they do relatively little testing or analyses of educational tasks and situations but devote most of their time to providing psychoanalytically oriented psychotherapy. A few apparently employ a systemic approach based on the work of A. Bandura at Stanford University in the United States.

To become a clinical psychologist generally involves five years of university training. The major theoretical orientation is psychoanalysis. Courses have to do with psychopathology, psychotherapy, and testing.

A small number of French psychologists work with infants in day nurseries and adolescents making the transition from school to employment. Their work may include vocational counseling. There is a need for more positions that allow psychologists to assist people not suffering from serious psychological and emotional problems.

A special five-year terminal degree program in child and adolescent psychology has recently been established in a few universities. It is hoped that a similar program for school psychologists will become available.

Major Research Interests

Purely structural (stage) conceptions of psychological development have been replaced by analyses of the relationships between structures and functions. A life-span perspective is emphasized and research revolves around the interaction between the subject and his or her environment, through which interaction cognitive and social structuring takes place. Both formal and informal social interactions, in school and other settings, are studied. Frequently simultaneous analyses of tasks, situations, and behaviors are involved. There is much concern with ecological validity.

Specific topics investigated are the development of early social and cognitive competencies, the development of psychomotor coordination, social interaction and communication, the acquisition of knowledge, the development of memory processes and metacognitive activities, cognitive dysfunctions and remedial procedures, and transitional periods (for example, from home to the nursery, from nursery school to elementary school). There have also been important cross-cultural studies of child development.

Michel Hurtig, Evelyne Cauzinille-Marmeche,
and Annick Weil-Barais

MAJOR JOURNALS

For each of the following journals, the date is the year in which the journal was first published.

L'Année Psychologique [This Year in Psychology]. Published by PUF, 12 rue Jean de Beauvais, 75005 Paris, English abstracts (1901).

Bulletin de Psychologie [Bulletin of Psychology]. 17 rue de la Sorbonne, 75005 Paris (1947).

Cahiers de Psychologie [Psychological Bulletin]. Published by the Université de Provence, 13621 Aix-en-Provence Cédex (1957).

Cahiers de Psychologie Cognitive [Bulletin of Cognitive Psychology]. IBHOP, rue des Géraniums, 13014 Marseille. English abstracts (1980).

Comportements [Behaviors]. Published by the CNRS, 15 quai Anatole France, 75007 Paris (1983).

Connexions [Connections]. Published by Epi, 6 bis rue Bachaumont, 75002 Paris. English abstracts (1970).

Enfance [Childhood]. Published with the help of CNRS, 41 rue Gay Lussac, 75005 Paris. English abstracts (1948).

Études Psychothérapiques [Psychotherapeutic Studies]. Published privately, 14 rue des Arts, 31068 Toulouse. English abstracts (1969).

Journal Européen de Psychologie de l'Education [European Journal of the Psychology of Education]. Instituto Superior de Psicologia Applicata, R. Jardim do Tabacco, 44, 1100 Lisboa-Portugal, M. Gilly, Editor, Aix-en-Provence, France. English abstracts.

La Psychiatrie de l'Enfant [Child Psychiatry]. Published by PUF, 12 rue Jean de Beauvais, 75005 Paris (1957).

Lieux de l'Enfance [Childhood Places]. Published privately, 14 rue des Arts, 31068 Toulouse (1985).

Neuro-psychiatrie de l'Enfant et de l'Adolescent [Child and Adolescent Neuropsychiatry]. Published by Expansion Scientifique Française, 15 rue St Benoît, 75278 Paris Cédex 06. English abstracts (1952).

L'Orientation Scolaire et Professionnelle [School and Vocational Counseling]. INETOP, 45 rue Gay Lussac, 75005 Paris.

Psychologie et Education [Psychology and Education]. Laboratoire Associé 259, 31081 Toulouse le Mirail. English abstracts (1976).

Psychologie Française [French Psychology]. Bulletin of the Société Française de Psychologie, Librairie Armand Colin, 103 bld St Michael, 75240 Paris Cédex 05 (1955).

Recherches de Psychologie Sociale [Social Psychology Research]. Published by Laboratoire de Psychologie Sociale de l'Université Paris VII (1979).

Revue de Psychologie Appliquée [Review of Applied Psychology]. Published by the Centre de Psychologie Appliquée, 48 avenue Victor Hugo, 75783 Paris Cédex 16. English abstracts and keywords (1950).

Sauvegarde de l'Enfance [Safeguarding Childhood]. Journal of the Association Française pour la Sauvegarde de l'Enfance, 28 place St Georges, 75442 Paris Cédex 09. English and Spanish abstracts (1945).

SUGGESTED READINGS

Debesse, M., & Mialaret, G. (Eds.). (1973–1974). *Traité des sciences pédagogiques* [Treatise on the pedagogical sciences] (Vols. 4–6). Paris: Presses Universitaire de France.

Fraisse, P. (1963–1969). L'Évolution de la psychologie expérimentale en France. In P. Fraisse & J. Piaget (Eds.), *Traité de psychologie expérimentale* [A treatise on experimental psychology] (9 vols.). Paris: Presses Universitaire de France.

Francès, R. (1976). Scientific psychology in France. *Annual Review of Psychology, 27,* 281–299.

Gratiot-Alphandery, H., & Zazzo, R. (Eds.). (1970–1976). *Traité de psychologie de l'enfant* [Treatise on the psychology of the child] (Vols. 1–6). Paris: Presses Universitaire de France.

Hurtig, M., & Rondal, J. A. (Eds.). (1981). *Introduction à la psychologie de l'enfant* [Introduction to child psychology] (Vols. 1–3). Liège: Mardaga.

Huteau, M., & Roubertoux, P. (1976). France. In V. S. Sexton & H. Misiak (Eds.), *Psychology around the world*. Monterey, CA: Brooks/Cole.

Reuchlin, M. (1966). The historical background for national trends in psychology: France. *Journal of the History of the Behavioral Sciences*, *1*, 115–123.

Reuchlin, M. (1974). *Histoire de la psychologie* [History of psychology]. Paris: Presses Universitaire de France.

Federal Republic of Germany

Carl F. Graumann and Alexandre Métraux

NATURE AND SCOPE OF THE DISCIPLINE

Definition(s) of Psychology

The conception of psychology adhered to in West Germany is similar to that found in other Western European countries. As the science of experience and behavior it would not even differ from occasional North American definitions. But two distinctions should be made. The German word *Wissenschaft* (translated here as "science") is not synonymous with that of natural science. The term *Wissenschaft* covers the various disciplines of the humanities, arts and letters as well as the natural and social sciences. The predominance of the experimental method in the study of cognition and motivation, rendering *Allgemeine Psychologie* (general experimental psychology), the basic and central discipline, a natural science, holds as well for the greater part of social and differential psychology but less so for developmental psychology. In other branches of psychology, the primacy of the experiment is balanced or outweighed by correlational and clinical procedures.

The decision as to whether psychology should be considered and taught mainly as a natural science or within a broader context has been, to some extent, a function of the faculty makeup of psychology institutes. After World War II most chairs and institutes of psychology belonged to the philosophical faculties; very few were part of the science faculties. Today, after the dissolution of the larger faculties, psychology is increasingly part of new social science faculties although its theoretical and methodological focus is on the individual person.

Organizational Structure

The oldest and internationally best-known professional organization is the Deutsche Gesellschaft für Psychologie [German Society for Psychology] (DGfPs). Founded in 1904 as Gesellschaft für experimentelle Psychologie [Society for

Experimental Psychology] and given its present name in 1929, it is the association of university psychologists active in research and/or teaching. One of its main functions is the organization of biennial congresses. Practitioners and other professionals of psychology are associated with the Berufsverband Deutscher Psychologen [Professional Organization of German Psychologists] (BDP), founded in 1947, the largest professional organization in Germany (Hauptgeschäftsstelle: Heilsbachstr. 22, D–5300 Bonn 1). Organized into a "federation," both DGfPs and BDP are members of the International Union of Psychological Science (IUPsyS). Besides these two, there are several professional organizations for clinical psychology and psychotherapy, such as the Deutsche Gesellschaft für Verhaltenstherapie [German Society for Behavior Therapy] (DGVT).

Major Programs and Laboratories Associated with Universities

Freie Universtät Berlin, Psychologisches Institut, Habelschwerdter Allee 45, 1000 Berlin 33.

Technische Universität Berlin, Institut für Psychologie, Dovestr. 1–5, 1000 Berlin 10.

Universität Bielefeld, Fakultät für Psychologie und Sportwissenchaft, Postfach 8640, 4800 Bielefeld.

Universität Bochum, Psychologisches Institute, Postfach 102148, 4630 Bochum.

Universität Bonn, Psychologisches Institut, Römerstr. 164, 5300 Bonn 1.

Universität Erlangen-Nürnberg, Institut für Psychologie, Bismarckstr. 1 and 6, 8520 Erlangen.

Universität Frankfurt/Main, Fachbereich 5 Psychologie, Postfach 11 19 32, 6000 Frankfurt/Main.

Universität Frankfurt/Main, Institut für Psychologie, Mertonstr. 17, 6000 Frankfurt/Main.

Universität Freiburg, Psychologisches Institut, Belfortstr. 18, 7800 Freiburg.

Universität Giessen, Fachbereich 06 Psychologie, Otto-Behagel-Str. 10, 6300 Giessen.

Universität Göttingen, Institut für Psychologie, Gosslerstr. 14, 3400 Gottingen.

Universität Hamburg, Fachbereich 16, Psychologisches Institut, Von-Melle-Park 5, 2000 Hamburg 13.

Universität Heidelberg, Psychologisches Institut, Hauptstr. 47–51, 6900 Heidelberg.

Universität Köln, Psychologisches Institut I, Hädenkampstr. 2, 5000 Köln 41.

Universität Konstanz, Fachgruppe Psychologie, Postfach 5560, 7750 Konstanz.

Universität Mainz, Psychologisches Institut, Postfach 3980, 6500 Mainz 1.

Universität Mannheim, Otto-Selz-Institut, Schlob, 6800 Mannheim.

Universität Marburg, Fachbereich Psychologie, Gutenbergstr. 18, 3550 Marburg/Lahn.

Universität München, Institut für Psychologie, Geschwister-Scholl-Platz 1, 8000 München 22.

Universität Münster, Psychologisches Institut, Schlaunstr. 2, 4400 Münster.

Universität Saarbrücken, Fachrichtung Psychologie im Fachbereich 6, Universitäts-Campus, Bau I, 6600 Saarbrücken.

Universität Trier, Fachbereich 1—Psychologie, Tarforst, Gebäude D, 5500 Trier.

Universität Tübingen, Psychologisches Institut, Friedrichstr. 21, 7400 Tübingen.

Universität Würzburg, Institut für Psychologie, Domerschulstr. 13, 8700 Würzburg.

Research Institutes

The institutes of the Max-Planck-Gesellschaft (MPG) are institutions of pure/basic research (no teaching). Institutes with research programs in psychology and with openings for visiting researchers are in Berlin, Munich, and Nijmegen. Their addresses are:

Max-Planck-Institut für Bildungsforschung, Forschungsbereich Psychologie und Humanentwicklung, Lentzeallee 94, 1000 Berlin 33.

Max-Planck-Institut für Psychologische Forschung, Leopoldstr. 24/26, 8000 München 40.

Max-Planck-Institut für Psycholinguistik, Berg en Dalsweg 79, NL–6522 BC Nijmegen.

Primary Functions of Psychologists

Psychological practitioners until the 1970s were principally engaged in testing and counseling; since then their activities have been extended to therapy (in a very broad sense). During the 1950–1975 period, the majority of professional psychologists worked in public and social services (education in general, schools for handicapped children, rehabilitation programs and clinics, the armed forces, and so forth) where funding was largely public (state or community). Increasingly, however, a large part of the profession is engaged in private psychological counseling and psychotherapy. It should be noted that since 1945 a relatively constant number of psychologists has worked in organizational and industrial psychology, marketing, management counseling, and forensic psychology as well as in psychiatric and gerontological (geriatric) institutions. A still relatively high, though steadily decreasing, percentage of psychologists is involved in basic research.

Funding of the Discipline

All major training programs and curricula are established by psychological institutes at universities. Practically all West German universities are state universities. Within the eleven *Länder* that make up the Federal Republic of Germany, the thirty-six existing programs or institutes are financially supported by the states. Their annual budgets are part of the university budgets appropriated by the state parliaments. According to Irle and Strack (1983), the average annual budget (excluding personnel costs) of an Institute of Psychology was DM 150,000 in 1978 (with a range, reflecting size and other criteria, of between roughly DM 50,000 and DM 386,000). Since then, the number of institutes and the average budget has increased slightly. Owing to cuts in public expenditures in the past few years, the steadily growing postwar curve of spending (and hence growth of funds for staff and equipment) has leveled off. For some facilities—for example, libraries—this has meant significantly fewer acquisitions. By far the largest part of an institute's budget has to be spent on books, journals, technical equipment, and maintenance. Funds for research have to be acquired mostly from grant-giving agencies.

Undergraduate and Graduate Curriculum Models

The curriculum model effective at most West German psychology departments is regulated by the *Diplomprüfungsordnung* (diploma examination regulations) of 1976. It subdivides the basic training leading to a diploma into three stages.

A first stage of two years (four terms) involves courses in general psychology (perception, cognition, memory and learning, motivation and emotion, and sometimes language), developmental psychology (sometimes life-span psychology), personality and differential psychology, social psychology, physiological psychology, and methodology (methods). This first stage is concluded by passing examinations in the above areas.

The second stage, again lasting two years, emphasizes specialization and practical training in three sets of subdisciplines. With local variations, the first set involves courses in social cognition, mathematical psychology, research methods, environmental psychology, and theoretical psychology. The second set emphasizes fields of application like educational, clinical, organizational, or industrial psychology. A third set offers training in clinical and educational testing, assessment, methods of interaction, and so forth. This second phase of training concludes with oral and written exminations in the various subdisciplines, many of which are optional within a fixed number of fields.

Passing the final diploma examination entitles the candidate to write an obligatory diploma thesis which, on the average, takes one more year. If accepted, the candidate is awarded his/her diploma and the academic degree of Dipl. Psych., which is roughly equivalent to the M.A. in the United States. Minimally, good overall performance at this level is the prerequisite for admission to doctoral candidacy. Most psychology students leave the university with only the diploma; about 10 percent earn a doctorate, which, on the average, can be attained in two to three years. Of those who are awarded the doctorate, a small percentage achieve candidacy for the *Habilitation*, a kind of higher-level doctorate, necessary for a university career.

Major Journals

Archiv für Psychology [Archives of Psychology]. Editors: O. Ewert; W. D. Fröhlich, Mainz (Editor-in-Chief); B. Foppa, Bern; G. Guttmann, Vienna; H. W. Krohne, Mainz; H. Thomae, Bonn. Publisher: Bouvier-Verlag H. Grundmann, Bonn.

Psychologische Rundschau [Psychological Review]. Edited for the Deutsche Gesellschaft für Psychologie by W. Prinz, Bielefeld, in cooperation with U. Baumann, Salzburg; D. Frey, Kiel. Publisher: Verlag für Psychologie, Dr. C. J. Hogrefe, Göttingen.

Sprache & Kognition. [Language and Cognition]. Editors: D. Dörner, Bamberg; J. Engelkamp, Saarbrücken; H. Grimm, Bielefeld. Publisher: Verlag Hans Huber, Bern.

Zeitschrift für Entwicklungspsychologie und Pädagogische Psychologie [Journal of Developmental Psychology and Educational Psychology]. Editors: O. Ewert, Mainz; H. Heckhausen, München; M. Mandl, Tübingen; F. E. Weinert, München. Publisher: Verlag für Psychologie, Dr. C. J. Hogrefe, Göttingen.

Zeitschrift für Experimentelle und Angewandte Psychologie [Journal of Experimental and Applied Psychology]. Editors: J. Drösler, Regensburg; K. Müller, München; F. Süllwold, Frankfurt/M. Publisher: Verlag für Psychologie, Dr. C. J. Hogrefe, Göttingen.

Zeitschrift für Klinische Psychologie, Forschung und Praxis [Journal of Clinical Psychology, Research, and Practice]. Editors: U. Baumann, Salzburg; B. Drahme, Hamburg; K. Grawe, Bern; H. Häfner, Mannheim; H. Remschmidt, Marburg; L. Schmidt, Trier. Publisher: Verlag für Psychologie, Dr. C. J. Hogrefe, Göttingen.

Zeitschrift für Sozialpsychologie [Journal of Social Psychology]. Editors: H. Feger, Hamburg; C. F. Graumann, Heidelberg; K. Holzkamp, Berlin; M. Irle, Mannheim. Publisher: Verlag Hans Huber, Bern.

Most Widely Used Introductory Textbooks

(1) Zimbardo, P. G. *Psychologie*. 3. neubearb. Aufl. Springer, 1978; 4. neubearb. Aufl. Springer, 1982. Bearbeitet und herausgegeben von W. F. Angermeier, J. C. Brengelmann, Th.J. Thiekötter. *Essentials of psychology and life* (Brief 10th Ed.). Glenview, IL: Scott, Foresman.

(2) Schönpflug, W., & Schönpflug, U. (1983). *Psychologie: Allgemeine Psychologie und ihre Verzweigungen in der Entwicklungs-, Persönlichkeits- und Sozialpsychologie. Ein Lehrbuch für das Grundstudium* [Psychology: General psychology and its ramifications in developmental, personality, and social psychology. A textbook for basic studies]. München: Urban & Schwarzenberg.

(3) Krech, D., Crutchfield, R. S., Livson, N., Wilson, W. A., Jr. & Parducci, A. (1985). *Grundlagen der Psychologie* [Fundamentals of psychology]. (Ed., H. Benesch). Weinheim/Basel: Beltz-Verlag.

Availability of *Psychological Abstracts* and Citation Indexes

Institutes of psychology have their own libraries. Since the majority of professional journals of psychology are published in English, institute as well as central university libraries carry the *Psychological Abstracts*. Citation indexes are normally kept by central university libraries.

Searching the literature for specific titles is facilitated by two agencies: (1) the Center for Psychological Information and Documentation at the University of Trier, which, besides keeping titles and abstracts on tape available for immediate retrieval, regularly issues *Psychological Indices* and bibliographies; and (2) the Center for Medical Documentation and Information (DIMDI), located in Cologne, which supplies most psychological titles. They can be accessed immediately from university libraries.

Major Needs

The first twenty-five years after World War II saw a period of reconstruction followed by growth and expansion. The increase in both the number of institutes and staff members was largely due to the unprecedented increase in psychology enrollment from 2,055 in 1960 to 18,574 in 1980, over 900 percent, while the average student increase in West Germany was only 340 percent (Heckhausen, 1983). It should be added that the student explosion in psychology came about in spite of very selective admission standards introduced at the federal level by the early 1970s.

During these years of expansion, top priority was given training programs rather than research projects. More resources and time for research are hence the major needs of psychologists at university institutes. There are signs that additional support from the government will be forthcoming in future years to strengthen the research capacity of university institutes. The number of students, however, is expected to go down.

Relationships with Other Disciplines

The relationships of psychology with other disciplines are influenced by two separate factors. On the one hand, such relationships are determined by common professional and practical interests; on the other hand, they result from shared theoretical interests or are deliberately established for interdisciplinary research purposes. Common professional interests, for example, have sustained more or less permanent relationships with psychiatry, psychosomatic medicine, and education. Shared theoretical interests, in contrast, exist between psychology and sociology, criminology, linguistics, and neurophysiology. Some ties are also intermittently maintained with philosophy because of a mutual interest in the theory or philosophy of science.

In recent years, interdisciplinary research projects have led to new institutional opportunities for cooperation among specialists of various disciplines. This is most conspicuous in the field of cognitive science, where experts in artificial intelligence, linguistics, semantics, and computer science have established a network fostering serious interaction with cognitive psychologists.

MAJOR TRENDS AND INFLUENCES SINCE
WORLD WAR II

Publication Trends

Two publication trends that are probably not unique to the West German scene should be noted. One is the increase in specialized professional journals. At the beginning of the postwar era there were in West Germany four comprehensive journals publishing articles in all fields of psychology: *Archiv für die gesamte Psychologie* [Archives of General Psychology] and *Psychologische Forschung* [Psychological Research] plus two new journals: *Psychologische Beiträge* [Psychological Contributions] and *Psychologische Rundschau* [Psychological Review], the latter similar to the *American Psychologist*. Since the 1950s journals have been added in animal psychology, social psychology, developmental and educational psychology, differential psychology, and most other areas. This process of specialization is still going on although the trend is being inhibited both by a restricted market limited to the German-speaking scientific community that is divided by the Iron Curtain and by the fact that many junior scientists write their research reports and other scientific articles in English and submit them to English-language (mostly North American) professional journals. This, unfortunately, fosters one-way scientific communication (Graumann, 1976).

Funding

The most important funding agency is the Deutsche Forschungsgemeinschaft [German Research Association] (DFG), a national science foundation supported by the Federal Government and the *Länder*. The DFG provides funds for peer-reviewed research projects, the organization of and participation in scientific conferences, postdoctoral and sabbatical research, and visiting professors. The printing of scientific publications (monographs and journals) is also sometimes subsidized by the DFG.

The second most significant funding sources are the various federal and state ministries, followed by grants from industry. While funds granted by government agencies are restricted to the solution of public problems, and those from industrial corporations and agencies aim at technological advances, public grant-giving agencies like DFG do not influence the choice of topics or the objectives of research.

Second largest among agencies providing monies for pure research is the Stiftung Volkswagenwerk [Volkswagen Foundation]. Proposals are required to fit into one of the major programs mainly in social and political science and history and other fields in the humanities.

Among the most important funding needs of a discipline like psychology is money for travel and scholarships for international academic exchange. Both the

Deutscher Akademischer Austauschdienst [German Academic Exchange Office] (DAAD) and Alexander-von-Humboldt-Stiftung help out here.

An excellent reference concerning West German funding agencies for psychology is A. Albert (1985), *Forschungsförderungsinformation Psychologie* [Information on research support in psychology], edited by Deutsche Gesellschaft für Psychologie.

Social Developments which Influenced the Discipline

Contrary to the widely held opinion that the end of World War II gave rebirth to a formerly politically corrupt and then socially rejected psychology, the field's history until the mid–1950s was marked by continuity relative to the pre–1945 period in terms of both doctrines and personnel. Indeed, very few academic psychologists who had been politically active during the National Socialist Regime were removed from their positions by the Allies during the denazification campaign. The vast majority of those holding academic positions in psychology continued to teach the theories that had been successfully established in the 1920s and 1930s, such as Ganzheit, Gestalt, and depth psychology; characterological and typological research in educational and industrial psychology also continued.

This continuity may be explained by various factors, among which we shall mention only two. Due to the relatively modest size of the discipline until the postwar period and the fact that the generation which had reached the age of twenty in 1939 was not given the chance to receive academic training under normal conditions, there was a lack of young academicians who could give new direction to the field after 1945. This explains why the first important social change within psychology did not take place until the mid–1950s when the first postwar generation of psychologists was ready to implant new ideas, new methods, and new approaches into the discipline.

A second factor responsible for the continuity of psychology was the minimal economic and social value of the research output throughout the first half of the century, unlike that of the natural sciences and medicine. Both before and directly after 1945 psychology was never in the center of public attention. Neither the political or social role nor the general aims of psychological research, teaching, and practice were widely discussed in the immediate post–World War II period in the three Western occupied zones that were to become the Federal Republic of Germany (FRG) in 1949. The situation was different in East Germany (GDR), where political debates about the past and present role of psychology took place after 1947–1948.

Seen against this historical background, the impact upon the science of psychology in the Federal Republic of Germany of two major changes caused by social developments is apparent. The first change occurred in the late 1960s and early 1970s; its immediate antecedent was the student movement, and its outlook was largely political. The second change appeared in the late 1970s and has not yet come to an end; it is linked with an internationally observed phenomenon, the "psycho-boom" and is primarily a function of social and economic dynamics.

Without doubt, the mandated ideal of scientific research in the postwar period was that of almost complete political and ideological neutrality. The demarcation between science and politics was regarded as a matter of principle which was reinforced first by the reaction against the political involvement of scientists during the Nazi period, then by the traditional division of labor between scientists and politicians, and finally by the rejection of what was seen as an antimodel, that is, the allegedly total takeover of social science by ideology in the German Democratic Republic. There is no question that these sociopolitical conditions favored the rise of an ivory-tower mentality in psychology. As has been pointed out, the main aim of psychology had become the production of verifiable knowledge *as such*, independent of possible political and other social concerns (Graumann, 1972, pp. 126–127).

The student movement in the FRG had at least one direct effect upon psychology in the sense that it generated controversy about the role of psychological research and practice in modern society. The argument did not concern psychology's past but rather its present and future; thus it induced the scientific community of psychologists, mainly the younger generation, to reflect critically upon the status of their field, either in order to justify the status quo or to change it.

This debate, however, had little impact on psychological theory. Suffice it to mention one example which shows a link between the political program of the New Left and the content of theories associated with the school of critical psychology, initiated by Klaus Holzkamp at the Free University of Berlin. Since psychology had been attracting an increasing number of students who believed the field to be of crucial importance for the solution of societal problems, and since the student movement had accelerated the reform of the university system that was already under way in the mid–1960s, the discipline finally came to be recognized as a socially relevant science and profession.

The second major change in psychology is more ambiguous and has not yet been systematically analyzed, although the overall impact upon the profession is rather pronounced. What is often referred to as the "psycho-boom" is a complex phenomenon. On the one hand, there is a socially based demand for psychotherapy on a large scale. On the other hand, there is a growing market for psychological services parallel to those offered by the medical profession. Here, supply and demand interact closely: growing demand seems to generate more therapies which, in turn, seem to enhance demand for therapeutic services. Hence, up to 70 percent of the professional practitioners of psychology specialize in psychotherapy and counseling (Geuter, 1984). In comparison with the 1960s, when the great majority of psychologists worked mainly in educational areas (and to a lesser degree in industrial consulting and management settings), contemporary curricula have been adapted to the needs of clinical psychology, and many practitioners are now in private practice. While educational psychology has been publicly funded for the most part, clinical psychology is supported primarily by the clients of private practitioners.

In response to these developments, some institutes of psychology have been transformed into training schools and thus have less significance as research institutions.

Research and Theory

Major Orientations and Assumptions

In terms of major orientations and assumptions, the profile of psychology from 1945 to the present is difficult to portray. The discipline has never acquired (nor could it acquire) theoretical and/or methodological homogeneity. We shall, therefore, present only a rough sketch of major trends.

In the immediate postwar period, a holistic approach was predominant. Its guiding ideas concerning the nature of human mental life as a nonquantifiable entity determined to a vast extent the contents of psychological theories, and in lesser measure the methods to be used (description and understanding). Simultaneously, a few institutes offered programs in experimental psychology, in line with psychological orientations such as Gestalt psychology which characterized the discipline during the Weimar Republic (1919–1933). This initial period was followed, upon adoption of American operationalism, by an era distinguished by a clearly method-oriented view of basic research. Consequently, formal and/or structural principles concerning the status of observables, variables, hypothetical relationships, and so forth were considered to be the factors determining not only the strength of psychological theories but also the range of phenomena amenable to psychological analysis (O'Connell, 1970).

From about 1970 to around 1980 specific research interests and concepts originating in the United States predominated. Cognitive dissonance and attribution theory are good examples.

The most recent phase (from 1980 to the present) is more European in outlook, based on a diversification of theoretical interests and more choice of research topics (regardless of whether such topics are favorably received in the United States or not). Indicative of this diversification is the role played by the theory of minorities, the theory of social representation, Piaget's theory of cognitive development, and the study of the phylogeny of memory and speech as developed in the Soviet Union.

Controversies and Limitations

As might be expected from a field of research like psychology with a rather indeterminate domain of reference where different trends and approaches coexist simultaneously, there are always controversies arising over specific issues of varying theoretical relevance. Rather than focus on these controversies, we will deal with two debates concerning the discipline as a whole.

By 1950, the main psychological approach was still based on a holistic, qualitative, descriptive, personality-centered theory inherited from the recent past. Emphasized were idiographic methodologies which, by definition, require special talents that are difficult to teach. This may explain to a certain extent the elitist character of some schools of traditional German psychology prior to the postwar era. It should be emphasized that, due to the Nazi regime and the war, the normal influx of information from abroad had been interrupted. German psychology became provincialized by isolation. As compared with international standards, psychology in Germany was lagging behind (Graumann, 1984).

Then, in the postwar period, the flow of information into the country began again, at first with the aid of the educational branches of the occupation forces. Psychologists from the United States and Great Britain traveled and lectured frequently in West Germany; growing numbers of German students and junior researchers were able to visit universities in the United States, England, and France. Hence, the information available increased exponentially after 1946–1947 and permitted the community of psychologists to compare various approaches and methods.

The resulting clash between the traditional (holistic-interpretative) approach and the "new" (operationalist and quantitative) orientation came to be known as the "methods controversy" (*Methodenstreit*) that reached its peak in the early 1950s. In a way, the methodological issue was inextricably interwoven with a conflict between two basic conceptions of psychology competing for both social recognition and power in the universities. That is why those involved in the controversy often referred to mutually exclusive value systems stressing quantification, physicalism, and materialism, on the one hand, and qualitative research and humanism on the other hand. On such grounds, the methodological controversy could not be settled. And yet, there is no doubt that the representatives of the quantitative approach (then simply and erroneously equated with operationalism and behaviorism) prevailed and determined the development of the discipline for the next two decades.

The second debate is usually referred to as the "positivist dispute" (Adorno, et al., 1976). It originally arose in sociology during the late 1960s as a clash between two antagonistic conceptions of social science: a scientific conception, broadly speaking, inspired by the Vienna Circle as well as by the falsificationism doctrine of Karl Popper, and a critical-emancipatory conception outlined by the Frankfurt School (Adorno, Horkheimer, Habermas) and the New Left. The debate was manifested in psychology in connection with an attempt to reformulate the discipline's main aims and research strategies along the lines of the critical-emancipatory conception (Graumann, 1970). This attempt, in turn, caused a number of metatheoretical reactions against the intended reformulations of the New Left. Although the positivist dispute was potentially of concern to the entire field, since it challenged nearly all features of psychology *as science*, and although its protagonists were among the leading figures of the discipline, its overall impact has remained minimal.

*Individuals Worldwide with the Most Influence on Psychology
during the 1945–1982 Period*

Individuals who, in our opinion, had the greatest impact on psychology worldwide include Gordon W. Allport, Leon Festinger, Sigmund Freud, Kurt Lewin,
Jean Piaget, Carl Rogers, and B. F. Skinner.

PERSPECTIVES ON PSYCHOLOGY IN OTHER COUNTRIES

The first two decades after 1945 have been both lauded and criticized as the
time when West German psychology was Americanized. It is true that after
almost complete isolation between 1933 and the late 1940s German psychologists, mainly junior scientists, rightly felt that they had a lot of catching up to
do. When travel became possible again, personal communications and contacts
were made mostly with psychologists in the United States. To adopt problems,
theories, and methods from American psychology made more sense to the majority of German psychologists than returning to pre–1933 approaches. Consequently, a strong bond was established between West German and North American
psychologists.

Beginning in the late 1960s and early 1970s, a serious reassessment took
place. This close relationship came to be seen partly as an uncritical emulation
of American modes of thought and partly as an undue dependence on American
scientific culture. Although critics are still a minority, they have found and
associate with like-minded psychologists in other West European countries. A
resulting Europeanization of the discipline is most conspicuous in social psychology. European psychologists from Western and Eastern Europe have, in
fact, united in a single group, called the European Association of Experimental
Social Psychology.

FUTURE DIRECTIONS

It is always difficult, if not foolhardy, to predict future developments in a
lively and growing field. All one can do is point to present trends that look
strong and promising enough to persevere, at least for a while.

First, there is a growing concern for ecological validity and representativeness
in psychological research. This has already generated increasing interest in nonexperimental, mainly field, studies and ecological problems. Action and interaction *in situ* will be the main challenge, not reactive behavior in the laboratory.
One aspect of this concern for ecological representativeness requires special
mention. It is the need to account more thoroughly for the social context of
human experience and behavior.

Again, related to the revival of interest in context is a growing concern for
the historical factors associated with the concerns of both psychological research

and the inquiry process itself. Also context-related is the increasing disregard of disciplinary boundaries. Neither reflection nor research is as easily stopped by boundaries between psychology and neighboring disciplines as once was the case. Concepts and methods from other social or natural sciences are more readily assimilated and integrated, and "synthetic" fields of investigation are opened as the new domain of cognitive science exemplifies. This may be a challenge to any conception of a unified psychology.

PSYCHOLOGICAL INSTITUTES AND PSYCHOLOGISTS WITH A STRONG INTEREST IN THE HISTORY OF PSYCHOLOGY

Archiv für Geschichte der Psychologie, Psychologisches Institut, Hauptstr. 47–51, 6900 Heidelberg (Prof. Dr. Carl F. Graumann; Dr. Alexandre Métraux).

Institut für die Geschichte der Neueren Psychologie, Schustergasse 21, 8390 Passau (Prof. Dr. Werner Traxel; Dr. Horst Gundlach; Dr. Gisela Schuster-Tyroller).

Dr. Ulfried Geuter, Martin-Luther-Str. 78, 1000 Berlin 62.

Dr. Siegfried Jaeger, Psychologische Institut der Freien Universität Berlin im Fachbereich Philosophie und Sozialwissenschaften I, Uferstr. 14, 1000 Berlin 65.

Prof. Dr. Helmut E. Lück, Arbeitsbereich Psychologie, Fern Universität Hagen, Postfach 940, 5800 Hagen 1.

Prof. Dr. Eckart Scheerer, Universität Oldenburg, Fach Psychologie im Fachbereich 5, Birkenweg 3, 2900 Oldenburg.

Prof. Dr. Irmingard Staeuble, Psychologisches Institut der Freien Universität Berlin im Fachbereich Philosophie und Sozialwissenschaften I, Uferstr. 14, 1000 Berlin 65.

REFERENCES

Adorno, T. W., Albert, H., Dahrendorf, R., Habermas, J., Pilot, H., & Popper, K. R. (1976). *The positivist dispute in German sociology*. New York: Harper & Row.
Albert, A. (1985). *Forschungsförderungsinformation Psychologie* [Information on research support in psychology]. Edited by Deutscshe Gesellschaft für Psychologie.
Geuter, U. (1984). Berufsfelder des Psychologen [Occupations in psychology]. In H. E. Lück (Ed.), *Geschichte der Psychologie. Ein Handbuck in Schlüsselbegriffen* [History of psychology: A handbook of key concepts] (pp. 49–55). München: Urban & Schwarzenberg.
Graumann, C. F. (1970). Conflicting and convergent trends in psychological theory. *Journal of Phenomenological Psychology*, *1*, 51–61.
Graumann, C. F. (1972). The state of psychology: Part I. *International Journal of Psychology*, *7*, 123–134.
Graumann, C. F. (1976). Modification by migration: Vicissitudes of cross-national communication. *Social Research*, *43*, 367–385.
Graumann, C. F. (Ed.). (1984). *Psychologie im Nationalsozialismus* [Psychology under National Socialism]. Heidelberg: Springer-Verlag.

Heckhausen, H. (1983). Zur Lage der Psychologie 1982 [The state of psychology in 1982]. *Psychologische Rundschau, 34*, 1–20.

Irle, M., & Strack, F. (1983). *Psychologie in Deutschland. Ein Bericht zur Lage von Forschung und Lehre* [Psychology in Germany: A report of the state of research and findings]. Weinheim: Verlag Chemie/edition psychologie.

O'Connell, D. C. (1970). *The changing faces of European psychology: Germany*. Paper presented at the meeting of the American Psychological Association, Miami Beach.

German Democratic Republic

Hans-Dieter Schmidt

NATURE AND SCOPE OF THE DISCIPLINE

Definition of Psychology

Most psychologists in the German Democratic Republic (GDR) assume that psychology is a science dealing with the phenomena, conditions, causes, and laws of the internal reflection of objective reality (nature, social interactions, society, and person) and the underlying patterns of information processing which serve as a basis for the orientation and regulation of action. Of particular concern are the structure, dynamics, and control of activities which are adaptive and ensure the maintenance, improvement, and development of human life.

In their study of behavior, psychologists take into account biological, interpersonal or social, and societal or cultural factors and contexts. Psychology, in other words, is neither a natural nor a social science. It is a hybrid discipline centered in those areas of intersection generated by the overlap and integration of the biological and sociocultural aspects of behavior. Consequently, prerequisite to successful psychological research and scientific progress in psychology as a whole are multiple relationships between psychology and the natural sciences as well as between psychology and those sciences concerned with the interpersonal and societal aspects of the human species. The necessity for such an integrated approach becomes apparent when we recognize the existence of three phenomena intrinsic to the human condition, namely, consciousness with language as its main support; reflection relative to external and internal objects, states, and events; and personality. None of these can be adequately described or explained if purely biological or sociocultural investigations are attempted.

Underlying psychological research in the GDR is the following principle: Whatever we are examining in the context of a specific situation, the psychological phenomenon in question is generated by an actively exploring, controlling person within a system of interactions which includes influencing the environment and processing the effects of action with the goal of adapting environmental conditions to human needs. This process, which continues throughout a person's life, results in changes of individual aptitudes and competencies. Abilities reflect both predispositions, acquired phylogenetically and ontogenetically, and environmental factors and events, including the natural surround and culture.

With this perspective on psychological research, psychologists in the GDR recognize that stimulus-response or stimulus-organism-response conceptions, which split the organic coherence or unity of these factors, are inappropriate. The main design problem for experimental psychologists is to preserve the biosocial unit of human behavior when generalizing from data (ecological validity is paramount). It is also essential when conducting psychological research to concentrate on both the semantic aspects and the structural features of cognition and motivation in addition to recognizing the unity of cognition, emotion, and motivation in human behavior.

Organizations and Institutions

In accordance with the principle of democratic-centralized management, psychological organizations and institutions are hierarchically arranged as depicted in Figure 1.

The planning and programming of higher education and research takes place within governmental departments with the Department of Higher Education playing the primary role. The professional staffs of these administrative units take into account both societal demands and the opinions and ideas of scientific experts. In psychology these include the members of the Scientific Council for Psychology (Wissenschaftlicher Rat für Psychologie) and the Board of the Society of Psychology of the GDR (Gesellschaft für Psychologie der DDR, DDR–1080 Berlin, Am Kupfergraben 7). The latter was founded in 1962 and has been a member of the International Union of Psychological Science (IUPsyS) since 1966. With regard to scientific and professional activities, the Society of Psychology is more autonomous than the university departments of psychology. The society is made up of "sections" having to do with major fields of psychology, that is, general psychology, clinical psychology, and educational psychology, and "working groups" focused on more topical concerns such as forensic psychology, personality research, and group psychotherapy.

The following six departments of psychology or laboratories are primarily responsible for instruction and research in the GDR. The four university departments both instruct and do research, while the two departments associated with government academies are essentially research facilities:

Department of Psychology, Humboldt University Berlin, GDR–1020 Berlin, Oranienburger Strasse 18. Cognitive psychology, developmental psychology, clinical psychology, industrial/engineering psychology.

Department of Psychology, Karl Marx University Leipzig, GDR–7030 Leipzig, Tieckstrasse 2. Psychology of personality, psychodiagnostics, educational psychology, clinical psychology, history of psychology.

Figure 1
Relationships among Psychological Organizations

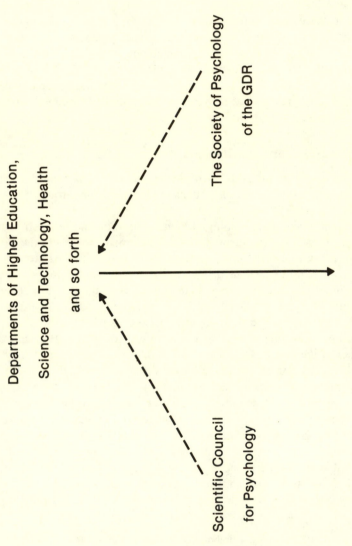

Departments of Higher Education,

Science and Technology, Health

and so forth

The Society of Psychology

of the GDR

Scientific Council

for Psychology

Departments of Psychology at

Universities and Academies

Department of Psychology, Friedrich Schiller University Jena, GDR–6900 Jena, Universitäts-Hochhaus. Social psychology (basic and applied research), history of psychology.

Department of Labor Sciences, Technical University Dresden, GDR–8027, Zellescher Weg 19. Cognitive psychology, psychology of action, industrial/engineering psychology.

Institute of Educational Psychology, Academy of Pedagogical Sciences of the GDR, GDR–1035 Berlin, Böcklinstrasse 1–3. Educational psychology, developmental psychology, developmental psychodiagnostics.

Department of Psychology, Central Institute of Cybernetics and Information Processes, Academy of Sciences of the GDR, GDR–1080 Berlin, Kurstrasse 33. General psychology, psychology of personality.

Considerable research also takes place in the following institutions:

Laboratory of Clinical Psychology, Wilhelm Pieck University Rostock (GDR–2500 Rostock, Gehlsheimer Strasse 20).

Department of Industrial Psychology, Central Institute of Occupational Medicine of the GDR (GDR–1134 Berlin, Nöldnerstrasse 40–42).

Central Institute of Youth Research Leipzig (GDR–7022 Leipzig, Stallbaumstrasse 9).

Institute of Psychology of Sports, Academy of Physical Culture and Sports Leipzig, (GDR–7010 Leipzig, Friedrich-Ludwig-Jahn-Allee 59).

Both basic and applied research is generally associated with interdisciplinary state research projects. Recently, for example, psychologists have been involved in a medical study of brain-damaged children and an industrial project concerning visual displays. Such work is supported financially by grants from various departments; the money appropriated in each case depends on its importance for society and on the quality of research already produced. All investigations, including pilot studies funded by universities, come under close scrutiny, thus assuring high-quality research.

Primary Functions of Psychologists

The functions of psychologists in the GDR relate to the tasks involved in developing a Socialist industrial society. Psychology, like other disciplines, is an autonomous scientific endeavor; however, psychological research is directed toward increasing productivity, facilitating physical and mental health, improving educational techniques, bettering management styles, and creating conditions for effective teamwork. Intrinsic to all this work is the general goal of promoting successful personality development. By successful personality development is meant self-realization through becoming an independent person with a strong sense of social responsibility.

Psychologists who earn diplomas are able to adapt their knowledge to the special demands and aims of their respective fields. They are capable of conducting applied research in a wide variety of settings, using appropriate procedures within a comprehensive theoretical framework based on dialectical materialism. Training, which is organized by the Society of Psychology, is a lifelong process. Continuing education helps psychologists in the GDR remain sensitive to new problems, be cognizant of new research methodologies, and develop the wherewithal to cooperate with nonpsychologists. Much of the work done in the GDR by psychologists in such specialized applied fields as clinical psychology, industrial psychology, and educational psychology differs little from that done by their counterparts in other industrialized nations.

In order to prevent the misuse of psychological knowledge, psychologists in the GDR are forbidden to engage in private practice. As is well known, there is considerable danger in capitalist countries that the profit motive can lead to unethical psychological practices. Misuse can also derive from the application of procedures based more on intuition than scientifically verified information. Furthermore, the negative view many people have of psychology makes it imperative that psychological applications occur under the scrutiny of peers.

Psychology Curricula

In the GDR, high-school students who pass their "leaving examinations" may enroll in five-year tuition-free courses of university study. All are eligible for grants. Students are required to take courses in the basic areas of kowledge and application (see Table 1). In contrast with other countries, though, undergraduates who want to become psychologists specialize in only one of the major applied fields of psychology. These are clinical psychology, industrial psychology, educational psychology, and social psychology. When demand justifies it, students may also earn a supplementary qualification in specialities such as forensic psychology or sports psychology.

Students who wish to train in clinical psychology may attend either Humboldt-University in Berlin or Karl Marx University in Leipzig. Those who want to become industrial/engineering psychologists go to Humboldt University or the Technical University in Dresden. Karl Marx University also offers a program in educational psychology while students seeking training in social psychology go to Friedrich Schiller University in Jena.

Approximately 180 psychologists graduate each year and there were in 1984 just over 3,800 psychologists in the GDR. The population of the country is about 17 million. The relatively small number of psychologists generally guarantees employment directly related to the competencies and personalities of each psychologist. About 5 percent of all graduates in psychology, only the best qualified and most gifted, are admitted to graduate programs which lead to a doctorate. This training is mandatory for those who plan to embark on scientific careers.

Most prominent psychologists in the GDR view the rapid growth in psychology in some Western countries as inflated and unproductive. Such expansion of the field has, it is felt, led to little genuine scientific progress, nor has it addressed real social needs. The high levels of anxiety and uncertainty experienced by the

Table 1
Curriculum at GDR Psychology Departments

Area	Special Orientation	Year/s Taken
Human Biology	functional anatomy, physical anthropology, behavior genetics, neurophysiology, psychophysiology	1st, 2nd Year
Philosophy, Social Sciences	fundamentals of Marxism-Leninism: theory of cognition, logic, political economy, scientific socialism; philosophical psychology, history of psychology	1st-4th Year
Foreign Languages	Russian, English (comprehension and production of psychological texts)	1st, 2nd Year
General Psychology	perception, cognitive processes (Information processing: memory and retention, concept formation, reasoning, problem solving), learning theories, emotional and motivational processes, mathematical psychology	1st-3rd Year
Developmental Psychology	human ethology, child psychology, psychology of adolescence, lifespan developmental psychology, aging processes	1st-3rd Year
Psychology of Personality, Social Psychology	differential psychology, structure and dynamics of personality, personality theories; social structures and processes, social cognition, group dynamics, experimental games, psychology of cooperation	2nd Year
Methodology and Methods	psychological methods, fundamentals of psychodiagnostics, psychological statistics, test theory	1st-4th Year
Clinical Psychology	general psychopathology, behavior deviations and neuroses, neuropsychiatry, psychotherapy and counseling, differential psychodiagnostics	3rd-5th Year
Industrial/Engineering Psychology	theory of action, psychological components of operator activity, psychological optimizing of means of production, decrease of loading, accident prevention, methods of operator training, vocational guidance, differential psychodiagnostics	3rd-5th Year
Applied Social Psychology	optimizing of social processes (cooperation, teamwork), behavior training of managers, psychological components of mass media effects, group diagnostics	3rd-5th Year
Educational Psychology	psychological components of educational and school learning processes, increase of productive/creative thinking, teacher-pupil interaction, psychodiagnostics of school achievement	3rd-5th Year

citizens of these countries will not be alleviated through more psychological services but rather through fundamental societal changes.

Major Journals, Textbooks, and Other Publications

There are two major psychological journals in the GDR: the *Zeitschrift für Psychologie* (one of the oldest psychological journals in the world, founded by Helmholtz, Ebbinghaus, and Stumpf in 1890, now edited by F. Klix, H.-D. Schmidt, and H. Sydow and published by Verlag Johann Ambrosius Barth, GDR–7010 Leipzig, Salomonstrasse 18) and *Probleme und Ergebnisse der Psychologie* (founded in 1960 and retitled, in 1983, *Psychologie für die Praxis*, edited by members of the Executive Committee of the Society of Psychology and published by VEB Deutscher Verlag der Wissenschaften, GDR–1080 Berlin, Postfach 1216). Psychologists, of course, also publish articles in many other journals.

The following textbooks serve to convey elementary psychological knowledge to undergraduate students and nonpsychologists in postgraduate training (for example, teachers, physicians, sociologists):

Claus, G., & Ebner, H. (1970). *Grundlagen der Statistik für Psychologen, Pädagogen und Soziologen* [Fundamentals of statistics for psychologists, educators and sociologists]. Berlin: Volk und Wissen Verlag.

Claus, G., et al. (Eds.). (1981). *Wörterbuch der Psychologie* [Dictionary of psychology] (3rd ed.). Leipzig: VEB Bibliogr. Inst.

Eckardt, G. (Ed.). (1979). *Zur Geschichte der Psychologie* [Toward a history of psychology]. Berlin: Dtsch. Verl. Wissensch.

Friedrich, W., & Mueller, H. (Eds.). (1980). *Zur Psychologie der 12- bis 22jährigen* [The psychology of the 12 to 22 year old]. Berlin: Dtsch. Verl. Wissensch.

Hacker, W. (1980). *Allgemeine Arbeits- und Ingenieurpsychologie* [General labor and engineering psychology] (3rd ed). Berlin: Dtsch. Verl. Wissensch.

Hacker, W. (Ed.). (1980). *Spezielle Arbeits- und Ingenieurpsychologie in Einzeldarstellungen* [Special labor and engineering psychology in isolated situations]. Band 1 und 2. Berlin: Dtsch. Verl. Wissensch.

Helm, J. (1978). *Gesprächspsychotherapie* [Talking psychotherapies]. Berlin: Dtsch. Verl. Wissensch.

Hiebsch, H., & Vorwerg, M. (Eds.). (1980). *Sozialpsychologie* [Social psychology]. Berlin: Dtsch. Verl. Wissensch.

Klix, F. (1971). *Information und Verhalten* [Information and behavior]. Berlin: Dtsch. Verl. Wissensch.

Klix, F., & Sydow, H. (Eds.). (1977). *Zur Psychologie des Gedächtnisses* [Toward a psychology of memory]. Berlin: Dtsch. Verl. Wissensch.

Kossakowski, A., et al. (Eds.). (1977). *Psychologische Grundlagen der Persönlichkeitsentwicklung im pädagogischen Prozess* [Psychological foundations of personality development in the context of the educational process]. Berlin: Volk u. Wissen Verlag.

Krause, B., & Metzler, P. (1983). *Angewandte Statistik* [Applied statistics]. Berlin: Dtsch. Verl. Wissensch.

Loewe, H., et al. (Eds.). (1983). *Psychologische Probleme des Erwachsenenalters* [Psychological problems of aging]. Berlin: Dtsch. Verl. Wissensch.

Schmidt, H.-D. (1970). *Allgemeine Entwicklungspsychologie* [General developmental psychology]. Berlin: Dtsch. Verl. Wissensch.

Schmidt, H.-D. (1982). *Grundriss der Persönlichkeitspsychologie* [An outline of personality psychology]. Berlin: Dtsch. Verl. Wissensch.

Sprung, L., & Sprung, H. (1984). *Grundlagen der psychologischen Methodologie und Methodik* [Fundamentals of psychological methods and methodological theory]. Berlin: Dtsch. Verl. Wissensch.

Sydow, H., & Paetzold, P. (1981). *Mathematische Psychologie* [Mathematical psychology]. Berlin: Dtsch. Verl. Wissensch.

Tembrock, G. (1980). *Grundriss der Verhaltenswissenschaften* [An outline of the behavioral sciences]. Jena: Gustav Fischer Verl.

Witzlack, G. (1977). *Grundlagen der Psychodiagnostik* [Fundamentals of psychodiagnostics]. Berlin: Dtsch. Verl. Wissensch.

Reviews providing information about the current needs, aims, problems, and contributions of psychology in the GDR can be found in the following sources:

Kossakowski, A. (Ed.). (1980). *Psychologie im Sozialismus* [Psychology under socialism]. Berlin: Dtsch. Verl. Wissensch.

Kossakowski, A. (Ed.). (1980). *Psychologie in der gesellschaftlichen Praxis* [Psychology practiced in social settings]. Berlin: Dtsch. Verl. Wissensch.

Schmidt, H.-D. (1980). Psychology in the German Democratic Republic. *Annual Review of Psychology, 31*, 195–209.

Edited by the Society of Psychology, annual bibliographical reviews of GDR publications have been available since 1978 (Address: GDR–1080 Berlin, Am Kupfergraben 7). The *German Journal of Psychology* (a quarterly of abstracts and review articles from Austria, FRG, GDR, and Switzerland, C. J. Hogrefe, Inc., Toronto/Canada) serves the same function.

Psychology and Other Disciplines

Psychologists in the GDR are very much interested in maintaining close relationships with professionals in other disciplines. As mentioned earlier, psychological research is, as a rule, embedded in interdisciplinary projects organized and funded by the state. Thus it is quite common for psychologists to work together with engineers, physicists, mathematicians, biologists, and physicians on problems requiring the expertise of all. Occasionally, although more rarely, psychologists also work cooperatively with educators, sociologists, and philosophers. It should be pointed out that some of the professionals in other disciplines have had graduate-level courses in psychology and, therefore, are familiar with psychological problems and methods. Interdisciplinary cooperation is also fostered in the GDR through conferences, symposia, and congresses. In addition, students, even during their undergraduate years, are made aware of the necessity of bringing many perspectives to bear on real-world problems.

There are, of course, impediments to interdisciplinary cooperation. Psychologists in certain fields tend to engender cooperation with the natural sciences while others are drawn more to the social sciences. These proclivities may not entirely reflect a natural closeness of respective subject matters. Cooperation also becomes difficult sometimes when the overlapping concerns of two or more disciplines go beyond a particular point, or when theoretical differences impede understanding. More can be done, in other words, to facilitate interdisciplinary efforts.

POST–WORLD WAR II PSYCHOLOGY

World War II left Germany in ruin materially, economically, morally, and in terms of manpower. There were few resources to rebuild the country and many of the best scientists had emigrated to escape Nazi oppression. German psychology lost Kurt Lewin, Heinz Werner, Wolfgang Köhler, William Stern, and many other promising psychologists. Nazi ideology had all but destroyed democratic traditions. Germany was divided into four zones of occupation, and in 1949, following the establishment of two independent German states, the Federal Republic of Germany and the German Democratic Republic, the task of building an anti-Fascist democratic society and transforming this society into a Socialist state commenced in the GDR.

Conditions were clearly not conducive for developing a new psychology. Funds that were available were mostly earmarked for disciplines such as physics, chemistry, engineering, and medicine, which were more directly involved in the reconstruction of the country, and for projects designed to improve public health services, upgrade education, and create full employment. In general, the disciplines most closely associated with the construction of a new industrial Socialist society were given the most financial support. The "Cold War" atmosphere also helped maintain the relatively low priority assigned to the funding of psychology during the immediate postwar period.

When it became apparent that psychological knowledge and techniques could facilitate societal progress, however, the fortunes of the discipline began to change. The support of the Socialist Unity party played an important role in bringing about the systematic advancement of psychology through government and party planning and financing.

In 1953, only about thirty psychologists graduated from universities in the GDR. Since 1970, between 150 and 200 graduate-level psychologists finished their training each year. During the same period the number of psychology professors increased from five to over sixty in 1983, and the membership of the Society of Psychology now stands at around 1,600.

The first national congress of the society was not held until 1964. Since then such gatherings have occurred every three or four years. In addition, since 1959 two to four symposia each year involving participants from other countries have been arranged by the society. A look at the programs of the national congresses indicates that psychologists in the GDR have been quick to recognize and contribute to significant new trends and to utilize new ideas for the betterment of society. The second national congress in 1968, for example, included important symposia on engineering psychology, psychometrics, programmed learning, criteria of success in psychotherapy, psychophysics, and cybernetics and cognitive psychology (see *Bericht über den 2. Kongress der Gesellschaft für Psychologie in der DDR* [Report on the Second Congress of the Society of Psychology in the DDR] edited by J. Siebenbrodt, Berlin: Deutscher Verlag der Wissenschaften, 1969).

Augmented by increasing exhanges of information, visiting lecturers, and fellowship programs for young scientists and undergraduates, the vitality of psychology is clearly apparent. The request by the International Union of Psychological Science to hold the 1972 International Congress in Leipzig reflected not merely an interest in honoring Wundt but was a recognition of the contributions contemporary psychologists in the GDR had been making.

Other indicators of progress are the growth of psychology departments in terms of staff and students; frequent salary increases for psychologists; the introduction of a state system of awards recognizing achievements in research, education, and management; the systematic extension of psychological services (clinical psychologists, for example, now work not only in neuropsychiatric facilities but also in pediatric, gerontological, and gynecological clinics as well as units concerned with internal medicine); and the increased representation of GDR psychologists on the boards of international psychological organizations.

In summary, the societal factors most responsible for the progress and growth of psychology in the GDR include the following:

1. A strengthening economy resulting from basic improvements in society during a period of peace and political stability.

2. A deeper understanding of the role that psychology can play in accelerating the building of a Socialist society. The discipline's primary function in this regard is to facilitate successful personality development and self-realization within a society which has learned to do without inhuman competition for the necessities and comforts of life.

3. Recognition that psychologists can contribute to the resolution of many important societal problems. These problems have to do with the incidence of psychogenic illnesses; motivation in the work place in the absence of competitive factors; the design of appropriate man-machine systems; the management of increasingly more extensive production facilities; adapting educational requirements to the abilities, needs, and motives of students; and ways to reduce the number of traffic accidents, suicides, divorces, and criminal acts arising from personal and social conflicts and crises.

Basic Research and Theory

The major approaches and assumptions of psychologists in the GDR can be understood only if one recognizes that psychological methodology and theory are directly or indirectly related to the axioms and principles of dialectical and historical materialism. A stimulating, progressive, and practical perspective on the human sciences, this philosophy provides a general frame of reference for psychological inquiry and application. Within this context, psychologists in the GDR stress the reflective function of cognitive processes which form the basis for the perception of the world; the regulatory function of decision making and motivation with regard to the adaptability of actions; the self-initiated components of behavior; the changeability of internal psychological states; personality as a biosocial unit; and the interdependence of personality, group dynamics, and the foundations of society. Basic research is being done on perceptual and cognitive processes, action theory, personality, human development, and the history of psychology.

Significant contributions in the area of perception and psychophysics include the work of H. G. Geissler and his coworkers, now at the Karl Marx University in Leipzig, on complex structures and classification procedures in vision, and the research of P. Petzold at the Friedrich Schiller University in Jena concerning decision rules involved in making judgments about both simple physical and more complex social stimuli. Perceptual studies are also intrinsic to certain applied research projects, particularly those conducted by engineering psychologists in Berlin and Dresden.

A major research focus in cognitive psychology is semantic information processing including the production and comprehension of language. Psychologists are working to identify the interconnections between the processes involved in the generation, use, and evalution of information, on the one hand, and memory, on the other. Promising work is also being done in investigating the relationships between physiological and cognitive processes. Prominent in this area are F. Klix, at Humboldt University, and J. Hoffmann, at the Academy of Sciences. Finally, important cognitive research concerning the problems of learning in school settings is being conducted by G. Clauss, at Karl Marx University, and J. Lompscher, at the Academy of Pedagogical Sciences.

The most prominent researcher in the area of psychological action theory is W. Hacker in Dresden. His theory combines elements of those processes involved in cognitive representation, decision making, and motivation in a cybernetic model which takes into account both internal and external activities. A. Kossakowski, at the Academy of Pedagogical Sciences, is engaged in similar research, but his primary interest at this time is the modeling of self-controlled human actions, particularly of children dealing with educational tasks.

Personality research and theory, too long a stepchild of basic research, is now an important aspect of psychological inquiry in the GDR. H. Hiebsch in Jena, M. Vorwerg at Karl Marx University, and H.-D. Schmidt at Humboldt University have been investigating the relationships between philosophical views of the human being and personality structure and function. In Leipzig, a research team led by H. Schroeder at Karl Marx University is examining the relevance of social competence and self-conceptualization for various theoretical explanations of the neuroses. Also at Karl Marx University, J. Guthke and his coworkers are searching for valid parameters of action sequences and the learning processes. Moreover, efforts are under way to integrate the psychology of personality with social psychology. There is considerable optimism that this development will lead to a new theory of personality which, *a priori*, takes into account the natural contexts of action. At this time H. Hiebsch's novel view of cooperation and role appears to be a particularly integrative conception.

Much of the developmental research conducted in the GDR centers on knowledge acquisition and utilization. H.-D. Schmidt and H. Sydow, for example, are concerned with various aspects of semantic information processing. W. Friedrich at the Central Institute of Youth Research, on the other hand, does longitudinal studies on the development of individual differences in cognitive functioning during adolescence. In addition to the work on knowledge acquisition and utilization, there is considerable interest in the compensation and decompensation effects brought about by the interaction of biological and psychosocial risk factors during human development. The studies of H.-D. Roesler and the Rostock team are noteworthy in this regard.

Much of the research on the history of psychology has been conducted by G. Eckardt in Jena, L. Sprung at Humboldt University, and W. Meischner at Karl Marx University. Important contributions have been made both with regard to the question of what constitutes appropriate frames of reference when conducting historical research and in terms of concrete studies concerning the work of Kant, Fechner, Wundt, Ebbinghaus, Preyer, and the Berlin Gestalt psychologists.

Applied Research

Applied research in the GDR is focused on major societal needs. A listing and brief discussion of some of the major contemporary work in the fields of clinical psychology, industrial/engineering psychology, educational psychology, and applied social psychology follow.

In clinical psychology, the classification of neurotic phenomena, individual and group therapy, the construction of psychodiagnostic techniques (for example, the studies done by W. Gutjahr at Humboldt University), and psychophysiological parameters of psychopathological phenomena have been primary concerns. Significant contributions include a psychologically determined clustering of neurotic types contrary to typologies generated by the usual neuropsychiatric approaches, statistical methods of measuring therapy-induced changes in personality structures, and the coherence of internal and external therapeutic variables (J. Helm, E. Kasielke, and their collaborators at Humboldt University).

Important projects in industrial/engineering psychology concern the development and implementation of working conditions simultaneously supportive of successful personality development and productivity, the design and testing of man-machine systems which allow for satisfying and efficient work in computerized and automated work settings, and physical and mental health in places of employment. Most of the significant contributions in the area of industrial/ engineering psychology have been made by research teams headed by W. Hacker in Dresden, K.-P. Timpe and R. Schindler at Humboldt University, and W. Bachmann, A. Seeber, and A. Meister at the Central Institute of Occupational Medicine (Berlin).

The leading center for research in educational psychology in the GDR is the Academy of Pedagogical Sciences in Berlin under the direction of A. Kossakowski, J. Lompscher, and G. Witzlack. Educational psychologists have worked to devise strategies that can be used to foster independence and a sense of responsibility in children learning to reason and solve problems. Major projects have also centered on group dynamics in the classroom, attitude formation favoring achievement motivation and moral development, and the development of tests facilitating the process of selecting children for various courses of study.

Research in applied social psychology, which takes place in Jena and Leipzig, deals with problems involved in training managers in all branches of industrial production, with group therapy and counseling, and through understanding the effects of mass media. Psychologists prominent in this area are H. Hiebsch and M. Vorwerg.

Major Influences on Psychology in the GDR

Developments in psychology in the GDR during the 1945–1983 period reflect not only the needs of society but also trends in psychology taking place in other countries. During the early period of reconstruction following World War II, the influence of S. Rubinstein, L. Vygotsky, A. Leontiev, B. Ananiev, P. Galperin, and other Soviet psychologists predominated. Even today, the Soviet influence, facilitated by increasing communication and cooperation, is strong, particularly within general psychology (for example, action theory), developmental psychology (for example, Leontiev's theory of "acquisition"), the psychology of personality, and educational psychology.

During the early period, the Pavlovian theory of higher nervous activity predominated. This orientation was misdirected because it favored a physiological definition of psychology and simple stimulus-response models. A more enlightened view emerged during the early 1960s as a consequence of such cybernetic conceptions as systems theory, control theory, information theory, and game theory. Since 1975, psychology in the GDR has been strongly influenced by semantic information theory. Statistical and structural approaches to information processing were supplemented by concepts of semantic networks and the psycholinguistic theory of semantics developed by American psychologists W. Kintsch, J. Bruner, H. Clark, and others. These new conceptions not only impacted on theory construction in cognitive, mathematical, and developmental areas of study but influenced engineering psychology as well.

Psychologists in the GDR have also been influenced by Piaget, life-span and ecological orientations, such as those proposed by U. Bronfenbrenner and P. Baltes, the critical psychology of K. Holzkamp, and C. Rogers's approach to psychotherapy. GDR psychologists are cognizant, too, of important new international developments in test theory, measures of change, and psychological statistics. The fact is that GDR psychologists have been and are receptive to ideas and findings from all sources provided that they are consonant with fundamental theoretical and methodological principles derived from dialectics, materialism, and Socialist humanism. Psychologists engage in neither parapsychology conceived of as having to do with supernatural events nor research which concerns psychological warfare.

The International Influence of GDR Psychology

While it is difficult to evaluate the influence of the work done by psychologists in the GDR on the psychologies of other countries, within German-speaking Europe the ideas and research of nearly all the leading representatives of GDR psychology are referenced and considered in relevant texts. The strength of scientific psychology in the GDR is also evidenced by the invitations extended to psychologists of our country by psychologists in other countries. The influence of GDR psychology is perhaps most apparent in the areas of cognitive psychology and action theory.

Though GDR psychology is well represented in the German literature, it is not well known by English-language psychologists. German authors in general, as well as those writing in Spanish and Russian, face the problem of underrepresentation in English-language publications. Philosophical and political factors also result in GDR psychology being favorably received by psychologists in other Socialist countries but often ignored by those in capitalist countries. It is unfortunate that such prejudices exist.

FUTURE DIRECTIONS

Scientific progress depends on open disagreement and discussion. This is certainly true with regard to psychology in the GDR. Developmental and educational psychologists frequently have different opinions as to the importance of internal and external determinants of human development and the significance of ethology. Cognitive psychologists are often accused of ignoring emotional or motivational factors. Action theorists debate the importance of a more formal approach (that is, systems theory) or an approach which places more emphasis on motivational factors. Clinical psychologists differ as to the relative appropriateness of individual and group therapy, particularly where neurosis is concerned, and there is strong disagreement among clinicians as to the efficacy of behavior therapy.

While one should always take a conservative approach when making predictions, the future of psychology in the GDR is likely to include many of the following developments. This forecast is based on what has already taken place in the discipline in this country and anticipation of certain new societal problems and trends.

In general psychology, there will probably be continuing concern with the interconnectedness of cognitive, emotional, and motivational processes; the modeling of perceptual and memory processes; computer simulations of cognitive processes which will help solve some problems in engineering psychology; and the reinterpretation of intelligence in the context of new principles of test-item design based on developments in cognitive psychology. Progress in cognitive psychology will, in particular, have wide-ranging implications.

In developmental psychology, there should be more support for research on such relatively neglected topics as the development of personality characteristics, infant psychology, the study of the aging processes, and the biology of behavior. In addition, developmental psychologists will likely investigate the rules governing the stages involved in cognitive and psycholinguistic development; motivation and moral development in general and in the context of educational demands; the formation of individual differences particularly during adolescence; the empirical foundations of socialization theory as it applies to both normal and abnormal development; and the compensation and decompensation of developmental risks. Finally, there should be continued interest in the construction of developmental tests useful for differential diagnoses and the implementation of longitudinal studies of individual aging styles (a differential gerontology will emerge).

The psychology of personality will become more integrated with differential psychology. Critical analyses and reinterpretations of theoretical trends abroad will intensify. More ideas and approaches usually associated with general psychology and social psychology will be imported into personality research and theory. As examples, the concept of social competence and action theory will increasingly be seen as having relevance for personality theory. More personality tests will be constructed, and through the use of statistics, more objective and valid typologies will be developed.

The social psychologists of the future will do more research on the effects of mass media; study and build models of social cognition, including self-conceptualization; examine the usefulness of various games as tools for investigating group dynamics; and devote more time to understanding the social development of children. There will also be systematic investigations of the relationships between fundamental assumptions of modern Marxist philosophy and sociology and social psychological theory.

Clinical psychologists will be concerned with the application of psychological principles and procedures in all areas of public health so that health services can be improved (medical psychology will expand). Furthermore, there will be increased research on psychopathological problems, the effectiveness of psychotherapies, relevant psychotherapeutic variables, and the problems of children. Research on the classification of neurotic phenomena should continue with the end in mind of linking therapy more closely with diagnosis. Efforts will also continue to construct instruments with enhanced differential validity.

In industrial/engineering psychology, more research will be done to identify and apply psychological criteria in the design of man-machine systems. This work takes into account the visual displays available to an operator, the interchanges required between operator and computers, and the general implications of highly automated work settings. Psychologists in this area will also be concerned with the reeducation of workers and ways to increase worker productivity, minimize the noxious effects of certain kinds of work, reduce the physical and mental demands of particular jobs, and decrease traffic accidents. Of continued importance, too, will be research designed to discover strategies to enrich work mentally in order to increase self-realization and motivation. Finally, the development of more valid aptitude tests will remain an important concern.

Educational psychologists will continue to do research to improve students' sense of independence and responsibility, which is obviously related to techniques for teaching problem solving. Also given priority will be studies having to do with the enhancement of cooperative tendencies, the motivation to achieve, and a moral sense. Relative to the educational enterprise or system, much work will be done to clarify the standards and developmental criteria that should be invoked when developing or modifying a curriculum. Research on the improvement of developmental tests will be encourged. The design and construction of diagnostic instruments is coordinated and supplemented by the recently founded Diagnostic Center under the direction of U. Schaarschmidt at Humboldt University. This facility is responsible for satisfying the ever-growing need for psychological tests in all applied fields of psychology.

SUGGESTED READINGS

Clauss, G., Guthke, J., & Lehwald, G. (Eds.). (1978). *Psychologie und Psychodiagnostik lernaktiven Verhaltens* [Psychology and psychodiagnostic learning behaviors]. Tagungsbericht. Berlin: Gesellsch. f. Psychologie d. DDR (Manuskriptdruck).

Dettenborn, H., Fröhlich, H. H., & Szewczyk, H. (1984). *Forensische Psychologie* [Forensic psychology]. Berlin: Dtsch. Verl. Wissensch.

Hoffmann, J. (1982). *Das aktive Gedächtnis* [Active memory]. Berlin: Dtsch. Verl. Wissensch.

Klix, F. (Ed.). (1984). *Gedächtnis, Wissen, Wissensnutzung* [Memory, knowing, and the benefits of knowing]. Berlin: Dtsch. Verl. Wissensch.

Psychologische Forschung und gesellschaftliche Praxis [Psychological research and social customs]. (1984). Sonderheft der Wiss. Zeitschr. der Humboldt Universität Berlin, Math.-Naturwiss. Reihe XXXIII, 6.

Schröder, H. (Ed.). (1982). *Psychologie der Persönlichkeit und Persönlichkeitsentwicklung* [Psychology of personality and personality development]. Tagungsbericht. Berlin, Leipzig: Gesellsch. f. Psychol. d. DDR, Karl Marx Universität Leipzig (Manuskriptdruck).

India

Durganand Sinha

HISTORICAL BACKGROUND

Psychology in India has ancient roots in a vast storehouse of religious and philosophical texts as well as in folklore. Many of the ancient systems of philosophy contain sophisticated analyses of perception, emotions, dreaming and wakefulness, and human behavior and personality. These analyses, however, are largely speculative and intuitive; they do not meet the modern scientific demands for objectivity of observation, repeatability, and verifiability. Nevertheless, there existed in the country a congenial intellectual climate so that modern psychology, when introduced from the West, grew rapidly.

Scientific psychology in India is a comparatively recent phenomenon whose birth can be traced to N. N. Sengupta's establishment of the first psychological laboratory in the country at Calcutta University in 1915. Having been trained at Harvard University under Professor Hugo Münsterberg, Dr. Sengupta brought with him the Wundtian and Titchenerian traditions, and Calcutta University became an active center for teaching and research. Early students of psychology there fully accepted the Wundtian approach. Many of them also received graduate training in London under C. B. Spearman and C. Burt, in Cambridge under F. C. Bartlett, or in Edinburgh under James Drever and G. H. Thomson. Others went on to study in Leipzig or in Chicago, Cornell, and other centers in the United States. These scholars pursued the lines of inquiry of their mentors; despite occasional brilliance and originality, their research projects were largely imitations and replications. As has been observed (Ramalingaswami, 1980, p. 48), the field of psychology began in India simply as a copy of the discipline that existed in Western countries during the early years of the twentieth century. This was true not only of experimental studies but also of the psychological tests that were developed.

In the initial phase, psychology, except at Calcutta University, was not taught as an independent discipline but was included as a subsidiary subject in undergraduate and graduate programs of philosophy and education (teacher-training courses). In the former, the coverage was theoretically oriented, consisting of one or more courses in general psychology, the history of psychology, psychopathology with emphasis on psychoanalysis, and sometimes social psychology. In the teacher-training programs, the orientation was more applied; the courses pertained to educational and developmental psychology and mental testing and measurement. It was only after independence that full-fledged master's programs in psychology at different universities and graduate colleges were introduced.

DEVELOPMENT SINCE INDEPENDENCE

Attainment of political independence from British rule in August 1947 closely followed the end of World War II. The period thereafter has been marked by rapid expansion in the teaching of psychology and a great upsurge of research. The expansion of teaching can be gauged from the increase in universities offering independent undergraduate and graduate courses in psychology. From only three at the time of independence (1947), they rose to nineteen in 1960, thirty-three in 1970, and fifty-two in 1982. In other words, during the course of three-and-a-half decades, the number of institutions offering independent courses in psychology multiplied almost twenty times.

Enrollment in programs leading to the M.A./M.Sc. and doctoral degrees has shown an extraordinary increase over the years. Precise data for the pre-independence period are not available. But it can be estimated that before 1947 there could not have been more than twenty or thirty holders of the master's degree in psychology throughout the country; there were probably a few hundred in the 1950s. Since the 1960s, however, the figures for enrollment in the subject have swelled from 1,122 in 1961–1962 to 4,194 for the year 1980–1981. Moreover, in 1961–1962, 543 master's degrees in psychology had been awarded, and the number reached 1,475 by 1978.

In the early days, Calcutta and Mysore universities were the only centers of research in India. Scholars received their advanced training in psychology abroad, mostly in British universities. Since independence the situation has changed. The number of students being trained in psychological research has risen steadily since 1961, from sixty-seven per year to 515 in 1981. Correspondingly, doctorates earned in psychology have shown an eightfold increase over the two decades, from twelve in 1961 to ninety-six in 1980–1981.

Though it is difficult to ascertain the total number of teachers of psychology in the country, various estimates indicate significant expansion. On the basis of information supplied by the Minisitry of Education, there were 213 faculty members teaching psychology in 1964–1965. According to the estimate of the University Grants Commission (UGC), the figure for teaching staff in psychology for the year 1980–1981 was 2,030, constituting 1 percent of all teachers at colleges and universities. If psychology teachers at professional institutions and intermediate (junior) colleges were included, the number would be much higher.

It is likewise difficult to determine with any degree of accuracy how many psychologists there are in India. The national association (Indian Psychological Association) has only a small and unsteady membership, due to frequent internal strife, and is no index of the overall number of psychologists in the country. A directory published in 1968 (Narain, 1968) had only 734 entries. This number was obviously too low because many psychologists known to the author were not listed. In a paper in the *International Journal of Psychology* (Rosenzweig, 1982), the total number of psychologists in 1975 was estimated to be 2,500.

The above figures constitute gross underestimates because they mainly include only those psychologists working in universities, degree-granting colleges, and research institutions. If those at junior colleges and in industries, hospitals, and other organizations were added and everyone with a graduate degree in the subject taken into consideration, the total number of psychologists in the country would most likely be over 4,000.

Recently, there has been a growing tendency for psychologists to work in diverse organizations beyond the confines of academia. The Defense Science Organization of the Ministry of Defense is by far the largest employer of trained psychologists outside the academic world. This organization is concerned not only with testing and selecting defense personnel but also with conducting research into psychological problems that relate to the military services, ranging from the design of equipment to projects concerned with stress, leadership, discipline, and rehabilitation. The report on the *Status of Psychology in Indian Universities* (UGC, 1982) summarizes the situation:

The largest number of trained psychologists find employment in teaching and research institutions. Service organizations, such as universities and private and government counseling and guidance centres recruit scholars for their specific needs. State governments and departments of education engage school psychologists in different sections for service and research. The Indian railways have psycho-technical cells. Some public and many private industries employ a certain number of psychologists to assist in human engineering, market research and human relations work. Some psychologists are called upon to collaborate with anthropologists and sociologists in studying problems of development, national integration, social change and tribals [tribes]. Psychological anthropology and rural psychology are gradually acquiring importance as problems of rural uplift, community development and tribal welfare are attracting increasing attention. (pp. 11–12)

The above statement gives an idea of the diverse areas that psychologists in India are entering. Although some are conventional, other fields like rural development and social change constitute new challenges.

APPLIED PSYCHOLOGY AND DEVELOPMENTS OUTSIDE ACADEMIA

The discipline as it developed in India from the beginning had an applied bent. Emphasis on practical applications is reflected by the establishment, in 1938 at Calcutta University on the advice of Charles S. Myers, C. Spearman, and Carl Jung, of the Section of Applied Psychology (now a full-fledged university department) designed to carry out studies primarily on mental tests and psychological problems related to industry, vocational guidance, education, and community service. The master's course in applied psychology (begun in 1952) offers specialization in industrial psychology, criminology, public opinion, and propaganda. In 1945 Patna University established the Institute of Psychological Research and Service which, apart from applied research, is engaged in counseling, individual therapeutic work, and child guidance. For a number of years, the institute also offered a master's program in applied psychology. Maharaja Sayajiraa (M. S.) University in Baroda has an active graduate center concentrating on applications of psychology to educational problems. The University of Bombay has a graduate department purporting to concentrate on applied psychology.

Beyond the university system, the earliest sign that psychology was having an impact on Indian society was the opening of a psychological clinic at the Carmichael Medical College and Hospital in Calcutta in 1928. This was followed by the establishment of a child and youth guidance clinic in Lahore (now in Pakistan) and then a home for feeble-minded children called Bodhana in 1933 in Bengal. In order to utilize psychological tests for personnel selection, the Defense Department established the Directorate of Selection and Personnel in 1942. It became the Psychological Research Wing of the Defense Science Organization in 1949 which, as indicated, is now the largest employer of psychologists in the country.

Sections/divisions of psychology concerned with both teaching and research are found at the All-India Institute of Hygiene and Public Health in Calcutta, the Indian Institute of Science in Bangalore, and the Agricultural Research Institute in New Delhi. Quite early, the discipline had discovered new areas of application in the training of health workers and administrators, managers, and agricultural extension workers. As teaching and research diversified, psychology took its place in major organizations such as the National Institute of Community (now Rural) Development in Hyderabad, the National Institute of Family Planning in New Delhi, the National Institute of Health Administration and Education in New Delhi, the National Institute of Mental Health and Neuro-sciences in Bangalore, the National Labor Institute in New Delhi, the Indian Institute of Mass Communication in New Delhi, the Sri Ram Centre of Industrial Relations in New Delhi, the Tata Institute of Social Sciences in Bombay, and the Institute of Criminology and Forensic Sciences in New Delhi.

In 1961, a development that significantly contributed to application of the discipline in various areas of education was the establishment of the National Council of Educational Research and Training (NCERT) in Delhi. NCERT not only employs a large number of psychologists but has extensive training and research programs and projects which apply to the field of education.

The area of vocational and educational guidance came into prominence when, on the recommendation of the Mudaliar Commission's report on secondary education in 1953, the decision was made to inaugurate multipurpose schools and channel students into humanities, science, and vocational streams following their eighth year of instruction. Providing vocational guidance and counseling services in schools became a necessity. The Uttar Pradesh (U.P.) Bureau of Psychology in Allahabad, established in 1947–1948, had already been engaged in developing intelligence and aptitude tests suitable for schools, offering vocational guidance and counseling and training career masters. It became the model for the bureaus of psychology that were established in most of the Indian states.

Demand for diagnostic and evaluative work in hospitals and recognition of the importance of psychological testing procedures in general as well as in psychiatric wards have stimulated the need for clinical psychologists. Advanced graduate training courses in clinical psychology leading to the Diploma in Medical and Social Psychology and a doctoral degree were started in 1955 at the All-India Institute of Mental Health (now designated as the National Institute of Mental Health and Neuro-sciences) in Bangalore, followed by the Hospital for Mental Diseases (now named the Central Institute of Psychiatry) in Ranchi in 1962; the B. M. Institute of Mental Health in Ahmedabad in 1973; and the Postgraduate Institute of Medical Education and Research in Chandigarh. It is estimated that there are at least 450 clinical psychologists in the country. According to a survey conducted by the Indian Council of Social Science Research (ICSSR), clinical psychologists constitute about 10 percent of psychologists working in India. Published research by clinical psychologists was found to be nearly a fifth of the total output of all psychologists in the country (Krishnan, 1972).

Psychologists work in a wide range of settings performing a variety of functions. They are involved in training, selection and placement, industrial production, marketing, advertising, labor, and employment. Distribution statistics and details of the exact work they do are not available. Yet it seems that there are more psychologists now working in specialized agencies, organizations, and institutions outside universities than there are those holding purely academic positions.

Thus, over the years, the areas of application have expanded and diversified. Mitra (1973) has observed that "the discipline is called upon to contribute its share to the solution of many problems in the all important spheres of national activity" (p. 5).

There is, however, a feeling of general dissatisfaction with the professional development of psychology in India. The UGC panel which reviewed the status of psychology up to 1976 (UGC, 1979), while emphasizing the unique position of the discipline among the social sciences in that it is both an academic field and a profession, felt that "as far as the professional side is concerned, the university courses have proved inadequate" (p. 24). The panel stated that the knowledge and training imparted were not of any particular relevance; therefore, "in India not only has psychology failed to develop as a profession, but very few psychology graduates are employed in professions where the knowledge and psychological skills acquired can be put to practical use. So the subject by and large continues to be an academic discipline'' (p. 24). A number of professional areas were emphasized, and the restructuring of courses in the universities was suggested. It was recommended that ''the content of psychology courses should be suitably modified to make it relevant to professional problems'' and that ''training in psychology should not be confined only to the classroom but should be linked to practical life situations'' (p. 25). Need for linking the teaching of psychology to work experience has also been stressed (p. 53). Today there is a strong desire among psychologists not only to develop the discipline so that is has greater application but also to make it more relevant to the many pressing problems of the country emerging in the wake of general socioeconomic development and social change.

PROFESSIONAL ASSOCIATIONS AND PUBLICATIONS

The influence that a discipline exerts on society can be judged from the state of its professional associations and the nature of its publications. Relative to both of these indexes, psychology in India is deficient. Professional bodies that often act as pressure groups constitute the usual channels of influence. If a professional association is weak or torn by internal conflicts, it ceases to have much impact on society. The history of the Indian Psychological Association (IPA) well illustrates this point.

In spite of the fact that the organization dates back to 1925, the IPA has not developed into a valid all-India body. Throughout the organization's long history, it has become both dissension-ridden and dormant from time to time. According to the electoral rolls for the 1984 and 1985 elections, only 226 and 437 members, respectively, were eligible to vote. Most of these individuals (over 190) are life members. The membership of the national association is no more than that of some state associations and the body as such is not truly ''national'' or ''representative'' in any sense. Notwithstanding its age, the group's official organ, the *Indian Journal of Psychology*, established in 1926, has appeared only irregularly. The articles it contains do not always meet high academic standards. The journal has not offered the best of Indian scholarship in psychology; many scholars prefer to have their most outstanding papers published in a foreign journal because of the accompanying prestige.

There are many special-interest groups. The traditional Indian concern with depth psychology and mental hygiene is congenial with psychoanalysis. Under the leadership of Professor G. Bose, who was analyzed through correspondence by Sigmund Freud himself, the Indian Psychoanalytic Association was formed in 1922 and its official journal *Samiksa* started in 1947. The association is affiliated with the International Psychoanalytic Society. It trains psychoanalysts and popularizes psychoanalysis. In its early phases, Freud, Jung, Jones, and many other analysts of international repute were associated with the organization's activities.

Impelled by the need for guidance in schools which the Mudaliar Commission on Secondary Education (1953) emphasized, the All-India Vocational and Educational Guidance Association was established in 1954. It founded its own journal and for many years organized national conventions attended by guidance and counseling psychologists, schoolmasters, and teachers. However, with the importance of the area declining by the late 1960s, the association has lost its original vigor, and the journal is no longer published on a regular basis.

A group of scholars in the south started the Indian Academy of Applied Psychology to foster interest in applied areas. The society is active and has held twenty-one annual all-Indian conventions. Though its membership is not very large, it has become a national body. It publishes the *Journal of the Indian Academy of Applied Psychology*.

The Indian Association of Clinical Psychologists was established in 1968. It is fairly representative of the clinical psychologists in the country and has so far held fifteen well-attended annual conventions. Its scope is rapidly expanding. The *Indian Journal of Clinical Psychology* first appeared in 1974 and is published regularly.

Apart from these national organizations, there are a number of regional and state associations which hold regular meetings and publish their own journals. The Madras Psychological Society, started by Professor G. D. Boaz in 1957, has been the most active regional association. Many members from outside the southern region belong, and it holds conventions regularly. Originally, it published three journals. As a result of escalating costs, however, it now publishes only two, the *Journal of Psychological Research* and the *Indian Journal of Applied Psychology*. Unlike other Indian journals of psychology, these have appeared fairly regularly during the last twenty-eight years.

Among the state associations, the Bombay Psychological Society seems to be the most active; it publishes the *Bombay Psychologist*. The state associations of Bihar and U.P. also have many members. Both of them have their own journals, though these do not appear very regularly. Their conventions, however, attract large attendance.

In addition to the national, regional, and state associations, there are many smaller bodies catering to local needs, often associated with particular departments or groups in universities and cities. In fact, some of the university departments of psychology publish their own journals. Among the more important of these are *Personality Study and Group Behaviour* (Guru Nanak Deo University, Amritsar) and the *Indian Psychologist* (Advanced Centre in Psychology, Utkal University). The most notable is *Psychology Studies*, founded in 1955 by Professor B. Krishnan of Mysore University. It is not only regular but maintains fairly high academic standards.

The *Journal of Indian Psychology* was started by the Department of Psychology and Parapsychology, Andhra University, under the leadership of Professor K. Ramakrishna Rao in 1978. This journal emphasizes classical ideas and current studies on the nature of man and psychological thought characteristic of the country; it also includes papers on paranormal and psychic phenomena, yogic practices, and non-Western perspectives in psychology. Andhra is the only center in the country engaged in large-scale scientific and systematic studies of paranormal and parapsychological phenomena.

Sponsored by the ICSSR, the *Indian Psychological Abstracts* is being published regularly. Containing lengthy summaries of studies in psychology and cognate areas conducted in the country, it has filled a serious communication gap among Indian scholars by making the detailed abstracts of published materials readily available to them.

In short, psychological journals which appear only sporadically are proliferating in India. Published papers are often substandard and not taken seriously by scholars. It was estimated in 1972 that about 200 papers were produced each year in India's twenty-six journals of psychology (ICSSR, 1973, p. 4). Nandy (1974) has observed that "these papers are rarely read by anyone except the authors . . . and their purpose is more ritualistic than scholarly. At the most their titles are invoked when someone applies for a job" (p. 5).

As for textbooks, in spite of almost four decades of independence and the policy of adopting Hindi or a regional language as the medium of instruction at least up to the undergraduate level, there is still a nearly total dependence on books published in the West, especially in the United States. The UGC report on *Reorientation of teaching and research in psychology in the Indian universities* (1979) laments the "almost complete dependence on foreign-produced textbooks and materials" (p. 9), which has adversely affected the standard of teaching. The situation is summarized as follows:

While most of the books used in Indian universities by the teachers of psychology are in themselves of a very high standard and of excellent calibre, they prove inadequate because of their foreign orientation and because they provide examples from a setting with which an average student is by and large unfamiliar. . . . On the other hand, there is hardly any textbook by Indian authors of the requisite standard with examples taken from the Indian context. Of late some good quality books dealing with studies conducted in India have been produced by Indian authors based on their own researches. But they are very seldom used or referred to in the normal classroom teaching in Indian universities. (p. 9)

Even when, out of necessity, Hindi or a regional language is adopted as the medium of instruction, the books in these languages are not original and are of indifferent quality, being mostly unsystematic compilations and poor translations of Western textbooks. The source materials used by advanced students and research scholars are almost entirely Western, as few original studies and books in the discipline are published by Indian scholars. One is, therefore, not surprised that the market is flooded with inexpensive Indian editions of foreign books. While it is laudable that, due to low prices, these books are easily available to Indian scholars and students, the situation has led to complete dependence in teaching and research on such sources; the overall effect has not proved beneficial.

It has acted against the fostering of originality among Indian scholars and kept psychology from addressing the problems of the country.

In the last decade or so, there has developed an awareness of the harm this Western orientation is causing, and efforts have been made by some scholars to produce "original" textbooks in Hindi and other regional languages. They have also started to publish original studies which can be referred to in teaching. The Indian Council of Social Science Research has brought out its first and second reviews surveying the investigations conducted since the beginning of scientific psychology in the country (Mitra, 1972; Pareek, 1980, 1981). Work on the third survey (1977–1982) is in progress. These surveys not only summarize the work done in different branches but also reflect the status of the discipline and the trends of research in the country. It is only gradually that these Indian materials are trickling into our classrooms. Until such time as teaching and research become "indigenized," the development of the subject will remain stunted with little relationship to the country's special needs.

Being conscious of this deficiency, the UGC organized four regional seminars involving psychologists from the entire country. Their deliberations formed the basis of a report directed toward the reorientation of teaching and research (UGC, 1979). A number of priority areas for research were enumerated. They comprised many phenomena and issues that are relevant to contemporary India: social change, rapid socioeconomic development, rural development, motivational and attitudinal dimensions of development, psychological problems of disadvantaged groups, minorities and youth, aggression and violence, intergroup relations, organizational behavior in Indian settings, institution building, socialization, psychodiagnostic tools to suit local conditions, unemployment, and poverty. The list given in the UGC report (pp. 37–39) is exhaustive.

The report also pinpointed a number of topics which should be included in the psychological curriculum. Some of these are psychology of social change and national development, social psychology of education, psychology of rural social problems, social skills and intervention techniques, youth and identity, population psychology, social research methodology in the Indian context, socialization in the Indian context, yogic psychology, parapsychology, and the psychology of religious experiences (pp. 51–52). A perusal of this list indicates definite effort on the part of Indian psychologists to emphasize Indian content and give a new orientation to the discipline, thereby making it more relevant to the needs of the country.

The situation concerning financial support for research during the years immediately following independence was quite bleak not only for psychology but for most social science disciplines. With the establishment of the ICSSR in 1969 and the government's policy of encouraging the social sciences, the outlook has improved considerably. In addition to funds available from the ICSSR, the UGC is encouraging and funding individual research projects. By establishing centers to provide special assistance and advanced facilities in different universities, the ICSSR is promoting research in a more organized way. So far it has recognized and is supporting two quality programs: one at Utkal University for advanced research in educational and social psychology, the other at Allahabad University for the psychological study of social change and development.

In addition to these sources, funds for research may be obtained from the Indian Council of Medical Research, the Council of Scientific and Industrial Research, different ministries of the government of India, and sometimes even the state governments. Some industries and private organizations are also beginning to sponsor and support projects, usually in special areas of interest to them.

MAJOR TRENDS SINCE INDEPENDENCE

The first ICSSR survey of research (Mitra, 1972), which covers the period from 1915 to 1969 and is based on over 3,300 references, points to the vigorous upsurge in psychological research, especially since independence. Almost 90 percent of the publications reviewed date from 1950; 62 percent appeared during the 1960s. On the average some 150 papers per year were published in the 1950s. The annual rate is now well over 250.

Various reviews of research have demonstrated the main trends. A review for the period from 1950 to 1960 (Krishnan, 1961) indicated that, in contrast with the pre-independence era when experimental studies were most prominent, the areas of educational, industrial, social, and personality psychology seemed to attract the greatest interest. A content analysis of articles appearing in the *Indian Journal of Psychology* during the years from 1964 to 1966 revealed that as many as 87 percent dealt with these areas.

In comparison, of the papers presented to the Section of Psychology and the Educational Sciences of the Indian Science Congress between 1925 and 1963, 27 percent were devoted to experimental studies; the rest were divided as follows: 14 percent, educational; 12 percent, general and theoretical; 11 percent, abnormal and clinical; 10 percent, psychometric; 9 percent, vocational and industrial; 6 percent, social; and 5 percent, personality. The remaining papers were on Indian psychology, criminal psychology, religion, and aesthetic psychology (Joshi, 1965). Analysis of publications in forty-three Indian and foreign journals (Ganguli, 1971) revealed that four areas, namely, social (16 percent), experimental (14 percent), mental testing (13 percent), and general (11 percent), accounted for more than half of the contributions of the period from 1920 to 1957.

Analysis of the publications for every five-year period since 1950 classified into ten different areas by the ICSSR survey (Mitra, 1972) showed that studies in clinical, social, and personality accounted for half of the total number of publications (Table 1). All the different trend analyses generally indicate that applications of psychology to social, industrial, organizational, and educational problems have interested Indian psychologists more than purely theoretical research.

Classifying 734 psychologists listed in a *Directory* (Narain, 1968), Ganguli

Table 1
Post–1950 Publications in Different Areas of Psychology

Areas	1951 -55	1956 -60	1961 -65	1962 -69	Total	%
Methodology	10	35	80	42	167	6
Experimental	21	64	91	112	288	10
Physiological & Comparative	3	12	18	49	82	3
Developmental	4	16	32	60	112	4
Social	41	94	100	167	402	13
Personality	20	71	173	261	525	18
Clinical	54	136	152	235	577	19
Educational	9	30	68	86	193	6
Industrial	51	84	96	122	353	12
Military	112	70	55	45	282	9

Source: Based on Mitra, 1972.

(1971) observed that while about 51 percent of the scholars identified themselves with traditional areas such as abnormal (and clinical), social, educational, industrial, personality, mental testing, and vocational guidance in percentages ranging from 5 to 13, nearly a third perceived themselves as working in the field of "general psychology." This indicated that the kind of specialization that is so typical of psychologists in the West is not characteristic of Indian psychologists. Indian psychologists frequently shift their areas of interest and are usually occupied with a wider range of issues and phenomena. Narrow specialization is rare.

Independence encouraged development of national pride and a search for identity among those Indian scholars not tied to Western scholarship. In psychology, it took almost twenty-five years for this trend to become noticeable, though it had started immediately.

The post–World War II period has seen phenomenal expansion worldwide in the field of psychology. India also witnessed tremendous growth in the subject; research interests diversified into various branches and directions as was also the case in Western countries. A perusal of the survey of research conducted by the ICSSR (Mitra, 1972) shows that Indian scholars were following closely in the footsteps of their Western colleagues. Working within the framework borrowed from the West and concentrating on almost the same topics, Indian psychologists made their analyses in Indian settings to see if similar factors were at work. Orientations, concepts, theories, and the tools of research remained Western, and topics for investigation were gathered from foreign sources popular at that time in the West. Commenting on this trend, D. Sinha (1973) observed that "there is a good deal of academic research that is traditional and conventional with very little relation to the realities of the contemporary situation" (p. 87).

Thus, in the area of testing, it became almost an obsession to adapt widely used Western tests with only minor variations or to develop Indian norms for established tests of intelligence, aptitude, and personality. Direct translations and crude adaptations were so ubiquitous that they have been described as "innumerable half-hearted replications, unending streams of adaptations and readaptations of western scales and tests" (Nandy, 1974, p. 3).

Replication characterized almost all the fields of psychology. To give some examples, anxiety scales were developed along the lines of the Taylor Manifest Anxiety scale. Preferred topics for experimentalists were retroactive inhibition, motivational factors governing perception and memory, verbal learning, and personality factors in learning. Industrial psychologists favored the study of job satisfaction, incentives, and styles of leadership and organizational problems. Human factors in designing aircraft displays and the influence of speed and work load on signal operators were explored. Social psychology gave so much attention to making attitude surveys with poorly developed schedules and questionnaires that it received the derogatory label of "questionnaire psychology" (D. Sinha, 1980).

Drawing inspiration from Murphy's *In the minds of men* (1953), which was the result of investigations of social tensions in Indian society conducted at the behest of the government of India, many Indian scholars began to study caste and national stereotypes and prejudices. But they leaned heavily on Western models and lacked an innovative approach suited to the Indian scene. As Nandy (1974) remarked, "All that has happened is that we have studied caste like race, communalism like anti-semitism and untouchables like American blacks" (p. 8).

In the field of personality, the construction and adaptation of different psychometric and projective measures constituted the primary work of Indian psychologists. Very little effort was made to clarify conceptual issues or make the tests appropriate to the sociocultural characteristics of the population. In fact, the underlying weakness of the research conducted during this period was its lack of a sound theoretical base. Indian scholars rarely made any effort to develop their own theoretical models or enunciate theory based on their findings. They followed the lines of their Western counterparts so closely that such research has been termed "Unitedstatean" or "Euro-American." Though it has been contended that psychology in India was "taking slowly a shape and a pattern of its own" (S. Sinha, 1963), the field remained largely Western despite efforts to give it an Indian content.

A distinct change occurred after the 1960s. Scholars not only realized the limitations of using theoretical approaches, models, and tools borrowed from the West but also felt the need for problem-oriented as opposed to purely theoretical research; that is, they recognized the need for conducting studies consciously directed toward solving problems the country was facing. There arose a general "concern about the foreignness of social science research in India today—in the field of psychology in particular" (ICSSR, 1973, p. 43). Awareness of this limitation led psychologists to seek research topics rooted in Indian settings which would make their findings relevant to contemporary problems. Thus, problems connected with the impact of rapid change and development posed a major challenge to psychologists and some researchers began to take up the task.

As defined by the International Labor Organization (ILO) in its *International standard classification of occupations*, social change and national development do not come strictly within the purview of psychology. In focusing their attention on problems arising from rapid social change and development, Indian psychologists thereby made a special contribution toward expanding the frontiers of the discipline through their effort to make it more "socially relevant." This ushered in the phase of indigenization of the discipline, when Indian psychologists started to display special interest in topics related to the needs of the country as distinct from what was fashionable in the West.

The variety of new themes that gained prominence and the directions which the discipline took in the 1970s can be gauged from the topics that constituted the second ICSSR survey of research for the period from 1971 to 1976 (Pareek, 1980, 1981). They included psychological theory and research methods, culture and personality, developmental processes, cognitive processes, deviance and pathology, counseling and therapy, processes of communication and social in-fluence, organizational dynamics, psychology of work, political processes and behavior, environmental psychology, and social issues (poverty, inequality, pop-ulation, and family planning), dynamics of social change, and other issues of relevance. These marked a clear departure from the ten conventional areas with which the first ICSSR survey was concerned.

Judged from the themes and number of research projects reported, the 1970s constituted not only a period of growth but of diversification for the discipline in India. This trend is most clearly visible in social, organizational, and clinical psychology, though traces of it can be discerned in other fields as well. The types of studies prevalent in the 1950s continued with greater vigor while new areas began to attain prominence. The Western influence remained strong and there were still many replicative studies, but, with curricular improvements which made courses in research methodology and quantitative techniques as well as the usual core courses compulsory, the volume of research increased and greater sophistication was displayed in the choice of topics, the design of research, and data analysis. Moreover, there were unmistakable signs of emerging lines of research. To give a few examples, realizing the key role of the agro-economic sphere in a country with over three-quarters of its population living in villages, Indian psychologists overcame their urban orientation and entered the rural scene to see if certain patterns of motivation and attitudes were associated with de-velopment. The nature of effective communication relative to health, family planning, and agricultural innovations was analyzed, and the impact on attitudes and behavior of the Satellite Instructional Television Experiment (SITE) program was studied. These and similar investigations not only represent a new direction in the field but, in a way, herald the beginning of a new subdiscipline, namely rural psychology.

The study of the psychological dimensions of poverty is another area of relevant research bearing on India's most pressing problem. Until recently, poverty was regarded as an exclusively economic issue. Psychologists have emphasized other aspects of the problem by analyzing the effects of poverty on perceptual and cognitive processes, language development, academic achievement, motivation, personality, and mental health. These studies have yielded data that are not only of theoretical interest but are useful for devising intervention strategies to ame-liorate poverty.

In the clinical field, investigations into the sociocultural context of pathology and epidemiological studies of morbidity have become frequent. There is also a sudden upsurge of interest in indigenous modes of health care and the rec-ognition of basic differences between Western and Indian approaches to psy-chotherapy (Kakar, 1982). Many Indian psychologists have emphasized local collective and contextual factors underlying personality formation and behavior rather than elements more common to Western society (Kakar, 1982; J. B. P. Sinha, 1982). A new paradigm for psychotherapeutic transactions appropriate to Indian sociocultural conditions based on the *guru-chela* (preceptor-pupil) relationship has even been suggested (Neki, 1976).

Turning to industrial and organizational psychology, while enthusiasm has not waned for the types of research projects conducted in the West, there is an evident tendency to investigate problems of organizations peculiar to the Indian setting. Thus, comparative analyses of psychological problems in the private and public sectors have been made (J. B. P. Sinha, 1973), and the pattern of leadership designated as the "nurturant task-leader" (J. B. P. Sinha, 1980) has been postulated to be the most effective in India. This pattern is distinct from the participative style found to be successful in the West in that it is task-oriented but at the same time draws upon cultural values like affection, dependency, and need for a personalized relationship.

So far as psychological assessment procedures are concerned, there is general dissatisfaction with indiscriminate borrowings from the West. Scholars have begun to forge their own tools for data gathering that are culturally appropriate for the Indian sociocultural context. This is true not only of questionnaires but also of projective and psychometric tests of abilities and personality.

INFLUENCE OF RELIGIOUS AND PHILOSOPHICAL THOUGHT

Doubts regarding the appropriateness of Western concepts, theories, and tools of research for Indian problems and the search for a new identity are evidenced in yet another way. India is one of the few countries with a rich religious and philosophical heritage continuous from ancient times. There has been a long-standing interest in analyzing human behavior and unraveling the nature of man, extending even to paranormal and psychic phenomena. The original reaction against the impact of psychology borrowed from the West was for some scholars to go back to the past, eulogize the old things, and cry out for "Indian psychology" as an alternative to modern scientific psychology. There was glib talk about everything that was psychological in the ancient texts from rebirth and the transmigration of the soul to paranormal perception and supernatural powers. A premium was put on the esoteric, and the scientism of modern psychology was decried.

Such revivalism did not sit well with the empirical and scientific ethos of modern psychology. The term "Indian psychology" soon acquired a pejorative connotation and was rejected by mainstream psychologists. However, in rejecting it outright, the baby was thrown out with the bath water. Very soon, many psychologists in the country began to realize the limitations of the modern Western approach in understanding the problems of "becoming" and development, integration of personality, and mental health and disease; they looked to Indian religious and philosophical systems for new conceptualizations and procedures. Akhilananda (1948, 1952) outlined the distinctive characteristics of

Hindu psychology and related them to mental health and psychotherapy. A famous practicing clinical psychologist asserted: "There is a wealth of applied clinical psychological concepts in the Yogic practices and philosophy which has yet to be explored and made to enrich modern science" (Dhairyan, 1961, p. 159).

As early as the 1950s, some effort had been made to assess the contributions which the psychological knowledge in ancient Indian texts could make to enriching modern psychology (Prabhu, 1976). Besides Akhilananda's two books, a comparative exposition of Indian and Western views of the nature, structure, dynamicis, transformations, and typologies of personality was attempted (Singh, 1972). Another endeavor tried to link the findings of the transactional psychology of perception to early Indian thinking (Prabhu, 1966).

Increasingly, there has emerged a tendency to achieve a synthesis by enriching modern psychology with certain concepts and procedures found in ancient Indian thought. Efforts have also been made to give these old concepts and procedures systematic scrutiny by utilizing scientific methodology and the sophisticated instruments that developments in electronics and computer science have provided. A plea for integrating modern psychology with Indian thought is being heard: "It is my feeling that there are numerous areas where the two lines can converge and integrate profitably. This would result in bridging many of the gaps that are too obvious in modern psychological theory of action, and at the same time interpret our philosophical thought in a scientific light" (D. Sinha, 1969, p. 278).

In fact, during the past few years, there has been a growing interest in psychological concepts and phenomena—for example, meditation, *samadhi*, and *guru* (preceptor)—that have their origins in the Eastern tradition. Systematic theoretical and empirical work is being conducted and published in psychological and medical journals both in India and in the West. The edited book *Altered states of consciousness* (Tart, 1972) includes a number of papers on meditation and yogic trance; it has become popular in many countries.

More recently, Paranjpe (1984) in his book *Theoretical psychology: The meeting of East and West* has, as the title indicates, not only made a formal comparison of Eastern and Western approaches to consciousness, self, and identity but tried to integrate the two traditions. Such a synthesis is being attempted not simply theoretically and conceptually. It also involves subjecting various yogic states, relaxation, and other psychological phenomena derived from ancient Indian religious and philosophical literature to systematic investigations and sorting out their physiological and psychological characteristics through the use of sophisticated equipment. Even indigenous healing practices have been subjected to rigorous analysis using the psychoanalytic perspective (Kakar, 1982). Institutions like the National Institute of Mental Health and Neuro-science in Bangalore, and the All-Indian Institute of Medical Sciences in New Delhi have become centers for studying such phenomena by employing modern experimental techniques.

CONCLUSIONS

A general review of the research done in psychology in India since independence reveals a definite "trend to outgrow the alien framework" (D. Sinha, 1980b) either by investigating problems that are relevant to the needs of the country rather than those that are significant to foreign scholars or by looking at the rich heritage of indigenous psychological thought and practices with a view to integrating them with modern scientific psychology. As a consequence, the field in India is becoming more problem-oriented, devoting more attention to culture-specific variables, and adopting a more macrocosmic and interdisciplinary perspective. The discipline has been consciously redirected to be concerned with social change and national development. Its impact on policy making, however, compared to that of the other social sciences, is still negligible. Some psychologists are even highly critical of this trend towards "social relevance." It has been dubbed a gambit that has only produced an "insipid watery brew which neither contributes to the growth of psychology nor proves useful to the policy-makers" (Nandy, 1974, p. 9). Despite these doubts and criticisms, it can safely be asserted that by taking up the challenge of problems resulting from social change and national development, psychologists in India have helped to extricate the discipline from the "narrow groove in which it seems to have got stuck" (Pareek, 1980, p. ix), and they have extended psychology's frontiers.

REFERENCES

Akhilananda, S. (1948). *Hindu psychology*. London: Allen & Unwin.

Akhilananda, S. (1952). *Mental Health and Hindu psychology*. London: Allen & Unwin.

Dhairyan, D. (1961). Research needs for development of psychotherapy in India. In T. K. N. Menon (Ed.), *Recent trends in psychology* (pp. 154–161). Bombay: Orient Longmans.

Ganguli, H. C. (1971). Psychological research in India: 1920–1967. *International Journal of Psychology, 6*, 165–177.

Indian Council of Social Science Review Committee. (1973). *A report on social science in India: Retrospective and prospective* (Vol. I). New Delhi: Author.

Joshi, M. C. (1965). Psychological research in India. In *Psychological research in India: A commemorative volume in honor of Professor S. Jalota* (pp. 25–34). Varanasi: Jalota Commemorative Volume Committee.

Kakar, S. (1982). *Shamans, mystics and doctors: A psychological enquiry into India and its healing traditions*. Delhi: Oxford University Press.

Krishnan, B. (1961). A review of contributions of Indian psychologists (1950–1960). In T. K. N. Menon (Ed.), *Recent trends in psychology*. Bombay: Orient Longmans.

Krishnan, B. (1972). Clinical psychology: A trend report. In S. K. Mitra (Ed.), *A survey of research in psychology*. New Delhi: Indian Council of Social Science Research.

Mitra, S. K. (Ed.). (1972). *A survey of research in psychology*. New Delhi: Indian Council of Social Science Research.

Mitra, S. K. (1973). Progress of psychology. In *A decade (1963–72) of science in India*. Calcutta: Indian Science Association.

Murphy, G. (1953). *In the minds of men*. New York: Basic Books.

Nandy, A. (1974). A non-paradigmatic crisis in Indian psychology: Reflections on a recipient culture of science. *Indian Journal of Psychology, 49*, 1–20.

Narain, R. (1968). *Directory of Indian psychologists*. Delhi: Manasayan.

Neki, J. S. (1976). An examination of the cultural relation of dependence as a dynamic of social and therapeutic relationships: I. Social development. *British Journal of Medical Psychology, 49*, 1–10.

Paranjpe, A. C. (1984). *Theoretical psychology: The meeting of East and West*. New York: Plenum.

Pareek, U. (Ed.). (1980). *A survey of research in psychology, 1971–76: Part I*. New Delhi: Indian Council of Social Science Research.

Pareek, U. (Ed.). (1981). *A survey of research in psychology, 1971–76: Part II*. New Delhi: Indian Council of Social Science Research.

Prabhu, P. H. (1966). Perception, personality and the Indian approach. *Special lecture*, Annamalai University, India.

Prabhu, P. H. (1976). India. In V. S. Sexton and H. K. Misiak (Eds.), *Psychology around the world* (pp. 190–203). Monterey, CA: Brooks/Cole.

Ramalingaswami, P. (1980). *Psychology in India: Challenge and opportunities*. New Delhi: Prachi Prakashan.

Rosenzweig, M. R. (1982). Trends in development and status of psychology in international perspective. *International Journal of Psychology, 17*, 117–140.

Singh, R. B. (1972). *A comparative study of Western and Indian thoughts and concepts of personality*. Unpublished doctoral dissertation, Jodhpur University, Jodhpur, India.

Sinha, D. (1969). Integration of modern psychology with Indian thought. In A. J. Sutich and M. A. Vich (Eds.), *Readings in humanistic psychology* (pp. 265–279). New York: Free Press. (Reprinted from *Journal of Humanistic Psychology*, 1965, Spring, 6–21).

Sinha, D. (1973). Applied social psychology in a developing country. *Journal of Social and Economic Studies, 1*, 81–92.

Sinha, D. (1980). Social psychology in India: A historical perspective. *Psychological studies, 25*, 157–163. (a)

Sinha, D. (1980). *Towards outgrowing the alien framework: Review of recent trends in psychological research in India*. Paper presented at the symposium, History of Psychology in Various Countries, XXII International Congress of Psychology, Leipzig, GDR. (b)

Sinha, J. B. P. (1973). *Some problems of public sector organisations*. Delhi: National Publishing House.

Sinha, J. B. P. (1980). *The nurturant task leaders*. New Delhi: Concept Publishing Company.

Sinha, J. B. P. (1982). The Hindu (Indian) identity. *Dynamische psychiatrie* [Dynamic Psychiatry]. 3/4 Hept.

Sinha, S. (1963). Progress of psychology. In *Fifty years of science in India*. Calcutta: Indian Science Congress Association.

Tart, C. T. (Ed.). (1972). *Altered states of consciousness*. Garden City, NY: Doubleday.

University Grants Commission. (1982). *Status of psychology in Indian universities*. New Delhi: Author.

University Grants Commission Panel on Psychology. (1979). *Reorientation of teaching and research in psychology in the Indian universities*. New Delhi: Author.

Israel

Esther Halpern

THE NATURE AND SCOPE OF THE DISCIPLINE

Overview

Psychology is defined in Israel as a science and profession along lines accepted by the international scientific community. This general definition, however, must be considered in the context of certain demographic factors if the special characteristics of the education of Israeli psychologists and the structure of the Israeli Psychological Association (IPA) are to be understood.

A good starting point is Rosenzweig's analysis of psychology in an international perspective (1984). He considers, among other things, such demographic information as the number of psychologists per million population, a useful framework in which to view the distribution of psychologists around the world. In surveying the forty-four countries which have national professional organizations, and therefore belong to the International Union of Psychological Science (IUPsyS), Rosenzweig reports a high concentration of psychologists in only ten countries. Israel, with a population of about 4 million and approximately 2,160 psychologists belonging to its national organization, the IPA, ranks among the five countries with the most psychologists on a per capita basis (1986). Psychology in Israel also meets a further international criterion, according to Rosenzweig, since IPA members have earned at least an M.A. and 25 percent hold a doctorate. Unlike the United States and some European countries, however, most psychologists in Israel engage in applied work.

Applied fields are popularized by news coverage in a country where the news in any media is the focus of daily attention. Programs on educational television and specials on regular television keep the public informed of the varieties of psychological practice which have a high level of acceptance. Employers of applied psychologists include the Labor Union's health group insurance facility; the Ministry of Health; the mental health network of the Ministry of Education; the education branches of urban councils; the Prison and Rehabilitation Services;

the Ministry of Absorption; the National Insurance, which cares for the handi-capped; the Ministry of Social Welfare; and the Ministry of Labor. Psychological services are also offered in the area of vocational guidance and by public and private facilities having to do with industrial psychology (Kugelmass, 1976). The psychological branch of the Israeli Defense Forces and the kibbutz com-munities and the Ministry of Education employ applied and research psychol-ogists to focus on some of their problems (Raviv, 1984a). Finally, private practice affords many clinicians lucrative work.

Academicians with teaching and research functions are found in the psychology and education departments of the five major universities and teachers' colleges. Some teach in medical schools and social work departments. Researchers in the field of education are associated with academic departments, the Ministry of Education's research units, or educational research institutes (Raviv, 1984a; Kaplan & Schnur, 1985).

Applied psychologists are accredited by divisions of the IPA and are licensed according to a law that came into effect in 1977, restricting the label of "psy-chologist" and defining and delineating the practices of each applied group. At present the IPA has divisions in the areas of clinical, educational, social, in-dustrial, and rehabilitation; a developmental section is planned.

Israeli psychologists are not provincial insofar as the associations they join. In spite of high dues and foreign currency restrictions, many are members of international associations or foreign affiliates of different national organizations. Among these are the Society for Research in Child Development, the American Society for Study of Behavioral Development, the American Orthopsychiatric Association, the International Society for the Study of Behavioral Development, the International Council of Psychologists, and the International Association of School Psychologists.

The Training of Psychologists

Five universities in Israel offer programs in psychology: Hebrew University in Jerusalem, Bar-Ilan University in Ramat-Gan, Tel-Aviv University in Tel-Aviv, Haifa University in the city of Haifa located in the northern region of the country, and Ben-Gurion University in the desert town of Beersheba. Most departments of psychology offer training and degrees in psychology at three levels leading respectively to the B.A., M.A., and Ph.D. degrees. Though there is a continuity in most curricula from the B.A. to the Ph.D., the requirements of these degrees, probably for historical reasons, evidence some organizational discontinuity (Halpern & Friedland, 1983).

The Bachelor of Arts, like a European degree, involves a three-year course of intensive study of the basic areas of psychology with an emphasis on exper-imental psychology, varying from university to university only in terms of the fields studied in depth. The traditional curriculum comprises compulsory courses in the basic psychology subjects: introductory psychology, learning theories, personality theories, perception, cognitive development, physiological psychology, social psychology, psychopathology, intelligence and personality testing, statistics, principles and research methods, and laboratory courses in most of these areas. Elective courses and seminars focus on current topics in psychology and/or on areas in which faculty members have particular interests or experiences. Psychology is taken as one of two majors (double major, D.M.) or as a single major (S.M.). An "empirical seminar" culminates in an original research paper similar to the honors thesis required by European universities. Additionally, a theoretical paper (two such works for S.M. students) are required for this first degree in psychology.

The Master of Arts, or "second degree," focuses on a specific field of psychology. This level of study was created to provide specialization in one particular research or applied area. Most universities offer specialization in experimental, social, cognitive, developmental, psychobiological, and physiological psychology. In the applied field the areas of specialization may include one or all of the following: clinical, educational/school rehabilitation, vocational/counseling/industrial, and clinical-child. The latter two, the most recently established areas of specialization at the M.A. level, are offered at one university only.

M.A. programs require at least two years of study. The common core of all master's programs includes courses in methodology and statistics; research seminars; a supervised theoretical paper; an original research project; and, finally, an original research thesis. Students attend five compulsory seminars or courses each year specific to their areas of specialization.

While M.A. programs in the experimental areas can be completed in two to three years, at least three, and up to five, years are needed to earn a master's in an applied field. The applied M.A. is usually a terminal degree and is recognized as sufficient for local accreditation/licensing.

Master's programs in clinical psychology (adult or clinical-child) closely resemble APA-approved Ph.D. programs in North America (Halpern & Friedland, 1983). The curriculum includes the two years of compulsory seminars and course work and, concomitantly, two years of supervised field work at accredited institutions. Elective courses and advanced clinical seminars follow completion of the compulsory work. Comprehensive examinations and an original research M.A. thesis complete the requirements for this second degree in psychology.

The discontinuity in university training manifests itself in the requirements for the third degree. The Ph.D. is a European degree par excellence in the sense that it is not awarded in a particular area of specialization (Sanua, 1971; Halpern & Friedland, 1983). It is bestowed either by a psychology department or a university as a whole. The Ph.D. in psychology was first offered in the 1970s and then by only a few university departments. Doctoral studies are undertaken by a select number of students each year. Emphasis is on the production of a scholarly work under the guidance of one of the senior faculty members; the time limit for its completion is flexible. The supervising professor and apprentice scientist collaborate until a satisfactory original scientific contribution is attained. Departmental committees and/or outside readers evaluate the work. All doctoral students take seminars in research, methodology, and computer programming as needed, in addition to a limited number of courses to broaden their background in the general field of psychology and/or to provide additional background in the area of their dissertation studies. Only candidates who have completed their second degree in psychology with an original experimental work of high quality for an M.A. thesis are ordinarily considered for admission to doctoral programs. The first one or two years represent a trial period during which an attempt is made to develop a comprehensive dissertation proposal and complete conclusive pilot studies.

The European and North American influences, which came with the faculty members of the original psychology departments, undoubtedly contributed to the structural discontinuity characterizing Israeli degree programs. This mixture of backgrounds is also reflected in the Israeli system of academic ranking. If correspondence exists between the Israeli system and any other, it is most closely manifested relative to some European academic institutions. However, in the applied fields, the Israeli system more closely approximates that found in the United States. The junior and untenured academic ranks are teacher and lecturer; in North American terms the approximate equivalents would be instructor and assitant professor, respectively. Senior lecturer is usually a tenured position; exact correspondence is difficult to find, but judging from ranks given to faculty arriving from the United States, this approximates the rank of associate professor. The rank of associate professor in Israel usually corresponds to that of full professor in North America; the full professor rank is given to only a few senior and prominent academicians. Endowed chairs are reserved for faculty of high distinction.

Before describing the undergraduate and graduate programs in psychology at Tel-Aviv University to illustrate the Israeli curriculum model, a few words should be said about research facilities. Psychology departments support research laboratories, institutes, and centers in many areas—for example, psychobiology, physiological and comparative psychology, child and adult development, human learning, perception, psychological stress, and information processing. There are also research institutes which are independent organizations servicing the behavioral sciences or focused on special tasks such as assembling bibliographic information and/or sponsoring research. Departmental computer systems, which are becoming increasingly available, are usually linked to universities' central computer facilities.

Israeli universities emphasize the social relevance of their academic endeavors. The undergraduate and graduate programs show how an attempt is made to integrate ivory tower strivings with the sociocultural realities of Israeli society.

The B.A. program at Tel-Aviv University, as well as the course work at all universities, requires that every student be involved in field studies. This aspect of the program, which adds an applied dimension to the academic experience, sensitizes students to human needs, teaches the social relevance of academic learning, and generally raises the social awareness of future psychologists. Students contribute their knowledge and services to society even at this early stage of their careers. First-year placement puts each student to work with a child from an impoverished neighborhood. The student tries to develop a "pal" relationship with the child. The focus is on problems related to matters of alienation and inadequate cognitive development. Weekly seminars integrate this experience into an academic-scientific framework.

Second-year field work involves working with the elderly or handicapped for at least two hours a week. Supervision of this practicum takes place through weekly group meetings, wherein experiential learning is placed in the context of theories of personality, social psychology, and psychobiology.

Third-year field work differs from that done during the first two years in that it is part of a compulsory course in psychopathology. Supervision is carried out by accredited clinical psychologists. Each student is assigned a patient in either a closed or an open ward of a mental-health institution; the apprentice psychologist offers social support and develops a professional relationship with the patient. This learning experience is integrated with the theoretical and clinical subject matter that comprises the formal part of the course (Halpern, 1987).

Tel-Aviv University is at present the only Israeli university to offer an M.A.-level specialization program in clinical-child psychology and was therefore chosen to illustrate a graduate-level degree curriculum (Sharabany, 1986). The curricular model exemplified takes into account the field requirements appropriate for Israeli society, while employing current thinking concerning the training of applied psychologists.

Clinical-child psychologists' functions were conceptualized using North American approaches as a guideline. Emphasis is placed on training clinicians for innovative roles (Halpern, 1967). This framework, however, was adapted to existing Israeli models of mental health delivery systems, particularly those serving school children (Halpern, 1981). North American innovations dealt with the various mental health services psychologists could deliver. The Israeli school system has offered a unique vehicle for providing help as an integral part of the educational process. Within this structure, there are channels for reaching 90 percent of children via mental health "stations," which are part of the educational network (Halpern, 1981; Raviv & Wiesner, 1985). As a result of integrating "what" mental health services are given with "how" they are delivered, the functions of clinical-child psychologists are to:

Promote the mental health of all children

Help the individual child through diagnosis and treatment (individual psychotherapy, family therapy)

Enhance the functioning of all adults involved in the care of children at school, in the community, and in the home

Invite, integrate, and encourage the work of allied professionals who seek to maximize the growth of children in schools. (Halpern, 1981)

In this context, the curriculum addresses both psychological issues associated with the community and the individual child's functioning. Therefore, the school becomes the primary locus for course work and field placements. To illustrate, the curriculum considers the school as an organization, primary and secondary intervention techniques, and the whole gamut of mental health consultative procedures adapted to practice in Israel (Raviv, 1979, 1984a). Students' practicum experiences include setting up innovative community programs originating in and involving the school. They may, for example, participate in establishing school-based emergency services, educating parents in teaching children cognitive skills through games, building playgrounds, using psychodrama, and helping families cope with life-cycle crises by consulting with health-promoting agencies such as well-baby clinics.

Children's psychological problems are viewed in developmental terms within the framework of individual and family dynamics. In course work and practice, human growth, psychopathology, assessment, and therapeutic techniques are integrated with teacher-oriented, as well as patient-oriented, services. A further step toward making training relevant to the needs of the field was taken in the way the curriculum was planned for the clinical-child master's program. A provision for periodic revision allows courses and projects to be designed in conjunction with a newly established mental health station located near Tel-Aviv University (Halpern, Raviv, & Ziv, 1973).

Needs

Identifying major needs in a developing country is a very subjective undertaking. It is difficult to compare objectively the situation in Israel with that of highly industrialized countries with their variety of institutions, wealth of human resources, and financial support for higher education.

The academic and applied training centers in Israel are all publicly funded, primarily through the Ministry of Education and Culture and additionally by funds from other ministries or public institutions. However, private fund-raising locally and abroad is always necessary for balancing budgets. Most research-oriented institutions maintain "research authorities," whose function it is to gather information concerning the availability of grants and to assist applicants with the required procedures. This is counterbalanced, however, by the increased difficulty in obtaining funds due to economic conditions. Support is even difficult to obtain in many instances for things taken for granted in most developed countries, such as research equipment, teaching aids, books, and journals. Financial help for students is almost nonexistent. Another problem in Israel is the fact that higher education for both women and men is delayed by three years when compared to most developed countries, because of the time given to national service. In addition, most Israelis get married relatively early and immediately start raising families, thus compounding the financial burdens for both partners. When financial aid is available for a few fortunate students, in the form of assistantships for teaching or research, the amounts awarded are so small that they have to be supplemented by income from outside jobs. These positions, therefore, do not always afford the opportunity for taking part fully in the academic life. The situation is most acute with students whose outside work is completely unrelated to the career for which they are training. Such obstacles, however, have not curtailed Israeli students' motivation to study psychology. Psychology still ranks among the five top areas in most universities in terms of enrollments.

Continued economic stress has affected psychology departments and applied centers alike. While psychology has increased its activities in depth and scope, most psychology department staffs have not grown proportionately nor have resources increased sufficiently during the past two to three years.

Another major issue for Israeli psychologists is the challenge of keeping abreast of developments in the discipline in other countries. There has been a concerted effort to be part of the international scene in order to guard against the provincialism and stagnation which would otherwise result from Israel's geopolitical isolation. International exposure has become increasingly sought, too, for economic reasons, since funding from outside the country is absolutely necessary. A look at periodicals and various editorial boards of international journals reveals a high level of participation in both published research and organizational matters by Israeli psychologists. Israel has hosted international conferences each year ranging from small groups to large organizations (Sanua, 1971; Raviv, 1984a).

There are, though, some negative aspects to these efforts to reach and stay in touch with the international psychological community. Publishing overseas has often led to the neglect of local journals. Books written by Israelis in English are only occasionally translated into Hebrew; one is more likely to find out about colleagues' work at meetings of the APA, the Society for Research in Child Development (SRCD), or international congresses than at national meetings. Thus one wonders about the cost of all these accomplishments within international forums. They may have inhibited the founding and nurturing of local scientific journals and publication of books that are readily available to Israeli psychologists.

This striving for recognition abroad, especially in the United States, is of course not unique to Israel. It is strongly felt by psychologists in most dveloping countries (Petzold, 1984). In the final analysis, the long-range goal of psychology in Israel should be to capitalize on the "natural laboratory" conditions of its society and strive to safeguard its uniqueness. At the same time Israeli psychologists should, of course, continue to look for commonalities with other psychological schools of thought. Ideally, and it is hoped, in the not too distant future, the discipline can make a significant contribution to the growth of the field in the Mediterranean or Middle East region.

MAJOR TRENDS AND INFLUENCES SINCE
WORLD WAR II

An objective, systematic history of the development of psychology in Israel has yet to be written. The discipline, however, has been periodically reviewed from a variety of perspectives and usually introduced by a brief historical background (Shannan & Weiss, 1963; Sanua, 1971; Weiss, 1975; Kugelmass, 1976; Pallak & Cole, 1977; Peleg & Adler, 1977; Amir & Ben-Ari, 1981; Halpern & Friedland, 1983; Raviv, 1984b). These historical overviews were the primary references for the comments which follow.

Heterogeneity of cultural background and a unique social setting (Peleg & Adler, 1977) colored the establishment of psychology as a discipline in Israel and the creation of psychology departments in Israeli universities. The field's development is inextricably intertwined with the inception and growth of the State of Israel as a nation (Kugelmass, 1976; Amir & Ben-Ari, 1981). At the time of statehood in 1948, psychology as a discipline was primarily applied (Shannan & Weiss, 1963; Sanua, 1971). It was closely linked with other "helping" professions, particularly psychiatry. As Gerald Caplan (1958) perceives it, during this era in which he himself briefly played a considerable part, psychiatry was innovative and characterized by an atmosphere of "recklessness in planning and brilliant improvisations." In accordance with the views of M. Petzold (1984), psychology as a science and profession was well suited to meet existing local needs of the late 1940s and early 1950s, a period when Israel was clearly a developing country.

The needs were acute at this period of Israel's early statehood. Mass immigration doubled and then quadrupled the host population within a short time span. The newcomers, who outnumbered the settlers, not only came from culturally different regions of the world, including Europe, North Africa, the Middle East, and Asia Minor, but had been through a variety of traumatic experiences. Many were abruptly dislocated, some were refugees and others survivors of the holocaust (Caplan, 1958; Kugelmass, 1976). Psychologists came from continental Europe, and later from England and North America, and worked primarily in applied settings. It is noteworthy that psychology became well enough established to warrant a national association before Israeli universities started training psychologists in their own departments. The Israeli Psychological Association was founded in the 1950s; by 1963 it numbered 170 members (Shannan & Weiss, 1963; Sanua, 1971; Weiss, 1975). School psychology also came into existence as a separate field without the benefit of formal university programs even earlier in 1936 when the first Educational Psychology Center was founded (Ziv, 1977). It continued to be the focus of much professional attention in the early years of Israel's statehood.

Formally, university training programs in psychology did not crystallize until 1957, following various attempts to teach the subject in institutions of higher

learning during the pre-state era and the late 1940s. According to Kugelmass
(1976), a course in psychology was offered from 1945 to 1947 at Hebrew
University's department of education by Professor Enzo Bonaventura, the eminent Italian psychologist. His untimely death at the hands of terrorists, however,
terminated that early effort at academic psychology (Amir & Ben-Ari, 1981).
A department of psychology opened in Jerusalem in 1950 but closed two years
later.

Thus in 1957 university departments were established against the background
of an active applied field. By then foreign-trained scientists, educational psychologists, clinicians, and other applied psychologists had already become
professionally established and a national association, the IPA, founded.

Hebrew University set up its psychology department with a clearly defined
program under Professor Sol Kugelmass. This was followed by Bar-Ilan University's psychology department in 1958, under Professor A. Siegman's chairmanship (Kugelmass, 1976) and Tel-Aviv University's program started by
Professor Hans Kreitler in 1961 (Halpern, 1987). Five universities in Israel now
grant degrees in psychology and educational school psychology and numerous
teachers' colleges and technical institutes offer courses in psychology. The universities with degree programs are Jerusalem's Hebrew University, Tel-Aviv
University, and Bar-Ilan University in the center of the country; Haifa University
in the north; and Ben-Gurion University in Beersheba, which attracts students
from the southern and desert regions.

The increase in universities granting degrees has been accompanied by the
expansion of programs. All offer bachelor's degrees in psychology and master's
degrees in at least four areas; most confer the Ph.D. This rapid growth in degree
programs is paralleled by a significant increase in the membership of the Israeli
Psychological Association (IPA) which now numbers 2,160 (Directory, 1986).
As Raviv (1984b) points out, the expansion in psychology occurred in the context
of dramatic population growth and an increasingly productive Israel.

As indicated before, the faculty members of Israeli psychology departments
originally came from a diversity of backgrounds. Those trained in North American universities included recent graduates and academics with considerable
experience. Concomitantly, all departments absorbed European psychologists
who took refuge in Israel before, during, and after World War II. More recently,
academicians have arrived from institutes of higher education in Eastern European countries and the Soviet Union. Today, one finds increasing numbers of
Israeli-trained psychologists who have spent sabbatical leaves abroad. In part
this is because Israeli departments of psychology became well established by
having faculty visit and learn from colleagues in long-standing departments in
other countries. The multiplicity of roots underlying academic thinking, in addition to ever-changing financial resources for training and research and changes
in employment opportunities for new graduates, constitutes a dynamic context
for academic life in Israel (Halpern & Friedland, 1983).

A great deal has been written about the societal influences on psychology's development in Israel since World War II (Sanua, 1970; Kugelmass, 1976; Ziv, 1977; Amir & Ben-Ari, 1981; Kaplan & Schnur, 1986). While World War II is used in this book as an important landmark, in many developing countries the establishment of an independent state is more of a milestone insofar as societal developments influencing the discipline are concerned. This becomes apparent when one reads the historical sketches of psychology's development in Israel. Most authors, when describing the beginnings of psychology, speak of a "mandate period" or "pre-statehood period" having to do with developments prior to 1947–1948 and the "statehood period" of "modern Israel" extending from the 1950s to the present (Sanua, 1970; Kugelmass, 1976; Amir & Ben-Ari, 1981).

In the pre-state period up to 1948, there was conflict between "European" psychology, particularly its psychoanalytic orientation, and the Socialist philosophy of the kibbutz which saw psychoanalysis as being too bourgeois. This situation has been viewed by some analysts as the major stumbling block to a potentially vigorous applied field (Amir & Ben-Ari, 1981). However, this view should be qualified by the fact that, until recently, certain historical accidents have influenced and determined the particular interactions that occurred between psychological schools of thought and societal developments. In the absence of an established discipline during the pre-state era, those schools of thought which could be influenced by the local society and which, in turn, had an impact on the field were those represented by the few psychologists who happened to come to this country. This certainly accounts for the high visibility of psychoanalysis in Israel during the 1930s. European psychology in the pre–World War II period was not primarily pyschoanalytic. It was, however, the psychological orientation with which Israel had a strong link. In the early 1930s, Freud was even a member of the board of directors of Hebrew University. His student, Max Eitinger, settled here and laid the foundations which led to the establishment in the early 1940s of the Palestine Institute of Psychoanalysis (Kugelmass, 1976). While the development of psychology in Israel may have been impeded by the clash between psychoanalytic and kibbutz Socialist perspectives, as Amir and Ben-Ari (1981) claim, the kibbutz movement soon became reconciled to psychodynamic concepts and "used psychoanalytic knowledge for the attainment of improved educational methods, healthy emotional development in children and better human relations in general," during the first years of statehood (Amir & Ben-Ari, 1981).

Psychoanalytic assumptions and concepts actually dominated early Israeli psychology, which was for the most part an applied field. The social and human problems associated with mass immigrations from a great variety of backgrounds and a population of traumatized refugees, in search of a home in a land that was just establishing its own identity, created an acute need for knowledgeable applied psychologists. The general tendency of Israelis to search for scientific and technological solutions to problems also accelerated the popular acceptance of psychology, as did the establishment of free education where psychological principles were first applied (Peleg & Adler, 1977).

Societal influences had changed by the late 1950s after statehood was secured. Formal frameworks for psychological work existed in the mental health field (Weiss, 1975; Berman, 1981), in education (Ziv, 1974; Raviv & Wiesner, 1985), and in various research institutes (see Appendix). This soon created a need for university-based psychology and education departments and attracted an increasing number of North American–trained psychologists and those from other English-speaking countries such as South Africa and England. As the discipline was being organized and academically structured and societal needs for survival were no longer so pressing, the field became more academic and diverse; with Israel's relative social stability and prosperity during the late 1960s and 1970s, psychologists turned to the whole range of contemporary theoretical issues.

Research and theories prevalent since the 1960s reflect developments in psychology worldwide, but the North American influence has been particularly strong. The relative luxury of building a few ivory towers has allowed Israeli psychologists to make contributions in all areas of study. They have, for example, done basic research in psychological, comparative, social, cognitive, and developmental psychology and on the psychological aspects of art, education, learning, linguistics, communication, and the mass media. At the same time, much work on real-world (applied) problems continues. Projects associated with societal needs tend to be funded. One finds relevance rather than theoretical interest generating research in many areas of investigation.

As indicated before, unique local conditions provide natural laboratories for research. There are, for instance, studies of the acculturation of immigrant populations; stress in times of security-related crises; socialization in kibbutz settings; educational variables in a school system that integrates a whole gamut of ethnic groups and sociocultural backgrounds; issues related to selection, vocational guidance, aptitude testing, and classification in the context of obligatory national service; economic conditions that have led to the rapid emancipation of women coming from various ethnic backgrounds; and studies of women's rights and self-concepts.

To conclude, psychology in Israel is pragmatic. At the same time, Israeli psychologists do stay abreast of and contribute to mainstream developments within the discipline. In the long run, the special characteristics and problems of Israel may determine the distinctive ways that its psychologists add to the body of psychological knowledge. It is hoped, as suggested earlier, that the Israeli perspective will become integral to Mediteranean or Middle Eastern psychology.

REFERENCES

Amir, Y., & Ben-Ari, R. (1981). Psychology and society in Israel. *International Journal of Psychology*, *16*, 239–247.

Berman, E. (1981). Growing pains of professional clinical psychology: A report from Israel. *Clinical Psychologist*, *34*, 6–8.

Caplan, G. (1958). *Some comments on problems of community psychiatry and technical cooperation in Israel*. Paper presented at the Conference on Economic Planning and Social Policy in Israel. Cambridge, MA: Harvard University Center for Middle Eastern Studies.

Directory. (1986). The Israeli Psychological Association. Tel Aviv, Israel: The Central Committee (in Hebrew).

Halpern, E. (1967). *Traditional and emerging roles in clinical psychology*. In E. C. Webster (Ed.), *The Couchiching conference on professional psychology*. Montreal, Canada: McGill University Press.

Halpern, E. (1981). Clinical services in Israeli schools: An issue of delivery systems and training. *International Journal of Group Tensions, 11*, 107–11.

Halpern, E. (Ed.). (1987). *The Department of Psychology at Tel Aviv University* (A brochure on its faculty composition and activities).

Halpern, E., & Friedland, N. (1983). Psychology in Israel. *International Psychologist, 24*, 19–21.

Halpern, E., Raviv, A., & Ziv, R. (1973). *Academic training and clinic grow together*. Paper prepared for the Israeli Psychological Association Meeting of October 1973 (canceled because of the Yom Kippur war).

Kaplan, M. S., & Schnur, M. (1985). School psychology in Israel. *School Psychology International, 6*, 95–100.

Kugelmass, S. (1976). Psychology in Israel. In V. S. Sexton and H. Misiak (Eds.), *Psychology around the world*. Monterey, CA: Brooks/Cole.

Pallak, M. S., & Cole, M. (Eds.). (1977). Special International Issue, *American Psychologist, 32*, 901–904.

Peleg, R., & Adler, C. (1977). Compensatory education in Israel: Conceptions, attitudes and trends. *American Psychologist, 32*, 945–958.

Petzold, M. (1984). Psychology and the developing world. *Society for the Study of Behavioral Development Newsletter, 5*, 5–6.

Psychologists' Law. (1977). *Official Gazette. The State of Israel* (in Hebrew).

Raviv, A. (1979). Reflections on the role of the school psychologist in Israel. *Professional Psychology, 10*, 820–826.

Raviv, A. (1984). School psychology in Israel. *Journal of School Psychology, 22*, 323–333. (a)

Raviv, A. (1984). Psychology in Israel. In R. J. Corsini (Ed.), *Encyclopedia of psychology*. New York: Wiley. (b)

Raviv, A., & Wiesner, E. (1985). School psychology in Israel: Some problems of the profession. *Journal of School Psychology, 23*, 113–119.

Rosenzweig, M. R. (1984). U.S. psychology and world psychology. *American Psychologist, 39*, 877–884.

Sanua, V. D. (1970). *Psychology programs and psychological research in Israel*. Paper presented at the Conference of the Founding Fellows, Center for Human Development, Hebrew University, Jerusalem.

Sanua, V. D. (1971). Psychology programs and psychological research in Israel. *American Psychologist, 26*, 602–605.

Shannan, L., & Weiss, A. A. (1963). Child psychology in Israel 1948–1963. *Israeli Annals of Psychiatry and Related Disciplines, 1*, 35–37.

Sharabany, R. (1986). Training in child clinical psychology: Identity and directions.

Israel Journal of Psychiatry. Unpublished manuscript, Department of Psychology, University of Haifa, Israel.

Weiss, A. (1975). Child psychology in Israel today. *Journal of Clinical Child Psychology*, *4* (2), 37–38.

Ziv, A. (1974). International aspects of school psychology. *Journal of School Psychology*, *12*, 31–39.

Ziv, A. (1977). School psychology in Israel. *Psychology in International Perspective*, *2*, 112–120.

SUGGESTED READINGS

Amir, Y. (1969). The effectiveness of the kibbutz-born soldier in the Israel defense forces. *Human Relations*, *22*, 333–334.

Aurback, H. A. (1953). Social stratification in the collective agricultural settlements in Israel. *Rural Sociology*, *18*, 25–34.

Ayalon, O. (1979). Community-oriented preparation for emergency (C.O.P.E.). *Journal of Death Education*, *3*, 227–244.

Ayalon, O. (1982). Children as hostages. *The Practitioner: Journal of Postgraduate Medicine*, *226*, 1773–1781.

Ayalon, O. (1983). Coping with terrorism: The Israeli scene. In S. Meichenbaum & M. Jaremko (Eds.), *Stress reduction and prevention*. New York: Plenum.

Ayalon, O. (1984). Children facing terrorists: Can they be helped? In O. Ayalon et al. (Eds.), *Holocaust and its perseverance: Sinai series*. Assen, Holland: Van Gorcum.

Ayalon, O. (1985). Resilience and vulnerability of children who were kept hostages by terrorists. In G. R. Anthony & C. Koupernik (Eds.), *The child and his family*. New York: Pergamon Press.

Bar, Y. (1959). The patterns of early socialization in the collective settlements in Israel. *Human Relations*, *12*, 345–360.

Barnett, L. D. (1965). The kibbutz as a child-rearing system: A review of the literature. *Journal of Marriage and the Family*, *27*, 348–349.

Beit-Hallahmi, B., Nevo, B., & Ragin, A. I. (1979). Family and communally raised children 20 years later: Biographical data. *International Journal of Psychology*, *14*, 215–223.

Berman, E. (1981). Growing pains of professional clinical psychology: A report from Israel. *Clinical Psychologist*, *34*, 6–8.

Betensky, M. (1967). The role of the adolescent in Israeli collectives. *Adolescence*, *2*(7), 335–344.

Brand, N. (1965). Collective agriculture settlements in Israel. *Psychiatria et Neurologia*, *150*, 1–7.

Breznitz, S. (1980). Stress in Israel. In H. Seyle (Ed.), *Seyle's guide to stress research*. New York: Van Nostrand Reinhold.

Breznitz, S. (Ed.). (1983). *Stress in Israel*. New York: Reinhold.

Caplan, G. (1954). Clinical observations on the emotional life of children in the communal settlements in Israel. In M. S. E. Senn (Ed.), *Problems of infancy and childhood*. Josiah Macy Foundation.

Cohen, E. (1968). "Social images" in an Israeli development town. *Human Relations*, *21* (2), 163–176.

Eisenberg, L., & Neubauer, P. B. (1965). Mental health issues in Israeli kibbutzim. *Journal of the American Academy of Child Psychiatry, 3*, 426–442.

Etzioni, A. (1957). Solidaric work-groups in collective settlements (kibbutzim). *Human Organization 16*, 2–6.

Faigin, H. (1957). Observation of babies: Social behavior in the kibbutz. *Journal of Abnormal and Social Psychology, 56* (1), 117–129.

Feuerstein, R., Rand, Y., Hoffman, M. B., & Miller, R. (1980). *Instrumental enrichment: An intervention program for cognitive modifiability.* Baltimore, MD: University Press.

Friedland, N. (1983). Hostage negotiations: Dilemmas about policy. In L. Z. Freedman & Y. Alexander (Eds.), *Perspectives on terrorism.* Wilmington, DE: Scholarly Resources.

Friedland, N. (1985). Political terrorism: A modern enigma. In W. Stoebe, A. Kruglanski, & D. Bar Tal (Eds.), *The social psychology of intergroup and international conflict: Theory, research and application.* New York: Springer.

Gerwirtz, H. B., & Gerwirtz, J. L. (1967). Caretaking and background patterns for kibbutz infants: Age and sex trends. *American Journal of Orthopsychiatry, 37*, 345–397.

Gerwirtz, H. B., & Gerwirtz, J. L. (1968). Visiting and caretaking patterns for kibbutz infants: Age and sex trends. *American Journal of Orthopsychiatry, 38*, 427–443.

Glick, Y., Rosner, M., & Avnat, A. (1980). *Satisfaction with consumption in the kibbutz as affected by economic, social and value factors.* Haifa: University of Haifa, IROK (in Hebrew and English).

Golan, S. (1958). Behavior research in collective settlements in Israel. *American Journal of Orthopsychiatry, 28*, 549–556.

Golan, S. (1959). Collective education in the kibbutz. *Psychiatry, 22*, 167–177.

Greenbaum, C. W., & Kugelmass, S. (1980). Human development and socialization in cross-cultural perspective: Issues from research in Israel. In N. Warren (Ed.), *Studies in Cross-Cultural Psychology* (Vol 2.). London: Academic Press.

Greenbaum, C. W., Rogovsky, I., & Shalit, B. (1977). The military psychologist during war-time: A model based on action research and crisis intervention. *Journal of Applied Behavioral Science, 13*, 7–21.

Halpern, E. (1974). Volunteering in times of community crisis: An integration within Caplan's theory of support systems. *Canadian Psychological Review, 15*, 242–250.

Halpern, E. (1985). Training family therapists in Israel: The necessity of indigenous models. *American Journal of Family Therapy, 13*, 56–61.

Halpern, E., & Schleifer, H. (1978). Volunteer deployment during community crises. *Journal of Crisis Intervention, 9*, 2–11.

Halpern, E., Schleifer, H., & Shillo, B. (1982). Children's support systems in coping with orphanhood: Child helps child in a natural setting. In N. A. Milgram, C. D. Spielberger, & I. Sarason (Eds.), *Stress and anxiety series. Vol 8.: Psychological stress and adjustment in time of war and peace: The Israeli experience.* New York: Wiley.

Irvine, E. E. (1966). Children in kibbutzim: Thirteen years after. *Journal of Child Psychology and Psychiatry, 7*, 167–178.

Jarus, A., Marcus, J., Oren, J., & Rapaport, C. (Eds.). (1970). *Children and families in Israel: Some mental health perspectives*. New York: Gordon and Breach, Science Publishers, Inc.

John, C., Young, L., Giles, H., & Hofman, J. E. (1985). Language, values, and intercultural differentiation in Israel. *Journal of Social Psychology, 125* (4), 527–529.

Kaffman, M. (1965). A comparison of psychopathology: Israeli children from kibbutz and from urban surroundings. *American Journal of Orthopsychiatry, 35*, 509–520.

Kaffman, M. (in press). Children of kibbutz: Clinical observations. In J. Masserman, *Current psychiatric therapies, 3*, 171–179. New York: Grune & Stratton.

Katz, E., & Floczower, A. (1961). Ethnic continuity in an Israeli town: Relations with parents. *Human Relations, 14* (4), 293–308.

Katz, E., & Floczower, A. (1961). Ethnic continuity in an Israeli town: Relations with peers. *Human Relations, 14* (4), 309–327.

Kav Venaki, S., Nadler, A., & Gersoni, H. (1985). Sharing the holocaust experience: Communication behaviors and their consequences in families of ex-partisans and ex-prisoners of concentration camps. *Family Process, 24*, 273–280.

Klein, L., & Eshel, Y. (1980). *Integrating Jerusalem schools*. New York: Academic Press.

Leviaton, U., & Rosner, M. (Eds.). (1980). *Work and organization in kibbutz industry*. Philadelphia: Norwood.

Lomeranz, J., Shmotkin, D., Zechovoy, A., & Rosenberg, E. (1985). Time orientation in Nazi concentration camp survivors: Forty years after. *American Journal of Orthopsychiatry, 55*, 230–236.

Luria, Z., Goldwasser, M., & Goldwasser, A. (1963). Response to transgression in stories by Israeli children. *Child Development, 34*, 271–280.

Merari, A. (1981). Political terrorism and Middle-Eastern instability. In N. Novik & J. Starr (Eds.), *Challenges in the Middle East*. New York: Praeger.

Merari, A., & Friedland, N. (1985). Social aspects of political terrorism. In S. Oskamp (Ed.), *Applied Social Psychology Annual*. New York: Sage.

Milgram, N. A., Spielberger, C. D., & Sarasan, J. (Eds.). (1982). *Psychological stress and adjustment in time of war and peace: The Israeli experience*. New York: Wiley.

Neubauer, B. (Ed.). (1965). *Children in collectives: Child rearing aims and practices in the kibbutz*. Springfield, IL: Charles G. Thomas.

Nevo, O. (1984). Appreciation and production of humor by Israeli Jews and Arabs. *Journal of Cross-Cultural Psychology, 15*, 181–198.

Nevo, O. (1985). Are there similarities between humor responses of men and women and Israeli Jews and Arabs? In M. Safir & M. Mednick (Eds.), *Women's Worlds New Scholarship*. New York: Praeger.

Nevo, O. (1985). Does one ever really laugh at one's own expense?: The case of Jews and Arabs in Israel. *Journal of Personality and Social Psychology, 49*, 799–807.

Palgi, M., & Rosner, M. (1980). *Family, familism and the equality between the sexes*. Haifa: University of Haifa, Kibbutz University Center, Institute for Research of the Kibbutz and the Cooperative Idea.

Palgi, M., et al. (Eds.). (1983). *Sexual equality: The Israeli kibbutz tests the theories*. Philadelphia: Norwood Press.

Pelled, N. (1964). On the formation of object-relations and identification of the kibbutz child. *Israel Annals of Psychiatry and Related Disciplines, 2*, 144–161.

Rabin, A. I., & Beit-Hallahmi, B. (1982). *Twenty years later: Kibbutz children grown up*. New York: Springer.

Regev, E., Beit-Hallahmi, B., & Sharabany, R. (1980). Affective expression in the kibbutz: Communal kibbutz families and family raised children in Israel. *Child Development, 51*, 232–237.

Safir, M., & Fragen, K. (1985). Battling the myths: Women's studies in Israel. *Canadian Women's Studies Journal, 6*, 50–52.

Sagi, A., et al. (1984). Security of infant-mother, -father, and -metapelet attachments among kibbutz-reared Israeli children. In I. Bretherton (Ed.), *The strange situation: New directions for research*. Society for Research on Child Development (Series: Monographs of the Society for Research on Child Development).

Shouval, R., Kav-Venaki, S., Bronfenbrenner, U., Devereux, E. C., & Kiely, E. (1975). Anomalous reactions to social pressure of Israeli and Soviet children raised in family versus collective settings. *Journal of Personality and Social Psychology, 32*, 477–489.

Shur, S., Beit-Hallahmi, B., Blasi, J. R., & Rabin, A. J. (1981). *The kibbutz: A bibliography of scientific and professional publications in English*. Philadelphia: Norwood.

APPENDIX: INDEPENDENT RESEARCH AND DEVELOPMENT INSTITUTES

Below are listed and described a few research and development institutes which are independent of universities but whose focus is psychology. The list is not exhaustive. It should be mentioned that the trend recently has been to open institutes within the academic framework rather than fund independent facilities.

The Israel Institute of Applied Social Research in Jerusalem focuses on interdisciplinary population studies and is concerned with such issues as immigration, sociocultural patterns of consumer preference, and sociocultural variables in health and disease (Sanua, 1970).

Henrietta Szold National Institute for Research in the Behavioral Services conducts research having to do with applied developmental issues, education, and welfare; maintains an extensive reference library of abstracts of relevant Israeli and foreign journals; and publishes its own Hebrew-language journal of psychology, *Megamot*. It is located in Jerusalem: 9 Columbia Street, Kiryat Menachem.

Institute of Research on Kibbutz Education coordinates and fosters educational and psychological research on kibbutz-related issues. It maintains an extensive collection of all relevant data and publications on kibbutz education (Sanua, 1970). It is located in Tivon: Kiryat Tivon (near Haifa).

National Institute for Educational Counseling, Testing and Evaluation is located in Jerusalem: 18 Bezalel Street.

Hadassah Vocational Guidance Institute is located in Jerusalem: 24 Strauss Street.

Japan

Takayoshi Kaneko

DEVELOPMENT AND PRESENT STATUS OF PSYCHOLOGY IN JAPAN

Definition of Psychology

With the end of the Tokugawa-shogunate in 1867, the new government rushed to Westernize Japan. Ever since, psychology as well as other disciplines in Japan have been influenced by the major Western trends. Thus, early in the twentieth century, Wundtian experimental psychology and British associationism were the main emphases. Around the 1930s, Gestalt psychology prevailed and after World War II, neobehaviorism.

A small percentage of Japanese psychologists are adherents of Russian materialistic psychology and some are disciples of French, particularly Piagetian, thought. A few are also concerned with bringing together scientific psychology and Oriental phylosophies such as Buddhistic Zen.

Historically, psychology's academic affiliation has been a matter of the way the field was defined. It was conventional in Japan, following the German tradition, that psychology departments belonged to the faculties of letters or humanities despite the field's strong scientific character. It was only after World War II that psychology became fully recognized as an experimental science.

Japanese Psychological Organizations

In the latter part of the nineteenth century, two eminent figures, Amane Nishi (1829–1897) and Yukichi Fukuzawa (1835–1901), brought scientific psychology and Western ideologies to Japan. Nishi, after returning from Europe, translated H. Haven's *Mental philosophy* in 1875. He coined the term *shinrigaku* (*shin* = psycho, *ri* = logical, *gaku* = study) and introduced other psychological nomenclature that is now well established in Japan. Fukuzawa opened the Keio

School of English (now Keio University) where psychology was added to the curriculum in 1881.

Yujiro Motora (1858–1912) assumed the lectureship in psychology at Japan's first governmental university, the University of Tokyo, which was founded in 1877, the year that the last Japanese civil war ended. Motora, the first fully accredited psychologist in Japan, studied in Boston in 1883 and earned his Ph.D. degree at Johns Hopkins University in Baltimore in 1885 under G. Stanley Hall.

Matataro Matsumoto (1865–1943), Motora's top student, was awarded the chair of psychology in the College of Humanities of Kyoto University, the second governmental university, founded in 1906, the year after the armistice of the Russo-Japanese war (1905). Around this time, two teacher-training colleges, Tokyo and Hiroshima Normal Schools, were also opened, thereby initiating another important epoch in the development of psychology in Japan.

The decade of the 1920s was a period of rapid growth for Japanese higher education, and psychological laboratories were established in many new universities: Tohoku in 1922, Kyushu in 1925, Keijo (now Seoul, Korea) in 1926, and Taihoku (now Taipei, Taiwan) in 1928. Nongovernmental universities, which emerged from existing schools, likewise created psychological laboratories: Keio in 1920, Rikkyo in 1922, Waseda in 1923, Nihon and Hosei in 1924, Doshisha in 1927, and Kwansei-gakuin in 1934. Faculties of literature and science were added to the normal schools of Tokyo and Hiroshima in 1929, creating universities of education.

The first psychological journal in Japan, *Shinri-kenkyu* [Psychological Research], edited by Yoichi Ueno (1883–1957), appeared in 1912. The Kyoto school also started *Nihon-shinrigaku-zasshi* [Japanese Psychological Journal] in 1919. In 1926, these two journals were combined to form a new journal, *Shinrigaku-kenkyu* [Japanese Journal of Psychology]. In 1927, the first annual psychological convention was held in Tokyo with 190 psychologists in attendance and sixty-six papers read. On the first day of the convention Nihon-shinrigaku-kai (the Japanese Psychological Association, JPA) was established and Matsumoto was elected the first president. Thus, in 1977, JPA marked its fiftieth anniversary. Psychology departments of the universities founded in the same period also celebrated with semicentenary memorial publications—for example, Hiroshima (1979), Nihon (1979), and Waseda (1981).

Although the economic boom after World War I facilitated the founding of the Japanese Psychological Association, deflation was already setting in by 1927, and Japan was gradually heading toward another war. The Association of Applied Psychology was founded in 1931, the Japanese Society of Animal Psychology followed in 1933, but then growth stopped.

The number of papers read at the JPA conventions rarely exceeded 100. As Japan became involved in World War II, all three of the psychological organizations were combined into one national union. In 1944 *Shinrigaku-kenkyu* suspended publication because of unfavorable wartime conditions.

Following the end of the war in 1945, however, Japanese psychology experienced another phase of development. Active interest in psychological research produced diversification and differentiation, which in turn led to the foundation of new professional organizations. Listed in the order of their inauguration (the year in parentheses) with addresses, they are as follows (the first three existed before the war):

Japanese Psychological Association (1927): 901 Yamazaki bldg., Hongo 2–40–14, Bunkyo-ku, Tokyo 113.

Japanese Association of Applied Psychology (1931): Psychology Department, Faculty of Arts and Sciences, Nihon University, Sakura-josui, Setagaya-ku, Tokyo 156.

Japanese Society of Animal Psychology (1933): Psychology Department, Faculty of Letters, University of Tokyo, Hongo, Bunkyo-ku, Tokyo 113.

Japanese Group Dynamics Association (1949): Japan Institute of Group Dynamics, Nishi-nippon Shinbun Kaikan bldg., Tenjin 1–4–1, Chuo-ku, Fukuoka 810.

Japanese Association of Educational Psychology (1952): Department of Educational Psychology, Faculty of Education, University of Tokyo, Hongo, Bunkyo-ku, Tokyo 113.

Japanese Society of Social Psychology (1960): Department of Social Psychology, Faculty of Letters, University of Tokyo, Hongo, Bunkyo-ku, Tokyo 113.

Japanese Association of Criminal Psychology (1963): Tokyo Juvenile Detention and Classification Home, Hikawadai 2–11–7, Nerima-Ku, Tokyo 176.

Japanese Society for Clinical Psychology (1964): National Institute of Mental Health, Konodai 1–7–3, Ichikawa-shi, Chiba 272.

These eight are pre–Tokyo-Congress societies which served as cohosts for the meetings. A liaison committee established in 1967 publishes a quarterly newsletter, *Saikologist* [Psychologist]. A more formally authorized Psychological Research Liaison Committee exists in the Japan Science Council.

In addition, there are regional and other specialized professional bodies. Regional associations have been formed in, from south to north, Okinawa, Kyushu, Chugoku-Shikoku, Okayama, Kansai, Tokai, Hokuriku, Niigata, Tohoku, and Hokkaido. The specialized organizations are as follows:

Japanese Society for Parapsychology (1953)

Japanese Society for Theoretical Psychology (1955)

Japanese Society for Hypnotical Psychology (1956)

Perception Psychologists Group (1960)

Society for Personality and Behavior Disorders (1960)

Japanese Association of Counseling Science (1967)

Japanese Biofeedback Research Society (1972)

Japanese Association of Behavior Therapy (1974)

Japanese Psychonomic Society (1982)

Japanese Society of Psychological Clinics (1982)

Japanese Society of Physiological Psychology and Psychophysiology (1982)

Japanese Society for Humanistic Psychology (1983)

There are other related interdisciplinary organizations and research groups. Among them are societies for psychoanalysis, aerospace medicine and psychology, psychosomatic medicine, special education, ergonomics, behaviormetrics, cognitive sciences, color science, sports psychology, and psychorehabilitation.

The Japanese Psychological Association belongs to the Union of Nine Societies. This organization consists of professional associations connected with the fields of religion, folklore, language, archaeology, music, sociology, anthropology, and geology. The union issues the journal *Jinrui-kagaku* [Anthropological Sciences]. JPA also has been a member of the Union of Literary Societies (literature, philosophy, and history) since 1951.

Laboratories and Research Institutes

Following World War II, the Japanese educational system was modeled after that in the United States. Several existing schools of higher education were transformed into universities and many new institutions were built. The *1982 JPA Directory* lists 106 universities and colleges with which JPA members are affiliated. The universities below now offer doctoral programs in psychology and are fully equipped with laboratory facilities:

Aichi-gakuin University, Faculty of Humanities: Nisshin-cho, Aichi-gun, Aichi 470–01.

Aoyama-gakuin University, College of Literature: Shibuya-ku, Tokyo 150.

Chukyo University, Faculty of Letters: Yagoto-hon-cho, Showa-ku, Nagoya 466.

Doshisha University, Faculty of Letters: Karasuma Imadegawa, Kamigyo-ku, Kyoto 602.

Hiroshima Shudo University, School of Human Sciences: Ohtsuka, Numata-cho, Asaminami-ku, Hiroshima 731–31.

Hiroshima University, Faculty of Integrated Arts and Sciences: Faculty of Education: Higashi-senda-cho, Hiroshima 730.

Hokkaido University, Faculty of Letters; Faculty of Education: Kita-ku, Sapporo 060.

Keio University, Faculty of Letters: Mita, Minatoku, Tokyo 108.

Komazawa University, Faculty of Literature: Komazawa, Setagaya-ku, Tokyo 154.

Kwansei-gakuin University, School of Humanities; School of Sociology: Uegahara, Nishinomiya-shi, Hyogo 662.

Kyoto University, Faculty of Letters; Faculty of Education: Yoshida-hon-cho, Sakyo-ku, Kyoto 606.

Kyoto University Primate Research Institute: Kanrin, Inuyama-shi, Aichi 484.

Kyushu University, Faculty of Letters; Faculty of Education: Hakozaki, Higashi-ku, Fukuoka 812.

Nagoya University, Faculty of Letters; Faculty of Education; Research Institute of Environmental Medicine: Furo-cho, Chikusa-ku, Nagoya 464.

Nihon University, College of Humanities and Sciences: Sakura-josui, Setagaya-ku, Tokyo 156.

Ochanomizu Women's University, Graduate School for Human Culture: Ohtsuka, Bunkyo-ku, Tokyo 112.

Osaka City University, Faculty of Letters: Sugimoto, Sumiyoshi-ku, Osaka 558.

Osaka University, Faculty of Human Sciences: Yamadagaoka, Suita-shi, Osaka 565.

Rikkyo University, College of Social Relations; Faculty of Literature: Nishi-ikebukuro, Toshima-ku, Tokyo 171.

Tohoku University, Faculty of Arts and Letters; Faculty of Education: Kawauchi, Sendai 980.

Tokyo Metropolitan University, Faculty of Social Science and Humanities: Yagumo, Meguro-ku, Tokyo 152.

University of Tokyo, Faculty of Letters; Faculty of Education, Hongo, Bunkyo-ku, Tokyo 113.

University of Tsukuba, Institute of Psychology: Tsukuba Science City, Ibaraki 305.

Waseda University, Faculty of Education: Nishiwaseda, Shinjuku-ku, Tokyo 160; School of Letters: Toyama-cho, Shinjuku-ku, Tokyo 162.

Governmental and private research institutes employing psychologists are listed below. Many of these facilities were established after World War II.

Aeromedical Laboratory, Japan Air Defense Force: Sakae-cho, Tachikawa-shi, Tokyo 190.

Industrial Products Research Institute: Yatabecho Higashi, Tsukuba-gun, Ibaraki 305.

Institute for Science of Labor: Sugao 1544, Miyamae-ku, Kawasaki-shi, Kanagawa 213.

Institute of Psychiatry: Komone 4–11–11, Itabashi-ku, Tokyo 173.

Japan Aiiku Child Care Research Center: Minamiazabu, 5–6–7, Minato-ku, Tokyo 106.

Japan Automobile Research Institute, Inc.: Yatabecho, Tsukuba-gun, Ibaraki 305.

Japan Broadcasting Corporation Research Institute, Division of Auditory and Visual Information Processing: Kinuta 1–10–11, Setagaya-ku, Tokyo 157; Public Opinion Research Center; Radio and Television Culture Research Center: Atago 2–1–1, Minato-ku, Tokyo 105.

Japan Color Research Institute: Roppongi-koyama bldg., Nishi-azabu 3–1–9, Minato-ku, Tokyo 106.

Japan Institute for Group Dynamics: Nishi-nippon Shinbun-kaikan, Tenjin 1–4–1, Chuo-ku, Fukuoka 810.

Japanese National Railway Labor Science Research Institute: Izumi-cho 2–5–6, Kokubunji-shi, Tokyo 185.

Japan Social Research Institute: Sendagaya 4–26–6, Shibuya-ku, Tokyo 151.

Mitsubishi Kasei Institute of Life Science: Minami-ohya 11, Machida-shi, Tokyo 194.

National Institute for Educational Research: Shimo-meguro 6–5–22, Meguro-ku, Tokyo 153.

National Institute of Mental Health: Konodai 1–7–3, Ichikawashi, Chiba 272.

National Institute of Special Education: Nobi 2360, Yokosuka-shi, Kanagawa 239.

National Institute of Statistics: Minami-azabu 4–6–7, Minato-ku, Tokyo 106.

National Institute of Vocational Research: Sun Plaza, Nakano 4–1–1, Nakano-ku, Tokyo 164.

National Language Research Institute: Nishigaoka 3–9–14, Kita-ku, Tokyo 115.

National Rehabilitation Center for the Physically Handicapped: Namiki 4–1, Tokorozawa-shi, Saitama 359.

National Research Institute of Police Science: Sanban-cho 6, Chiyoda-ku, Tokyo 102.

Psychiatric Research Institute of Tokyo: Kamikitazawa 2–1–8, Setagaya-ku, Tokyo 156.

Research Center for Education of the Multihandicapped: Nishikata 2–8–20, Bunkyo-ku, Tokyo 113.

Tanaka Institute for Educational Research: Ishibashi bldg., Kita-otsuka 3–1–2, Toshima-ku, Tokyo 170.

Tokyo Metropolitan Institute for Neurosciences: Musashidai 2–6, Fuchu-shi, Tokyo 183.

Tokyo Metropolitan Institute of Gerontology: Sakae-cho 35–2, Itabashi-ku, Tokyo 173.

Primary Functions of Psychologists

The occupational distribution of JPA members gives some idea as to the primary functions of psychologists in Japan. Table 1 shows the number of psychologists in various professional areas and postwar trends. The membership of JPA has increased considerably, but the occupational settings have remained proportionally constant. As can be seen, about half the members are associated with universities and colleges. The need to offer psychology courses in general education and teacher-training programs in universities and colleges, including two-year junior colleges, has sustained the demand for psychologists in academic positions. The others are in nonacademic fields; however, it must be noted that many psychologists in applied work may not affiliate with JPA.

Research Funding for Psychology

Psychologists' routine research is supported by the institutes with which they are affiliated. The amounts vary depending on the financial situation of the institutes or on the national budget. While the budget for research and teaching

Table 1
Distribution of JPA Members According to Work Settings: 1958, 1970, 1982

Work Settings	1958*	1970**	1982***
Universities and colleges	780	1120	2214
Graduate students	267	460	675
Government and public services (Ministry of Justice, defense forces, police and others)	244	250	116
Hospitals and welfare institutes	103	405	461
Research institutes	118	90	192
Schools	124	85	93
Business and Industry	37	120	121
No occupation or unspecifiable	145	---	190
Foreign countries	---	---	65
TOTAL	1818	2530	4127

*Adapted from *JJP* (1958), 29, 415.
**Adapted from JPA, 1972.
***Based on the *JPA Directory*, 1982.

in the governmental universities and colleges is controlled by Mombu-sho (Ministry of Education), funds for scientific or experimental psychological research have been approved by Mombu-sho only since World War II.

Researchers also look for sources of additional funding. For psychologists in academic institutions, the Mombu-sho's Kagaku-kenkyu-hi or Kaken-hi (scientific research fund) is the primary source of extramural funds. Table 2 shows the amounts the Kaken-hi fund appropriated for psychological research every fifth year from 1957 on. The fund approximately doubled each half decade until 1977, reflecting the growth of the Japanese economy as well as monetary inflation during this period.

In addition, large industrial firms are investing in scientific research. For example, the Toyota Foundation, sponsored by the Toyota Motor Company, provided 274,090,000 yen (about $168,000,000) in 1983 for ninety-seven projects, five of which were conducted by psychologists with a funding of 9,800,000 yen (about $6,000,000). The projects concerned traffic problems and youth, vocabularies of sensory defective children, the diagnosis of people with defective color vision, assistance to severely handicapped children, and the treatment of pain in cancer patients.

Curriculum in Universities and Colleges

All four-year university and college students are required to take two-year preliminary courses in general education before advancing to their majors. General psychology is favored by many students regardless of their eventual majors. Statistics, computer programming, data analysis, and basic experimental psychology are usually prerequisites for the psychology major. Courses in foreign languages are also required. Students study English and German, or English and French. For psychology students, German was indispensable before World War II; now English suffices.

Many universities and colleges offer majors in psychology involving lectures, seminars, and courses in research methodology. Seminars often require reading foreign psychological articles. A thesis is required at the end of the fourth year for a bachelor's degree in psychology. In Japan, the academic year ends in March and the next year starts in April. Unfortunately, many undergraduate psychology majors leave school after graduation for jobs unrelated to psychology and only a small percentage advance to graduate training.

As indicated earlier, some twenty universities offer graduate programs leading to both master's and doctoral degrees. Many more offer terminal master's programs. The master's degree may be conferred upon a student who has completed two years of course requirements and a thesis. For the doctoral degree, a candidate must hold a master's degree and complete another three years of course work plus research and a dissertation. The University of Tsukuba, founded in 1973, offers a five-year doctoral program emphasizing research during the last three years. Many candidates, of course, spend more than three years earning their

Table 2
Governmental Funding Trends: Kaken-Hi Fund Grants for Psychological Research Projects Every Fifth Year from 1957

Year	Number of research awards	Approximate total amount in yen*	Approximate amount per award in yen
1957	36	7,860,000	218,000
1962	43	12,080,000	281,000
1967	78	35,830,000	459,000
1972	49	53,780,000	1,097,000
1977	100	165,080,000	1,650,000
1982	84	170,680,000	2,103,000

*The postwar international money exchange rate was 360 yen for one U.S. dollar. Currently, it is about 240 yen for one U.S. dollar.

Source: Based on *JJP* news announcements.

doctoral degrees. Two-year terminal master's programs train applied professionals such as school psychologists.

Journals, Research Reports, and Bibliographical Lists

Shinrigaku-kenkyu [Japanese Journal of Psychology], a JPA journal which was discontinued in the confusion at the end of the war, resumed publication in 1949. It has appeared bimonthly since 1955. Other JPA journals are *Japanese Psychological Research*, a quarterly published in English since 1954, and *Shinrigaku monograf* [Psychological Monograph], published irregularly since 1965.

Psychologia: An International Journal of Psychology in the Orient, founded in 1957 and edited by the Psychologia Society, Kyoto University, is an English journal. Other English journals or research reports are *Tohoku psychologica folia*, published annually since 1933 by the Psychology Department, Tohoku University; *Hiroshima Forum for Psychology*, published annually by the Psychology Department, Hiroshima University since 1975; *Journal of Child Development*, published by the Department of Educational Psychology, Waseda University since 1965; *Primates: Journal of Primatology*, published by the Japan Monkey Center, Inuyama-shi, Aichi 484 since 1958; and *Behaviormetrika*, published by the Behaviormetric Society of Japan, National Institute of Statistics since 1974. In addition, the *Japanese Journal of Psychonomic Science*, appearing semiannually since 1982 and published by the Japanese Psychonomic Society, Keio University, includes English articles.

There are dozens of journals and periodicals put out by psychological societies and associations as well as a variety of research reports and bulletins released by psychological departments of universities and research institutes. They are usually in Japanese though they often include a table of contents and article abstracts in English.

To the author's knowledge, the following Japanese journals are covered by the *Psychological Abstracts* of the American Psychological Association:

Annals of the Japan Association for the Philosophy of Science (since 1967)

Annual Report on Mental Health, Japan (1967)

Bulletin of the Faculty of Education, University of Nagoya (1956)*

Bulletin of Tokyo Kasei Daigaku (1974)

Folia Primatologia (1963)*

Hiroshima Forum for Psychology (1975)*

Japanese Journal of Aerospace and Environmental Medicine (1967)

Japanese Journal of Child and Adolescent Psychiatry (1960)*

Japanese Journal of Criminal Psychology (1965)

Japanese Journal of Educational Psychology (1956)

Japanese Journal of Experimental Social Psychology (1972)

Japanese Journal of Psychology (1929)

Japanese Journal of Special Education (1970)

Japanese Psychological Research (1954)*

Japanese Psychological Review (1969)

Primates (1966)

Psychologia: An International Journal of Psychology in the Orient (1957)

Research Bulletin of the National Institute for Educational Research, Tokyo (1963)

Tohoku Psychologica Folia (1933)*

The asterisked journals are those covered beginning with the first volume. Japanese psychologists owe much to *Psychological Abstracts*. There is, unfortunately, no Japanese counterpart for comprehensive coverage of Japanese literature. *Igaku-chuo-zasshi* [Japana Centro Revuo Medicina], a counterpart of *Excerpta Medica of U.S.*, covers only a limited number of psychological articles.

The Psychological Research Liaison Committee of the Japan Science Council has published the *Bibliographical Index 1967*, covering psychological articles during the 1962–1966 period, *Index 1981* for the 1975–1979 period, and *Index 1983* for the 1980–1982 period. *Index 1983* lists 821 articles published in twenty-one psychological and related journals. There is no Japanese citation index.

Introductory Textbooks

Older textbooks for general psychology courses in Japan tend to emphasize sensory and perceptual processes. Recent books, however, place more emphasis on the biological and social aspects or dimensions of the field. The following table of contents of *The essentials of modern psychology* (Kaneko, 1982, in Japanese) illustrates the contemporary organization of psychological subject matter:

1. Development of modern psychology: *Historical Background of Psychology* (rationalism vs. empiricism, psychology, and positivism); *Schools of Modern Psychology* (Gestalt psychology, behaviorism, neobehaviorism, psychoanalysis, Soviet psychology)

2. Biosocial bases of man: *Physiological Bases of Psychology* (systems of neurons and internal secretions, central nervous system, and brain as a system, behavior and the brain); *Genesis and Development of Behavior and Its Modification* (ontogenesis and phylogenesis of behavior and learning); *Theories of Personality and Man and Society* (social cognition, social attitudes, group behavior)

3. Man as an information-processing system: *Sensorial and Perceptual Processes* (sensing systems, selective processing of information, interaction and integration of information, learning factors); *Control of Motion* (feedback control of motion, feedback in man-machine systems, control characteristics of sensorimotor circuits); *Cognition, Memory, and Learning; Symbolic Behavior and Thinking*

4. Psychological measurement: *Psychophysics and Scaling; Individual Differences and Test Theories*

Many introductory textbooks on psychology are now published. Over 200 such texts have been produced since 1980. Currently well over 100 are still available. Most of the books are between 200 and 300 pages in length and by multiple authors. This means that quite a number of psychologists who teach psychology are involved in writing textbooks, too. Naturally they tend to adopt their own books for the courses they teach. It is difficult to determine which books are most widely used.

MAJOR TRENDS SINCE WORLD WAR II

Demographic Trends

The first postwar meeting of the Japanese Psychological Association was held on September 22, 1946, and annual JPA conventions resumed in 1947. As Table 3 indicates, JPA membership has increased by approximately 1,000 each decade.

Table 4 shows the distribution of JPA members in terms of their primary research interests. Table 4 also presents the percentages of articles published in the *Japanese Journal of Psychology (JJP)* and *Japanese Psychological Research (JPR)* by psychologists in each division. It can be seen that, despite the comparatively large memberships of Divisions I, II, and III, the two JPA journals have been strongly biased toward experimental studies done by members of Division I. This bias is partly due to the experimental heritage of JPA, but it also results from the fact that psychologists in the nonexperimental divisions are affiliated with specialized associations which publish their own journals. Experimentalists did not have their own specialized organization until the Japanese Psychonomic Society was founded in 1982. Moreover, the slow growth of the memberships of Divisions III, IV, and V is probably due to the fact that psychologists in these areas are affiliated with associations related to their specific subfields.

Research and Theory

A review of trends in research and theory up to the early 1970s was done by Iwahara (1976) for every area, namely, experimental (perception, learning, memory, physiological, psychopharmacological), quantitative and mathematical, developmental, educational, personality, clinical, social, industrial, and criminal. Excellent reviews of developments in Japanese psychology were also written by Tanaka (1966), Tanaka and England (1972), Hidano (1980), and Miki and Hidano (1982). The latter two publications are available only in Japanese.

Table 5 demonstrates research trends as reflected by papers read at selected JPA conventions since 1951. Growing interest in physiological psychology and cognitive studies is evident as is the fact that sensation and perception have always been the main research concerns of Japanese psychologists. Develop-

Table 3

Demographic Trends of the Annual Conventions of the Japanese Psychological Association after World War II

Convention Number	Year	Number of papers read	Number in attendance	Membership (approx.)
11	1947	110	---	---
15	1951	283	460	812
20	1956	481	1299	1363
25	1961	491	1245	2103
30	1966	485	1016	2563
35	1971	313	1001	2937
40	1976	624	1445	3272
45	1981	820	2111	4058
47	1983	871	2058	4207

Source: Based on *JJP* news reports.

Table 4

Approximate Number of JPA Members in Five Research Divisions for 1970 and 1980 and the Percentages of Articles in *JJP* and *JPR* during the 1975–1979 Period Published by the Members of These Divisions

Divisions	Members		Percentages	
	1970*	1980**	*JJP***	*JPR***
Perception, Physiological, Learning and Thinking	540	1275	60	66
Developmental and Educational	550	966	16	14
Clinical and Personality, Criminal and Correctional	950	1043	12	6
Social, Industrial and Cultural	400	502	10	11
Methodology, Theoretical, Historical and General	90	77	2	3
Total	2530	3863	100	100

*Adapted from JPA, 1972.
**JJP (1980) 52, 192.

287

Table 5
Trends in Research Interests According to Number of Papers Read in Respective Research Divisions at JPA Conventions

Divisions	1951	1961	1970	1982	1983
Theory, Method, Mathematical and General	12	8	21	24	21
Physiological	14	22	31	84	85
Sensation & Perception	37	74	74	100	107
Cognition, Memory, Thinking and Language	22	48	75	176	188
Emotion, Motivation, Behavior and Instinct	23	14	29	39	40
Development	20	49	53	131	121
Personality	16	22	33	62	63
Educational, Intelligence, Evaluation, Special Education	38	43	39	45	35
Social and Cultural	23	58	59	118	83
Clinical, Abnormal, Counseling and Diagnostic	40	75	51	94	83
Criminal and Correctional	20	45	11	8	7
Industrial, Vocational and Traffic	18	33	46	34	38
TOTAL	283	491	522	915	871

Some entries are only approximate because of unavoidable arbitrariness in classification.
Source: Adapted from *JJP* news reports.

mental studies are also popular. On the other hand, interest in criminal and industrial psychology is waning.

Polygraphic instruments were first introduced into psychological laboratories early in the 1950s. From then on, physiological psychology has been steadily advancing, facilitated by the development of medical electronics and, more recently, computerized data processing. Brain surgery on experimental animals is conducted in many psychological laboratories. Psychopharmacology is gaining in importance. Because of growth in this area, the Japanese Association of Physiological Psychology and Psychophysiology was organized in 1982.

Research on sensation and perception in Japan followed the tradition first of Wundtian and later Gestalt psychology. Experimental studies on geometric illusions and figural processes have been particularly favored (Sagara & Oyama, 1957; in Appendix, see Oyama, 1960, and Noguchi, 1965). The most original contribution in this area was Obonai's psychophysiological induction theory which was largely systematized in his posthumous *Perception, learning and thinking* (Obonai, 1977, in English; for articles on the late Obonai, see Sato, 1969, and Kaneko, 1969, both in Appendix). Motokawa (1903–1971) was primarily a physiologist but his theory of retinal induction (see Ogasawara, 1958, in Appendix, for Motokawa's theory) and his *Physiology of color and pattern vision* (Motokawa, 1970, in English) had a great deal to do with the psychology of vision. The study of perceptual constancies has also been prominent with the work of Y. Akishige being most comprehensive and systematic (see Appendix for Akishige, 1968; JPA, 1979, for the late Akishige). *Tohoku psychologica folia* publishes studies of the Tohoku school such as a series on sensory deprivation. Electronics and computerization have, of course, greatly influenced perceptual research. Since the 1970s, the human being is even conceived by many psychologists as an information-processing system. Paradoxically, at the same time, European phenomenology has been attracting the attention of Japanese perceptual researchers. The Perception Psychologists Group has been meeting several times each year since 1960 and holds an annual colloquium.

Postwar memory research started in 1951 with the measurement of associative values of Japanese syllables (Umemoto, 1959, in Appendix). Contrary to the Wundtian tradition which focused on sensory and perceptual processes, some psychologists have been attracted to other processes such as memory, attention, and thinking. Their studies are stimulated by the resurgence of cognitive psychology in America. The dual system of Japanese characters, phonetic and ideographic, has provided a unique tool for the study of cerebral laterality in both perceptual and memorial information processing. Work on artificial intelligence was largely responsible for the emergence of the cognitive sciences in Japan; the Japanese Association of Cognitive Sciences, and interdisciplinary organization, was founded in 1983.

In educational psychology, the Piagetian cognitive and developmental framework has been replacing stimulus-response (S-R) paradigms. Developmental studies are more likely to be reported at conventions of the Japanese Association of Educational Psychology (JAEP), where they accounted for 20 to 40 percent of papers read in the 1970s, than at meetings of JPA. However, the criticism is sometimes made by educational psychologists themselves that many of these studies have little to do with classroom practice since they are conducted in artificial laboratory settings.

Insofar as mathematical psychology is concerned, prewar Japanese psychologists were already vigorously involved in introducing statistics into psychology. Postwar psychologists were quick to see the relevance of stochastics in the field and to use multivariate methods, factor analysis, and multidimensional scaling. The work of Tarow Indow of Keio University (now at University of California, Irvine) was particularly distinguished. Mathematical models of psychological processes such as sensation, perception, and learning have been developed. Theories concerning the analysis of categorical data have been developed and widely used in social psychology. Sensory processes involved in the quality control of industrial products have been extensively studied, and there has been much work in the area of psychometrics. A 920-page volume, *Sensory evaluation handbook* (JUSE, 1973), is acclaimed worldwide.

We see in mathematical psychology in Japan typical examples of scientific contributions which represent elaborations and extensions of existing techniques and ideas. This is also true of some experimental studies, especially in the area of perception. Although Japanese psychologists are proud of their achievements, little is known about their work outside Japan, solely because of language barriers.

Social Psychology and Other Applied Areas

Table 6 shows current trends in social psychology as evidenced by papers presented at conventions of the Japanese Society of Social Psychology (JSSP). Studies of cognitive behavior and social consciousness are increasing while there is less concern with group processes and collective behavior. A remarkable increase in research concerning language and culture and related topics is due to the emergence of interest in prosocial behavior, nonverbal communication, cross-cultural studies, and so forth.

The Japanese Group Dynamics Association, led by J. Misumi, who became a leading figure in Japan in leadership research with his performance-maintenance theory (Misumi, 1978), was the first new psychological society organized after the war. Nearly 50 percent of the articles published in *Journal of Experimental Social Psychology*, the society's journal, during the 1960–1977 period, were on leadership. Psychological problems associated with socioeconomic crises and natural disasters are, however, gaining in urgency. People are increasingly concerned with sociopolitical affairs and the nuclear threat.

The Japanese Association of Applied Psychology resumed its conventions after the war in 1949 with 114 papers being presented in that year. The association was most active in the mid–1950s with about 300 papers scheduled for each convention. But then participation and membership declined rapidly because of

Table 6
Number of Papers Read at the Conventions of the Japanese Society of Social Psychology for the 1967–1972 and 1973–1978 Periods Classified by Research Area

Research Areas	1967–1972	1973–1978
Cognition and attitudes	52	89
Group processes	40	12
Language and culture	20	54
Collective behavior	56	15
Social consciousness	60	42
Other	58	134
TOTAL	286	346

Source: Adapted from Hoshino, 1979.

the emergence of more specialized societies in educational, criminal, clinical, and other applied areas. Interest in vocational guidance and aptitude testing has remained strong throughout the postwar period. With the advent of commercial television and the spectacular economic growth of the 1950s, interest in advertising and consumer behavior emerged. Another feature of postwar industrial psychology has been its concern with social factors, human relations and adjustment, and motivation and job satisfaction. Recently there has been an increase of interest in the study of aging.

Human engineering and ergonomics were pursued in labor research institutes and the armed forces technical laboratories before the war. The research continued after the war in reorganized institutes of labor sciences and laboratories of the Self-Defense Forces. The Japan Ergonomic Research Society was organized in 1964 with Motokawa the first president. *Ningen-kogaku* [Human Engineering] has been its official journal since 1965. About 20 percent of the members of the society are psychologists. Sadao Sugiyama, a psychologist at Kwansei-gakuin University, is currently president of the International Ergonomic Society. The Japan Society of Traffic Psychology was organized in 1975.

Clinical psychology in Japan is almost entirely a postwar phenomenon even though Yuzaburo Uchida (1894–1966), known for his Uchida-Kraepelin work test, and Kan-ichi Tanaka (1882–1962) (see Nakano, 1963, in Appendix, for Tanaka), with his Tanaka-Binet Intelligence Test, were prewar pioneers in this field. Around 1950, new diagnostic intelligence tests, such as the WISC and WAIS, and personality inventories, such as the MMPI, were introduced along with projective tests. The Rorschach test was made available for use by Japanese psychologists by Kodama (1957b, in Appendix) and others. Japanese versions of the TAT and other projective instruments soon were developed. In the 1960s, training in counseling and psychotherapeutic theory and practice became part of graduate programs in clinical psychology. Rogerian theory was the most influential, but hypnotic approaches, psychodrama, existential analysis, psychoanalysis, and Jungian analysis were also investigated and utilized.

While the Japanese Association of Clinical Psychology was founded in 1964, the Japanese Society of Psychological Clinics was independently organized in 1982 with a different ideology. Behavior therapy has been represented by the Japanese Association of Behavior Psychotherapy since 1974. At present, clinical practice by psychologists has not yet achieved full social recognition and legal protection. Legislation authorizing the psychotherapeutic work of psychologists is clearly needed.

New legislation in 1949 concerning the status and treatment of juvenile delinquents created a great demand for professionals able to classify errant youths. This promoted the development of postwar criminal psychology in Japan. Societies for correctional medicine and correctional psychology were started in 1951; one of them became the Japanese Association of Criminal Psychology in 1963. Currently about 60 percent of its approximately 700 members are engaged in correctional service, and 15 percent are employed by the courts and police departments. The convention papers of this association concern both the psychological states and processes of delinquents and criminals, correctional treatment, the prognosis of particular types of criminals, ways to prevent crime, the psychology of justice, and policies toward criminals.

Postwar social changes have brought new dimensions to crime and juvenile delinquency. Whether or not to lower the age limit with regard to juvenile law is now a salient issue. Also of increasing concern are the increase in the number of crimes being committed by women and the elderly than previously and burgeoning traffic offenses.

JAPANESE PSYCHOLOGY IN THE INTERNATIONAL ARENA

Throughout a century of Japanese contact with Western psychology, international exchanges with other countries have been inexcusably one-sided. Too few of Japan's psychologists have taken part in international meetings.

The first Japanese psychologist to attend an International Congress of Psychology (ICP) was Y. Motora, who gave a presentation entitled *Idea of ego: An essay on Eastern philosophy* in Rome in 1905. In 1951, When IUPS (now IUPsyS—International Union of Psychological Science) was established, Japan was one of the original members. Koji Sato (1905–1971), one of the most active Japanese psychologists in internationalizing Japanese and Oriental psychology, the founder of *Psychologia*, and a member of the executive board of IUPS from 1960 until 1969, helped organize the Tokyo Congress, the first ICP held in the Orient; however, he died before the meeting took place.

Yoshihisa Tanaka (for information on the late Tanaka, see JPA, 1977) succeeded Sato on the executive board of IUPS and was vice-president for the 1972–1976 period. He died in Uppsala, Sweden, on his way home from the IUPS executive committee meeting in Windsor, England. Presently, Hiroshi Azuma is on the board. Owing to the efforts of these people, the Tokyo Congress Memorial Fund for International Exchange was established in 1972. This fund covers expenses for foreign scholars who are invited to take part in Japanese conventions. Most of the following foreign guest speakers at JPA conventions were, for example, supported by the fund:

W. Metzger (Münster University), *Do schools of psychology still exist?*; and H. Thomae (Bonn University), *Cognition and motivation: Modern aspects of an ancient problem* (36th convention in 1972 in Osaka)

P. Chauchard (Université de Paris à la Sorbonne), *Le mécanismes cérébraux de la volonté* (41st convention in 1977 in Tokyo)

E. T. Gendlin (University of Chicago), *Experiential therapy and focusing* (42nd convention in 1978 in Fukuoka)

B. F. Skinner (Harvard University), *Selection by consequences* (43rd convention in 1979 in Tokyo)

A. Zander (University of Chicago), *Expectancy of group achievement*; and G. B. Flores d'Arcais (Leyden University), *Perception and language* (44th convention in 1980 in Sappro)

Xu Liang Cang (Chinese Academy of Science), *Development of psychology in China* (45th convention in 1981 in Tokyo)

A. Bandura (Stanford University), *Model of causality in social learning* (46th convention in 1982 in Kyoto)

R. S. Lazarus (University of California, Berkeley), *Stress and coping in aging* (47th convention in 1983 in Tokyo)

Japanese delegates for the ICP Young Psychologists Program have been supported by the Memorial Fund. The Japan Society for the Promotion of Science, a semigovernmental organization, also supports international exchange programs for scientists including psychologists.

PSYCHOLOGISTS WITH A STRONG INTEREST IN THE HISTORY OF PSYCHOLOGY

The semicentennial history of the Japanese Psychological Association was edited by JPA under the leadership of then-president Gen-ichi Hagino and the able coeditorship of Taketoshi Takuma (Tokyo Metropolitan University). Another coeditor, Seiji Kodama (Nihon University), is currently interested in the comparison of Chinese and Japanese psychological terms used during the late nineteenth century.

Mioko Takahashi (Senshu University, Higashi-ikuta, Tama-ku, Kawasaki-shi 214), a psychologist with strong training in the philosophy of science, is now investigating Wundt and his era. M. Wertheimer's *A brief history of psychology* (Holt, Rinehart & Winston, 1970) has been translated into Japanese by Takayuki Funatsu (Kyushu University). Masaaki Yoshida (School of Science and Engineering, Chuoh University, Bunkyo-ku, Tokyo 112) has published biographical essays on renowned Western psychologists (Yoshida, 1983). Tadasu Oyama of the University of Tokyo has written a small book on the history of psychology with Takahashi and others (Oyama, et al., 1977). Junkichi Abe (Kokusai College of Commerce, Kawagoe-shi, Saitama 350) has presented at JPA conventions a series of reports on social psychology in Japan during the late nineteenth century. The late Imada's *History of psychology*, a counterpart of Boring's *History of experimental psychology*, is the most reliable Japanese book on the history of psychology currently on the market (for Imada, see Imada & Kotake, 1971, in Appendix).

REFERENCES

Fujisawa, K., & Naitoh, P. (1980). Shinkuro Iwahara: 1927–1978 (Part 1). *Perceptual and Motor Skills, 50*, 245–246.

Hidano, T. (Ed.). (1980). *Trends of modern psychology: 1946–1980*. Tokyo: Kawashima-shoten (in Japanese).

Hiroshima University, Psychology Department. (1979). *Semicentenary history of Psychology Department of Hiroshima University* (in Japanese).

Iwahara, S. (1973). Oriental psychology. In M. H. Marx & W. A. Hillix (Eds.), *Systems and theories in psychology* (2nd ed.). New York: McGraw-Hill.

Iwahara, S. (1976). Japan. In V. S. Sexton & H. Misiak (Eds.), *Psychology around the world*. Monterey, CA: Brooks/Cole.

JPA. (1964). Shiro Morinaga (1908–1964). *Japanese Psychological Research, 6*, 185.

JPA. (1972). *A guide to psychological institutions in Japan*. Japanese Psychological Association.

JPA. (1977). Necrology: Yoshihisa Tanaka (1917–1977). *Japanese Psychological Research, 19*, 204.

JPA. (1979). Necrology: Yoshiharu Akishige (1904–1979). *Japanese Psychological Research, 21*, 208.

JPA. (1979). *Psychological institutions in Japan*. Japanese Psychological Association.

JPA. (1980). *Semicentennial history of the Japanese Psychological Association* (Part 1). Tokyo: Kaneko-shobo (in Japanese).

JSSP. (1972). *Social psychology in Japan: A brief guide*. Japanese Society of Social Psychology.

JUSE. (1973). *Sensory evaluation handbook*. Tokyo: JUSE (Union of Japanese Scientists and Engineers Press) (in Japanese).

Kaneko, T. (1982). *The essentials of modern psychology*. Tokyo: Kyoiku-shuppan (in Japanese).

Marx, M. H., et al. (1980). Shinkuro Iwahara: 1923–1978 (Part 2). *Perceptual and Motor Skills, 50*, 260–270.

Miki, Y., & Hidano, T. (Ed.). (1982). *Psychology in Japan*. Tokyo: Nihon-bunka-kagaku-sha (in Japanese).

Misumi, J. (Ed.). (1978). *Social psychology in Japan*. Department of Social Psychology, Osaka University.

Motokawa, K. (1970). *Physiology of color and pattern vision*. Tokyo: Igaku-shoin.

Nihon University, Psychology Department. (1979). *Fifty years of the Psychology Department of Nihon University* (in Japanese).

Obonai, T. (1977). *Perception, learning and thinking: Psychophysiological induction theory*. Tokyo: Hokuseido-press.

Oyama, T., et al. (1977). *The progress of psychological history*. Tokyo: Yuhi-kaku (in Japanese.

Sagara, M., & Oyama, T. (1957). Experimental studies on figural after-effects in Japan. *Psychological Bulletin, 54*, 327–338.

Tanaka, Y. (1966). Status of Japanese experimental psychology. *Annual Review of Psychology, 17*, 233–272.

Tanaka, Y., & England, G. W. (1972). Psychology in Japan. *Annual Review of Psychology, 23*, 695–732.

Waseda University, Psychology Department. (1981). *Semicentennial history of the Psychology Department of Waseda University* (in Japanese).

Yoshida, M. (1983). *Episodes from the history of psychology*. Tokyo: Saiens-sha (in Japanese).

APPENDIX

Articles about Japanese psychology and psychologists which have appeared in *Psychologia* are listed below in chronological order.

Sato, K. (1957). Japanese studies on the transposition problem, *1*, 22–29.

Kodama, H. (1957). In memory of Dr. Tohru Watanabe, *1*, 63–64.

Kodama, H. (1957). Personality tests in Japan, *1*, 92–103.

Kotake, Y., & Miyake, Y. (1958). Our seventeen years of research on conditioned responses in man, *1*, 158–166.

Ogasawara, J. (1958). Motokawa's induction theory and form perception, *1*, 182–184.

Hake, H. W. (1958). Japanese experimental psychology viewed from America, *1*, 184–186.

Umemoto, T. (1959). Japanese studies in verbal learning and memory, *2*, 1–19.

Yoda, A., & Hidano, T. (1959). Development of educational psychology in Japan, *2*, 137–149.

Tachibana, K. (1959). Trends in gerontology in Japan, *2*, 150–156.

Hirota, K. (1959). Development of social psychology in Japan, *2*, 216–228.

Oyama, T. (1960). Japanese studies on the so-called geometrical optical illusions, *3*, 7–20.

Motoyoshi, R., & Iwahara, S. (1960). Japanese studies on animal behavior in the last decade, *3*, 135–148.

Sawada, A., Amano, T., & Maeda, Y. (1960). Study of acceleration phenomena in Japan, *3*, 222–233.

Kido, M. (1961). Origin of Japanese psychology and its development, *4*, 1–10.

Osaka, R. (1961). Intelligence tests in Japan, *4*, 218–234.

Oba, S. (1962). Programmed learning movement in Japan, *5*, 88–92.

Sato, K. (1963). Gestalt psychology in Japan, *6*, 7–10.

Nozawa, S., & Iritani, T. (1963). A review of Gestalt studies in Japan: Development of studies on form perception, *6*, 22–45.

Iwahara, S., & Fujita, O. (1963). Behaviorism in Japan, *6*, 59–65.

Miki, T. (1963). Measures for helping the mentally retarded in Japan, *6*, 165–170.

Nakano, S. (1963). Professor Kan-ichi Tanaka (1882–1962) and his contribution to educational measurement, *6*, 171–172.

Noguchi, K. (1965). Necrology: Shiro Morinaga (1908–1964), *8*, 120–121.

Indow, T. (1966). Professor Matsusaburo Yokoyama (1890–1966), *9*, 185–186.

Tsuru, H. (1967). Youth problems and adolescent psychology in Japan, *10*, 19–24.

Otani, S. (1967). History of parapsychology in Japan, *10*, 51–57.

Akishige, Y. (1968). Studies on the constancy problem in Japan: I & II, *11*, 3–45, 127–139.

Sato, K. (1969). Professor Torao Obonai (1899–1968), *12*, 63–64.

Kaneko, T. (1969). The late Professor Torao Obonai and his psychological works, *12*, 186–188.

Akishige, Y. (1970). In memory of the late Professor Kanae Sakuma, *13*, 161–162.

Yagi, B., & Torii, S. (1971). Celebrating the seventy-eighth birthday of Professor Sadaji Takagi, *14*, 50–51.

Umemoto, T. (1971). Progress in Japanese studies in verbal learning and memory, *14*, 77–82.

Imada, H., & Kotake, Y. (1971). Dr. Megumi Imada (1894–1970), his life and work, *14*, 112–113.

Editors of *Psychologia*. (1972). Research psychologists in Japanese universities and institutes: I, II & III, *15*, 1–14, 65–75, 191–197.

Hoshino, A. (1979). Current major trends in psychology in Japan, *22*, 1–20.

Mexico

Rolando Diaz-Loving and Adrian Medina-Liberty

FOUNDATIONS OF MEXICAN PSYCHOLOGY

For most Mexican psychologists the Aztec word "Tonalpouhqui" has no meaning. However, during the Pre-Hispanic period the Tonalpouhqui represented a central and highly influential personage who constituted the antecedent of clinical psychologists in Mexico (León-Sanchez & Patiño-Muñoz, 1984). These individuals were priests whose activities were similar to those of the modern psychotherapist; their main function was to restore the spiritual balance of the Aztecs by means of a "long talk."

Many aspects of the Aztec culture either disappeared or changed when the Spaniards conquered Mexico and imposed their own culture and religion. During the colonial period, which extended from the fifteenth to the eighteenth century, although science was marked by a narrow and scholastic tradition, there were several important contributions which influenced the later development of psychology.

In 1557, *Physica speculatio* was published in Mexico and represented the first attempt to describe and explain behavioral changes. This treatise was written by Fray Alonso de la Veracruz, who presented an Aristotelian perspective on certain psychological matters. Among other things, he advanced some interesting premises concerning the relationships between climatic changes and mental states. Fray Alonso also discussed the effects of ingesting hallucinogenic mushrooms by some Mexicans.

Another priest, Fray Bernardino de Sahagún, studied the Aztec culture from a naturalistic perspective. He investigated the everyday Aztec way of life and systematized it by making careful descriptions of Aztec beliefs and customs. His observational techniques were similar to those of contemporary anthropologists.

In 1567, the first mental hospital on the American continent was founded in Mexico City by Fray Bernardino Alvarez. The San Hipólito Hospital, as it was called, was created to care for and protect the mentally disabled.

During 1773, physiology was introduced into the classrooms and laboratories of the Faculty of Medicine at the University of Mexico. The man responsible for this innovation was the brilliant physician José Ignacio Bartolache, who made systematic observations and conducted experiments directed at discovering the organic functions of animals. According to Robles (1952), Bartolache also conducted the first study of hysteria in Mexico and probably on the entire continent. In his work, Bartolache reported some interesting findings about the differential appearance of hysterical symptoms in high and middle socioeconomic classes, particularly in "spoiled" girls. Moreover, he also described very accurately the symptoms that are presently known to be associated with psychoneurotics: anxiety, fixed ideas, headaches, crying crises, anesthesias, and functional paralysis.

In 1835, José Ramon Pacheco, a member of the Societé de Phrénologie de Paris, published in Mexico his work entitled *Exposición sumaria del sistema frenológico del Dr. Gall* [A brief exposition of the phrenological system of Dr. Gall]. This book generated many passionate debates within academic circles. In 1884, Rafael Serrano's *Psiquiatría optica* [Optic phychiatry] was published. This book is a monograph about psychiatry and offered a new perspective on psychiatric diagnosis which included psychophysical techniques.

During 1901 and 1902, two important works appeared: *Las localizaciones cerebrales y la psicología* [Brain localizations and psychology] and *Enumenración y clasificación de las formas de sensibilidad* [Enumeration and classification of sensibility forms]. Both monographs were written by Porfirio Parra, an eminent physician and philosopher who stimulated interest in psychological topics in academic institutions. Finally, in 1907, Juan N. Cordero wrote a voluminous book which appears to have been the first psychology text in Mexico: *La vida psíquica* [The psychic life] (see Diaz-Guerrero, 1976).

Probably the most important fact to be discerned from the history of psychology in Mexico up to the early 1900s is the recurring emphasis on clinical topics. This could help explain the current interest of students in the clinical area.

THE BEGINNING OF THE TWENTIETH CENTURY

Between 1910 and 1950, knowledge of psychology expanded greatly. In this period psychology grew mostly because of the efforts of three enthusiastic scientists: Dr. Ezequiel Chavez, Dr. José Meza y Gutierrez, and Dr. Enrique O. Aragón.

Dr. Chavez devoted his life to improving education and psychology in Mexico. He wrote many books and essays about psychology, among which *Ensayo de psicología de la adolescencia* [Essay on the psychology of adolescence] (1928) and *Ensayo de psicología de Sor Juana Inés de la Cruz* [Essay on the psychology of Sor Juana Inés de la Cruz] (1931) were the most significant. In 1896 he taught the first course ever offered in experimental psychology at the Escuela Preparatoria (high school). In order to teach this course, he translated E. B. Titchener's *Elements of psychology* and later used translations of the works of W. James,

J. Baldwin, and W. Wundt in his course. Dr. Chavez also invited Baldwin to lecture at the University of Mexico several times between 1909 and 1913.

Dr. Meza y Gutierrez was one of the pioneers of clinical psychology who organized the Manicomio General (General Mental Hospital). He was an excellent teacher with an extraordinary memory and keen clinical judgmental skills. Among his many works, two monographs deserve special attention: *Ficción de locura* [Fiction of madness] (1911) and *Paranoia y psicosis de obsesión* [Paranoia and obsessive psychosis] (1912).

The third eminent figure in the history of early Mexican psychology was Dr. Enrique O. Aragón. Robles (1952) has pointed out that Aragón was one of the most prolific psychological writers in Mexico. He wrote many articles in educational and medical journals, but his most outstanding work was *La psicología* [Psychology] published in 1902. He taught psychology for twenty-six years in the Faculty of Philosophy and Letters at the National University of Mexico and in 1916 founded the first psychological laboratory in Mexico modeled after Wundt's facility. He died in 1942 just when his efforts and those of his students were about to culminate in the creation of a department of psychology within the Faculty of Philosophy.

In 1945, an independent Department of Psychology in the Faculty of Philosophy and Letters was created at the National University of Mexico. In this department students could obtain a master's degree after three years of study, provided they had earned a Licenciate in Philosophy diploma. By 1956, new regulations were approved; the Department of Psychology became the School of Psychology and the Ph.D. degree was introduced. Two years later, a group of professors designed a new degree program which was approved in 1960. Under this new program, students had to study four years and write a thesis in order to obtain the degree of Licenciate in Psychology. After completing this program, students were able to work toward master's and doctoral degrees.

THE MODERN ERA

The creation, during the early 1960s, of the School of Psychology within the Faculty of Philosophy and Letters at the National University of Mexico marks the beginning of the emancipation of Mexican psychology from psychiatry and philosophy. This movement, which was accompanied by dramatic changes in teaching, research, and practice in psychology culminated in the formation in 1973 of the first independent faculty of psychology in Mexico.

A number of events interacted with and contributed to the changes observed during the decade of the 1960s. The continuous academic exchange with the departments of psychology and educational psychology of the University of Texas at Austin, in which large groups of Mexican students participated (Holtzman, Iscoe, & Neal, 1964; Holtzman, 1970), was one of the most important sources of psychological knowledge during this period. Besides those who attended the University of Texas, many young Mexican psychologists obtained doctoral degrees from the National University of Mexico and other universities in the United States, Canada, and Europe. Following their training, they demanded radical changes in the curriculum; these changes formed the basis of the current four-and-a-half-year professional psychology program. Master's and doctoral programs in clinical, experimental, and social psychology, and the experimental analysis of behavior were also established.

A second conceptual revolution of this era, based on a dogmatic Skinnerian approach, provided an alternative to the prevailing psychoanalytic perspective. Once psychology, as an area of study, became fully accepted, the behaviorist approach subsided giving way to a more eclectic orientation which included behavioral, cognitive, psychodynamic, and social-psychological approaches. In the move toward an eclectic perspective, the group of assistants and researchers associated first with the Centro de Investigación en Ciencias del Comportamiento (CICC) and later with the Instituto Nacional de Ciencias del Comportamiento y Actitud Publica A.C. (INCCAPAC) [Institute for the Behavioral Sciences and Public Opinion] were very influential.

Research during the 1960s centered primarily around Hernández-Peón and his followers in the field of neuropsychology and Diaz-Guerrero and his colleagues in the field of personality development and cross-cultural research. Hernández-Peón, who died in 1968, conducted research on sleep and dreaming, sensory-evoked potentials, wakefulness, and attention (Morgane, 1970). Diaz-Guerrero and his group, working at INCCAPAC, have been actively involved in cross-cultural research in child development (Holtzman, Diaz-Guerrero, & Swartz, 1975), styles of coping (Diaz-Guerrero & Peck, 1963; Diaz-Guerrero, 1973, 1979), and affective meaning (Diaz-Guerrero & Salas, 1975).

A third group, organized by Erich Fromm, Guillermo Dávila, Alfonso Millán, and M. Maccoby, engaged in behavioral research in rural areas (Fromm & Maccoby, 1973).

The growth of teaching and research in Mexican psychology following the creation of the Faculty of Psychology in 1973 has been dramatic. The student population has grown from 200 in 1956 to over 20,000 presently enrolled in more than forty Mexican universities. A survey of the institutions, research, and publications generated in the last decade is presented in the following sections.

PROGRAMS AND DEGREES

Once students have completed their basic education (six years in elementary school plus six years in high school), they may begin training for a professional career. At present, there are more than sixty Mexican universities that offer degrees in psychology. In Mexico, as in most of Latin America, there are three degrees offered in the field: the Licenciate (the professional degree), the M.A. degree, and the Ph.D. degree.

The Professional Degree

The professional degree program was designed to train students for professional practice. Although there are small variations among Mexican universities, the programs are similar and are designed to be completed in five years in two stages: basic training and area specialization. Basic training includes general studies in theoretical and methodological issues and takes the first six semesters (three years). During the remaining three semesters, specialization in one of the following six areas of psychology is possible: psychophysiology, experimental, industrial, clinical, educational, and social. Almost all subjects include applied work and research. Finally, the students have to present a thesis in order to obtain the degree of Licenciado en Psicología (Licenciate in Psychology).

Table 1 shows the number of students registered in each area of specialization offered by the Faculty of Psychology at the National University of Mexico during the period from 1972 through 1982. As shown in the table, the most popular area is clinical psychology followed by industrial and educational. The areas with fewer students are experimental psychology and psychophysiology. Psychologists in the latter two specialties, however, are productive researchers.

Master's and Doctoral Degrees

The master's and doctoral degrees each take at least two years of study. Both degrees require courses in theoretical subjects and methodological issues, research seminars, and a dissertation. The master's program was designed basically for the teaching of psychology, while the main objective of the doctoral program is to enable graduates to do research in their fields. At present, master's degrees are offered in the following areas: educational, psychophysiological, social, clinical, experimental, and the experimental analysis of behavior. Doctoral degrees are available only in the last four areas.

Table 2 lists some of the most important departments of psychology in Mexico and provides relevant information. The letter *D* indicates graduate work at the doctoral level, the letter *M* indicates graduate work at the master's level, and the letter *L* indicates professional training at the licenciate level. It is important to note that these data were collected in 1982 and some slight changes have occurred since then. New information and details concerning entrance requirements and contents of programs offered may be obtained by writing department chairmen.

JOURNALS

A large number of journals related to psychology have been published in Mexico. Some of them, like *Psicología Dialéctica* [Dialectical Psychology] and the *Revista Mexicana de Psicología* [Mexican Journal of Psychology] have been discontinued. According to Diaz-Guerrero (1984), this is due to the fact that

Table 1
Students Registered in Each Specialty

AREAS \ YEARS	1972	1973	1974	1975	1976	1977	1978	1979	1980	1981	1982
Clinical Psychology	316	232	335	423	551	847	895	877	854	834	820
Educational Psychology	171	199	367	394	403	472	452	389	326	210	186
Experimental Psychology			48	126	148	186	139	98	58	56	35
Psycho-physiology		6	8	19	15	24	48	51	29	24	35
Social Psychology	112	170	153	196	200	167	341	295	255	163	128
Industrial Psychology		226	302	323	499	471	465	475	465	498	470

Source: Data provided by the Planning and Evaluation Department of the Faculty of Psychology at the National University of Mexico.

Table 2
Departments of Psychology in Mexico

University and Location	Areas of Specialization	Number of Academic Staff	Degree/s Offered
Cuernavaca			
Universidad Autónoma del Edo. de Morelos	Social, Clinical Educational, Industrial	15	L.
Guadalajara			
Universidad Autónoma de Guadalajara	Social, Clinical Educational, Industrial	38	L.
Universidad de Guadalajara	Social, Clinical, Educational, Industrial	68	L.
Instituto Tecnológico de Estudios Superiores de Occidente	Social, Clinical Educational, Industrial	32	L.
Jalapa			
Universidad Veracruzana	Social, Clinical, Educational, Experimental Industrial	30	L.
Mexico			
Universidad Anahuca	Clinical, Educational, Industrial, Psycho-physiology	46	L.

303

Table 2 (*continued*)

University and Location	Areas of Specialization	Number of Academic Staff	Degree/s Offered
Universidad Autónoma Metropolitana Iztapalapa	Social	18	L.
Universidad Autónoma Metropolitana Xochimilco	Social, Educational	30	L.
Universidad Nacional Autónoma de México (UNAM)	Social, Clinical, Industrial, Educational, Experimental, Psychophysiology	550	L.,M.,D.
UNAM, Escuela Nacional de Estudios Profesionales Iztacala	Social, Clinical, Experimental, Behavior Modification, Behavioral Pharmacology	180	L.,M.
UNAM, Escuela Nacional de Estudios Profesionales Zaragoza	Social, Clinical Educational	120	L.
Universidad Femenina de Mexico	Clinical, Industrial	30	L.
Universidad Iberoamericana	Clinical, Educational, Industrial	69	L.,M.,D.
Universidad Intercontinental	Social, Clinical, Educational, Industrial	18	L.

Table 2 (*continued*)

Monterrey

Universidad Autónoma de Nuevo León	Social, Clinical, Industrial, Human Development, Analysis of Behavior	78	L.,M.
Universidad Reglomontana	General, Industrial	19	L.
Universidad de Monterrey	Social, Clinical, Educational, Industrial, Analysis of Behavior	35	L.

Cd. Obregon

Instituto Tecnológico de Sonora	Social, Clinical, Educational, Industrial	18	L.

Puebla

Universidad de las Américas	Social, Clinical, Educational, Experimental	18	L.,M.
Universidad Autónoma de Puebla	Social, Clinical, Educational, Experimental	35	L.

Querétaro, Oro.

Universidad Autónoma de Querétaro	Social, Clinical, Educational, Industrial	25	L.,M.

Table 2 (*continued*)

University and Location	Areas of Specialization	Number of Academic Staff	Degree/s Offered
Saltillo			
Universidad Autónoma de Coahuila	Social, Clinical, Educational, Industrial	22	L.
Universidad Autónoma del Noreste	General	85	L.
Tampico			
Universidad del Noroeste	Clinical, Educational, Industrial	25	L.
Toluca			
Universidad Autónoma del Edo, de México	Social, Clinical, Educational, Industrial		

Mexican journals often depend solely on the economic resources and efforts of their editors. A list of some of the most important current journals in Mexico follows.

Acta Psicológica Mexicana [Journal of the Faculty of Psychology at the National University of Mexico]. Edited by Jorge Peralta. Three volumes since 1981. Facultad de Psicología, UNAM. Ciudad Universitaria, 04510 México, D.F.

Aletheia [Journal of the Institute for Research in Clinical and Social Psychology]. Edited by Marilú Diaz-Fuentes. Three volumes since 1980.

Cuadernos de Psicoanálisis [Journal of the Mexican Psychoanalytic Association]. Edited by Francisco T. Cantú. Nine volumes since 1975.

Enseñanza e Investigación en Psicología [Journal of the National Council for Teaching and Research in Psychology]. Edited by Humberto Ponce Talancón. Nine volumes since 1975. Apartado Postal No. 19–174. México 19, D.F.

Métodos Docentes [Journal of the Faculty of Psychology at the National University of Mexico]. Edited by Jorge Peralta. Three volumes since 1979. Facultad de Psicología, UNAM. Ciudad Universitaria. 04510 México, D.F.

Psicología [Psychology]. Edited by Gabriel Barrera. Thirty-six issues since 1975.

Revista de la Asociación Latinoamericana de Psicología Social [Journal of the Latin American Association of Social Psychology]. Edited by Susan Pick. Two volumes since 1981. Bosque de Avellanos No. 156 México 10, D.F.

Revista Mexicana de Análisis de la Conducta [Journal of the Mexican Society of Analysis of Behavior]. Edited by Victor Colotla. Eight volumes since 1975. Facultad de Psicología, UNAM. Ciudad Universitaria. 04510, México, D.F.

Revista Mexicana de Psicología [Journal of the Mexican Society of Psychology]. Edited by Juan Lafarga. Two volumes since 1984. Sociedad Mexicana de Psicología, Av. Río Mixcoac 66–101 Col. del Valle 03940, México, D.F.

Revista de Psicoanálisis, Psiquiatría y Psicología [Journal of Psychoanalysis, Psychiatry, and Psychology] (Mexican Psychoanalytic Society and Mexican Institute of Psychoanalysis). Edited by Jorge Silva García. Eight volumes since 1965. Calle de Odontología No. 9. Copilco Universidad. México 21, D.F.

Revista de Psicología Social y de Personalidad [Journal of Social Psychology and Personality]. Edited by Rolando Diaz-Loving and Patricia Andrade Palos. First number July 1985. Apartado 70–342, Admon. 70, 04510, México, D.F.

PROFESSIONAL ASSOCIATIONS

In 1951, Werner Wolf (United States), Rogelio Diaz-Guerrero (Mexico), Oswaldo Robles (Mexico), Eduardo Draff (Argentina), and others founded the Sociedad Interamericana de Psicología (SIP) [Interamerican Society of Psychology]. The Mexican Psychological Association was founded simultaneously as a branch of SIP. The first president was Manuel Falcón-Guerrero, who was followed by Guillermo Dávila, Rafael Nuñez, Rogelio Diaz-Guerrero, Angel San Román, and Mario Cicero, the current president.

There are at present many psychological associations in Mexico. Among the most important are:

Asociación Latinoamericana de Psicología Social [Latin American Association of Social Psychology], President: Dr. Hector Manuel Capello, Facultad de Psicología, Departamento de Psicología Social Posgrado, Universidad Nacional Autónoma de México, México, D.F.

Asociación Mexicana de Psicología Social [Mexican Social Psychology Society], President: Dr. Rogelio Diaz-Guerrero, Apartado 70–342 Admon. 70, 04510 México, D.F.

Consejo Nacional para la Enseñanza e Investigación en Psicología [National Council for Teaching and Research in Psychology], Dr. Juan Lafarga, Departamento de Psicología, Universidad Iberoamericana, México, D.F.

INCCAPAC, President: Dr. Rogelio Diaz-Guerrero, Retorno Cerro de Acapulco #18. Col. Oxtopulco-Universidad, 04310 México, D.F.

Instituto Mexicano de Psiquiatría [Mexican Institute of Psychiatry], Calz. México-Xochimilco No. 101, Col. San Lorenzo Huipulco, Delegación Tlalpan, 14370 México, D.F.

Sociedad Mexicana de Análisis de la Conducta [Mexican Society for the Analysis of Behavior], Dr. Arturo Bousas, Fernández Leal No. 55 Altos, Coyoacán, México 20, D.F.

Sociedad Mexicana de Psicología [Mexican Society of Psychology], Director: Dr. Mario Cicero, Río Mixcoac No. 66–101, Colonia del Valle, México, D.F.

RESEARCH AND APPLIED PSYCHOLOGY

In this section, the main areas of psychological research and application of Mexican psychology are presented. An attempt has been made by reviewing the literature to present a representative overview of what has been achieved in each area.

The Experimental Analysis of Behavior

Extensive experimental analyses of behavior have been conducted. A. Bouzas (1976: Bouzas & Baum, 1976) has investigated problems of behavioral contrast, while J. C. Todorov (1977; Todorov & Gragas de Souza, 1978) has done exhaustive research on the effects on response patterns of using concurrent reinforcement schedules. López and Ribes (1974) studied the relationships between contingency of reinforcement and level of conceptualization. They applied Skinner's model to conceptual behavior in an experiment that employed a variable ratio reinforcement schedule with a group of school children, in order to determine whether or not levels of functional and concrete conceptual responses could be changed. The results obtained confirmed this hypothesis. Ribes (1977) investigated the relationships among behavior theory, experimental research, and behavior modification techniques; he has also discussed the status of private experience in a science of behavior (1982). Alcaraz (1980), in his book on the synthetic function of language, raises some interesting issues about psychohphysiology, operant conditioning, and language. Bruner (1981, 1982) has focused his attention on the phenomena of autoshaping and automaintenance. In the field of behavioral pharmacology, Colotla has conducted research concerning the effects of amphetamines on schedule-induced drinking in rats (1977) and shed new light on the properties of polydipsia (Colotla & Beaton, 1971; Colotla, 1981). There are many others such as E. Rayek, V. García, F. Cabrer, and C. Santoyo who have contributed to the experimental analysis of behavior.

General Experimental Psychology

Research concerning general experimental psychology in Mexico is so broad that it is impossible to give a reasonable summary. Table 3 lists the most frequently studied topics and provides estimates of the numbers of investigations conducted. The data for this table were collected between 1978 and 1982 by the Department of General Experimental Psychology of the Faculty of Psychology at the National University of Mexico.

For those who are interested in contacting researchers, a brief account of the main areas of interest of some experimentally oriented psychologists at the Facultad de Psicología, Universidad Nacional Autónoma de México, follows:

Cognitive Psychology: Javier Aguilar, Cecilia Mora, Carolina Díaz, Joaquín Figueroa, Victor Solís, Miguel Kasén, Serafín Mercado, and Naum Martinez.

Therapy and Personality: Benjamín Rodriguez, Juan José Sanchez Sosa, Hector Ayala, Graciela Rodriguez de Arizmendi, and Rogelio Diaz-Guerrero.

Psychophysiology of Dreams and Biofeedback: María Corci-Cabrera, Jacobo Grimberg, Xochitl Gallegos, and Victor Alcaraz.

Animal Behavior and Reinforcement Programs: Florente López, Arturo Bouzas, Carlos Bruner, Carlos Santoyo, F. Cabrer, and Jorge Martinez-Stack.

Ecological Psychology: G. Alvarez, B. Dominguez, Ma. Enedina Montero, Serafín Mercado, Carlos Santoyo, and Javier Urbina.

Arithemetic Behavior: Vicente García and Emilio Ribes.

Behavior Modification

From 1960 to 1980 a firm tradition of behavior modification applications and research emerged and consolidated as a result of the work of F. López-Rodriguez, J. Molina, H. Ayala, B. Dominguez, G. Fernandez, E. Ribes, and V. García among others.

In 1967, the Eleventh Interamerican Congress of Psychology took place in Mexico. It was at this meeting that the first study of behavior modification in Mexico, and perhaps in all of Latin America, was presented. In this study, Jorge Molina and Hector Ayala applied behavioral principles to rehabilitate learning-

Table 3
Research Articles by Area

Research Topic	1978	1979	1980	1981	1982	Total
Therapy	9	1		1	1	12
Personality	2				1	3
Disabled Children	2	4	4	4	2	16
Addictive Behavior	3				2	5
Education	2	4	5	5	2	18
Reading	9	1	1		10	21
Cognition	10	5	6	6	10	37
Methodology	9	12	8	12	6	47
Reinforcement Programs	4	6	2	4	4	20
Animal Behavior	3	4	3	2	2	14
Computation				3	2	5
Ecological Psychology	2	2		5	3	12
Behavioral Pharmacology		1	1	2	1	5
Psychophysiology of Dreams	4	4	4	3	3	18
Biofeedback	4	1	1	1	1	8
Human Development		1		2	1	4
Arithmetic Behavior	1	1	1			3
TOTAL	64	47	36	50	51	248

disabled children. Hector Ayala and his colleagues have since been working extensively on applications of behavioral principles to problems such as drug addiction and delinquency. In August of the same year (1967), Florente López created the Center for Operant Studies at the Universidad Veracruzana, the first facility of its kind in Mexico. This center was designed to study and train students in the area of special education.

Dominguez in 1982 published a book on ecological psychology, concerned with behavior analysis and modification in custodial institutions, which is a synthesis of work done over ten years. Emilio Ribes has worked vigorously to disseminate behavior modification techniques; much of this research is reported by Keller and Ribes (1974) and Bijou and Ribes (1972). Ribes (1976) has also published a book on the applications of behavioral techniques to learning-disabled children. Additional information about behavior modification research conducted in Mexico can be found in Pablo Speller's book *Análisis de la conducta* [Behavioral analysis] (1978).

Educational Psychology

As is the case with experimental psychology, the research conducted in the educational area is so broad that it is almost impossible to present a fair review. Therefore, only a sample of highlights and contributors is presented.

A group of young psychologists from the National University of Mexico has been studying the way practica are organized at the professional level. Training in the model they have derived is organized into four levels. The first two are devoted to psychological approaches to the study of basic processes (for example, motivation, perception, and learning) combined with different orientations (for example, behavioral, Piagetian, or human information processing.) The last two levels deal with phenomena that result from human interactions such as group behavior, attitudes, and communication. At all four levels, students are gradually introduced to theoretical, methodological, and technical matters. The foundations for this model can be found in López (1978) and Medina-Liberty and López (1981); information concerning its evaluation is presented by Santoyo and Cedeño (1981) and Cedeño and Ruiz (1982).

Solano-Flores (1983) has recently proposed in his book *Principles of educational structural analysis, methodology, and techniques for education* a set of reasoning techniques and algorithms to deal with various educational issues by means of a methodology based on graph theory and linear and Boolean algebra. Apparently, this procedure offers the advantage of formalizing many educational problems in such a way that it becomes possible to deal with the use of computers and mathematics.

Javier Aguilar (1982) has studied the relationship between cognitive theory and educational processes, especially those concerned with reading comprehension. José Huerta has dedicated his efforts to the study of the logical organization of learning experiences (1977) and has also dealt with the organization of educational objectives and goals (1983). Ely Rayek, who has been a consistent researcher in education (Rayek & Ribes, 1977), is presently editing the "Sesame Street" children's television program in Mexico.

Other psychologists who have been working in this field are Fernando García, Margarita Castañeda, Antonio Gago, Juan Lafarga, Ezequiel Nieto, Ma. Teresa Lartigue, Sylvia Rojas, Frida Diaz, and Ma. de Lourdes Lule among many others.

Psychophysiology

Undoubtedly, the leader in the field of psychophysiology in Mexico was Raúl Hernández-Peón (1924–1968). According to Morgane (1970), Hernández-Peón "was generally recognized as the foremost investigator in the neurological sciences in Mexico and one of the leading world investigators in the field of neurophysiological mechanisms of sleep" (p. 379).

His research in psychophysiology, reported in more than 120 articles, deals with many topics including habituation, attention, facilitation, and sleep mechanisms. After studying the phenomenon of habituation and dishabituation (1956), he reported some interesting characteristics of temporary inhibitions by showing that evoked responses to click stimuli disappear during the presentation of visual or olfactory stimuli. In 1961, Hernández-Peón postulated that when an animal attends to a given stimulus, input to other sensory modalities is filtered out or attenuated by peripheral gating mechanisms in such a way that the animal can remain maximally sensitive to input from the attention-evoking stimulus. Hernández-Peón's work stimulated many investigators to continue doing research in this field. Among his most eminent students and colleagues are A. Fernández-Guardiola, H. Brust, René Druker-Colin, and J. Antonio Rojas.

Currently, psychophysiological research in Mexico emphasizes several problems. Corsí-Cabrera and his colleagues (1975) have found that caudate nucleus lesions selectively increase paradoxial sleep episodes in the rat; they have also studied the effect of light deprivation on sleep in the rat (Corsí-Cabrera, et al., 1982). Ostrosky and his colleagues (in press) compared the cognitive strategies used by normal and dyslexic children in exploratory and verbal tasks; they found that learning-disabled children require more time, commit more mistakes, and make inefficient movements. Valencia and Velázquez (1982) explored the effect of reinforcement programs on the phenomenon of superreactivity and demonstrated that the effect of drugs on a given variable, such as weight, could be modified dramatically. They also discovered that this behavioral intervention could modify qualitatively the effect of amphetamines and similar drugs on urinal excretion. Other investigators presently engaged in psychophysiological research are H. Lara-Tapia, J. Palacios, D. Rodriguez, and C. Contreras.

History and Philosophy of Psychology

There is a growing body of research on the roots and epistemological foundations of psychology in Mexico. This area of study can be traced to the work of Oswaldo Robles who in 1952 conducted the first systematic study on the history of Mexican psychology. In recent years, many other psychologists have been searching for the roots of Mexican psychology (Ribes, 1968, 1979; Colotla & Gallegos, 1978; Gallegos, 1980; Diaz-Guerrero, 1976, 1984; Alvarez & Ramirez, 1979).

During the early 1970s, psychologists from the National University of Mexico assembled a group which adopted a critical perspective toward the history and philosophy of psychology. For these individuals, the development of psychology is not only based on technical and methodological improvements but requires a redefinition of the field's foundations. The members of this group have been working on a variety of topics: R. León-Sanchez and G. Patiño-Muñoz (1984), P. Valderrama and F. Rivero del Pozo (1983), and Alvarez and coworkers (1979, 1981) concentrate on historical studies; J. Molina (1980) has analyzed the relationships among education, psychology, and ideology; Medina-Liberty has studied methodological issues (1978, 1981a) and some problems related to the construction of objective psychological knowledge (1981b, 1984); Pérez-Cota (1981) has discussed social influences on the selection of psychological theories; and Corres (1983) has conducted an investigation of the scientific policies underlying Mexican research during the 1970s. Finally, Z. Monroy Nase has studied the influence of rationalism and empiricism on the makeup of scientific psychology (1983). Other colleagues such as Carolina Diaz and Cecilia Mora have been working intensively on topics such as cognition, subjectivity, and epistemology.

Clinical Psychology

Most of the research in clinical psychology has emphasized different therapeutic orientations currently prevalent in Mexico. Within a client-centered conception of therapy, Lafarga (1976, 1978a, 1978b) has studied the development and growth of human potential. From an encounter-group position, Mouret (1976) and Velasco (1978) have evaluated the changes produced by encounters. Reviews and discussions of the social impact and uses of behavioral therapy can be found in the papers of Colotla and Ribes (1981) and Rayek and Ribes (1977). Cueli and his colleagues (Cueli & Biro, 1975; Cueli, 1976; Lartigue, 1976) have developed a psychoanalytic model of community psychology and are in the process of evaluating it in Mexico City. Employing a more general approach, Nuñez (1968), with the help of Hathaway, introduced and psychometrically adapted the MMPI to a Mexican population.

Lara-Tapia and Velez (1975) and Medina-Mora and colleagues (1981) have

done research on psychopharmacology, mental health, drug addiction, and alcoholism. Diaz-Guerrero (Diaz-Guerrero, Lichtszajn, & Reyes-Lagunes, 1979)
found that the subjective meaning of "insults to the mother" was strongly related
to twenty clinically critical concepts. More recently, Diaz-Guerrero (1982a) has
demonstrated how the sources of anxiety for given populations in certain cultures
can be identified using a correlational method involving economic data. Special
mention should be given to Santiago Ramírez (1984) who has incorporated a
historical and cultural perspective within psychoanalytic theory. Other researchers in the clinical area are Victor Castillo-Vales, Blanca Chavez, Raymundo
Macías, Bertha Fortes, Abraham Fortes, José Lichtszajn, and Julian MacGregor.

Social and Personality Psychology

The traditional diversity of phenomena and factors included in the definition
of social and personality psychology is even greater than usual in Mexico. Here
the field extends from a pure sociological and structural position to a functional
social-experimental orientation. Topics of study include physical and mental
health, interpersonal relationships, attitudes, opinions, ideologies, politics, demographic variables, migration, nutrition, organization, and labor; research
methods include participant-observation, unobtrusive measures, interviews,
questionnaires, surveys, and physiological measures. Topics and research strategies depend also on the theoretical orientation assumed which may be Freudian,
Skinnerian, even Marxist, or derived from field theory, communication theories,
and so forth.

Due to the importance of solving a growing number of social problems, there
is much interest in conducting applied research. For example, because of the
population growth in Mexico, several researchers (Pick de Weiss, 1978, 1980;
Diaz-Guerrero & Morales, 1976, 1977; Diaz-Guerrero, et al., 1977) have been
engaged in exploring the social, demographic, and personality factors conducive
to family planning. More recently, Covarrubias (1981) applied principles from
Bandura's social learning theory to create and later evaluate the impact of a
television soap opera designed to change attitudes toward family planning in
rural areas.

An interdisciplinary group has been working for several years in the mountains
of Puebla, Mexico, with Indian communities (Almeida, 1982). Several of Almeida's students have also been engaged in participant-observer studies and
action research in other rural areas. Sanguineti (1984), for example, has helped
communities in Michcacán, Mexico, preserve their heritage.

Dominguez (Dominguez, 1974; Dominguez & García, 1979) and Nadelsticher
(Del Pont & Nadelsticher, 1982; Cosacov, Gorenec, & Nadelsticher, 1984), who
introduced criminological psychology into Mexico, have been evaluating the
Mexican penal system. Flores and Rivera (1984), on the other hand, have studied
the stereotype of the Mexican politician.

A growing number of psychologists have become interested in the psychology of women. A program in this area has, in fact, recently been established at the Faculty of Psychology of the National University of Mexico under the direction of Bustos and the guidance of Sanchez-Bedolla. Some of the interest in the psychology of women was generated by cross-cultural research on women's sex-role behavior and its correlates, as well as the work concerned with the quality of health services offered to women in Mexico (Rodríguez de Arizmendi, 1980). Other investigators have studied the influence of family variables on women's work satisfaction (Ito Sugiyama, 1984), psychosocial characteristics of women working in paid jobs (Campos, García, & Bedolla, 1984), and problems of Mexican-American working couples (Hernández-Holtzman, 1984). The Spence and Helmreich Personal Attribute Questionnaire, which was psychometrically adapted to a Mexican population and measures masculininty and femininity traits, has been widely used for studies in this area (Diaz-Loving, Diaz-Guerrero, Helmreich, & Spence, 1981).

Several personality inventories have been developed in recent years. The most extensively used instrument was constructed by Diaz-Guerrero (1973, 1976, 1977) who created a series of scales to measure the degree of flexibility-rigidity to which sociocultural norms are adhered. The diverse factorial dimensions of the historic sociocultural premises (HSCPs) of this instrument measure, among other things, machismo, affiliative obedience, abnegation, fear of authority, and family status. Based on the realization that there are certain sociocultural premises that dictate the strategies Mexicans use to cope with problems (Diaz-Guerrero, 1976), a new instrument, the "Filosofía de Vida," was designed (Diaz-Guerrero, 1973, 1976, 1977). In a U.S.–Mexican transcultural study using this scale (Diaz-Guerrero, 1982b) it was found that Mexicans prefer a "self-modifying" coping style, while American children preferred an "other-modifying" style.

Self-esteem personality inventories have also proliferated. In the early 1980s Gilda Gomez and Reidel de Aguilar proposed two different measures, while La Rosa is currently refining a multidimensional self-esteem inventory.

Choynowski (1977, 1978), who has systematically worked on aggression in Mexican adolescents, developed an excellent multidimensional measure of this tendency. He translated this instrument into English in order to work with Eysenck on a cross-cultural program of aggression research.

Diaz-Loving and Andrade-Palos (1984) have constructed a locus of control scale for children that incorporates a second form of internal control not contemplated by Rotter (1966). These researchers found that children believe they can modify their environment indirectly through affiliative relations. More recently, Andrade-Palos (1984) found a strong relationship between locus of control and children's perceptions of their parents' child-rearing style.

Diaz-Loving also initiated an ongoing research program related to empathy and prosocial behavior (Archer, et al., 1981; Diaz-Loving, Earle, & Archer, 1981; Nadelsticher, Diaz-Loving, & Nina, 1983; Diaz-Loving, 1984). Diaz-Loving is also engaged in self-disclosure research within Mexican culture (Diaz-Loving & Nina-Estrella, 1982; Diaz-Loving & González Varela, 1984). Finally,

Reyes-Lagunes (1982) and Capello (1975) pioneered research on attitude scale construction in Mexico, while Calleja (1984) has introduced research on personal and vital space.

REFERENCES

Aguilar, J. (1982). El enfoque cognoscitivo contemporáneo: Alcances y perspectivas [Contemporary cognitive focus: Pursuits and perspectives]. *Enseñanza e Investigación en Psicología*, *8*, 171–187.

Alcaraz, V. M. (1980). *La función de síntesis del lenguaje* [The synthesis function of language]. México: Trillas.

Alcaraz, V. M., Castro, V. I., De la Cruz, S., & Del Valle, G. (1981). Conditioning and recovery of functions lost by brain damage. *Neuroscience and Behavioral Reviews*, *5*, 371–383.

Almeida, E. (1982). Investigación participativa en San Miguel Tzinacapan [Participative research in San Miguel Tzinacapan]. *Memorias del encuentro sobre investigación participativa en el medio rural*. Morelia, Mich.

Alvarez, G., & Molina, J. (Eds). (1981). *Psicología e Historia* [History and psychology]. México: UNAM.

Alvarez, G., & Ramírez, M. (1979). En busca del tiempo perdido [In search of the lost period]. *Enseñanza e Investigación en Psicología*, *5*, 386–391.

Andrade-Palos, P. (1984). Influencia de los padres en el locus de control de los hijos [Parental influence on locus of control of their children]. In *Proc. of 23rd International Congress of Psychology*, Acapulco, México.

Archer, R., Diaz-Loving, R., Grollwitzer, P., Davis, M., & Foushee, C. (1981). The role of dispositional empathy and social evaluation in the empathic mediation of helping. *Journal of Personality and Social Psychology*, *40*, 786–796.

Ayala, H., Chism, S. K., Cardenas, G., Rodríguez, M., Cervantes, L., & Caballero, P. (1982). Una alternativa al tratamiento y rehabilitación de enfermos mentales crónicos [An alternative to the treatment and rehabilitation of chronic mental patients]. *Salud Mental*, *5*, 87–93.

Ayala, H., & Molina, J. (1967). Modificación de la conducta de auto-estimulación en niños con retardo en el desarrollo. [Behavior modification of the self-confidence of retarded children]. Paper presented at the Eleventh Interamerican Congress of Psychology, Mexico City.

Ayala, H., Quiroga, H., & Mata, A. (1981). La familia enseñante: Evaluación del modelo en México, en términos de reincidencia en su applicacion a una muestra de niños inhaladores de solventes industriales. [The teaching family: Evaluation of the Mexican model in terms of reoccurrence in its application to a sample of children who have inhaled industrial solvents]. *Salud Mental*, *4*, 4–15.

Bandura, A., & Ribes, E. (1977). *Modificación de conducta, análisis de la agresión y la delincuencia* [Behavior modification and analysis of aggression and delinquency]. México: Trillas.

Bijou, S., & Ribes, E. (1972). *Modificación de conducta: Problemas y extensiones* [Behavior modification: Problems and extensions]. México: Trillas.

Bouzas, A. (1976). Contraste conductual con señales remotas [Behavioral contrast with remote signals]. *Revista Mexicana de Análisis de la Conducta*, *2* (2), 149–164.

Bouzas, A., & Baum, W. H. (1976). Behavioral contrast of time allocation. *Journal of Experimental Analysis of Behavior, 25*, 179–184.

Bruner, C. (1981). The effect of cycle length, interstimulus interval and probability of reinforcement in autoshaping. *Revista Mexicana de Análisis de la Conducta, 7*, 149–158.

Bruner, C. (1982). The effect of varying the stimulus probability in "autoshaping/automaintenance." *Revista Mexicana de Análisis de la Conducta, 8*, 47–58.

Cabrer, F. (Coord.). (1983). Una década en la psicología experimental [A decade of experimental psychology]. In F. García and J. Molina (Eds.), *Una década de la Facultad de Psicología, 1973–1983*. México: UNAM.

Calleja, B. N. (1984). *Medición e invasión de espacio personal en ambientes naturales* [Measurement and the invasion of personal space in natural environments]. Unpublished master's thesis, Universidad Nacional Autónoma de México.

Campos, M., García, B., & Bedolla, P. (1984). La mujer trabajadora: Dos aspectos psicológicos vinculados a su situación laboral [The working woman: Two aspects related to the place of work]. In *Proc. of 23rd International Congress of Psychology*, Acapulco, México.

Capello, H. M. (1975). Tensión internacional como una función de la reducción en comunicación [International tension as a function of reduced communication]. In G. Marin (Ed.), *La psicología social en Latinoamérica*. México: Trillas.

Cedeño Aguirre, M. L., & Ruiz Primo, A. (1982). *Una estrategia para evaluar habilidades metodológico-conceptuales* [A strategy to evaluate conceptual methodological skills]. Professional dissertation. Facultad de Psicología, UNAM.

Choynowski, M. (1977). Estudio de la agresividad en adolecentes mexicanos [The study of aggression in Mexican adolescents]. *Enseñanza e Investigación en Psicología, III*, 2.

Choynowski, M. (1978). Estudio de la agresividad en adolecentes mexicanos (II) [The study of aggression in Mexican adolescents II]. *Enseñanza e investigación en Psicología, IV*, 1 (7).

Colotla, V. (1977). Effects of amphetamine on schedule induced drink duration in rats. *Revista Mexicana de Análisis de la Conducta, 3* (1), 29–38.

Colotla, V. (1981). Adjunctive polydipsia as a model of alcoholism. *Neuroscience and Biobehavioral Reviews, 5*, 335–342.

Colotla, V., & Beaton, J. M. (1971). Concurrent palatability-induced and schedule-induced polydipsia in rats. *Psychological Record, 21*, 145–150.

Colotla, V., & Gallegos, X. (1978). La psicología en México [Psychology in Mexico]. In R. Ardila (Ed.), *La profesión del psicólogo*. México: Trillas.

Colotla, V., & Ribes, E. (1981). Behavior analysis in Latin America. *Spanish Language Psychology, 1*, 121–136.

Corres, P. (1983). *Politique scientifique et recherche sociologique au Mexique dendant les années 70's*. Paris, France: Université de Paris.

Corsi-Cabrera, M., Blazeuz, N., Galarraga, E., Signoret, L., & Valle, P. (1982). Effect of light deprivation on sleep in the rat. *Physiology and Behavior, 28*, 437–440.

Corsi-Cabrera, M., Grinberg, Z. J., & Ardity, L. S. (1975). Caudate nucleus lesion selectively increases paradoxical sleep episodes in the rat. *Physiology and Behavior, 14*, 7–11.

Cosacov, G., Gorenec, K., & Nadelsticher, M. A. (1984). *Duración del proceso penal en México* [Duration of the penal process in Mexico]. México: INACIPE.

Covarrubias, A. C. (1981). Educación no formal a través de la television [Informal education through television]. *Revista de la Asociación Latinoamericana de Psicología Social, 1* (1), 39–56.

Cueli, J. (1976). Psicocomunidad [Psyco-community]. *Enseñanza e Investigación en Psicología, 2* (2), 78–86.

Cueli, J., & Biro, C. (1975). *Psicocomunidad* [Psycho-community]. Englewood Cliffs: N.J.: Prentice-Hall International.

Del Pont, M., & Nadelsticher, M. A. (1982). *Delitos de cuello blanco y reacción social* [White-collar crime and social reactions]. México: INACIPE.

Diaz-Guerrero, R. (1973). Interpreting coping styles across nations from sex and social class differences. *Journal Internationale Psychologíe, 8,* 193–203.

Diaz-Guerrero, R. (1974). El psicólogo mexicano ayer, hoy y mañana [The Mexican psychologist yesterday, today, and tomorrow]. In L. Lara Tapia (Ed.), *Memorias del Primer Congreso Mexicana de psicología.* México: Imprenta Univ. U.N.A.M.

Diaz-Guerrero, R. (1976). Mexico. In V. Sexton & H. Misiak (Eds.), *Psychology around the world* (pp. 280–292). Monterey, CA: Brooks/Cole.

Diaz-Guerrero, R. (1977). A Mexican psychology. *American Psychologist, 32* (11), 934–944.

Diaz-Guerrero, R. (1979). The development of coping styles in humans. *Development, 22,* 320–331.

Diaz-Guerrero, R. (1982). Fuentes de ansiedad en la cultura mexicana [Sources of anxiety in Mexican culture]. *Enseñanza e Investigación en Psicología, 8* (1), 65–75. (a)

Diaz-Guerrero, R. (1982). *Psicología del Mexicano* [Psychology of the Mexican]. México: Trillas. (b)

Diaz-Guerrero, R. (1984). Contemporary psychology in Mexico. *Annual Review of Psychology, 35,* 83–112.

Diaz-Guerrero, R., Kye Choon, A., Subhas, C., Davidson, A., Dubey, D. C., & Mehryar, A. (1977). *Acceptability of new antifertility methods for men: Highlighting results for Mexico.* México: INCCAPAC.

Diaz-Guerrero, R., Lichtszajn, J. L., & Reyes-Lagunes, I. (1979). Alienación de la madres, psicopatología y la práctica clínica en México [The alienation of mothers, psychopathology, and clinical practice in Mexico]. *Hispanic Journal of Behavior Sciences, 1* (2), 117–133.

Diaz-Guerrero, R., & Morales, M. L. (1976). La paternidad responsable y las actitudes hacia la procreación [Paternal responsibility and attitudes toward procreation]. *Neurology Neurocir. Psiquiatry 17* (2), 103–114.

Diaz-Guerrero, R., & Morales, M. L. (1977). *La contribución de INCCAPAC respecto al problema de la planificación familiar* [The contribution of INCCAPAC with respect to the family-planning problem]. México: Ediciones INCCAPAC.

Diaz-Guerrero, R., & Peck, R. F. (1963). Respecto y posición social en dos culturas [Relations and social positions in two cultures]. In *Séptimo Congreso Interamericano de Psicología* (Ed. by the Interamerican Society of Psychology). Mexico City.

Diaz-Guerrero, R., & Salas, M. (1975). *El diferencial semántico del idioma español* [The semantic differential of the Spanish language]. México: Trillas.

Diaz-Loving, R. (1984). The effects of mood and nature of appeal on helping: A need for control explanation. In *Proc. of 23rd International Congress of Psychology,* Acapulco, México.

Diaz-Loving, R., & Andrade-Palos, P. (1984). Una escala de locus de control para niños [Locus of control scale for children]. *Revista Interamericana de Psicología, 18* (1–2), 21–33.

Diaz-Loving. R., Diaz-Guerrero, R., Helmreich, R. L., & Spence, J. T. (1981). Comparación transcultural y análisis psicometrico de una medida de rasgos masculinos (instrumentales) y femeninos (expresivos) [Transcultural psychometric analysis of facial expressions in males (instrumental) and females (expressive)]. *Revista de la Asociación Latinoamericana de Psicología Social, 1* (1), 3–38.

Diaz-Loving, R., Earle, W., & Archer, R. L. (1981). *Empathy and morality as precursors of altruism.* Unpublished manuscript. University of Texas.

Diaz-Loving, R., & González Varela, M. (1984). Explaining self-disclosure sex differences: If you are expressive your sex is not important. In *Proc. of 23rd International Congress of Psychology*, Acapulco, México.

Diaz-Loving, R., & Nina-Estrella, R. (1982). Factores que influyen en la reciprocidad de autodivulgación [Factors influencing reciprocity in self-revelation]. *Revista de la Asociación Latinoamericana de Psicología, 2* (2), 91–110.

Domínguez, B. (1974). Contingencias aplicables al control de grupos institucionalizados [Contingencies applicable to institutionalized control groups]. In Ardila, R. (Ed.), *El análisis experimental del comportamiento: La contribución Latinoamericana.* México: Trillas.

Domínguez, B. (1982). *Psicología ecológica, análisis y modificación de la conducta humana en instituciones de custodia* (Ecological psychology: Analysis and behavior modification in custodial institutions]. México: UNAM.

Domínguez, B., & García, V. M. (1979). Ambientes educativos en instituciones de custodia [Educational environments and custodial institutions]. *Enseñanza e Investigación en Psicología, 5* (1), 424–436.

Flores, M. M., & Rivera, S. (1984). Estereotipo del político mexicano [The stereotype of the Mexican politician]. In *Proc. of 23rd International Congress Psychology*, Acapulco, México.

Fromm, E., & Maccoby, M. (1973). *Sociopsicoanálisis del campesino mexicano* [Sociopsychoanalysis of the Mexican peasant]. México: Fondo de Cultura Económica.

Gallegos, X. (1980). James M. Baldwin's visits to Mexico. *American Psychologist, 35*, 772–773.

García, V., & Rayek, E. (1978). Análisis experimental de la conducta aritmética: Componentes de dos clases de respuestas en problemas aritméticos de suma [Experimental analysis of arithmetic behavior: Components of two types of answers to arithmetic problems]. *Revista Mexicana de Análisis de la Conducta, 4*, 41–58.

Grinberg-Zylberbaum, J. (1980). Correlatos electrofisiológicos de la experiencia subjetiva [Electrophysiological correlates of subjective experience]. *Enseñanza e Investigación en Psicología, 6*, 44–52.

Grinberg-Zylberbaum, J., & John, E. R. (1981). Evoked potentials and concept formation in man. *Physiology and Behavior, 27*, 749–751.

Hernández-Holtzman, E. (1984). Relationship between social network support and psychological functioning among dual working Mexican American parents. In *Proc. of 23rd International Congress of Psychology*, Acapulco, México.

Hernández-Peón, R. (1961). Reticular mechanisms of sensory control. In Walter A. Rosenblith (Ed.), *Sensory communication* (pp. 497–520). New York: MIT Press/Wiley.

Hernández-Peón, R., Scherrer, H., & Jouvet, M. (1956). Modification of electric activity in cochlear nucleus during "attention" in unanesthetized cats. *Science, 126*, 331–332.

Holtzman, W. H. (1970). Los seminarios internacionales de psicología en Texas: Un experimento en intercambio transcultural en psicología [International seminars in psychology in Texas: An experiment in transcultural exchange in psychology]. *Revista Interamericana de Psicología, 4* (3–4), 279–282.

Holtzman, W. H., Diaz-Guerrero, R., & Swartz, J. D. (1975). *Personality development in two cultures.* Austin: University of Texas Press.

Holtzman, W. H., Iscoe, I., & Neal, J. W. (1964). *Final report, Mexican psychology student seminar*, January 5–25. Austin: University of Texas.

Huerta, J. (1977). *Organización lógica de las experiencias del aprendizaje* [The logical organization of learning experiences]. México: Trillas.

Huerta, J. (1983). *Fines, metas y objetivos* [Purposes, goals, and objectives]. México: Trillas.

Ito Sugiyama, M. E. (1984). Influencia de variables familiares en la satisfacción de mujeres profesionales con su trabajo [The influence of known variables in the job satisfaction of professional women]. In *Proc. of 23rd International Congress of Psychology*, Acapulco, México.

Keller, F. S., & Ribes, E. (1974). *Behavior modification applications to education.* New York: Academic Press.

Lafarga, J. (1976). Experiencia y crecimiento personal en la psicoterapia y en la educación [Experience and personal development in psychotherapy and education]. *Enseñanza e Investigación en Psicología, 2* (1), 29–38.

Lafarga, J. (1978). *Desarrollo del potencial humano* [Development of human potential] (Vol. 1). México: Trillas. (a)

Lafarga, J. (1978). El sistema centrado en la persona en psicoterapia y educación [The central system in the person in psychotherapy and education]. *Enseñanza e Investigación en Psicología, 4* (2), 200–216. (b)

Lara Tapia, H., & Velez, J. (1975). Alcoholismo y farmacodependencia en un sistema de seguridad social: Un estudio epidemiológico [Alcoholism and drug dependency in the security system: An epidemiological study]. *Salud Pública México, 16* (3), 387–395.

Lartigue, T. (1976). Entrenamiento para supervisores de trabajo de comunidad [Supervisors' training for community jobs]. *Enseñanza e Investigación en Psicología, 2* (1), 15–18.

León-Sanchez, R., & Patiño-Muñoz, G. (1984). *Historia de la psicología en México: La época prehispánica* [The history of psychology in Mexico: The pre-Hispanic era]. Professional thesis, Fac. de Psicología, UNAM.

López, F. (1977). Programas de tiempo fijo: manipulación del programa de mantenimiento precedente [Fixed-interval schedules: Manipulation of preceding maintenance schedules]. *Revista Mexicana de Análisis de la Conducta, 3*, 39–52.

López, F. (1978). Consideraciones sobre las prácticas básicas en Psicología [Considerations concerning the basic practices in psychology]. *Enseñanza e Investigación en Psicología, 4*, 217–222.

López, F. (1980). Notas sobre el desarrollo conceptual y metodológico del análisis experimental de la conducta [Notes on conceptual development and the methodology of the experimental analysis of behavior]. *Revista Mexicana de Análisis de la Conducta, 6,* 185–200.

López, F., & Ribes, E. (1974). El nivel de conceptualización: Una clase de respuestas verbales controladas por las contengencias de reforzamientos [The conceptualization level: One class of verbal answers controlled by reinforcement contingencies]. *Memorias del I Congreso Mexicana de Psicología.* México: UNAM, 119–124.

Medina-Liberty, A. (1978). Acerca del uso del método experimental en psicología [Uses of the experimental method in psychology]. *Enseñanza e Investigación en Psicología, 4,* 137–141.

Medina-Liberty, A. (1981). Psicología, método experimental y construcción de conocimientos [Psychology, the experimental method, and the structure of consciousness]. In G. Alvarez & J. Molina (Eds.), *Psicología e historia.* México: UNAM. (a)

Medina-Liberty, A. (1981). Psicología, método experimental y el problema de la objetividad [Psychology, the experimental method, and the objectivity problem]. *Acta Psicológica Mexicana, 1,* 47–56. (b)

Medina-Liberty, A. (1984). Psicología y verdad: En torno al problema de la objetividad [Psychology and truth: Toward the objectivity problem]. In *Proc. of 23rd International Congress of Psychology,* Acapulco, México.

Medina-Liberty, A., & Lopez, F. (1981). *La enseñanza de la psicología: Un modelo integrativo* [The teaching of psychology: An integrative model]. Paper presented at the Terceras Jornadas Nacionales de Psicología Social. Mérida, Venezuela.

Medina-Mora, M. E., Castro, M. E., Campillo Serrani, C., & Gomez Mont, F. (1981). Validity and reliability of a high school drug use questionnaire among Mexican students. *Bulletin of Narcotics, 33* (4), 67–76.

Molina, J. (1980). Ideología y educación: El ejemplo de la instrucción personalizada [Ideology and education: A sample of personalized instruction]. *Enseñanza e Investigación en Psicología, 1,* 101–108.

Monroy Nase, Z. (1983). *Racionalismo e empirismo naconstitufao da psicología científica* [Rationalism and empiricism: Constituents of scientific psychology]. Brasil: Univ. Fed. de Rio de Janeiro.

Morgane, P. J. (1970). Raúl Hernández-Peón (1924–1968). *Physiology and Behavior, 5,* 379–388.

Mouret, Eduardo. (1976). *Grupos de encuentro, una evaluación práctica* [Encounter groups, a practical evaluation]. Unpublished licenciate thesis. Mexico, UIA.

Nadelsticher, A., Diaz-Loving, R., & Nina, R. (1983). La empatía: Unidimensional o multidimensional? [Empathy: Unidimensional or multidimensional?]. *Enseñanza e Investigación en Psicología,* IX, 2 (18).

Nuñez, R. (1968). *Aplicación del Inventario Multifásico de la Personalidad (MMPI) a la psicopatología* [Application of the Minnesota Multiphasic Personality Inventory (MMPI) to psychopathology]. México: El Manual Moderno, S.A.

Ostrosky, F., Canseco, E., Navarro, E., & Jones, D. (in press). Cortical evoked potentials by verbal information in normal and dyslexic children. *EEG Journal.*

Pérez-Cota, F. (1981). Sobre la selección de teorías [Concerning the selection of theories]. In G. Alvarez & J. Molina (Eds.), *Psicologia e historia.* México: UNAM.

Pérez-Mitre, G. (1981). Autoestima: Expectativas de éxito o de fracaso en la realización de una tarea [Self-esteem: Expections of success or failure in task completion]. *Revista de la Asociación Latinoamericana de Psicología Social, 1* (1), 135–156.

Pick de Weiss, S. (1978). *A social-psychological study of family planning in Mexico City.* Unpublished doctoral dissertation, London University.

Pick de Weiss, S. (1980). *Estudio social psicológico de la planificación familiar* [A social-psychological study of family planning]. México: Siglo XXI Editores.

Ramírez, S. (1984). La psicología del mexicano actual a la luz de los mitos prehispánicos [The psychology of the contemporary Mexican in the light of pre-Hispanic myths]. *Comunidad CONACYT, 116,* 52–53.

Rayek, E., & Ribes, E. (1977). The development of behavior analysis in Mexico: Sidney W. Bijou's contribution. In B. Etzel, J. Le Blanc, & D. Baer (Eds.), *New developments in behavioral research theory, method and application.* Hillsdale, NJ: LEA.

Reidel de Aguilar, L. (1981). Atracción, semejanza e influencia personal [Attraction, resemblance, and personal influence]. *Revista de la Asociación Latinoamericana de Psicología Social, 1* (1), 93–108.

Reyes-Lagunes, I. (1982). *Actitudes de los maestros hacia la profesión magisterial y su contexto* [Teacher's attitudes toward the teaching profession and its context]. Ph.D. thesis, Universidad Nacional Autónoma de México.

Ribes, E. (1968). Psychology in Mexico. *American Psychologist, 23,* 565–566.

Ribes, E. (1976). *Técnicas de modificación de conducta: su aplicación al retardo en el desarrollo* [Behavior modification techniques: Applications to cases of retarded development]. México: Trillas.

Ribes, E. (1977). Relationships among behavior theory, experimental research, and behavior modification. *Psychological Record, 27,* 417–424.

Ribes, E. (1979). Some recent developments in psychology in Mexico. *American Psychologist, 30,* 774–776.

Ribes, E. (1980). Consideraciones metodológicas y professionales sobre el análisis conductual aplicado [Methodological and professional considerations concerning applied behavioral analysis]. *Revista Mexicana de Análisis de la Conducta, 6,* 89–102.

Ribes, E. (1982). Los eventos privados: Un problema para la ciencia de la conducta? [Private events: A problem for the behavioral sciences?]. *Revista Mexicana de Análisis de la Conducta, 8,* 11–30.

Rivero del Pozo, F. (1983). La Frenologia en México: intento de sintesis historica (1835–1907) [Phrenology in Mexico: An attempt at a historical synthesis (1835–1907)]. Trabajo presentado en la mesa redonda "Historia de la psicología en México." Fac. de Psicología. UNAM.

Robles, O. (1952). Panorama de la psicología en México, pasado y presente [A perspective on psychology in Mexico, past and present]. *Filosofía y Letras, 23* (45–46), 239–263.

Rodríguez de Arizmendi, G. (1980). Assumptions about sex role behaviors and their effects. Abstract Guide, 2 (p. 473). In *Proc. of 22nd International Congress of Psychology,* Leipzig, GDR.

Rotter, J. B. (1966). Generalized expectancies for internal vs. external control of reinforcement. *Psychological Monographs, 80* (1), 609 (entire issue).

Sanguineti, Y. (1984). *La psicología social y la metodología participativa en los procesos de desarrollo, en la década de los 80* [Social psychology and participative methodologies in the developmental processes, during the decade of the 1980s]. Unpublished doctoral dissertation, National University of México.

Santoyo, C., & Cedeño Aguirre, M. L. (1981). *Una estrategia para el desarrollo de un modelo taxonómico de evaluación e intervención para un sistema de prácticas* [A strategy for the development of a taxonomic model of evaluation and intervention for a practica system]. *Métodos Docentes, 2*, 23–39.

Solano-Flores, G. (1983). *Principios de análisis estructural educativo, metodología y técnicas para la educación* [Principles of educational structural analysis, methodology, and techniques for education]. México: Trillas.

Speller, P. (Ed.) (1978). *Análisis de la conducta: Trabajos de investigación en Latinoamerica* [Behavioral analysis: Investigations in Latin America]. México: Trillas.

Todorov, J. C. (1977). Effects of punishments of main key responding in concurrent schedules. *Revista Mexicana de Análisis de la Conducta, 3* (1), 17–28.

Todorov, J. C., & Gragas de Souza, D. (1978). Minimum interchange over intervals in concurrent schedules. *Revista Mexicana de Análisis de la Conducta, 4* (1), 17–28.

Valderrama, P., & Rivero del Pozo, F. (1983). *Ensayos de historia de la psicología en Mexico* [Historical essays on psychology in Mexico]. Professional thesis, Facultad de Psicología, UNAM.

Valencia, M., & Velázquez, D. N. (1982). Discriminative stimulus properties of Tr3369, a new antihypertensive compound. *Psychopharmacology, 76*, A1–A5.

Velasco, M. G. (1978). Medición del cambio en los grupos de encuentro [Measurement of change in encounter groups]. *Enseñanza e Investigación en Psicología, 4* (1), 126–131.

SUGGESTED READINGS

Diaz-Guerrero, R. (1984). Contemporary psychology in Mexico. *Annual Review of Psychology, 35*, 83–112.

García, F., & Molina, J. (1983). *Una década de la Facultad de Psicología* [One decade of the Faculty of Psychology]. 1973–1983. México, UNAM.

Pick de Weiss, S., & Diaz-Loving, R. (1986). Applied psychology in Mexico. *International Review of Applied Psychology, 35*, 577–598.

Ribes, E. (1975). Some recent developments in psychology in Mexico. *American Psychologist, 30*, 774–776.

The Netherlands

Pieter J. van Strien, Charles J. de Wolff, and Roelf J. Takens

HISTORICAL BACKGROUND

The Pre–World War II Period

The roots of Dutch psychology extend back to the early physiological work of F. C. Donders (1818–1889) and H. Zwaardemaker (1857–1930) as well as to the psychological experiments conducted by philosopher Gerard Heymans (1857–1930). Donders pioneered reaction-time studies (1860); Zwaardemaker was an authority on the psychology of smell; and Heymans, whose theory of knowledge, metaphysics, and ethics were based on an inductive approach, founded the first psychological laboratory in Groningen in 1892. His studies on optical illusions, psychological inhibition, and differential psychology were published in international scientific journals.

Whereas psychology had become a respected scientific discipline in the universities of Germany, France, and the United States by the early twentieth century, the only center of scientific psychological research in the Netherlands during World War I was the Groningen laboratory. Psychological inquiry remained largely the concern of philosophers, psychiatrists, pedagogues, and theologians. Most of them were interested in practical rather than theoretical matters and valued psychology as a new tool for understanding and guiding human beings. Old formulas and certainties had by then lost much of their cogency.

In an effort to counter the liberal thinking of the time, Protestant and Catholic scholars each developed their own type of psychology. As a result, problems associated with marriage, mental health, education, religion, and interpersonal relations at work were psychologically discussed and analyzed in both popular magazines and pedagogical journals.

Heymans' interests also changed. His research became centered upon classifying human psychological differences. In his famous rectorial address of 1909, for example, he expounded upon his view of the "forthcoming age of psychology." As he saw it, social problems would be solved, and personal needs met, by the growing insight provided by psychological research into human intellectual capabilities and limitations. Heymans and his generation, however, believed psychology's influence upon society would come primarily through the diffusion of psychological information rather than the direct application of psychological principles and procedures to societal problems.

In contrast, the next generation of Dutch psychologists sought to apply their psychological knowledge toward improving society. Although the Netherlands was not directly involved in World War I, there was a strong desire for both socioeconomic and cultural renewal following the conflict. As part of this viewpoint, there were great hopes that applied psychology, or psychotechnics as it was referred to by German-American psychologist Hugo Munsterberg, would contribute innovative solutions to the problems and challenges the country faced.

During the 1920s and 1930s, vocational counseling and industrial psychology burgeoned. In line with the denominational segregation ("pillarization") which was typical of Dutch society as of the late 1800s, Catholic, Protestant, and secular vocational counseling agencies and pedagogical institutes were founded, for example, the Pedagogical Institute at the Free University in Amsterdam (1931). In 1924, the Philips Corporation became the first large firm in the Netherlands to employ a psychologist. The postal service followed in 1929. During the 1930s, psychologists were hired by Rotterdam Harbor and the state mines. And as early as 1922, the army utilized the services of several university psychologists.

In 1921, as the result of a new educational act, philosophy departments were able to offer doctoral programs in psychology. In 1922, the University of Utrecht established a full professorship in psychology (F.J.M.A. Roels), making it the first university to do so. Similar positions were soon created at other Dutch universities: Groningen (H.J.F.W. Brugmans, 1928); Free University, Amsterdam (J. Waterink, 1929); Catholic University, Nijmegen (F. J. Th. Rutten, 1931); and University of Amsterdam (G. Révèsz, 1933). In Leyden, the oldest university in the Netherlands, it was only after World War II that a full professorship in psychology was created (A. M. J. Chorus). Most of the men who assumed these positions during the 1920s and 1930s were associated with a certain religious denomination, and each geared the new science toward the views prevailing at his university.

As evidence of the recognition of Dutch psychology, the Eighth International Psychological Conference, presided over by Heymans, took place in 1926 in Groningen. In 1928, the Fifth International Association of Applied Psychology assembled in Utrecht under Roels' presidency. Although educational and philosophical journals had for some time been publishing psychological articles, the first Dutch psychological journal, *Het Nederlands Tijdschrift voor de Psychologie en haar Grensgebiden* [The Dutch Journal of Psychology and Its Cognate Fields], was founded in 1933. In 1935, Geza Révèsz, a Hungarian-born professor at the University of Amsterdam, founded the European journal *Acta Psychologica*. Several multidisciplinary societies for the study of psychology were also established, but most did not survive after the Netherlands Institute of Practicing Psychology (NIPP) was founded in 1938 by approximately a dozen pioneers of applied psychology.

Consolidating the Profession (1945–1965)

During the period of recovery and rebuilding after World War II, Dutch psychologists consolidated and expanded the discipline. A growing number of students were attracted to the field and new faculty positions were created. In 1950, approximately 200 students were majoring in psychology programs, and by 1960 the number had grown to more than 2,000. Jobs were plentiful that many had secured positions before graduation. Personnel selection, vocational counseling, and child psychology offered the greatest opportunities during the 1950s. In the 1960s, however, the demand for clinical psychologists began to surpass that of all the other areas, as clinicians assumed a larger share of the diagnostic function in mental health settings and increasingly took part in providing psychotherapy.

The membership of NIPP grew from thirty-six in 1946 to nearly 300 in 1960. From the beginning, the association worked for the legal recognition of the title "psychologist" and legal protection of the professional activities of psychologists. A code of conduct and a disciplinary board to deal with members transgressing the code were established in 1961. Additionally, a small bureau to promote the interests of psychologists was set up, as were a variety of committees to deal with both the internal and external affairs of the organization. It was not until 1970 that NIPP's efforts to obtain legal protection of the designation "psychologist" succeeded.

Until the middle of the twentieth century, Dutch psychology was primarily German in orientation. German and Swiss characterology and holistic assessment techniques were particularly influential. Psychoanalysis also had its adherents, especially among psychiatrists. Influenced by German and French existentialism as well as anthropological psychiatry, the University of Utrecht became an internationally renowned center of phenomenological-existential psychology and philosophy in the 1950s (F. J. J. Buytendijk, M. J. Langeveld, and D. J. van Lennep). This orientation predominated until the retirement of Buytendijk, the intellectual leader of this perspective, and the apostasy of his successor, J. Linschoten, in the early 1960s.

The Discipline Becomes More Empirical and Analytical (Since 1960)

Psychology continued to grow during the 1960s and 1970s as psychological services became intrinsic to the Dutch welfare state. The number of newly enrolled students increased from 308 in 1960 to 1,377 in 1970. The number of individuals with graduate degrees in psychology increased from about 250 in 1960 to approximately 2,500 in 1970.

During the 1960s, the intellectual climate changed. The reliance upon characterology and the phenomenological-existential orientation was gradually replaced by a vigorous Anglo-American empirical-analytical tradition. University of Amsterdam professor Adriaan de Groot, a defender of this perspective, published a book in 1961 entitled *Methodology*, which became a landmark work. In the applied areas, the empirical-analytical approach resulted in the gradual supplementation or replacement of holistic assessment techniques (the clinical method) by psychometric procedures. Interestingly, this change in assessment procedures first occurred within military psychology. Industrial psychologists and those in other applied fields gradually followed suit.

The new empiricism was most pronounced in the universities. Most of the younger faculty members were preparing for scientific, rather than applied, careers. In this spirit, the Foundation for Psychonomics was established in 1968. In the same year, "Practicing" was dropped from the name of NIPP, and the association became the Netherlands Institute of Psychologists (NIP). Two years earlier, the news bulletin had been restructured into a professional journal, *De Psycholoog* [The Psychologist] which published articles of general scientific interest. The previously mentioned *Het Nederlands Tijdschrift voor de Psychologie en haar Grensgebiden*, which had primarily served as a forum for analytical essays directed at psychologists and other scholars, became a scientific journal specifically written by, and geared toward, psychologists. In 1970, a new journal, *Gedrag* [Behavior], was established. It flourished, as did several specialized journals, all of which featured scientific articles.

THE CONTEMPORARY SITUATION

The number of psychologists currently employed in the Netherlands is estimated at approximately 8,000. Along with the United States and Sweden, the Netherlands is among the countries with the highest number of psychologists per capita (Rosenzweig, 1982). The training of psychologists as well as most scientific psychological research takes place in the psychology departments of universities. These include the state universities in Leyden, Groningen, and Utrecht; the University of Amsterdam; the Free University in Amsterdam; the Catholic University in Nijmegen; and the Catholic University in Tilburg. All universities, the "religious" as well as the state ones, are fully financed by the Dutch government. There is not a marked difference in quality and standing among the universities. Some opportunities for psychological research and training also exist at the technical universities located in Delft, Eindhoven, and Twente; the Agricultural University in Wageningen; the University of Limburg in Maastricht; the Erasmus University in Rotterdam; and the business schools of Rotterdam/Delft and Nijenrode in Breukelen. Moreover, psychologists have been given the opportunity to participate in government-sponsored research pro-

The Netherlands

jects at independent research institutes. Practice-oriented studies are also taking place in the social research departments of large companies (for example, Philips, Dutch State Mines, Dutch Steel Company, Postal Services, Dutch Railways) as well as some psychiatric hospitals and institutions.

University Departments and Curricula

Following World War II, most university psychology departments consisted of one full professor (ordinarius) and one assistant. Today, however, each psychology department is staffed by approximately ten full professors representing the various areas of psychology. On the average, a teaching and research staff of seven or eight people is associated with each full professor. The most common full professorships are in experimental psychology, developmental psychology, social psychology, personality psychology, clinical psychology, and work-and-organizational psychology. Some universities also have full professorships in methodology and the theory and history of psychology. Others have them in mathematical psychology, educational psychology, ergonomics, cultural psychology, the psychology of religion, economic psychology, and other areas. Doctoral students concentrate in one of the major areas.

In 1964, psychology became a department within the school of social sciences. The other departments are sociology and pedagogics/andragology. Andragology includes social pedagogics, adult education, and community development. At some universities the school of social sciences also encompasses the political sciences. Relationships among the disciplines within each school have primarily been administrative. Since 1983, however, the Ministry of Education has been exerting pressure on the various subfaculties in an effort to get them to integrate. This initiative has been strongly opposed by most psychologists as they fear that the professional identity of their discipline will be lost in such a reorganization. The main subjects or fields covered by each department are presented in Table 1.

Prior to a major revision of university curricula in 1982, students were required to follow a five- to six-year program leading to a doctorandus certificate. Most students, in fact, took from seven to nine years to complete this course of study. The achievement of the doctorandus certificate enabled a student to submit a dissertation for a doctoral degree. About 10 percent of those achieving doctorandus status actually went on to prepare a dissertation. Since the doctorandus certificate is sufficient for recognition as a psychologist in the Netherlands, most psychologists have used this credential as the basis for obtaining work as practicing psychologists.

The revised curriculum includes an introductory year, at the end of which students must pass the "propædeutic examination" in order to begin a three-year program leading to the doctorandus title. Students failing to pass the doctorandus examination within six years are discontinued. Only a restricted number of students who have passed this test are admitted to the doctoral program. Under

Table 1
Major Subjects Covered by Psychology Departments

BASIC SUBJECTS	THEORY AND METHODS*	APPLIED PSYCHOLOGY	AUXILIARY SUBJECTS
1. BASIC FUNCTIONS (exp. psych.) (cognition, learning, performance, motivation, emotion, language)	1. THEORETICAL PSYCHOLOGY (general theory, methods and history of psych., incl. general intro.)	1. WORK-AND-ORGANIZATIONAL PSYCHOLOGY	1. PHILOSOPHICAL AND/OR ANTHROPOLOGICAL PSYCH; THEORY OF SCIENCE
2. DEVELOPMENTAL PSYCHOLOGY (development of functions, individuality, life phases, socialization)	2. DIAGNOSTIC AND RESEARCH METHODS (psychodiagnostics, tests, interview, observation, inventories, experimental methods)	2. CLINICAL PSYCHOLOGY AND PSYCHOTHERAPY	2. SOCIOLOGY OF PSYCHOLOGY OF CULTURE; HISTORICAL PSYCHOLOGY
3. PSYCHOLOGY OF PERSONALITY (individuality, intra-indiv. consistency and inter-indiv. differences)	3. STATISTICS AND PSYCHOMETRICS AND MATHEMATICAL PSYCH. (data models and data analysis)	3. CHILD AND JUVENILE PSYCHOLOGY (applied developmental psychology)	3. BIO-PSYCHOLOGY; PHYSIOLOGICAL PSYCHOLOGY; COMPARATIVE PSYCHOLOGY
4. SOCIAL PSYCHOLOGY (social interaction, cognition, attribution)		4. EDUCATIONAL PSYCHOLOGY	
		5. PSYCHO-GERONTOLOGY	
		6. ERGONOMICS/TECHNO-PSYCHOLOGY	
		7. APPLIED PSYCHO-LINGUISTICS	
		8. ECONOMIC PSYCHOLOGY	
		9. PASTORAL PSYCHOLOGY	
		10....................	

*The first three fields are part of the curriculum of all psychology departments; the auxiliary subjects are taught at some universities.

the new curriculum, the title psychologist and accreditation are still available to those who have earned only the doctorandus certificate. Those who wish to practice psychotherapy, however, must first work under supervision for a number of years. As continuing professional education is not required of practicing psychologists in the Netherlands, plans are under way to introduce more in-service training.

The propædeutic year consists mostly of a general survey of psychological theories and methods largely based on American or American-style introductory material. An emphasis on statistics and the analysis of data represents a stumbling block for many of the students. The first year of the doctoral program also focuses on basics, and students are only allowed a few optional courses. During the remainder of the program, students specialize in one of the principal areas of psychology.

Basic Areas of Study

Experimental Psychology

Each university department of psychology has its own laboratory for experimental research and pursues its own research interests. The University of Amsterdam is known for its research on the thought processes, a tradition which dates back to De Groot's well-known study on thought and choice in chess (1946, translated into English in 1965). De Groot derived some of his inspiration from the German-Jewish refugee O. Selz (a pupil of Külpe), who spent the last years of his life in Amsterdam. N. H. Frijda and J. J. Elshout are currently carrying on with this tradition.

Meanwhile, at Catholic University in Nijmegen, some interesting work on artificial intelligence is taking place (G. A. M. Kempen). Nijmegen is also where W. J. M. Levelt is conducting a number of outstanding psycholinguistic investigations. In 1980, Levelt's institute became the seat of the International Research Center for Psycholinguistics of the Max Planck Foundation, a German research foundation. Furthermore, significant psycholinguistic studies have been conducted at the University of Leyden (G. B. Flores d'Arcais), where comparative psychology is also of special importance. And at the University of Utrecht, C. F. Van Parreren, who studied the work of Soviet psychologists, initiated an experimental research program on human learning. Utrecht is the site of research in sensory psychology, too.

Physiological psychology plays a strong role in Amsterdam (Free University's J. F. Orlebeke) and Nijmegen (J. M. H. Vossen) as well as in Utrecht (J. L. Slangen) and Tilburg (C. H. M. Brunia). In Groningen, J. A. Michon, who founded a laboratory for both basic and applied research in traffic psychology, is conducting studies on the psychology of time. Other prominent individuals in applied research are H. Bouma, A. F. Sanders, and W. A. Wagenaar.

Additionally, research in ergonomics is taking place at the Institute for the

Physiology of the Senses in Soesterberg, the Institute for Perpetual Research in Eindhoven, the Postal Service, and various industries in the private sector. The above, of course, is only a sampling of Dutch experimental research, but it illustrates the broad scope of the discipline in the Netherlands.

In 1968 experimental psychologists, in conjunction with a number of researchers from other sciences, founded the Dutch Foundation for Psychonomics. This eventually led to the *Handbook of Psychonomics*, edited by Michon and his colleagues. The book was published in 1976 and translated into English in 1979.

Developmental Psychology

Until 1970, developmental psychology in the Netherlands for the most part consisted of applied child psychology. In the listing of areas in Table 1, the practice of child psychology and the practice of psychogerontology are classified as applied fields. The applied aspects of developmental psychology are detailed later within the context of the psychology of mental health.

During the initial period, much attention was devoted to children's play. Particularly of interest was the influence of limited opportunities for play and exploration in urban environments upon intellectual and emotional development. The work of W. J. Bladergroen is representative of this focus.

Basic research in developmental psychology was given a new impetus in the early 1970s by the theories of Piaget. While the major emphasis now is on cognitive processes, research is also being done on social and emotional development. In Leyden, emotional development is being studied from the perspective of J. Bowlby's attachment theory. Adolescence is an important area of research at the Free University in Amsterdam, in Groningen, and in Nijmegen. Nijmegen is also prominent in gerontology (J. M. A. Munnichs).

It is difficult to distinguish between psychological and pedagogical practice. Much of the work which could be done by psychologists is performed by educational specialists called orthopedagogues. These practitioners are engaged in diagnostic work and in the treatment of learning and other disabilities. At Leyden there is in this respect a most promising cooperation between psychologists and orthopedagogues, while in Amsterdam at the Free University both disciplines work within one department.

Personality Psychology

Personality psychology has experienced a period of crisis in the Netherlands. Both trait theory and German-Swiss characterology have been strongly criticized. Attention has shifted to a variety of new developments and orientations, including psychometrics, judgmental and attributional processes, Kelly's personal construct theory, the self-confrontation method, and a new synthesis of trait and attribution dynamics. Especially noteworthy in psychometrics is the work of J. Th. Snijders and W. K. B. Hofstee in Groningen and P. J. D. Drenth at the Free University in Amsterdam. Hofstee is also known for his work on attribution theory. Others who should be mentioned are Amsterdam-based J. T. Barendregt, who has done significant work in clinical diagnostics, and J. C. J. Bonarius in Utrecht, who has carried out psychological studies based upon Kelly's personal construct theory.

Also of importance is the self-confrontation method, a combined diagnostic and therapeutic procedure developed by H. J. M. Hermans in Nijmegen. Recent efforts to synthesize trait and attribution processes, in line with work of Swedish psychologist D. Magnusson, have been made by P. J. Hettema (in Tilburg) and others. Lastly, Dutch personality psychologists have played an active role in establishing the European Research Group on Personality.

Social Psychology

Before World War II there were some publications on imitation, suggestion, mass behavior, and propaganda and also on national and regional characteristics. After the war, there was a general shift in psychology from explanations based on individual characteristics to situational explanations (Rutten, 1958).

Contemporary social psychology emerged from the influence of American group dynamics; the work of H. A. Hutte and J. Koekebakker is representative. With the exception of a few early studies, little progress was made in experimental social psychology until the 1960s. Initially, attitudes and social perception were the primary research topics (H. E. J. Duijker, N. H. Frijda, and J. M. F. Jaspars). Subsequent studies concerned power, social comparison, coalition formation, and the perception of risk and its influence on behavior (M. Mulder in Rotterdam, J. M. Rabbie in Utrecht, J. B. Rijsman in Tilburg, and H. A. M. Wilke in Groningen).

Social psychology in the Netherlands has always had a strong practical orientation. Research on leadership and organization, multicultural cooperation (minorities), ways of fostering the economical use of energy, and so forth are representative of this practical orientation. While some areas of application, such as social planning, community development, and adult education, constitute a part of applied social psychology in most other countries, in the Netherlands these areas are the domain of andragology. Criticisms of the quality of research done in this specialty, and doubts as to whether its theoretical concerns warrant an independent discipline, have put andragology under heavy pressure. With budgetary cutbacks in the universities, the "science of andragogics" is currently being organized as a subdiscipline of pedagogics and psychology.

Closely related to social psychology is a relatively new field, cross-cultural psychology (in Tilburg). Other related areas, with longer traditions, are the psychology of culture, the psychology of religion, and pastoral psychology (in Nijmegen). H. M. M. Fortmann has been this field's central figure. There is currently considerable interest on the part of researchers in the surfacing of neofacism among modern youth.

Dutch social psychologists have their own research organization and play an active role in the international network of social psychologists, particularly in Europe.

Theory, Methodology, and History

In this section we shall concern ourselves only with theoretical issues that transcend the boundaries of specific subdisciplines, the history of psychology, general methodology, methods and theories of data analysis, and mathematical psychology. More specifically related subjects, mentioned in Table 1 under theory and methods, are not reviewed.

Theoretical Psychology and the Foundations and History of Psychology. When each university department of psychology consisted of only one or two full professorships, theory building and the history of the discipline were the concerns of a few "generalist" professors. As the differentiation of the discipline progressed, special professorships for theoretical psychology were created. The first psychologist appointed in this area was C. Sanders at the Free University of Amsterdam (1962). Several university departments currently have a section concerned with theoretical psychology or the foundations and history of psychology. Contemporary work in these areas centers upon the role of models, metaphors, and perspectives in psychological theory and methodology (P. Vroon, J. F. H. van Rappard, P. J. van Strien). These studies also take into account the influence of societal factors upon the inquiry process.

Interest in the history of psychology is a very recent development in the Netherlands. The best-known Dutch historians of psychology are probably W. van Hoorn, L. K. A. Eisenga, and Van Rappard, who is especially concerned with the philosophical roots of the discipline. Studies concerning the history of Dutch psychology have recently been initiated by Eisenga, R. Abma, R. Ter Meulen, and Van Strien. Additionally, H. F. M. Peeters in Tilburg is studying long-term changes in human behavior within historical perspectives.

Methodology, Data Analysis, Mathematical Psychology, and Decision Theory. As mentioned earlier, empirical-analytic methodology became the dominant approach during the 1960s. De Groot, while focusing upon the psychology of thinking, emphasized the "forum function" of science. By this he meant that there should be a consensus among experts in the field as a criterion of truth. His view can be considered a modification of Popper's falsificationism. In 1980 Hofstee modified this point of view by insisting that rival predictions be specified by the scientists in a particular field. His modification is known as an adversary model.

Statistics and data theory have achieved high status in the Netherlands. The same is true of mathematical psychology and psychometrics (J. P. van de Geer in Leyden; Hofstee, W. Molenaar, and J. M. F. ten Berge in Groningen; E. Ch. J. Roskam and Th. G. G. Bezembinder in Nijmegen; and G. J. Mellenbergh in Amsterdam). Topics of concern include Bayesian statistics, nonlinear multivariate analyses, and multidimensional scaling. Internationally recognized work in decision theory is being conducted by C. A. J. Vlek (Groningen).

Applied Psychology

Although Table 1 lists nine fields of applied psychology, applied psychological research can be organized into three major categories: work-and-organizational psychology, which includes ergonomics and applied social psychology; mental health, which includes clinical psychology and the clinical study of children and youth as well as psychogerontology; and educational psychology, which includes school psychology.

Work-and-Organizational Psychology

There has always been an interest in work-and-organizational psychology in the Netherlands, not only in the universities but also within governmental and private organizations. As far back as the 1920s, professors of psychology were deeply concerned with industrial psychology, and large corporations established psychological services departments. Today many businesses employ psychologists.

Professorships in work-and-organizational psychology were established at all universities, including the technical ones, during the 1960s. At most universities, work-and-organizational psychology departments are combined with their social psychology counterparts.

Until the early 1960s, work-and-organizational psychologists were almost exclusively concerned with personnel selection. Since then, however, the field has rapidly branched out, with ergonomics and organizational psychology receiving much attention. These psychologists generally work on projects concerning organizational change, industrial democracy, workers' councils, the structuring of work, and the training of groups. At the end of the 1960s, the name of this area was changed from industrial psychology to work-and-organizational psychology, indicating that research and other activities were not restricted to industrial firms but were also relevant to such entities as government agencies and hospitals. Perhaps more than is the case in other countries, Dutch work-and-organizational psychology places considerable emphasis upon organizational matters. This is reflected in a recent handbook (Drenth, et al., 1984), which features many chapters on organizational issues.

Although work-and-organizational psychology has always been a popular specialization for students and psychologists in the Netherlands, there was a considerable decline of interest in this field during the late 1960s and 1970s. This was probably due to changes in Dutch society's perspectives on the role of industry within the country (De Wolff, in Drenth, et al., 1984). During this decade, however, interest in the field has been actively renewed, in part because of employment opportunities. Many new psychologists are now finding positions as organizational consultants and personnel management specialists.

A number of research areas which were originally considered part of work-and-organizational psychology have developed into separate subfields. Economic psychology (in Tilburg and Rotterdam), traffic psychology (in Groningen), and ergonomics (in Tilburg) illustrate this trend.

Among the most prominent psychologists in work-and-organizational psychology are: P. J. D. Drenth, who has primarily been interested in industrial democracy and the meaning of work; H. Thierry, whose chief concern is worker compensation and shift work; Ch. J. de Wolff, who has investigated organizational stress; R. A. Roe, who is investigating personnel selection, and P. J. Willems (Drenth, et al., 1984), who conducted research in ergonomics.

Mental Health

It is estimated that more than 4,000 psychologists in the Netherlands are working in the clinical field. This means that nearly half of all employed Dutch psychologists are engaged in clinical work. Clinical psychologists did not begin working in psychiatric hospitals until after World War II. Today, though, they participate in nearly every segment of the Dutch health care system.

Initially, clinical psychologists operated primarily as psychodiagnosticians. Then, in the late 1960s and early 1970s, a shift toward more therapeutic work became apparent. As clinical psychologists became increasingly involved with the treatment of patients both in and out of hospitals, their professional status increased (as did their salaries). This was furthered by the introduction by the NIP of a register of clinical psychologists and by the Netherlands Association of Psychotherapy (NVP) of a register of psychotherapists. An upcoming bill in the Netherlands will legalize the titles of clinical psychologist and psychotherapist, respectively.

Most of the clinical psychologists are employed by psychiatric hospitals, mental health centers, and general hospitals. Private practice in conjunction with general practitioners is rapidly increasing in popularity among younger colleagues who cannot find jobs elsewhere.

Due to the educational work load at the universities as a result of the large number of clinical psychology students, academic research in this field has not really flourished. J. T. Barendregt's well-known work on psychodiagnostics (1961) and his later work on phobic disorders (1975) are exceptions. Worth mentioning also are the research on depressive illnesses and suicidal behavior being conducted by R. F. W. Diekstra at the University of Leyden and the experimental clinical research being done by A. F. Kalverboer and others in Groningen, in which biological and neurophysiological variables are related to behavioral disorders. At this same university, P. M. G. Emmelkamp is conducting research in the field of behavior therapy.

Educational Psychology

The field of psychology devoted to educational matters has been known by several names. It was originally referred to as pedagogical psychology, went on to be called school psychology after World War II, and is now identified as educational psychology. Although the problems of the individual child were previously emphasized, the educational situation in general has become the focal point. Pupil, teacher, subject matter, teaching method, school organization, and fellow students are regarded as interacting variables within educational settings. Most educational psychologists are affiliated with school guidance and advisory centers. Due to the increased complexity of the work, cooperation with educators, sociologists, didactic experts, remedial teachers, physicians, social workers, and other specialists is, of course, necessary. Presently, the science of education is essentially an interdisciplinary field of study. There has always been a particularly close association between educational psychology and orthopedagogics. This is demonstrated by the joint research programs which have taken place at a number of universities, for example, the Free University in Amsterdam and the University of Leyden.

Academic research in educational psychology has branched out in two directions. Some psychologists study the educational learning process (for example, the recently retired C. F. van Parreren while at the University of Utrecht); others concentrate upon the cognitive and social development of students and their motivation relative to educational matters (C. F. M. van Lieshout and M. Boekaerts, at the Catholic University at Nijmegen, and De Groot, who was at the University of Amsterdam until 1980). Particularly since the establishment of the Stichting voor Veevoedings Onderzoek (SVO) [Foundation for the Advancement of Educational Research] in 1966, educational research has acquired a prominent position. As a result of De Groot's influence, a Central Educational Institute for the Development of Educational Tests (Centraal Instituut voor Toets Ontwikkeling) was founded in 1968. This institute is concerned with instruments used to measure school achievement.

The Organization of Research

Funding

There are three sources of financial support for psychological research in the Netherlands. The first of these stems from the Ministry of Education and Science, which provides funds for research directly to the universities (see Table 2).

Researchers at the universities have to make their research plans known every five years. When the ministry approves a program, funds are allocated for the next period. Through this "conditional financing" policy, which was recently introduced, the government is attempting to increase its control of the way research money at the universities is spent.

The second source of funding involves the same ministry, but in this case the money is channeled through the Netherlands Organization for the Advancement of Pure Research (ZWO). Authorized individuals draw up priority lists of research proposals submitted to them. For psychology, this task is accomplished by a committee from Psychon, a newly founded organization which has its roots in the former Netherlands Psychonomics Foundation (Nederlandse Stichting voor

Table 2
Volume of Research in the Social Sciences in Terms of Man-Year Equivalents, Differentiated According to Disciplines and Noting the Sources of Funding at the Universities and the Research Centers Allied to the Universities in 1981

	1st Source	2nd Source	3rd Source	TOTAL
Law	315 (87)	10 (3)	38 (10)	363 (100)
Economics, including the science of industrial organization	269 (86)	6 (2)	39 (12)	314 (100)
Social Sciences:	718 (58)	89 (7)	435 (35)	1242 (100)
- social cultural sciences	249 (68)	27 (7.5)	86 (24.5)	362 (100)
- psychology	254 (70)	45 (12)	66 (18)	365 (100)
- pedagogical and andragogical sciences including the science of education	195 (69)	12 (4)	74 (27)	281 (100)
- others, mainly in institutes charged with university assignments	20 (8)	5 (2)	209 (89)	234 (100)
Total	1302 (68)	105 (5)	512 (27)	1919 (100)

The numbers in parentheses refer to percentages. The figures for the Agricultural University in Wageningen and the State University of Limburg are not included in this survey.
Source: Wetenschapsverslag [Science Report], 1981.

Psychonomie) and the Foundation for the Advancement of Research in Psychology (Stichting voor Wetenschappelijk Onderzoek in de Psychologie). Psychon has some fifteen divisions (*werkgemeenschappen*) that unite researchers with common interests. It is expected that this second source of support will become even more important in the future.

The third source includes all other sponsors of psychological research. These are governmental institutions, industrial concerns, and private foundations such as Praeventiefonds and the Dutch Heart Foundation.

Publication Trends

The leading periodicals include *Het Nederlands Tijdschrift voor de Psychologie* [The Dutch Journal of Psychology], *Acta Psychologica* (European, but publishing many Dutch articles and edited by a largely Dutch editorial board), *De Psycholoog* [The Psychologist], *Gedrad* [Behavior], *Psychologie en Maatschappij* [Psychology and Society], and the magazine *Psychologie* [Psychology]. Psychologists also frequently publish in multidisciplinary Dutch journals such as *Tijdschrift voor Psychotherapie* [Journal of Psychotherapy], *Tijdschrift voor Onderwijsresearch* [Journal of Educational Research], *Tijdschrift voor Orthopedagogiek* [Journal of Orthopedagogics], *Kennis en Methode* [Knowledge and Method], *Mens en Organisatie* [Men and Organizations], and *Grafiet*.

Two interesting trends are taking place at the present time. First, psychologists are more often writing for broader audiences by publishing articles in newspapers, weeklies, and various popular magazines including *Psychologie*, the Dutch equivalent of *Psychology Today*. Secondly, there has been an increase in the number of specialized periodicals devoted to specific issues. These include *De Eerste Lijn* [The First Echelon], which concentrates on primary health care, as well as *Tijdschrift voor Gedragstherapie* [Journal of Behavior Therapy], *Tijdschrift voor Seksuologie* [Journal of Sexology], and *Tijdschrift voor Relatieproblematiek*, which is concerned with interpersonal relations.

Although Dutch psychological abstracts or citation indexes do not exist, literature surveys are available on a variety of subjects. The Center for Information and Documentation in the Social Sciences (SWIDOC) publishes *Titles of Studies in the Social Sciences*, while the Netherlands Center for Mental Health (Nederlands Centrum voor Geestelijke Volksgezondheid) publishes a *Bulletin of Literature on Mental Health*. For additional material, one must look to foreign periodicals such as *Psychological Abstracts* and the *Psychological Reader's Guide*. (Interestingly, the *Psychological Reader's Guide* is published by a Dutch firm.)

Dutch psychologists also publish in many international journals, of which the English-language ones are by far the most preferred. Often dissertations appear in English, partly because a publish-or-perish mentality currently pervades the Netherlands. Since Dutch universities claim to be very demanding, applying high standards to dissertations, the publication of a dissertation is viewed as a way of demonstrating one's professional or academic competency.

International Contacts

American influence on Dutch psychology has been very strong during the past twenty-five years. This influence is evidenced not only by the extensive use of American textbooks and professional literature at Dutch universities but also by the referencing of American publications. Moreover, many Dutch psychologists have visited the United States, either to receive part of their training there or for purposes of scientific exchange and international cooperation. In recent years, European collaboration, much of it initiated by Dutch psychologists, has become more pronounced. In 1981, the European Federation of Professional Psychologists Associations (EFPPA) was founded. Stuyling de Lange, a former director of NIP, was instrumental in establishing this organization. Eleven countries were represented at the first general meeting in Heidelberg. At present, twenty-four associations are members.

The Netherlands has been the host country of many international conferences, the largest of which, to date, was the International Association of Applied Psychology (IAAP) Conference in Amsterdam in 1968. In 1982, the first European convention of the International Society for the History of the Behavioral and Social Sciences (Cheiron) took place in Amsterdam. The following year the first Northwest European Congress of Work-and-Organizational Psychologists met in Nijmegen. Networks consisting of prominent researchers have also been established in recent years. Not only is there now such a network in the area of work-and-organizational psychology (ENOP), but similar organizations exist for social as well as personality psychologists.

The relationships between psychologists in the Netherlands and their counterparts in developing countries should also be mentioned. Both Drenth, of Free University, and F. J. Mönks, a professor at Catholic University in Nijmegen, have had extensive experience working in several developing nations. The Dutch government has sponsored training programs for psychologists from Indonesian universities who come to the Netherlands to study for their doctorates. Located in Wassenaar is the Netherlands Institute for Advanced Studies in Humanities and Social Science (NIAS, Meyboomlaan 1, 2242 PR Wassenaar), an organization which supports research for periods of one year. Approximately two-thirds of the scientists who take advantage of this opportunity are from the Netherlands; the others come from abroad.

The Practice of Psychology

Het Nederlands Instituut van Psychologen [*The Netherlands Institute for Psychologists*]

As previously noted, the Netherlands Institute for Psychologists (NIP) is the national professional association. Its current membership of 4,500 includes 600 student members. Approximately 40 percent of Dutch psychologists are members of this association. The NIP has a dual purpose. On the one hand, it tries to promote the application of psychological knowledge; on the other hand, it seeks to serve the professional interests of its members. This is achieved through meetings, conferences, and courses. The association also sets standards for professional practice, negotiates collective labor agreements for psychologists, and provides legal aid to members.

Those who belong to NIP must adhere to its code of professional ethics. A specific code of behavior was first established in 1961 and later modified and enlarged. The current code was formulated in 1976 and a new version is in preparation. Before being registered as a member of the NIP, each applicant is required to sign a statement declaring his or her adherence to the code. A disciplinary committee was instituted to handle complaints.

One of the association's major achievements has been the launching of a successful campaign for the recognition of the title "psychologist." Two registration procedures exist within the NIP, one for clinical psychologists and the other for psychologist-psychotherapists. The association also plays an important role in the training and registering of psychological paraprofessionals classified either as psychological assistants or psychological coworkers. The NIP places a great deal of emphasis upon the responsible use of tests and has created a special board to examine new tests and determine their reliability and validity. A review of new tests is published regularly, and every few years this information is assembled into a book entitled *Tests and test research in the Netherlands*.

Many NIP activities are organized at the divisional level. Within each division, colleagues with similar interests and backgrounds congregate to share ideas and discuss common interests. There are currently seven divisions: psychology of work and organizations (formerly industrial psychology), vocational psychology, child psychology, clinical psychology and psychotherapy, educational psychology (formerly school psychology), social psychology, and social gerontology. In addition to these divisions there are various work groups, some of which concern special areas such as forensic psychology. Other work groups focus upon topics such as the early recognition of learning disabilities, training and career development in organizations, and employment opportunities for psychologists.

One of the NIP's major tasks is to communicate with other disciplines and government agencies about such issues as professional standards and academic training. As mentioned earlier, the association publishes a journal, *De Psycholoog* [The Psychologist].

The Registration of Professional Psychologists

A new act to regulate health care professions is currently being drawn up in the Netherlands. If approved, this act will do away with the current system, which gives legal recognition to the various professional activities, and will replace it with a system based on the recognition of specific titles people have earned. Only titles that warrant a sufficient level of training will be acknowledged. As a particular professional title may only be used by those who satisfy the legally determined competency requirements, consumers of health care services will be able to identify qualified practitioners.

This new regulation is compatible with registration procedures employed by the NIP since 1967 for clinical psychologists and since 1980 for psychologist-psychotherapists. Different requirements must be met by the two types of professionals. The most important condition of registration for a clinical psychologist is full-time work for at least three years under the supervision of a registered colleague in a relevant setting. Psychologist-psychotherapists must demonstrate knowledge and practical skills and practice psychotherapeutic techniques under supervision. The latter requisites are also necessary for membership in the Netherlands Association for Psychotherapy (Nederlandse Vereniging voor Psychotherapie, NVP) which, in turn, promotes psychotherapy and bestows unofficial recognition upon psychotherapists.

The NVP represents a conglomeration of several psychotherapy associations, including the Netherlands Association for Psychoanalysis, the Association for Rogerian Therapy, and the Netherlands Association for Behavioral Therapy. As it does not limit itself exclusively to clinical psychologists, membership is open to therapists from other disciplines. The association originally consisted primarily of psychiatrists, but now clinical psychologists predominate. Few social workers and pedagogues belong to the association. The purposes of the organization are to promote psychotherapy in the Netherlands and to serve the interests of psychotherapists. It has also developed guidelines for the training of psychotherapists. In the last ten years membership in the NVP has dramatically increased, in part because of the semiofficial status that membership implies.

At the present time, the profession of psychotherapy is not legally protected in the Netherlands. As a result, the label psychotherapist may be used by anyone. There is evidence that this situation will soon be changed, making it impossible for poorly trained individuals to practice. When psychotherapeutic treatments are given in the context of the service rendered by the official Mental Health Institutes, its costs are paid by the government by way of the Exceptional Medical Expenses Act. Some private health insurance companies also provide financial support.

The Health Service System in the Netherlands

Health services in the Netherlands are organized into three levels. First, there is the family physician or general practitioner, who is increasingly working in cooperation with other trained professionals such as district nurses, social workers, and physiotherapists. A few psychologists also provide primary mental health care, usually as independent practitioners. Only a small number of health insurance companies pay for psychological services at this level. Young, recently graduated psychologists who have problems finding employment will occasionally take the financial risk and go into private practice.

The second level of service, referred to as ambulant mental health care, is for the most part organized around Regional Mental Health Care Centers (Regionale

Instellingen voor Ambulante Gestelijke Gezondheidszorg). These regional centers usually provide services for areas with a population of about 200,000 residents. There are separate teams to work with the young, with adults, and with the elderly. In addition, there are units for psychotherapy (Organisatorische Eenheden voor Psychotherapie) and for preventive care. Psychologists, psychiatrists, social-psychiatric nurses, social workers, and other professionals all work together in a multidisciplinary effort to provide the necessary assistance. The problems that prompt people to present themselves for treatment vary from all kinds of psychiatric disorders to psycho-social problems concerning marriage and interpersonal relations, education, crises associated with various stages of life, and addictions. Some staff members also serve as consultants to family doctors, social workers, and teachers. Although most services are provided during office hours, someone is always on call to deal with emergency cases. The work of these regional centers is financed entirely by the government. However, employees have to pay a social insurance premium for the support of this medical program.

General psychiatric hospitals and facilities that serve particular groups of patients comprise the third level of mental health care services in the Netherlands. Included in this category are rehabilitation centers, addiction clinics, and geriatric nursing homes. Clinical psychologists are employed in all of these institutions, especially in psychiatric hospitals.

Most of the patients in the mental hospitals are there of their own volition; some, however, are there involuntarily. Dutch law specifies that individuals can be committed against their will when they constitute a danger to themselves or to society and when there is good reason to believe that this danger is related to some mental problem.

The number of clinical psychologists working in general hospitals and geriatric nursing homes continues to increase. In the Netherlands it is possible to buy insurance protection against the high cost of staying in such facilities. Most of these costs, however, are paid by the government.

Employment Opportunities

During the last few decades, the number of Doctorandi (Drs.) in psychology has increased dramatically. There were approximately 100 psychologists in 1950, 600 in 1960, 2,500 in 1970, 8,000 in 1980, and 11,500 in 1985. It is estimated that in 1990 there will be more than 15,000 psychology Drs. in the Netherlands. Whether the number of jobs will increase at the same rate is questionable (see Figure 1). Not all of those with a Drs. diploma in psychology seek employment as psychologists, however. In the past this was primarily the case with women who dropped out of the work force after they married. Now most of these married women are seeking at least a part-time position. Nevertheless, several hundred of those who have completed their studies in psychology choose to accept work in a different field. Despite this, there are approximately 1,800 psychologists in

Figure 1
Unemployed Psychologists

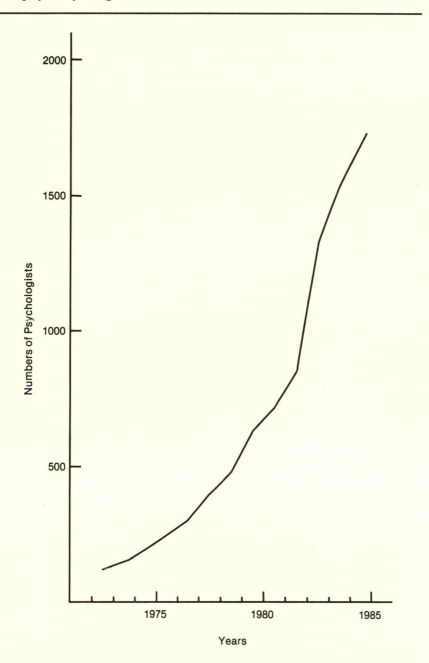

Table 3
Newly Enrolled Psychology Students and Students Completing Their Drs. Degrees (Differentiated by Sex)

Year	Newly Enrolled	% Female	Drs. Degree	% Female
1960/61	268	* 44	84	* 30
1965/66	656	* 39	144	* 33
1970/71	1,377	* 38	319	* 34
1971/72	1,118	* 39	433	* 35
1972/73	1,175	42.6	431	38.3
1973/74	1,230	43.9	490	35.9
1974/75	1,287	45.1	552	36.1
1975/76	1,107	48.0	609	37.6
1976/77	1,223	49.6	679	37.7
1977/78	1,210	50.0	748	35.8
1978/79	1,258	53.8	695	38.1
1979/80	1,227	58.6	745	40.7
1980/81	1,223	56.4	803	43.5
1981/82	1,136	57.7	779	48.2
1982/83	1,029	62.8	777	47.9
1983/84	1,235	61.9	777	49.2
1984/85	1,234	61.0	787	48.7

*Estimates based on data for three-year intervals.

the Netherlands who are unable to find work in their chosen profession. Table 3 presents the number of psychologists graduating from the universities each year. It is apparent from the data that, after a significant increase during the 1960s and 1970s, the number of new doctorates in psychology has stabilized at between 750 and 800 each year.

During the 1960s, many psychologists were hired by universities. In 1963 there were about ninety psychologists employed by universities, but by 1972 this number had increased to nearly 600, 32 percent of all psychologists (Krijnen, 1975). As university growth leveled off in the early 1970s and was followed by a decline in the late 1970s and 1980s, institutions of higher learning were forced to economize and thus reduce their faculties. The new generation of psychologists therefore looked for work in applied settings but experienced only limited success, especially in the clinical area. Out of 1,535 registered unemployed psychologists in 1983, 727 were clinicians. The situation for work-and-organizational psychologists was somewhat better. It has been of little comfort that the unemployment problems of the last ten years or so were predicted by a government study in 1958 and another study in 1968.

The NIP conducted a study in 1972 which demonstrated that the domain of professional psychology has become less exclusive (Krijnen, 1976). Many psychologists now believe that the particular positions they hold could reasonably well be filled by professionals from other social science disciplines. As a matter of fact, nearly 50 percent of psychologists shared this belief in 1972. In 1954, the figure was only 25 percent. There is clearly a substantial overlap among many disciplines.

Current enrollment figures indicate that the number of psychologists in the Netherlands will increase substantially during the 1980s, despite employment problems. In 1983, for example, 8,150 students were preparing to become psychologists; the figures for 1984 were even higher. These strong enrollments reflect the fact that, while employment opportunities are limited at this time, the situation is even more depressed in other related fields such as pedagogics and andragogics.

CONCLUSION

It is now almost 100 years since Heymans founded his laboratory in Groningen, and about eighty years since he presented his rectorial address in which he envisaged the forthcoming age of psychology. Heymans' high expectations about psychologists solving social problems and meeting personal needs have not come true, and psychology is not the dominant science he predicted. Nevertheless, psychology as a discipline and as a profession is today well established. The number of psychologists per capita is higher in the Netherlands than in almost any other country. Since so many students have enrolled in psychology, however, there is now a serious unemployment problem and the advancement of employment opportunities will need to be given top priority by the NIP in the next decade.

Dutch psychologists have a strong international orientation. In 1989, NIP and Psychon (in collaboration with EFPPA) will organize the first European Congress of Psychology in Amsterdam to stimulate scientific and professional communication among European psychologists.

REFERENCES

Abma, R. (1983). Psychology between science and society: Development of psychology at the Catholic University of Nijmegen. In S. Bem, H. van Rappard, & W. van Hoorn (Eds.), *Studies in the history of psychology and the social sciences.* Proceedings of the First European Meeting of Cheiron (Amsterdam, September 1982), Leyden.

Dijkhuis, J. J. (Ed.). (1968). Psychology in the Netherlands. Special issue of *De Psycholoog, 3*, 431–475 (on the occasion of the XVIth Congress of Applied Psychology, Amsterdam, 1968).

Drenth, P. J. D., Thierry, H., Willems, P. J., & Wolff, Ch. J. de (Eds.). (1984). *Handbook of work and organizational psychology.* Chichester: Wiley.

Eisenga, L. K. A. (1978). *Geschiedenis van de Nederlandse Psychologie* [History of psychology in the Netherlands]. Deventer: Van Loghum Slaterus.

Groot, A. D. de (1946). *Het denken van den schaker, een experimenteel-psychologische studie* [The thinking of chess players, an experimental-psychological study]. Amsterdam: Noord-Hollandishe Uitgevers Maatschappij.

Hoorn, W. van. (1976). Psychology in the Netherlands. In A. Misiak and V. Sexton (Eds.), *Psychology around the World* (pp. 293–316). Monterey, CA: Brooks/Cole.

Krijnen, G. (1975). *Ontwikkeling functievervulling van psychologen* [Functional development of psychologists] (Part I). Nijmegen: Institute of Applied Psychology.

Krijnen, G. (1976). *Ontwikkeling functievervulling van psychologen* [Functional development of psychologists] (Part II). Nijmegen: Institute of Applied Psychology.

Michon, J. A., Eykman, E. G. J., & de Klerk, L. F. W. (1979). *Handbook of psychonomics* (2 vols.). Amsterdam: North Holland.

Netherlands Institute for Psychologists. (1975). Professional code for psychologists. *De Psycholoog, 10*, 179–285.

Rosenzweig, M. R. (1982). Trends in development and status of psychology: An international perspective. *International Journal of Psychology, 17*, 117–140.

Rutten, F. J. Th. (1958). De geschiedkundige ontwikkeling der sociale psychologie in Nederland [The historical development of social psychology in the Netherlands]. *Nederl. T. v. Psychologie, 13*, 89–110.

Strien, P. J. van. (1984). Psychology and its social legitimation: The case of the Netherlands. *Proceedings of the Second Meeting of Cheiron-Europe*, Heidelberg, 1983. Leiden, pp. 80–99.

Wolff, Ch. J. de (1984). The role of the work- and organizational psychologist. In P. J. D. Drenth et al. *Handbook of work and organizational psychology.* Chichester: Wiley, pp. 51–79.

Norway

Holger Ursin

NATURE AND SCOPE OF THE DISCIPLINE

It is easy to specify what a psychologist is in Norway. Since 1973 the profession of psychology has been regulated by law. Authorization is issued by the Governmental Health Authority and based on well-defined exams administered by the University of Oslo and the University of Bergen. There is some governmental influence on the exams, since changes in the psychology curriculum require changes in the law. This does not affect academic freedom in teaching and research, but the national standards guarantee a core of knowledge common for all psychologists trained by the two universities.

The simplest way to define psychology is to state that psychology is whatever psychologists are doing professionally. This definition, however, excludes some of the activities within academic psychology involving nonpsychologists. Many engaged in psychological research are, in fact, trained in medicine (the present author included), education, or social science.

This review covers research taking place within psychological laboratories, departments, institutes, or faculties even though the research is also part of neurophysiology, sociology, behavioral medicine, psychiatry, or education. Only work that has attained international prominence is considered. Adequate recognition is not given to those who devoted much of their professional careers to translating and transforming psychological literature written in foreign languages into Norwegian; their efforts in large measure made contemporary Norwegian psychology possible.

Organizations

Close to 90 percent of Norwegian psychologists are members of the Norsk Psykologforening [Norwegian Psychological Association]. This organization functions both as a professional society and as a trade union, negotiating salaries and working conditions (secretariat: Bjørn Farmandsgate 16, Oslo 2). Negotiations with state and local governments on these matters go primarily through a larger organization, the Akademikernes Fellesforbund (AF) [Academicians Central Organization], which is made up of academically trained professionals from several disciplines. The organization that represents scientists including psychologists employed by the universities or research organizations is also a member of AF. This organization is known as the Norsk Forskerforbund [Norwegian Association for Research Workers]. The chairman was for several years Per Schioldborg, a psychologist.

The Norwegian Psychological Association in collaboration with health authorities licenses specialists in clinical psychology. The arrangement is analogous to that of the medical profession for its specialists. The association has a permanent committee for ethical issues regarding both clinical work and research. Serious complaints which may impact on licensing are handled by the State Psychology Board (Psykologrådet, chairman: Professor Bjørn Christiansen, Bergen) appointed by the national government.

Within the various applied fields there are groups, some rather informal, which arrange for collaborative efforts among colleagues. Such groups exist for clinical psychologists and for psychologists concerned with mental retardation, alcohol and drug abuse, educational psychology, hypnosis, and industrial and organizational psychology. Some involve psychological researchers from all the Scandinavian countries. This is the case for those working in the areas of physiology and behavior (Holger Ursin, Department of Physiological Psychology, University of Bergen) and cognitive and sensory psychology (Per Saugstad, Institute of Psychology, Oslo).

Major Programs and Laboratories

In Norway, research and teaching programs are separate because the two major universities, at Bergen and Oslo, train their psychologists for applied or professional careers. Preprofessional and professional training is provided by separate departments or institutes. In Bergen, these units constitute a faculty within the university, just as there are faculties for medicine, law, social science, and so forth. In Oslo, the Institute of Psychology is a part of the Social Science Faculty. Teaching is handled by four separate groups with instructional responsibilities at all levels. The various units in Bergen and Oslo are also engaged, at least in principle, in providing research training in their particular fields. Further information may be obtained by writing either the Faculty of Psychology in Bergen (University of Bergen, N–5014 Bergen) or the Institute of Psychology in Oslo (University of Oslo, P.O. Box 1094, Blindern, Oslo 3) (see also Hassel (1983), who describes Norwegian and other European programs).

University of Bergen

In Bergen the preprofessional departments are separate units with their own budgets, grants, and research programs. Each department has to do with a major area of psychology and is generally staffed by one professor and two or more lecturers (*lektors*). In addition, there are usually one or more postcandidate research fellows, supported primarily by grants from the Norwegian Research Council for Science and the Humanities or other extramural sources. The university itself offers a few fellowships.

The program at Bergen in physiological psychology is supervised by Professor Holger Ursin. The initial research focus of this group was limbic structures and behavior based on the pioneer work of B. Kaada and R. McCleary. At present, projects range from the neurobiology of hippocampus slices to collaborative studies with the Norwegian Navy and the Norwegian Underwater Technology Center concerning neuropsychological changes in the same brain structures following exposure to high atmospheric pressures.

The oil discoveries in the North Sea have stimulated research on the physiological and psychological effects of deep diving and ways to improve safety on ships and oil platforms. Another major research interest of this group is stress-related disorders in animals and humans. Based on an animal model of endocrine changes during coping, proposed by G. D. Coover, H. Ursin, and S. Levine in 1964, a series of human psychoendocrine studies were conducted by Ursin, Levine, and E. Baade. A specific psychosomatic model for gastrointestinal and cardiovascular diseases and psychiatric conditions was also worked out recently by Ursin and R. C. C. Murison. The importance of defense mechanisms for performing dangerous tasks was demonstrated by R. Vaernes in 1983 confirming work by Swedish researcher U. Kragh. Linkages between defense mechanisms and the immunological system in personnel with low coping capacity and high levels of reported stress have also been suggested by studies done in the early 1980s by Ursin and his coworkers.

The first research group in psychology at the University of Bergen had to do with cognitive psychology. The unit is now under the leadership of Professor Kjell Raaheim whose primary interests concern problem solving and intelligence. D. Svendsen, who died in 1981, was very active with cognitive developmental psychology and also much interested in epidemiological approaches to psychosocial health problems. K. H. Teigen had published a series of studies on the psychology of judgment and preferences. T. Dalland, whose original work was in animal neuropsychology (hippocampus and septum), is currently applying models from this area to developmental studies of human learning and memory. And, finally, T. Helstrup has studied various forms of memory.

In the social psychological area at the University of Bergen, Professor Julius Marek is engaged in research on problems connected with environmental safety. In the field of traffic safety, he has collaborated with T. Steen in Trondheim; in the area of industrial safety, particularly with regard to oil platforms, he has done research with L. E. Aarø. Aarø is also conducting studies on health education and is engaged in behavioral epidemiology. He has, for example, studied smoking in medical doctors and in children and been actively involved in the antismoking program for the World Health Organization.

In personality psychology, Professor Dan Olweus is well-known for his pioneering studies on aggression in boys; his findings have been important in a national campaign against bullying in Norwegian schools. D. Olweus and his coworkers have also found relationships between plasma testosterone levels and aggression in boys, related, in particular, to lack of frustration tolerance and a defensive type of aggression. F. Vollmer has worked on achievement motivation in children, students, and parachutist trainees.

Arne Øhman, who was professor of somatic psychology, or psychophysiology, in Bergen, has returned to Sweden for a professorship in Uppsala. Øhman, the president-elect of the Society for Psychophysiological Research in 1983, developed a very active laboratory. R. Eide has studied psychosocial risk factors for cardiovascular disease, in particular hypertension, in western Norway. S. Svebak is using traditional psychophysiological methods to study "mirthfulness" and the relationships between motivational states, emotional load, and information load. Together with J. Stoyva he recently published a theoretical paper on the pleasurable effects of high arousal.

The faculty runs its own outpatient clinics for children, adults, and the elderly in addition to a neuropsychological clinic and a facility devoted to psychodiagnostic and psychotherapeutic research. Some patients are referred by medical staff, and a degree of collaboration exists with medical departments. There is, for instance, a project concerning parents of seriously ill children being conducted by M. Raundalen and A. Dyregrov, as well as a study by O. Havik concerning patients who have gone through myocardial infarctions.

The Department of Clinical Neuropsychology at Bergen under the leadership of Professor Hallgrim Kløve focuses on Kløve's work on the Halstead-Reitan test batteries. The department also studies the relationships between the pharmacological treatment of hyperactive children and a psychophysiological classification of patients. This approach is partially based on an animal model developed by neurophysiologist Kjell Hole at the Institute of Physiology in Bergen. B. Ellertsen and D. Hammerborg are also working on a system of classifying and measuring headaches based on psychophysiological measurements. Biofeedback has been used for several problems, including epilepsy. Basic research on epilepsy is carried out through joint projects with R. Ursin and S. Grahnstedt at the Sleep Laboratory of the Institute of Physiology.

Moreover, the clinic is collaborating on a research program for alcoholics with Hjellestad-Klinikken, probably the best facility for the treatment of alcoholism in Norway. T. Løberg has examined the neuropsychological profiles and MMPI response patterns of alcoholics. The latter are remarkably similar to those reported by psychologists in the United States. Løberg has also studied violence in alcoholics.

Professor Bjørn Christiansen has a key position within the community psychology program at Bergen. Christiansen was the founder of the program and held the chairmanship of the institute (now faculty) for many years. The public perception of psychology in Norway as a credible, academically based profession and the achievement by the discipline of a strong administrative structure and legal status may be credited in large part to the vision and persistence of Christiansen. The transition from intense controversy to creative collaboration and cooperation within Norwegian psychology may be due to the open and enlightened climate created in psychology at Bergen during the late 1960s. Christiansen has written extensively on Norwegian psychology, from both a local and an international perspective. The community psychology program is currently engaged in gerontopsychological research and in crisis intervention and network building for widowers and widows.

Educational psychology is important at Bergen since many psychology graduates work in schools. Professor Hans-Jørgen Gjessing, who heads this program, has been working mainly on learning disorders; he is in charge of a large Nordic study of children with learning disabilities.

In the area of organizational psychology, work is being done at Bergen by Professor Svein Kile on group processes in industrial and business settings. Kile, who heads this unit, has been a central figure in the development of organizational psychology in Norway. His research, emphasizing psychosocial factors and health in the textile industry, has had a positive impact on working conditions in Norway. Organizational psychology is now a significant growth area within the discipline.

Most students who study psychology at Bergen receive assistance with their research projects from the Department of Psychometrics. Professor Hans Magne Eikeland, who heads the department, has, in collaboration with Bertheussen, provided a rationale for estimating generalizability coefficients in multifactorial designs. He has also worked with the univariate eta concept. T. B. Johnson developed a useful multipurpose program and several innovative applications of multivariate methods. K. Hagtvet studies the relationships between worry, emotionality, and fear of failure and test anxiety.

University of Oslo

Relative to the psychology department at Bergen, there is less integration of the research and teaching functions of the psychological institute at the University of Oslo. As a consequence, there is more flexibility, with each instructor being assigned to one of four instructional programs: personality and clinical psychology (coordinator: Leif J. Braaten), developmental and social-cognitive psychology (coordinator: Lars Smith), biological and clinical neuropsychology (coordinator: Carl Erik Grenness), and methods (coordinator: Thorleif Lund). These sections are responsible for instruction at all levels of the preprofessional and professional programs. Research groups comprise smaller units within the instructional programs.

The institute is well known for its research on perception, especially visual perception. Professor Ivar Lie, for example, has done basic work on rod-and-cone interactions, color contrast, perceptual constancies, and visual detection. He has also conducted applied research on visual impairments and ways to help the visually handicapped. Some of his studies have taken him into the field of ergonomics. S. Magnussen has been a prolific investigator of the visual processes having done research with many collaborators. S. Krekling has focused on binocular depth discrimination.

Perhaps the most significant contribution of this group is the work on color vision by brothers B. and U. Stabell, inspired by the studies of Per Saugstad and I. Lie on duplicity theory. P. Schioldborg investigates attention and visual perception and has done applied work on the relevance of perceptual theory for children's traffic safety. It should be noted that much of the empirical research of this group of investigators derives from ideas and theoretical positions originally developed by Saugstad. Saugstad's interests have more recently turned to psycholinguistics.

Other programs in Oslo include a small, but active, group concerned with animal learning and limbic neuropsychology (T. Sagvolden). There is also a well-equipped psychophysiology laboratory (F. Sagberg and K. B. Kveim). D. Smørvik and L. Smith study the behavior of babies and small children experimentally; E. Hartman and H. Haavind, with a more applied emphasis, investigate how mothers function as teachers for their children.

Professor Jan Smedslund, who is among the most highly cited Norwegian psychologists, has worked on a variety of problems (see Table 1). Initially he did experimental work inspired by Egon Brunswik on multiple-probability learning. Later he worked with both J. Piaget and J. Bruner on the cognitive development of children. His writings on applications of Piaget's psychology are available in English, French, and Norwegian. A specialist in clinical psychology since 1977, he has worked with young drug addicts and also has a private practice. He has proposed a set of basic "rules" of psychological treatment and developed a controversial "common sense psychology."

The studies of social interaction and communication by Professor Ragnar Rommetveit comprise the focus and foundation for one of the most influential research groups in Oslo. He and his coworkers have developed a social-cognitive theory of communication which has generated many investigations. In these studies, researchers have been able to combine field observations with laboratory experiments. R. M. Blakar is the most active of Rommetveit's younger colleagues. He has published extensively and coauthored an interesting review of Norwegian social psychology with H. E. Nafstad in 1982.

Research on the career problems of women has been augmented by the theoretical and empirical work of Rommetveit and Blakar. This area of study started in the early 1970s inspired by the work of H. Holter, who now heads a group that specializes in investigating this issue.

Related to the Oslo Institute, but apart from it, is the Center for Research in Clinical Psychology established by the Norwegian Research Council for Science and the Humanities. The director of this center is Svenn Torgersen, who has for the last fifteen years conducted twin studies on the relationships between blood pressure and anxiety disorders, phobic fears, and neurosis. He was trained by

Table 1
Most Frequently Cited Norwegian Authors in Psychology, 1975–1982

		Number of quotations				
		1975–79	1980	1981	1982	Total
B. Kaada	Brain and behavior	407	69	57	63	596
C. Kohler	Brain, behavior, neurochemistry	58	46	100	114	318
J. Smedslund	Developmental, cognitive	131	28	68	55	282
H. Ursin	Brain and behavior, stress	117	43	62	35	257
A. Øhman	Psychophysiology	113	58	27	30	228
C. Astrup	Psychiatry, conditioning	140	32	17	34	223
K. Hole	Behavioral neurochemistry	128	27	25	14	194
R. Ursin	Sleep, brain and behavior	97	20	25	21	163
E. Kringlen	Psychiatry, genetics	81	31	26	14	152
H. Kløve	Clinical neuropsychology	80	20	31	11	142
K.-G.Gøtestam	Learning, psychiatry	93	16	7	16	132
U. Stabell	Vision	68	16	5	18	107
D. Olweus	Aggression	17	39	13	30	99
R. Rommetveit	Psycholinguistics, social	55	15	6	4	80
B. Stabell	Vision	49	9	5	17	80

Source: Science Citation Index and Social Science Index (first authors only).

Einar Kringlen who was professor of clinical psychology in Bergen for several years. He then held a position in behavioral medicine in Oslo and is currently in psychiatry in Oslo. Kringlen is known for his work on twins and psychosis; he has written textbooks in psychiatry and behavioral medicine.

There are several active clinical researchers in Oslo. A.-L. Løvlie has studied the ego functions of psychotherapists. L. Braaten, originally trained by Carl Rogers, has written about a wide range of clinical problems including student mental health and group psychotherapy. Several projects at the center have focused on psychological factors involved in diseases such as asthma and diabetes mellitus and the family situation of children with leukemia. Involved in this research have been A. Faleide, L. K. Thulesius, and J. Haug and his collaborators.

Finn Tschudi and Gudrun Eckblad, psychometricians in Oslo, developed computer programs for the behavioral sciences in the late 1960s. These programs were important for the development of modern computer science in Norwegian psychology. Eckblad developed a "curvex structure" for the relationship between ratings of interestingness, task complexity, pleasantness, and happiness. T. Lund made important contributions in the area of multidimensional scaling, and J. M. Sundet has done heritability studies as a means of analyzing the effect of the environment on IQ scores.

Educational psychology is taught at a separate institute in Oslo where students do not receive the regular psychology degree. The emphasis is on the practical applications of educational psychology, and some research has been published internationally. Professor Eva Nordland, for example, studies psychosomatic and electroencephalographic abnormalities in boys with behavioral disturbances. O. O. Bø investigates the relationship between brain damage and perception and learning. T. Gjesme works on achievement motivation, test anxiety, and time perspective. R. Nygård and P. Rand likewise study achievement motivation. Finally, S. E. Ulvund does research on the influence of the physical environment on early cognitive and motivational development.

University of Trondheim

Graduate-level psychology is taught at the University of Trondheim, too, but according to a Ph.D. model which does not lead to a psychologist license. This program focuses on human learning, with clinical and educational emphases (Professor Ivar Bjørgen), and on the neurobiology of vision (Professor Paul Heggelund). Heggelund developed a laboratory for single-cell studies of the cat striate cortex. Professor Per Olav Tiller, who is responsible for the training of social workers, is also associated with the university.

The Department of Psychiatry at Østmarka Hospital in Trondheim, under the direction of Professor K. Gunnar Gøtestam, has offered postgraduate training for psychologists and physicians since 1977. Research here is concerned with psychological and biological treatment approaches. Gøtestam, who is trained both as a psychologist and a physician, is well known for his applications of learning theory within psychiatry.

Regional Colleges

Regional "colleges" (*distriktshøyskoler*) are a new development in Norway. Originally, they were intended to provide abbreviated and more job-oriented training than the universities. Now, it is possible to earn university degrees in fine arts, natural science, and political science. Most of these colleges do not have psychology departments. In Stavanger, however, where psychology is taught at the introductory level, there is an active research program in psychosocial stress factors and biofeedback as well as an animal laboratory (Odd Harald Zahl Begnum, Rogaland Distriktshøgskole, P.O. Box 2540, Ullandhaug, N–4001 Stavanger). Jo Kleiven at the regional college in Lillehammer investigates communication and social psychology in collaboration with the Rommetveit group.

Other Research Programs

Several national research centers are located in Oslo. These include institutes dealing with occupational and organizational psychology (Work Research Institutes, P.O. Box 8149, Oslo 1), problems associated with drugs and alcohol, and gerontology. The Norwegian College of Physical Education and Sports has an active psychology program (Professor A. Morgan Olsen, Professor W. S. Railo).

The Norwegian Research Council for Science and the Humanities has three programs for the development of special competencies relevant to psychology. The programs for clinical research and for the role of women in society have been mentioned. A third program concerned with interdisciplinary research on children and located in Trondheim (NAVF's senter for barneforskning, N–7055 Dragvoll) was started in 1982.

Primary Functions of Psychologists

Nearly 50 percent of Norwegian psychologists work within the public health system and about 25 percent are employed by the school system. The rest do research, teach, consult, serve as administrators, or are involved with industrial, military, occupational, or rehabilitation psychology.

Funding of the Discipline

School psychologists are paid by local governments which are partially reimbursed by the national government. Salary and working conditions are determined by negotiations on the national level. Clinical psychologists are most often employed by mental health facilities and hospitals. Their salaries are also negotiated nationally and paid by county governments. Those in private practice receive reimbursement from the compulsory health insurance system with fixed rates per patient per treatment hour, or per diagnostic procedure.

Research in psychology is funded by universities, the government directly, or the Norwegian Research Council for Science and the Humanities, which is funded by the government. University funds tend to be granted without any serious peer review of research proposals. Monies are dispensed on a per capita basis rather than on the basis of merit. The Research Council, on the other hand, reviews proposals carefully.

University support for laboratory research is generally insufficient. The growth in funding which occurred during the early 1970s has ended. Many researchers must find monies from external sources. This has led to an emphasis on applied studies and there is some concern that basic research is suffering as a consequence.

The Royal Norwegian Council for Scientific and Industrial Research also funds some psychological studies. This support, however, is for applied rather than basic research. At present the council is funding research on safety and psychological stress in various work environments. Several of the governmental ministries have research and development programs that provide monies to the universities. University research budgets are further augmented by donations from private foundations (the Meltzer Foundation in Bergen; Anders Jahres Fund in Oslo). Finally, some psychologists do applied research for private industries.

Curriculum Models

There is no undergraduate college system in Norway. After students complete twelve years of schooling, the last three years within a gymnasium program, they may enroll in one of the four universities (Bergen, Oslo, Tromsø, or Trondheim) or one of the regional colleges (*distriktshøyskoler*). The student who elects psychology as his or her main field has to complete the general introductory course, which usually takes from one to one-and-a-half years. Students with top marks (approximately the upper 20 percent) may then enter the psychology "school" for an additional five years of training. There is limited admission in Bergen and Oslo, with a waiting period of a year or more. After successful completion of the final examination, the student has earned the academic title of Candidate of Psychology. The candidate title is common to all the learned professions, including medicine and law.

For a scientific career, the candidate degree must be supplemented by research training and a thesis leading to the doctorate. The thesis requirement generally involves three or four published papers relating to one common problem, or the equivalent in manuscripts or a monograph. There are stipends available for some students, generally with a limit of three years.

The clearest difference between psychological and medical training is the emphasis on research that is characteristic of the former. Research papers are required both in the preprofessional and the professional part of the curriculum. This necessitates a relatively high number of teachers per student. In Bergen, students have to complete one project per term for five terms, each term lasting approximately eighteen weeks. The marks given are based partly on performance on theoretical exams and partly on the quality of the project report. A dissertation must also be submitted at the end of the professional phase of the program.

Journals

The Norwegian Psychological Association has its own monthly journal, *Tidsskrift for Norsk Psykologforening* [Journal of the Norwegian Psychological Association], with abstracts in English (Sigrid Sandsberg, N–1560, Larkollen). There is one journal for school psychology, *Skolepsykologi* [School Psychology] (P.O. Box 121, N–2760 Brandbu), and one for education, *Norsk Pedagogisk Tidsskrift* [Norwegian Pedagogical Journal] (Oppland distriktshøgskole, avd. Wiese, P.O. Box 1004, N–2601 Lillehammer).

The Nordic psychological associations publish two journals in collaboration, *Nordisk Psykologi* [Nordic Psychology] and *Scandinavian Journal of Psychology*. Other journals include *Scandinavian Journal of Educational Research* and *Scandinavian Journal of Behavior Therapy* as well as several other Scandinavian publications in fields in which psychologists also publish.

Introductory Textbooks and Library Services

There are a number of Norwegian textbooks. The most widely used international texts are those by Krech, Crutchfield, and Livson and Hilgard, Atkinson, and Atkinson, both published in the United States.

Psychological abstracts, citation indexes, and computer-assisted literature searches are available at university libraries. Most international journals are on file in Bergen, Oslo, and Trondheim. Those not kept in local libraries can be accessed through a national and a European library network. The current situation is in stark contrast with that right after World War II when only one complete series of an international journal could be found at the Institute of Psychology in Oslo, and books were donated by colleagues in the United States.

Major Needs

It is probably a good sign that the most common complaints among colleagues responding to the question of needs were insufficient time, too few personal resources, and not enough training opportunities. While it is true that research funds for basic research have diminished, most laboratories have been able to survive the crisis through reallocation and more emphasis on applied research. These readjustments are not entirely negative, but basic research must be sustained in order to maintain quality programs.

Relationships with Other Disciplines

Since the health-care aspect of psychology is emphasized in Norway, the discipline maintains a close relationship with medicine. This relationship has been mutually beneficial, resulting in increased research and professional competence among psychologists and a heightened awareness of the importance of psychology and behavioral medicine among medical doctors. There is some conflict between psychologists and those trained in education because both qualify for jobs in the school system. In Bergen, there was also tension between psychologists and social scientists until they were organized into two faculties. Limited employment opportunities may, unfortunately, intensify interprofessional conflicts in the future, particularly insofar as psychology and medicine are concerned.

MAJOR TRENDS AND INFLUENCES SINCE WORLD WAR II

Demographic and Organizational Aspects

When the University of Oslo reopened in 1945 following the German occupation, the Institute of Psychology had a staff of one professor, H. Schjelderup, and one docent, Å. G. Skard. There were only fifteen psychologists in the country. By 1980, approximately 1,300 authorized psychologists were registered in Norway, and 100 or so new psychologists are graduating each year. Because of the age distribution, only a few retire each year. As a consequence, the annual increase in the number of psychologists is presently close to 8 percent. During the middle 1970s the growth rate reached 15 percent per year.

The initial phase of this period of rapid growth, which lasted until 1970, has been described by Å. G. Skard (1976), who was very much a part of that era. She was the third student to major in psychology (the year was 1930). She functioned as chairman of the Institute of Psychology in Oslo a number of times during the postwar period.

There are now thirty-two psychologists per 100,000 inhabitants in Norway. This is slightly lower than the thirty-seven to forty-three per 100,000 inhabitants in the United States, Denmark, Sweden, and the Netherlands. Unlike Norway, however, these countries report that some of their psychologists are unemployed. (Christiansen, 1981). Psychologists show the same preference for urban life as the members of other professions. Close to 40 percent live in Oslo. About 90 percent of Norwegian psychologists receive their salaries from the national government or local governmental sources.

A new degree program in psychology was introduced at the University of Oslo in 1948 and revised in 1956. In 1969, the University of Bergen initiated a program in psychology. In 1973, the Norwegian parliament approved a new law pertaining to the profession, providing a legal basis for the authorization of psychologists, and standards of training were developed. To some extent the Bergen curriculum became the national model. Previous conflicts between schools and orientations within psychology have diminished or entirely disappeared.

Research and Theory

Social Psychology

An extensive review of social psychology in Norway is available (Nafstad & Blakar, 1982). The prominence of this field in Norwegian research is due mainly to the founding with private funds of the Institute for Social Research in Oslo, in 1951, independent of the University of Oslo. For two decades this unique private facility was the center for modern social and psychological research in Norway. The institute supported the applied social sciences in general and there was enough academic freedom in addition to funding and competence to generate a broad and interdisciplinary research environment. Many American psychologists spent their sabbaticals here including J. Block, J. French, E. Frenkel Brunswik, E. Haggard, H. Hyman, I. L. Janis, D. Katz, and D. Krech. Funds came initially from the Fulbright program and other U.S. sources. American professors had a profound influence on the young Norwegian research fellows at the institute. Many of the men and women who built Norwegian psychology developed essential research skills here. These include B. Christiansen, S. B. Gulbrandsen, H. Holter, S. Lysgaard, R. Rommetveit, J. Smedslund, and P. O. Tiller. Since the late 1960s, several of the functions of the institute have been gradually taken over by governmental agencies, research institutes, or the universities.

The most productive social psychologist in Norway is R. Rommetveit. Many Norwegian psychologists regard him as the most creative psychologist in Norway. His major contribution, which is psycholinguistic in nature, concerns the hierarchical structure of language, the influence on communication of context and social factors, and the relationship between message structure and the structure of sentences. This work is the basis for a social-cognitive theory of communication. His first research on social norms and roles, conducted during the early 1950s, offered precise definitions of these terms, operationalizing the concepts as measurements of expectancies. His book on ego psychology published in 1958 had an important impact in Norway, Denmark, and Sweden. He has been active internationally and participated in an early cross-cultural investigation of threats and rejection involving some of the best social psychologists in the United States and Europe.

Psychoanalysis

Freud in his *Interpretation of dreams*, published in 1900, acknowledged the dream research reported by the Norwegian professor of philosophy J. M. Vold in the 1890s. In literature, Ibsen's writings clearly deal with dynamic processes antedating those analyzed by Freud. Even so, the impact of psychoanalysis on Norwegian cultural life in the late 1920s and the 1930s was remarkable, having a profound influence on literature, the fine arts, medicine, philosophy, and psychology.

Alnaes (1980) has recently reviewed the history of psychoanalysis in Norway. Both before and after World War II, Harald Schjelderup was a central figure in academic psychoanalytic research. He combined an empirical and scientific approach with psychoanalytic interests. He did not, however, compromise his academic standards in times rife with fads, fraudulent claims, and severe criticism by academicians of some of his work. In the middle 1950s, he published a review of the long-term effects of analysis on twenty-eight of his patients over a period of fifteen years. Even though there was no control group, this study represents a unique early investigation still worthy of attention.

Characteristic of Norwegian psychoanalytical thinking during the 1930s was a strong interest in the postural and muscular concomitants of ego defense. Nonetheless, this special focus was never well founded scientifically and has been a controversial issue since its inception. During the 1930s, many German scientists including Wilhelm Reich moved to Norway. Reich came in 1934, but in 1939 his residence permit was not renewed as a result of fraud charges stemming from his claims of "spontaneous life" in a contaminated bottle and "orgons" as energizers. He then moved to the United States where he died in prison. Some therapists, though, remained loyal to Reich despite legal, scientific, and ethical problems. Both physicians and psychologists use "characteranalytic vegetotherapy" based on Reichian prescriptions.

There is no doubt that Reich's influence set back Norwegian psychoanalysis. Norwegian analysts were ostracized from the International Psychoanalytic Association until 1975. On the surface the dispute seemed to concern the number of hours of analysis per week mandated, but at least initially the real issue had to do with whether or not Norwegian analysts were theoretically "pure."

Psychoanalysis does not command the same interest today, nor have the same status, it once did in Norwegian clinical psychology. In 1980 there were only forty members of the Norwegian Psychoanalytic Society, most of whom live in Oslo and are psychiatrists.

Skeletomuscular Psychophysiology

The psychological aspects of the skeletomuscular system have been emphasized in Norwegian psychology for many years. This is due, in part, to the influence of Trygve Braatøy, a psychiatrist. He was eclectic in his approach to therapy and collaborated extensively with physiotherapists. While Braatøy was not a scientific researcher, during the 1940s and early 1950s, J. Clausen, one of the analysts he trained, studied the differences in the respiration patterns among normal, neurotic, and psychotic subjects. Clausen soon turned to experimental psychology (vision and psychophysiology) and moved to the United States in 1952. Some of Braatøy's works were published in English posthumously in 1954.

Bjørn Christiansen perpetuated the Norwegian interest in somatic psychology. He studied respiration patterns with Gardner Murphy at the Menninger Foundation during the early 1960s and with Arthur Shapiro in New York in the mid–

1960s. Much of his empirical work has never been published but his theoretical perspective is portrayed in a book, *Thus speaks the body* (1972). Christiansen's viewpoints have been reflected both in the curriculum he organized in Bergen and through the personal care he took in establishing a special Department of Somatic Psychology. S. Svebak, who has published extensively on the contraction patterns in muscles as a function of psychological dynamics, is now in charge of this unit.

Biological Psychology

Brain science developed early in Norway. Fridtjof Nansen, for example, introduced Golgi's neuroanatomical silver-staining techniques into the country in the 1880s. The related clinical disciplines also developed vigorously. Following World War II, neurophysiology became a significant field. Birger Kaada, trained by J. Fulton at Yale, started his pioneer work on limbic structures in the Yale laboratory in the early 1950s. His most important contribution to behavioral research concerns the psychological aspects of the limbic structures of the brain. He published the first paper on hippocampus in rats and recent memory deficits in 1960 in collaboration with Wulff Rasmussen. Rasmussen set up the first laboratory for the study of rat behavior in Norway at the Institute of Psychology in Oslo.

The most cited studies ever conducted in Norwegian behavior research, even more so than the well-known Schjelderup-Ebbe pecking order research reported in 1921, were the Kaada and McCleary investigations of limbic structures and the inhibition/facilitation of behavior. Robert McCleary spent a year at the Anatomical Institute in Oslo, in 1957, before he became professor of psychology at the University of Chicago. The model proposed by Kaada and McCleary was based on Kaada's neurophysiological work and H. Mowrer's model for avoidance behavior. H. Ursin, trained by both Kaada and McCleary, spent the next twenty years working on this model before discarding it. In its stead T. Dalland and C. Kohler and H. Sundberg proposed a set of cognitive hypotheses, and T. Sagvolden offered an explanation based on an arousal model.

Kaada's work on limbic structures was also the starting point for neuroethological research by Ursin and his collaborators in the 1960s on temporal lobe structures and their importance for flight, defense and avoidance behavior and, in the 1970s, on coping strategies. The model derived from this experimental animal research by Ursin and R. C. C. Murison, in the early 1980s, predicts rather well the relationships between psychological strain, level of control, and somatic disease in humans.

Ethology

In addition to the neuroethological studies mentioned above, psychologists and zoologists have observed animal behavior in the hostile arctic environment. These investigations are part of an extensive research program in arctic biology started by Professor Johan B. Steen and now headed by Professor A. S. Blix at the University of Tromsø. H. Allen recently examined the relationships between hen and chick in the arctic grouse, including the learning that takes place while the chick is still in the egg. G. Myhre, on the other hand, has investigated how social structure influences the physiological state of the same species. In Trondheim there is a new ethology research group. Professor Y. Espmark, a zoologist, is an expert on deer behavior, and T. Bjerke, a psychologist, is examining imprinting in several species of birds.

Learning

Standard operant conditioning techniques have been used extensively in the neurophysiological and neuropsychological laboratories in Bergen and Oslo. They are also employed in the research on grouse being conducted in Tromsø. Only T. Sagvolden in Oslo does research on the learning processes per se. T. Bjørgen and his collaborators in Trondheim have, however, investigated human learning for many years, and C. Astrup has studied classical conditioning phenomena in psychiatric patients.

Interest in the practical applications of learning theory has increased. There are now several laboratories and clinics using procedures based on learning principles to treat behavioral problems and somatic complaints. The leading researcher in Norway in this field is K. Gunnar Gøtestam. His applications of learning theory range from traditional psychiatric care to the treatment of alcoholism and pain. He has also established an animal laboratory in Trondheim for the study of basal mechanisms. His group has recently investigated the effects of diazepam on both discrimination and conditioned emotional responses and conducted research on the reinforcing effects of amphetamines.

Common-sense Psychology

Jan Smedslund advocates a set of common-sense theorems which he claims represent relationships among concepts embedded in ordinary language. A rather unsettling conclusion reached by Smedslund in 1978 was that much psychological research is pointless since it attempts to verify logically necessary statements rather than test empirically open questions where more than one possibility is predicted by common sense. This controversial position has been questioned by Albert Bandura and many other psychologists. Smedslund's present stance seems more generally acceptable. He now claims that since common-sense assumptions are shared by all members of a culture, they can be empirically tested. His research on a system of thirty-six psychological theorems derived from Brandura's theory of self-efficacy seems to support his position.

Applied Areas

Child and School Psychology

From the beginning, educational psychology in Norway had two roots, one related to the educational process, the other to clinical problems. Each tradition was pioneered by a woman.

Åse Gruda Skard was the first clinical child psychologist in Norway. Her work became known internationally, some of her publications being translated into Danish, English, Eskimo, Finnish, Korean, Swahili, and Swedish. She has received numerous awards. Her interests range from animal research to systematic observations of behavior in children and longitudinal follow-up studies of small cohorts.

Helga Eng was the first professor of educational psychology in Norway. She was appointed in 1938, after many years of work in experimental psychology and education. She was trained by Wundt, though initially rejected by him because she was a woman ("die mannlichen mussen der Vorzug haben"). During the 1920s, she preceded Darrow and Lacey in finding differences in physiological responses relative to the stimulus situation. Her main contribution to Norwegian psychology, however, was in educational psychology. Unfortunately, the close contact between basic and applied research which she advocated failed to continue.

Clinical Research

Although both Bergen and Oslo train their psychologists for applied or professional careers, most of the research is nonclinical. It has been difficult to fill the top positions of the clinical departments with people who have both clinical and academic competencies. To counter this, the Norwegian Research Council for Science and the Humanities has made an effort to upgrade clinical research. Two centers have been established, one in Bergen and one in Oslo, headed, respectively, by Geir Nielsen and Svenn Torgersen. Fellowships have been granted and foreign guest professors invited for prolonged visits.

The conventional way of stimulating and expanding applied research is to support productive researchers who have the experience to train others. Fortunately such individuals exist and progress has been made in the areas of learning theory, biological psychology, biological technology, and new therapeutic techniques.

The curriculum facilitates cooperation between traditionally separated disciplines. There are, for example, cooperative programs in clinical neuropsychology in Bergen and psychiatry in Trondheim. These programs combine basic and clinical research and use psychological and biological methods, both in testing and in therapy.

Social psychology, a well-developed field, has also facilitated clinical research and practice. R. M. Blakar and his students have contributed to the understanding of schizophrenia and psychopathological processes in general. Labeling theory has been used by R. Ommundsen and T. J. Ekeland and by P. Gjerde, R. Sand, and J. Kleiven to investigate the process of psychiatric diagnosis. The effects of modeling, feedback, and experimental factors on counselor empathy have been studied by H. M. Rønnestad.

Drug Addiction Studies

The most serious addiction problem in Norway is alcoholism. Considerable research has been done in this area, notably by social psychologists such as S.

Bruun-Gulbrandsen. In recent years, the issue of controlled drinking has been a much debated topic in Norway.

N. Bejerot, a Swedish alcoholism expert, wrote a provocative paper in 1971 on drug addiction as a biological phenomenon involving "short-circuiting" of reward systems in the brain. Physiological psychologists H. Ursin and H. Sundberg rejected his speculations, contending that learning in general and state-dependent learning, in particular, were important factors in any drug dependency. The role of learning in drug dependency is now a topic of considerable interest within the curriculum at the University of Bergen, and a number of graduates of this program are doing research in the area at the Hjellestad Clinic. Postgraduate training at Trondheim also benefits from K. G. Gøtestam's combined basic and applied research approach. Finally, the fact that a NATO conference on drug dependency was held in Norway in 1977 is further evidence of the importance Norwegian psychologists place in the study of drug dependency.

Military Psychology

Since 1946, a small number of psychologists have worked in the Norwegian Armed Forces being involved in personnel selection, psychiatric treatment, and research of interest to the military. There is considerable collaboration in this field among psychologists in the Scandinavian and NATO countries and even among psychologists in nations not part of NATO.

Much of the research associated with personnel selection, which extends back to the immediate postwar period, has had to do with the performance and safety of pilots and other high-risk personnel (see, for example, the work of R. Gerhardt, V. C. Jarl, and E. Riis, published during the mid–1950s). Gerhardt also investigated the relationships between hemispheric laterality and performance in pilots. U. Kragh, in 1960, developed a defense mechanism test which appears to have considerable usefulness in selecting people for dangerous tasks. More recently, E. Baade examined the correspondence among psychological test scores, performance, and physiological responses in parachutist trainees.

PERSPECTIVES ON PSYCHOLOGY IN OTHER COUNTRIES

Norwegian psychology, which emerged early in the twentieth century, has its origins in the scholarly and scientific developments in Germany, Austria, and, to some extent, France and Switzerland. Much later, the intellectual exodus from Germany during the 1930s had an important impact. After World War II, the main developments in psychology took place in the United States and there was much collaborative work with American psychologists. The assistance given Norwegian psychology by the U.S. government and American colleagues had a profound effect on the postwar reemergence of the discipline in Norway.

While the American connection remains reasonably strong, European cooperative efforts have increased. This is especially the case in social psychology and biological psychology. The Piagetian influence has, of course, been substantial for some time, and British contributions to learning theory, personality theory, perception, and human factors research have grown in significance. In matters having to do with the professionalization of the discipline, the influence of U.S. psychology remains primary. Norway has perhaps the most effective and enlightened legal underpinnings for psychology in Europe (Fichter & Wittchen, 1980; Hassel, 1983).

Psychology seems to have less to offer developing countries than other social science disciplines. Psychology tends to be viewed as a luxury when there is not enough food to go around. Since malnutrition has behavioral consequences, however, it should be recognized that familiarity with psychological knowledge and procedures might help change attitudes and habits that create and sustain the problem. Population control, for example, depends quite directly on an understanding of complex and interrelated psychological factors. Norwegian psychologists who have tried to provide assistance to underdeveloped societies include Arvid Ås, who died on a trip to Uganda in 1970.

NOTE ON THE FUTURE

The future of Norwegian psychology looks bright, in part because psychologists are trained according to a science-based professional model which prepares them for applied work. This strengthens psychology both as a basic science and as an applied art or craft. Collaborative research with other European countries will probably continue to expand. While fewer young psychologists from Canada and the United States have been coming to Norway in recent years, partly because of economic reasons, it is hoped that the situation will soon change. It would be a shame if psychologists from North America had less interchange with European psychologists just when psychologists from Europe have much more to share.

PSYCHOLOGISTS WITH A STRONG INTEREST IN THE HISTORY OF PSYCHOLOGY

Ivar Bjørgen, Institute of Psychology, University of Trondheim, N–7000 Trondheim.

Bjørn Christiansen, Department of Community Psychology, University of Bergen, N–5000 Bergen.

Carl Erik Grennes, Institute of Psychology, University of Oslo, Postboks 1094, Blindern-Oslo 3.

Per Saugstad, Institute of Psychology, University of Oslo, Postboks 1094, Blindern-Oslo 3.

Karl Halvor Teigen, Department of Cognitive Psychology, University of Bergen, N–5000 Bergen.

Holger Ursin, Department of Physiological Psychology, Arstadveien 21, 5000 Bergen.

NOTE

Several colleagues have been very helpful by answering my questionnaires, reading through parts of the chapter, and furnishing me with references and literature. I apologize for not being able to give them all the credit they deserve. Some helped substantially more than others, in particular Bjørn Christiansen, K. Gunnar Gøtestam, Knut A. Hagtvet, Tor Løberg, Robert C. C. Murison, Åse Gruda Skard, and Sven Svebak. In spite of their generous efforts, I remain solely responsible for all opinions and evaluatory statements in the text, as well as any errors that exist.

REFERENCES

Alnaes, R. (1980). The development of psychoanalysis in Norway. *Scandinavian Psychoanalysis, 3*, 55–101.

Christiansen, B. (1972). *Thus speaks the body.* New York: Arno Press.

Christiansen, B. (1981). Norsk psykologi i verdensperspektiv [Norwegian psychology in various perspectives]. *Tidsskrift for Norsk Psykologiforening, 18*, 621–636.

Fichter, M. M., & Wittchen, H. U. (1980). Clinical psychology and psychotherapy: A survey of the present state of professionalism in 23 countries. *American Psychologist, 35*, 16–25.

Hassel, K. (1983). Clinical psychology in other European countries. In A. Liddel (Ed.), *The practice of clinical psychology.* Chichester: Wiley.

Nafstad, H. E., & Blakar, R. M. (1982). Current trends in Norwegian social psychology: A brief review. *European Journal of Social Psychology, 12*, 195–212.

Skard, Å. G. (1976). Norway. In V. S. Sexton & H. Misiak (Eds.), *Psychology around the world* (pp. 317–28). Monterey, CA: Brooks/Cole.

SUGGESTED READINGS

Bandura, A. (1978). On distinguishing between logical and empirical verification: A comment on Smedslund. *Scandinavian Journal of Psychology, 19*, 97–99.

Braatøy, T. (1954). *Fundamentals of psychoanalytic techniques.* New York: Wiley.

Eckblad, G. (1980). The curve: Simple order structure revealed in ratings of complexity, interestingness, and pleasantness. *Scandinavian Journal of Psychology, 21*, 1–16.

Gerhardt, R., Jarl, V. C., & Riis, E. (1975). Étude du probleme de la sécurité en vol. *Revue de Psychologie Appliqué, 7*, 137–143.

Raknes, O. (1970). *Wilhelm Reich and orgonomy.* Oslo: Scandinavian University Books.

Rommetveit, R. (1978). Language and thought. *Cornell Review, 2*, 91–114.

Saugstad, P. (1965). *An inquiry into the foundations of psychology.* Oslo: Universitetsforlaget.

Schjelderup, H. (1955). Lasting effects of psychoanalytic treatment. *Psychiatry, 18*, 109–133.

Smedslund, J. (1982). Revising explications of common sense through dialogue: Thirty-six psychological theorems. *Scandinavian Journal of Psychology, 23*, 299–305.

Svebak, S. (1983). Helga Eng: A Norwegian precursor to Darrow and Lacey. *Psychophysiology, 20,* 600–601.

Ursin, H., & Murison, R. (Eds.). (1983). *Biological and psychological basis of psychosomatic disease.* Oxford: Pergamon Press.

Poland

Lidia Grzesiuk

NATURE AND SCOPE OF THE DISCIPLINE

Definition of Psychology

The psychologist whose perspective has had the greatest influence on psychological research in Poland is T. Tomaszewski (1975) who views psychology as both a scientific discipline and an applied profession. The focus of psychology as science is human purposive behavior, that is, actions directed toward the achievement of particular goals. Such behavior is referred to specifically as activity by Tomaszewski. Man's actions are always oriented toward particular objectives which undergo changes as a consequence of these activities. A human being is distinguished from other living organisms by his or her constant pursuit of certain goals and the accomplishment of definite tasks. Psychological knowledge is useful when it helps us understand how a person undertakes and fulfills such tasks. In this context, psychology is defined as the scientific study of human activity.

Overall Organizational Structure

Research

Research is carried out mainly at the psychology department of Warsaw University (ul. Stawki 5/7, 00–183 Warszawa) and at psychological institutes associated with Gdansk University (ul. Krzywoustego 19, 80–953 Gdansk), Jagiellonian University (ul. Golebia 13, 31–007 Krakow), Lodz University (ul. Uniwersytecka 3, 90–137 Lodz), Maria Curie-Sklodowska University (ul. Narutowicza 12, 20–004 Lublin), Adam Mickiewicz University (ul. Szamarzewskiego 89, 60–569 Poznan), Silesian University (ul. Tyszki 53, 40–126 Katowice), and Boleslaw Bierut University (ul. Dawida 1, 50–527 Wroclaw). Research is also conducted in the context of the Mikolaj Kopernik University Psychology

Chair in Torun (Fosa Staromiejska 3, 87–100 Torun). These facilities are all responsible to the Ministry of Higher Education and Technology (MHET) as are the psychology divisions or laboratories at higher pedagogical schools in Bydgoszcz, Czestochowa, Kielce, Krakow, Olsztyn, Rzeszow, Slupsk, Szczecin, and Zielona Gora. The psychology section of Catholic University in Lublin (Al. Raclawickie 14, 20–950 Lublin), which is independent of the MHET, carries out psychological studies as well.

At the Polish Academy of Sciences (PAS), psychological research is chiefly the responsibility of the psychology division (Plac Malachowskiego 1, 00–063 Warszawa) and its affiliated center in Poznan. Psychological departments and laboratories are connected, too, with other government agencies. For example, studies having to do with health care are conducted at medical academies (Gdansk, Krakow, Warszawa), the Psychoneurological Institute, the Mother and Child Institute, and the Institute of Labor Medicine and Hygiene. Educational research takes place at the Teachers' Training Institute, the Institute of Research on Youth, and the Institute of School Syllabuses. Various psychological projects are also carried out at the Academy of Internal Affairs, the Academy of Physical Training, the Central Institute of Labor Protection, the Main Institute of Mining, the Maritime Institute, the Institute of Delinquency Problems, the Sports Institute, the Institute of Industrial Design, the Military Institute of Aerial Medicine, and the Higher Navy School.

The PAS Psychological Sciences Committee, made up of representatives appointed by independent research psychologists, coordinates and supervises scientific projects. The committee assures that essential research is conducted in Poland.

Education

The education of psychologists takes place in the above-mentioned universities, whose graduates earn master's and doctoral degrees and assistant and associate professorships. Some university centers provide postgraduate courses aimed at the improvement of professional qualifications. Postgraduate training is also available outside the purvue of MHET, for instance, at the Medical Education Center.

Professional Activity

Clinical psychologists work primarily in institutions responsible to the Ministry of Health and Welfare, such as medical academies, hospitals, health care dispensaries, and centers offering psychotherapy. Educational psychologists are associated with agencies run by the Ministry of Learning and Education, particularly career guidance facilities. Work psychologists are employed by enterprises regulated by government departments having to do with building, mining, transportation, and so forth. Both applied and research psychologists belong to the Polish Psychological Society. Only a few psychologists are in private practice.

Major Programs and Laboratories

Research is carried out by psychologists in universities and the Polish Academy of Sciences. One of the major research projects recently undertaken is entitled "Diagnosis of the effectiveness of the educational system." It involves over twenty psychologists headed by Professor A. Gurycka of the Warsaw University psychology department (ul. Stawki 5/7, 00–183 Warszawa). Another project called "Changes of the personalities of individuals and changes in cultural life under the conditions of social reforms" is carried out by a team from the PAS psychology division (Pl. Malachowskiego 1, 00–063 Warszawa) under the direction of Professor J. Reykowski.

Primary Functions of Psychologists

Psychologists working at universities and other institutions of higher learning both teach and do research. Those at other scientific centers are almost entirely involved in research. Applied psychologists render a variety of services to the public. However, the professional status of psychologists is not adequately specified in all the areas of the field (there is no law having to do specifically with the profession of psychology in Poland).

Most clearly defined is the role and professional status of clinical psychologists. A special regulation issued by the Ministry of Health and Welfare, analogous to those operative in medicine, now provides clinical psychologists with two levels of specialization. Recently, clinical psychologists have become more than psychodiagnosticians and are increasingly involved in doing psychotherapy. Many are also beginning to take part in community and preventative projects. Psychologists doing educational counseling primarily do testing. In addition, they render preventive and corrective services for children and youth in need of psychological assistance. The functions of work psychologists are least well defined. They give tests, teach, serve as mediators, and provide practical advice in work settings. Overall, applied psychologists do relatively little research and teaching.

Funding of the Discipline

Instruction provided by universities under the auspices of the Ministry of Higher Education and Technology is paid for by the state. Catholic University in Lublin is the only institution of higher learning supported by public donations. Research is financed mainly by the government. Applied services are funded by various state agencies such as the Ministry of Health and Welfare and the Ministry of Learning and Education. A small number of psychologists are associated with units and laboratories sponsored by the Polish Psychological Society or work in medical cooperatives where fees are paid by their patients.

Curriculum Model

The training of psychologists in universities leading to the master's degree is designed to take five years. All university departments (with the one exception of Catholic University in Lublin) use the same MHET-approved curriculum. What is taught is determined to some degree by the instructors associated with each department. Three major categories of subjects are included:

1. Methods courses—taught in the initial period of study and covering the principles of data collection, the classification of information, and rudimentary statistical techniques
2. Courses on the major content areas—taught so as to present an integrated conception of the human species
3. Applied courses—designed to introduce students to the problems of applied psychology.

The syllabus includes courses on the history of psychology, cognitive processes, learning and memory, emotion and motivation, personality, the psychology of individual differences, methods of empirical research in psychology, statistical methods in psychology, foundations of diagnosis in psychology, biological mechanisms of behavior, social psychology, the psychology of human development, applied psychology, clinical psychology, educational psychology, and organizational psychology. Work for the master's degree concludes with the successful completion of a thesis and the passing of an examination.

In order to earn a doctorate, a university graduate has to write a dissertation under the guidance of a sponsor and then pass two examinations: one in psychology, the other in philosophy or economics. A positively reviewed dissertation is then subject to a public hearing before the faculty of the psychology department involved or an appropriate scientific council. If the candidate successfully defends his or her dissertation, the review board confers the Ph.D. degree, which must then be confirmed by the MHET.

The highest scientific degree is the degree of habilitated doctor which can be attempted by anyone holding a doctorate. This degree is earned by presenting any of the following: an original independent research study, a monograph published in book form, a concise scientific dissertation on a selected topic, or a series of published articles. If the work is approved by three reviewers, the candidate has to successfully present a colloquium before the psychology department council (or the institute's scientific council). A positive outcome is followed by a motion to confer the degree of habilitated doctor which must then be approved by the Central Qualifying Commission.

Major Journals

There are four major psychological periodicals in Poland:

Polish Psychological Bulletin, a quarterly published in English, carrying works by Polish psychologists. It appears under the auspices of the Polish Psychological Society and under the imprimatur of the PAS Psychological Sciences Committee.

Przeglad Psychologiczny [Psychological Review], a quarterly concerned with all fields of psychology except educational and teaching psychology, following trends in theoretical, empirical, and applied psychology in Poland and other countries. It also covers the professional affairs of psychological organizations (includes foreign summaries) and is published by the Polish Psychological Society.

Psychologia Wychowawcza [Educational Psychology], a bimonthly publication on theoretical and empirical research related to education, personality development, and the social environment. It also presents book reviews, reviews of Polish and foreign periodicals, and deals with the problems of psychological practice (includes foreign summaries). It is published under the auspices of the Ministry of Learning and Education.

Studia Psychologiczne [Psychological Studies], a biquarterly journal reporting empirical studies, published by the PAS Psychological Sciences Committee (includes foreign summaries).

The Most Widely Used Introductory Textbooks

The basic introductory textbook is *Psychologia* [Psychology] edited by T. Tomaszewski (1975). It defines psychology as a science of human activity. The subject matter of the book is drawn from domestic and foreign literature and covers the following topics: man and the environment, biological foundations of behavior, social foundations of behavior, consciousness, orientation in the environment, learning and memory, thought processes, language and speech, and the structure and regulating mechanisms of human actions and personality.

Psychologia spoleczna [Social psychology] by S. Mika (1982) spans theoretical and empirical achievements of world and Polish psychology. The book deals with the influence of social situations on psychic processes in man, human behavior, attitudes, interactions and interpersonal perception, and the group as a system of individuals in a state of interaction.

Psychologia kliniczna [Clinical psychology], edited by A. Lewicki (1969), is not systematically organized but reflects different theoretical foundations of clinical psychology as well as differences in clinical practice. The book presents an outline of clinical psychology by Lewicki and then deals with psychologists' tasks in psychiatric units, clinical and educational problems associated with children and youth, the role of psychologists in clinics dealing with the brain-damaged, and the foundations of criminal psychology.

Also used in the education of psychologists is a textbook edited by M. Zebrowska (1966), *Psychologia rozwoju dzieci i mlodziezy* [The psychology of developing children and youth], which presents a synthesis of psychological research from a dialectical conception of psychological development. Another textbook, *Podstawy rozwoju psychicznego dzieci i mlodziezy* [Foundations of the mental development of children and youth] by M. Przetacznikowa (1973), covers such issues as the objectives and tasks of developmental psychology, the concept of mental development, maturational process, the role of early experience in development, stages and factors in mental development, and indicators and mechanisms relative to the development of children and youth.

A handbook, *Stosowana psychologia wychowawcza* [Applied educational psychology] edited by A. Gurycka (1980), provides information about the professional training of psychologists concerned with assisting students. The book considers foundations of applied educational psychology, educational counseling, professional orientation and guidance, reeducation and therapy, psychodidactics, and psychological expertise relative to education.

Psychologia pracy [The psychology of work], a handbook edited by X. Gliszczynska (1979), is an introduction to professional issues of concern to psychologists doing research on work. The following topics are covered: the psychology of personnel selection, engineering psychology, management psychology, the social psychology of work, the utilization of decision theory for the psychology of work, and motivation and creativity.

The Availability of *Psychological Abstracts* and Citation Indexes

The basic sources of bibliographic information are two books edited by L. Woloszynowa (1974, 1977). The first is a bibliography of psychological writings published in Poland from 1946 to 1968; the other lists works published from 1969 to 1973.

Information on foreign publications is drawn from *Psychological Abstracts, Bulletin Signalitique, Child Development Abstracts and Bibliography, Deafness, Speech and Hearing Abstracts*, and *Current Contents*.

Major Needs

Not all the psychological specialties have achieved a clear professional status.

Psychologists have limited access to world literature.

Articles take more and more time to be published.

Research laboratories are frequently poorly equipped.

There is a lack of modern Polish textbooks in a number of psychological subjects.

Teaching aids lag far behind needs.

Few original psychodiagnostic instruments are available at university centers.

Graduate and postgraduate training is insufficient.

A large number of psychologists are not suitably prepared to offer psychotherapy, rehabilitation, and counseling; they are engaged only in diagnostic work.

Relations with Other Disciplines

The development of research in psychology is reflected in the increasing pursuit of complex studies which overlap the concerns of other disciplines. Hence new fields are formed at the interfaces between psychology and physiology (psychophysiology), neurophysiology (neuropsychology), and linguistics (psycholinguistics).

Psychological training also extends to many nonpsychologists. Psychology courses, for example, are included in the professional training of engineers, physicians, educators, and even agricultural specialists. The Institute of Social Prevention and Rehabilitation (Warsaw University), for instance, teaches clinical psychology as one of its professional specializations. Pedagogical programs provide courses on the developmental and clinical aspects of children. Medical studies include clinical and medical psychology.

The practical work of psychologists tends more and more to involve teams consisting of psychiatrists, social workers, and other specialists. This is particularly the case with regard to psychotherapy or projects having to do with community problems.

MAJOR TRENDS AND INFLUENCES SINCE WORLD WAR II

Organizations and Membership Trends

The Polish Psychological Society (PPS), founded in 1949, aims to promote theoretical and applied psychology by means of scientific meetings, lectures, workshops, publications, and scientific awards. In 1957 the society became a member of the International Union of Psychological Science (IUPsyS).

Since 1950 the membership of PPS has grown from 224 to 3,500. The society is made up of divisions, each representing a major city. There were seventeen such divisions in 1975; there are now twenty associated with the following cities: Bialystok, Bydgoszcz, Czestochowa, Gdansk, Katowice, Kielce, Koszalin, Krakow, Lublin, Lodz, Olsztyn, Opole, Poznan, Rzeszow, Szczecin, Siedlce, Torun, Warszawa, Wroclaw, and Zielona Gora.

Leadership of the society resides in the general assembly and the main board. The board appoints groups with the responsibility of working on particular problems. Operating currently are the following such units: Diagnostic Techniques Laboratory at the psychology department of Warsaw University; Psychoeducational Laboratory; Youth Psychotherapeutical Center; Educational Skills Development Center; Center for Psychological Family Assistance; Publishing Workshop; Psychotherapy and Prevention Workshop; Organizational Counseling Workshop; Prenatal Psychology Workshop; Consulting-Educational Workshop; Children and Youth Therapy Section; Somatic Patients Psychology Section; Children, Youth, and Family Psychological Therapy Section; and Psychological Assistance Section to help people with alcohol-related problems.

In order to understand the growth of Polish psychology since World War II, we need briefly to review the history of graduate education in Poland. In the 1950s, a course of study leading to the M.A. degree in psychology was inititated at the universities in Warsaw, Krakow, and Poznan. These institutions started to train psychologists within faculties independent from philosophy or pedagogy. In 1963, two clinical specializations were introduced: clinical psychology of adults and clinical educational psychology. In 1968, psychological studies were initiated in Katowice, Lodz, and Wroclaw, and, in 1978, a separate Institute of Psychology was founded at Warsaw University. These were eventually followed by independent institutes within pedagogical or philosophico-historical departments at other universities. The country's first department of psychology has been in existence at Warsaw University since 1981. Most university centers have institutes of psychology. A psychometric unit was established at the Polish Academy of Sciences in 1959 but closed ten years later. Since 1980 the PAS has included a psychology division.

In 1956, the number of clinical psychologists working in various divisions of the health service was 200. The agency currently employs over 1,500 psychologists, with some 900 working in psychiatric and neurological centers.

Educational and professional guidance centers for children and youth, established after World War II, were closed in 1953. Reinstated in 1956, they now number more than 500. Over 1,900 psychologists work at these facilities.

Data on work psychologists are scarce. In 1968, the mining and metallurgic industries operated twenty-one psychological laboratories. By 1976, the automobile transport industry employed over 160 psychologists, most of them young women. In 1976, about 600 work psychologists were employed in various national industries.

Publication Trends

The bibliography of psychological publications edited by L. Woloszynowa (1974, 1977) covers books and articles from professional and nonprofessional periodicals. Approximately 6,000 publications are listed in the first volume (1946–1968) and about five thousand in the second (1969–1973).

Most of the studies in psychology during the immediate postwar years were based on introspective approaches. Applied research focused on psychometric issues. Articles written in the 1950s were primarily about applications of Pavlov's theory of higher nervous system activity to theoretical and practical psychology.

During the 1960s, work centered on learning theory and the regulation theories of Polish psychologists. Tomaszewski (1963), for example, defined psychology as the science concerned with the regulation of mutual relations between living organisms and their environments. He considered the term "action" the basic concept in psychology. J. Reykowski defined personality as a central system of behavior regulation (see Maruszewski, Reykowski, & Tomaszewski, 1967). A. Lewicki (1969), on the other hand, proposed that clinical psychology had to do with goal-oriented activities governed by internal regulative mechanisms. And in the 1970s, J. Strelau's theory of temperament (1974), emphasizing regulative functions, was formulated. T. Tomaszewski's theory (1963) was used to analyze the mechanisms regulating the aggressive, decision-making, and linguistic activities of human beings (I. Kurcz & J. Reykowski, 1975). During the same decade, humanistic perspectives influenced clinical psychology.

By the late 1970s much interest had emerged in cognitive psychology, and psychological research in the 1980s has been dominated by cognitive theories. This is particularly true in social psychology, clinical psychology, and areas having to do with personality and decision making.

Societal Developments That Influenced the Discipline

During the 1950s, Polish psychology was strongly influenced by Marxist philosophy, Socialist ideology, and Soviet psychology. Introspective psychology and testing were strongly criticized by some psychologists. New conceptions, based on the principle of dialectical materialism were formulated. Psychology became the study of higher nervous activity, which led to the closure of mental health centers modeled after prewar American facilities along with a ban on tests. These centers were replaced by dispensaries whose employees, forbidden to use the title "psychologist," were essentially psychiatric assistants. In 1953, guidance centers for youth and children were also closed. The period of criticism of introspective psychology and testing yielded fruit in the form of an independent Polish theory of human functioning (regulation theory) and the utilization of clinical experiments in research (especially in neuropsychology).

Following sociopolitical changes in 1956, new opportunities for psychologists were created, particularly in applied psychology. Career and educational guidance centers, staffed by educational psychologists, reopened; clinical psychologists started to work out an approach to clinical diagnosis separate from the psychiatric model.

After 1956, psychologists (mainly scholars and researchers) had wider access to world science through travel and the availability of more foreign psychological literature. In the 1960s, scientific staff positions were significantly increased (at present Warsaw University's psychology department has over 100 faculty members), and the number of research projects and publications grew as well.

In the 1970s, increasing contact with psychologists in other countries facilitated the influence of humanistic psychology, particularly on clinical psychology. The principle of therapeutic community was introduced into hospital wards and psychotherapy extended to psychotics and their families. Group training techniques were also employed in both clinical and work settings.

Educational reforms, initiated during the 1970s, in primary and secondary education broadened the scope of educational psychology with psychologists now working directly in the schools. The restoration of industries destroyed by the war also created a demand for the services of work psychologists. Emphasis in this area shifted from the study of individuals to organizational research.

Research and Theory

The psychological literature in Poland is extensive and diverse. The theory of regulation, however, provides an integrative framework. The starting point is the action theory of T. Tomaszewski (1963, 1975) which provides a set of general assumptions about psychology as a science. Fundamental to the theory is the fact that man (and woman) has to regulate his relationships with his physical and social environment and in the process develop a personalized adaptive mode of functioning. All human behaviors serve regulatory functions but are also influenced by other processes. The simplest form of behavior is reactive, or stimulus-response (S-R). The activities most characteristic of humans, however, are goal-oriented and are referred to specifically as "actions." An action is a process directed toward the attainment of an effect (E) or goal whose structure is shaped by existing conditions. If in a specific situation a person identifies a goal to be achieved and a program to be implemented, he or she is said to be setting a task. Action is a reaction to a task situation (T) which is symbolically presented as T-E.

Goal-oriented behavior of the T-E type is a higher form of behavior than the S-R type. These types of behavior involve two different levels of organization: reactive reflexes, which operate in keeping with previous experience, and goal-oriented behavior, which reflects anticipation of the future. These two organizational processes are not mutually exclusive; hence a more detailed representation of goal-oriented behavior is T(S-R)E. Reactive activities, in other words, operate within goal-oriented actions.

The regulative functions of cognitive processes were stressed by A. Lewicki (1960). In the context of Pavlovian theory, Lewicki claimed that, from a functional point of view, cognitive processes have to be seen as mechanisms which enable an organism to adjust to the environment. These processes, he contended, play an essential role in determining our orientation to the environment by providing information about the value of objects and the activity relevant to particular objects. Lewicki, as part of his research on the ways new conceptions are formed, proposed that cognitive activities require both positive and negative abstraction. Positive abstraction is related to perception and the integration of the relevant features of a concept. Negative abstraction, on the other hand, eliminates irrelevant features and random background distractions.

The general theory of action was supplemented by concepts concerning specific types of situations, that is, tasks, problems, decisions, conflicts, and risks (see Nosal, 1979). J. Kozielecki (1968, 1969, 1975), the author of the theory of optimal decisions, made extensive studies of hypothesis formation and decision making which he saw as complex and directed actions of a phasic character allowing a person to use various strategies which were, however, vulnerable to the distortion of information. Kozielecki showed that the reception of information depends not only on the reliability of the source but also on its compatibility with previously acquired knowledge. His studies proved that individuals rarely use nondeceptive strategies in making decisions and formulating hypotheses. T. Tyszka (1973, 1978) studied the uses of game theory for the analysis of conflicts of interest and applied strategies.

Studies dealing with cognition also include a model worked out by J. Trzebinski (1981) of the structure, origins, and functioning of naturally occurring conceptions in developing human beings. From this perspective, the information constituting an idea determines the core and potential extent of its transformation. Every idea or notion is considered to have a center which is the syndrome of individual values associated with each of the significant dimensions of the notion. The process of transforming core information involves the gradual modification of the values connected with all of its dimensions. Trzebinski examined how the extent of potential transformations of cognitive structures affects human creative capabilities. In general, his research confirmed his theoretical assumptions.

The development of psycholinguistics in Poland is associated first of all with studies by I. Kurcz (1976). Her experiments examined the connections between cognitive processes and the structure of language. Her early surveys dealt with semantic memory and revealed functional differences between sensory and semantic generalization. Further research was inspired by N. Chomsky's theory which is consonant with regulation theory in that it proposes that speaking is not a sequence of acquired reactions but a system of goal-oriented activities. Kurcz's research in this field also dealt with differences in the forgetting of phonetic, syntactic, and semantic aspects of linguistic utterances. In addition, she studied differences in syntactic transformations with the same meaning (affirmative and negative sentences containing the same information). Kurcz confirmed that affirmative sentences provide the building blocks of human knowledge and that verbal information is most likely coded in the human mind in the form of affirmative sentences.

Studies by W. G. Shugar (1976) deal with the regulatory functions of the speech of small children insofar as communication in situations requiring cooperation is concerned. Her approach involves naturalistic observations and behavior stream unitization procedures. She found that linguistic functioning in small children depends both on the organization of their sphere of activity and on the partner who communicates with them. These factors determine the type of paradigmatic-functional context in which a child's utterances appear, providing their meanings and defining their effectiveness.

Studies on memory and learning processes in children have been conducted by Z. Wlodarski (1964, 1979). He examined the dependency of learning on the characteristics of the material taught and the way it is presented. His initial investigations provided data on the relationships between the sensory form of memorized material and the sensory modality through which it reaches the sub-

ject. He found, among other things, that the duration of traces of nonverbal
stimuli is specific to each sensory modality (there is no general sensory memory).
It also appears that the memorization of material via one sensory system is poorer
when learning effectiveness is measured using another sense. In a study on
learning extending over several years, he undermined the traditional view that
maximally organized knowledge is functionaly optimal. He found that the degree
of organization that most facilitates learning depends on the purpose the information or knowledge to be assimilated is to serve.

The "code-emotions" theory of K. Obuchowski (1982) presents an integration
of affective and cognitive functioning. He assumes that human psychological
processes, which are conditioned by anticipations of events and the accommo-
dation of programs of activity, serve survival. The human brain, he believes, is
capable of representing the world in various codes. There are separate systems
for the reception and processing of information. Concrete codes underlie automatic anticipation processes while abstract codes serve creative or constructive
anticipations. The first category includes a code through which an individual
registers statistical correlations of events and a code to register reality in the
form of images. Among abstract codes, the author distinguishes a semantic code
(to represent reality in the form of models with unrestricted degrees of generalization) from a creative code (to enable the simulataneous spatial processing
of information). The employment of a code in a given situation is determined
by emotional processes which serve both signifying and activating functions.
Negative emotions elicit concrete codes and positive emotions trigger abstract
codes. The intensity of the positive and negative properties of situations determines the level of activation. High activation levels block cognitive processes
while low levels induce transitions to the concrete code.

J. Reykowski's regulatory personality theory (1966) also combines cognitive
and emotional mechanisms. His theory assumes that the regulation of behavior
is qualified by the interaction of three structures: impulsive and emotional mechanisms, a cognitive network, and an operational network. Impulsive and emotional mechanisms result from learning both to avoid negative emotions and to
intensify positive emotions produced by internal stimuli and stimuli which are
a function of the external surround. A cognitive network represents the physical
and social surroundings of the subject and is arranged in a twofold way: as a
multidimensional psychological space representing mutual relations between objects and phenomena and as a structure classifying objects and phenomena according to their values. A distinctive place is occupied in the cognitive network
by the self-structure which is a reflection of the entirety of individual experience.
An operational network results in the internalization of practical actions and their
transformations into symbolic processes. Adaptive techniques involving symbolic transformations serve to achieve cognitive and practical control over the
environment. The regulatory functions of personality depend on the intercorre-
lations among its individual structures and mechanisms.

Much of the research done by Reykowski and his coworkers (1979, 1980) has had to do with the role of personality (the self-structure in particular, M. Jarymowicz, 1979) in prosocial behavior associated with the protection and development of other people or social institutions. The research proves that the motivation underlying prosocial behavior depends on the position of the self-structure in a network of values and the distance between self and non-self in the cognitive network.

W. Lukaszewski (1974) conceives of personality as evolving from learning and the restructuring of experience. Personality, he maintains, is a synthesis of the outcomes of learning (the accumulation of individual and social experiences combined with the effects of restructuring and processing of experience). This synthesis regulates individual actions, that is, it is instrumental in directing, motivating, and programming behavior. The information involved has to do with the environment, one's self, relationships between self and environment, and personal actions. Each of these realms is divided into information about real and ideal states. The mutual relationship between the two provides a basis for activities which lead from the real to the ideal state. The whole system functions according to a principle based on the informational discordance which can occur between the models of reality and the visions of reality. This discordance triggers human activity. Lukaszewski's studies (1978) and those of his associates have confirmed this proposition.

J. Strelau's regulatory theory of temperament (1974, 1985), based on empirical findings, shows that temperamental features perform regulatory functions in human behavior. He defines temperament as a set of formal and relatively constant behavior patterns manifested in both the energy level and the time-related characteristics of reactions. Two features are distinguished insofar as the energy level of behavior is concerned: reactiveness and activeness. Reactiveness refers to the intensity with which individuals respond to stimuli. Activeness concerns the intensity of or frequency with which individuals undertake specific tasks. Individuals with high reactiveness avoid stituations and actions that result in strong stimulation (individuals low in reactiveness do the opposite). Persons with low reactivity demonstrate a high level of activity and those with high reactivity show a low level of activity. Low-reactive individuals in comparison with high-reactive people, for example, tend to focus more on principal actions than on auxiliary maneuvers. When an individual acts, the level of reactiveness does not have a bearing on effectiveness if the person behaves in a typical way. In difficult situations, however, particularly those which require behavior not compatible with an individual's style of activity, the effectiveness of action depends on the level of reactiveness. In surveys on the regulatory function of temperament, diagnosis is essential. For such diagnostic purposes Strelau developed his Temperament Inventory. Matysiak's work (1980) on the need for stimulation of animals also relates to this research area.

The regulatory conception of temperament is based on Pavlov's theory of higher nervous system activity. Studies carried out by H. Budohoska (1979), for instance, were inspired by Konorski's (1969) integrational theory of brain functioning. This theory concerns multilevel analyzers and those areas of the brain that generate fixed perceptual patterns. Budohoska's studies dealt with the interactions between new and unfamiliar perceptual patterns and underlying brain structures. In one of these projects examining the interactions associated with the elements of compound stimuli, it was shown that differences between the perception of familiar and new stimuli involves the facilitation of the elements of the pattern in the former and negative interactions relative to the latter. Further studies indicated that interactions occur at the preparatory stage of visual information processing involving the synthesis of physical features of the pattern. In right-handed people this process most likely takes place in the projection regions of the visual cortex in the left cortical hemisphere.

Some studies in social psychology also focus on human cognitive functioning. K. Skarzynska (1981), in her book about person perception, adopts a theoretical approach illustrating the roles our views of others play in the process of regulating social interactions. She has been particularly interested in the factors important in our assessment of the people with whom we interact. In her educational research, she found pupils' motivation for task performance and talent to be the things a teacher considers most in assessing students. In other projects, Skarzynska examined the effect of rewards and punishments on behavior. Her findings indicate that severe punishment brings immediate and short-lived effects but generates negative attitudes toward the punisher while strong rewards produce more enduring results and lead to the formation of positive attitudes.

The effects of punishment have also been examined by S. Mika (1975). He and his associates have shown that, in educational situations, the effectiveness of punishment is not a simple function of the strength of the penalties applied but depends on whether the person punished and the punisher accept the same social-moral norms. A survey involving school children, their mothers, and headmasters demonstrated that ineffectively punished pupils (as opposed to those punished effectively) have negative attitudes toward the punisher.

J. Grzelak (1974) through his work in industrial settings found the following factors were relevant insofar as the effectiveness of punishment is concerned: the punisher's attitude toward the punished and the compatibility of the punishment with accepted norms. Grzelak (1978) also analysed the process of human interaction. In his experimental studies on conflicting interests, he found that in group situations instilling cooperation or rivalry the choices made depend on the structure of rewards, the level of payments, the strategy adopted by each person involved, whether or not communication between partners is possible, and personality features and attitudes.

The problems associated with social interactions are also intrinsic to the concept of equalization of attitudes proposed by Z. Zaborowski (1967), who claims that whenever relations develop between two persons, the phenomenon of equalization of attitudes or the attainment of cognitive equilibrium must occur. According to Zaborowski, this phenomenon is founded on our perception of the attitudes of those with whom we interact.

This problem was dealt with, too, by Z. Necki (1975) who attempted to determine whether similarity or complementariness of personality features brings people together. He found that in male-female pairing, the choice of a partner can be based on either similarity or complementarity. His findings were, therefore, not compatible with Zaborowski's theory.

Polish social psychologists have also studied aggressive behavior. The most significant and original research on this topic has been conducted by A. Fraczek (1979) and his coworkers. They established a distinction between reactive type of aggression (due to the stimulation of appropriate subcortical centers) and instrumental aggression (intentional actions consciously directed toward causing others harm).

The most important developmental theory in Polish psychology is the four-factor theory of M. Zebrowska (1966). This perspective conceives of mind as a brain function reflecting objective reality and defines mental development as a sequence of qualitative changes (self-improvement of the reflective functioning of the developing individual) accompanying growth. It proposes that mental development is determined by the following factors: inborn organic predispositions based on the structure and characteristics of the nervous and hormonal systems; the subject's own level of activity; the environment; and education, meaning the organization of specific situations and contents of experience.

Developmental research is focused on the problems in children and adolescents associated with mental development. The emotional and psychological development of adults and the psychology of old age have received much less emphasis. Studies by S. Szuman (1955) demonstrated a close relationship between thinking and level of activity in early childhood. The author isolated two basic forms of adaptive functions: adaptation of the individual through internal changes and adaptation through actions on the part of the child transforming things and other organisms according to his or her needs.

Moreover, accomplishments in developmental psychology include studies on speech and social-emotional development, research on personality development as well as behavior in difficult situations, and investigations of mental deficiencies. M. Przetacznikowa (1963) found that differences in the psychomotor development of children with different backgrounds increase with age. Studies in educational psychology mainly concern the educational process relative to various types of pupils. A. Gurycka and her associates (1979, 1980) studied educational situations in the classroom. They found that the interaction between educator and student is oriented toward whatever intentional influence obtains. The structure of such an interaction reflects the educational goal, the educational situations created by the teacher and their influence on the children, and changes in the personalities of the pupils. These factors are interconnected and interdependent. One of Gurycka's studies designed to identify optimal educational situations was a factor analytic investigation. The analysis considered many factors grouped into the following categories: character of the task, the pupils working on the task, and pupils' perceptions of the situation. The findings indicated that the nature of the task was the most influential factor and that it is very difficult to control students' perceptions of the educational situation.

M. Wosinski (1978) analyzed the didactic functioning of teachers in the context of various classroom situations. He concluded that teachers, without realizing it, tend to favor and positively reward pupils who are best at posing problems or summing up the work of the class. They tend to expect little of pupils who do not perform such functions. Therefore, teachers' behavior reinforces the existing behavior of individual pupils and their status relative to their classmates.

Studying shyness in children, M. Tyszkowa (1978) found that shyness derives from high standards of value and behavior in conjunction with dissonance between real and ideal self. A. Gurycka (1970) reported that social passivity in children results from a sense of insecurity in social situations. Gurycka claims that training children to be part of the center of group attention plays a vital part in increasing social involvement. I. Borzym (1979) found that gifted children tend to come from cultured and well-to-do families where approval and close attachments are the basis of all relationships. Many gifted pupils, however, manifested symptoms of socio-emotional maladjustment and neurosis; they engendered little popularity and prestige among their less-gifted classmates.

Clinical research on children owes much to the thinking of H. Spionek (1973). Inspired by the need to help children who have trouble adjusting to school settings, her orientation is based on a neurophysiological interpretation of childhood disorders. Spionek examined the pathogenesis and mechanisms of such problems in terms of the dynamics of neurophysiological processes and a typology of the nervous system. As pathological developments occur, the intensity of nervous activity is believed to decrease, thereby upsetting a natural balance. This process is mostly a function of defects at the micro level which obstruct harmonious nervous system development. Social factors are also involved.

Spionek's associates have modified her theory placing stronger emphasis on the role of personality and social factors. Their studies concentrate on motorically oversensitive, psychomotorically retarded, epileptic, and mentally retarded children. For instance, M. Koscielska (1984) studied the problems of moral responsibility. She worked on the question of whether children with limited mental capability demonstrate unique patterns of social development relative to school adjustment, self-reliance, and interpersonal competence. The findings indicate that the lowering of mental capability can be variously correlated with social functioning; this suggests that nonintellectual factors may affect social development more than intellectual dexterity.

The general theoretical orientation of the clinical psychology of adults in Poland was devised by A. Lewicki (1969). Clinical psychology, he claimed, is the science concerned with behavioral disorders. These, in turn, have to do with goal-oriented factors which are a function of internal regulatory mechanisms. An activity is disturbed when it fails to fulfill regulatory functions, that is, when it does not satisfy personal needs or fails to meet the demands of everyday life associated with the requirements of the environment.

Most scientific studies in clinical psychology focus on disorders in processes regulating human behavior in the context of difficult social conditions. J. Rey-kowski's investigations (1966) offer a typology of stressful situations and de-scribe accompanying changes in mental processes as well as different types and stages of reaction to stress. Research was also done applying cognitive categories to the functioning of people under stress.

In recent years there has been an increase in theoretical and experimental research on the affective and descriptive aspects of social perception in various forms of pathology. H. Sek (1980), defining the orientation problems in social situations, distinguishes three groups of disorders. In schizophrenic disorders the author found a lowering of perceptive sensitivity to social objects and limited evaluations of situations. Depressive patients were highly sensitive to social cues. And neurotics displayed intensified affect.

Interpersonal communication styles have been dealt with by L. Grzesiuk (1979). In the process of communication, psychologically healthy people tend to con-centrate on themselves as well as their partners. Neurotics concentrate on them-selves *or* the other person involved in the interaction. In schizophrenics the latter strategy predominates, manifested as passive withdrawal, egocentrism, or a tend-ency to manipulate.

K. Jankowski and his associates (1970) studied the psychophysiological effects of long-term psychiatric hospitalization. Their findings led Jankowski to propose a new explanation of, and treatment for, mental disorders which provides an alternative to hospital treatment. Jankowski claimed that the inertia of patients resulting from hospitalization and neuroleptization is reversible through psycho-social means. His postulates have generated widespread controversy in the bi-ologically oriented medical community.

Another controversial concept is K. Dabrowski's positive disintegration theory (1979). He views integration as a function of consolidated structures and factors subordinated to a controlling center. Dabrowski claims that excitability and neurotic symptoms and crises are signs of disintegration. This, he argues, can be considered positive evidence of human developmental potential. He distin-guishes two mechanisms of positive disintegration: horizontal disintegration, involving breakdown and harmony, and stratified disintegration, when an indi-vidual, aware of the many levels of his own mental structure, seeks to transform himself to a more ideal state and, as a consequence, undergoes secondary in-tegration. Dabrowski's theory was vigorously rejected by clinicians who treated disintegrative states as symptoms of pathology requiring treatment.

The most important studies in medical psychology investigated links between psychological agents and somatic disorders. Z. Pleszewski (1977) analyzed the emotional functioning of patients prior to and after a heart attack. He found that in the period before trauma his subjects sought success; were socially active; behaved dynamically; were able to resist fatigue, internal conflicts, and protracted difficulties; and demonstrated a high level of excitability but were able to control emotional expression and suppress tension. Immediately after the attack subjects were very anxious about new situations they encountered. Though the anxiety eventually subsided, the pursuit of professional and personal goals diminished.

Research in medical psychology centers on the theory of regulation applied to people suffering from illnesses. I. Heszen-Klemens (1979), for example, studied the consequences of informing patients about having to undergo a surgical operation. The patients who were told appeared to be in a better mood before the surgery and showed less anxiety and aggression than the uninformed patients. After the surgery the informed patients reacted with less fear of subsequent treatments and were more ready to resume everyday activities on their own. Prior to leaving the hospital they were more optimistic about their condition and gave hospital personnel higher assessments than did the uninformed patients.

Neuropsychology, an important area of study for clinical psychologists, was founded in Poland by M. Maruszewski (1966). He developed an approach to the psychological diagnosis of organic brain disorders which he felt could contribute to the rehabilitation of patients. Maruszewski's approach also applied to speech therapy (his main field of inquiry), which he employed in cases of aphasia for the reconstruction of patients' linguistic communication. In his studies of aphasia he concentrated on disorders in verbal communication programing mechanisms. D. Kadzielawa (1983), who continued Maruszewski's research in neurophysiology, used a neurolinguistic perspective to analyze the utterances of aphasics. Her aim was to detect empirically the neuropsychological mechanism of speech comprehension. She gathered data on the reception of human utterances, the syntactic transformations of utterance structure, and the interpretation of the meanings of the auditory productions of aphasics.

Some clinical psychologists have studied human behavior in penitentiaries. B. Waligora (1974) investigated behavioral disorders in prisoners; his findings suggest that problem behaviors such as hunger strikes and self-mutilations reflect both personality disorders and the conditions associated with repressive confinement. In the field of legal psychology, A. Sokolowska's (1977) work demonstrates how psychological expertise can be used in the courts.

Work psychology has benefited from the contributions of Z. Ratajczak (1979), based on T. Tomaszewski's theory of action, to understanding employees who bring new ideas to their occupational fields, and of X. Gliszczynska (1971) whose theory of motivation utilizes a decision-making model. Other studies in this area analyze work in the context of various professions, job stability, adaptations to work, occupations and their respective work places, the physical conditions of work, and disorders in the work environment.

Methodological problems are also of concern to Polish psychologists. J. Brzezinski (1976, 1980, 1984), for example, has worked on the structure of the research procedures involved in the behavioral sciences, the methodology of psychological studies, and the use of variance analysis in experimental psychological investigations.

There are only a few works on the history of psychology. Most noteworthy, of those is a book written by W. Bobrowska-Nowak (1973) at the Silesian

University. Finally, Polish psychologists do research on the psychology of sports, the arts, and aesthetics and are involved in ecological studies.

As can be seen from this review of Polish psychology, polemics have been rare in theoretical and empirical work (aside from the controversies over introspective psychology and test method in the postwar period). Nor has there been much critical analysis of other psychologists' theories. Polish psychologists, however, often discuss views presented in foreign publications. For instance, A. Malewski (1961) took issue with M. Rokeach's explanation of the origins of dogmatism. A list of the psychologists whose theoretical or empirical accomplishments contributed most to the development of Polish psychology and inspired further research should include Tomaszewski, Lewicki, Reykowski, Spionek, Strelau, and Kozielecki.

Research and Responsibilities of Applied Psychologists

Clinical psychologists work primarily in health-service institutions. Clinical psychologists dealing with adults are most often employed in outpatient clinics, hospitals, and psychiatric clinics. Significant changes occurred within this field in the 1970s as diagnostic techniques shifted from a descriptive-differential to a more dynamic approach which took into account the functions of the entire human personality. Clinical psychologists also became involved in psychotherapy. These developments generated more interest in humanistic psychology. Psychotherapy is now usually carried out on an individual basis rather than with groups. Most psychotherapists use an eclectic approach and treat more neurotic than psychotic patients.

With the advancement of medical psychology, especially in the 1980s, an increasing number of psychologists began to work with somatic patients. These psychologists are employed by hospitals, clinics, and facilities having to do with a variety of physical ailments. Their activity is more often diagnostic than therapeutic.

Child specialists in clinical psychology work in units responsible to the ministries of health, education, and justice. In health service units (hospitals, clinics, pediatric and obstetric counseling centers) and institutions for the blind, deaf, and mentally retarded children, they act as consultants to doctors, advise parents, and serve as members of therapeutic teams. Their activity, too, is diagnostic rather than therapeutic.

Neuropsychologists are essentially diagnostic consultants to medical doctors in hospitals, clinics, and neurosurgical and neurological outpatient centers. Since the 1970s, they have been involved in the rehabilitation of some patients, mainly aphasics. Some clinical psychologists specialize in the rehabilitation of disabled individuals. Again they perform mostly diagnostic functions but do participate in the process of occupational training and helping people readjust to normal life.

Court psychologists cooperate with prosecutors' offices and the courts as experts in divorce cases and other cases involving children. Correctional psychologists perform diagnostic tasks for prisons and participate in the resocialization of inmates.

The basic task of educational psychologists is to ensure the psychological well-being of pupils and disseminate psychological knowledge. However, they also have prophylactic, diagnostic, and corrective functions. Their specific responsibilities include preventing school failures, determining the sources of difficulty in implementing school policies and appropriate educational environments, reducing the causes of social maladjustment, selecting students for special schools, helping teachers work out better study habits for pupils, and reeducating children with special deficiencies. Psychotherapy with children and their families is seldom practiced. The use of psychotherapy to improve educational skills is a new development.

Work psychologists do not have a well-defined professional model. They are employed by industries having to do with mining and metallurgy, energy production, engineering, and transportation. They examine the professional fitness for those seeking work as bus drivers and railroad engineers and participate in the recruitment of employees. They also examine the causes of labor accidents (especially when casualties are involved), train engineering personnel, and analyze labor mobility. In the 1970s, work psychologists started to use group methods in training managerial staffs.

Polish Psychologists Who Influenced Psychology Worldwide

During the period from 1945 to 1982, Polish psychology did not significantly influence psychology in most other countries. Its impact was limited chiefly to European countries where Polish publications sometimes appear. To some degree, psychologists outside of Poland are made aware of the work being done in Poland via international conferences and the membership of Polish psychologists in international scientific psychological societies. The psychologists who have had the greatest impact on world psychology are Reykowski, Strelau, Kozielecki, Kurcz, Fraczek, Obuchowski, and Przetacznikowa.

FUTURE DIRECTIONS

The analysis of the psychological sciences conducted by the Psychological Sciences Committee of the Polish Academy of Sciences leads to the following conclusions. There are signs that the number of persons with the degree of doctor or habilitated doctor in psychology will continue to increase. Instruction should improve because of a wider availability of textbooks and teaching aids. However, the development of the psychological sciences may be hampered by limited technological and laboratory equipment, insufficient access to world literature, and increasing publication lag time.

The PAS Psychological Sciences Committee plans to continue discussing the status and direction of psychological research in the country and the progress of Polish psychology relative to achievements in other countries. The Polish Psychological Society is also continuing its efforts to bring about legislation strengthening the profession of psychology and increasing postgraduate psychological research opportunities for psychologists. Universities and other institutions are involved, as well, in the latter task.

REFERENCES

Bobrowska-Nowak, W. (1973). *Poczatki polskiej psychologii* [The beginnings of Polish psychology]. Wroclaw: Ossolineum.

Borzym, I. (1979). *Uczniowie zdolni* [Gifted pupils]. Warsaw: Panstwowe Wydawnictwo Naukowe.

Brzezinski, J. (1976). *Struktury procesu badawczego w naukach behawioralynch* [Structures of the research process in the behavioral sciences]. Warsaw: Panstwowe Wydawnictwo Naukowe.

Brzezinski, J. (1980). *Elementy metodologii badan psychologicznych* [Elements of methodology in psychological research]. Warsaw: Panstwowe Wydawnictwo Naukowe.

Brzezinski, J. (1984). *Zastosowania analizy wariancji w eksperymentalnych badaniach psychologicznych* [The use of variance analysis in experimental psychological studies]. Warsaw: Panstwowe Wydawnictwo Naukowe.

Budohoska, H., Grabowska, A., & Jablonowska, K. (1979). The effect of interaction between elements of familiar and unfamiliar patterns. *Polish Psychological Bulletin, 10*, 2.

Dabrowski, K. (1979). *Dezintegracja pozytytwna* [Positive disintegration]. Warsaw: Panstwowy Instytut Wydawniczy.

Fraczek, A. (1979). *Studia nad psychologicznymi mechanizmami czynnosci agresywnych* [Studies on the psychological mechanisms of aggressive actions]. Wroclaw: Ossolineum.

Franus, E. (1978). *Myslenie techniczne* [Technical thinking]. Wroclaw: Ossolineum.

Gliszczynska, X. (1971). *Psychologiczne badania motywacji w srodowisku pracy* [Psychological studies on motivation in work environment]. Warsaw: Ksiazka i Wieda.

Gliszczynska, X. (1979). *Psychologia pracy* [The psychology of work]. Warsaw: Panstwowe Wydawnictwo Naukowe.

Grzelak, J. (1974). *Empiryczne przeslanki skutecznosci karania* [Empirical assumptions of punishment effectiveness]. Wroclaw: Ossolineum.

Grzelak, J. (1978). *Konflikt interesow* [Conflict of interests]. Warsaw: Panstwowe Wydawnictwo Naukowe.

Grzesiuk, L. (1979). *Style komunikacji interpersonalnej* [Styles of interpersonal communication]. Warsaw: Wydawnictwo Uniwersytetu Warszawskiego.

Gurycka, A. (1970). *Dzieci bierne spolecznie* [Socially passive children]. Wroclaw: Ossolineum.

Gurycka, A. (1979). *Struktura i dynamika procesu wychowawczego* [The structure and dynamics of the educational process]. Warsaw: Panstwowe Wydawnictwo Naukowe.

Gurycka, A. (Ed.). (1980). *Stosowana psychologia wychowawcza* [Applied educational psychology]. Warsaw: Panstwowe Wydawnictwo Naukowe.

Heszen-Klemens, I. (1979). *Poznawcze uwarunkowania zachowania sie wobec vlasnej choroby* [Cognitive conditioning of an individual's behavior toward his own disease]. Wroclaw: Ossolineum.

Jankowski, K., Grzesiuk, L., & Markiewicz, L. (1970). *Psychophysiological aftereffects of prolonged stay in a psychiatric hospital.* Warsaw: State Sanatorium for Nervous Diseases.

Jarymowicz, M. (1979). *Modyfikowanie wyobrazen dotyczacych "ja" dla zwiekszania gotowosci do zachowan prospolecznych* [The modification of the self-image in order to increase the readiness for prosocial behavior]. Wroclaw: Ossolineum.

Kadzielawa, D. (1983). *Czynnosc rozumienia mowy* [Speech comprehension activity]. Wroclaw: Ossolineum.

Konorski, J. (1969). *Integracyjna dzialalnosc mozgu* [Integrational activity of the brain]. Warsaw: Panstwowe Wydawnictwo Naukowe.

Koscielska, M. (1984). *Uposledzenia umyslowe a rozwoj spoleczny* [Mental retardation and social development]. Warsaw: Panstwowe Wydawnictwo Naukowe.

Kozielecki, J. (1968). *Zagadnienia psychologii myslenia* [Selected aspects of the psychology of thinking]. Warsaw: Panstwowe Wydawnictwo Naukowe.

Kozielecki, J. (1969). *Psychologia procesow przeddecyzyjnych* [Psychology of pre-decision-making processes]. Warsaw: Panstwowe Wydawnictwo Naukowe.

Kozielecki, J. (1975). *Psychologiczna teoria decyzji* [Psychological theory of decisions]. Warsaw: Panstwowe Wydawnictwo Naukowe.

Kurcz, I. (1976). *Psycholingwistyka* [Psycholinguistics]. Warsaw: Panstwowe Wydawnictwo Naukowe.

Kurcz, I., & Reykowski, J. (Eds.). (1975). *Studia nad teoria czynnosci ludzkich* [Studies of the theory of human actions]. Warsaw: Panstwowe Wydawnictwo Naukowe.

Lewicki, A. (1960). *Procesy poznawcze i orientacja w otoczeniu* [Cognitive processes and orientation in the environment]. Warsaw: Panstwowe Wydawnictwo Naukowe.

Lewicki, A. (Ed.). (1969). *Psychologia kliniczna* [Clinical psychology]. Warsaw: Panstwowe Wydawnictwo Naukowe.

Lukaszewski, W. (1974). *Osobowosc: struktura i funkcje regulacyjne* [Personality: Structure and regulative functions]. Warsaw: Panstwowe Wydawnictwo Naukowe.

Lukaszewski, W. (1978). *Struktura Ja a dzialanie w sytuacjach zadaniowych* [Self-structure and task situations]. Wroclaw: Wydawnictwa Uniwersytetu im. B. Bieruta.

Malewski, A. (1961). *Rozdzwiek miedzy przekonaniami a jego konsekwencje* [Dissonance between convictions and their consequences]. *Studia Socjologiczne, 1*, 63–91.

Maruszewski, M. (1966). *Afazja, zagadnienia teorii i terapii* [Aphasia: theory and therapy]. Warsaw: Panstwowe Wydawnictwo Naukowe.

Maruszewski, M., Reykowski, J., & Tomaszewski, T. (Eds.). (1967). *Psychologia jako nauka o czlowieku* [Psychology as a science of the human being]. Warsaw: Ksiazka i Wiedza.

Matysiak, J. (1980). *Roznice indywidualne w zachowaniu zwierzat w swietle koncepcji zapotrzebowania na stymulacje* [Individual differences in animal behavior and the stimulation need]. Wroclaw: Ossolineum.

Mika, S. (1969) *Skutecznosc kar w wychowaniu* [The effectiveness of punishment in education]. Warsaw: Panstwowe Wydawnictwo Naukowe.

Mika S. (1975). *Spoleczne podstawy zachowania* [Social behavior foundations]. In T. Tomaszewski (Ed.), *Psychologia* [Psychology]. Warsaw: Panstwowe Wydawnictwo Naukowe.

Mika, S. (1982). *Psychologia spolezcna* [Social psychology]. Warsaw: Panstwowe Wydawnictwo Naukowe.

Necki, Z. (1975). *Psychologiczne uwarunkowania wzajemnej atrakcyjnosci* [Psychological conditioning of mutual attraction]. Wroclaw: Ossolineum.

Nosal, Cz. (1979). *Mechanizmy funkcjonowania intelektu: zdolnosci, style poznawcze, przetwarzanie informacji* [Mechanisms of intellectual functioning: Talent, cognitive styles, information processing]. Wroclaw: Wydawnictwa Politechniki.

Obuchowski, K. (1982). *Kody orientacyjne i struktura procesow emocjonalnych* [Orientation codes and the structure of emotional processes]. Warsaw: Panstwowe Wydawnictwo Naukowe.

Pleszewski, Z. (1977). *Funkcjonowanie emocjonalne pacjentow przed i po zawale serca* [Emotional functioning of patients prior to and after heart attacks]. Poznan: Wydawnictwa Uniwersytetu im. Adama Mickiewicza.

Przetacznikowa, M. (1973). *Podstawy rozwoju psychicznego dzieci i mlodziezy* [Foundations of the mental development of children and youth]. Warsaw: Panstwowe Zaklady Wydawnictwo Szkolnych.

Przetacznikowa, M., Butlerowicz, H., & Chrzanowska, D. (1963). *Rozwoj psychiczny dzieci od 9 miesiecy do 3 lat wychowywanych w zlobkach i w srodowisku domowyn* [Mental development of children 9 months to 3 years of age reared in nurseries and at home]. *Psychologia Wychowawcz, 1*, 2–16.

Ratajczak, Z. (1979). *Psychologia organizacji* [Organizational psychology]. Katowice: Wydawnictwa Uniwersytetu Slaskiego.

Reykowski, J. (1966). *Funkcjonowanie osobowosci w warunkach stressu psychologicznego* [The functioning of personality under psychological stress]. Warsaw: Panstwowe Wydawnictwo Naukowe.

Reykowski, J. (1979). *Motywacja: postawy prospoleczne a osobowosc* [Motivation: Prosocial behavior and personality]. Warsaw: Panstwowe Wydawnictwo Naukowe.

Reykowski, J. (1980). *Osobowosc a spoleczne zachowanie sie ludzi* [Personality and social behavior of people]. Warsaw: Ksiazka i Wiedza.

Sek, H. (1980). *Orientacja w sytuacjach spolecznych* [Orientation in social situations].Poznan: Wydawnictwa Uniwersytetu im. Adama Mickiewicza.

Shugar, W. G. (1976). Behavior stream organization during early language acquisition. *Polish Psychological Bulletin, 7*, 1.

Skarzynska, K. (1981). *Spostrzeganie ludzi* [Perception of people]. Warsaw: Panstwowe Wydawnictwo Naukowe.

Sokolowska, A. (1977). *Psychologiczna ekspertyza sadowa w sprawach dzieci i mlodziezy* [Psychological expertise in court cases involving children and youth]. Warsaw: Panstwowe Wydawnictwo Naukowe.

Spionek, H. (1973). *Zaburzenia rozwoju uczniow a niepowodzenia szkolne* [Disorders in pupils' development and school failures]. Warsaw: Panstwowe Wydawnictwo Naukowe.

Strelau, J. (1974). *Temperament i typ ukladu nerwowego* [Temperament and type of nervous system]. Warsaw: Panstwowe Wydawnictwo Naukowe.

Strelau, J. (Ed.). (1985). *Temperamental bases of behavior: Warsaw studies on individual differences*. Lisse: Swets a. Teitlinger.

Szuman, S. (1955). *Rola dzialania w rozwoju umyslowym malego dziecka* [The role of activity in the mental development of small children]. Wroclaw: Ossolineum.

Tomaszewski, T. (1963). *Wstep do psychologii* [An introduction to psychology]. Warsaw: Panstwowe Wydawnictwo Naukowe.

Tomaszewski, T. (Ed.). (1975). *Psychologia* [Psychology]. Warsaw: Panstwowe Wydawnictwo Naukowe.

Trzebinski, J. (1981). *Tworczosc a struktura pojec* [The creation and structure of notions]. Warsaw: Panstwowe Wydawnictwo Naukowe.

Tyszka, T. (1973). *Maksymalizacja oczekiwanej uzytecznosci jako kryterium wyboru w warunkach niepewnosci* [Maximization of anticipated utility as optimal criterion in conditions of uncertainty]. *Studia Psychologiczne, 11*, 83–119.

Tyszka, T. (1978). *Konflikty i strategie. Niektore zastosowania teorii gier* [Conflicts and strategies: Some applications of game theory]. Warsaw: Wydawnictwa Naukowo-Techniczne.

Tyszkowa, M. (1978). *Osobowosciowe podstawy syndromu niemialosci* [Personality-related foundations of the shyness syndrome]. *Psychologia Wychowawcza, 3*, 230–242.

Waligora, B. (1974). *Funkcjonowanie czlowieka w warunkach izolacji wieziennej* [The functioning of man in prison isolation]. Poznan: Wydawnictwa Uniwersytetu im. A. Mickiewicza.

Wlodarski, Z. (1964). *Pamiec jako wlasciwosc poszczegolnych analizatorow* [Memory as a property of individual analyzers]. Warsaw: Panstwowe Wydawnictwo Naukowe.

Wlodarski, Z. (1979). *Wplyw organizacji i prezentacji tresci naucznaia na uczenie sie* [The influence on learning of the organization and the presentation of material by teachers]. Warsaw: Panstwowe Wydawnictwo Naukowe.

Woloszynowa, L. (1974). *Bibliografia prac psychologicznych wydanych w Polsce w latach 1946–1968* [Bibliography of psychological works published in Poland from 1946 to 1968]. Wroclaw: Ossolineum.

Woloszynowa, L. (1977). *Bibliografia prac psychologicznych wydanych w Polsce w latach 1969–1973* [Bibliography of psychological works published in Poland from 1969 to 1973]. Wroclaw: Ossolineum.

Wosinski, M. (1978). *Wspoldzialanie nauczyciela z uczniem* [Teacher-pupil cooperation] Katowice: Wydawnictwa Uniwersytetu Slaskiego.

Zaborowski, Z. (1967). *Koncepcja wyrownywania postaw w stosunkach miedzyosobniczych* [The concept of leveling of attitudes in interpersonal relations]. *Studia Socjologiczne, 3*, 171–195.

Zebrowska, M. (Ed.). (1966). *Psychologia rozwojowa dzieci i mlodziezy* [The psychology of developing children and youth]. Warsaw: Panstwowe Wydawnictwo Naukowe.

SUGGESTED READING

Tomaszewski, T. (1984). *Glowne idee wspolczesnej psychologii* [General ideas of contemporary psychology]. Warsaw: Wiedze Powszechna.

South Africa

I. van W. Raubenheimer

INTRODUCTION

A review of the history of psychology in South Africa shows that impressive progress has been made over the years in the academic, research, and professional spheres. Psychology has become a major field of study and practice in this country. The reasons for this are tied to the composition and dynamics of South African society.

South Africa is often regarded as a microcosm of the world since in most aspects of life the influence of many parts of the globe can be observed. This is no less true of a scientific discipline such as psychology. Diverse influences have placed psychology on a strong, broadly based footing. Thus the discipline has the potential of contributing to a thorough understanding of the psychodynamics of people in a Third World subcontinent which is rapidly developing into a First World community. These circumstances have frequently resulted in a freshness of orientation and approach. Yet, as many psychologists realize, the multitude of opportunities that present themselves for psychological study create challenges that can hardly be met in a single lifetime.

NATURE AND SCOPE OF THE DISCIPLINE

Definitions of Psychology

It is impossible to provide one comprehensive definition of psychology which reflects the orientation and trends in the varied and extensive activities of psychologists in South Africa. While most psychologists claim to be eclectic, major influences from abroad can be observed in their teaching and research. At some universities neobehaviorism flourishes while at others psychodynamics, humanism, or phenomenology prevail. As far as research is concerned, a functional spirit, with its emphasis on activity, can be discerned in much of the work being done. However, a growing dissatisfaction with the inability of these orientations to provide an integrated system of knowledge of human behavior is evident among the younger generation of psychologists. This has led to the exploration of promising new avenues in theory building. Research interests extend from comparative psychology, which embraces extensive research on primates, to industrial/organizational psychology, which involves studies of organizational design and managerial strategies.

Organizational Structure

Universities

Psychology is taught at seventeen universities in South Africa at both the undergraduate and graduate levels. Two of these universities, the University of South Africa and, to a lesser extent, Vista University, are so-called nonresidential institutions which, like the Open University in London, provide instruction via correspondence courses and lectures to small groups of students at different localities across the country. In addition to its correspondence section, Vista University also provides instruction mainly to Black students on five campuses in metropolitan areas.

In South Africa it usually takes three years to earn a bachelor's degree with an additional year of study necessary for an honors degree. Two more years of study can lead to a master's degree. A doctorate can be earned after from two to five years of study and research beyond the master's degree. At the under-graduate level students can major in several areas. In addition, they can take courses in sociology, anthropology, geology, criminology, history, economics, accounting, mathematics, philosophy, political science, statistics, law, physics, languages, and so forth.

Unlike most universities in other countries, the majority of South African universities provide training in industrial psychology outside the ordinary psychology curriculum. Some universities have separate departments of industrial psychology while others offer industrial psychology courses in their psychology departments. This arrangement, which started in the early 1940s, has probably been necessitated by a strong demand by South African industry for people professionally trained and skilled in dealing with human behavior in occupational settings.

According to Ebersohn (personal communication, 1985), *The National Register of Physical and Human Scientists* (which has been updated annually since 1965) shows that in 1982 there were approximately 40,500 people with degrees in psychology. Over 84 percent had bachelors' degrees, 11.3 percent had honors degrees, 3.5 percent had master's degrees, and 1 percent had doctorates.

Professional Associations

During the 1960s and 1970s there were two professional associations in South Africa, the South African Psychological Association and the Psychological Institute of the Republic of South Africa. These two organizations were discontinued in 1982, however, and the Psychological Association of South Africa (PASA) established. This organization is made up of five institutes concerned with the following fields: academic and research psychology, industrial psychology, counseling psychology, clinical psychology, and educational psychology. PASA consists of a number of branches and each institute has representative groups in the various regions of the country. These local bodies play an important role in advancing psychology and providing assistance to their communities. Table 1 indicates the membership of the various institutes in 1985. Membership in PASA is a function of academic and professional qualifications. Simultaneous membership in more than one institute is possible.

PASA, which is affiliated with the International Union of Psychological Science (IUPsyS), has a joint responsibility with the Professional Board for Psychology, the licensing body for psychologists in South Africa, to promote psychology as a science, that is, to stimulate research, training, and professional practice; to disseminate information; and to counteract abuse and misconduct in the field. Although close cooperation and liaison exist between PASA and the Professional Board for Psychology, not all psychologists registered with the Professional Board are members of PASA. In fact, in 1984 only 52 percent of licensed psychologists were members.

Professional Registration (Licensing)

Statutory recognition of psychology as a profession in South Africa is granted by Act 56 (1974) which provides for the establishment of a Professional Board for Psychology under the auspices of the South African Medical and Dental Council. The main function of the board is to instill high standards of professional training and conduct among members of the profession. In doing so the board protects the public against unqualified "psychologists" and misconduct by registered psychologists. Psychologists are registered in the following categories: clinical, counseling, educational, industrial, and research.

In order to qualify for registration with the Professional Board a candidate should have a master's degree (or equivalent) in psychology and complete a formal internship of one year or eighteen months, depending on the nature and scope of the master's degree training. All university training programs leading to registration as a psychologist are approved by the Professional Board. Internship training is presently provided by 121 accredited institutions including hospitals (mental and general), clinics, education departments of universities, research institutes, industrial organizations, and the like. An accredited institution takes responsibility for the training of its interns according to a predetermined and approved program. Continuous supervision is provided by a registered psychologist employed by the institution in cooperation with a registered psychologist associated with a university.

In view of the limited number of accredited institutions, the board allows individuals (frequently industrial psychologists) to complete an internship pro-

Table 1
Institute Memberships, 1985

	Full	Associate	Student	Honorary	Total
Institute for Academic and Research Psychology	185	41	20	6	252
Institute for Clinical Psychology	387	–	5	2	394
Institute for Counselling Psychology	235	54	23	1	313
Institute for Educational Psychology	166	49	8	1	224
Institute for Industrial Psychology	160	135	61	5	361
	1,133	279	117	15	1,544

gram which can be undertaken while performing their normal work. Such individualized programs need to be approved in advance by the board. All the supervisory requirements for the accredited institutions also apply to these individualized programs.

In addition, the board makes provision for the registration of psychometrists (after they have obtained an accredited honors degree or an ordinary honors degree plus six months supervised experience in the use of psychometric techniques) and psychotechnicians (after they have obtained a bachelor's degree and gained six months supervised experience in psychometric techniques). Psychometrists may administer and interpret what are classified as A-, B-, and C-level tests under the supervision of a registered psychologist, and psychotechnicians may do the same with A- and B-level tests, also under supervision of a registered psychologist.

Not all people in possession of a master's degree in psychology, however, are registered with the Professional Board, most probably because they do not, strictly speaking, perform the activities explicitly reserved for psychologists by law. The time and effort involved in internship training could be another reason. In 1983, a total of 1,495 psychologists were registered with the Professional Board in the following categories: clinical (39 percent), counseling (21 percent), educational (14 percent), industrial (19 percent), and research (7 percent). Psychometrists and psychotechnicians registered with the Professional Board totaled 577 and 497, respectively. In 1984, the number of psychologists registered increased to 1,624.

Psychologists registered with the Professional Board may have their names entered in the *International Directory of Psychologists*. Most psychologists avail themselves of this opportunity as a means of making contact with psychologists in other countries.

Closely linked to the activities of the Professional Board is the Test Commission of the Republic of South Africa (TCRSA) which was established and affiliated with the International Test Commission in 1975. The main objective of the TCRSA is "to advance professional test development—to guard against the use of inadequate psycho-diagnostic procedures and the use of tests by unqualified persons and to ensure that tests are not used in a manner that is objectionable on scientific or ethical grounds" (Prinsloo, 1982, p. 110). In its capacity as the recognized body for the control and use of psychological tests, it advises the Professional Board on these matters.

Research Institutes

The Human Sciences Research Council (HSRC), established in 1969, is a major research institute in South Africa. It has a long history, starting in 1917, and had its primary origins in the former National Bureau of Educational Research, the National Bureau of Educational and Social Research, and the National Council for Social Research. The HSRC is a corporate body established by statute outside the public services, although most of its funding comes from the state. The primary task of the HSRC (according to Act 23 of 1968) is to make provision for the advancement of research and the expansion of knowledge in the domain of the human sciences.

At present the HSRC has a staff of more than 900 (of whom approximately 300 are graduates in the different fields of the human sciences). It is organized into eleven research institutes concerned, respectively, with communication processes, educational matters, historical studies, language and the arts, manpower, psychological and edumetric processes and issues, the development of new research projects, sociological and demographic studies, statistical investigations and research support services, and personnel research under the auspices of the National Institute of Personnel Research.

Prior to 1969 its research activities were directed toward problems such as the selection and coordination of statistical and educational data, vocational guidance, the effective utilization of manpower, and ways to improve the training of teachers. It also sponsored research projects at universities by means of scholarships and public grants.

An imaginative expansion of the HSRC's involvement in human science research in South Africa started with the South African Plan for Research in the Human Sciences (SAPRHS) in May 1980. This plan "contains a modus operandi through which the human sciences research community, collectively and in close collaboration with the users of Human Sciences research findings, can help find solutions to national problems in South African society, without thereby inhibiting self-initiated research by individuals or groups of human scientists" (HSRC, 1980, p. 3).

The SAPRHS makes provision for two distinct budgets, one for self-initiated research (such as that done by researchers at universities) and one for research on national problem areas (usually performed by multidisciplinary teams of researchers from universities, research institutes, and the private sector). Some of the largest projects completed under this scheme concern education, sports, intergroup relations, manpower issues, and research methodology.

The scope and emphasis of the investigation into education, for example, can be gleaned from the government's request for recommendations to the cabinet on "a) guiding principles for a feasible education policy in South Africa, b) the organization, controlling structure and financing of education, c) machinery for consultation and decision-making in education, d) an education infrastructure to provide for the manpower requirements of the RSA, and e) a program for making available education of the same quality for all population groups" (HSRC, 1980, p. 5).

Important results accrue from these national projects which will undoubtedly have a marked influence on South African society. In all its research programs the HSRC draws heavily upon the advice and expertise of university staffs.

Apart from the national research programs, numerous other programs are under way within the different institutes of the HSRC. The institute whose activities have the most direct bearing on psychology is the Institute for Psychological and Edumetric Research. Among the psychometric instruments developed by this institute are the New South African Group Test and the New South African Individual Scale which are the officially sanctioned tests for use in South African schools. At present this institute consists of sixteen divisions and has a staff of 125, of which seventy-two are researchers. A wide range of topics are studied such as personality factors associated with aggression; maladjustments within the family context; child education and parental guidance; selection for training as artisans; personnel classification for air force jobs; computerized career counseling; the development of new tests for issuing drivers' licenses; the use of joint tests for different population groups; compilation and standardization of a common group intelligence test for use by whites, coloreds, and Asians; learning problems and reading dysfunction; attitudes toward studying mathematics in school; the functional analysis of the Guidance Battery for Secondary Pupils used by national and independent Black states; school readiness; and the compilation of test-item banks for school subjects.

The National Institute for Personnel Research (NIPR), established in 1946 as one of several laboratories controlled by the South African Council for Scientific and Industrial Research (CSIR), has over the years made an invaluable contribution to the development of psychology in South Africa. Since its foundation, the NIPR has produced more than 850 research reports and publications (Raubenheimer, 1981; Pearl Labuschagne, personal communication, 1985) covering a wide spectrum of applied topics such as absenteeism; accident proneness; alcoholism in industry; consumer behavior; labor turnover; leadership; manpower management; job analysis and description; selection and training of bus drivers, managers, clerical workers, and army personnel; female workers; T-group training; vocational interests; and test construction and validation.

Apart from applied research, basic studies are also done in or on such areas, processes, and procedures as anesthesia, anxiety, auditory and visual perception, cognition, communication, neuropsychology, extrasensory perception, information theory, methods and techniques in mathematical statistics, mental deficiency, homosexuality, and personality. The NIPR consists of the following research divisions: personnel assessment and counseling psychology, training studies, management studies, psychometric methods, test construction, computer services, neuropsychology, sensory-motor research, ergonomics, applied research, human development, and industrial relations. It boasts a staff of 155 of which about two-thirds are graduates in different fields of psychology and mathematical statistics. The NIPR at present conducts about eighty research projects and has regional offices in all major centers of the country.

A great deal of emphasis is placed on African studies. A large portion of the aforementioned research has been performed on Black subjects, and a wealth of information on the aptitudes, abilities, needs, motives, and attitudes of Black people has been accumulated over the years (Andor, 1983). Indeed the most notable contribution of the NIPR to the advancement of psychological knowledge lies in the area of cross-cultural research.

In July 1984, the NIPR was transferred from the Council for Scientific and Industrial Research to the Human Sciences Research Council as one of the latter's institutes. This organizational restructuring is not expected to hamper the activities of the NIPR in any way. On the contrary, having the infrastructure of the HSRC at its disposal, it can be expected to render an even greater variety of services and increasingly sophisticated assistance to government, industry, and commerce.

The Human Resources Laboratory of the Chamber of Mines of South Africa is the only research body of its kind and scope funded by a private concern, namely the Chamber of Mines of South Africa, in contrast with the aforementioned research institutes whose activities are funded to a very large extent by the state. While it has roots dating back to 1946, and has worn different hats over the years, it was formally established in 1974 as the Human Resources Laboratory. Research was initially directed toward problems of personnel placement and applied physiology, but its investigatory activities have been expanded (especially since 1964) to include human productivity, particularly in the mining industry. Specific attention is devoted to manpower planning, quality of life, work performance, and health and safety. The laboratory has also made contributions to the field of ergonomics (human factors engineering) in South Africa. Over the last few years, the laboratory has developed along multidisciplinary lines. Its present staff includes thirty-six professional and fifteen administrative workers. This facility along with the HSRC and NIPR is accredited by the Professional Board for Psychology to provide internship training.

Major Programs/Laboratories

The training programs at the different universities in South Africa are quite similar. Specialization in particular professional fields usually starts at the graduate level. Undergraduate work generally provides a basic orientation and knowledge of psychology. There are a few exceptions, though, in that specialized training in counseling and clinical psychology starts during the third year of study for the bachelor's degree at some universities. By the end of master's work, however, the extent and depth of training received are much the same in all universities. Virtually all departments of psychology have laboratories for practical work by their students. These laboratories are also used to some extent for research.

Training in industrial psychology tends to be more professionally oriented and problem-directed even at the undergraduate level. Basic psychological principles are studied and applied within the framework of practical, real-life situations likely to be encountered in the occupational world. As a result, a major part of the practical work is done in organizations outside the university rather than in laboratories.

In addition to the work done in psychology department laboratories, there are units at some universities doing research in specialized fields. At the University of South Africa, for example, the Institute for Behavioral Sciences runs a neuropsychological research unit for the study of child development. The unit has an impressive research program which concentrates on the study of the social and neuropsychological development of young Black children (Griesel, 1985, pp. 21–23). The Primate Behaviour Research Group of the University of the Witwatersrand was formally established in 1974. It grew out of the animal behavior laboratory established in 1965 to investigate the behavioral biology of prosimian primates, the lesser bush baby, and the thick-tailed bush baby indigenous to South Africa.

Primary Functions of Psychologists

Psychologists are found in a wide range of occupations. In an extensive study of South African psychologists, Ebersohn (1981) found that psychologists work in hospitals (9.4 percent), clinics (child guidance, study counseling, etc.) (28.6 percent), research organizations (8.8 percent), schools (17.4 percent), business and industry (15.0 percent), government departments (military, penal, etc.) (6.0 percent), and private practice (14.8 percent).

The work of psychologists is broad and diverse. Psychologists are involved in child guidance; family, pastoral, marriage, student, and occupational counseling; psychodiagnosis; psychotherapy; education; manpower management; and research. According to the survey by Ebersohn, at least 68 percent of individuals with graduate training in psychology are in occupations where they can utilize their knowledge and skills.

Job opportunities for psychologists have increased considerably. Ebersohn reports a composite growth of 11.3 percent for the 1965–1981 period. This compares favorably with a projected growth of 2.8 percent in the demand for White manpower from 1977 through 1987 (Terblanche, 1983). The demand for qualified psychologists encourages students to pursue psychology as a career. This is evidenced by the fact that the number of psychologists registered with the Professional Board for Psychology increased from 168 in 1973 to 1,624 in 1984, which represents an average growth rate of 87.9 percent per year.

Funding of the Discipline

In the 1981–1982 fiscal year, South Africa spent approximately 0.74 percent of the country's gross national product on research and development. (The USA spent 2.4 percent, Britain 2.1 percent, and Japan 2.0 percent during the same period.) Of the total amount, R497 million, the human sciences received R57.2 million or 11.5 percent. This figure includes all the human sciences. The 11.5 percent is divided into the following categories: basic research (5.1 percent), applied research (4.6 percent), and development (1.8 percent) (Garbers & Smit, 1984).

Psychological training, research, and practice in South Africa are funded by a variety of institutions in both the public and private sectors. Many government departments, national and local, and private organizations employ psychologists to perform psychological work and to do applied research directed toward specific work-related problems. Moreover, imaginative graduate programs and research projects by graduate students or university staff, which may be of value to state departments and organizations in the private sector, are frequently sponsored. Nevertheless, the bulk of research in psychology, basic and applied, is funded by the Human Sciences Research Council. This does not include the provision of buildings, facilities, and salaries of teaching and research staff which are funded by the government and private patrons.

Apart from funding the South African Plan for Research in the Human Sciences, scholarships and grants are awarded by the HSRC for study in South Africa, for study and research abroad, for independent research, for the establishment of research units, for foreign researchers, for attending international conferences and workshops, and for publishing scholarly works.

Curriculum Models

Course work at both the undergraduate and graduate levels is more or less the same at all South African universities. It typically starts with an introductory course in the first year covering the physiological and cognitive aspects of human behavior, with some attention given to personality and motivation. Developmental, social, and abnormal psychology form the core of the second-year course. In the third year, topics studied during the first two years are expanded upon, while areas such as psychological testing, research methodology and experimental design, history and systems of psychology, and therapeutic and counseling procedures are added.

The honors course requires five or six papers. Students may usually choose topics from such areas as social psychology, psychopathology, developmental psychology, differential psychology, personality, perception, psycholinguistics, neuropsychology, psychological assessment, history and systems of psychology, research methodology and experimental design, clinical psychology, counseling psychology, and environmental psychology.

Study at the master's level offers a thesis or a nonthesis option. The thesis option entails independent research on an approved topic. The nonthesis option requires extensive course work, practica, and an advanced research paper in either clinical psychology, counseling psychology, or educational psychology.

The training program for industrial psychology is unique. In the first year general principles of individual and group behavior are normally studied. In the second and third years students focus on personnel psychology, organizational psychology, psychometrics, consumer psychology, ergonomics, and occupational psychology. Each of these includes, as an introduction, the study of the basic principles of human behavior relating to the particular field. In the honors course these topics are dealt with at an advanced level. At the master's level there is a thesis and a nonthesis option.

All universities provide training at the doctoral level, which typically consists of a dissertation based on an advanced research project. Some universities also expect their candidates to present a number of seminars (usually four) based on their research and may require an oral examination.

Journals

Until recently a number of South African journals published articles on psychology. Then, in 1976, the government-sponsored Bureau for Scientific Publications was established. This institution provides both funds and a sophisticated infrastructure for the publication of scientific journals; as a result, several journals devoted to psychology were discontinued. The bureau, however, sponsors the *South African Journal of Psychology*, which is the official journal of the Psychological Association of South Africa. It enjoys a wide circulation abroad and is listed in citation indexes such as *Biosciences Information Service, Sociology of Education Abstracts, International Bibliografie der Zeitschriftenliteratur*, and *Internationale Bibliografie der Reprits*. It is abstracted in *Psychological Abstracts*. Since its establishment in 1971, the *South African Journal of Psychology* has incorporated the following journals: *South African Psychologist, South African Journal of Psychology, Journal of Behavioural Science*, and *Psychologia Africana*.

Perspectives in Industrial Psychology, an independent journal for scientific contributions to the field of industrial psychology, and sponsored solely by its subscribers, was established in 1975. The journal enjoys a substantial readership in South Africa. Distribution abroad, though, is limited due to a lack of funds.

The Human Sciences Research Council publishes a *Research Bulletin* which, apart from carrying interesting articles on topical research developments, informs readers about national research projects and research trends in South Africa and elsewhere. It also publishes a register of new, current, and recently completed studies in South Africa.

Apart from the aforementioned journals, a score of in-house publications, annual reports, and newsletters is published by university departments, research institutes, and the institutes of the Psychological Association of South Africa. Some of these publications have an extensive readership in South Africa, and some are circulated abroad. South African psychologists are in the fortunate position of having virtually all the acknowledged international journals of psychology available in their libraries. Many South Africans publish in these journals.

The Most Widely Used Introductory Textbooks

The 1970s and 1980s have witnessed an upsurge in psychology textbook writing in South Africa. These books cover a wide spectrum of topics. The majority are written in Afrikaans and are prescribed at Afrikaans universities, particularly at the undergraduate level. English-speaking universities tend to use British and American textbooks, although a number of their prescribed books are written in English by South Africans.

As far as introductory textbooks are concerned, the following are at present most widely used at South African universities (they are, in fact, prescribed at eleven universities):

Atkinson, R. A., Atkinson, R.C., & Hilgard, E. R. (1983). *Introduction to psychology*. New York: Harcourt Brace Jovanovich.

Louw, D. A. (1982). *Inleiding tot die psigologie* [Introduction to psychology]. Johannesburg: McGraw-Hill.

Silverman, R. E. (1982). *Psychology*. Englewood Cliffs, NJ: Prentice-Hall.

Major Needs

Although there has lately been a significant increase in funds made available for research in the human sciences (of which only a portion goes to research in psychology), much more should be allotted since the natural sciences receive about 90 percent of the research and development funds in South Africa. Additional money for research in psychology, however, will not necessarily generate more high-quality studies. Universities, and perhaps the community of psychologists in general, have the responsibility of educating and inspiring young researchers to investigate creatively the phenomena of relevance around them. At the same time, governmental support for research in psychology seems to be a mixed blessing. The necessary control that accompanies such funding may inhibit the work of some individuals.

The new Psychological Association of South Africa and its five institutes are now well-established, although only 52 percent of the psychologists registered with the Professional Board for Psychology belongs to the association. Increased membership is clearly necessary. The newly formed association could also do a great deal to inform South Africans about the expertise and services provided by the profession. Many people suffer unnecessarily because of inaccurate information or from a lack of knowledge concerning services psychologists can provide. Charlatanism, in South Africa as well as other countries, has always impeded the development of psychology as a profession. Much more can be done by both the Professional Board and the association to exercise stricter control of practitioners. The legislation prohibiting unqualified people from performing psychological services does exist.

The division of South African universities into predominantly English-speaking and Afrikaans-speaking institutions inhibits communication, so that psychologists are not always aware of the programs and projects run by colleagues at other universities. The annual conferences held by the new psychological association should reduce this problem.

Most South African psychologists are insensitive to the historical development of psychology in their own country. Perhaps they are too busy trying to establish psychology as a science and profession in a rapidly developing country.

Very few Blacks are found in psychology despite the fact that the field seems to be a popular subject among Black undergraduates. A few psychologists have addressed themselves to this problem. For example, Strumpfer (1981) pleads for a more socially responsive psychology in South Africa. Holdstock (1979) concludes that psychology in South Africa belongs to the colonial era, and Kruger (1981), writing about psychology in general but still from within a South African framework, asks whether psychology has not failed as a scientific enterprise.

South Africans, however, have not turned a deaf ear to these issues. Interesting research is being done on the role of the *izangoma*, or indigenous healer, in rendering health services to his community. In addition, Raubenheimer and Kotzé (1984) have tried to integrate the cultural values of the rural Black and the work values of a Westernized occupational world by developing a system of personnel management for Black workers.

Although the establishment of the Professional Board for Psychology is a very important milestone in the history of psychology in South Africa, psychologists are wary of the possibility that legislation governing the activities of the board may curtail development of the discipline to some extent. The debate is still going on and may result in a number of minor alterations to the relevant laws.

As is probably the case in most countries around the world, large student enrollments and a shortage of faculty members restrict the time available for research. Most of the investigations at the universities have to be done after hours and during vacations. Taking into account all the needs and difficulties mentioned above, however, South African psychology is surprisingly sophisticated and well developed.

Relationships with Other Disciplines

Behavioral and social scientists in South Africa have long been aware of the value of interdisciplinary approaches to research problems. Some of the earliest and most important works in this country—for example, the development of an individual intelligence scale (Coetzee, 1931) and the investigations of the Carnegie Poor White Commission which started in 1928 (Malherbe, 1981)—support this claim. Today an interdisciplinary approach is intrinsic to many research programs. Virtually all the national programs under the auspices of the South African Plan for Research in the Human Sciences of the Human Sciences Research Council are interdisciplinary in nature.

At the university level, however, fewer of the studies performed are interdisciplinary. Practical considerations and the absence of well-developed and sustained infrastructures could be responsible for this. Although in all undergraduate training in South Africa students are required to combine psychology with courses in other fields of study, an interdisciplinary orientation toward solving problems is seldom encouraged.

Another development (still in the planning stage) at one or two universities concerns the establishment of so-called schools of psychology, which will provide for more specialized training in psychology earlier in students' programs of study. This will further reduce opportunities for interdisciplinary studies. Time will tell whether these plans come to fruition or not.

MAJOR TRENDS AND INFLUENCES SINCE WORLD WAR II

Although World War II is generally considered to have had a profound effect on developments in many countries, it would be an overstatement to ascribe all progress in South Africa after 1945 directly to the war. South Africa sided with the Allied Forces and contributed to ultimate victory, yet it escaped virtually all the destruction that went along with the conflict. South Africans were therefore not compelled to rebuild their country, a program which required a major human effort in most other nations. Nevertheless, the war effort stimulated many changes, especially in South African industry and the armed forces, including utilizing manpower scientifically. The establishment of the National Bureau for Personnel Research in 1946, which later became the National Institute for Personnel Research, resulted directly from work done during the war.

Demographic and Organizational Developments

Universities

The first university in South Africa, the University of the Cape of Good Hope (UCGH), was established in 1873 and patterned after the University of London. Initially the university was purely an examining body. In 1916 the UCGH was reconstructed to form the University of South Africa (Unisa), a federal organization consisting of six constituent colleges with its headquarters in Pretoria. By the end of World War II, there were five autonomous universities in South Africa and six university colleges affiliated with the University of South Africa. In 1946 an additional constituent college was established known as the Division of External Studies of Unisa. Meanwhile the number of constituent colleges grew and they eventually developed into independent universities.

In 1985 there were eighteen universities in the Republic of South Africa. By 1980 a total of 159,572 students had received instruction at South African universities. As can be seen from the following dates and figures, enrollments since 1910 have increased dramatically: 1910 (1,171), 1920 (3,211), 1930 (8,232), 1940 (13,253), 1946 (23,989), 1950 (23,103), 1960 (42,308), 1970 (82,909), and 1980 (159,572) (Louw, 1982). All the universities have psychology departments except the Medical University of South Africa which specializes in the training of Black physicians. Twelve universities have industrial psychology departments in addition to their departments of psychology. The establishment of independent departments of industrial psychology can perhaps be considered the most important development at South African universities in the field of psychology since World War II.

Industrial psychology in this country has shown a remarkable growth over the last two decades (Raubenheimer, 1982). Six out of sixteen unversities had separate departments of industrial psychology by 1972. This number increased to twelve out of seventeen by 1985; another three may be established in the near future. There has, naturally, been a substantial increase in the number of students studying industrial psychology. From 3,147 in 1972 to 5,757 in 1981, there was an increase of 83 percent in ten years. Also interesting is the fact that the percentage increase for most levels of training in industrial psychology is larger than for the total university student population over the same period (Raubenheimer, 1981).

As far as psychology per se is concerned, the number of students who complete a bachelor's degree each year with psychology as a major subject is increasing. In 1970, there were 729 and in 1975, 1,044. Data for graduate study and research reveal the same trend. The number of theses and dissertations in psychology completed since 1961 (expressed as a percentage of all theses and dissertations in all disciplines) increased from 4.2 percent in 1961 to 9.9 percent in 1978. The number of theses and dissertations in psychology submitted annually to South African universities has increased appreciably in recent years. Thirty-seven theses and dissertations were submitted in 1968, 135 in 1978, and 141 in 1981, an increase of 281 percent over thirteen years.

The development of psychology since the postwar years as far as training programs and fields of research are concerned was more or less the same as that in Britain, the United States, and Europe, differing only in degree of specialization. It seems that there is much less opportunity for specialization in South Africa than in other countries, probably because of the different demands and priorities characterizing a developing country.

Membership Trends

There were two psychological associations in South Africa until 1982, namely the South African Psychological Association (SAPA), organized in 1948, and the Psychological Institute of the Republic of South Africa (PIRSA), established in 1962. PIRSA was formed after a dispute within SAPA regarding membership of Black psychologists. In retrospect, this division both stimulated and hampered the development of psychology in South Africa.

Both associations aimed at, and succeeded in, furthering the academic and professional interests of psychologists in South Africa. Each sponsored a scientific journal, held annual conventions, and kept a professional register of members. In 1980, SAPA and PIRSA had memberships of 525 and 372, respectively (Raubenheimer, 1981). However, the vigor of the groups was gradually lost because of growing disinterest among younger psychologists and a questioning of the need for two similar associations serving the needs of no more than 2,000 psychologists.

By 1982 this uneasiness resulted in the abolition of the two associations and the establishment of the Psychological Association of South Africa. Membership in the new association is open to all population groups. Much support has been forthcoming from the community of psychologists in South Africa for the new association since it has proved that it can and will serve the academic and professional needs of its members. In 1985 the total membership of the new association was 1,544, whereas the association started with 891 members in 1982. This represents an average growth rate of 57.8 percent per year.

Statutory Recognition

Another major development in the history of psychology in South Africa since World War II was the establishment of the Professional Board for Psychology in 1974. Psychologists have for many years striven for statutory recognition. The first effort in this regard was made in 1946 when the South African Medical Association proposed that so-called medical psychologists be registered. In February 1948, the South African Medical and Dental Council (SAMDC) invited a representative group of psychologists to discuss the registration of psychologists. At this meeting psychologists realized that they needed a professional body to further their professional interests. Hence the South African Psychological Association was formed in July 1948. Further negotiations with the SAMDC followed which resulted in important concessions. In 1964, the SAMDC recognized the newly formed Psychological Institute of the Republic of South Africa and a joint advisory committee representing both psychological associations was established to advise the SAMDC on matters related to the registration of psychologists. Due to sustained effort by the two psychological associations, legislation was passed in 1974 (Act No. 56) to consolidate and amend the laws governing the South African Medical and Dental Council so as to make provision for the establishment of a Professional Board for Psychology. The number of psychologists registered with the Professional Board has increased spectacularly since its inception. In 1974, 233 psychologists were registered with the board; by 1984 there were 1,624.

The statutory recognition of psychologists gave significant impetus to the academic and professional development of psychology in South Africa. The board convenes at regular intervals to review training standards and to take disciplinary action in cases of improper or disgraceful conduct by registered psychologists. A strong liaison exists between the Board for Psychology, the South African Medical and Dental Council, and the Council of the Psychological Association, assuring proper monitoring of the training and professional conduct of psychologists.

Publication Trends

Publication of psychological literature in professional journals in South Africa had a modest beginning in 1932 with the establishment of the *Suid-Afrikaanse*

Tydskrif vir Sielkunde en Opvoedkunde [South African Journal for Psychology and Education]. Despite the enthusiasm displayed by its founder, Dr. P. R. Skawran, the journal ceased publication shortly afterward. Before then, and for some time thereafter, psychological material was published in newspapers, magazines, annual reports of state departments, annals of universities, in-house journals, newsletters of organizations, student magazines, and so forth. Although professional journals eventually appeared, these other publications are still widely used by psychologists.

In 1957 *Psychologia Africana* was launched by the National Institute for Personnel Research as the first professional journal of psychology in the country. (Its predecessor was the *Journal of the National Institute for Personnel Research* which was actually an in-house publication with a limited readership.) The 1970s saw the launching of many more professional journals. The *South African Journal of Psychology*, the *Journal of Behavioural Science*, and *Humanitas* were all launched in 1971, and *Perspectives in Industrial Psychology* appeared in 1975. In 1977, the *South African Journal of Psychology* came under the auspices of the Bureau for Scientific Publications which henceforth subsidized and published the journal. This had a marked effect on the other journals. In 1979, the *Journal of Behavioural Science* was subsumed by the *South African Journal of Psychology*. In 1983 *Humanitas* was terminated. *Psychologia Africana*, which had for a quarter of a century been the house organ of the National Institute for Personnel Research and which had been listed in the *Science Citation Index* of the Institute for Scientific Information, ceased publication in the same year. Today two journals exist which publish exclusively psychological articles, namely the *South African Journal of Psychology* and *Perspectives in Industrial Psychology*.

A topical analysis of the articles published in *Psychologia Africana* and the *South African Journal of Psychology* reveals interesting trends. Since the late 1950s cross-cultural issues and psychometrics have received the most attention by far. Then follow studies on personality, attitudes, psychopathology, and therapy, more or less in this order, and each of equal importance. In the past five to seven years, language, communications, and research methodology have received more attention. Perceptual and neuropsychological studies, however, have been less emphasized. In addition to these major emphases, the articles published cover an impressive array of topics in virtually all fields of psychology.

Funding Trends

Although the human sciences are lagging far behind the natural sciences as far as research and development support is concerned, there has been an improvement in the proportion of funds allotted to the human sciences. Whereas in 1977–1978 the human sciences received 9.3 percent of the total amount spent on research and development in South Africa, this figure increased to 11.2 percent in 1981–1982.

The absolute amount of money spent on research and development in the human sciences has also increased in recent years (see Table 2). Agency funds

Table 2
Funding of Research and Development in the Human Sciences in South Africa

Category[1]	1977/78	1979/80
Total	R21,510,308[2]	R33,225,730
Humanities	13,212,553	19,969,105
Psychology	3,845,366	4,043,536
Education	2,091,848	4,938,282
Sociology	1,190,126	1,519,498
Law	1,184,045	1,657,163
History	1,115,949	2,016,344

[1]Not all categories are listed.
[2]R refers to the South African unit of money, the Rand.

for self-initiated research administered by the Human Sciences Research Council have also increased considerably over the past six years. Puth (1985) reports an average annual increase of 39 percent. Although readily available funds tend to stimulate research, more money will not necessarily result in significantly more research in psychology at this time because of a limited number of qualified investigators.

Societal Developments That Influenced the Discipline

South Africa is often hailed as the most interesting laboratory of human behavior in the world because of the extensive differences in culture, language, and socioeconomic development encompassed within its borders. This diversity, however, has a marked effect on the development of societal structures, procedures, regulations, and so forth in all spheres of life including the fields of education and scientific development.

Universities are predominantly Afrikaans- or English-speaking institutions. This cultural division undoubtedly creates differences in orientation toward the role and function of the university in general and the scientist and researcher in particular. Where psychologists at English-speaking universities tend to concern themselves with basic research along traditional experimental lines, their colleagues at Afrikaans' institutions tend to do applied research based on surveys and *a posteriori* models. English-speaking psychologists, furthermore, tend to communicate with the world at large through their publications, and they therefore address themselves to problems and topics entertained by their fellow psychologists abroad. Afrikaans-speaking psychologists, however, tend to focus more on research problems generated in and by their immediate environment. Their work is usually published in Afrikaans (despite the fact that most Afrikaans-speaking people have a good command of English) and is therefore seldom read by psychologists in other countries.

The fact that many South Africans have always been keenly aware of the needs and opportunities for research in their immediate environment has resulted in a number of major research projects. The development and standardization of a variety of psychological tests which started in 1961 and continues even now, the investigation by the Carnegie Poor White Commission which was completed in 1932, the South African Talent Survey initiated in 1960, and the National Investigation into Intergroup Relations completed in 1985 are examples of such projects.

As far as the practice of psychology is concerned, the 1970s and 1980s have seen what could certainly be described as an explosion in the demand for psychological services in all walks of life. The increase in the number of graduate students at the different universities and the increase in the number of psychologists registering every year with the Professional Board for Psychology show that this demand is being met.

Developments in the field of labor in recent years have brought more lenient legislation as far as labor unions are concerned. The resulting rise in the number of strikes and the importance of negotiation provide new opportunities for the application of psychological knowledge and expertise in dealing with conflict and grievances to help management and workers reach satisfactory agreements.

Although one could conclude that psychological training, research, and practice are on a sound footing in South Africa, it is a matter of concern that relatively few Blacks are psychologists even though nothing formally bars them from receiving the necessary professional training and engaging in psychological research and practice. Some eminent South African psychologists have consequently argued for the abandonment of an obsolete Westernized model of psychology in this part of the world. Instead, a more Africanized conception of human behavior is being propagated which, among other things, makes provision for the role of the indigenous Black (spiritual) healer in the treatment of "abnormal" behavior.

Trends and Influences in Theory and Research

Major Orientations and Assumptions

Psychology in South Africa reflects the full spectrum of the psychologies of the Western world. This can most probably be ascribed to the fact that many psychologists seek to establish and maintain links with other countries in order to keep abreast of developments abroad. Many psychologists go abroad for graduate studies and postdoctoral research, bringing home perspectives and orientations prevalent at the institutions where they studied. The most significant influence comes from the United States, Great Britain, the Netherlands, and Germany.

Although some departments of psychology are behavioristically oriented and others tend toward a humanistic/phenomenological approach, it is not uncommon to find American, British, and Dutch textbooks prescribed for a particular course. The eclecticism of most South African psychologists brings with it certain disadvantages; for instance, the approach necessitates a loosely integrated system of scientific knowledge that does not enhance the development of psychology as a science. Here, as in other countries, psychology as a body of knowledge has a tendency, by and large, to be an uncoordinated collection of facts. Yet anyone seriously involved in basic psychological research endorses the fundamental view that the eventual aim of the scientific endeavor is to provide relational constructs that form a framework within which natural phenomena (and thus human behavior) can be explained and predicted.

Against this background, important work has been launched in recent years with a view to creating integrated systems of human behavior. Jordaan and Jordaan (1980) promote a metatheory which they call a sixth force in psychology. From this standpoint man is seen as a system within a total ecosystem in which he functions in a hierarchically integrated fashion. This involves the interaction of certain subsystems on different levels, which to be understood requires an interdisciplinary corpus of knowledge. One must, for example, have some understanding of biological, intrapsychological, physical, interpersonal, social-psychological, and sociological perspectives. A particularly salient feature of this approach is that it comprises a broad outlook which provides for the integration of knowledge across a wide range of fields. A second contribution involves the studies of Augustyn (1978) and De Jager (1979) aimed at verifying a four-dimensional theory of human behavior (Raubenheimer, 1978) which is essentially a classification theory deriving certain basic concepts from the natural sciences. It is envisaged that more psychologists will in the near future come up with new orientations, models, and assumptions which should furnish a better understanding of the complexities of human behavior in an extremely heterogenous society.

As far as research is concerned, the following observations were made by the Human Sciences Research Council after soliciting the opinions of a number of specialists in their respective fields (*Research Bulletin* [Journal of the SAPRHS], 1985, *15* (1), 32–37). First, although psychology accounted for 20% of all research expenditures in the human sciences in 1981–1982, it may lose its prominent position as a research discipline. Appreciably more scholarships and grants are awarded annually for honors and master's study than for doctoral study and self-initiated research. The future of the discipline is largely dependent upon the latter type of research. It is suspected that the professionalization of psychology, especially registration with the Board for Psychology, has lured people away from research beyond the master's degree. Probably also as a result of the professionalization of psychology, only a small percentage of the studies done in recent years can be considered basic research. Second, based on a reasonably sound data base, it is estimated that approximately 66 percent of all studies over the past few years are quantitative in nature, while 21 percent are qualitative and 6 percent theoretical. Third, there is a tendency for psychologists to avoid interdisciplinary research, and, finally, the work of research institutes is to some extent handicapped by a shortage of trained research psychologists.

Questions of Most Concern

South Africa is in many ways both a developing, and in some respects under-developed, Third World country and a highly developed First World country. Nowhere is this more clearly demonstrated than in the professional and occupational realms. On the one hand, many South Africans are industriously seeking to keep abreast of and contribute to the development and application of science and technology. At the same time, many South Africans, usually Blacks, find it difficult to adapt to and keep pace with the ever-changing demands of their work environments.

There are various cultural, political, educational, and other reasons for this. Social scientists and psychologists, in particular, are much concerned that an unbridgeable gap, involving virtually all dimensions of modern life, formed between different socioeconomic groups within a relatively short period of time. It represents a challenge to many psychologists who see numerous opportunities for doing research and providing help in the acculturalization of people with diverse backgrounds who find themselves in a rapidly developing and highly demanding society. This does not necessarily imply the abolition of traditional cultural values in favor of imported Western ones. Many psychologists are keenly aware of the stability that stems from maintaining cultural ties and the therapeutic importance of sustaining cultural continuity.

Major Contributions

Listing major contributions of South African psychologists is a function of personal orientation and depends on whether one has the local or the international community in mind. A number of South Africans conducted their initial work here and then emigrated to expand their knowledge and make their contributions abroad.

Major contributions to psychology in South Africa per se should be seen in terms of the work done by the Human Sciences Research Council (and its predecessors) on the development of psychological measurement techniques and the furnishing of a wide variety of psychometric instruments for practical application in many spheres. The work done by the National Institute for Personnel Research on the abilities of Blacks in Africa (and the measurement of these abilities), for example, is original and significant (Andor, 1983).

Individual contributions cover a wide spectrum. These include J. G. Taylor's work on the behavioral basis of perception; H. F. E. Reuning's studies of the abilities, temperament, interests, and creativity of the Kalahari Bushmen; W.

Hudson's studies on the perceptual abilities of Blacks; J. Wolpe's and A. Lazarus' work in the field of behavior therapy; F. W. Blignaut's study on alcohol addiction in white mice; and S. Biescheuvel's research on intelligence and abilities of different population groups in South Africa. Among earlier contributions, the following are particularly noteworthy: R. W. Wilcocks' development of intelligence and special-aptitude tests in the 1930s; P. R. Shawran's early work on the selection of pilots for the armed forces; and I. D. MacCrone's study of racial attitudes in South Africa.

Most Creative Psychologists

Naming the most creative individuals in the history of psychology in South Africa is a difficult and tentative exercise. Creativity is not reflected only in published research work. In a developing country like South Africa, it also entails original ideas and insights for building the necessary educational and professional infrastructures. Ultimately, it is also a function of the evaluator's own bias and orientation.

Nevertheless, viewing creativity as being reflected by original contributions in a variety of contexts, the following eminent names can be mentioned: P. R. Shawran (early applied work in industrial/occupational psychology), R. W. Wilcocks (development of special ability and trade tests), I. D. MacCrone (work on race attitudes), S. Biesheuvel (founding of the National Institute for Personnel Research and studies on the abilities of Blacks), A. J. la Grange (establishment of the first psychological association), J. G. Taylor (research on the behavioral basis of perception), A. Lazarus and J. Wolpe (contributions in the field of behavior modification), H. F. Verwoerd (first courses in commercial psychology in the early 1930s which heralded the establishment of industrial psychology in South Africa), and E. G. Malherbe (one of the initiators and first head of the National Bureau for Educational and Social Research which later became the Human Sciences Research Council).

Controversies and Limitations

In a rapidly developing society there does not seem to be much room for explicit controversies among psychologists. Since South African psychologists tend to be eclectic to a large degree, different approaches and points of view are tolerated. South Africans seem to have come to accept the notion that an aggregation of different points of view or schools of thought contributes to a better conception and understanding of behavioral phenomena.

On the other hand, while much has been done in recent years to provide effective professional, organizational, and funding infrastructures, psychologists are overburdened, especially at educational institutions, because much of their time is spent doing advisory work for the public and private sectors. This leaves them insufficient time for their instructional duties and research.

Trends in Applied Areas

It is difficult to single out major contributions in applied areas. Applied psychology flourishes in many settings including schools, parent and child guidance clinics, psychiatric hospitals, vocational bureaus, industrial organizations, and private practice. All these activities are to some extent supported by applied research conducted at universities and research institutes.

The measuring devices developed over the years by the Human Sciences Research Council and by the National Institute for Personnel Research are widely used. The General Adaptability Battery, developed by the NIPR for use on illiterates as well as people speaking many languages and dialects and utilized successfully for many years in the mining industry and industrial organizations, is a typical example of such research (Biesheuvel, 1976).

Contributions to Other Disciplines and Society

Contributions to other disciplines by psychologists cannot be readily identified. However, psychologists are frequently highly esteemed members of university faculties. Their ways of thinking undoubtedly have an effect on those with whom they interact. Over the years at least four psychologists have become presidents (vice-chancellors) of their universities, C. H. Rautenbach (University of Pretoria), E. G. Malherbe (University of Natal), R. W. Wilcocks (University of Stellenbosch), and I. D. MacCrone (University of the Witwatersrand), while a former prime minister of South Africa, H. F. Verwoerd, had been a professor of applied psychology at the University of Stellenbosch. It is also evident that the vigorous and systematic orientation of psychologists toward research has had a marked influence on colleagues in sociology, education, economics, and management.

Foreign Psychologists with the Most Influence on South African Psychology

To single out all the individuals who have influenced South African psychology would be an almost impossible task. As indicated earlier, over the years many South Africans have traveled abroad for graduate and postdoctoral study which brought them into contact with a score of eminent foreign psychologists. Many psychologists from other countries have also paid visits to South African institutions for varying periods of time. Psychologists who spent some time in South Africa include J. Dewey (U.S.), J. Waterink (Netherlands), V. Frankl (U.S.), G. W. Allport (U.S.), T. F. Pettigrew (U.S.), C. R. Rogers (U.S.), M. Argyle (England), J. H. van den Berg (Netherlands), R. H. Thouless (England), E. H. Erikson (U.S.), H. H. Leavitt (U.S.), F. Herzberg (U.S.), A. Tomatis (France), and J. van der Leeuw (Netherlands).

Perspectives on Psychology in Other Countries

Virtually all the neighboring states of South Africa have their own universities. In many of them South Africans play a leading role in administration, management, and instruction. Some universities, however, tend to be oriented toward Great Britain and have obtained expertise from there. In view of the fact that these universities (there are ten in the immediate neighborhood of South Africa) are of recent origin, independent contributions to the field of psychology seem unlikely.

FUTURE DIRECTIONS

Predicting the directions which psychology in South Africa will take in the future is certainly no easy task. One would prefer to refrain from doing so. Yet, the following developments are likely to occur. As far as training (or course content) is concerned, South Africans will not deviate dramatically from what is offered in Western countries, the primary reason being that most prescribed books and study material originate in these countries. South African psychologists may, however, add new information and meaning to major Western psychological conceptions in order to describe psychological phenomena and orientations springing from a hybrid of Western and African cultures.

A great deal of the research done in South Africa will in all probability be focused on problems in South African society and thus be applied in nature. With the necessary infrastructure already in place, professionalism is bound to flourish. This no doubt will lead to a better control of charlatanism and lay "psychologists." Most professional activities will probably continue to take place under the auspices of the Psychological Association of South Africa. Yet it is possible that small interest groups (loosely attached to PASA) will be formed to allow certain psychologists to pursue their own specialized interests. By and large, it seems that psychology in South Africa is at the threshold of an exciting and stimulating era.

PSYCHOLOGISTS WITH A STRONG INTEREST IN THE HISTORY OF PSYCHOLOGY

Dr. D. H. Forster, Department of Psychology, University of Cape Town, Private Bag, Rondebosch, 7700.

Dr. S. J. Louw, Department of Psychology, University of Durban-Westville, Private Bag X54001, Durban, 4000.

Mr. J. O. Meara, Department of Psychology, Rhodes University, P.O. Box 94, Grahamstown, 6140.

Dr. V. Nell, Department of Psychology, University of South Africa, P.O. Box 392, Pretoria, 0001.

Dr. I. van W. Raubenheimer, Department of Industrial Psychology, Rand Afrikaans University, P. O. Box 524, Johannesburg, 2000.

ADDRESSES OF INSTITUTES AND ASSOCIATIONS

Human Resources Laboratory of the Chamber of Mines of S.A., The Director, P.O. Box 91230, Aucklandpark, 2006.

Human Sciences Research Council, The President, Private Bag X41, Pretoria, 0001.

National Institute for Personnel Research, The Director, P.O. Box 32410, Braamfontein, 2017.

Perspectives in Industrial Psychology, The Editor in Chief, P.O. Box 524, Johannesburg, 2000.

Professional Board for Psychology, The Registrar, S.A. Medical and Dental Council, P.O. Box 205, Pretoria, 0001.

Psychological Association of South Africa (and all its institutes), The Secretariate, P.O. Box 2729, Pretoria, 0001.

South African Journal of Psychology, The Editor, Bureau for Scientific Publications, P.O. Box 1758, Pretoria, 0001.

Universities—addresses of all universities in South Africa can be obtained by writing: The Chief Public Relations Officer, Human Sciences Research Council, Private Bag X41, Pretoria, 0001.

REFERENCES

Andor, L. E. (1983). *Psychological and sociological studies of the Black people of Africa, south of the Sahara, 1960–1975: An annotated select bibliography*. Johannesburg: National Institute for Personnel Research.

Augustyn, J. C. D. (1978). *Tyd as n fundamentele konsep in menslike gedrag* [Time as a fundamental concept in human behavior]. D.Com. dissertation, University of Stellenbosch.

Biesheuvel, S. (1976). South Africa. In V. Sexton & M. Misiak (Eds.), *Psychology around the world* (pp. 357–369). Monterey, CA: Brooks/Cole.

Coetzee, J. C. (1931). *Verstandsmeting* [Mental measurement]. Pretoria: Van Schaik.

De Jager, L. C. (1979). *Sielkundige diepte-orientasie as determinant van menslike gedrag* [Psychological depth orientation as a determinant of human behavior]. D.Com. dissertation, Johannesburg: Rand Afrikaanse University.

Ebersohn, D. (1981). *Die sielkundiges van die R.S.A.* [The psychologists of the R.S.A.]. Institute for Manpower Research, HSRC. Versiag MM–92.

Garbers, J. G., & Smit, P. (1984). Opleiding en navorsingstendense in die geesteswetenskappe [Training and research trends in the human sciences]. *Research Bulletin* (Journal of the SAPRHS), *14* (9), 1–8.

Griesel, R. D. (1985). Neuropsychological research unit for the study of child development. *Research Bulletin* (Journal of the SAPRHS), *15* (4), 21–23.

Holdstock, T. L. (1979). Indigenous healing in South Africa: A neglected potential. *South African Journal of Psychology*, *9* (3), 118–124.

Human Sciences Research Council. (1980). *Eleventh Annual Report.*

Jordaan, W. J., & Jordaan, J. J. (1980). Metateorie: n Sesde "krag" in die sielkunde [Metatheory: A sixth "force" in psychology]. *South African Journal of Psychology, 10* (1), 28–41.

Kruger, D. (1981). Het die sielkunde as n wetenskaplike projek misluk? [Has psychology failed as a scientific project?]. *South African Journal of Psychology, 11* (1), 6–17.

Louw, J. B. Z. (1982). *Statistiek van ingeskrewe studente aan universitere onderwys-inrigtings vir die jare 1910–1980* [Statistics of students enrolled at teacher-training universities between 1910 and 1980]. Verslag: SANSO–204, Macro Education Policy Directorate, Department of Education, Republic of South Africa.

Malherbe, E. G. (1981). *Never a dull moment.* Cape Town: Howard Timmins.

Prinsloo, R. J. (1982). The control of psychologial tests by the Test Commission of the Republic of South Africa (TCRSA). *South African Journal of Psychology, 12* (4), 106–110.

Puth, G. (1985). Applications for research funds: Guidelines for writing and procedures for submitting research proposals. *Research Bulletin* (Journal of the SAPRHS), *15* (4), 1.

Raubenheimer, I. van W. (1978). Raamwerk vir die ontwikkeling van n 4-dimensionele teorie van menslike gedrag [Framework for the development of a 4-dimensional theory of human behavior]. *Perspectives in Industrial Psychology, 4* (5), 33–72.

Raubenheimer, I. van W. (1981). Psychology in South Africa: Development trends and future perspectives. *South African Journal of Psychology, 11* (1), 1–5.

Raubenheimer, I. van W. (1982). Some facts and thoughts on the training and practice of industrial psychologists. *Perspectives in Industrial Psychology, 8* (1), 1–16.

Raubenheimer, I. van W., & Kotzé, J. C. (1984). *Personeelbestuur en die Swart werker* [Personnel management and the Black worker]. Durban: Butterworth.

Research Bulletin (Journal of the SAPRHS). (1985). *15* (1), 32–37.

Strumpfer, D. J. W. (1981). Towards a more socially responsive psychology. *South African Journal of Psychology, 11* (1), 18–28.

Terblanche, S. S. (1983). *An analysis of the macro manpower demand and supply situation (1977–1987) in the R.S.A.: Aid to manpower planning at the organizational level.* South African Institute for Manpower Research, HSRC, Report MM–83.

The National Register of Physical and Human Scientists. (1983).

Soviet Union

Boris F. Lomov

It is not possible in a short chapter to provide a complete characterization of Soviet psychology, rooted as it is in ancient traditions and formed by diverse needs and influences. Instead, I shall sketch its background, summarize the principles guiding theory and research, identify the major centers of research, discuss the training of psychologists, and make a few comments about the USSR Society of Psychologists.

A BRIEF HISTORY OF PSYCHOLOGY IN RUSSIA AND THE USSR

Early Developments

Interest in psychological phenomena extends back to ancient times. Russian folktales, bylinas (saga-like narratives), legends, and proverbs are rich with material for psychological study. In an unsophisticated way they indicate an awareness of many of the issues associated with perception, memory, emotions, and personality. The same is true of manuscripts written several centuries ago.

The first relatively comprehensive explications of basic mental or psychological[1] concepts, however, took place within philosophical thought. A number of seventeenth- and eighteenth-century treatises were devoted to the nature and essence of mental phenomena. The Russian philosopher I. P. Kozelsky, for example, attributed these phenomena to the functioning of the brain and raised a very important question: How is it possible to incorporate the whole world in something as small as the human brain? A contemporary version of the question might be: In what kind of information processing must the brain engage to reflect the environment? Since Kozelsky, many philosophers and psychologists have been concerned with this problem.

A momentous event in the history of Russian science was the establishment of the Russian Academy of Sciences in 1724 by Peter the Great. The primary goals of the academy were to develop science, educate young men, and spread knowledge. Originally, the academy included Russia's first university, but the university later became a separate institution. There was no department of psychology within the academy, but at that time psychology as a branch of science did not exist. Later, when psychology did emerge as a distinct field in Russia, it was considered a science, as opposed to one of the arts.

After the academy was founded, psychological research was conducted, but it was done by scientists in other disciplines. Scholars on geographic or geological expeditions, for example, also observed and described the ways of life, customs, and patterns of behavior of peoples living in the regions they visited. Today we would say they were engaged in cross-cultural research. Christian von Wolff, a well-known philosopher and member of the academy, was the first to propose the subdivision of psychological studies into rational and empirical psychology. This organization was eventually adopted by scholars all across Europe.

The most prominent Russian scientist of the eighteenth century was Mikhail Vasilyevich Lomonosov (1711–1765). Lomonosov's scientific interests were so broad that Alexander Pushkin, the great Russian poet, called him "the first Russian university." Lomonosov contributed importantly to the development of physics, chemistry, geology, geography, linguistics, and poetics. He also addressed some psychological topics. He proposed, for instance, that all color sensations result from combinations of yellow, green, and violet, anticipating the trichromatic theory of color vision. He also investigated the interactive processes associated with thought and language and stressed the idea that human mental development is dependent upon proper human action.

Until the second half of the nineteenth century, psychological ideas developed mainly within the framework of philosophy. The mind-body problem was the central issue and thinkers were divided into two camps. There were the idealists who believed in the primacy of mind and the materialists who asserted the primacy of matter. Introspective psychology developed within the confines of idealism, with proponents attempting to understand psychological processes in and of themselves, that is, as unrelated to either brain processes or material reality.

Materialists considered mind and consciousness to be functions of the brain and in the realm of natural science. They insisted that the psychological domain was subject to objective laws and regularities and should be studied using scientific or objective procedures. Propagating materialist approaches to psychological inquiry during the nineteenth century was a group of influential Russian philosophers including A. I. Herzen, V. G. Belinsky, N. G. Chernyshevsky, N. A. Dobroliubov, and D. I. Pisarev. They all agreed that the mental does not exist apart from the material world. During the nineteenth century the natural sciences in general were rapidly developing.[2] This was particularly true of biology which was much influenced by Darwin's theory of evolution. Materialism and progress in the natural sciences laid the foundation for the emergence of psychology as an independent science in Russia. Ivan Mikhailovich Sechenov (1829–1905) is generally considered the founder of the discipline.

Within the context of the debate between idealism and materialism, Sechenov developed his theory of reflection. According to this theory, psychological, or mental, functions are controlled by the brain which, through its activities, generates a subjective reflection of the objective world. In his published works, including *Impression and reality*, *Elements of thinking*, and *Reflexes of the brain*, Sechenov demonstrated that sensation, perception, memory, and thinking are different forms of reflection. He made an attempt to identify the physiological mechanisms underlying these processes and considered the reflex to be such a mechanism. In Sechenov's view, psychological events are not epiphenomenal relative to physiological processes but are directly involved in regulating behavior; this they do by relating human and animal action appropriately to the environment. He also viewed proprioceptive signals produced by the movements of people and animals as taking part in the process of reflection, a proposal which is particularly relevant for the perception of time and space.

The Emergence of Experimental Psychology

Vladimir Mikhailovich Bekhterev (1856–1927), another great Russian scientist, had research interests similar to Sechenov and, in 1885, he founded the first Russian laboratory of experimental psychology in Kazan. Although Bekhterev is frequently remembered only for his theory of reflexology and study of reflexes, his scientific concerns were actually much broader. He began, for example, to study experimentally the influence of communication (*obschenie*)[3] on perception, memory, and thought. He also wrote a number of articles on problems associated with social psychology and conducted experiments in psychopharmacology, psychotherapy, and hypnosis. He advocated both biological, particularly physiological, and pedogogical studies of the human being.

Another scientist of some consequence for experimental psychology was Nikolay Nikolaevich Lange (1858–1921). Lange elaborated the idea, proposed by Sechenov, that perception is a developing process rather than one which produces instant copies of the world-out-there. According to Lange, perception involves a rapidly changing series of stages with each preceding stage being more global and undifferentiated than the next. Perception, in other words, is a sort of refinement process (*Psychological Research*, Odessa, 1893).

The most well-known follower of Sechenov was Ivan Petrovich Pavlov (1849–1936). Pavlov developed precise techniques for the study of reflexes and formulated a theory of the functioning of the higher nervous system that is universally recognized. His primary objective was to explain the neurophysiological mechanisms of the mind. Pavlov affirmed that the main function of the nervous system is signaling and that this process involves a variety of signals and mechanisms. Most of his experimental findings derive from animal research, but late in life he began to study human behavior. It was in the context of this work that he proposed the first and second signal systems. The first system has to do with the reflection of the environment and includes sensory and perceptual processes. Both animals and humans have such a system. The second signal system has evolved only in humans as an "extraordinary addition" to neurological activity. This system is concerned with language and speech, which are, in turn, socially determined.

Alexey Alexeyevich Uhktomsky (1875–1942), who also followed in Sechenov's footsteps, proposed that there is a primary or dominant center of excitation in the brain. This center "attracts" all other excitation and provides a powerful explanation for the attentional processes.

During the nineteenth and early twentieth centuries experimental psychology progressed rapidly. In 1912, Georgy Ivanovich Chelpanov (1862–1936) organized the first institute of experimental psychology. The institute was affiliated with Moscow University. Chelpanov, an idealist and existentialist, was also a strong supporter of experimental psychology. The approach to psychological inquiry represented by Sechenov and his followers ran contrary to idealism, but an idealistic psychology was supported by both the tsarist government and the church.

Following the Great October Revolution of 1917

The Great October Socialist Revolution of 1917 significantly changed living conditions in the Russian and other parts of the country. Industries, banks, and transportation systems were nationalized. The economy was reconstructed on the principle that the means of production are common property. New forms of political power, new principles and procedures for organizing society, and a new ideology were systematically instituted.

The Soviet government immediately placed a high priority on developing the sciences. Even during the difficult years of the Civil War, economic dislocation, and military intervention by other countries, several new research institutes were founded. In 1918, for example, the Institute of Brain Research, headed by Bekhterev, was established in Petrograd (Leningrad). Staffed by specialists in biological evolution, neuroanatomy, physiology, and psychology, this facility was the first to initiate comprehensive studies of the human species.[4]

The need to restructure the economy and educate the people stimulated the growth of labor psychology and educational psychology in the 1920s. Laboratories to develop and apply psychological procedures were established in factories and schools. Tests were widely used and empirical research flourished. There was keen interest among Soviet psychologists in behaviorism and psychoanalysis, which had recently become fashionable in Western psychology.

It soon became clear, however, that these orientations were of little help in solving the problems of Soviet society. Critical analyses of existing paradigms and the working out of new ones were necessary. Soviet psychologists looked to Marxism for answers. Konstantin Nikolaevich Kornilov, in 1921, and Pavel Petrovich Blonsky, in 1923, introduced dialectical materialism into psychology. Articles by Kornilov and Blonsky were republished in the *Psychological Journal* in 1981 and 1983. The very essence of the human being was questioned. The conception of man as merely a highly developed animal along with belief in a primordial antagonism between individuals and society came into conflict with the realities involved in building a Socialist society.

The 1930s were characterized by intense debate and discussion concerning the future development of psychology and the philosophical problems besetting the discipline. Several orientations emerged during this decade. The prominent psychologists of the time included Lev Semenovich Vygotsky (1896–1934), Sergei Leonidovich Rubinstein (1889–1960), Dimitry Nicolaevich Uznadze (1887–1950), and Vladimir Nikolaevich Myasischev (1893–1973).

Vygotsky, who was in Kharkov, established a school for the study of cultural-historical development and initiated research on higher mental functioning. Influenced by French sociological perspectives and the work of Piaget, which focused on patterns of human activity, Vygotsky affirmed that words or signs are the key determinants underlying the development of the higher mental functions, that is, those psychological capabilities unique to humans. Words (signs) are the means by which people control their actions. Alexey Nikolaevich Leontiev (1903–1979) and Alexander Romanovich Luria (1902–1977), two other prominent members of this school, sought to demonstrate that human mental functioning is determined by historical events.

Rubinstein and his followers worked on philosophical problems associated with psychology. Proceeding from Marxist assumptions and Lenin's theory of reflection, Rubinstein viewed psychological phenomena as different forms and levels of the subjective reflection of objective reality. This same general idea had earlier been proposed by Sechenov. For Rubinstein, the subjective was not an immaterial self-contained substance but rather represented an aspect of human action and thought within the societal context. Rubinstein, in other words, proclaimed that human consciousness and activity are unified, with the psychological or mental being formed, developed, and maintained through activity (performance), primarily work.

Uznadze is best known for his concept of set (*ustanovka*). Set, according to Uznadze, is a primary modifier of personality and is manifested in all human activities. His work and thought led to the development of an important school of psychology in Soviet Georgia.

Myasischev, a disciple of Bekhterev, elaborated a perspective on psychological relationships (*psychologicheskie otnosheniya*) originated by A. F. Lazursky (also one of Bekhterev's followers) in 1907 and similar to the concept of attitude proposed by American researchers W. I. Thomas and F. Znaniecki in 1918. Myasischev proposed that psychological relationships are real phenomena with their foundations in social relations rather than mere theoretical constructs. He stressed that consciousness is simultaneously a reflection of reality and an attitude, and that personality develops and is sustained within socially based psychological relationships. Myasischev's conception was consonant with the Marxist view that a person's consciousness is his or her attitude toward the environment.

In the 1940s the Ananiev school emerged. Boris Gerasimovich Ananiev (1907–1972), another disciple of Bekhterev who proselytized for comprehensive studies of the human being, was primarily concerned with developmental research. He devoted many years to the study of sensation and perception, proposing a theory of sensory functioning which took into account all sense modalities. He was the first to study the interactions between activities in the cerebral hemispheres of the human brain and the sense organs considered as bilateral analyzers. He was also the first to recognize the functional asymmetry of the brain. His developmental investigations of memory and thinking, which focused on microdevelopmental processes, resulted in his law of heterochronistic development insofar as mental functioning is concerned.

The research of many psychologists was, of course, involved in the formation of the theoretical foundations of Soviet psychology during the 1940s and 1950s. In the tradition of Sechenov, for example, B. M. Teplov, A. A. Smirnov, P. A. Shevarev, V. J. Kaufman, A. I. Bogoslovsky, and A. J. Zotov studied the dynamics of sensory processes and such aspects of perception as the constancies. F. N. Shemyakin did research on the perception and mental representation of space, D. G. Elkin investigated time perception, and S. V. Kravkov studied the development of the sense organs in the course of biological evolution. One of Kravkov's major contributions was his formal recognition of the fact that the sensory systems interact.

Out of this research developed the conception that sensation is the subjective reflection of the separate properties of objects acting on the sense organs, whereas perception involves the reflection of objects as a whole. Mental representation, memory, and thinking were also studied within the theory of reflection. This led to a totally new approach to psychological inquiry, one which recognized that sensory, perceptual, and cognitive processes must be studied in the context of real-world human activity. This perspective brought with it the need to investigate the origins and development of the psychological domain within the process of biological evolution. Zoological and comparative psychological research, as exemplified by N. D. Ladygina-Kots's longitudinal study comparing the development of a human child and a chimpanzee infant, was undertaken.

Starting in the 1920s, considerable psychological research was done in the fields of labor and education. Tests were used in factories and schools to select workers and students for occupations and courses of study, respectively. The new theoretical approach to psychology, however, soon cast doubt on the placement of people on the basis of test results because this procedure seemed incompatible with the principle of social equality. As a consequence, standard psychological techniques were strongly criticized.

Psychologists in schools and industries turned their attention to problems associated with human development, teaching, learning, and creativity. S. M.

Vasileysky, through investigating the activities of designers and inventors, identified the main stages of the creative process and developed strategies of creative decision making. Selection procedures were studied only in connection with such specialized occupations as airplane pilot and, later, cosmonaut.

Much research also centered on blind, deaf, and mute children. I. A. Sokolyansky worked out a system for teaching such youngsters and many of his pupils became successful adults. Olga Skorokhodova, for example, who was blind, deaf, and dumb, attained a Ph.D. and wrote a much praised book entitled *How I perceive and understand the world*. Later, A. I. Mecheryakov continued Sokolyansky's work helping many children to become highly educated. Both psychologists were honored formally by the government.

Psychology during World War II

The period of aggression by Nazi Germany against the Soviet Union (1941 to 1945) interrupted the many constructive programs which were well under way by the 1930s. As was true of all the scientific disciplines, psychology was redirected to work on wartime matters. Psychologists conducted research concerned with the training of military personnel; the camouflage of cities, towns, and villages; and the rehabilitation of the wounded. Teplov wrote an insightful article entitled "The mind of a general" based on the psychological analysis of documents from the War of 1812. As the war went on, everyone became involved and worked for victory. Many psychologists joined the army and the Corps of People's Volunteers. Unfortunately, a large number of scientists were killed, and almost all scientific institutions have a memorial dedicated to colleagues killed during this terrible conflict.

Because the Nazis occupied most of the European territory of the USSR, they were in control of many cities with scientific institutions such as Kiev, Minsk, Tallin, Riga, Tartu, Kharkhov, Novgorod, Pskov, and Odessa. In addition, Leningrad was blockaded for nearly three years. But the development of Soviet science, including psychology, continued. Before the end of the war, academic units of psychology were established at Moscow University and Leningrad University. In 1944, the RSFSR (Russian Soviet Federated Socialist Republic) Academy of Pedagogical Sciences was founded. The academy included the Research Institute of Psychology. In 1970, the academy was transformed into the Academy of Pedagogical Sciences of the USSR, and the Institute of Psychology became the Institute of General and Educational Psychology.

Psychology since World War II

After the war, many Soviet psychologists returned to basic research. Developmental studies were particularly encouraged during the 1940s and 1950s because intrinsic to dialectical materialism is the principle that to understand an event one must consider its development. Furthermore, it is recognized that development involves qualitative as well as quantitative changes and that contradiction provides the motivational force. How the mental or psychological emerged and developed during the course of biological evolution and how consciousness arose and changed throughout human history were questions of much importance to Soviet psychologists.[5]

Interest focused on both the evolution of the species (phylogenesis) and the development of individual human beings (ontogenesis). The most important task for psychologists came to be understanding how a newborn, helpless "lump of living matter" is transformed into a socially active person having consciousness, will, intelligence, and a complex spectrum of emotions. In the 1950s and 1960s research on child development had top priority. Child psychology emerged as a separate field and research on the development of cognitive processes, abilities, temperament, and character burgeoned. Stage theories were proposed and hypotheses attempting to explain the motivating forces underlying mental development were investigated. After considerable research, play, learning, and labor, in that order, were shown to be the activities (*deyatelnost*) that are the primary determinants of mental development.[6] As the human being plays, learns, and works, psychological growth takes place. Perception, memory, attention, will, thought, and imagination, as well as abilities, mature. Activities of individuals are shaped by sociohistorical factors, and people are shaped by the activities which characterize their time and place.

The mental development of an individual is not spontaneous but is regulated by systems of education. The relationship between psychological development and education, however, is not clear. Some psychologists and educators maintain that development is totally determined by formal education, while others believe that education has to adapt to developmental processes. Both are extreme positions, and establishing a harmonious and balanced perspective became an important goal for Soviet psychologists. Ukrainian psychologist G. S. Kostyuk is noted for his contribution with regard to this issue. Educational psychology is the most highly developed specialty within Soviet psychology and is closely associated with child psychology.

Research on the neurophysiological mechanisms associated with psychological phenomena continued vigorously during the 1950s and 1960s. Because of the work of Pavlov and his followers, there has always been a strong interaction between psychological and physiological research. Within the Pavlovian tradition, E. N. Sokolov investigated perception, and E. I. Boiko the complexities of behavioral reactions. Also within this tradition, A. R. Luria, T. N. Ushakova, and others studied the interactions between the first and second signal systems, focusing on the roles played by words in cognition. B. M. Teplov and V. D. Nebylitsin conducted research on individual differences based on Pavlov's theory of nervous-system functioning. Out of this work emerged the new and promising field of differential psychophysiology. Recently, work in this specialty has included the study of genetic factors that may relate to psychophysiological abnormalities.

In the 1960s, P. K. Anokhin expanded on a theory of functional systems which he had worked out in the 1930s. Anokhin's theory resolved some of the fundamental issues concerning the relationships between psychology and physiology by demonstrating the limitations of the concept of reflex arc as the mechanism underlying behavioral acts. A functional system for Anokhin is a complex organized whole involving motivation, afferentiated syntheses, decisional processes, programming, and a system receiving feedback from those actions performed. The latter system is important because it reflects information relevant to future activities and allows for comparison of the proposed or planned result with what is actually achieved. Consequently, Anokhin's theory provided investigators with an interpretation of the neurophysiological mechanisms associated with goal-directed behavior and anticipated some of the thinking of A. R. Luria and N. A. Bernstein. Even more significantly, his theory provided a new perspective on the ancient mind-body problem. Mental and psychological processes were no longer related to separate neurophysiological processes but were rather related to the arrangement of these processes.

The theory of functional systems is being elaborated by neurophysiologists K. V. Sudakov and V. B. Shvyrkov in collaboration with a number of psychologists. In addition, V. M. Rusalov is working on a new approach to the psychophysiological study of interpersonal differences.

Before turning our attention to developments during the 1950s and 1960s in engineering psychology and social psychology, it is important to point out that interest in the history of Russian psychology was also emerging. B. G. Ananiev, B. M. Teplov, and later E. A. Boudilova, M. G. Yaroshevsky, A. V. Petrovsky, and E. S. Kouzmin, to name but a few, published significant historical studies.

The mechanization and automation of industries, the availability of computers, new transportation modalities and systems such as space vehicles, and technological developments in general served as catalysts for the study of human activities in a variety of new settings. The need for engineering psychology quickly became apparent, and in 1959 the first Laboratory of Engineering Psychology was established at Leningrad University. Shortly thereafter, similar laboratories were founded at other universities, including those in Moscow and Kharkov, and at the Institute of Psychology of the RSFSR Academy of Pedagogical Sciences.[7]

In the 1960s, social psychology reappeared as a separate area of study. While social psychology was recognized as a legitimate field during the 1920s and 1930s, the need for such a specialty was subsequently questioned because it was contended that all mental phenomena are socially determined. In that case, there would be no reason for a separate field of social psychology. Social psychological research, of course, continued in the 1940s and 1950s, but it took place in educational and other fields. For instance, a renowned teacher, A. S. Makarenko, studied problems experienced by people working together in collectives. A collective is a group, such as an industrial team, united by a common goal.

In order to understand the history of social psychology in the Soviet Union during the period from the 1920s to the 1960s, it is necessary to add a brief historical note. Near the end of the nineteenth and the beginning of the twentieth centuries, G. V. Plekhanov, the first Marxist propagandist in Russia, played a role in the development of social psychology. While many in the West think that Marx reduced all of life to economic processes and states, this is a misconception. Marx considered society as a complex system of social relations with economic, civil, political, ethical, aesthetic, legal, and other dimensions. The production of goods provides the foundation of society and supports a societal superstructure made up of legal norms and ethics, social institutions, the government, science, the ideology of the group, and so forth. Marx stressed that consciousness as well as human mentality, in general, is determined by social reality but that consciousness is not a passive reflection of the social realm. Social consciousness, he proposed, strongly influences the development of society.

Guided by the ideas of Marx, Plekhanov contended that in order to study society it is necessary to begin with an analysis of the factors associated with the production of goods. The analysis, however, cannot end there but must determine how the "bare economic skeleton" acquires its cultural superstructure. Plekhanov was particularly interested in the processes by which people develop social consciousness, and he urged that research be done to identify social psychological laws and principles. He himself analyzed some case studies of sociopsychological phenomena and demonstrated that the process of imitation manifests itself uniquely in different sociohistorical periods. Furthermore, he believed that imitation brings with it a counterimitative tendency.

V. M. Bekhterev, discussed earlier, also conducted social psychological studies. He was the first to use experimental techniques to investigate imitation, suggestion, and the spread of feelings within groups.

To return to the 1960s, let us provide a few details concerning the reemergence of social psychology as a distinct specialty. A. G. Kovalev wrote an influential paper[8] in which he insisted that this field has its own subject matter, problems, and methodology. Social psychology, he proclaimed, studies a special class of phenomena such as shared feelings, imitation, suggestion, common opinions, and, in a more general sense, psychological climates arising out of social interactions. Later, B. D. Parygin published a book entitled *Social psychology as a science* (1965) concerned with social psychological theory, and E. S. Kouzmin empirically studied workers' groups, or collectives. In 1961, the first sociopsychological laboratory was founded at Leningrad University. Since then, similar facilities have been established at other centers of psychological research.

In the 1960s, the nature and functions of clinical psychology were also seriously reviewed. During the same period, the fields of neuropsychology, juridical (legal) psychology, organizational psychology, and cross-cultural psychology became established, and research in psycholinguistics accelerated. Overall, the credibility of psychology improved for two reasons: because it was increasingly

recognized that psychologists could help solve social problems and because it
became apparent that psychology, as a bridge between the natural and social
sciences, was essential for a unified science of the human being.

In 1971, the Presidium of the Academy of Sciences established the Institute
of Psychology. Of considerable significance is the fact that the decision to set
up this new research institution was supported by three departments of the
academy: the Department of Philosophy and Law, which includes sociology; the
Department of Mechanics and Control Processes; and the Department of Physiology. It was also supported by the Scientific Council for Cybernetics. The
function of the institute has been to unite the major fields of psychology which
had been developing in the USSR; these are general psychology, social psychology, engineering psychology, the psychology of labor, and psychophysics.
All the major schools of psychology in the USSR, including the perspectives of
Ananyev, Anokhin, Leontiev, Luria, Rubinstein, and Teplov-Nebylitsin, are
represented at the institute. The primary goal of psychologists connected with
the institute is to integrate and synthesize the knowledge acquired by researchers
working within the contexts of these orientations. The overriding theoretical
outlook is a systems approach derived from the principles of dialectical materialism. This approach requires that human life be examined on several levels.

The first level concerns the human being as an element of society. The focus
is on social relations within the cultural context. These social relations form the
objective background for a person's attitudes, interests, motivations, sympathies,
antipathies, attachments, affections, and so forth. Social relations, however, are
not viewed as external coordinates of life, but are, as Lenin stressed, made up
of the concrete actions of individuals.

The main objective of level-one analyses is to determine the systematic relationships between societal development, the development of personalities, with
personality considered to be a manifestation of human performance (*deyatelnost*),
and interactions (*obschenie*) with other people.[9] Here psychology overlaps with
the social sciences. Research focuses on sociopsychological phenomena and the
indentification of the laws of development of different types of communities
(primarily small groups and collectives).

While personality, performance, communication, and, in fact, behavior as a
whole are viewed globally in level-one studies, it is also necessary to investigate
the structure and dynamics of personality, performance, and communication.
This is where level-two analyses enter the picture.

One way or another, a person reflects his or her social environment, thereby
forming the basis for subjective attitudes toward different aspects of society,
such as its economic and political structure. Psychologists investigate the scope,
stability, and interrelationships of these attitudes. Of particular importance is the
motivational sphere of personality. Most psychologists, quite correctly, connect
motives with needs. Some consider a motive to be a reflection of a need.

When dealing with needs, however, one must keep in mind not only individual
requirements but the needs of society as well. Both are reflected in the motives

of individuals. Motives oriented toward individual and societal needs, that is, production and consumption, are combined in the motivational dynamics of personality. A person's attitudes and motives, in turn, determine the course of personality development.

The study of attitudes and motives helps clarify what it is a person wants or wishes. But the question then arises: What is he or she able to do? Level-two research must, therefore, also be concerned with human capabilities, or abilities. In Soviet psychology, capabilities are considered properties of personality that form as the individual develops. Genetically determined predispositions are viewed as prerequisites, but not simple determiners, of abilities. The relationships between these predispositions or inclinations and capabilities are complex. Similar abilities may develop in the context of different predispositions, or very different abilities may form in the context of similar predispositions. The human species is characterized by tremendous genetic polymorphism and every person is genetically unique. Everyone has a particular system of genetically determined predispositions which allows for the development of a personal set of interrelated capabilities. Whether or not a certain ability develops depends on the social relationships an individual experiences.

In Soviet psychology there are several theoretical perspectives on human performance, or action. Each offers its own set of principles for dividing performance into simpler elements. One theory proposes that the basic components are actions and operations; another contends that habits and creative actions are the basic elements; and still another assumes that planning, decision making, and the evaluation of results are intrinsic to performance. All agree that goals and motives play key roles in determining human actions, although there are different opinions as to the ways in which goals and motives interact.

There are also several different views as to the nature of communication. Some investigators try to apply to the process of communication the same approaches and assumptions used for the analysis of performance or activity. Others look for components specific to communication. Psychologists who view communication as a special form of activity, different from performance, propose that the concept "performance" represents an interpretation of subject-object relationships, while the concept "communication" depicts the subject-subject relationship.

Level-three analyses concern psychological processes, such as perception, attention, memory, thought, and emotion, which are involved in performance and communication. Much experimental data concerning these processes has been obtained by psychologists in many countries. What is unusual about Soviet psychology, however, is that Soviet psychologists conceive of these processes as different forms of subjective reflection of reality which control human activities, or, more specifically, regulate performance and communication.

At the fourth level, research concerns the relationships between psychological and physiological processes. The physiological mechanisms associated with perception, memory, thinking, and emotion have been extensively studied in the

USSR. The primary aim is to determine the interrelationships among these mechanisms, and research is centered on the organism as a whole. Investigations do not concern only the functioning of the nervous system but the activities of the cardiovascular, the hormonal, the muscle, and other physiological systems as well. Psychologists studying emotions, for example, record not only electroencephalographic activity but also heart rate, blood pressure, and amount of perspiration.

In summary, the establishment of the Institute of Psychology of the Academy of Sciences in the USSR in 1971 contributed to the development of Soviet psychology in a number of important ways. Two contributions, however, stand out. First, communication (*obshenie*) was more thoroughly studied, and the influence of communication on the cognitive processes has been extensively investigated experimentally. It has been found, for example, that individuals perceive, think, and use mnemonics differently when communication is possible than when they work independently. Creative decision making also proceeds differently when people are allowed to communicate with each other than when they have to solve problems without sharing information. Related studies by A. A. Bodalev have centered on social perception. Others have studied ways to improve the organization of projects worked on jointly by a number of individuals. The problems associated with communication, have, in fact, become a major new focus of research relevant to many fields of psychology. Second, there has been much interest in determining the interaction among all psychological processes and phenomena. At present, for instance, research on anticipation as an integrative process is receiving considerable attention.

THE MAIN PRINCIPLES UNDERLYING SOVIET PSYCHOLOGY

As Soviet psychology developed, several basic principles were established. While the various schools of psychology and scientific disciplines implement these principles differently, they constitute a basic common theoretical foundation.

Principle of Determinism

The principle of determinism is at the foundation of every science. In psychological inquiry, however, it took a long time before this principle was seen as relevant. For centuries it was believed that psychological phenomena were independent of objective laws and had no connection with the material world. Such phenomena were said to exist in their own space or realm.

Psychology emerged as a science when it adopted the principle of determinism. Originally, however, scientific psychology was characterized by overly simple deterministic explanations that were modeled after classical mechanics. Cause and effect were viewed as being manifested in straightforward linear chains of events. The most radical version of linear determinism proclaims that a particular stimulus always produces the same response and a particular response is always caused by the same stimulus.

It soon became clear, however, that behavior, particularly human behavior, involves a much more complicated set of dynamics. According to the principle of dialectics, the relationships between cause and effect are not straightforward, rigid, or simple. In nature, an effect may be transformed into a cause and a cause may become an effect. Cause and effect may also be separated by long time intervals, and, sometimes, cause is cumulative, that is, an outcome results from an accumulation of a number of antecedent factors or events.

It is important to keep in mind that behavior, especially that of people, is self-determined in the sense that when a person acts, he or she changes the environment and therefore the determinants of behavior. Mind and human action cannot be reduced to simple causal relationships. One must consider many internal and external factors and a system of complex links. In short, psychological determinism is of a systemic character, it involves a complex of many different elements and events.

Principle of Reflection

Soviet psychologists consider psychological phenomena to be different levels and types of subjective reflection of objective reality. While the psychological or mental realm has at various times been viewed as a separate substance, a special form of matter in motion, and even as a unique material realm (vulgar materialism), Soviet psychologists conceive of the mental as a quality of matter in motion, not as a substance or a movement. This quality is manifested in different forms of subjective reflection and arises in life forms at a particular stage of evolution. We do not know, at this time, what conditions must obtain for reflection to evolve or for nonsensitive matter to be transformed into sensitive matter, because this issue is as fundamental and complex as the origins of life itself.

Like any other quality, reflection is a function of the movement and interaction of material bodies. In the course of these interactions, bodies inform each other. The action of object A, for example, produces particular changes in object B. Subjective reflection, however is a quality only of living organisms. Living entities, of course, need to orient themselves adaptively to their surrounds. They need, in other words, to act in ways that will take into account their interests as total organisms. In order to provide the necessary guidance, reflection cannot passively mirror environmental changes; it must transcend these changes to some degree. Subjective reflection is, thus, an active process within which information is selected, transformed, and stored, and wherein the direction of changes is noted so that some anticipation (foresight) of future events is possible. Each moment of the reflective process involves information of the present and past and is relevant, to some extent, for the future. As P. K. Anokhin has emphasized and experimental work in perception, memory, and thinking has verified, subjective reflection is forward-directed.

Insofar as psychological inquiry is concerned, the study of sensation, perception, cognition, and concept formation has to do with the relationships between reflection and the objects reflected. This is the psychophysical dimension of the problem. Psychophysiological research, on the other hand, has to do with the relationships between reflection and its "bearer," the brain. Finally, the relationships between reflection and behavior focus on the problem of how reflection directs the actions of people and other life forms.

Principle of Development

As was briefly pointed out, a particular phenomenon or event can be understood only when considered in the context of its development. In the Soviet Union a developmental approach is utilized both when studying the phylogenesis of mind in the human species and when investigating mental development in individuals (ontogenesis). The approach is, of course, also used when conducting research on specific psychological processes such as perception or cognition.

A key issue in developmental research is the question of what changes should be observed and monitored. It is clear that human development is not a monotonic process characterized only by quantitative changes such as an increasingly larger memory; important qualitative changes also take place. For example, perceptual strategies change, and there is a transition from image memory to verbal memory as children learn a language.

Phylogenetically, the most important qualitative change in psychological development occurred when the human species and human society emerged. Within the evolutionary process, the formation of the animal "mind" was determined by biological factors and can be explained by invoking biological laws. When the human species evolved, however, social factors and laws became primary. Human labor transformed nature, social relations arose, and language appeared. These developments brought with them new psychological phenomena, namely, conceptual thinking, creative imagery, the voluntary regulation of behavior, and so forth. Reflection, as manifested in human consciousness, was perfected.

While the essence of humankind is found in the complex of social relationships that people weave, biological laws are still relevant. Their control, however, is mediated by sociohistorical laws. Man's nature is a product of history.

On the whole, psychological development is an elaborate process beset by contradictions, deviations, and regressions. There are contradictions between different motives, between goals, between motives and goals, and among different forms and levels of reflection. During every stage of development, however, one contradictory situation or set of dynamics predominates, and the resolution of this conflict serves as a transition to a new stage which is qualitatively different from the former stage. The laws of human development manifest themselves in specific ways within each person. This means that the formation of each personality, while following certain general principles, is still a process in some ways unique to every human being.

Principle of the Unity of Activity (*deyatelnost*) and Consciousness

The mental or psychological is not some kind of self-contained reality. It has what Soviet psychologists refer to as a concrete subjectivity. By subjectivity or the subjective is not meant an immaterial, incorporeal, ideal state inaccessible to scrutiny. Rather the concept derives from the recognition that the subject, as a corporeal, material being, is actively included in the process of living. In the context of this process, each person, through his or her activities, changes the environment which in turn changes the person.

The principle of the unity of activity and consciousness contends that consciousness, and indeed the psychological dimension in general, is generated, structured, and manifested in activity or human performance. In the process, an individual becomes part of the system of social relations, which, in turn, determines the person's motives, goals, and distinctive personality. These then influence attention, memory, style of thinking, and emotional characteristics.

The complexity of the concept *deyatelnost* (activity or performance) is demonstrated by the diverse research that this concept has generated in the Soviet Union. Some psychologists study activity as a manifestation of social interactions and are interested in such issues as the strategies individuals employ in becoming part of the social system and the role of human actions in personality formation. Others investigate the structure of activities and are frequently concerned with ways to organize work rationally or with the learning processes in general. And still others inquire into the relationships between activity and such psychological processes as perception, memory, and thought. Interest centers both on determining how psychological processes influence activity and how activity is involved in the development of specific psychological processes.

Principle of Communication or Social Interaction (*obshenie*)

The concept of *obshenie* is difficult to translate into English because it concerns both communication processes and modalities, and the social interactions made possible by people communicating with each other. The more cumbersome English equivalent will therefore defer to the Russian transliteration. Since *obshenie* has to do with the characteristic ways that individuals in particular societies communicate with each other, the concept has a sociohistorical dimension. This means that there are interconnections among modes of communication, styles of social interaction, and human activity (*deyatelnost*) in general. The concepts of *obshenie* and *deyatelnost*, in fact, have much in common.

During human history, many forms and techniques of communication developed. While verbal communication became the primary mode, much information is exchanged nonverbally. Human gestures and actions of all types serve a communicative function.

Through the exchange of opinions, ideas, information, and feelings, communication allows people to reveal to each other aspects of their inner or subjective worlds. More specifically, the functions of *obshenie* are to exchange information (cognitive function), to insure the mutual control of behavior or activity (regulative function), and to bring about emotional states or their reduction (affective function). This makes possible the sharing of plans, the coordination of labor, the mutual understanding of people, and the development of interpersonal relationships. As there is unity between consciousness and activity, insofar as subject-object relationships are concerned, so *obshenie* makes possible a unity of consciousness and activity in subject-subject relationships.

As was mentioned when discussing the contributions of the Institute of Psychology of the USSR Academy of Sciences, the study of *obshenie*, or the communication processes, has, since the early 1970s, become one of the central concerns of Soviet research psychology. The many studies in this area include the investigation of the interrelationships among communication, activity, and social behavior; the structure and dynamics of communication; the involvement of the various psychological processes, such as perception and cognition in different forms of communication; and the interplay among communication processes, personality development, learning, and the mastery of social norms.

Principle of Personality

When scientific psychology became a separate field of study, there was a tendency to investigate perception, cognition, and other psychological processes as though each was self-contained and independent. The interrelationships between these processes and the functioning of the person as a whole was ignored. While it is appropriate to investigate the dynamics of specific dimensions of psychological functioning, we must remember that sensations, perceptions, and emotions do not exist in themselves but are mere abstractions. Research on these abstracted processes has succeeded in identifying some general laws but has told us little about the ways that sensory, perceptual, and affective functioning manifests itself in particular human beings, each of whom is unique.

Here we are faced with an important philosophical problem: What are the interrelationships between the general and the particular? According to dialectics, the general does not exist apart from the particular. At the same time, in any specific instance, there is evident both what is general and what is distinctive.

The goal of psychological research, then, is twofold. First, it is necessary to identify the general qualities and laws associated with individual processes, phenomena, or behavioral acts. In other words, we have to move from the concrete to the abstract. After that, we need to test our abstractions by attempting to predict specific situations. This step is difficult but it is essential, particularly when we are trying to make use of psychological knowledge and laws in applied situations. The principle or concept of personality which requires that we acknowledge the interrelationships among all the psychological processes and the peculiarities of each person reminds us that we must always be simultaneously concerned in our research with general processes and laws and with individual human beings.

Principle of Integration

Since the mental or psychological, as a quality of living matter in motion, is an organized whole, all of the aforementioned principles must be integrated into a single system of laws. This essentially holistic approach, shared in principle by the Gestalt psychologists, Piaget, and others, not only stresses the unified nature of the mental but contends that the mental cannot be meaningfully studied by breaking it into separate processes and states. Holistic, however, does not imply that the psychological is amorphous or without order but rather recognizes that there exists a very complex set of dynamics among those aspects that can be differentiated. In order to conduct psychological research it is necessary to study a large number of phenomena and their interrelationships in real-world situations.

The principle of integration demands that we investigate a particular psychological phenomenon within the following contexts: as a qualitatively unique process, in relation to other systems of phenomena (the macro context), and in relation to relevant microsystems. Psychological research thus generates laws, each of which establishes linkages among particular factors, phenomena, and processes. None, however, is comprehensive or all-encompassing. It is only a system made up of these and other laws that can reveal the essence of the mental as an organized whole.

The systemic or integrative approach also has broader implications. If we look at science in its entirety, we find three main types of qualities: the material-structural, the functional, and the systemic. Experience has shown that progress in science requires that all three categories of qualities and their interrelationships be investigated. It behooves us, therefore, to organize our research so that the hierarchy of psychological qualities, from the structural to the systemic, can be worked out. Structural and functional approaches are by themselves insufficient. In this way, we shall also be able to discover the interconnection between the biological and the social relative to the psychological development of the human species.

Unity of Theory, Experimentation, and Praxis Principle

Theory does not develop in isolation. It is closely connected not only with research but also with applied work. A good theory allows us to solve practical problems, and fruitful applied efforts produce new theoretical ideas. If we examine the history of any scientific field, we find that often a societal need generates a new scientific problem or perhaps a whole new set of problems. At other times, practical needs of a society, which on the surface appear to be completely unrelated, form the basis for a new scientific research project. Once events suggest a new issue to be explored, the need for experimental and theoretical work begins; hypotheses are formulated and checked out and theories are verified, modified, or rejected. Successful theories are then used to guide the solution of societal problems. The results of these efforts provide an ongoing check of theoretical formulations and, as new questions arise, suggest further research. This endless process is what brings about scientific progress.

RESEARCH CENTERS AND FACILITIES

Research in the USSR is planned and organized in accordance with government five-year plans. Scientific councils, made up of leading scientists from research institutes, universities, educational institutions, and professional societies, put forward proposals which are summarized for consideration by the presidium of the USSR Academy of Sciences and Ministries. A draft is then prepared and published for public review. This leads to a state plan and funding by the government of relevant research projects.

The major scientific research center in the Soviet Union is the USSR Academy of Sciences (AS USSR). Sometimes referred to as the "Big Academy," it includes more than 200 research institutes extending across all of the natural and social sciences and technological fields. Each republic also has its own Academy of Science with the exception of the RSFSR (Russia). In addition, there are specialized academies of medicine, education, and agriculture. All of these engage in both basic and applied research. Several government ministries also include research institutes, but they primarily work on applied projects. And both basic and applied research is conducted in the more than fifty universities and 200 other institutions of higher education in the Soviet Union. The scientific enterprise in the USSR is systematically organized but takes place in a wide diversity of settings.

The Institute of Psychology, founded in 1971 as part of the USSR Academy of Sciences, not only conducts research but also coordinates scientific investigations at other psychological facilities throughout the country. Moreover, the institute has cooperative agreements with psychological centers in all the Socialist countries as well as Canada, Finland, France, Norway, and the United States.

In addition to conducting and coordinating research, the Institute annually publishes summaries of theoretical, experimental, and applied work in a ten- to fifteen-volume set of books; organizes international conferences and seminars; and publishes the *Psychological Journal*, which is considered the leading journal of scientific psychology in the USSR. The journal highlights information about psychology in the Soviet Union and elsewhere and also publishes articles by foreign authors. All papers include an English summary.

The only Academy of Sciences in the Soviet Union associated with a particular republic having an Institiute of Psychology is in the Georgian Soviet Socialist Republic. Founded in 1941 by Uznadze, psychologists at this institute do experimental work in general, social, engineering, educational, and child psychology. The guiding theoretical formulation is Uznadze's concept of set (*ustanovka*). In the academies of science in the other Soviet republics, psychological research takes place in the context of the institutes of philosophy, sociology, biology, or physiology. In the Ukrainian Republic, there is a Research Institute of Psychology, but it is part of the Ministry of Education. Established in 1945, it is concerned with child and educational psychology, although some work is also conducted in social psychology, engineering psychology, and the psychology of labor.

The USSR Academy of Pedagogical Sciences (a specialized academy) has its own Institute of General and Educational Psychology. It is concerned with mental development, personality development, genetic psychophysiology, labor psychology, and work psychology.

Departments of psychology exist at the Institute of Preschool Education and the Institute of Defectology of the USSR Academy of Pedagogical Sciences. This academy publishes the journal *Voprosy Psychologii* [Problems of Psychology] founded in 1955, which included a broad spectrum of information until 1980 when the *Psychological Journal* was established; now most articles have to do with child and educational psychology. Psychological papers also appear in the journal *Defectology*, published by the academy.

A number of industries have laboratories of engineering psychology and social psychology. Psychologists at these facilities mostly conduct applied research and help make decisions concerning the selection and training of personnel, the performance of work groups, the organization of work spaces, and the human factors involved in the design of new technology.

THE EDUCATION OF PSYCHOLOGISTS

There are departments of psychology at Moscow University, Leningrad University, and Yaroslavl University. At the universities in Kiev, Tbilisi, Tashkent, Yerevan, Tartu, Kazan, Saratov, Rostov, and Kharkhov, psychology courses are part of the curricula of other departments, especially the departments of philosophy, history, and biology.

During their first two years, university students seeking a diploma in psychology take courses in all the major academic areas, including mathematics, history, biology, philosophy, and physiology, as well as courses in social psychology, child psychology, educational psychology, engineering psychology, psychophysiology, the psychology of labor, and the history of psychology. In their third year, students of psychology begin to specialize and experimental psychology is emphasized. It takes five years to obtain a diploma in psychology and during the last year of training students are required to design and carry out an original theoretical, experimental, or applied research project and, finally, to defend a thesis.

At teacher-training institutions there are chairs of psychology, or pedagogy and psychology. Students enrolled in these schools take courses in general, educational, and child psychology. Some students conduct experimental research in fulfillment of the thesis requirement.

Courses in engineering psychology and the psychology of labor are offered at some technical schools, while social and organizational psychology are usually part of the curriculum at institutes specializing in economics. Psychology is also taught at the Academy of National Economics where high-level managers, including ministers and deputy ministers, take advanced courses. Organizational, social, and engineering psychology are emphasized at this academy.

THE USSR SOCIETY OF PSYCHOLOGISTS

Many of the more than 5,000 psychologists in the Soviet Union are members of the USSR Society of Psychologists. Founded in 1957, the society was originally affiliated with the Academy of Pedagogical Sciences. In 1975, it came under the auspices of the USSR Academy of Sciences. The main objectives of the society are to play an active role in the social life of the country, to develop psychological theory, to contribute to the development of the various fields of psychology, to assure the unity of research and work in applied settings, to help members of the society with their work, to improve professional skills, to propagate psychological information, to maintain relations with other scientific societies, and to publish psychological articles and books.

The Society arranges the all-union congresses which take place every five years. At these meetings, participants discuss research projects and findings, make plans for the future, and elect the president and members of the Central Council of the society. Some sense of the scope of Soviet psychological research is indicated by the fact that for the sixth congress, which took place in 1983, twenty volumes were required to publish the abstracts (more than 4,000 of them) associated with the event.

In addition to the congresses, the society organizes four to five all-union conferences and twelve to fifteen regional conferences every year on specific topics. The Central Council is also involved in an ongoing seminar concerning theoretical problems of the discipline. Finally, the society is a member of the International Union of Psychological Science.

NOTES

1. In Russian the terms *psychica* and *psychicheski* are used to denote the total field of psychological events and phenomena. In this chapter, the terms *mental* and *psychological* are used interchangeably.
2. The social sciences and the humanities were also expanding significantly in the

nineteenth century. The Russian linguist A. A. Potebnya (1835–1891), for instance, stressed the importance of the psychological aspects of language. He was, in particular, interested in the relationships between image and reality and between language and thought. He noted that words reflect thought while at the same time influencing the thinking and behavior of others. His conceptions, as well as those of K. D. Ushinsky, an educator, and G. V. Plekhanov, a sociological scholar, influenced later thinking in psychology.

3. The term *obschenie* is difficult to translate into English. In Russian it is etymologically associated with such words as common, community, society, general, and joint. In the psychological context, the closest meanings are communication, social interaction, and interaction. Contextually relevant translations have been used to the extent possible.

4. In the 1950s, this institute was united with the Institute of Higher Nervous Activity named after Pavlov. Lenin signed a decree in 1921 in support of Pavlov's laboratory.

5. During 1910–1913, V. A. Vagner put forth a theory of mental development based on the theory of evolution. In 1922, N. A. Severtsov published an article, entitled "Evolution and mentality," in which he demonstrated that the emergence of mentality in the course of evolution is a natural outcome of the development of living organisms. He also proposed that once the psychological realm comes into being it is the major factor insofar as future development is concerned.

6. The word *deyatelnost* has no exact English equivalent. It is often translated as "activity" or as "performance." Neither is a precise definition. When the term is used, it is important to keep in mind the active goal-directed transformation of an object (material or ideal) by a subject in accordance with a premeditated purpose.

7. Research concerning the arrangement of industrial work places and man-machine systems was first done in the 1920s, but there was at that time no separate field of engineering psychology.

8. Kovalev, A. G. (1962). Subject-matter and problems of social psychology. In *Problems of Marxist sociology*.

9. See notes 6 and 3 for explanations of the concepts, *deyatelnost* and *obschenie*.

SUGGESTED READINGS (IN ENGLISH)

Cole, M., & Maltzman, I. (Eds.). (1969). *Handbook of contemporary Soviet psychology*. New York: Basic Books.

Lomov, B. F. (1983). Soviet psychology: Its historical origins and contemporary status. *American Psychologist 37*, 580–586.

Lomov, B. F. (1984). Scientific law as the link between pure and applied research: A Soviet perspective. *Australian Psychologist, 19*, 345–352.

Lomov, B. F., & Bertone, C. M. (1969). The Soviet view of engineering psychology. *Human Factors, 11* (1), 69–74.

Strickland, L. H. (Ed.). (1979). *Soviet and Western perspectives in social psychology*. New York: Pergamon Press.

See also many articles published in the *Psychological Journal*, and see *Psychological Research in the USSR* (Vol. 1) published in Moscow in 1966 by Progress Publishing.

Spain

Mariano Yela

HISTORICAL OVERVIEW

There is in Spain a very old and rich tradition made up of philosophical, medical, historical, and literary approaches to psychological inquiry. From Roman times through the Middle Ages the general orientation, with autochthonous Stoic and Christian variations, was Platonic, Aristotelian, Augustinian, and Thomist scholasticism, augmented by Hippocratic and Galenic medicine, Arabian and Jewish thought, and the writings of Seneca. This tradition is embodied in many books on man's fortunes and misfortunes, on religious and profane love, and on human nature and *de anima*. It is also evident in numerous biographical sketches and descriptions of rural and court life. The works of Ramón Llull, in the late Middle Ages, and Suárez, in Baroque metaphysics, are the most original and outstanding examples of psychologically relevant philosophical writings (Cruz Hernández, 1977; Siguán, 1981b). From the Renaissance on there is an increasing empirical emphasis. Luis Vives (1492–1540) and Huarte de San Juan (1530–1588) are considered by most to be the fathers of modern (including general, differential, and applied) psychology (Bonilla, 1903; Siguán, 1981b; Pinillos, 1983a).

By the end of the nineteenth century, the polemics on the mind-body problem, the influence of philosophical empiricism, and the success of the experimental method generated a serious interest in what was referred to as the "New Psychology."

Francisco Giner de los Ríos, in his *Lecciones sumarias de psicología* [Brief lectures on psychology] (Madrid, 1874, 1877), demonstrated familiarity with the then recent work of Helmholtz, Fechner, and Wundt (Carpintero, 1981; Díaz, 1973; Lafuente Niño, 1980, 1982; Viqueira, 1930). In 1902 Luis Simarro, a psychiatrist, neurologist, and versatile scholar, was appointed professor of experimental psychology at the University of Madrid. He was probably the first in the world to occupy a chair of experimental psychology in a department of natural and physical sciences (Campos, 1983; Carreras Artau, 1952; Kaplan,

1969; Viqueira, 1930). Under the leadership of Simarro and Ramón y Cajal, a group of neurologists, psychiatrists, and psychologists including Achúcarro, Río Ortega, Lafora, Sacristán, Viqueira, Rodríguez Lavín, Barnés, Navarro Flores, Herrero Bahíllo, and Verdes Montenegro, opened the way for the emergence of scientific psychology in Spain (Campos, 1983; Carpintero, 1980a, 1981, 1982; Germain, 1954, 1981; Kaplan, 1969; López Piñero, et al., 1983; Mallart, 1981; Mestre, 1982; Valenciano, 1977; Viqueira, 1930; Yela, 1982a).

Nevertheless, experimental research in psychology really begins with Ramón Turró (1854–1926) and Emilio Mira (1896–1964) along with their colleagues and disciples in Barcelona (Cardoner, 1950; Carpintero, 1980a; Germain, 1954; Kircher, 1981; Mallart, 1981; Mira, 1920; Miralles, 1980a; Siguán, 1981b), and with César Madariaga, José Germain, José Mallart, and Mercedes Rodrigo, and their coworkers in Madrid (Germain, 1981; Mallart, 1981; Yela, 1982a). Although several of them, especially Turró and Mira, also worked in basic research, the focus during this period, extending until the outbreak of the Spanish Civil War (1936), was on applied psychology, particularly individual differences, testing, industrial and educational psychology, and vocational guidance.

Through the work done at the Institutes of Psychotechnology in Barcelona (Mira) and Madrid (Germain), Spanish scientific psychology grew and gained international recognition. The Second (1921) and Sixth (1930) International Conferences of Psychotechnology took place in Barcelona, and Madrid was selected for the Eleventh International Congress of Psychology. First Ramón y Cajal, until his death, and then Ortega y Gasset were chosen president of the congress with Mira the executive president, Lafora the vice-president, Germain the secretary, and Mallart the treasurer. Spain's Civil War (1936–1939), however, made it impossible to hold the congress and disrupted the development of psychology in Spain (Montoro & Quintanilla, 1982; Siguán, 1981b).

Slowly and with difficulty psychology recovered from the Civil War and World War II which followed. Despite some official aloofness toward experimental psychology, the interest in the sciences that came from the neoscholastic movement of Louvain led by Juan Zaragueta, Fernando M. Palmés (Siguán, 1981b), and Manuel Barbado (Barbado, 1943; Zanón & Carpintero, 1981), the great prewar philosophical contributions of Unamuno and Ortega y Gasset, Spain's eminent neurological and psychiatric tradition, and the competent direction of Germain sparked the renewal of psychology. The pioneers were José Luis Pinillos, Miguel Siguán, Manuel Ubeda, and Mariano Yela. Their common outlook was both experimental and philosophically sophisticated. Pinillos had worked with Eysenck; Siguán had been at the British Institute of Industrial Psychology; Ubeda belonged to the school of Ramón y Cajal; and Yela had spent several years with Thurstone and Neff, at Chicago, and Michotte, at Louvain. We all enjoyed a number of delightful years at the Department of Experimental Psychology of the Higher Council for Scientific Research which we organized under the leadership of Germain in 1948. That work represented a new starting point.

Since then, slowly at first but eventually more rapidly, psychology in Spain has grown and achieved a fairly high level of sophistication both as a science and as a profession.

NATURE AND SCOPE OF THE DISCIPLINE

Definitions

Psychology in Spain is a multiparadigmatic and, to some extent, a preparadigmatic science. In general, it has a positive image. The field has clinical, cultural, and humanistic as well as experimental, quantitative, and natural-science dimensions, but in most research and thinking both perspectives are manifested. Empirical verification is usually the final proof of whatever claims are made. According to Pinillos: "The subject matter of psychology is the activity by which organisms exist in their respective environments, making responses to their stimulations and operating upon them in a purposive and to some extent conscious way" (Pinillos, 1975, p. 692; 1964; 1982). For my part, I define our science as the biosocial study of behavior, behavior being conceptualized as a physical pattern of biological and, in the case of man, meaningful biographical events. The aim of psychology is both to explain the functional structure of behavior and to understand the subject's action in his biophysical environment and in his social and cultural world. (Yela, 1982a). These views of psychology are, I think, representative of Spanish psychologists' perspectives on the discipline.

Universities

Most teaching and research take place in the universities. A listing of the state and private universities which have departments of psychology and the university colleges which offer the first phase of psychological study follows.

State Universities

Universities with Autonomous Departments of Psychology: Universidad Complutense, Campus de Somosaguas, Madrid 11; Universidad Autónoma, Campus de Cantoblanco, Madrid 34; Universidad Nacional de Educación a Distancia, Ciudad Universitaria, Madrid 3; Universidad de Barcelona, Gran Vía de las Cortes Catalanas, 585, Barcelona 11; and Universidad de Valencia, Paseo de Valencia al Mar, Valencia.

Universities with Departments of Psychology within More General Fields: Universidad Autónoma, Campus de Bellaterra, Barcelona; Campus Universitario de la Cartuja, Granada; Avda. de la Universidad, La Laguna, Tenerife; Complejo Residencia Espinardo, Murcia; Valdés Salas, Oviedo; Universidad de Palma de Mallorca, Gregorio Marañón, Palma de Mallorca; Universidad de Salamanca, Plaza de Anaya, 1. Salamanca; Universidad del Pais Vasco, Alto de Zorroaga,

San Sebastián; Avda. de Juan XXIII, Santiago de Compostela, La Coruña; Universidad de Sevilla, Dña. María de Padilla, Sevilla; and Universidad de Barcelona, Plaza Imperial Tarraco.

University Colleges: "Abad Oliva" registered in the Universidad Central de Barcelona, Avda. Pearson, 9, Barcelona; Castellón de la Plana, registered in the Universidad de Valencia, Carretera de Barcelona, Km. 72; Gerona, registered in the Universidad Autónoma de Barcelona, Plaza Obispo Lorenzano; La Coruña, registered in the Universidad de Santiago, Almirante Lángara; "Cardenal Cisneros," registered in the Universidad Complutense, Maldonado, 48, Madrid; "San Pablo," registered in the Universidad Complutense, Julián Romea, 23, Madrid; "Luis Vives," registered in the Universidad Autónoma de Madrid, Gaztambide, 65, Madrid; and Orense, registered in the Universidad de Santiago.

Private Universities

There are psychological units at the following universities: Pontificia de Salamanca in Salamanca, Deusto in Bilbao, Comillas in Madrid, and Navarra in Pamplona.

Curricula

Psychology curricula usually consist of three levels of instruction. The first includes three years of basic studies. The second offers two years of advanced courses and initial specialization mainly in the fields of clinical, industrial, and educational psychology, although more specific training in such areas as child psychology, family dynamics, psycholinguistics, social, or theoretical-experimental may be offered. The third level embraces two years of Ph.D. studies, made up of advanced courses and research. The current and the newly proposed curricula of the Complutensis University of Madrid are detailed.

Current Curriculum

Basic cycle. First year: anthropology, logic and theory of science, general psychology I: foundations of mathematical psychology, sociology, philosophical systems. Second year: general psychology II: biological foundations of behavior, mathematical psychology I (statistics), history of psychology, social psychology. Third year: developmental psychology, mathematical psychology II (psychometrics), psychometric tests, projective tests, physiological psychology.

Second cycle. Fourth year: experimental psychology (laboratory), differential psychology, pathological psychology, learning, one of the following: psychoanalysis, data processing, group dynamics. Fifth year: personality, thinking and language, psychodiagnosis, perception, motivation; one of the following: behavior modification, counseling, communication.

Third cycle. Two years; four courses each year, chosen among those offered. In 1982–1983, for instance, the following courses were available: factor analysis and the structure of verbal intelligence, multivariate techniques in the human sciences, formal models in psychology, item-response theory, anthropology and symbolic construction of reality, psychochemistry, contemporary models in psychopathology, social change and ethics, automata theory and artificial intelligence, the Rorschach as nonprojective technique, dyslexias, psycholinguistics of the metaphor, personality and aging, epistemological status of psychology, the problem of value judgments in psychology, recent advances in classical conditioning, psychology as a basis for the human sciences, evaluation of anxiety, applied research in psychology, bilingualism: a psychological approach, memory and knowledge processing in animal experimentation.

Proposed Curriculum

Basic cycle. First year: introduction to psychology, foundations of mathematical psychology, learning, biological foundations of psychology, sociology, anthropology, logic and methodology of science. Second year: social psychology, physiological psychology, mathematical psychology I (statistics), perception, motivation and emotion, human learning and memory. Third year: thinking and language, developmental psychology I, psychopathology I, mathematical psychology II (psychometrics), experimental psychology (laboratory).

Second cycle. (I) *Common disciplines*: differential psychology, personality, history of psychology, philosophy of psychology. (II) *Specific disciplines*: Clinical Section: psychopathology II, psychological evaluation, psychotherapy, behavior therapy, psychodiagnosis. Educational Section: developmental psychology II: guidance, psychology of teaching, educational intervention, psychosociology of education. Industrial Section: psychosociology of work, business psychology, ergonomics, selection and training, problems of adjustment. Social Section: methods of social research, group dynamics, applied social psychology, psychology of the community, environmental psychology. Theoretical-Experimental Section: multivariate analysis, basic processes, design and analysis of data, cognitive psychology, neuropsychology. (III) *Optional disciplines*: mental disturbances, differential education, language disturbances, simulation, behavior modification, ethology.

Third cycle: Same as current curriculum.

Other Organizations

In addition to the departments of psychology in the universities and colleges, there is the Institute of Applied Psychology (Escuela de Psicología y Psicotecnia) at the Complutense University of Madrid, where students with the master's degree in psychology (Licenciados en Psicología) are offered professional training in clinical, educational, and industrial psychology. There are also institutes of medical psychology (Escuelas de Psiquiatría y Psicología Médica) in some departments of medicine and numerous centers and associations concerned in different ways and to differing degrees with teaching, research, organizing and conducting meetings and congresses, publishing, professional work, and so forth.

The primary psychological organizations in Spain are the Spanish Psychological Association (Sociedad Española de Psicología), Isaac Peral, Ciudad Universitaria, Madrid, 3; and the Professional Union of Psychologists (Colegio Oficial de Psicólogos), Fernández de los Ríos, 87, Madrid, 15. The Spanish Psychological Association, the "mother organization," was founded in 1952 and its presidents have been José Germain (1952–1973) and Mariano Yela (1973–   ). The best sources for psychological and historical studies of the association are *Revista de Psicología General y Aplicada* [Journal of General and Applied Psychology] and the various documents and proceedings published by the organization.

The Colegio Oficial de Psicólogos was founded in 1980. Its present dean is Carlos Camarero. With a membership of about 6,000 and delegations all over Spain, it is the best source of documentation on psychological activities in the country, especially through its *Papeles del Colegio* [Papers of the Union] and its *Guía del Psicólogo* [Psychologist's Guide].

More information about universities, teaching and training, publishing, students, and psychological organizations in Spain can be found in publications by Blanco Villaseñor, 1983; Colegio Oficial de Psicólogos, 1983; Fernández Seara, et al., 1983; Fundación Universidad-Empresa, 1980; García Yague, et al., 1975; Ortega and Fernández Dols, 1980; Bayés, 1978, 1983; Delval, 1980b; Pascual, 1983; Rivas, et al., 1976; Siguán, 1978.

The following organizations are also related to scientific psychology in Spain:

Asociación Española de Psicoterapia y Psicología de la Infancia, Atocha 20, Madrid, 12.

Asociación Española de Terapia del Comportamiento, apartado 9209, Madrid.

Asociación Iberoamericana de Análisis Transaccional, Avda. Madrid 133, Barcelona, 28.

Colegio Oficial de Psicólogos, Fernández de los Ríos 87, Madrid, 15.

Escuela de Psicomotricidad, Londres 41, Madrid, 28.

Instituto de Orientación Educativa y Professional (formerly, National Institute of Applied Psychology), Isaac Peral, Ciudad Universitaria, Madrid, 3.

Instituto de Salud Mental, García de paredes 65, Madrid, 3.

Instituto Municipal de Educación, Mejía Lequerica 21, Madrid, 4.

Instituto Municipal de Educación, Valencia.

Instituto Municipal de Investigación en Psicología Aplicada a la Educación, Ayuntamiento de Barcelona, Barcelona.

Instituto Nacional de Asistencia Social, José Abascal 39, Madrid, 3.

Instituto Nacional de Pedagogía Terapéutica, General Oráa 39, Madrid, 6.

Instituto Psicotécnico de la Generalidad, Ayuntamiento de Barcelona, Barcelona.

MEPSA, Franco Rodríguez 47, Madrid, 20.

Sociedad Española de Parapsicología, Belén 15, Madrid, 4.

Sociedad Española de Psicoanálisis, Barcelona.

Sociedad Española de Psicología, Isaac Peral, Ciudad Universitaria, Madrid, 3.

Sociedad Española de Rorschach y Métodos Proyectivos, Delegación Central, Madrid.

Sociedad Valenciana de Análisis y Cambio de Conducta, Universidad de Valencia, Valencia.

Técnicos Especialistas Asociados, T.E.A., Fray Bernardino de Shahgún 24, Madrid, 16.

Journals

The primary references for psychological research are *Revista de Psicología General y Aplicada* [Journal of General and Applied Psychology], first founded and edited by José Germain and now directed by José L. Fernández Trespalacios, and *Investigaciones Psicológicas* [Psychological Research], edited by the Facultad de Psicología of the Complutense University, both published in Madrid; and *Anuario de Psicología* [Yearbook of Psychology], edited by Miguel Siguán, and *Cuadernos de Psicología* [Papers on Psychology], edited by Jordi Bachs, both published in Barcelona. More specific fields are covered by *Análisis y Modificación de Conducta* [Behavior Analysis and Modification], founded and edited by Vicente Pelechano, and *Revista de Historia de la Psicología* [Journal of the History of Psychology], founded and edited by Helio Carpintero, both at the University of Valencia. For current topical information and documentation consult the already mentioned *Papeles del Colegio* and *Guía del Psicólogo*, published by the Colegio Oficial de Psicólogos.

There are also many psychological and psychiatric journals, newsletters, and bulletins published by universities and various agencies. These concern both research and applied areas.

Introductory Textbooks, Abstracts, and Indexes

There are many standard textbooks written by Spanish psychologists (i.e., books by Alonso Fernández, Amón, Arnau, Ballús, Caparrós, Carpintero, Cruz Hernández, Fernández Trespalacios, Fernández Ballesteros, Genovard, Guillamón, Jiménez-Burillo, Martínez Arias, Mayor, Pérez y Pérez, Pelechano, Seoane, Simón, Vega, and Yela). A representative series of books is published by the Open University (Universidad Nacional de Educación a Distancia, Ciudad Universitaria, Madrid, 3).

The most widely used introductory textbook in general psychology written by a Spanish psychologist is J. L. Pinillos' *Principios de psicología* [Principles of psychology], Madrid, Alianza Editorial, 1975 and successive editions. Among those translated into Spanish the most popular include:

Fraisse, P., and Piaget, J. (1973). *Tratado de psicología experimental* [Treatise on experimental psychology]. Buenos Aires: Paidós.

Hebb, D. O. (1975). *Psicología* [Psychology]. México City: Interamericana.

Hilgard, E. R. (1969). *Introducción a la psicología* [Introduction to psychology]. Madrid: Morata.

Lindsay, P. H., and Norman, D. A. (1983). *Procesamiento de información humana: Una introducción a la psicología* [Human information processing: an introduction to psychology]. Madrid: Tecnos.

Morgan, C. T. (1978). *Introducción a la psicología* [Introduction to psychology]. Madrid: Aguilar.

Neisser, U. (1976). *Psicología cognoscitiva* [Cognitive psychology]. México: Trillas.

Osgood, C. E. (1971). *Psicología experimental* [Experimental psychology]. México: Trillas.

Reuchlin, M. (1980). *Psicología* [Psychology]. Madrid: Morata.

Whittaker, J. O. (1968). *Psicología* [Psychology]. México: Interamericana.

Wolman, B. (1979–1980). *Manual de psicología* [Manual of psychology]. Barcelona: Martínez Roca.

Students can also consult books of readings in most psychological fields. They have access not only to Spanish sources but to many of the basic and current books and papers published in other major languages, especially English and French.

In addition to the standard bibliographic sources, in English and other languages, and the abstracts published by Spanish journals (Ferrándiz, 1980; Ortega & Fernández Dols, 1980), there are three main indexes of Spanish psychological literature: *Spanish Language Psychology*, Interamerican Society of Psychology and International Union of Psychological Science, Amsterdam: North-Holland; *Indice Español de Ciencias Sociales* [Spanish Index for the Social Sciences], Instituto de Información y Documentación en Ciencias Sociales y Humanidades, Consejo Superior de Investigaciones Científicas, Madrid; and *Indice Médico Español* [Spanish Medical Index], Centro de Documentación e Informática Biomédica, Valencia.

There are several centers connected with national and international networks of computerized data banks. Perhaps the best source of information concerning such resources if FUNDESCO, Fundación par el Desarrollo Social de las Comunicaciones, Serrano 187, Madrid, 2.

Functions of Psychologists

The primary functions of psychologists in Spain are teaching, research, and administrative and professional work in a variety of organizational, educational, and clinical settings, both in private and public institutions, and for some private practice. There is a growing demand for psychologists to work in centers concerned with family and community planning and counseling, health and sanitation programs, the armed forces, and to do forensic consulting and provide psychological care in prisons.

Funding for Research

Financial support for research, most of which is done in university departments and laboratories, is rather scarce. It normally comes from the state (Ministerio de Educación y Ciencia) in the form of small annual allocations for full professors (Catedráticos y Agregados) and, in more substantial amounts, for special research projects previously approved by the National Research Commission (Comisión Asesora de Investigación Científica y Técnica, Ministerio de Educación y Ciencia, Rosario Pino 14, Madrid). There are also a number of national, international, and private foundations that provide funds for research, scholarships, and scientific cooperation and exchanges with psychologists in most Western countries.

Financial aid, though small, is increasing. From 1965 to 1982, about 12 billion pesetas were distributed by the National Research Commission to support research projects. In 1965, the amount was 28 million; in 1982, 3.5 billion. Only about 8 percent of these funds have, however, been allocated for social and human science research programs (Proyectos de Investigación, 1965–1982, Comisión Asesora de Investigación Científica y Técnica, Ministerio de Educación y Ciencia, Madrid, 1983).

Needs

The major needs at this time are better equipment and more funding for basic and applied research; fuller acceptance of the discipline by society; more jobs; continuing education programs for young professors and professionals; and improved cooperation between departments of psychology and hospitals, clinics, schools, and social and industrial organizations.

Relationships with Other Disciplines

In the instructional field, there are opportunities for psychologists to teach courses in teachers' colleges, business and vocational schools, medical departments, and the fields of journalism, sociology, philosophy, and criminology. There are many interrelationships between psychological training, research, and application, on the one hand, and philosophical, medical, educational, sociological, mathematical, and natural science disciplines, on the other.

MAJOR TRENDS AND INFLUENCES SINCE WORLD WAR II

Demographic and Organizational Aspects

In 1946, Germain founded the *Revista de Psicología General y Aplicada* [Journal of General and Applied Psychology]. It was then the only psychological journal and has been one of the integrating factors in Spanish psychology through-out the years.

In 1948, Germain and Yela founded the Department of Experimental Psychology within the Higher Council for Scientific Research. A small group of young psychologists devoted to experimental work was soon assembled. The group included Ubeda, Siguán, Pinillos, Secadas, Pertejo, Alvarez Villar, and García Yague.

In 1952, the Spanish Psychological Association (Sociedad Española de Psicología) was organized. Its founders were Germain, J. López Ibor, Zaragueta, Yela, Pinillos, Ibarrola, J. Marías, Lafora, J. Mallart, Vallejo-Nágera, Gil Fagoaga, Romero, Sacristán, Lavín, Ubeda, and Alvarez de Linera. Membership has grown from 16 members in 1952, to 189 in 1962, 709 in 1972, and 1,500 in 1982. The association now has four national divisions, namely theoretical-experimental, educational, industrial, and clinical, and three regional ones, Cataluña, Valencia, and Galicia. The divisions hold monthly scientific sessions, and the association has organized twenty-seven national meetings and seven national congresses. The Seventh National Congress, held in 1982 in Santiago de Compostela, was attended by about 1,600 participants and included two plenary sessions, forty round tables and numerous sessions for the presentation of papers, films, and so forth. The XXVII National Meeting took place in 1983 in Madrid, with several workshops and two round tables, each lasting two days. One concerned drugs and therapy, the other psychology and the computer.

In 1953, the Institute of Applied Psychology (Escuela de Psicología y Psicotecnia) was founded at the University of Madrid, with Zaragueta as president and Yela as secretary. The institute is a graduate training center for professional psychologists, the first in Spain to grant a university degree in psychology. About 10,000 students have graduated from the institute.

In the early 1950s, Germain was reappointed director of the National Institute of Applied Psychology, which he had organized and directed before the Spanish Civil War. There, senior psychologists such as Mallart and Vázquez and some of their younger colleagues, for example, Pinillos and Yela, reestablished interest in test development, industrial psychology, and vocational guidance. At the same time the Institute of Barcelona undertook similar tasks under the direction of Borrás with the help of Soler Dopff, Cerdá, and other psychologists. Numerous guidance centers were also founded in different cities.

In 1969, the first Section of Psychology was organized as part of the Facultad de Filosofía y Letras of the Complutense University of Madrid, with Yela as president. Soon new sections of psychology were founded in other universities, beginning with the one organized by Siguán in Barcelona. In 1969, there were 2,435 students of psychology. By 1977 this number had increased to about 20,000. Since then there has been little change.

In 1980, the Professional Union of Psychologists (Colegio Oficial de Psicólogos) was founded. With a membership of about 6,000, it keeps in touch with some 30,000 psychologists throughout the country. The professional Colegio, the association, and the universities have worked together on several projects. For example, in 1983 they organized the First National Congress of the Psychology of Work, attended by more than 600 industrial and organizational psychologists and supported by many employers', managers', and workers' organizations.

The rapid economic development of Spain since the 1960s has created a growing demand for facilities concerned with education, health, and personnel selection. The trend toward democracy stimulated interest in psychology and the growth of unrestricted research and applied work (Pelechano, 1982). Since the end of World War II, most Spanish psychologists have established collaborative relationships with the outstanding professors, laboratories, and clinics in Europe, Latin America, and the United States. There are now between 2,000 and 3,000 psychological experts, several hundred professors and instructors, and a few dozen high-level research psychologists in Spain.

Research and Theory: Major Orientations and Programs

The major orientations of psychology in Spain are much the same as in other countries. It is more difficult to summarize the concrete programs and contributions. They are many and varied, and some are of questionable importance. The major research centers are located at the universities of Madrid, Barcelona, Valencia, and Granada.

The predominant orientation is the conceptualization of psychology as an empirical, experimental, and often mathematical and quantitative study of behavior. The purposive and cognitive dimensions as well as the biological and social components are also commonly emphasized (Pelechano, 1972, 1973; Pinillos, 1964, 1975; Siguán, 1977, 1981b; Yela, 1963, 1974, 1980, 1982a). A good description of contemporary orientations may be found in an issue of *Análisis y Modificación de Conducta* edited by Pinillos (1980) on current problems of scientific psychology, entitled *Problemas actuales de la psicologiá científica*.

Behavioristic, mostly Skinnerian, viewpoints are represented, too, both in basic research and in applied behavior modification (Bayés, 1979, 1983), although in the latter case there is a growing eclecticism (Avia & Kanfer, 1980; Fernández Ballesteros & Carrobles, 1981; Mayor & Labrador, 1983; Pelechano, 1978, 1980).

There are also cognitive approaches. Some are based on information-processing conceptions and computer analogs, some are Piagetian, and others derive from Soviet perspectives (Delclaux & Seoane, 1982; Delval, 1973, 1978, 1980a; Jáñez, 1981; Fernández Trespalacios, 1978; Siguán, 1981a, 1981b, 1982. See a special issue devoted to Piaget of the *Revista de Psicología General y Aplicada*, edited by Yela [1982b]).

There is also a personalistic and humanistic orientation. This perspective is somewhat unique in the sense that it places emphasis on careful empirical verification, especially in applied psychology (Gondra, 1975).

There are many approaches which are more or less psychoanalytic (Rof-Carballo, 1952, 1971, 1972, 1975; Villamarzo, 1982) but are also related to existential or Marxist philosophy as well (Ayestarán, 1980; Castilla del Pino, 1969, 1972).

And, finally, there is a rich tradition of psychoneurological research (Gonzálo, 1945; Rodríguez Delgado, 1972), many contributions to psychiatry (Alonso-Fernández, 1976–1977, 1978; López Ibor, 1964, 1966, 1969, 1974; Rey-Ardid, 1964; Sarró 1940), and important phenomenological and anthropological analyses of human life (see, for example, Lain Entralgo, 1964, 1968, 1972–1975, 1978, 1982; Marías, 1970; Zubiri, 1963, 1964).

The most influential and world-renowned contributions of Spanish psychology are those of the Ramón y Cajal school of neuropsychology, the endocrinological studies of emotions by the school of Marañón, and the philosophical analyses of human life done by Ortega y Gasset and his followers. Of increasing significance are the efforts of present-day psychologists to coordinate the differential and general approaches to psychological phenomena and to demonstrate the interconnection of experimental and quantitative methodology with the purposive, cognitive, conscious, social, cultural, and biographical aspects of human behavior. I also detect a growing interest in employing psychological techniques to further individual human development and to improve society.

PSYCHOLOGISTS WITH A SPECIAL INTEREST IN THE HISTORY OF PSYCHOLOGY

There are two groups of psychologists working on historical topics. One is led by Dr. Helio Carpintero at the University of Valencia, which specializes in bibliometric approaches. Most of this group's work has appeared in the *Revista de Historia de la Psicología*, founded and edited by Dr. Carpintero. The other group works at the University of Barcelona and has a more epistemological slant. Most representative is Dr. Antonio Caparrós.

Analyses of psychology in other countries and in Spain are included in the references. For convenience, those having to do with Spanish psychology are identified in the following listings.

General Analyses

Bayés, 1984; Carpintero, 1980a, 1981, 1982; Fernández-Zúñiga & García Tuñón, 1976; Finisson, 1977; Germain, 1954, 1981; León & Brozek, 1980; Mallart, 1981; Peiró & Carpintero, 1981, 1983; Pinillos, 1980, 1982; Rodríguez, 1981; Siguán, 1977, 1981b; Ullesperger, 1954; Viqueira, 1930; Yela, 1975, 1982a.

Analyses of Trends, Schools, and Authors

Campos, 1983, on Simarro; Cardoner, 1950, on Turró; Carpintero, 1981, on Wundt and Spanish psychology; Carreras Artau, 1952, on the nineteenth century; Delval, 1980a, on Piaget; Díaz, 1973, on social philosophy; Jiménez-Burillo, 1976, on social psychology; Kaplan, 1969, on Simarro; Kircher, 1981, on Mira; Lafuente Niño, 1980, 1982, on Giner de los Ríos; Lison, 1971, on anthropology; Mestre, 1982, on Viqueira; Mestre & Carpintero, 1983, on the introduction of Freud to Spain; Pascual, 1983, on the armed forces; Pinillos, 1965, on social psychology, 1983a, on Huarte, psychoanalysis, and personality, and 1983b, on the American influence; Sahagún, 1976, on twentieth-century anthropology; Siguán, 1981a, 1982, on Piaget in Spain, 1981b, on psychology in Catalonia; Valenciano, 1977, on Lafora; Zanón & Carpintero, 1981, on Barbado.

Analyses of Journals, Textbooks, and Congresses

Barberá & Pastor, 1981; García, et al., 1981; González, et al., 1981; Luque, et al., 1981; Mallart, 1983; Martínez, 1978; Maso, et al., 1981; Montoro & Quintanilla, 1982; Navarro, et al., 1981; Pastor, 1960; Pastor-Carballo & Carpintero, 1980; Peiró & Carpintero, 1981; Tortosa & Carpintero, 1980.

Analyses of Teaching, Training, and Research

Bayés, 1978, 1983; Bayés & Garau, 1982; Campos & Aguado, 1977; Delval, 1980b; Miralles, 1980a, 1980b; Rivas, et al., 1976; Siguán, 1978; Yela, 1982a.

CONCLUSION

Scientific psychology has achieved a relatively high status in Spain. It is characterized by multiple, sometimes antagonistic, orientations but is generally rooted in empirical and experimental traditions. Its major challenges are to integrate internal and external validity, make basic research relevant to human behavior, conduct studies which are both precise and meaningful, and recognize that values must not be sacrificed in the pursuit of efficiency.

REFERENCES

Alcaín, M. D., & Sánchez, J. M. (1983). Análisis bibliométrico de las búsquedas retrospectivas on-line y de fotodocumentación en Psicología [Bibliometric analysis of retrospective on-line searching and photo-documentation in psychology]. *Guía del Psicólogo, 7,* 10–29.

Alonso-Fernández, F. (1976–1977). *Fundamentos de la Psiquiatría actual* [Foundations of contemporary psychiatry]. Madrid: Paz Montalvo.

Alonso-Fernández, F. (1978). *Psicología médica y social* [Medical and social psychology]. Madrid: Paz Montalvo.

Avia, M. D., & Kanfer, F. H. (1980). Coping with aversive stimulation: The effects on training in a self-management context. *Cognitive Therapy and Research, 4* (1), 73–81.

Ayestarán, S. (1980). *Manual de psicoterapia de grupo* [Manual of group psychotherapy]. Salamanca: Universidad Pontifica.

Barbado, M. (1943). *Introducción a la psicología experimental* [Introduction to experimental psychology]. Madrid: C.S.I.C.

Barberá, E., & Pastor, R. (1981). Estudio bibliométrico de la *Revista Cuadernos de Psicología* 3 (1975–1977) [Bibliometric study of the *Journal of Psychology* 3 (1975–1977)]. *Revista Historia de la Psicología, 2* (4), 361–374.

Bayés, R. (1978). Evolución de las preferencias de los estudiantes de Psicología en Barcelona entre 1967 y 1977 [Evolution of preferences among psychology students in Barcelona between 1967 and 1977]. *Revista Psicología General y Aplicada, 33*, 915–923.

Bayés, R. (1979). *Psicología y mediciana* [Psychology and medicine]. Barcelona: Fontanella.

Bayés, R. (1983). Enseñanza y ejercicio profesional del análisis de la conducta en España [The teaching and professional use of behavioral analysis in Spain]. *Revista Psicología General y Aplicada, 38*, 232–245.

Bayés, R. (1984). Psychology in Spain. In R. J. Corsini (Ed.), *Encyclopedia of psychology* (Vol. 3, pp. 155–157). New York: Wiley.

Bayés, R., & Garau, A. (1982). Investigación en psicología experimental en la Universidad Autónoma de Barcelona [Experimental psychological research at the Autonomous University of Barcelona]. *Revista Historia de la Psicología, 3* (1), 73–84.

Blanco, L. (1972). *El concepto de conducta en Tolman* [The concept of behavior according to Tolman]. Madrid: Prial.

Blanco Villaseñor, A. (1983). *Guía documental en psicología y educación* [A guide to documents in psychology and education]. Barcelona: Departamento de Psicología Experimental, Universidad de Barcelona.

Blas Aritio, F. (1980). Problemas y tareas de la historia de la psicología [Problems and tasks associated with the history of psychology]. *Revista Psicología General y Aplicada, 35*, 751–767.

Blas Aritio, F. (1982). El desarrollo "reformista" de la psicología [The "reformist" movement in psychology]. *Revista Historia de la Psicología, 4*, 333–366.

Bonilla y San Martín, A. (1903). *Luis Vives*. Madrid: Real Academia de Ciencias Morales y Políticas.

Campos, J. J. (1983). El Dr. Simarro y la tradición experimental en la psicología española [Dr. Simarro and the experimental tradition in Spanish psychology]. *Informes de Psicología, 2* (2), 109–131.

Campos, J. J., & Aguado, L. (1977). La investigación psicológica en España [Psychological research in Spain]. *Cuadernos de Psicología, 3* (6–7), 16–27.

Caparrós, A. (1975). Apuntes históricos al freudo marxismo [Historical notes on Freudian Marxism]. *Anuario de Psicología, 13*, 5–35.

Caparrós, A. (1977). Neoconductismo y psicoanálisis [Neobehaviorism and psychoanalysis]. *Anuario de Psicología, 17*, 56–86.

Caparrós, A. (1979). *Introducción histórica a la psicología contemporánea* [Historical introduction to contemporary psychology]. Barcelona: Rol.

Caparrós, A. (1980). *Los paradigmas en psicología* [Paradigms in psychology]. Barcelona: Horsori. (a)

Caparrós, A. (1980). Problemas historiográficos de la historia de la psicología [Historiographic problems in the history of psychology]. *Revista Historia de la Psicología, 1* (3–4), 393–414. (b)

Caparrós, A., & Siguán, M., et al. (1981). *La psicología genética de Jean Piaget* [The genetic psychology of Jean Piaget]. Barcelona: Universidad de Barcelona.

Cardoner, A. (1950). *Estudi critic de l'obra cientifica de Ramón Turró* [A critical study of the outstanding scientific contribution of Ramón Turró]. Barcelona: Institut d'Estudis Catalans.

Carpintero, H. (1976). *Historia de la psicología* [History of psychology]. Madrid: UNED.

Carpintero, H. (1979). Algunas dimensiones institucionales de la psicología [Some institutional dimensions of psychology]. *Boletín Informativo*, Fundación March, *82*, 3–14.

Carpintero, H. (1980). La psicología española: Pasado, presente y futuro [Spanish psychology: Past, present, and future]. *Revista Historia de la Psicología, 1* (1), 33–58.(a)

Carpintero, H. (1980). La psicología actual desde una perspectiva bibliométrica [Contemporary psychology from a bibliometric perspective]. *Análisis y Modificación de Conducta, 6* (11–12), 9–23.(b)

Carpintero, H. (1981). Wundt y la psicología en España [Wundt and psychology in Spain]. *Revista Historia de la Psicología, 2* (1), 37–56.

Carpintero, H. (1982). The introduction of scientific psychology in Spain, 1875–1900. In W. R. Woodward & M. G. Ash (Eds.), *The problematic science: Psychology in nineteenth-century thought*. New York: Praeger.

Carpintero, H., Pascual, J., & Peiró, J. M. (1977). La psicología a través de sus textos: Análisis del manual de E. R. Hilgard [Psychology through its tests: Analysis of E. R. Hilgard's manual]. *Análisis y Modificación de Conducta, 3*, 111–125.

Carpintero, H., & Peiró, J. M. (1978). Un método sociométrico de análisis de contenido: Su aplicación a la investigación actual sobre "generaciones" [A sociometric method of restraint analysis: Its application to current research on "generations"]. *Análisis y Modificación de Conducta, 4* (6), 111–126.

Carpintero, H., & Peiró, J. M. (1980). Una perspectiva bibliométrica sobre la modificación de conducta [A bibliometric perspective on behavior modification]. *Revista Historia de la Psicología, 1* (3–4), 283–322.

Carpintero, H., & Peiró, J. M. (Eds.). (1981). *Psicología contemporánea. Teoría y métodos cuantitativos para el estudio de su literatura* [Contemporary psychology. Theory and quantitative methods for the study of scientific literature]. Valencia: Alfaplus.

Carpintero, H., & Peiro, J. M. (1983). Aplicaciones de la metodología bibliométrica a los estudios de historia de la psicología [Applications of bibliometric methodologies to the study of the history of psychology]. *Revista Historia de la Psicología, 4* (1), 21–32.

Carreras Artau, T. (1952). *Estudios sobre médicos filósofos españoles del siglo XIX* [Studies of Spanish medical philosophers of the nineteenth century]. Barcelona: C.S.I.C.

Castilla del Pino, C. (1969). *Psicoanálisis y marxismo* [Psychoanalysis and Marxism]. Madrid: Alianza Editorial.

Castilla del Pino, C. (1972). *Introducción a la hermenéutica del lenguaje* [Introduction to the hermeneutics of language]. Barcelona: Península.

Colegio Oficial de Psicólogos. (1983). *Guía de recursos asistenciales en psicología clínica en la Provincia de Madrid* [Guide to the resources in clinical psychology in the Province of Madrid]. Madrid: Author.

Cruz Hernández, M. (1953). *Francisco Brentano* (Franz Brentano]. Salamanca: Universidad de Salamanca.

Cruz Hernández, M. (1977). *El pensamiento de Ramón Llull* [The thoughts of Ramón Llull]. Madrid: Fundación.

Delclaux, I., & Seoane, J. (Eds.). (1982). *Psicología cognitiva y procesamiento de la información* [Cognitive psychology and information processing]. Madrid: Pirámide.

Delval, J. (1973). *La bibliografía en castellano sobre Piaget* [Spanish bibliography on Piaget]. *Revista Psicología General y Aplicada, 28* (122), 333–358.

Delval, J. (1978). Piaget y la psicología cognitiva [Piaget and cognitive psychology]. *Boletín Informativo*, Fundación March, *72*, 3–16.

Delval, J. (1980). *La herencia de Jean Piaget* [The heritage of Jean Piaget]. *Revista Psicología General y Aplicada, 35* (167), 1123–1133.(a)

Delval, J. (1980). Observaciones sobre la teoría psicológica y su enseñanza [Observations on psychological theory and its teaching]. *Estudios de Psicología, 1*, 124–137.(b)

Díaz, E. (1973). *La filosofía social del krausismo español* [The social philosophy of Spanish Krausism]. Madrid: Edicusa.

Fernández Ballesteros, R., & Carrobles, J. A. I. (Eds.). (1981). *Evaluación conductual* [Behavioral evaluation]. Madrid: Pirámide.

Fernández Seara, J. L., et al. (1983). *Status de la psicología en la universidad española* [The status of psychology in the Spanish university]. Salamanca: Universidad de Salamanca.

Fernández Trespalacios, J. L. (1978). *La psicología soviética en contradistinción con la psicología norteamericana* [Soviet psychology in contrast to North American psychology]. *Boletín Informativo*, Fundación, 77, 3–16.

Fernández-Zúñiga, A., & García Tuñón, R. (1976). Apuntes para una historia de la psicología en España [Historical notes on Spanish psychology]. *Cuadernos de Psicología 3, 4*, 26–30.

Ferrándiz, P. (1980). Fuentes bibliográficas en psicología [Bibliographic sources in psychology]. *Informes de Departamento de Psicología General* (Madrid), *4*, 221–233.

Finisson, L. J. (1977). Psychologists and Spain: A historical note. *American Psychologist, 32*, 1080–1084.

Fundación Universidad-Empresa (1980). *Los estudios de Psicología* [Studies in psychology]. Madrid: Author.

García, B., et al. (1981). Autores citados en la *Revista de Psicología General y Aplicada (1946–1979)* [Authors cited in the *Journal of General and Applied Psychology* (1946–1979)]. Reunión Internacional de Psicología Científica, Alicante.

García Vega, L. (1977). *Historia de la psicología* [History of psychology]. Madrid: Seteco.

García Yague, J., et al. (1975). *Tests empleados en España* [Tests used in Spain]. Madrid: Instituto Nacional de Psicología Aplicada y Psicotecnia.

Genovard, C. (1980). *Vocabulario básico trilingue de psicología científica* (Ingléscastellano-catalán) [Basic trilingual vocabulary of scientific psychology]. Barcelona: Fontanella.(a)

Genovard, C. (1980). *Diccionrio de psicología* [Dictionary of psychology]. Barcelona: Elicien.(b)

Germain, J. (1954). Para la pequeña historia de la psicología en España [A short history of Spanish psychology]. *Revista Psicología General y Aplicada, 9* (32), 633–642.

Germain, J. (1981). Número homenaje con su autobiografía [Autobiography of Germain]. *Revista Psicología General y Aplicada, 36,* (6), 1001–1186.

Gondra, J. M. (1975). La psicoterapia de Carl Rogers [The psychotherapy of Carl Rogers]. Bilbao: Desclée de Brower.

Gondra, J. M. (1982). *La psicología moderna* [Modern psychology]. Bilbao: Desclée de Brower.

González, J., Peiró, J. M., & Carpintero, H. (1981). La psicología en los *Archivos de Neurobiología* [Psychology in the *Archives of Neurobiology*]. Reunión Internacional de Psicología Científica, Alicante.

Gonzálo, J. (1945). *Investigaciones sobre la neuva dinámica cerebral* [Research on the new cerebral dynamics]. Madrid: Consejo Superior de Investigaciones Científicas.

Jáñez, L. (Ed.). (1981). *Simulación en psicología* [Simulation in psychology]. Madrid: Departamento de Psicología Matemática, Universidad Complutense.

Jiménez-Burillo, F. (1976). Psicología social en España: Notas para una historia de las ciencias sociales [Social psychology in Spain: Notes on the history of the social sciences]. *Revista Psicología General y Aplicada, 31* (139), 235–284.

Kaplan, T. (1969). Luis Simarro's psychological theories. *Actas, III Congreso Nacional de Historia de la Medicina,* Valencia, 523–533.

Kircher, M. (1981). La obra de Emilio Mira en el Instituto de Orientación Profesional de Barcelona (1919–1939) [The work of Emilio Mira at the Professional Institute of Barcelona (1919–1939)]. *Revista Historia de la Psicología, 2* (3), 225–246.

Lafuente Niño, E. (1980). Sobre los orígenes de la psicología científica en España: El papel del movimiento krausista [Origins of scientific psychology in Spain: A paper on the Krausist movement]. *Estudios de Psicología, 1,* 138–147.

Lafuente Niño, E. (1982). La psicología de Giner de los Ríos y sus fundamentos krausistas [The psychology of Giner de los Ríos and its Krausist foundations]. *Revista Historia de la Psicología, 3* (3), 247–270.

Lain Entralgo, P. (1964). La relación médico-enfermo [The doctor-patient relationship]. Madrid: Revista de Occidente.

Lain Entralgo, P. (1968). *Teoría y realidad del otro* [Theory and reality of the other]. Madrid: Revista de Occidente.

Lain Entralgo, P. (Ed.). (1972–1975). *Historia universal de la medicina* [Universal history of medicine] (Vols. 1–7). Barcelona: Salvat.

Lain Entralgo, P. (1978). *Antropología de la esperanza* [Anthropology of hope]. Barcelona: Labor.

Lain Entralgo, P. (1982). *El diagnóstico médico* [Medical diagnosis]. Barcelona: Salvat.

León, R., & Brozek, J. (1980). Historiography of psychology in Spain: Bibliography with comment. In J. Brozek & L. J. Pongratz (Eds.), *Historiography of modern psychology* (pp. 141–151). Toronto: Hogrefe.

Lison, C. (1971). *Antropología social en España* [Social anthropology in Spain]. Madrid: Siglo XXI.

López Ibor, J. (1964). *Lecciones de psicología médica* [Lessons on medical psychology]. Madrid: Paz Montalvo.

López Ibor, J. (1966). *Las neurosis como enfermedades del ámino* [The neuroses as illnesses of the soul]. Madrid: Gredos.

López Ibor, J. (1969). *La angustia vital: Patología general psicosomática* [The vital anguish: General pathology of psychosomatic problems]. Madrid: Paz Montalvo.

López Ibor, J. (1974). *El cuerpo y la corporalidad* [The body and the physical realm]. Madrid: Gredos.

López Piñero, J. M., & Morales Mesequer, J. M. (1970). *Neurosis y psicoterapia: Un estudio histórico* [Neurosis and psychotherapy: A historical study]. Madrid: Espasa-Calpe.

López Piñero, J. M., et al. (1983). *Diccionario histórico de la ciencia moderna en España* [Historical dictionary of modern science in Spain]. Barcelona: Peninsula.

Luque, O., Peiró, J. M., & Carpintero, H. (1981). *Autores citados en Anuario de Psicología (1964–1979)* [Authors cited in the *Annual Review of Psychology* (1964–1979)]. Reunión Internacional de Psicología Científica, Alicante.

Mallart, J. (1981). Autobiografía [Autobiography]. *Revista Historica Psicología, 2,* 91–122.

Mallart, J. (1983). Una nota sobre la reanudación de actividades de psicólogos españoles en congresos internacionales después de la segunda guerra mundial [Notes on the resumption of participation of Spanish psychologists in international congresses after World War II]. *Revista Psicología General y Aplicada, 181,* 247–250.

Marías, J. (1970). *Antropología metafísica: La estructura empírica de la vida humana* [Metaphysical anthropology: The empirical structure of human life]. Madrid: Revista Occidente.

Martínez, F. (1978). *La neuropsiquiatría española vista a través de* Archivos de Neurobiología [Neuropsychiatry in Spain as revealed by the *Archives of Neurobiology*]. Madrid: Garsi.

Maso, M., Peiró, J. M., & Carpintero, H. (1981). *La psicología en la* Revista Española de Psicoterapia analítica [Psychology in the *Journal of Spanish Analytic Psychotherapy*]. Reunión Internacional Psicología Científica, Alicante.

Mayor, J., & Labrador, F. J. (Eds.). (1983). *Manual de modificación de conducta* [Manual of behavior modification]. Madrid: Alhambra.

Mestre, M. V. (1982). Psicólogos españoles: Juan Vicente Viqueira (1886–1924) [Spanish psychologists: Juan Vicente Viqueira (1886–1924)]. *Revista Historia de la Psicología, 3* (2), 133–156.

Mestre, M. V., & Carpintero, H. (1983). Enrique Fernández Sanz y la introducción de las ideas de Freud en España [Enrique Fernández Sanz and the introduction of Freudian ideas in Spain]. *Revista Historia de la Psicología, 4* (1) 69–84.

Mira, E. (1920). El Funcionamiento del Laboratorio de Psicología Profesional del Instituto de Orientación Profesional de Barcelona [Function of the Laboratory of Professional Psychology of the Professional Institute of Barcelona]. *Archivos de Neurobiología, 1,* 129–147, 356–380.

Miralles, J. L. (1980). Antecedentes de la obra de E. Mira y López en la fisiología catalana del siglo XIX [Antecendents of E. Mira and López's book on the Catalan physiology of the nineteenth century]. *Revista Historia de la Psicología, 1* (1), 59–88.(a)

Miralles, J. L. (1980). Análisis bibliométrico de la producción científica en psicología:

Perspectivas españolas [Bibliometric analysis of scientific productivity in psychology: Spanish perspectives]. *Análisis y Modificación de Conducta, 6* (11–12), 65–75.(b)

Montoro, L., & Quintanilla, I. (1982). El Congreso Internacional de Psicología de Madrid [The International Congress of Psychology in Spain]. *Revista Historia de la Psicología, 3,* 223–230.

Navarro, M. M., Peiró, J. M., & Carpintero, H. (1981). *La Psicología en la* Revista de Psiquiatría y Psicología Médica [Psychology in the *Journal of Psychiatry and Medical Psychology*]. Reunión Internacional de Psicología Científica, Alicante.

Ortega, J. E., & Fernández Dols, J. M. (1980). *Fuentes documentales en psicología* [Documented sources in psychology]. Madrid: Debate.

Pascual, M. (1983). Pasado, presente y futuro de la psicología aeronáutica militar en España [Past, present, and future of the psychology of military aeronautics in Spain]. *Revista Psicología General y Aplicada, 38* (2), 349–378.

Pastor, R. (1960). *Estudios bibliométricos y sociométricos sobre revistas de psicología en España* [Bibliometric and sociometric studies of psychological journals in Spain]. XII Reunión Sociedad Española de Psicología, Madrid.

Pastor-Carballo, R., & Carpintero, H. (1980). Análisis de la *Revista de Psicología General y Aplicada* (1946–1970) [Analysis of the *Journal of General and Applied Psychology* (1946–1970)]. *Revista Historia de la Psicología, 1* (2), 199–214.

Peiró, J. M., & Carpintero, H. (1981). Historia de la psicología en España a través de sus revistas especializadas [The history of psychology in Spain as revealed by specialized journals]. *Revista Historia de la Psicología, 2* (2), 143–182.

Peiró, J. M., & Carpintero, H. (1983). History of psychology in Spain through its journals. In G. Eckardt & L. Sprung (Eds.), *Advances in historiography of psychology*. Berlin: VEB Deutscher Verlag.

Pelechano, V. (1972). *Adaptación y conducta* [Adaptation and behavior]. Madrid: Marova.

Pelechano, V. (1973). *Personalidad y parámetros* [Personality and parameters]. Barcelona: Vicens-Vives.

Pelechano, V. (1978). Formulación y panorama actual de la psicología de la modificación de conducta [Formulation and present perspective on behavior modification]. *Análisis y Modificación de Conducta, 4* (5), 63–88.

Pelechano, V. (1980). *Terapia familiar comunitaria* [Community family therapy]. Valencia: Alfaplus.

Pelechano, V. (1982). Unas notas en torno a la psicología y el mundo social [Notes about psychology and the social world]. *Análisis y Modificación de Conducta, 18,* 139–164.

Pinillos, J. L. (1964). *Introducción a la psicología contemporánea* [Introduction to contemporary psychology]. Madrid: C.S.I.C.

Pinillos, J. L. (1965). La psychologie sociale en Espagne [Social psychology in Spain]. *Social Sciences, 4,* 23–39.

Pinillos, J. L. (1975). *Principios de psicología* [Principles of psychology]. Madrid: Alianza Editorial.

Pinillos, J. L. (Ed.). (1980). Problemas actuales de la psicología científica [Contemporary problems of scientific psychology]. *Número Especial de Análisis y Modificación de Conducta, 6,* 11–12.

Pinillos, J. L. (1982). Autobiografía [Autobiography]. *Revista Historia de la Psicología, 3,* 185–207.

Pinillos, J. L. (1983). *La psicología y el hombre de hoy* [Psychology and today's man]. México: Trillas.(a)

Pinillos, J. L. (1983). Influencia de los Estados Unidos en las ciencias del hombre [The influence of the United States in the sciences of man]. In R. Bela, et al. (Eds.), *Influencia Norteamericana en el desarrollo científico español* [The North American influence on the development of Spanish science] (pp. 105–128). Madrid: Asociación Cultural Hispano-Norteamericana.(b)

Rey-Ardid, R. (1964). *Psicología médica* [Medical psychology]. Zaragoza: Heraldo de Aragón.

Rivas, F., et al. (1976). Estudio de los intereses específicos dentro de la carrera de psicología y las influencias motivacionales de los estudiantes [Study of the specific interests within psychology and the motivational influences on students]. *Revista de Psicología y Pedagogía Aplicadas*, 17–18, 181–197.

Rodríguez, S. (1981). Esquema para una historia de la psicología en España [A scheme for the history of psychology in Spain]. *Revista Psicología General y Aplicada*, 36 (172), 881–891.

Rodríguez Delgado, J. M. (1972). *Control físico de la mente* [Physical control of the mind]. Madrid: Espasa Calpe.

Rof-Carballo, J. (1952). *Cerebro interno y mundo emocional* [The internal brain and the emotional world]. Barcelona: Labor.

Rof-Carballo, J. (1971). *Patología psicosomática* [Psychosomatic pathology]. Madrid: Paz Montalvo.

Rof-Carballo, J. (1972). *Biología y psicoanálisis* [Biology and psychoanalysis]. Bilbao: Desclée de Brower.

Rof-Carballo, J. (1975). *Fronteras vivas del psicoanálisis* [Important frontiers of psychoanalysis]. Madrid: Karpos.

Sahagún, J. (Ed.). (1976). *Antropologías del siglo XX* [Anthropology of the twentieth century]. Salamanca: Sígueme.

Sarró, R. (1940). *Tratamiento moderno de las esquizofrenias* [Modern treatment of schizophrenia]. Barcelona: Bosa y Pagés.

Siguán, M. (1977). La psicología en España [Psychology in Spain]. *Anuario de Psicología*, 1, 5–22.

Siguán, M. (1978). La enseñanza universitaria de la psicologia en España: Notas para su historia [Teaching of psychology in the universities of Spain: Historical notes]. *Anuaria de Psicología*, 19, 125–137.

Siguán, M. (1981). Piaget en Cataluña [Piaget in Catalonia]. *Anuario de Psicología*, 25, 5–16.(a)

Siguán, M. (1981). *La psicología a Cataluña* [The psychology of Catalonia]. Barcelona: Edicions.(b)

Siguán, M. (1982). Piaget en España [Piaget in Spain]. *Revista Psicología General y Aplicada*, 175, 275–283.

Tortosa, F. M., & Carpintero, H. (1980). Evolución de la psicología en España en el siglo XX: Un estudio sobre manuales introductorios [Evolution of psychology in Spain in the twentieth century: A study of introductory manuals]. *Revista Historia de la Psicología*, 1 (3–4), 353–392.

Tortosa, F. M., Carpintero, H., & Peiró, J. M. (1981). Introducción de la psicología europea en U.S.A. a través del *American Journal of Psychology* (1887–1945)

[Introduction to psychology in Europe and the U.S.A. through an analysis of the *American Journal of Psychology* (1887–1945)]. *Revista Historia de la Psicología, 2* (4), 289–336.

Ullesperger, J. B. (1954). *Historia de la psiquiatría y de la psicología en España* [History of psychiatry and psychology in Spain]. Madrid: Alhambra.

Valenciano, L. (1977). *El doctor Lafora y su época* [Doctor Lafora and his time]. Madrid: Morata.

Villamarzo, P. F. (1982). *Frustración pulsional y cultura en Freud* [Instinct and culture in Freud]. Salamanca: Universidad Pontifica.

Viqueira, J. V. (1930). *La psicología contemporánea* [Contemporary psychology]. Barcelona: Labor.

Yela, M. (1963). Conciencia, cuerpo y conducta: Reflexiones sobre el sentido de la psicología contemporánea [Consciousness, body, and behavior: Reflections on the meaning of contemporary psychology]. *Revista Universidad Madrid, 11* (41), 7–29.

Yela, M. (1974). *La estructura de la conducta: Estímulo, situación y conciencia* [The structure of behavior: Stimuli, situations, and consciousness]. Madrid: Real Academia de Ciencias Morales y Políticas.

Yela, M. (1975). "Psicología", en la obra *Historia Universal de la Medicina*, dirigida por P. Laín [Psychology in the work reported in the *Universal History of Medicine*, directed by P. Lain]. Barcelona: Salvat.

Yela, M. (1980). La evolución del conductismo [The evolution of behaviorism]. *Interdisciplinaria* (Buenos Aires), *1* (1), 43–65.

Yela, M. (1982). Esbozo de autobiografía [Autobiographical sketch]. *Revista de Historia de la Psicología* (Valencia), *3* (4), 281–332.(a)

Yela, M. (Ed.). (1982). Homenaje a Piaget [A tribute to Piaget]. *Revista Psicología General y Aplicada, 37*, 2.(b)

Zanón, J. L., & Carpintero, H. (1981). El Padre Manuel Barbado y su introducción a la psicología experimental [Father Manuel Barbado and his introduction to experimental psychology]. *Revista Historia de la Psicología, 2* (3), 189–224.

Zubiri, X. (1963). El hombre, realidad personal [The personal reality of men]. *Revista de Occidente, 1*, 5–29.

Zubiri, X. (1964). El origen del hombre [The origin of man]. *Revista de Occidente, 17*, 146–173.

Sweden

Kenneth Hugdahl and Arne Öhman

INTRODUCTION: EARLY HISTORY (1910–1950)

The Early Chairs in Pedagogy and Psychology

The history of psychology in Sweden is in a restricted sense very short (see Dahllöf, 1984; Künnapas, 1976; Sandström, 1969, for an outline of the early history of Swedish psychology). If the existence of psychology is established by the founding of a professorial chair, then psychology in Sweden did not begin until 1948 when the first professor of psychology was appointed in Uppsala. However, professorial chairs in pedagogy and psychology had existed since 1910 when Bertil Hammer was appointed in Uppsala. In 1912, Lund had its first professorship in pedagogy and psychology, with Axel Herrlin occupying the position. The third chair was appointed in Gothenburg in 1919, and the scholar who received that distinction was G. A. Jaederholm. Stockholm did not get such a chair until 1937 when the German psychologist David Katz was appointed professor of pedagogy.

From 1948 to 1953 all four chairs of pedagogy and psychology were split into separate professorships, one in psychology, the other in pedagogy. Thus, by the end of 1953 Sweden had four full professors of psychology: Rudolf Anderberg in Uppsala, Herman Siegwald in Lund, John Elmgren in Gothenburg, and Gösta Ekman in Stockholm. Mats Björkman was later appointed to the fifth chair in 1966 at the University of Umeå.

It should be pointed out that although there was an official bias toward pedagogy during the first decades of the century, the research interests of the professors were mainly psychological. This was also reflected in the fact that when their successors in the early 1950s were asked to choose between becoming professors of psychology or pedagogy, all four chose chairs in psychology.

Early Differential Psychology

The study of individual differences, particularly in intelligence, was of prime interest to the early pedagogy professors. In Gothenburg, G. A. Jaederholm wrote a Ph.D. thesis in 1914 entitled *Intelligensmätningarnas teori och praxis* [The theory and practice of intelligence measurement]. According to Dahllöf (1984), Jaederholm's thesis was "not only a translation into Swedish of the method of Binet and Simon, but it was also an important theoretical contribution concerning the nature of intelligence from the perspective of a Gaussian distribution" (p. 18, our translation). Jaederholm had studied in London under K. Pearson and retained a lifelong interest in the genetics of intelligence.

During the 1940s, the study of individual differences and intelligence was taken up by Rudolf Anderberg in Uppsala, by Herman Siegwald in Lund, and by John Elmgren in Gothenburg, who also brought factor analysis and the use of the electroencephalogram (EEG) to Swedish psychology. Siegwald was appointed to the chair in Lund in 1947; Elmgren had replaced Jaederholm in Gothenburg in 1939.

Applied Differential Psychology

Psychologists were recruited to apply their knowledge about differential psychology in the armed forces during World War II. As pointed out by Sandström (1969), this provided the first opportunity for psychology to be applied to practical problems on a large scale. Test methods for the selection of army personnel were rapidly developed within the subfield of psychotechnics, and several talented young psychologists were encouraged to study differential psychology. A special section for testing military personnel was formed in Stockholm in 1944 with the distinguished scholar Torsten Husen as scientific advisor (Künnapas, 1976). Among his collaborators was a student from Lund, Gösta Ekman, who later became the leading early Swedish researcher in psychophysics and scaling. As a continuation of the work done by psychologists in the army during the war, the *Militärpsykologiska institutet* (MPI) [Institute of Military Psychology], was founded with Jan Agrell as its head. Another independent institute for the study of individual differences was the *Psykotekniska institutet* (PTI) [Psychotechnic Institute] which was also founded in 1944. The PTI was, from the beginning, concerned primarily with aptitude tests. In 1949, a similar institute was established in Gothenburg, under the leadership of Professor Elmgren, dealing with problems of working conditions.

Physiological Psychology

Sidney Alrutz conducted experimental psychological research as early as 1892. Therefore, he predated most of the other people mentioned so far. The remarkable fact is that Alrutz seems to have been mainly an autodidact, without any formal teachers. He was initially allowed to work at the Physiological Institute in Uppsala, studying the psychological dimensions of skin sensations. Among other things, he developed a well-known apparatus for demonstrating "hot-cold" experiences. The setup consists of two intertwisted pipes, one with running hot water, the other with cold water. Several other ingenious apparati of his are exhibited at the library of the psychology department in Uppsala. His contributions to sensory physiology were published in 1897 under the title *Zu den Kälte- unde Wärmepunkten* [About the cold and warm points]. Alrutz also had a lively interest in hypnosis and hypnotizability.

It is interesting to note that a number of additional physiological discoveries of some consequence were made by Swedes about the same time Alrutz started his career. For example, in 1882 Magnus Blix published his discoveries of the specific energies of the skin nerves. In 1891, Öhrwall published the now classic account of the basic qualities of good taste, and later the same year Torsten Thunberg uncovered the basics of the skin senses.

The Experimental Orientation

In summarizing the early efforts of Swedish psychological researchers, one is struck by the experimental orientation of the persons involved. To some extent this orientation was due to international influences and the influence of physiology. For example, Axel Herrlin, the first professor in Lund, had studied under Georg Elias Müller in Göttingen. As previously mentioned, G. A. Jaederholm of Gothenburg had visited Pearson in London, and Alrutz in Uppsala had worked in close collaboration with physiologists. Finally, Elmgren, Anderberg, and especially David Katz were all committed to experimental work.

However, in spite of strong experimental leanings, which have in many respects persisted, Swedish psychologists have been more inclined to study verbal reports of subjective experiences than overt behavior. In fact, neither classical behaviorism (Watson, 1913) nor neobehaviorism (Hull, 1943) have had a particular impact on Swedish psychology. Behavioristic influences were not strongly felt in Swedish psychology until the late 1960s when Sten Rönnberg in Stockholm and Lars-Göran Öst, Lennart Melin, and K.-G. Götestam in Uppsala (Öst, 1981) used behavior therapy for the treatment of various clinical disorders.

Although many of the persons involved with pedagogy and psychology during this early era were experimentally oriented, one notable exception was John Landquist, professor in Lund from 1936 to 1947. Landquist was the successor to Herrlin and had been a political editor for one of the major Swedish newspapers before becoming professor of pedagogy and psychology in Lund. He was influenced by psychoanalytic theory and, in fact, had been analyzed by Freud himself. Landquist was a humanistic scholar with a broad knowledge of the cultural history of Europe. His interest in psychoanalysis may have been instrumental for later developments at the psychology department in Lund. In contrast with the other major psychology departments in Sweden, the department in Lund has continued to emphasize psychoanalytic theory (Sjöbäck, 1984).

Psychological Periodicals

Alrutz, a remarkable man in many respects, included among his accomplishments the publication of the first Swedish psychological journal, *Psyke* [The Psyche], from 1906 to 1920. It was not until 1949 that a new journal, *Nordisk Psykologi* [Nordic Psychology], was published. *Nordisk Psykologi*, however, was not originally a journal for scientists. It was a joint project of the Scandinavian organizations of professional psychologists. Thus, it contained job announcements, notices of course offerings, and so forth for professional psychologists, in addition to scientific articles. Sweden and the other Scandinavian countries had their first "pure" scientific journal in psychology when the *Scandinavian Journal of Psychology* began publication in 1960. It was the product of several persons including Gösta Ekman and especially Carl-Ivar Sandström, who served as the first editor. Although Sweden, and Scandinavia, lacked a scientific journal of their own until 1960, many Scandinavians published in *Acta Psychologica*, a Dutch journal founded in 1935 by Geza Révèsz and David Katz. Katz became professor of pedagogy in Stockholm two years later.

Among recent Swedish periodicals, the *Scandinavian Journal of Behaviour Therapy* is now an international journal. From 1971 until 1974, it was a newsletter entitled *Beteendeterapi* [Behavior Therapy]. In 1974, the newly appointed editor, K.-G. Götestam, gave the publication its present name and made it into a scientific journal.

DEVELOPMENTS AFTER 1950

Perception

The first professor of pedagogy in Stockholm was David Katz, appointed in 1937. Originally a student of Müller in Göttingen, Katz was therefore well acquainted with the psychophysical tradition derived from Fechner and Weber and carried on by Müller. Sandström (1969) suggests that Katz was probably introduced to the study of psychology as a subject in an experiment on the scaling of weights. The weights lifted by Katz had previously belonged to Fechner and even Weber himself might have started his experimental career with these particular weights. However, although Katz had trained in the classic continental tradition of psychophysics and introspection, it was his successor, Ekman, whose research brought Swedish psychology international prominence in the area of psychophysics.

Perhaps because Katz was not a Swede, but a German, his work brought a more international orientation to Swedish psychology. He initiated research in many different fields of inquiry. His main interests, however, were perception, especially color perception (Katz, 1935), and the development of psychological methods. Both in his theoretical and in his methodological orientation he stayed close to the Gestalt school (Katz, 1950), although he was influenced, as well, by phenomenology, especially the work of Edmund Husserl. He also did research on taste and vibrations (Katz, 1925) and conducted comparative studies (Katz, 1937).

The international status Katz attained is perhaps best evidenced by the wide recognition of his death in 1953. For the first time, a Swedish psychologist was honored by obituaries in such major journals as the *British Journal of Psychology*, *Psychological Review*, and *American Journal of Psychology*. His international reputation was instrumental in bringing the Thirteenth International Congress of Psychology to Stockholm in 1951. As noted by Sandström (1969), "without [Katz], nobody would ever have thought of Sweden as the place for the congress" (p. 213, our translation).

Katz not only experimented in color perception and related areas, he also gathered around himself a small group of talented students who later made substantial contributions to the field of perception. Among these were Carl-Ivar Sandström and Gunnar Johansson, whose Ph.D. theses Katz supervised.

Gunnar Johansson received his Ph.D. in 1950. His thesis concerned configurations in event perception. In the opinion of Künnapas (1976), "Johansson's doctoral work pioneered the field of event perception, [and] belongs among the first and best examples of the new Swedish experimental psychology. [It made] use of technical aids and physical measurement procedures that were practically unknown in Swedish psychology" (p. 409).

In 1957, Johansson succeeded Rudolf Anderberg as professor of psychology at Uppsala University. His determination to develop a technically sophisticated experimental department was immediately apparent. He startled his colleagues in the faculty of philosophy when he requested money to purchase a lathe for his department. This piece of equipment was placed in a workshop that grew into an important resource not only for Uppsala but for many other places in the country. It became particularly well known for the ingenious high-precision equipment built by Gunnar Ågren and Lärs-Erik Larsson. Johansson also quickly recognized the revolutionary importance of computers for psychological research. He was one of the first psychologists to make a computer an integral part of his laboratory when he installed a DEC LINC–8 in 1968. Lars Bäckström's original and sophisticated programming skills in conjunction with this system soon attracted American psychologists who came to learn the new procedures.

Johansson's contributions to the understanding of visual perception took place in three areas, the first being event perception where motion and change are considered the normal and functionally basic conditions for visual perception. The perceived motion of moving dots is analyzed in terms of the common and individual components of movement using a vector-analysis model developed in 1950.

In the early 1960s, Johansson next turned to depth perception and the analysis of three-dimensional percepts (Johansson, 1964). Using a similar vector model, he managed to show that size and form changes in three-dimensional perception can be described in terms of common and individual components. This work brought Johansson close to some of the assumptions concerning depth perception advocated by James Gibson in the United States (Gibson, 1979). Johansson and Gibson subsequently had a close professional relationship until Gibson's death.

Finally, in the early 1970s, Johansson delved into biological motion (Johansson, 1973). Inspired by his dissertation work, he developed a model and a technique for the analysis of biological motion. His technique became widely used. Johansson simply filmed, in darkness, people who were visible only because a dozen lights were attached to their main joints. When in motion, these lights were perceived as vivid images of humans in action. Later, this study led to a fresh perspective on social perception, persuasively represented by one of Johansson's students, Sverker Runesson.

Johansson's research was also the impetus for several applied projects including studies in traffic psychology on night driving and the design of automobile headlamps. This work was later carried on by another one of Johansson's students, Kåre Rumar.

Among the ''first-generation'' students who worked in Johansson's laboratory in the 1960s were Sten Sture Bergström, Sture Eriksson, Göte Hansson, and Gunnar Jansson. In the 1970s, Erik Börjesson, Alf Gabrielsson, Claes von Hofsten, Hans Marmolin, and Sverker Runesson worked in Johansson's laboratory. Von Hofsten has recently turned to developmental psychology, investigating the reaching behavior of infants. Sture Eriksson is now involved in basic research on the neurophysiology of visual perception, and Gunnar Jansson is directing a research project on the development of aids for the visually handicapped. Alf Gabrielsson's interests have remained unchanged; he continues to do research on auditory perception, particularly the perception of rhythm.

In summary, then, it is evident that the Uppsala school of perceptual research has been instrumental in bringing Swedish psychology to the attention of psychologists in other countries. Evidence of this international recognition is readily provided by invitations extended to Johansson and coworkers to contribute to the *Annual Review of Psychology* (Johansson, von Hofsten, & Jansson, 1980) and to the *Handbook of sensory physiology* (Johansson, 1978).

However, it should be remembered that the study of perception was carried out in several other universities in Sweden during this period. For example, Gösta Ekman's investigations in Stockholm inspired several perceptual research projects. Among his students, Madjid Mashour, who studied the perception of velocity, and Gunnar Goude, who was interested in the perception of art, should be mentioned. Theodore Künnapas did research on the perception of distance, auditory perception, and the perception of the vertical-horizontal illusion. Later, Ulf and Birgitta Berglund initiated an elegant study of the perception of odor. Others interested in perceptual research include David Magnusson and Lars

Nystedt in Stockholm, who have been studying person perception; Tommy Gär-ling, now at the University of Umeå, who has studied the perception of archi-tecture; and Ingvar Bokander in Lund, who has studied perceptual conflict induced by stereoscopic presentations. Magnusson has lately turned to the study of per-sonality and interactionalism, whereas Gärling has been interested in environ-mental psychology, including the study of orientation in space (see Gärling, 1982, for a review of Swedish environmental psychology).

Psychophysics and Scaling

A second major area of Swedish psychological inquiry is psychophysics and sensory scaling. Psychophysics is linked primarily to Gösta Ekman in Stockholm. Ekman followed Katz in 1952 as professor of pedagogy. One year later he chose to become professor of psychology when the chair was divided into psychology and pedagogy. In addition to his outstanding scientific merits, Ekman had the personal qualities to create an outstanding intellectual milieu in his department. He managed to transform the rather small Stockholm department into one of Europe's largest and most productive during his tenure as chairman.

Ekman started his career as a student of individual differences. Among other things, he made important contributions, within the then-prevailing mainstream of Swedish psychology, to the theory of reliability (Ekman, 1947) and the relationships between typologies and dimensional analyses. He further published a textbook on differential psychology that is still well worth reading (Ekman, 1952). Later he turned his psychometric skills to the problem of sensory scaling.

Two contributions mark the beginning of the Stockholm school of psycho-physics. The first was Ekman's idea that judgments of similarity between two stimuli (transformed to numbers between 0 and 1) were analogous to correlation coefficients. In one study, Ekman had subjects perform estimates of similarity between colors of varying wavelength. The matrix of averaged similarities was then factor analyzed. The outcome was five color factors with different "load-ings" along the continuum of wavelength. The similarity judgments were com-pared with physiological data on color vision.

The second contribution, according to Mats Björkman, one of Ekman's stu-dents, arose as a result of a seminar on Guilford's *Psychometric methods* (personal communication). During the seminar, some of the participants voiced skepticism about the possibility of having subjects assign numbers to pairs of stimuli in the form of ratio judgments. Ekman's answer typically reflects his empirical approach to scientific problems: "Let me do a few experiments to see if subjective scales can be established on the basis of ratio judgments."

These initial experiments inspired intensive research during the next fifteen years. Of particular importance was the work on different scaling methods. Among the first techniques to be studied were estimation methods or, as they are sometimes called, "direct methods." Ekman and Sjöberg (1965) explained the rationale behind estimation methods as follows: "On the basic assumption that the subject behaves according to instructions, the scale construction is a straightforward procedure essentially consisting of averaging experimental data, and for such reasons the methods may be considered as direct. Since they are all based on the individual subject's quantitative estimates of subjective relations, they form a class of estimation methods'' (p. 452). Ekman and his group kept in close contact with S. S. Stevens of Harvard concerning problems of ratio scaling and estimation methods. As noted by Björkman (personal communication), the Stockholm-Harvard connection was an important source of inspiration for the students in Ekman's laboratory.

Other scaling techniques studied in Ekman's laboratory were Thurstonian, or "indirect" methods. Thurstonian scaling is based on ordinal judgments (rank order), and a basic assumption concerns the use of variability across subjects, or trials, as the unit of measurement. Thus, what is regarded as error in the direct methods is the very basis of the scaling procedure in the indirect methods. Indirect methods were studied by Sjöberg (1962) and by Björkman (1958) who used these methods to measure associative strength in paired-associate learning.

A third aspect of research on scaling methods concerned multidimensional methods and work on multidimensional similarity. In studies where multidimensional ratio estimation is used (so-called content methods), the subject is typically instructed to estimate how much of a stimulus a is contained in stimulus b. He then also estimates how much of b is contained in a. The two percepts corresponding to a and b are represented in multidimensional space by percept vectors. Different mathematical procedures are then used to describe the vectors. The Stockholm group developed several variants of content models (see Sjöberg, 1975, for a review).

The scaling methods developed by Ekman were later applied to different areas of research. Among these were studies related to Stevens' psychophysical law (Hannes Eisler), time estimation (Marianne Frankenhaeuser), and intrasubjective relations (Ekman, 1961).

During the 1930s, a discussion was initiated in Great Britain concerning the issue of so-called fundamental measurement in psychology, that is, the possibility of measuring subjective magnitudes in a way corresponding to measurement procedures employed in physics. One of the students of the Ekman group, Gunnar Goude, made an important contribution within this subfield by introducing additive methods and comparing them with other approaches used in psychophysics and psychological measurement in general. Because both internal consistency and agreement between methods based on addition and the others were satisfactory, Goude concluded that fundamental measurement in psychology is possible.

Ekman resigned his chair in psychology in 1969 when he was awarded a personal professorship in psychological scaling methods. Since his untimely death in 1971, the Stockholm school has been sustained by the work of Birgitta Berglund on the use of direct methods in solving various environmental problems and by the investigations of Hannes Eisler (1982), who perhaps more than anyone else personifies the Stockholm school of psychophysics after thirty years of research. In addition, Åke Hellström (1985) has recently published a major review on studies of time-order errors.

Many students were drawn to the exciting atmosphere of Ekman's department in Stockholm. Among the first were Mats Björkman, Hannes Eisler, Marianne Frankenhaeuser, Gunnar Goude, Theodore Künnapas, David Magnusson, and Lennart Sjöberg.

Other work carried out in Stockholm, and related to the psychophysics tradition of Ekman, is the research of Gunnar Borg on the development of a scale for the subjective rating of exercise intensity. The scale is now widely used in cardiac programs. Oswald Bratfish and Ulf Lundberg have studied the relationships between temporal and geographical distance and emotional involvement. Finally, Ove Franzen has investigated the neurophysiological correlates of subjective estimates.

In retrospect, two characteristics of the Stockholm school stand out. First of all, there has been a strong positivistic attitude underlying the research. Introspective reports have been regarded as unscientific and mostly discarded. However, as pointed out by Björkman (personal communication): "Having subjects assign numbers to their experiences is a form of introspection, numerical introspection if you like." Second, research has centered on attempts to find simple relationships. Interestingly, this emphasis has had an aesthetic quality to it which was particularly apparent in much of Ekman's work.

Finally, it is interesting to note that many of Gösta Ekman's students, as well as Gunnar Johansson's, later became professors and scientific leaders in different parts of the country. Thus, the influence of Ekman and of Johansson on Swedish psychology is not only reflected by their own achievements but is also manifested in the positions now occupied by their former students.

Percept-Genesis: Experimental Psychoanalysis

Another important area of perceptual research in Sweden is that of percept-genesis carried out mainly in Lund (summarized in Smith & Westerlundh, 1980; Westerlundh & Smith, 1983). However, in contrast to the perceptual studies conducted in Uppsala and Stockholm, this work is not directed at perceptual processes per se but uses perceptual techniques to investigate the organization of personality within a psychodynamic frame of reference.

The theory and methods of percept-genesis are intimately linked to Ulf Kragh and Gudmund Smith. Smith became professor of psychology in Lund in 1960 (after Herman Siegwald). Following a period as professor of clinical psychology at the University of Oslo, Kragh returned to become professor of applied psychology in Lund in the late 1970s.

The percept-genesis approach is based on the psychodynamic theory of neuroses, especially with regard to defense mechanisms. Mental images and processes that represent threats or dangers to the individual are postulated to evoke anxiety as a signal for the activation of defense mechanisms which protect the ego from becoming flooded by anxiety. The various techniques developed in Lund attempt to reveal the activation of such defense mechanisms. Apart from being a research tool, these techniques have also been successfully used in the clinical field and to select air force pilots.

Two of the most well-known methods developed by Kragh and Smith (the Defense Mechanism Test, DMT; the Meta-Contrast Test, MCT) involve presenting complex pictures tachistoscopically with increasing duration times. Each stimulus includes at its center a neutral or positive figure, such as a child, and in the periphery a threatening, or anxiety-provoking, figure, such as an angry-looking male. The subject is asked to report what he or she sees in the picture on the basis of the initial very brief presentations and subsequently as the picture is increasingly more clearly perceived because of longer exposure times. By assuming that the factors determining perceptions of the stimuli presented reflect salient events during ontogenesis, responses are interpreted as reflecting subjects' conflicts and dominant defenses.

Research on percept-genesis has been carried out in Sweden since the mid–1950s. The DMT was developed by Ulf Kragh (1959), and the MCT method was developed by Gudmund Smith (Smith & Hendriksson, 1956). The meta-contrast (MCT) technique is closely related to the DMT but is based on the assumed subliminal perception of the threatening element in the stimulus. Other techniques employed in Lund involve aftereffects which are a function of the threatening aspects of the presentations (Smith & Kragh, 1967).

Alf Andersson and his coworkers have done research using the spiral aftereffect technique, a special variant of the serial afterimage test. Other students of Kragh and Smith who should be mentioned are Bert Westerlundh and Alf Nilsson. Nilsson has used the above-mentioned techniques in his studies of obsessive neurotics and hysterics. Westerlundh recently developed a method that involves experimentally manipulating anxiety to detect repression within defensive mechanisms. Furthermore, Olof Ryden uses tachistoscopic presentations in his therapy with diabetic children, and Anna Danielsson in collaboration with Smith has investigated the development of defense mechanisms in children and adolescents.

The Interactional Perspective on Personality

David Magnusson, a student of Gösta Ekman, continued his mentor's work in classical psychometrics and wrote a textbook on test theory that has been widely translated (Magnusson, 1966). When Ekman was awarded a personal professorship at the Social Science Research Council in 1970, Magnusson became his successor as professor in Stockholm. Over the years, Magnusson developed a metatheoretical position on personality research which has had a larger international impact than the work of most other contemporary Swedish psychologists. Known as an interactional approach to personality, it has been expounded and analyzed in a series of international conferences in Stockholm directed by Magnusson and various coworkers (Magnusson & Endler, 1977; Magnusson, 1981; Magnusson & Allen, 1983; Magnusson & Öhman, 1985).

Central to Magnusson's point of view is the conviction that *situations* are critical but neglected prerequisites for psychological functioning. According to Magnusson, psychological events are always inextricably tied to particular situations. Neither person nor situational variables are sufficient by themselves to explain psychological events. Only by jointly considering person and situation, preferably in a developmental perspective, can we hope to account for what is taking place.

Recently Magnusson has also stressed the importance of interactions among subsystems within the individual (Öhman & Magnusson, 1985). For example, it is argued that various physiological systems within the person interact with the psychological level to determine thoughts and actions.

Magnusson has not been content with developing a specific theoretical perspective, but he has demonstrated that his approach is useful in a variety of empirical settings. In collaboration with some of his students (Anders Dunér, Bo Ekehammar, Lars Nystedt, Håkan Stattin, Bertil Törestad, and Lars Bergman), he has, for instance, analyzed anxiety and anger from interactional cross-cultural perspectives. Furthermore, he launched a major longitudinal study of 2,000 Swedish children twenty years ago which is still ongoing.

Magnusson has also been an outstanding administrator. He represents psychology in the Swedish Council for Humanities and Social Sciences and is currently the Swedish delegate in the governing body of the European Science Foundation. Finally, Magnusson is the only psychologist to be elected to the Swedish Royal Academy of Sciences.

Cognitive Psychology

Although research on cognition has been conducted at essentially all psychology departments in Sweden, the department in Umeå has, ever since it was started in 1966, been almost exclusively devoted to cognitive psychology. First the department was directed by Mats Björkman and Berndt Brehmer; more recently it has been under the direction of Lars-Göran Nilsson. Thus, our review of cognitive psychology will start at the most northern of Sweden's universities, then turn south to Gothenburg and the group under professor Lennart Sjöberg, and end up in Stockholm in central Sweden with the research done by Stanislav Dornic, Yvonne Waern, and Ola Svensson.

Cognitive Psychology in Umeå

Inference and decision making. In 1966, Mats Björkman became the first professor of psychology at the University of Umeå. Björkman came originally from Stockholm where he studied with Gösta Ekman, focusing on the measurement of learning. Björkman did his Ph.D. thesis on verbal rote learning. This work was based on Hull's influential theorizing (1943) and utilized sophisticated measurement techniques to quantify evocation potential, the central dependent variable in Hull's theory. When Björkman moved to Umeå in 1966, his research interests shifted toward human inference and decision making. Theoretically, the research was based on Brunswik's probabilistic functionalism (Brunswik, 1952), which was applied to the study of decisions and social judgments (Björkman, 1973).

However, while Björkman initiated research based on Brunswik's theory, Berndt Brehmer's investigations in this area during the 1970s developed it and produced a major international impact. The theory of "probabilistic functionalism" deals with the relationships between distal and proximal stimulation, that is, between objects in the real world (the distal stimuli) and the information available to the organism about these objects (the proximal stimuli). These relationships being at best probabilistic, a major task for the psychologist is to reveal the strategies used by subjects to make inferences about distal events. Brehmer has made extensive use of social judgment theory (SJT) (Hammond, Stewart, Brehmer, & Steinmann, 1975) in his studies of inferential processes. The SJT is essentially a general theoretical framework for the study of human judgment derived from the functionalistic probabilism of Brunswik. This research is well summarized by Brehmer (1979).

Brehmer and his many students have researched the process of inference in several applied settings. For example, they studied inferential processes in the context of interpersonal conflict (Brehmer, 1976). Moreover, the process of clinical inference has been investigated (Brehmer, 1980). Recently, Brehmer has made important theoretical contributions to cognitive psychology by pointing out the necessity for "ecological validity" in psychological research (Brehmer, 1984).

Both Björkman and Brehmer attracted many students to the growing psychology department in Umeå during the 1970s. Among them, Håkan Andersson, Kerstin and Bengt-Åke Armelius, Lars Lindberg, Roger Hagafors, and Håkan Alm should be mentioned. The strong research tradition developed in Umeå was transplanted to Uppsala in 1977 when Brehmer took over Gunnar Johansson's chair following his retirement and Björkman was awarded a personal professorial chair in the same department.

Memory research. Interest in the study of memory and memory functioning has a long history in Swedish psychology. As previously mentioned, both Herrlin in Lund and Elmgren in Gothenburg initiated research in this area during the early decades of the twentieth century. In Gothenburg, Elmgren's tradition has been carried on by Lars Alin and Erland Hjelmquist in psychology and by Ference Marton in pedagogy.

However, perhaps the most influential contemporary research in memory has been that done by Ronald Cohen in Uppsala (Cohen & Johansson, 1967), who introduced the information-processing perspective (Atkinson & Shifrin, 1971) to memory research in Sweden. Cohen left Sweden for Canada in the early 1970s, but two of his former students, Bo Johansson and especially Lars-Göran

Nilsson (1979), continued his work. Nilsson succeeded Björkman as professor of psychology at Umeå University in 1981 and has, during a relatively short time period, developed a very productive research unit for the study of memory. In addition to his theoretical contributions, Nilsson's recent publications concern research findings which help us understand better the memory processes of the elderly (Bäckman & Nilsson, 1984) and memory disturbances in epilepsy (Nilsson, 1980) as well as studies of the modality effect (Nilsson, Ohlsson, & Rönnberg, 1980). In one of his most recent publications he made an important theoretical contribution by presenting a functionalistic view of memory as an alternative to the information-processing model (Nilsson, 1984).

The cognitive basis of dyslexia. Ingvar Lundberg, a senior researcher in Umeå, is working on a large-scale Scandinavian epidemiologic study of childhood dyslexia, the "Bergen project" (Lundberg, 1983). He has developed the concept of linguistic awareness as an important characteristic of the ability to read (Lundberg, 1978). Linguistic awareness means that when a child starts to read, his or her attitude toward language must change. Although most of the words a child encounters in reading are well known, other aspects of language, such as ability to divide words into syllables or phonemes, now require attention.

Cognitive Psychology in Gothenburg

In 1970, John Elmgren retired from his chair in Gothenburg, and the chair was assumed by another of Ekman's former students and collaborators, Lennart Sjöberg. Of all contemporary Swedish psychologists, Sjöberg probably has the most diversified research profile. He has published extensively in almost every area of cognitive psychology, and in social and theoretical psychology as well. Space limitations permit only a selective account of his many important contributions. As mentioned before, Sjöberg initially worked with Ekman in the 1950s on indirect scaling and later turned his attention to multidimensional scaling (Sjöberg, 1975). He also collaborated with Carl-Otto Johnson on research concerned with the measurement of mood while in Stockholm. In Gothenburg, he worked with Erland Svensson on the development of a reliable model for the measurement of mood and mood changes which could be used for testing the effects of psychopharmacological drugs (Sjöberg, Svensson, & Persson, 1979).

Sjöberg also did studies on decision making wherein he related the cognitive processes involved to both the elicited emotional states and the attitudes individuals have toward the focus of the decision (Sjöberg, 1980). As a result of recognizing the affective processes intrinsic to decision making, his group recently studied decision making in relation to breaking addictions (Sjörberg, 1980). Finally, he has investigated the importance of interest to the act of studying.

In addition to Sjöberg's research in Gothenburg, Henry Montgomery has been concerned with the relationships between category scales and magnitude scales. He and Carl-Martin Allwood have also studied problem solving from an information-processing perspective. Stig Fhaner has made psychometric analyses of achievement testing and published several books on psychological metatheory. Olof Östberg has done work on diurnial rhythms in shift workers. Ann Frodi wrote a Ph.D. thesis on aggression examined within the framework of experimental social psychology. Frodi left Gothenburg in 1974 for a postdoctoral position at the University of Wisconsin with Leonard Berkowitz; she subsequently occupied a faculty position at the University of Northern Iowa and is now at the University of Rochester (New York).

Psycholinguistic research has been conducted in Gothenburg during the last decade by Erland Hjelmquist and a number of collaborators and by Sten-Olof Brenner. Brenner, however, is now in Luleå where he is professor of technical psychology. Hjelmquist's investigations in actuality fall within the field of "language psychology," which is somewhat different than traditional psycholinguistics. Hjelmquist and his group have emphasized a functional communicative perspective on language and the use of language. A major contention of theirs is that language must be studied in an interactional context involving both situational and individual cues. This view differs from traditional psycholinguistics which emphasizes the study of language in isolation from the environment.

Cognitive Psychology in Stockholm

Cognitive psychology in Stockholm during the last two decades includes the work of Stanislav Dornic on the perceived effort associated with tasks varying in terms of their demands on attention and memory. He recently initiated research on individual differences in information-processing capacity. In 1975, Dornic, with P. Rabbit, coedited a volume of the internationally respected series *Attention and performance* (Rabbitt & Dornic, 1975).

Yvonne Waern has been interested in reading problems associated with text meaning and comprehension. She has furthermore used Piaget's theory to analyze children's experiences and explanations of others' behavior. Since Swedish psychologists have been relatively uninterested in developmental psychology, Waern's research is an interesting exception although Ola Svensson has also investigated how children solve mathematical problems. Recently, however, he has turned his attention to risks and decisions in the traffic environment. Finally, Lars Nystedt has conducted studies of judgments we make of others using the concept of "cognitive complexity," in addition to work on the role of casual attribution in decisions and decision making.

CLINICAL PSYCHOLOGY

From what has been said so far, it should be obvious that the mainstream of Swedish academic psychology has been primarily directed toward basic research favoring experimental and quantitative methods. Given this context, it is perhaps not surprising that clinical psychology remained a neglected area for a long time. A few investigators have, nevertheless, been able to make substantive contributions to this area throughout the years.

Ingmar Dureman, the first professor of applied psychology in Uppsala (1969–1979), was a pioneer of clinical psychology in Sweden. In the early 1950s, he worked as a clinical psychologist at the Department of Psychiatry of the University Hospital of Uppsala. In collaboration with a psychiatrist, Henry Sälde, he applied his knowledge of psychometrics and experimental methods to clinical diagnosis. These two investigators developed a battery of intelligence tests for clinical populations with particular emphasis on the diagnosis of brain damage. Dureman also applied various experimental techniques involving critical flicker fusion, threshold measurements, and visual movement aftereffects to clinical diagnosis and the evaluation of psychopharmacological drugs. Perhaps most important, he was one of the first psychologists in Sweden to become interested in the use of psychophysiological methods in clinical settings. For instance, he evaluated the effects of various drugs (Dureman, 1963). In collaboration with another psychophysiologist, Torkel Scholander, he established a psychophysiological laboratory, which, among other things, was equipped to measure pupillary activity using procedures considered very sophisticated at that time. In his doctoral thesis work in 1959, Dureman compared the effects of amphetamine and chlorpromazin on the conditioned and unconditioned autonomic activity in humans.

Moreover, Dureman introduced several students to psychophysiology. Among them was Arne Öhman, who joined Dureman's group in the mid–1960s. In 1982, Öhman was appointed to the professorship (now in clinical psychology) which Dureman had held until 1979 when he died. Within clinical psychology, Öhman has studied psychophysiological factors related to the acquisition of phobias (for example, Öhman, 1979b) and the subtyping of schizophrenia (Öhman, 1981). He has recently initiated research in Uppsala on the relationships between Type-A "coronary-prone" behavior and cardiovascular disorders.

Dureman's interest in psychopharmacology prompted him to develop an animal laboratory in the early 1960s. Under the leadership of two of his students, Bengt Henriksson and Torbjörn Järbe, this laboratory became extremely efficient and productive. The number of international publications deriving from research done in this facility over the years is in the hundreds. The laboratory is particularly well known internationally because of Järbe's work on drug discrimination. Dureman also supervised the doctoral work by Carl-Erik Brattemo on proverb understanding in schizophrenics. Brattemo was later given a professorial position in Uppsala. At the Ulleråker University Hospital in Uppsala, Lars Kebbon initiated a broad research program on mental retardation and the care of the mentally handicapped in the mid–1960s.

Turning our attention to developments in Stockholm, psychophysiological techniques were applied to clinical problems by Daisy Schalling and her co-workers. Originally interested in clinical neuropsychology and the psychology of personality, Schalling in the mid–1960s began a research project on psychopathy in collaboration with forensic psychiatrists, particularly Sten Levander and Lars Lidberg. This project brought Schalling international recognition within the field (Hare & Schalling, 1978). More recently, Schalling has collaborated with Marie Åsberg to study relationships between physiological variables and brain transmitter activity.

Work in human psychopharmacology was performed in Stockholm by Carl-Otto Johnsson and his group. In the 1970s Johnsson, who is professor of applied psychology in the Department of Psychology, published a series of papers on the psychological aspects of senile dementia. Currently he is engaged in research on early symbiosis and separation. Hans Bergman became professor of psychological alcohol research at the Karolinska Hospital in Stockholm in 1980, after a research career focused on the personality profiles and neuropsychological characteristics of chronic alcoholics. Among the handful of investigators who have been able to transform psychodynamic theorizing into solid empirical research are Kristina Humble and Gitte Settergren in Stockholm, who analyzed personality and social psychological factors in young criminals from an ego-psychological perspective.

While research on the diagnosis and etiology of psychopathology spans several decades, much less has been done with regard to psychological treatment. Until the 1970s, there were few practicing psychotherapists in Sweden, and the training of psychologists in treatment techniques was virtually nonexistent. Academic psychology's inability to provide such training opportunities was an important factor underlying practicing psychologists' discontent with university programs during the early 1970s. Regular training in psychotherapy became available in Umeå and Stockholm in the late 1970s, but it was not based on academic psychology nor on research. In spite of widespread interest in psychotherapy research among psychologists, very little investigatory work has been done in this field. An exception is in the area of behavior therapy, where important contributions have been made by Lars-Göran Öst, Lennart Melin, K.-G. Götestam, and P. O. Sjöden in Uppsala, and by Sten Rönnberg and Ola Nordlund in Stockholm.

PSYCHOBIOLOGY

As indicated before, Sidney Alrutz, who had strong physiological interests, was outside mainstream pedagogy and psychology at the turn of the century. This situation still prevails in the sense that biologically oriented psychology has never been central to Swedish psychology. Ironically, though, there has been much high-quality research in this area. In fact, this research includes the most internationally acclaimed contributions to Swedish psychology.

Psychophysiology

Psychophysiologists observe the physiological correlates of psychological states or manipulations in humans. Typically, peripheral physiological activity such as the electroencephalogram (EEG), muscle activity (electromyography, EMG), or various types of autonomic activity (such as heart rate, blood pressure, and electrodermal activity) are measured in response to external stimulation.

Psychophysiology was introduced into Sweden by Ingmar Dureman in Uppsala, primarily in a clinical context. However, he also had an interest in basic research in psychophysiology. Dureman's interest in autonomic conditioning was later assumed by Arne Öhman, who both extensively analyzed the orienting response (OR) in conditioning (Öhman, 1983) and developed an influential information-processing theory concerning the role of the OR in attention and learning (Öhman, 1979a). Öhman's work on conditioning and on the acquisition of phobic fears (Öhman, 1979b) has met with international acclaim. This research also provided the starting point for the doctoral work of several students. Kenneth Hugdahl made important contributions to this area before he turned to psychophysiological analyses of lateralized stimulus input and hemispheric differences. Hugdahl recently succeeded Öhman as professor of somatic psychology at the University of Bergen in Norway. Mats Fredrikson turned to experimental work on hypertension after a dissertation which compared physiological responses in phobics with those in conditioned normals. Staffan Hygge did his dissertation work on vicarious conditioning, and Ulf Dimbeg studied the psychophysiological effects of stimulating the face. The international impact of the psychophysiological work of Öhman and his students is perhaps best illustrated by Öhman's election in 1983 as the first non-native English-speaking president of the Society for Psychophysiological Research in the United States.

Dureman also conducted sleep research and inspired Gunilla Bohlin to do her dissertation work on the relationship between the habituation of the OR and sleep onset. Bohlin continued to investigate the OR with Frances Graham at the University of Wisconsin. However, she is now engaged in a developmental project on infant temperament in collaboration with Berit Hagekull.

Other psychophysiological research in Sweden includes the studies on the habituation of the OR and problems measuring the OR, published by Schalling and Levander in Stockholm, and work on using biofeedback to control heart rate by Aleksander Perski.

Finally, the use of measures of cerebral blood flow during various psychological manipulations by David Ingvar and Jarl Risberg in Lund is another example of Swedish psychophysiological research which is frequently cited worldwide. (A more detailed review of Swedish psychophysiological research is provided by Hugdahl [1984].)

Psychoneuroendocrinology

Swedish researchers have made conspicuous contributions to psychobiologically oriented stress research (see Lundberg, 1984, for a summary). To a considerable extent, this research draws on the physiological work on noradrenalin by the Nobel laureate Ulf von Euler, who developed methods to measure catecholamines in urine. This provided an important starting point for the research of Lennart Levi. Levi is now the head of the Swedish Institute for Environmental Medicine in Stockholm.

Another influential group is headed by Marianne Frankenhaeuser at the Department of Psychiatry and Medical Psychology at the Karolinska Institute in Stockholm. Originally a student of Ekman's, Frankenhaeuser was given a professorship in medical psychology at the Karolinska Instituute after an extended period as professor of experimental psychology at the Swedish Medical Research Council.

Frankenhaeuser's research in psychoneuroendocrinology (Frankenhaeuser, 1979, 1983) began in the 1960s with studies examining both the effects of various types of physical and psychological stress on catecholamine excretion and the effects of the infusion of adrenaline on psychological states. This work then expanded into an extensive research program on the relationship between stress and coping, on the one hand, and excretion of adrenaline and noradrenaline, on the other hand. Frankenhaeuser first worked within the tradition of Walter Cannon, focusing on the emergency function of the sympatho-adrenal medullary axis. More recently, Frankenhaeuser's group has begun to take into account measurements, particularly of cortisol, from the pituitary-adrenal cortex axis. On the basis of their findings, they have argued that these two axes are related to different types of psychological states. Whereas catecholamine secretion is primarily related to effort spent in coping, cortisol secretion is viewed as primarily related to states of distress. Thus, the two types of hormones can be dissociated, for example, in situations involving effort without distress or distress without effort. Other findings from Frankenhaeuser's program show that adrenaline is more related to mental, and noradrenaline to physical, stress. Systematic sex differences have been observed, with males appearing to exhibit a much stronger physiological response during effort-related stress than females. Women in male occupations, however, show a hormonal activation pattern more similar to that typical of men.

Frankenhaeuser has supervised many doctoral students. Among those active in basic science settings are Paul Patkai, Torbjörn Åkerstedt, and Mats Gillberg, who have all done research on circadian rhythms. Her most longstanding collaborator, Ulf Lundberg, took his Ph.D. with Gösta Ekman, and went on to work with Frankenhaeuser on various stress problems. He has recently made independent contributions relative to the stress of crowding and of commuting and on Type-A behavior, particularly from a developmental perspective.

As an extension of her work on stress, Frankenhaeuser joined Bertil Gardell, professor of social psychology in Stockholm, in a research program to discover the relationships between psychological adjustment and stress, on the one hand, and working life environments, on the other. This work led to studies by another Frankenhaeuser-trained psychologist, Gunn Johansson, who is investigating the effects of computerization in work settings on life in Sweden.

Work environment research is done, too, at the National Board of Occupational Safety and Health in Stockholm where Lennart Lennerlöf heads a work psychology unit. The unit includes Fransisco Gamberale, Anders Kjellberg, Heinz Leymann, and Gunnela Westlander. Finally, organizational psychologist Sigvard Rubinowitz, professor of applied psychology at the University of Gothenburg, has been investigating aspects of concern in the work place, principally job satisfaction and the prevention of absenteeism.

Physiological Psychology

Physiological psychology, or behavioral neuroscience, represents a strong interdisciplinary tradition in Sweden. Key contributions have come as frequently from medical as from psychological researchers. The scope of contemporary Swedish behavioral neuroscience can be found in a recent volume edited by Per Södersten (1982).

Among medical contributors to physiological psychology in Sweden, Bengt Andersson deserves special mention for his pioneering discovery of a hypothalamic mechanism for the control of thirst in goats. This finding set the stage for important advances in the understanding of the neural control of motivated behavior. Similarly, using the Swedish Falck-Hillarp neuroanatomical method to visualize biogenic amines in the nervous system, Urban Ungerstedt revolutionized thinking about the neurobiology of motivation by demonstrating dopamine involvement in the loss of appetite after lateral hypothalamic lesions.

Knut Larsson, a physiological psychologist at the University of Gothenburg, has for a long time been in the forefront of Swedish neuroscience and international research relative to the neural control of sexual behavior. Around 1960, in collaboration with neuroanatomist Lennart Heimer, he initiated an impressive research program on the neural regulation of male sexual behavior in the rat. This program provided evidence for excitatory as well as inhibitory neural mechanisms in sexual behavior. In an often-cited study, Heimer and Larsson (1966–1967) unequivocally demonstrated the importance of the preoptic-anterior hypothalamic area in the control of male sexual behavior.

The neural and hormonal analysis of sexual behavior has been extended by Larsson's student, Per Södersten, who has published extensively on the neuroendocrine control of sexuality (for example, Södersten, 1985). Among other things, he and his coworkers have related the hormonal function of the endocrine system to the development and display of sexual behavior.

The findings of Södersten's group suggest that the traditional assumption that sex differences in behavior are primarily due to hormone sensitivity is at least partly incorrect. Instead, Södersten and his collaborators proposed that differences between male and female rodents relate primarily to the differential sensitivty to diurnal rhythm mechanisms exhibited by the two sexes. The work of Larsson and Södersten has been extended by Södersten's student, Stefan Hansen, who, among other things, analyzed the effects of preoptic lesions in relation to motivational theory. Further contributions to the understanding of the role of biogenic amines in the control of sexual behavior were made by Bengt Meyersson, professor of medical behavior research in Uppsala, who suggested that serotonergic mechanisms are inhibitory to sexual behavior.

A final example of biologically oriented psychology in Sweden is the work done in the mid–1970s by Per-Olof Sjöden in Uppsala and his student, Trevor Archer, on the conditioning of taste aversion in rats. Sjöden and Archer showed that such conditioning is dependent on contextual cues in the environment. This was contrary to the predominant view a decade ago that taste-aversion learning was independent of external cues. Archer has also demonstrated the involvement of noradrenalin in avoidance conditioning through the use of a selective noradrenergic neurotoxin, DSP4.

REFERENCES

Atkinson, R. C., & Shifrin, R. M. (1971). The control of short-term memory. In R. C. Atkinson (Ed.), *Psychology in progress: Readings from* Scientific American. San Francisco: Freeman.

Bäckman, L., & Nilsson, L.-G. (1984). Aging differences in free recall: An exception to the rule. *Human Learning, 3,* 53–56.

Björkman, M. (1958). *Measurement of learning: A study of verbal rote learning.* Stockholm: Almqvist & Wiksell.

Björkman, M. (1973). Inference behavior in nonmetric ecologies. In L. Rappoport & D. Summers (Eds.), *Human judgement and social interaction.* New York: Holt, Rinehart & Winston.

Brehmer, B. (1976). Social judgement theory and the analysis of interpersonal conflict. *Psychological Bulletin, 83,* 985–1003.

Brehmer, B. (1979). Preliminaries to a psychology of inference. *Scandinavian Journal of Psychology, 20,* 193–210.

Brehmer, B. (1980). In one word: Not from experience. *Acta Psychologica, 45,* 223–241.

Brehmer, B. (1984). Brunswikian psychology for the 1990's. In K. M. J. Lagerspetz & P. Niemi (Eds.), *Psychology in the 1990's.* Amsterdam: Elsevier Science Publishers (North-Holland).

Brunswik, F. (1952). *Conceptual framework of psychology.* Chicago: University of Chicago Press.

Cohen, R., & Johansson, B. S. (1967). The activity trace in immediate memory: A reevaluation. *Journal of Verbal Learning and Verbal Behavior, 6,* 139–143.

Dahllöf, U. (1984). *Pedagogik ämnet, disputationerna och arbetsmarknaden for doktorerna fram till slutet av 1940-talet* [The discipline of pedagogy, debates and the job market for physicians since the 1940s]. Arbetsrapporter från Pedagogiska institutionen, Uppsala Universitet, Nr 94.

Dureman, I. (1959). *Drugs and autonomic conditioning. The effects of amphetamine and chlorpromazine on the simultaneous conditioning of pupillary and electrodermal response elements.* Stockholm: Almqvist & Wiksell.

Dureman, I. (1963). Psycho-physiological methods applied in studies of effect of psychotropic drugs in men. *Revue de Psychologie Appliquée, 11,* 403–415.

Eisler, H. (1982). On the nature of subjective scales. *Scandinavian Journal of Psychology, 23,* 161–171.

Ekman, G. (1947). *Reliabilitet och konstans. Ett bidrag till testpsykologiens metodologi* [Reliability and constancy: A contribution to psychometric theory]. Uppsala: Almqvist & Wiksell.

Ekman, G. (1952). *Differentiell psykologi* [Differential psychology]. Stockholm: Almqvist & Wiksell.

Ekman, G. (1961). Some aspects of psychophysical research. In W. A. Rosenblith (Ed.), *Sensory communication*. New York: Wiley.

Ekman, G., Engen, T., Künnapas, T., & Lindman, R. (1964). A quantitative principle of qualitative similarity. *Journal of Experimental Psychology, 68*, 530–536.

Ekman, G., & Sjöberg, L. (1965). Scaling. *Annual Review of Psychology, 68*, 530–536.

Frankenhaeuser, M. (1979). Psychoneuroendocrine approaches to the study of emotion as related to stress and coping. In H. E. Howe & R. A. Dienstbier (Eds.), *Nebraska symposium on motivation 1978*. Lincoln: University of Nebraska Press.

Frankenhaeuser, M. (1983). The sympathetic-adrenal and pituitary-adrenal response to challenge: Comparison between the sexes. In T. M. Dembroski, T. H. Schmidt, & G. Blumchen (Eds.), *Biobehavioral bases of coronary heart disease*. Basel: Karger Press.

Gärling, T. (1982). Swedish environmental psychology. *Journal of Environmental Psychology, 2*, 233–251.

Gibson, J. J. (1979). *The ecological approach to visual perception*. Boston: Houghton Mifflin.

Hammond, K. R., Stewart, T. R., Brehmer, B., & Steinman, D. O. (1975). Social judgement theory. In M. Kaplan & S. Schwartz (Eds.), *Human judgement and decision processes*. New York: Academic Press.

Hare, R. D., & Schalling, D. (Eds.). (1978). *Psychopathic behavior: Approaches to research*. New York: Wiley.

Heimer, L., & Larsson, K. (1966/67). Impairment of mating behavior in male rats following lesions in the preoptic-anterior hypothalamic continuum. *Brain Research, 3*, 248–263.

Hellström, Å. (1985). The time-order error and its relatives: Mirrors of cognitive processes in comparing. *Psychological Bulletin, 97*, 35–61.

Hugdahl, K. (1984). Human psychobiology in Scandinavia: I. Psychophysiology—Theory, method, and empirical research. *Scandinavian Journal of Psychology, 25*, 194–213.

Hull, C. L. (1943). *Principles of behavior*. New York: Appleton-Century.

Johansson, G. (1950). *Configurations in event perception*. Uppsala: Almqvist & Wiksell.

Johansson, G. (1964). Perception of motion and changing form. *Scandinavian Journal of Psychology, 5*, 181–208.

Johansson, G. (1973). Visual perception of biological motion, and a model for its analysis. *Perception and Psychophysics, 14*, 201–211.

Johansson, G. (1978). Visual event perception. In R. Held, H. W. Leibowitz, & H.-L. Teuber (Eds.), *Handbook of sensory physiology, Vol. VII; Perception*. New York: Springer-Verlag.

Johansson, G., Hofsten, C. von, & Jansson, G. (1980). Event perception. *Annual Review of Psychology, 31*, 27–63.

Katz, D. (1925). *Der Aufbau der Tastwelt* [Construction of the tactile world]. Leipzig: Barth.

Katz, D. (1935). *The world of colour*. London: Kegan, Paul, Trench, Truber, & Co.

Katz, D. (1937). *Animals and men.* New York: Longmans & Green.

Katz, D. (1950). *Gestalt psychology.* New York: Ronald Press.

Kragh, U. (1959). Type of precognitive defensive organization in a tachistoscopic experiment. *Journal of Projective Techniques, 23,* 315–322.

Künnapas, T. (1976). Sweden. In V. S. Sexton & H. Misiak (Eds.), *Psychology around the world* (pp. 405–417). Monterey, CA: Brooks/Cole.

Lundberg, I. (1978). Linguistic awareness as related to reading. In A. Sinclair, R. J. Jarvella, & W. M. Levelt (Eds.), *The child's conception of language.* New York: Springer-Verlag.

Lundberg, I. (1983). *Läs och skrivsvårigheter i ljuset av aktuell forskning* [Reading and writing difficulties in the light of current research]. Stockholm: Skolöverstyrelsen.

Lundberg, U. (1984). Human psychobiology in Scandinavia: II. Psychoneuroendocrinology—Human stress and coping processes. *Scandinavian Journal of Psychology, 25,* 214–226.

Magnusson, D. (1966). *Testteori* [Test theory]. Stockholm: Almqvist & Wiksell.

Magnusson, D. (Ed.), (1981). *Toward a psychology of situations: An interactional perspective.* Hillside, NJ: Lawrence Erlbaum Associates.

Magnusson, D., & Allen, V. L. (Eds.), (1983). *Human development: An interactional perspective.* New York: Academic Press.

Magnusson, D., & Endler, N. S. (Eds.). (1977). *Personality at the crossroads: Current issues in interactional psychology.* Hillsdale, NJ: Lawrence Erlbaum Associates.

Magnusson, D., & Öhman, A. (Eds.). (1985). *Psychopathology: An interactional perspective.* New York: Academic Press.

Nilsson, L.-G. (Ed.). (1979). *Perspectives on memory research. Hillsdale, NJ: Lawrence Erlbaum Associates.*

Nilsson, L.-G. (1980). Methodological and theoretical considerations as a basis for an integration of research on memory functions in epileptic patients. *Acta Neurologica Scandinavica, 62,* (Supplementum 80), 62–74.

Nilsson, L.-G. (1984). New functionalism in memory research. In K. M. J. Lagerspetz & P. Niemi (Eds.), *Psychology in the 1990's.* Amsterdam: Elsevier Science Publishers (North-Holland).

Nilsson, L.-G., Ohlsson, K., & Rönnberg, J. (1980). Processing and storage explanations of the modality effect. *Acta Psychologica, 44,* 41–50.

Öhman, A. (1979). The orienting response, attention, and learning: An information-processing perspective. In H. D. Kimmel, E. H. van Olst, & J. F. Orlebeke (Eds.), *The orienting reflex in humans.* Hillsdale, NJ: Lawrence Erlbaum Associates. (a)

Öhman, A. (1979). Fear-relevance, autonomic conditioning, and phobias: A laboratory model. In P. O. Sjödén, S. Bates, & W. S. Dockens III (Eds.), *Trends in behavior therapy.* New York: Academic Press. (b)

Öhman, A. (1981). Electrodermal activity and vulnerability to schizophrenia: A review. *Biological Psychology, 12,* 87–145.

Öhman, A. (1983). The orienting response during Pavlovian conditioning. In D. A. T. Siddle (Ed.), *Orienting and habituation: Perspectives in human research.* Chichester: Wiley.

Öhman, A., & Magnusson, D. (1985). An interactional paradigm for research on psychopathology. In D. Magnusson & A. Öhman (Eds.), *Psychopathology: An interactional perspective.* New York: Academic Press.

Öst, L.-G. (1981). Beteendeterapin i Sverige–En historisk tillbakablick [Behavior therapy in Sweden: A historical review]. *Scandinavian Journal of Behavior Therapy, 10,* 153–172.

Rabbitt, P. M. A., & Dornic, S. (Eds.), (1975). *Attention and performance* (Vol. 5). London: Academic Press.

Sandström, C.-I. (1969). *Lakttagelse och upplevelse* [Observation and experience]. Stockholm: Almqvist & Wiksell.

Sjöbäck, H. (1984). *Psykoanalytisk forsvarsteori* [Psychoanalytic theory of defense mechanisms]. Lund: Studentlitteratur.

Sjöberg, L. (1962). The law of comparative judgement: A case not assuming equal variances and covariances. *Scandinavian Journal of Psychology, 3,* 219–225.

Sjöberg, L. (1975). Models of similarity and intensity. *Psychological Bulletin, 82,* 191–206.

Sjöberg, L. (1980). The risk of risk analysis. *Acta Psychologica, 45,* 301–321.

Sjöberg, L., Svensson, E., & Persson, L.-O. (1979). The measurement of mood. *Scandinavian Journal of Psychology, 20,* 1–18.

Smith, G. J. W., & Hendriksson, M. (1956). Studies in the development of a percept within various contexts of perceived reality. *Acta Psychologica, 12,* 263–281.

Smith, G. J. W., & Kragh, U. (1967). A serial afterimage experiment in clinical diagnostics. *Scandinavian Journal of Psychology, 8,* 52–64.

Smith, G. J. W., & Westerlundh, B. (1980). Perceptgenesis: A process perspective on perception—personality. In L. Wheeler (Ed.), *Review of personality and social psychology.* Beverly Hills, CA: Sage.

Södersten, P. (Ed.), (1982). Behavioral neuroscience in Scandinavia. *Scandinavian Journal of Psychology* (Supplementum 1), 1–181.

Södersten, P. (1985). Estradiol-progesterone interactions in the reproductive behavior of female rats. In D. W. Pfaff (Ed.), *Current topics in neuroendocrinology* (Vol. 5). New York: Springer-Verlag.

Watson, J. B. (1913). Psychology as the behaviorist views it. *Psychological Review, 20,* 158–177.

Westerlundh, B., & Smith, G. J. W. (1983). Perceptgenesis and the psychodynamics of perception. *Psychoanalysis and Contemporary Thought, 6,* 597–640.

Turkey

Gündüz Y. H. Vassaf

THE FACTS-AND-FIGURES APPROACH TO HISTORY AND TURKISH PSYCHOLOGY

Most histories of psychology and the other social sciences in the Third World deal with developments that can be quantified. At the other extreme, a few analyses consider only the theoretical characteristics of the field with no reference to organizational structure and development (Ari, in press). Both approaches generally ignore the relationships between scientific events and overall societal developments. In quantitative studies, one is usually confronted with an array of statistics and figures purporting to depict the growth of psychology in terms of a rise in the number of psychology departments, practicing psychologists, and publications. Although such data can be of immense importance, they can also be misleading or meaningless if not evaluated qualitatively within a historical framework.

The growth of modern psychology and other contemporary social sciences in Turkey, as in the rest of the Third World, has not been like that in the West. However, a dominant school of thought in the West views progress in the Third World as, primarily, a catching-up process. This viewpoint is based on the premise that Third World countries will go through the same processes of modernization experienced by Western countries (Eisenstadt, 1966; Morse, 1969; McClelland, 1967). Thus, modernization is defined by one chief proponent of this perspective as a "process of social change whereby less developed societies acquire characteristics common to the more developed societies" (Lerner, 1964). Modernizationists see all aspects of society ranging from economic development to the achievement of a contemporary democracy and the institutions of twentieth-century Western society in terms of learning from the West. Social change in the Third World is to be brought about by a Westernized elite who control and direct the government, businesses, the military, and the universities and who are dependent on foreign experts and consultants. According to modernization theorists, traditions and the lack of a trained elite have prevented the Third World from achieving modern societies. The development in the Third World of universities in general and the social sciences in particular has usually been considered in the context of modernization; historical analyses of Turkish psychology have emphasized the facts-and-figures approach.

To illustrate, a modernizationist's brief quantitative account of Turkish psychology might be as follows. There are officially twenty-seven universities in Turkey, all established by the government.[1] Undergraduate departments of psychology have been given official sanction to open at all Turkish universities. Graduate studies in psychology are offered at five universities. There are two psychological associations.[2] Türk Psikoloji Derneği (Turkish Psychologists Association), founded over thirty years ago in Istanbul, has a membership of approximately 200. It represents Turkey at the International Union of Psychological Science meetings. The more recent Psikologlar Derneği (Psychologists Association) has approximately 500 members. Since its founding in 1976 it has published the quarterly *Psikologlar Derneği Dergisi* [Psychologists Association Journal] with a circulation of about 750. Another journal, *Tecrübi Psikoloji Calismalari* [Studies in Experimental Psychology] has been published by Istanbul University since 1936. For the past three years, the Psychologists Association in Ankara has also organized annual congresses of psychology, marking the first time that psychologists have met independently of the National Psychiatric and Neurological Association.

Over the past fifteen years, many new employment opportunities have been created for psychologists. They work as clinical psychologists in the psychiatry departments of all university hospitals as well as at the four mental hospitals in Turkey. In Ankara, the capital, there are a total of twenty-two psychologists employed at four hospitals: Hacettepe University Hospital has six; Ankara University Hospital, eight, Gülhane Military Hospital, six; and Golbaşi Psychiatric Hospital, two full-time psychologists. The number of psychologists working at hospitals in Istanbul is about fifty. Many are employed as counselors at secondary schools throughout the country, and many others teach both psychology and philosophy which are mandatory courses in all Turkish lycées.

The number of psychologists in private practice, especially those who administer psychological tests to children, is increasing. Works of Freud, Fromm, Reich, Foucault, Adler, Jung, and Piaget are all available in Turkish. The first translation of the Stanford-Binet appeared in Turkey a few years after the United States edition was published (Tunç, 1948, p. 3). Most widely used psychological tests in the United States are available to psychologists in both Turkish and English.

With time and more resources, it is anticipated that Turkey will have more periodicals, graduate departments, books, conferences, and so forth. It is expected that development will be a function of the modernization or Westernization of Turkey, the two terms often used synonymously (Black, 1967, p. 6). Of the two leading articles concerned with the history of psychology in Turkey, one by McKinney (1960) looks upon the rather low numbers of psychologists and psychology departments in Turkey as characteristic of an underdeveloped country with non-Western traditions. The other study, carried out twenty years later (LeCompte, 1980), though much wider in scope and a significant contribution, follows the same approach.

Öztürk and Volkan (1971), in a landmark article dealing with the theory and practice of psychiatry in Turkey, provide a detailed and informative perspective on Turkish history and culture. Nevertheless, they do not analyze the interactional relationship between the recent imposition of Western models (ranging from the Swiss civil code to the practice of psychiatry) and society. Along the same lines as the two articles on Turkish psychology, their account is another example of the modernizationist approach. Thus, custom and tradition are viewed as impediments to progress and Westernization while no mention at all is made of the fact that rapidly imposed Westernization could be disruptive. The suitability of the Western approach to psychology for Turkish society is not taken into account, and traditional belief systems and practices relative to treatment are completely ignored. The important role of traditional practice is, however, taken up in another article by Öztürk (1964).

In summary, the Western and traditional conceptions of psychology, psychiatry, and mental health are generally treated as mutually exclusive and competing systems without considering the potential of mutual enrichment, which could perhaps lead to a new synthesis and a pluralistic model.

SOCIETAL CHANGE AND THE DEVELOPMENT OF PSYCHOLOGY

The main shortcoming of the above approach is a tendency to assume that the Western model of development holds universal applicability. Western psychology has been shaped by centuries of cultural development and technological innovation. Especially in this century, psychology has been formed by the demands of Western society, which has then been influenced by psychology.

The origin of psychological testing is a case in point, with the Paris school system requesting help from Binet and Simon to separate the "normal" learners from the "slow" learners so that all could benefit from public education. It was capitalism and the industrial revolution that led to individual competition and specialization, in turn creating the need to ascertain individual differences through tests for the sake of the efficiency of large enterprises, a mechanized military, and a mass educational system. The ensuing rapid development of technology and increasing emphasis on merit also required the assessment of individual abilities. Mandated by Western society, the test movement ultimately exercised a profound influence on that parent society.

Like testing, many other developments such as industrial psychology, T-groups, human engineering, Synanon, and computer therapy have resulted from changes in and demands of Western society, now in its postindustrial phase. On the other hand, psychology in Turkey and many other Third World countries has not developed through such a dialectical interaction between science and society. Rather, it is the result of an "export-import" relationship between the industrialized and urbanized countries of the West and the peripheral Third World, a dependency-promoting relationship that continues to be encouraged by the present state of affairs (Wallerstein, 1976).

The export-import process in Turkey not only has led to a severing of contemporary cultural and social ties with the country's heritage but has brought in irrelevant ideas and information from Western psychology. The imported paradigms concerning psychological health and applied psychology may inhibit independent thinking and have an adverse effect on the welfare of the population as a whole. Furthermore, Western psychology suffers too in the sense that it becomes export-oriented rather than integration-seeking with regard to research, publications, the exchange of scholars, and, most important, the search for universal principles, theories, and ethics.

Forced upon Turkish psychology through historical circumstances, the export-import relationship has been fostered by Turkish psychologists. The change from dependence to independence in the development of psychology in a Third World country under normal conditions would be twofold. One aspect involves gaining independence from other disciplines, especially philosophy and psychiatry. The other entails gaining independence from Western psychology whose roots are firmly set in Judeo-Christian thought and, more recently, capitalism, in the process establishing a separate identity. It is my thesis that psychology in Turkey has experienced abnormal development relative to both of these requisites for successful maturation (Vassaf, 1983). Let me provide a little historical background.

Asia Minor, situated at the crossroads of Europe, Africa, and Asia and for centuries the center of the Mediterranean world, gave rise to civilizations that served as a foundation for contemporary societies in both the West and the East: the Hittites, the Greeks, the Romans, the Persians, the Byzantines, and, for the past 600 years, the Ottoman Empire and the Turks. Anatolia is central to the cultural heritage of all these civilizations.

Before the establishment in the sixteenth century of the mercantilist world economic system that eventually replaced Ottoman domination, there had been in Turkey a strong classical Greek and Islamic-Ottoman tradition with respect to the study of both individual and social behavior. Some of this is still preserved and reflected in the works of İbn-Sina (Avicenna) and İbn-Khaldun.

The Turkish republic was built on the remnants of the Ottoman Empire which fell to the major victorious powers of World War I. The leader of Turkey's war of liberation, Mustafa Kemal (Atatürk), is looked upon by his most noted biographers as a man "who uprooted the traditions of centuries" to create a new society in which many Western institutions and habits ranging from the creation of a secular state to the wearing of the hat (instead of the fez) were officially adopted (Kinross, 1965; Lewis, 1965). Thus, the change from empire to republic can be viewed as an attempt to replace one civilization with another rather than as a mere transition from one political system to another. Therefore, within a few years after the declaration of the republic in 1923, all religious institutions of higher learning (*medrese*) were abolished and replaced by universities fashioned after those in the West. During the 1930s many of these were staffed by German professors who, fleeing racist Nazi ideology, settled in Turkey and in many instances became Turkish citizens. Psychology in Turkey was strongly influenced by European philosophical orientations.

It was not until a close military and political relationship between Turkey and the United States evolved, especially after the Korean War and Turkish entry into NATO, that American influence manifested itself within Turkish education and applied social science. Accompanying this development came intellectual domination by the United States, reinforced by American global superiority after World War II and the dependency of other countries on American technology and knowledge. The dependency was not only the result of objective conditions but was actively sought by those who were dominated. The example presented in the following section indicates the numerous factors that reinforce such a dependent relationship.

THE EXPORT-IMPORT MODEL AND THE DEPENDENT DEVELOPMENT OF TURKISH PSYCHOLOGY

The first major exportation of applied psychology from the United States to Turkey occurred in the early 1950s. In accordance with an agreement between the two governments, American psychologists arrived as experts at the Turkish Ministry of Education and the main teachers' training school, Gazi Eğitim Enstitüsü. Their aim was to set up guidance and counseling programs for the educational system. Turkish students were given scholarships to study psychology at universities in the United States. This led to the use of intelligence tests in schools for the first time. Nevertheless, it is in the universities themselves rather than in specific government-initiated programs that the dependency relationship is best seen.

Hacettepe University, a modern Turkish university founded in 1966 with the help of various institutions in the United States, included in its curriculum a four-year program in psychology leading to a bachelor's degree. The goals were to create a psychology department in keeping with American standards and, eventually, to develop a staff made up of its own graduates, thereby eliminating the need for further outside support. Another hope was that Turkish society would benefit from the university's graduates through their work on applied problems. To this end, catalogues of American universities were used as guides for the creation of a department of psychology. The Fulbright program played a key role in enabling psychologists from the United States to teach and conduct research in Turkey. An astonishingly large number of Turkish psychologists received support from Fulbright funds (LeCompte, 1980).

After four years, the department graduated its first class of fifteen. But none could find a job. The entire group went back for a fifth year so that they could qualify for certificates as secondary-school teachers. The establishment of this psychology department did not end the dependency on the West as initially envisioned by some. Rather, it promoted further dependency. Although the department became the largest of its kind in Turkey and was at one time a showcase for psychology, fourteen years after it was founded, "out of eleven faculty members who had doctorates all but two had received their degrees either in England or the United States" (LeCompte, 1980, p. 746). All psychology textbooks were American. Not one textbook during all of that time had been written in Turkish. Psychological concepts, many of questionable applicability and validity even in Western countries, were discussed and used in research without consideration of their relevance to Turkish culture and society.

The development of psychology at Istanbul University, which has a much older history than Hacettepe, serves as another example of the dependency model underlying the development of psychology in Turkey. In spite of remarkable efforts by both the Turkish and foreign scholars who devoted a lifetime to developing psychology in Turkey, their goals have not been reached, mainly because of the unsuitability of their assumptions concerning what psychology should be.

Psychology was first offered as a course at Istanbul University in 1915 when Professor G. Anschütz from Germany came with his laboratory equipment to teach experimental psychology for three years. Then in 1919 a young Turkish psychologist, Sekip Tunc, educated at the Jean Jacques Rousseau Institute in Geneva, was appointed chair of general psychology. Although unfamiliar to most psychologists in Turkey today, he is generally regarded as having founded psychology in Turkey. In 1937, along with other prominent German professors fleeing Nazi oppression, Wilhelm Peters came to Turkey and became chair of experimental psychology. For over fifteen years Peters worked almost single-handedly setting up an Institute of Psychology, a psychology library, and a psychology laboratory and helping found the Turkish Psychological Association and a journal of psychology (Toğrol, 1983). Such outstanding individual effort led to the establishment of a formal structure in which psychology took root as an academic discipline. All these developments, however, reflected a continuing dependency on Western psychology. The following observations with respect to the development of psychology at Istanbul University give clear support to the argument that it is more the country's foreign policy and the world's economic situation than the interests of science that have determined particular developments in scientific disciplines.

An examination of the card catalog at the psychology library at Istanbul University illustrates this contention. Between 1920 and 1950 approximately 80 percent of the books at the library came from either Germany or France. Turkey's abandonment of a neutral foreign policy in favor of a pro-American stance after 1947 and the emerging world dominance of the United States are clearly reflected in the psychology books acquired after that period. Since then, publications have come mainly from the United States. The library now has approximately 1,300 books. The intellectual tradition based on a closeness to France and Germany ceased abruptly and was replaced by the American connection. It is obvious that such dependencies cannot form the basis of traditions necessary for the pursuit of scientific knowledge. Furthermore, the books in Turkish libraries are kept in locked cabinets and rarely used since most students cannot speak or read foreign languages.

The libraries of the other universities are also stocked mainly with American publications, and the purchase of books has been severely curtailed as a result of the world economic crisis. The Istanbul University library, for instance, could only acquire five psychology books from 1983 through 1985. Though *Psychological Abstracts* and citation indexes are available in Istanbul and Ankara, many journal subscriptions have been canceled in recent years. Thus, another drawback to intellectual dependency is that it is closely linked to economic conditions. Nevertheless, it is largely because of Western books that psychology in Turkey exists at all since Turkish faculty members publish very little.

Over the forty-five-year period following 1928, members of the psychology department at Istanbul University wrote or translated a mere fifty-five books listed as university publications (Orhan, 1974). Of these, twenty-eight are translations and twenty-seven are original works. This amounts to one original work every two years by a department with an average size of approximately seven academicians. Furthermore, over one-third of all the books that were either translated or written during this period were the products of only three individuals, namely Mustafa Şekip Tunç, Mümtaz Turhan, and Selmin Evrim, all of whom are now dead.

Lack of original contributions on the part of the faculty and the dependency on Western books, paradigms, and issues are reflected also in the thesis research of undergraduate psychology students. Between 1934 and 1972, 450 theses were written (Togrol, 1972). Of these, nearly half (196) merely reported the results of administering American psychological tests to Turkish students. During the 1962–1972 period, 163 works dealt with the administration of tests and only 85 with other topics. The faculty encourages psychometric studies and is not at all critical of this situation (Canitez & Toğrol, 1983).

In looking over the psychological literature one gets the impression that the cart has been put before the horse and that the sole raison d'être is to use Western instruments such as IQ tests and attitude surveys. It is important to emphasize that these instruments, which are unreliable and unvalidated in Turkey, are not employed to develop or test theory. They are not even used to conduct cross-cultural research. They are merely empirical investigations devoid of any intrinsic or contextual importance. The article referred to above by Canitez and Toğrol (1983) on the student dissertations they have supervised over the years supports this argument. There is no reference in their paper to any possible relationships between test results and theory. The authors merely report IQ scores based on invalid and unreliable tests administered by unqualified and unsupervised undergraduate students.

This trend is also apparent in the changing characteristics of the psychology textbooks used in Turkey before and after the 1950s, when American influence became dominant upon Turkish entry into NATO. The three main textbooks of the previous period (Hasan, 1923; Sarp, 1932; Tunç, 1948) all indicate a strong concern with theory and a sensitivity to the dangers of emphasizing empirical research without an adequate theoretical foundation.

In the foreword of his textbook *Psikoloji'ye giriş* [Introduction to psychology], Tunç (1948) states that he followed the lead of psychologists such as Ribot, James, and Ebbinghaus who refused to stay within the confines of the laboratory. The organization of his textbook also reflects the importance of theory over methodology, with the scientific method discussed last rather than first as is done in most American textbooks. It is also significant that since the publication of Tunç's book the only comprehensive university-level text to appear in Turkish has been a translation of Morgan's *Introduction to psychology* (1981). In part this may have been a result of the transition from attempts at bringing about political and economic independence in the early days of the republic to the abandonment of self-sufficiency following World War II due to the availability of Marshall Plan funds (Sertel, 1969).

An overview of the psychological literature illustrates that dependency is manifested also in the usage of inappropriate Western social science terminology to describe and interpret behavior in Turkey. One such example is the use of the term "juvenile delinquency" which is appropriate when referring to certain behaviors in capitalist, urban cultures characterized by nuclear families, but it is inappropriate when referring to activities of youth who take part in traditional blood feuds which have their roots in feudalism and clanlike families (Yavuzer, 1984).

Another significant characteristic of the psychological literature in the republican period is that there is seldom any reference to Ottoman and Islamic scholars. The rupture with the past by a republic embarked on modernization through Westernization is a basic cause of Turkish psychology's dependence on Western thought.

DEPENDENCY AND ETHICAL ISSUES

The dependency relationship has become increasingly entrenched. This has curtailed the development of an indigenous psychology in Turkey, impeded the creation of adequate public and community mental health services, and led to gross violations of basic professional ethical principles. Over the years, more and more students have graduated with bachelor's degrees in psychology. In the 1983–1984 academic year, for instance, seventy-two students received their bachelor's degrees in psychology from the three universities in Ankara. The yearly average for the past five years for all Turkish universities is approximately 100. Some graduates, through persistence, have managed to obtain positions for which they are not qualified in various university and government hospitals

offering psychiatric services. Calling themselves clinical psychologists, they
were asked by psychiatrists what they could do. "Give tests" was the answer
(though most only had a two-semester course in testing), and, as is the case in
most Third World countries, psychology and psychologists became associated
solely with testing.

The only tests available, however, were the Stanford-Binet, the Wechslers,
and the MMPI. These American tests, without being adapted or standardized,
became widely used in hospitals and schools (Öner & Özge, 1983). Now, over
twenty years later, no psychological tests used in Turkey meet minimum psychometric standards (Vassaf, 1982). The same situation exists in other Third
World countries (Drenth, 1975).

Recently, as a field project, my students visited various institutions and offices
in Istanbul where psychologists are employed. They found that all psychologists
use and rely on tests with very little or no knowledge of test norms, and most
had no formal training in testing. A report with most disturbing findings shows
that 35 percent of the students placed in special classes for the mentally retarded
in the Ankara school system were improperly classified (Çağlar, 1977).

The demand for tests continues to grow with parents eager to have their
children's IQs determined. Public demand has led to the opening of private
offices by many unqualified individuals professing the expertise to measure
intelligence, personality, and so forth. There is no board or organization authorized to license or control the practices of this new and growing "profession,"
and even bookstores can order psychological tests from distributors in the United
States, making tests available to anyone wanting to use them.[3] Psychologists as
recently as 1984 were still not clear as to what their official job description
should be (Arkun, 1984).

Through the years, the dependency relationship between Turkish psychology
and the West has been perpetuated both because of the dynamics set in motion
in Turkey and because of ties with the West. Thus, psychologists who would
be expected to object to the misuse of tests on ethical and scientific grounds
remain silent and passively collaborate with the system by translating tests and
teaching their use to those who will inevitably misuse them. Professional psychological associations on the national level offer no criticism of the situation
and prevent open discussion of the problem out of fear that, because psychologists
are associated with tests, the young profession could be blemished in the eyes
of the public. Those who object to the status quo are immediately ostracized.
Some educators and psychologists fail to raise objections because they derive
their income from tests. The Turkish people, many of whom are adversely
affected because their children are unjustly labeled mentally retarded, do not
protest because they have respect for science and scientists. Thus, Fulbright
exchange professors continue to come to Turkey and lecture at Turkish universities on the finer points of testing, and the Psychological Corporation continues to sell ever newer and more expensive editions of its tests. The situation
thereby perpetuates itself, with those who have the greatest knowledge of psy-

chometric techniques, and the greatest power to stop the misuse of tests, failing to protest (Vassaf, 1982).

THE LIMITS OF MODERNIZATION

What modernization has meant with respect to the development of psychology in Turkey is a feeble attempt to imitate the West, brought about mostly by those who received their doctorates in the United States or Europe. Until their retirement they teach what they learned as graduate students with little change. The average monthly salary of a full professor in Turkey is approximately $300. Therefore, they can do virtually nothing to update their knowledge as it is economically unfeasible for them to continue their contacts with the West in terms of attending international scientific meetings, keeping up with the literature, ordering books, and subscribing to journals.

The continuance of dependence on Western psychology is protracted by succeeding generations who go abroad to study. However, because of changing historical conditions in both Turkish and international politics, each generation comes back with the perspectives of different Western countries. This explains the influence, in turn, on Turkish psychology of French, German, and eventually American psychology. For example, my mother (Belkis Vassaf) who studied psychology with Tunç at Istanbul University between 1928 and 1932 was thoroughly exposed to Piaget's work. When she went to Smith College in the United States for graduate work in 1936, however, she found that no one there had even heard of the Swiss psychologist. By the 1950s, Piaget was no longer important in Turkish psychology, but as the discipline came under U.S. influence during the 1950s the Piagetian orientation was reintroduced. Such dependency shifts have prevented the formation in Turkey of an intellectual tradition characterized by continuity.

The case of Turkey is a clear example of the theory of modernization in practice implemented by a local elite with the support of Western institutions and experts. Turkey has, perhaps, the longest experience of any Third World country with respect to modernization. Attempts at Westernization first began under the Ottoman Empire. Yet, a century later, and after fifty years of an explicitly formulated policy of planned modernization, Turkey is still underdeveloped (Koopmans, 1978, p. 76). The same applies with regard to the development of the social sciences in general and psychology in particular. In spite of all efforts by Turkish and prominent Western psychologists, the gap between Western science and Turkish scholarship has widened to such a degree that academicians in Turkey are unaware of most recent issues in psychology. Still, progress in psychology is expected to take place in the context of modernization. Hence, people like McKinney can claim that psychology in Turkey has failed to develop because the East is not accustomed to rational thought. Some Turkish psychologists as well argue that education, birth control, and similar innovations will contribute to the development of the country even though their cross-cultural studies show that Turks still do not have a Western mentality (Kağitçibaşi, 1981). Consequently, a vicious circle is reinforced. Even more importance is ascribed to Westernization so that the country can develop, but increased Westernization leads to greater dependency and underdevelopment.

Ironically, Turkish psychology is less developed now then when it first embarked upon importing the Western model in the sense that the discrepancy between the West and Turkey in terms of knowledge accumulation is greater. Modernization has led to a reinforcement of dependency and perpetuated underdevelopment. Yet, Western universities and experts continue to export bits and pieces of their specialties to a receptive local elite.

Critics of modernization theory ascribe the differences between developed and underdeveloped countries to the emergence of capitalism in the sixteenth century. The resulting international division of labor has since then powerfully molded the experience of the non-Western countries while inhibiting the natural development of their inherent characteristics (Turner, 1979; İslamoğlu, 1983). Modernizationists, on the other hand, believe that the stunting of progress in the Western sense is due to cultural differences and the lack of a modernizing elite. The basis of their argument, for Moslem countries especially, is provided by Max Weber who sees the irrationality in Islam as the main impediment to the formation of capitalist societies based on rationalism. The same argument is made by others to explain the slow progress made by societal institutions, including the university and its departments. A brief look at the contributions of science and medicine in the Ottoman Empire before and after the sixteenth century, however, demonstrates that science gradually declined, in part at least because of Western economic domination.

THE OTTOMAN-ISLAMIC HERITAGE AND WESTERN DOMINATION

A whole body of scientific knowledge stemming from Islamic medical and behavioral research (scholarship which led to the founding of the first European universities in the middle of the twelfth century) and institutions founded during the Ottoman Empire have nearly been forgotten. Contemporary psychologists and psychiatrists in Turkey either take no account of the past or regard it, along with the modernizationists, as an impediment to progress. Mazhar Osman Usman, the founder of modern Turkish psychiatry, makes no reference to Islamic scholars and Ottoman medicine in his classical text *Psychiatrica*. In the foreword of his book he clearly manifests a negative attitude toward the past when he states, "Psychiatry is a new science. For thousands of years it was in the hands of 'hodja's' [learned religious men in Islam] and priests. Mental illness is the business of doctors only. It can only be taught in the classroom and in the laboratory" (Usman, 1947, p. 3).

Although I cannot do justice to the history of medicine under the Ottoman Empire, a few brief examples illustrate the reasons for looking at scientific development in a historical rather than the modernizationist context. The history of medicine with respect to mental illness in the Seljuk Turks (1071–1308) and the Ottoman Empire (1298–1923) is replete with cases showing that the humanistic approaches of the founders of modern psychiatry in the United States (Rush) and Europe (Pinel, Connoly, Simon) had ancient precedents. During the twelfth century there were already at least seven hospitals in Anatolia, with the two in Kayseri and Sivas attached to medical schools (Şehsuvaroğlu, 1984, p. 17). The architecture of the hospitals shows that they were designed with the mentally ill in mind and manifested an understanding of ecological psychology. There were also facilities for both recreational and occupational therapy (Şehsuvaroğlu, 1984, pp. 17–18). Something akin to the community mental health movement could also be seen in certain Anatolian villages which were exempt from paying taxes, in return for the service that they rendered. The villagers would look after the mentally ill in their own houses and at the same time encourage their participation in the life and work of the community (Ünver). Passages about social hierarchies in *Kutadgu-Bilig*, a Turkish book written in 1069, with reference to the *otakçi* who treated physical illness and the *efsuncu* who treated mental illness, suggest that even then a differentiation was made between positivist and spiritualist approaches to treatment.

It is clear that long before the Western-style insane asylums were established in the Ottoman Empire toward the end of the nineteenth century there were many centers where those who showed a disharmony in their behavior were treated humanely. Today, not even small traces of these centers exist. The deterioration of mental health services began with the decline of the Ottoman Empire in the sixteenth century.

Not only have institutions disappeared, but entire philosophies and medical advances have been overshadowed. This is true to some extent even with regard to the contributions of the famous philosopher-scientist of Islam, İbn-Sina (980–1037), known in the West as Avicenna. His two major works are *Kitab Ash-Shifa* [Book of healing], a philosophical and scientific encyclopedia, and *Quanum fi at-tibb* [Canon of Medicine], which according to the *Encyclopedia Britannica* is the most important book in the early history of medicine in both the East and West. İbn-Sina's and Zekeriya Razi's (854–932) books were translated into Latin and taught at medical schools in Europe until the eighteenth century. The greatest social scientist of Islam was İbn Khaldun (1332–1401), a sociologist and philospher of history, whose major work, the *Muqaddimah* [Introduction to history] deals with historiography and the study of the nature of society and social change. With respect to the above he is credited with the founding of a new branch of the social sciences, *ilm al-umran* [the science of culture], whose subject matter he defined as human society and social transformations. The *Muqaddimah* is integrated around İbn Khaldun's concept of *asabiyah* [social cohesion] as affected by psychological, sociological, economic, and political factors, all of which he analyzes in detail.

These two scholars along with the physician İbn-Rushd (1126–1198), referred to in Western literature as Averroës, are acknowledged in the West for their contributions to the development of Aristotelian philosophy and their being conveyors of classical Greek philosophy to Europe before the Renaissance. Because they are known in the West, they have been rediscovered to some extent in countries like Turkey. Scores of non-Aristotelian Islamic and Ottoman scholars who studied behavior and medicine, however, wait to be recognized by their own society.

It should be noted that the present-day achievement of Western science has been facilitated by the fact that it is an autonomous enterprise relative to formal religion. Islamic-Ottoman science, on the other hand, was never secular. Ottoman scientists did not go through a period of Renaissance and enlightenment with logic and method taking precedence over faith. Rather, science and education remained under the control of the ruling elite. Any questioning of this elite's teachings was looked upon as a form of seditious behavior and also as an act of heresy. In fact, even Ottoman sultans met with strong resistance when they tried to establish schools of medicine that would allow for systematic observation, experimentation, dissection, and autopsy. Thus Selim III (1789–1807) could manage to open a modern school of medicine only for the Greeks in the empire, because reactionary forces would not allow Moslem students to attend. The school founded in Kuruçeşme in Istanbul in 1805 had to be closed in 1820 in reaction to the Greek independence movement. It was not until 1839 that the first dissection of a human cadaver could be carried out in a Turkish medical school. Even that was done under the guidance of an Austrian physician, C. A. Bernard, who is looked upon as the founder of modern medicine in Turkey (Şehsuvaroğlu, 1984, pp. 203–205).

Thus, both science and art remained distant from the changing conditions, while the West after the Renaissance embarked on the path of scientific inquiry, even trying to prove the existence of God through logic, as in the case of Descartes. Öztürk sees the present-day dominance of Western science in Turkey not only in terms of Western domination but emphasizes the fact that the Islamic-Ottoman tradition is not compatible with contemporary science (personal communication).

In spite of the widespread propagation of Western conceptions of human behavior and mental health through educational institutions and the popular media in Turkey, a relatively recent study (Savaşir, 1969) shows that a stark contrast still exists between Western and Turkish views of mental illness. Savaşir compared the attitudes of people in rural villages and urban settings with regard to their perceptions of mental illness based on the symptomatic conception of current Western psychiatry and found that many "psychiatric entities" were not recognized by either group. One interpretation of these findings would be that the study demonstrates the persistence of traditional cultural norms in Turkish society despite manifest urbanization, an increase in the level of education, and closer ties with Western society. Therefore, modernization may not have the destructive effect on tradition which is often assumed. Such findings suggest new possibilities for the future.

TOWARD A NEW PSYCHOLOGY

There are many psychologists throughout the world who are striving to arrive at a new synthesis in the study and understanding of human thought and behavior. This synthesis is being sought outside of the dominant Western paradigms but is still very much dependent on Western culture and intellectual traditions. No personality theory, for example, can ignore the significance of Judeo-Christian thought. But, for personality theory to claim universality, it must also take into account, for example, Taoism, the Aztec-Mayan culture, Buddhism, Marxism, and Islamic thought. Furthermore, no understanding of humankind can be developed through an exchange of ideas only by Westernized scholarly elites in various countries separated from their respective societies and cultures. If we are to consider the human condition in its universality, we cannot overlook cultural diversity. It is through an understanding of the heterogenity of our species that we can derive a sense of our uniqueness.

A universal model of psychology and accompanying new paradigms will not exclude Western perspectives, as the thrust of this chapter may have unintentionally suggested. Intellectual traditions and practice cast aside in the West in favor of positivism, however, need to be reevaluated. At the same time, we also must be aware of and avoid romanticized emotional attachments with the Third World which are sometimes perpetuated by both Third World and Western scholars.

The new psychology should not be expected to forge a mechanical synthesis of current Western psychology and Third World culture. Rather, devoid of all ethnocentricism and bias toward contemporary trends, we need to be able to distinguish the particular aspects of people in their changing historical contexts while trying to gain understanding in the light of universal principles. The aim of this effort should not be to control and predict behavior but rather to enhance human potential by promoting diversity.

An independent scientific field, especially in the social sciences, is similar to an independent person or an independent country. In a Third World country like Turkey, psychology, to be independent, should be in a position to define its own problem areas, both in the light of overall developments in the field and with respect to its particular historical and cultural circumstances.

Psychological research in Turkey, for instance, has not been concerned with the lives of the Turkish masses. In a country where over half the people are peasants and workers, the only significant studies of these groups have been done by Kağitçibaşi (1981), Vassaf (1983), Gitmez (1979), and many years ago Sherif (1948). Muzafer Sherif, one of the founders of social psychology, has been in the United States for the past forty years. Like Tunç in Istanbul, Sherif founded psychology as an independent academic discipline at Ankara University in 1937. He was forced to leave Turkey in 1945, after being imprisoned and spending a short time in solitary confinement. Though he was not charged with anything, the authorities of the one-party regime in power at the time were not pleased with his research. His classical text, *Outline of social psychology*, was mostly based on his research in Turkey.

It is not only for political reasons that faculty and students are still discouraged and prevented from carrying out research in factories and villages on workers and peasants. Class prejudices and elitism also inhibit "bourgeois" university scholars from "getting their feet dirty" by going to the people. In fact it is only recently in India, one of the few neutral and democratic Third World countries, where peasants have been studied systematically. A promising development is the expected publication of a book on rural psychology in which peasants are dealt with as persons in their own right and relative to their own needs, rather than within the context of a deficiency model wherein they are compared with Westernized urban residents (Sinha, 1984).

Another important trend emanating from the Third World is the establishment of a field of psychology concerned with the effects of a country's policies for economic development on the individual, the family, and the community. Both the theory and the practice of psychology are influenced by internal as well as external factors (Licuanan, 1984). The social sciences, as a function of their socioeconomic, political, and cultural environments, have the potential to develop in many directions. At the core of this potentiality is the interactive and dialectical relationship between society and science and between theory and practice. The specific characteristics of a society cannot only lead to new paradigms and research methodologies but also contribute to the universal understanding of humanity.

Third World social scientists have little to offer science by merely replicating research carried out in the West. Scientific progress requires originality, and originality is a function of researchers conducting studies generated by their own contexts. Blindly imported concepts, assumptions, theories, and findings are detrimental to the development of psychology as is the search for a solely Islamic or a Third World psychology (Kutup, 1984). Any ethnocentric approach makes difficult the search for universal principles of behavior.

We are, however, as a result of Western-capitalistic-cultural imperialism, face-to-face with either an eradication of other cultures or chauvinistic reactions on the part of Third World countries to Western domination. Both alternatives impede the development of science and culture. Psychologists have unwittingly become politicized to such a degree that their familiarity with international scientific literature is more a function of their governments' foreign policies than the interests of science. The relationships between psychologists in the United States and the Soviet Union and their knowledge of each other's work serve as prime examples.

The trend toward the Westernization of psychology inevitably promotes the standardization of humankind throughout the world. Of all the sciences, psychology, founded on the importance and the value of individual differences, has a key role to play in countering this dangerous trend. It can best be achieved through an awareness of the heterogeneity of the human species and cultures in combination with an eradication of the ethnocentricism prevailing in Western psychology.

NOTES

This article is an extended version of a paper presented at the symposium entitled "International Perspectives" at the 92nd Annual Convention of the American Psychological Association, Toronto, Canada, August 24–28, 1984. I am very grateful to the following persons for their comments and help with respect to the preparation of this article: Zuhal Baltas, Resit Canbeyli, Albert Gilgen, Carol Gilgen, Huricihan İslamoğlu-Inan, Orhan Öztürk, Harun Turgan, Perin Uçman, and William Woodward.

1. The Higher Council of Education, set up after the military intervention of 1980, controls academic life in all the universities with everyone being subject to the same set of regulations ranging from a dress code for students and faculty banning trousers for women and beards for men to the determination of what courses should be taught. Not only have many academicians resigned in protest of the new university law but the universities are also no longer able to attract new staff. In the meantime the student quotas have been increased on average 25 percent at all universities resulting in a very unfavorable student/teacher ratio and a decline in the quality of education. The reader should consider the present situation in light of the recent crisis in Turkish higher education.

2. The addresses of the two associations and journals are: Psikologlar Derneği, P.K. 117, Küçükesat, Ankara; Türk Psikoloji Derneği, P.K. 407, Aksaray, İstanbul.

3. At one point I wrote a personal letter to David Wechsler requesting him to do all in his power to curtail the misuse of his tests in Turkey. I received no reply but rather a reaction from the Psychological Corporation in New York asking for information on tests being used in Turkey as copyright laws were apparently being disregarded. There was no indication in the response that this deplorable situation would be rectified. In the six years since nothing has been done.

REFERENCES

Ari, O. (in press). History of sociology in Turkey. In A. Emmanuel (Ed.), *Sociology in the Balkan States*.

Arkun, N. (1984). Psychology, psychiatry, and clinical psychology. *Journal of Pedagogy* (Istanbul University Publications), 65–69.

Black, C. E. (1967). *The dynamics of modernization*. New York: Norton.

Çağlar, D. (1977). Problems in diagnosing mentally retarded children in the educational system. *Ankara University Faculty of Education Journal, 9*, 446–464 (in Turkish).

Canitez, E., & Toğrol, B. (1983). Findings about some tests used in Turkey. In N. Bilgin (Ed.), *Proceedings of the First National Congress of Psychology*. İzmir: Aegean University Faculty of Literature Publications (No. 1987) (in Turkish).

Drenth, P. (1975). Psychological tests for developing countries: Rationale and objectives. *Nederlands Tijdscrift voor de Psychologie, 30,* 5–22.

Eisenstadt, S. N. (1966). *Modernization, protest, and change.* Englewood Cliffs, NJ: Prentice-Hall.

Gitmez, A. (1979). *The story of migration.* Ankara: MAYA (in Turkish).

Hasan, A. (1923). *Psychology.* Istanbul: Muallim Ahmet Halit Publications (in Turkish).

Islamoglu. H. (1983). Ottoman history and the world-system: An evaluation. *Society and Science, 23.*

Kağitçibaşi, C. (1981). *Values of children: Values and fertility in Turkey.* Istanbul: Boğaziçi University Press.

Kinross, L. (1965). *Atatürk.* New York: Morrow.

Koopmans, R. (1978). *The limits of modernization: Turkey.* Unpublished manuscript, University of Amsterdam.

Kutup, M. (1984). *Psychology according to Islam.* Istanbul: Hicret Publications (in Turkish).

LeCompte, A. (1980). Some recent trends in Turkish psychology. *American Psychologist, 8,* 745–749.

Lerner, D. (1964). *The passing of traditional society: Modernizing the Middle East.* New York: Glencoe.

Lewis, G. (1965). *Turkey.* London: Ernst Benn.

Licuanan, P. (1984). [Interview with F. Culbertson]. *International Psychologist* (Quarterly publication of the International Council of Psychologists), *35* (3).

McClelland, D. (1967). *The achieving society.* New York: Glencoe.

McKinney, F. (1960). Psychology in Turkey: Speculation concerning psychology's growth and area culture. *American Psychologist, 15,* 717–723.

Morgan, C. T. (1981). *Introduction to psychology.* Ankara: Hacettepe University (in Turkish).

Morse, C. (Ed.). (1969). *Modernization by design.* Ithaca: Cornell University Press.

Öner, N., & Özge, S. (1983). Psychological tests used in Turkey. In N. Bilgin (Ed.), *Proceedings of the First National Congress of Psychology.* Izmir: Aegean University Faculty of Literature Publications (No. 1987) (in Turkish).

Orhan, G. (1974). *A bibliography of Istanbul University Faculty of Literature publications.* Istanbul: Istanbul University Faculty of Literature Publications (No. 1987) (in Turkish).

Öztürk, O. (1964). Folk treatment of mental illness in Turkey. In A. Kiev (Ed.), *Magic, faith, and healing: Studies in primitive psychiatry today.* New York: Free Press.

Öztürk, O., & Volkan, V. (1971). The theory and practice of psychiatry in Turkey. *American Journal of Psychotherapy, 15,* 240–271.

Sarp, H. S. (1932). *Psychology.* Istanbul: Ikbal (in Turkish).

Savaşir, Y. (1969). *Attitudes and beliefs toward mental illness and the mentally ill.* Unpublished manuscript, Hacettepe University Medical School, Ankara (in Turkish).

Şehsuvaroğlu, B. (1984). *History of Turkish medicine.* Bursa: Tas Yayincilik (in Turkish).

Sertel, Y. (1969). *Progressive movements in Turkey.* Ankara: Ant Publications (in Turkish).

Sherif, M. (1948). *Outline of social psychology.* New York: Harper.

Sinha, D. (1984, September). Psychology in rural areas: The case of a developing country. *Invited address.* Presented at the XXIII International Congress of Psychology, Acapulco, Mexico.

Toğrol, B. (1972). Department of Psychology and the Institute of Experimental Psychology, 1937–1972. *Works of Experimental Psychology Supplement*, *3*, 1–7 (in Turkish).

Toğrol, B. (1983). Development of psychology in Turkey. In N. Bilgin (Ed.), *Proceedings of the First National Congress of Psychology*. Izmir: Aegean University Faculty of Literature Publications (No. 1983) (in Turkish).

Tunç, M. S. (1948). *Introduction to psychology*. Istanbul: Istanbul University Faculty of Literature Publications (in Turkish).

Turner, B. (1979). Marx and the end of Orientalism. In Talad Asad (Ed.), *Anthropology and the colonial encounter*. London: Humanities.

Ünver, S. (Undated). *Onocak Mental Health House*. Istanbul: Chair of the History of Medicine, Cerrahpaşa Medical Faculty (in Turkish).

Usman, M. O. (1947). *Psychiatrica*. Istanbul: Kader (in Turkish).

Vassaf, G. (1982). Mental massacre: The use of psychological tests in the Third World. *School Psychology International*, *2*, 43–48.

Vassaf, G. (1983). Psychology from yesterday to tomorrow. In N. Bilgin (Ed.), *Proceedings of the First National Congress of Psychology*. Izmir: Aegean University Faculty of Literature Publications (No. 1987) (in Turkish).

Vassaf, G. (1985). *Wir haben unsere Stimme noch nicht laut gemacht. Turkische Arbeitskinder in Europa* [We have as yet not raised our voices. Turkish worker's children]. Felsberg: Res Publicae (originally published in Turkish in 1983).

Wallerstein, I. (1976). *The modern world system*. New York: Academic Press.

Yavuzer, H. (1984). Intelligence, personality, and environmental traits of Turkish juvenile delinquents. *Journal of Pedagogy*, *2*.

United Kingdom

Ian J. Donald and David Canter

INTRODUCTION

Psychology in the United Kingdom has evolved as a result of a complex interplay among political, social, and economic factors in conjunction with the efforts of outstanding individuals. Fashion and attitude have also played their part. In our account we focus on the sociopolitical and economic influences that have made British psychology what it is today. We do, of course, mention people who have played a role in giving psychology in the United Kingdom its distinct character but do not emphasize their contributions. When considering more contemporary aspects of the discipline, we look at factors such as government policy, the relevance of training, and the growing professionalism of the field. We have chosen this course because we believe that what gives a country's psychology its national character, in a time when international communication is so well developed, is its unique sociopolitical context. The work of major internationally known figures is already well documented. What is not readily available to an international audience is information about the discipline as it is taught, practiced, and experienced by psychologists in the United Kingdom.

Before reviewing the early history of the discipline and its current developments, we should briefly mention a few of the British scientists and psychologists who have achieved international status in psychology. Among the better known are P. L. Broadhurst for psychogenetic studies of emotional reactivity in animals; J. Bowlby, M. Rutter, and A. M. and A. D. B. Clarke who have done considerable research on the effects of environmental and maternal deprivation on children; R. D. Laing for his work on schizophrenia and the family; R. L. Gregory for his writings on perceptual organization and his theory of constancy scaling; Judith Greene for her investigations of language and cognition; and R. A. Fisher for his contributions to statistics, especially the development of analysis of variance. The work of H. Eysenck, D. Broadbent, M. Argyle, D. Shapiro, and a handful of others is so influential in current British psychology that we shall say more about their contributions later.

The United Kingdom provided the philosophical roots for empirical psychology. The great traditions established by empiricist and associationist philosophers such as Bacon, Locke, Berkeley, Mill, Hume, Reid, and Bain led the French psychologist Ribot to remark, in 1870, that it was Britain "which has done most for psychology" (Misiak & Sexton, 1966). Edwin G. Boring, the notable American historian of psychology, credited British empiricism and associationism with furnishing "a full half of the preparation for experimental psychology" (Boring, 1950, p. 462). Indeed the acknowledged founder of modern psychology, Wilhelm Wundt, derived many of his ideas from British works (Hearnshaw, 1979), although he has had less direct reciprocal influence on British psychology.

In the stimulating intellectual climate which existed in Britain at the turn of the twentieth century, one would expect scientific psychology to have flourished. Unfortunately, while British psychologists did take up the challenge of the new science, progress in the first decades of the twentieth century was not as rapid as might have been predicted. In the main this can be traced to a reluctance within the British academic community to embrace new approaches and ideas.

During the latter half of the nineteenth century, British universities were still few in number and conservative in outlook. New civic universities had been established, but they were overshadowed by the traditions of the much older institutions. Indeed, at the beginning of the nineteenth century, England had but two universities, Oxford and Cambridge; in Scotland there were only four. Because of the reluctance of Oxford and Cambridge to accept "the new," it was not until the mid- to late 1800s that the natural sciences were incorporated into the university system and scientific laboratories established. Britain had achieved fundamental and revolutionary discoveries in the natural sciences for a number of centuries; however, these were often made by individuals working independently of academic institutions. Initial progress in psychology followed a similar pattern.

This feature of British science, the virtual independence of eminent scientists from the constraints of academic institutions, played an essential role in shaping the unique character of psychology in the United Kingdom. By way of contrast, in Germany and the United States science was institutionalized creating the conditions for schools to emerge. The fact that British scientists were free to pursue their own personal and sometimes idiosyncratic interests gave psychology in the United Kingdom its own, often eccentric, stamp.

EARLY HISTORY

The evolutionary theories proposed by Charles Darwin and others had a direct and lasting influence on British psychology. They eventually led to the establishment in the United Kingdom of one of the major streams of psychological research, namely comparative psychology. Darwin's *The descent of man* (1871), in particular, provided an intellectual justification for comparative psychology. In this landmark publication, Darwin argued that the intellectual powers of man and animals varied by degree rather than kind and were located on a continuum, with man and other vertebrates being fundamentally similar.

In the late nineteenth century, G. J. Romanes, a Darwinian, published *Animal intelligence* (Romanes, 1883) which discussed work based to some degree on experimental techniques. More important, the book provided a useful conceptual framework within which comparative psychology could grow. Romanes was directly followed by C. Lloyd Morgan and L. T. Hobhouse, both of whom made significant contributions to comparative psychology. Morgan was well received in the United States although his associationist ideas were out of fashion in the United Kingdom and the vigor of British comparative psychology was short-lived. As domination of the field moved to the Soviet Union and the United States, interest in the United Kingdom waned. Morgan and Hobhouse represented the last important comparative psychologists in Britain until well after World War II.

Herbert Spencer borrowed from Darwin, though he contributed to evolutionary theory as well. Spencer hypothesized that it would be possible to understand the mind by showing how it evolved. He was essentially a philosopher but did have an influence on other psychological pioneers. A course taught by William James at Harvard became known as the "Spencer elective" due to James' reliance on Spencer's "synthetic philosophy."

Darwin's contributions to social psychology were also strong but less often recognized perhaps because they were rather indirect. Wundt's much neglected *Volkpsychologie* [Folk psychology] demonstrates Darwin's influence on the German psychologist. Additionally, George Herbert Mead considered Darwin's work to be the most important contribution to the psychology of his day (Farr, 1983a). Darwin's impact on psychology, however, was manifested primarily through the work of his cousin, Sir Francis Galton, and his successors who formed what eventually became one of the most consequential and distinct schools of psychology in the United Kingdom.

Francis Galton and the London School

From Darwin's theories, Sir Francis Galton developed his conception of eugenics with the aim of improving the general quality of the population. In order to support his position, Galton conducted one of the first genealogical studies, which involved tracing the family trees of prominent families.

Galton furthermore attempted to measure variations within populations, thereby taking British psychology in a direction different from Wundt's. In 1884, Galton set up an anthropometric laboratory to conduct measurements of the physical and mental characteristics of a vast number of people. In all, he subjected some 9,337 paying customers to his measurements. In this way the field of individual differences was established, and the statistical techniques he developed for the analysis of his data represent the genesis of psychometrics.

In 1886, Galton published a paper on regression, followed by another in 1888 that led to the concept of correlation. In 1892 it was renamed the coefficient of correlation by F. Y. Edgeworth. K. Pearson, one of Galton's students, went on to provide the mathematical foundation for this coefficient, which has become one of the most important statistical tools in all fields of science.

In 1897, one of the first psychological laboratories in the United Kingdom was founded at University College in London by J. Sully using some funds provided by Galton. Sully is recognized mostly as a textbook writer and for his early work on educational and child psychology (see, for example, Sully, 1895). His work helped establish two important and ongoing fields of British psychology.

In 1906, Charles Spearman assumed leadership of the London laboratory and the "London school" was born. Spearman's main interests were intelligence and its measurement. While in Germany, and immediately prior to his return to the United Kingdom, Spearman published what Hearnshaw (1964) described as an epoch-making article. Entitled "General intelligence objectively determined and measured" (Spearman, 1904), the article concerned Spearman's famous two-factor theory of intelligence which generated a new approach to mental testing. Spearman's work contributed, as well, to the development of factor analysis, though factorial concepts were clearly evident in the work of Karl Pearson who had held the chair in eugenics in London. Spearman also developed other important statistics such as Rho. Misiak and Sexton call him "one of the greatest figures in the history of psychology" (Misiak & Sexton, 1966, p. 228).

Cyril Burt succeeded Spearman to the chair at University College in 1931. While at Liverpool University, Burt had already published articles and conducted research on intelligence, and over the years he developed numerous IQ and scholastic tests. Some of these were employed by Yerkes in the United States. Additionally, he revised such tests as the Binet-Simon scale and, with G. H. Thomson (Thomson, 1939), made contributions to factor analysis (Burt, 1940). Burt was perhaps the last British pioneer in this area. The initiative then went to Thurston in Chicago. Burt further achieved distinction as Britain's first full-time applied psychologist when he was appointed to the position of psychologist by the London County Council.

In recent years Burt's theory of mental abilities and his establishment of an educational psychology service, for which he was knighted, have been over-shadowed by charges of fraud relative to some of his empirical research. Although reprehensible, this unfortunate shortcoming in his work does not negate his other contributions. The psychometric tradition remains strong in British psychology.

Applied Psychology and the Cambridge School

In 1877, W. H. Rivers unsuccessfully attempted to establish a psychology laboratory at Cambridge. At that time the university senate described psychology as an "insult [to] religion by putting the human soul on a pair of scales" (Hearnshaw, 1964). In 1897, however, Rivers achieved success. During World War I, he worked for the British Army helping treat war neuroses.

In 1912, the directorship of the Cambridge laboratory went to C. S. Myers. Myers was also appointed psychological consultant to the British armies in France. His major concern was the phenomenon then known as "shell shock." Interest in clinical psychology was developing rapidly in the United Kingdom, and in 1914 a hospital for the treatment of war neuroses was established at Maghull. The hospital had a significant impact on psychology in the United Kingdom primarily due to the work of a number of prominent psychologists who received their grounding in psychotherapy there. Included were W. H. Rivers, William McDougall, and William Brown.

The context in which British clinical psychology developed is perhaps one reason why psychoanalytic theories failed to have much impact on British psychology. The war-induced psychopathologies challenged comprehensive theories, including Freud's. To this day, psychoanalysis has not had much influence on British psychology though the orientation has affected the course of other social sciences in the United Kingdom.

At the same time that these developments in clinical psychology were taking place, progress was being made in industrial psychology. The first incursions of psychologists into industry resulted from the government's concern over the productivity of munitions workers. In 1915, the Health of Munitions Workers' Committee was established to consider fatigue relative to hours worked. The wide-ranging issues which this committee considered included hours of work and productivity, fatigue, environmental issues such as ventilation and lighting in factories, and industrial accidents and other factors relating to health and well-being. The field investigations that resulted are among the most important pioneering studies of workers in an industrial context conducted in the United Kingdom. While the Fatigue Research Board had been established in 1914 and in 1928 became the broader Industrial Health Research Board, the work done in the munitions industry resulted in the establishment of the influental National Institute of Industrial Psychology (NIIP) in 1921.

Following C. S. Myers' departure from Cambridge to assume the directorship of the NIIP, F. C. Bartlett took up the chair there. Bartlett has had an enormous impact on psychology. Two of his cognitively oriented books, *Remembering* (1932) and *Thinking* (1958), are still widely read by students. Moreover, an extremely important role was played by Bartlett in promoting an applied psychology relevant to everyday issues. For a relatively short time he was director of the Cambridge Medical Research Council Applied Psychology Unit, where Kenneth Craik and Donald Broadbent both worked. Bartlett's approach to psychology was exemplified in his 1951 presidential address to the British Psychological Society when he stated that "the old puppet subjects of the early German psychologists have had their time . . . and they can be put away in their boxes. In their places we will have real people." Bartlett also had a distrust of quantification and statistics, which he considered "scientific make-shifts" (Hearnshaw, 1964). This attitude clearly revealed the divergent interests of London and Cambridge. As Eysenck and Broadbent both note, the two schools had a rivalry that hindered the cross-fertilization of ideas. The complementary nature of their divergence was not recognized (Broadbent, 1980; Eysenck, 1980).

Thus, by the end of World War II, there were two major departments of psychology in Britain. It is impossible to know fully the role played by Bartlett and others as external examiners or referees for the appointment of British professors. However, for a number of years before and after World War II, it was rather unusual for any British professor not to have studied with the heads of one or the other of these departments. Indeed, in 1960, two-thirds of the chairs in British universities were held by Bartlett's former students.

Early Psychology in English Universities Other Than Cambridge and London

While psychology at Cambridge got off to a strong start with the work of Myers and Bartlett, psychology at Oxford began slowly. Some would say that, with the exception of the social psychology of M. Argyle and his colleagues, Oxford has yet to make its mark on British psychology. In the early days there seemed an almost hostile reaction to the "new science" by this most traditional of universities. William McDougall arrived at Oxford in 1904 to lecture in psychology, but he was not allowed to conduct experiments. He did, however, manage to perform experimental studies in a private laboratory. Dissatisfied with the attitude toward psychology in the United Kingdom, he left for the United States. In 1936, an Institute of Experimental Psychology was established, partially due to the efforts of William Brown, a clinical psychologist. It was not until 1947 that a chair, first held by George Humphrey, was created.

Outside Cambridge it was probably the University of Manchester which took the lead in recognizing psychology as a discipline in its own right. The chair in psychology, initiated in 1919 and originally held by T. H. Pear, was the first "real chair" in psychology in the United Kingdom though there was a chair in "mind and logic" at University College in London. Starting in 1913, Manchester offered a full undergraduate honors degree in psychology. Three years earlier, a diploma in the psychology of medicine had been introduced there. The principle orientation of psychology at Manchester, which lacked the constraints imposed by centuries of tradition, was the "social psychology of everyday life."

By British standards, the University of Reading developed an interest in psychology quite rapidly. In 1910 a laboratory, which quickly became one of the finest in the country, was established; by 1920, the university possessed an independent department of psychology. A chair, first held by A. W. P. Wolters, was instituted in 1943.

Scottish Universities and Psychology

Whereas psychology slowly and modestly gained acceptance in other English universities—for example, Liverpool—in Scotland, away from the domination of Cambridge and the inhibiting influence of Oxford, psychology experienced its most rapid progress within the walls of academia. The University of Edinburgh was only nine years behind London and Cambridge in establishing a psychological laboratory. Under the directorship of D. G. Smith, the facility grew quickly to a position overshadowed only by the Cambridge laboratory. Smith, who had studied philosophy at Edinburgh, had worked at Leipzig and in the United States. A year after Smith's death in 1918, James Drever, Sr., headed the laboratory and the directorship became a chair in psychology. Among Drever's accomplishments was a particularly well-received textbook *The psychology of everyday life* (Drever, 1921). His son, James Drever, Jr., succeeded to the chair in 1944.

As was the case at other British universities, the psychology program at Edinburgh presented good and extensive coverage of experimental work and theory. However, a balance was also struck with the practical applications of psychology. Such a mixture made Edinburgh an attractive institution in which to conduct psychological work. The establishment of Moray House Training College in 1912, famous as the home of the Moray House School Tests, with a laboratory of experimental education, turned the city into one of the main centers of psychology in the country (Hearnshaw, 1964).

Even though the University of Aberdeen had established a lectureship in comparative psychology in the department of moral philosophy as early as 1896 (first held by G. F. Stout), it did not institute a chair until 1946. The main areas of psychological work at Aberdeen were sensation, memory, and association. In addition, child and abnormal psychology were taught. Despite having a lectureship in the discipline in 1907, Glasgow University did not establish a psychology chair until 1955. It is surprising that a chair was not forthcoming earlier, since Glasgow employed a number of prominent psychologists, including cognitive psychologist H. J. Waft, "one of our most eminent academic psychologists of the first part of the century" (Hearnshaw, 1964, p. 178).

THE BRITISH PSYCHOLOGICAL SOCIETY

The British Psychological Society (BPS) was founded October 24, 1901, during a meeting held appropriately at University College in London. Among the ten participants were Sully, Rivers, and McDougall. The society was formed in order to provide a forum for the discussion of both psychological research and professional aspects of the emerging discipline. By 1905 the society had admitted as honorary fellows William James, Wundt, Ribot, and other non-British psychologists. Its founding marked the recognition of psychology as a distinct discipline rather than as a branch of moral or empirical philosophy.

Increases in membership were initially small. By 1918 there were fewer than 100 members and the society faced financial difficulties. Partly to raise funds, it was decided in 1919 to open the society to any member of the public who had an interest in psychology. Fueled by the work of psychologists during World

War I and a strong general interest in psychology, the society subsequently flourished.

In 1941, the BPS was incorporated and took the first steps toward accepting professional responsibility for its practicing members. By 1958, all new members had to have a professional qualification, usually a university degree, in psychology. The society, however, still allowed nonpsychologists to belong as "subscribers," these usually being undergraduate psychology students. This policy has promoted the injection of new blood into the BPS.

The society won formal recognition as the official British organization of psychologists when it was incorporated by Royal Charter in 1965, giving it the right to carry out regulatory and disciplinary functions. Shortly thereafter, the BPS started lobbying for legislation to establish a registration process for psychologists. This goal has not yet been achieved although, in 1985, the appropriate legislation was set in motion and registration will be required in the near future. This being so, it is worth briefly discussing the form such registration will probably take.

In a departure from typical professional regulation in Britain, the registration procedures will be administered by the BPS itself. Registration will not require membership in the society; however, individuals wishing to represent themselves as psychologists will need to register. Those registered will be given the title of "chartered psychologist" and be subject to the codes of practice and disciplinary action of a council consisting of a committee of psychologists empowered to decide on eligibility for membership and a body, constituted of psychologists and nonpsychologists, which will enforce the codes of practice and take any necessary disciplinary action.

Eligibility will require both professional training and some formal qualification as well as approximately three years of extensive practical experience. Clients will most likely be able to request information regarding a practitioner's skills, qualifications, and affiliations. It has also been proposed that titles such as "psychiatrist," "parapsychologist," "psychotherapist," "psychoanalyst," and so forth be used without registration.

During the 1980s, 400 to 500 new members joined the BPS. Total membership in 1983 was 9,368 (10,838 if subscribers and foreign affiliates are included).

The BPS is made up of the following divisions (membership in parentheses): clinical psychology (1,341), educational and child psychology (662), occupational psychology (294), criminological and legal psychology (167), and the Scottish Division of Educational and Child Psychology (101). In addition, there are ten sections concerned with occupational psychology (598), education (545), social psychology (484), medical psychology (273), counseling (237), cognitive psychology (217), mathematics and statistics (208), history and philosophy (92), and psychobiology (72). The latter two are the newest sections.

The BPS publishes the *British Journal of Psychology*, the *British Journal of Medical Psychology*, the *British Journal of Social Psychology*, the *British Journal of Clinical Psychology*, the *British Journal of Mathematical and Statistical*

Psychology, the *Journal of Occupational Psychology,* and the *British Journal of Developmental Psychology.* The *British Journal of Educational Psychology* is under separate ownership.

Furthermore, the society commissions and publishes books on topics related to the field. Practicing professional psychologists have recently become more involved as educators, helping others to carry out work previously performed by psychologists. Reflecting this trend, the BPS published a number of successful books on psychology specifically tailored for other professional groups including managers, teachers, social workers, nurses, speech therapists, career counselors, physiotherapists, occupational therapists, and medical practitioners. Also published have been books on statistics and social policy in relation to child development. A series of volumes entitled *Psychology Survey* provides reviews of various areas within psychology. The series is probably of greatest value to undergraduates (see, for example, Foss, 1978). Finally, the BPS maintains a large library and archives of psychology at the University of Liverpool.

FINANCING PSYCHOLOGICAL RESEARCH

Research in the United Kingdom is financed by public and private sources. At the present time more reductions are being made in the allocation of public funds to research than is the case with private donations. Additionally, collaborative projects, financed by both the government and private contributors, are being encouraged. The principal public financing bodies most relevant to psychology are the University Grants Committee (UGC) and the government research councils, which include the Medical Research Council (MRC), the Economic and Social Research Council (ESRC), and the Science and Engineering Research Council (SERC). Moreover, Local Education Authorities (LEAs) provide money for polytechnics, and other regional agencies offer funds for educational purposes such as graduate training in clinical psychology.

University Grants Committee (UGC)

The UGC is an independent body responsible for allocating monies to universities. All British universities are supported primarily by public funds, and it is the UGC that distributes these funds nationally. Overall, the UGC makes the largest single contribution to universities, which in theory enjoy considerable freedom as to how they use these funds. However, there is an increasing trend for the government to specify areas in which research grants should be spent.

There are about forty British universities that offer psychology courses. Thirty or so degree programs are also offered by polytechnics, which are institutions of higher education funded by local authorities (such as a city council).

Medical Research Council (MRC)

The MRC has played a key role in the development of psychology, especially applied psychology. This council provides funds for individual research projects in many areas of psychology including nonclinical fields. In perhaps its most important function, the MRC finances a number of research facilities throughout the United Kingdom, especially applied psychology units. We have already mentioned the MRC Applied Psychology Unit at the University of Cambridge. Additionally, it finances the Applied Psychology Unit at Sussex; the Brain Metabolism Unit at the Royal Edinburgh Hospital; and the Social and Applied Psychology Unit, jointly funded with the Economic and Social Research Council at the University of Sheffield.

Economic and Social Research Council (ESRC)

The ESRC was originally named the Social Science Research Council (SSRC). The name change was a direct consequence of a Conservative minister of education being skeptical that there was a viable social science or that, if there was, it should be supported by the government. This change reflects the continuing pressures under which British social science has always existed. Recently, for example, there has been a severe reduction of the funds allocated to the council. Nevertheless, the council is still extremely important to psychological research. A study by Haggard and Shackel in 1978, while the ESRC was still the SSRC, indicated that the principal areas of psychology financed by the council were educational, developmental, social, experimental, personality, and occupational. Methodological research was also well funded.

Science and Engineering Research Council (SERC)

Although SERC provides less support for psychological research than the MRC and ESRC, its contributions are still significant. The principal areas financed (Haggard & Shackel, 1978) have been comparative and physiological psychology, methodology, and experimental/cognitive psychology.

FINANCING TRAINING IN PSYCHOLOGY

All individuals admitted to an undergraduate program have a statutory right to a grant, subject to a means test, to cover tuition, fees, and living expenses for three years. Undergraduate grants are provided by the local education authorities. Grants for graduate students in psychology are usually provided by the research councils; these awards are not statutory, and the decision whether or not to make them depends upon the judged value of the course of study or research proposed. At present, there is a severe reduction in support for graduate training in psychology.

TRAINING PROGRAMS

Undergraduate Training

Psychology may be read as a first degree at about seventy institutions throughout the United Kingdom. Most such degrees are offered by universities, though not always by psychology departments. First degrees are also offered by the polytechnics that were established in the 1960s as alternatives to universities in order to provide more applied courses. While polytechnics have to some extent fulfilled their mission, their single honors programs in psychology show a striking similarity to those found in the universities. The awarding of degrees by polytechnics is under the auspices of the Council for National Academic Awards (CNAA), and the degrees which they award are, at least theoretically, given equal status to those of the universities.

A third means of obtaining a first degree in psychology is through the Open University, which is a "university of the air." Students study by correspondence, observe television lectures, and frequently attend summer school courses offered by university departments.

A survey of examination questions set by British university departments of psychology in 1975 gives some indication of the areas emphasized in the teaching of undergraduate psychology in the United Kingdom (Lowe, et al., 1977). Table 1 provides a summary of the findings.

Clearly, the emphasis has been on traditional areas of psychology such as learning, motivation, perception, and physiology rather than the applied fields. These findings are supported by those of Vine (1977). A content analysis of the examination questions performed by Lowe and his colleagues indicated that the American *Psychological Abstracts* classification categories were inappropriate for the analysis of British psychology, suggesting that while common material may be studied on both sides of the Atlantic, the way in which it is presented and grouped may be somewhat different.

Graduate Education and Training

First degrees in psychology provide graduates with extensive knowledge of the discipline useful in many areas of work; nevertheless, before entering the profession in the majority of its principal fields, it is necessary, or at least helpful, to undertake further graduate study. In 1982, of the psychology graduates whose "first destinations" after graduating were known to have been research and further academic study, the percentages were 12 percent for university graduates and 10 percent for those graduating from polytechnics. Of course, others reenter academia after a period of work (or unemployment).

Graduate courses vary in the extent to which they are vocational. Individuals studying educational psychology are likely to work in schools or education in

Table 1
Topic Areas of British University Examinations in Psychology

Category	% of all categories	Largest sub-divisions of category	% of category
Biological	23.5	Physiology/psychophysiology	22.8
		Learning	19.2
		Animal behaviour/comparative	17.9
		Perception	9.4
Developmental	18.5	Child development	27.7
		Language	22.7
		Personality	17.2
		Thinking/learning	15.7
Experimental	16.6	Perception	29.2
		Memory	14.2
		Learning	13.8
		Information processing	8.8
Social	13.1	Social processes	30.9
		Groups	25.3
		Learning	13.8
		Information processing	9.9
Applied	10.7	Abnormal/clinical	38.9
		Assessment	23.6
		Occupational	23.6
		Educational	13.1
Method	9.7	Statistics	45.3
		Experimental methodology	27.0
		Mathematical psychology	10.5
		Analysis of behaviour	10.2
General	7.9	Theoretical, conceptual	48.7
		Historical	21.6
		Philosophical	17.7

Source: Based on Lowe et al., 1977.

some capacity, while those taking, for example, environmental psychology may follow a more diverse career path. Graduate education leading to an M.A. or M.Sc. usually involves taking courses and completing a short dissertation. The degrees of M.Phil. and Ph.D. are earned by conducting research. Let us briefly consider the necessary routes for entry into the areas of clinical, educational, and occupational psychology.

Clinical Psychology

To become a clinical psychologist requires taking a two- or three-year master's degree program in the subject. Students train in the field and take required courses. This is then followed by a probationary period of supervised work as a clinical psychologist. An alternative route, developed initially in response to a shortage of clinical psychologists, is two or three years of supervised in-service training and the BPS diploma in clinical psychology.

A Ph.D. or M.Phil., which requires research in a clinical area, does not exempt the holder from the requirement of the M.Sc. diploma. It may, however, be helpful in obtaining desirable employment in what is a very competitive marketplace.

Educational Psychology

To be admitted to a master's program in educational psychology, an individual is usually required to have at least two years experience working with children. Generally, experience means teaching, and to teach one must obtain a Post Graduate Certificate of Education (PGCE). To earn this certificate takes about one year. It is becoming increasingly difficult for students who hope to become educational psychologists to be admitted to the PGCE program, because colleges offering such courses are actively being discouraged by the present government from enrolling social science graduates.

Occupational Psychology

Occupational psychology is less formalized than other applied fields in psychology. Professional training may be achieved either through a graduate program—for example, the M.Sc. program in occupational psychology offered by Queens University in Belfast—or by a specially adapted first degree program. Occupational psychologists are also expected to have three years of relevant and varied experience. However, five years of similar experience may be accepted. About eleven universities now offer programs for individuals who want to work as occupational psychologists.

A number of other career opportunities are open to psychologists; however, there are no formal qualification standards. Graduate courses which may be useful include those having to do with psychotherapy; dyslexia; reading; mental retardation; research methods; and social, mathematical, environmental, experimental, and developmental psychology.

Degrees by Research

The British Ph.D. degree differs from the Ph.D. typically earned in the United States. Although a few courses, generally in research methods, may be required, the degree involves two or three years of supervised research in one specialized area. The investigations undertaken are usually in keeping with the interests of the particular department in which the degree is being taken. When the research is completed, the candidate submits a thesis which has to represent an "original contribution" to the particular field in which she or he has studied. The thesis is then examined by both an internal examiner (often the student's supervisor) and an external examiner who is a recognized expert in the field of study. Finally, the candidate is examined orally on the research.

POLITICS AND BRITISH PSYCHOLOGY

As in most other countries, the relationship between politics and psychology as both a discipline and a profession is manifested in a number of ways. The important issues seem to emerge over where the particular emphasis is placed in the relationship. In the United Kingdom, the government through the civil service is often the client for research. Therefore, the government has little direct influence on the epistemological base of the subject.

The most partisan use to which a political party has put psychological services is in marketing election campaigns. Ironically, it was the British Conservative party that, in 1959, first used an advertising company to change, promote, and improve the image of the party. The result probably contributed to a large shift in favor of the Conservatives, who won the election. It is perhaps a case of "chickens coming home to roost" that the Conservatives are presently seeking to introduce legislation to prevent the Labor Local Authorities from using advertising to promote their cause, and it is under the Conservative party that funding and support for the social sciences has been severely cut.

The government also acts as client in commissioning expert evidence or advice from psychologists. Psychologists are, of course, at liberty to refuse to provide research evidence to government departments. However, since much of the work is apolitical, in that it supports no party but is rather for the "common good," psychologists generally comply. Evidence has been given, for example, by the BPS in regard to the Mental Health Bill (1959), Training Centers for Handicapped School-Leavers (1962), and the administrative structure of the medical and related services (1968). The BPS also has representatives on a few parliamentary committees. In this context psychologists have acted as expert witnesses with regard to the effects of airport expansions in relation to noise and local resident well-being. One of the most recent contributions by psychologists has been to provide evidence to the Popplewell inquiry into crowd safety at soccer games.

There are, however, some worrisome asides to the question of so-called apolitical research. First, one can argue that the preservation of the status quo is itself a political act. Second, the legislation to which psychologists contribute may be used in oppressive ways; a good example of this was the Mental Health Act of 1959. Third, it is often difficult for the researcher to understand fully the political implications of his or her findings. In a country that has no Freedom of Information Act but does have an Official Secrets Act, it is possible for an investigator to lose control of what is or is not published. Fortunately, however, with an active free press there is little evidence that the worst-case possibilities inherent in this system ever actually occur. Indeed British television has a long record of making public research findings of general interest, often before they are published, and British psychologists seem to have ready access to newspapers, radio, and television.

Another way psychology can be used for political means is by providing scientific or at least pseudoscientific support for particular ideologies or policies. The closest British psychology has come to doing this was the study of eugenics. As was noted earlier, Galton started the eugenics movement and founded a chair in eugenics at University College. Since then some of the themes evident in Galton's writings on the subject have been apparent in the work of certain psychologists in the United Kingdom, the United States, and Germany. With a few notable exceptions (for example, Billig, 1982), however, psychologists tend to brush rather lighty over the subject.

Galton defined eugenics as "the study of agencies under social control which may improve or impair the *racial* [our emphasis] qualities of future generations either physically or mentally." That statement appears to be both racist and in support of a Fascist ideology. It has been argued, in the United Kingdom and the United States, that the eugenics movement in those countries remained detached from direct political involvement (Billig, 1982). This is certainly true when compared to Germany under National Socialism, where the German Eugenic Society's journal, *Archiv für Rassen—und Gesellschaftsbiologie* [Archive for Race- and Sociobiology], took a pro-Nazi stance. Billig argues that it is misleading, however, to suggest, as some have done, that Lorenz' use of Nazi terminology in defending a scientifically based policy to preserve racial purity was involved in the genesis of any political ideology. Quite simply, Billig contends, Lorenz found an orientation that was both powerful and receptive. The eugenics movement in the United States, though, was at least as instrumental in bringing about racist legislation as it was in Germany (see, for example, the account by Angela Davis, 1982). Nor should it be forgotten that the British psychologist McDougall (1931) was concerned about "a swamping of the white 'race' by the swarming multitudes of other races" (p. 23). Such sentiments may seem less than relevant to us today; nevertheless, Billig counters that aspects of eugenic theory are still present in contemporary British psychology. He cites as a prime example some of the thinking of Hans Eysenck.

A group established by the Professional Affairs Board of the BPS concerned with the abuse of psychology for political purposes recommended that members should take no part in the use of psychology to subordinate individual well-being to political belief; refuse to advise, train, and supply information to anyone wishing to use the information politically; report and draw attention to inappropriate uses of psychological expertise and information to the society; and refuse to take part in the diagnosis of "abnormality" for political purposes or punishment for political activity and report such cases to the society (BPS, 1978). It is clear that this set of recommendations is a reaction to psychological abuses in oppressive regimes. Although the United Kingdom has always had its element of totalitarian politicians and leaders, there is no indication of any organized movement to harness all academic and professional activities for the work of the state. Such aspirations are not gaining any more ground in Britain today than they did in Victorian times.

EMPLOYMENT OF PSYCHOLOGISTS

Along with the rapid expansion of psychology as a recognized area of study in the 1960s came an equally enthusiastic injection of funding into the universities. The consequence of this for the "new" discipline of psychology was a marked increase in the number of academic posts available to psychologists. As the demand for people to fill these posts could not be met by the number of established psychologists, many newly graduated individuals were recruited. Thus by 1981 the mean age of the 606 full-time academic staff members in British psychology departments was thirty-eight, with 35 percent being under thirty-five and only 9 percent being over fifty-five. By the year 2010 fewer than one in three of them will have reached normal retirement age (Over, 1984).

The severe financial reductions imposed on universities more recently have limited the number of posts. At this time about twenty chairs in psychology remain unfilled for economic reasons. As it is unlikely that significant numbers of full-time academics will leave voluntarily and few will retire before the twenty-first century, a whole new generation of psychologists will be denied access to academic positions at a time when their numbers are rising.

The potential results of this are wide-ranging and varied. First there is the issue of academic standards. Evidence, reviewed by Over (1984), suggests that past performance of academics is more predictive of future performance than age. However, attitudes and values are developed within a particular ethos. As the nature of the discipline changes, it is possible that the values and attitudes of academics may become outdated. Additionally, the widening generation gap between student and teacher may lead to academics providing less effective role models. Finally, there is some doubt that the aging population of academics will be able to keep up with developments in the settings outside the universities wherein most young psychologists will be working.

A second problem which has arisen out of the conditions described above is the underrepresentation of women psychologists in academic departments. In 1969, 51 percent of psychology graduates were female; by 1979, the figure had increased to 65 percent. Concomitantly, while 20 percent of Ph.D.s were awarded to females in 1969, by 1979, 40 percent of graduates awarded this degree were women. In spite of this development, only 14 percent of full-time positions in psychology departments are held by women (Over, 1984). The consequences of institutionalized sexism in British psychology must be faced.

During the 1960s and more especially the 1970s, an increasing number of women became involved in women's studies. The work produced by many of the scholars working within this multidisciplinary field provided strong evidence for the inadequacies of male-dominated science. These inadequacies not only bias the subject matter of psychological analysis but have critical implications for the epistemological and philosophical structure on which psychology is built. The underrepresentation of women cannot be redressed by men teaching a different form of psychology outside the experience of women. Removing masculine pronouns from the literature is not enough (the BPS recently recognized that it should pay particular attention to this type of sexism when considering publication material). The establishment of organizations of women psychologists and the holding of conferences to address the problems of women in the field are certainly steps in the right direction. More must be done to cope with the problem of employment in academia for all British psychologists.

The BPS *Bulletin* of February 1986 published its first article recognizing lesbian and gay psychology as a neglected area of British research (Furnell, 1986). Certainly British psychologists are beginning to recognize that the dominant, establishment view on the subject is outdated and inappropriate. Nonetheless, it is still difficult to find any recognition of the heterogeneity of British society in the papers presented at annual BPS conventions.

Employment as a member of the research staff of an academic institution was at one time viewed as a step toward a teaching career. This is no longer the case. Senior researchers tend to retain their positions. Unless policies are adopted to keep people in such posts for limited periods of time, new graduates may be prevented from entering research positions. Furthermore, the employment practices regarding junior research staff are often archaic and possibly questionable on ethical grounds. Typically, an investigator is employed to work on a specific project and may be dismissed when the project is completed. There is no possibility of tenure except in the few research institutes. The future of a researcher depends on the good will of the academic who may (or may not) obtain sufficient funds to reemploy the members of his or her research staff. A number of proposals have been tabled by more senior academics in order to limit the employment period of investigators. While such actions do provide openings for the younger psychologist, they reduce the level of expertise. Morale among researchers also falls and perhaps with it a commitment to produce high-quality work. Thus, while economic benefits which accrue from employing fewer qualified and more inexperienced researchers may help in the short-term, the long-term consequences are damaging to the quality and progress of psychology in the United Kingdom.

A recent review by Canter and Canter (1983) of employment trends of psychology graduates revealed both that psychology is becoming a profession to a greater extent than it is remaining a predominantly academic field and that many graduates are unemployed. In 1966, 101 graduates entered research or academic study and 161 went into permanent employment. In 1979, those entering research and academic study had risen to 192; however, the number going into permanent employment had increased dramatically to 485. At the same time the number of graduates entering all forms of educational employment had fallen from 75 to 51, while those going into industry and commerce had risen from 55 to 253. These employment statistics have important implications for the education and training of psychologists.

THE RELEVANCE OF ACADEMIC PROGRAMS FOR THE WORK OF BRITISH PSYCHOLOGISTS

Given the employment settings of psychology graduates and the increasing professionalization of the field, the content and structure of undergraduate psychology curricula may not provide as relevant and useful a training as might be wished (see Canter & Canter, 1982). Progams remain academically oriented while the demand is for applied professional competencies.

As we noted earlier, most required courses are in the classical areas of psychology such as learning, perception, memory, and so forth. In many areas of the psychological profession, only a minority of practitioners report using such subject matter (Canter & Canter, 1982). More often utilized are the methods, concepts, and findings of social, organizational, and clinical psychology.

A further difficulty lies in the research procedures taught undergraduates. The well-controlled, laboratory-based experiment is still predominant. In psychological practice, however, field studies rather than field experiments are increasingly found to be most useful in addressing clients' problems. The need to adopt a field research approach is only gradually becoming recognized in academic psychology. Many applied psychologists, of course, have long recognized the need for such an approach; others, including social psychologists, have begun to express considerable dissatisfaction with the laboratory, either as an actual research setting or as a metaphor. Related to the use of experimental approaches to psychological inquiry is professional jargon which distances psychology graduates from their future clients.

British psychologists need more training in descriptive techniques. A number of authors have pointed out that an essential early descriptive stage is often lacking in psychological research. While this is a serious omission in academic research, when attempting to solve real-world problems, description and clarification may often be absolutely essential. New research approaches and techniques of analysis are, fortunately, leading to progress with respect to this issue.

Finally, it should be realized that British psychology graduates need, increasingly, to survive in a competitive world. It ought to be well within the abilities of psychologists to teach the necessary communication, interpersonal, management, and other skills necessary for their students to merchandise their competencies. The state of the British economy and political traditions have probably led to a deemphasizing of the value of these skills. Psychologists in the United States appear to do a better job in this regard. However, in the present economic climate, communicating effectively with managers and decision makers in business and government is as important as knowing how to increase the efficiency of a rat running a maze.

Within the framework of a traditional university and employment in academic circles, the British Ph.D. degree was generally useful in former times. This is less the case today. It has been contended that the Ph.D. does not provide the necessary background for professional practice and may even be counterproductive (Baddeley, 1979, 1983; Morris, 1984). Besides, the focus on a narrow and circumscribed area with little formal course work may fail to provide not only the student but the discipline with a firm foundation for future growth.

In an article on the training of professional psychologists, Pearson and Howarth (1982) argue for a system of education which would, seemingly, be more relevant to professional practice. They propose that psychologists be taught to identify a problem area and clarify the goals; survey the resources; devise a strategy for the use of available resources; and, ultimately, implement and evaluate the strategy. Once individuals have a grasp of the expertise necessary to perform these activities, they can then, it is contended, specialize in the "context" or "knowledge" base of a particular area.

Such an approach has many advantages and also shifts the emphasis from knowledge of the so-called basics of psychology (perception, memory, and so forth) to methods and techniques that psychologists must master for the actual problems they encounter. This methodological orientation also has the advantage of allowing greater cross-fertilization among the various areas of the discipline, which is necessary for the successful practice of psychology.

Whether there will be any significant curricular changes instituted in the traditionally conservative universities, particularly during these hard times, is yet to be seen. However, if psychology in the United Kingdom is to flourish, change will need to be more rapid than was the case during the early days of psychology in Great Britain.

DEVELOPMENTS IN RESEARCH METHODOLOGIES

British psychology has been theoretically eclectic; no single metatheory has emerged. The general orientation has been cognitive, probably as a consequence of Galton's, Burt's, and Bartlett's influence, but there is great diversity within this framework. There has been no overall sociopolitical ideology into which theories are forced as has been the case, for example, in the Soviet Union. The historical conditions which underlie the characteristics of British psychology are complex. To a large extent psychology in the United Kingdom grew out of a need to solve societal problems such as those resulting from World War II; therefore, whatever means or theories were necessary for their solution were employed. Nevertheless, psychology in this country has always been predominantly experimental, modeled after procedures used in the natural sciences. This, in part, resulted from a desire to disassociate the emerging discipline from its philosophical foundations. However, the experimental approach is now being challenged by British psychologists, ironically, because of their involvement in solving real-world problems.

One of the more promising recent approaches to psychological inquiry is "new paradigm" research (Reason & Rowan, 1981). The variety of specific procedures which make up this orientation incorporate many methodological tactics and strategies but are united in their rejection of a psychology that treats people as experimental subjects. Research is conducted with, rather than on, people. The new paradigm approach has obvious links to the phenomenological tradition found in continental Europe and is a sign that British psychology is drawing closer to European thinkers and away from the influence of North American psychologists.

On the other hand, an American who has had a special influence on psychological methodology in the United Kingdom is George Kelly. Kelly's Personal Construct Theory fits well with both the cognitive orientation of British psychology and new paradigm research (see, for example, Bannister, 1981). The Repertory Grid technique has been employed in a number of areas including environmental perception (Riley & Palmer, 1976), design participation (Stringer, 1974), children's self-perceptions (Bannister & Agnew, 1977), and education (Pope & Keen, 1981), as well as in the clinical field. Among the principal British protagonists of this approach are Donald Bannister and Fay Fransella.

Important developments have also taken place in data analysis. The United Kingdom has had a strong tradition in statistics since the pioneering work of Galton, Pearson, Spearman, Fisher, and others. However, conventional statistics are now being questioned. Under critical review, for example, are the arbitrary significance levels of inferential statistics and the use of the null hypothesis. Multidimensional scaling techniques are increasingly being seen as better suited to data analysis and they are more appropriate for new paradigm research. A library of multidimensional programs, MDS(x), has been developed by A. Coxon and his colleagues at the universities of Wales and Edinburgh (Coxon, 1982).

Allied with the growth of multidimensional scaling techniques has been the increased use of facet theory developed by L. Guttman in Israel. This approach more precisely relates a research domain to empirical observations and has been particularly fruitful in applied fields. Recent publications (for example, Canter, 1985) and the First International Conference on Facet Theory at the University of Surrey in 1984 have begun to alert a wider audience to this approach which seems poised for much more use in the near future. There is still, however, some resistance on the part of academic psychologists to embracing these new methodologies. Funds for research associated with new paradigm approaches are also difficult to obtain (Fineman, 1981). In our opinion, many of the problems and inadequacies of undergraduate programs could be remedied by more acceptance of these orientations which would better prepare graduates to conduct meaningful studies as professional psychologists.

DEVELOPMENTS IN SPECIFIC FIELDS

Clinical Psychology

Since the end of World War II and psychologists' early incursions into the field of mental disorder, most clinical psychologists have worked within the National Health Service (NHS) established by the government in 1948. Clinical psychologists do not usually operate in a free-market context and as a consequence do not have to sell their wares to the general public. Formerly, this lack of independence reduced them to testers or assistants to psychiatrists. Now they have become part of health-care teams.

While there may be some epistemological and regional variation in the activities of individual clinical psychologists, their work is similar wherever they are employed. Being employed by a public health agency, ultimately under the auspices of the government, clinical psychologists have a direct link to national policy formulation and implementation and do not often have to justify their work, for example, to the insurance companies who pay patients' bills.

The development of clinical psychology as a profession has been reviewed at length by Hetherington (1981) and Reavley (1982). Plainly there has been a steady increase in the demand for the services of clinical psychologists and change in the nature of the tasks they perform. According to Barden (1979), there was an 8 percent annual increase in the number of practitioners between 1957 and 1978.

Although some of the tests in wide use in Britain are American in origin, a large number are "homegrown." Among the latter are the Maudsley Personality Inventory and others developed by Eysenck at the Institute of Psychiatry associated with the University of London and the Maudsley and Bethlehem Royal Hospitals.

Eysenck has played a central role in the development of clinical psychology in the United Kingdom, although his work and theories are certainly not endorsed by all British clinical psychologists and he never worked solely as a clinical practitioner. The Institute of Psychiatry, where he had the chair until his retirement, has been one of the national centers for research and teaching (Eysenck, 1980). Eysenck's internationally renowned research and theory of personality have helped broaden the role of clinical psychologists. Indeed it has been said that his early publication, *Dimensions of personality* (1947), has been the most universally read and influential book in clinical psychology (Hetherington, 1981). The increased use of tests covering a range of human psychological functions, which was stimulated in part by theories of personality, allowed psychologists in the 1950s to produce profiles of clients' psychological functioning.

By the 1960s British psychologists were doing psychotherapy. Initially their approach was based primarily on learning theory and concentrated almost exclusively on overt behavior. Again the Institute of Psychiatry played a central role in this development.

This rather quantitative, essentially nomothetic, approach to clinical research and practice, wherein the patient is treated as being typical of a particular class of patients and assessable relative to characteristics of that class, has been challenged in recent years. Approaches that owe more to Kelly's Personal Construct Theory (1955) and other more individual-oriented, humanistic frameworks have grown in favor. This general outlook has always been present at the Tavistock Clinic in London, established in 1920. In the 1960s, Eysenck's polemical writings contrasted the Maudsley work with that conducted at Tavistock. Whereas the establishment NHS psychologists adopted Eysenck's perspective in the early days of this debate, there is growing evidence that the Tavistock view is now being drawn on increasingly by clinicians in public as well as private practice.

An interesting and controversial recent development has been the opening of the first for-profit psychiatric hospital for patients committed by the state ("Profit-making," 1985). Only time will tell if the concerns expressed by some are justified.

Educational Psychology

Educational psychology has strong academic roots in Britain. Alexander Bain, for example, published widely on education, and Sully organized the British Association for Child Study in 1895. The most significant early contributions came from Burt as well as G. H. Thomson, who published a seminal work, *The factorial analysis of human ability* (1939), and helped develop the Moray House tests. Charles Valentine was one of the most significant figures in the history of educational psychology in the United Kingdom while holding the chair in education at Birmingham University (still an important center in the field). He founded the *British Journal of Educational Psychology* in 1931 and published widely on psychology and education, continuing to write until his death in 1964.

Burt, the first British applied educational psychologist, was appointed by the London County Council in 1913 as advisor to the education department. The original job description for the post he took was ambiguous in the extreme, giving him an opportunity to do much testing. The work of educational psychologists has broadened and increased considerably since these early days; there are now some 1,000 such specialists working for Local Education Authorities (LEAs) in England and Wales.

The functions of educational or school psychologists fall into five broad, though not mutually exclusive, categories: individual case work, in-service training, consultation on organizational issues, research and evaluation, and policy formulation (Topping, 1982). The nature of the work undertaken depends to a large extent on the particular LEA employing the psychologist and whether the setting is urban or rural.

Earlier, the major role of applied educational psychologists was that of "ancillary technician," serving as diagnosticians for teachers and medical doctors (Topping, 1982). As was the case with clinical psychologists, a medical model dominated, and problems were seen as located within the child rather than as products of the social environment, a context which is in vogue currently. Today, case work includes recommending changes in the behavior of significant others associated with the child. There is increasing overlap between the roles of educational and clinical psychologists.

Case work now occupies the largest proportion of the educational psychologist's time (40 to 80 percent). Research has, however, cast some doubt on the usefulness of such work (Shepherd, et al., 1971); Wright & Payne, 1979). Since the 1960s, the National Foundation for Educational Research has designed and conducted studies dealing directly with the role of teachers. A recent survey (Wolfendale, 1980) has shown that educational psychologists contribute a great deal to the in-service training of teachers. It is likely that such training, which is supported by the government, will occupy more of educational psychologists' time. This extra work will probably lead to a reduction in case work, but enlightened teachers may reduce the need for this professional intervention.

As emphasized by Canter and Canter (1982), organizational issues are intrinsic to the work of applied psychologists, including educational psychologists. Their role may be essentially supportive, helping management clarify problems and make decisions.

Research conducted by psychologists in educational settings is beset with problems because the traditional experimental approach is of little use (Topping, 1982). Research must be made more relevant for action or policy formulation.

At present there seems insufficient involvement on the part of psychologists in policy formulation at either the local or national level (Raven, 1977; Topping, 1982), although the BPS does submit evidence to government committees which often include psychologists. Topping (1982) has compiled a list of areas in which psychologists have been involved. These include the reorganization of special schools, the design of screening techniques to uncover those in need of special help, curriculum development, multicultural education, and job creation and youth opportunities programs.

The future of educational psychology depends on the political philosophy of the government. The present right-wing government has already begun to emphasize discipline and standards. Both the evaluation of children and teachers' pay, it is proposed, should be linked to results. The 1981 Education Act is also likely to affect psychologists though it is too soon to predict the long-term consequences of the legislation.

Social Psychology

The roots of social psychology in Britain are to be found in McDougall's early "hormic" psychology. In 1908, McDougall published his textbook *Social psy-*

chology, which has gone through many revisions and editions and is still in use today. The ethos prevalent at the time *Social psychology* first appeared was Social Darwinism and thus biological in orientation. Today, the emphasis in British social psychology has shifted to the social influences on behavior. Aspects of McDougall's approach are, however, still evident.

In general, social psychology in the United Kingdom has been an applied discipline. Social psychologists have been involved, for example, in the advertising campaigns of political parties (Butler & Rose, 1960). They are also making significant contributions to the general field of advertising and other areas of consumer psychology (Frost & Canter, 1982).

Within the universities, among the most influential and productive social psychologists have been H. Tajfel, Michael Argyle, Rom Harré, and G. Jahoda. Tajfel held the chair at Bristol until his recent death. His last work was in the field of intergroup relations (Tajfel, 1978). He also wrote or edited widely used texts in social psychology (Tajfel & Fraser, 1978; Israel & Tajfel, 1972). Michael Argyle, at the University of Oxford, has been a particularly productive scholar. He and his research team have been influential in the areas of social skills and nonverbal communication. More recently, they have been studying the social psychology of situations (Argyle, 1979) and analyzing what they call episodes. Their research has included such real-world problems as football (soccer) violence. Related to Argyle's approach is the work of Rom Harré, also at Oxford in the philosophy department. He has written a number of important social psychological books (Harré & Secord, 1972; Harré, 1979) in which he attempts to explain people's behavior using an "ethogenic" approach. Another characteristic of much of his work has been the use of "accounts" for data collection. Other institutions with distinctive orientations toward social psychology include the University of Sussex, where Jahoda held a chair until the 1970s, and the London School of Economics.

In general, social psychology in the United Kingdom has been moving away from the experimental approach. Researchers are striving for external validity and adequate models of social action. In taking this direction it seems likely that British and American social psychological emphases will continue to diverge.

Occupational Psychology

In the United Kingdom, psychological inquiry in the work context has, from its beginning, gone beyond the confines of what is usually recognized as industrial psychology (Rodger & Guest, 1969). Indeed the official publication of the National Institute of Industrial Psychology (NIIP) has, since 1938, been the *Journal of Occupational Psychology*. The first manifestation of industrial psychology was the government's Health of Munitions Workers' Committee (1915–1917). Through the years, the NIIP's investigations have ranged from environmental conditions to worker selection and assessment.

The Medical Research Council's Applied Psychology Unit (APU) at Cambridge has made major contributions to the psychological study of people in the work place. The APU has emphasized research in the area of ergonomics (*ergos*, meaning work, and *nomos*, natural laws), the British equivalent of human factors. Much research was initiated under the directorship of K. Craik, a brilliant psychologist with a thorough understanding of engineering. The unit was until recently led by Donald Broadbent who, after twenty-five years as director, moved to Oxford. A. D. Badeley, who has written extensively on memory, now heads the facility. Significant contributions to ergonomics have also been made by researchers at the University of Birmingham, the University of Loughborough, and the Ergonomics Research Unit at the University of Aston in Birmingham. The Ergonomics Research Society (later the Ergonomics Society) was founded in 1949.

Early in the twentieth century the work of Frederick Taylor in the United States was very influential in Britain. Later, as a more humanistic orientation swept the field of organizational psychology, competing theories emerged. The Tavistock Institute of Human Relations, established in 1947, made important contributions to the field. Of particular significance was the notion of the "autonomous working group" (AWG) with its foundations in human relations and humanistic principles which came from Tavistock in the 1950s and 1960s. The AWG approach to job design was intended to redress the problems at work which grew from Taylor's approach.

In the 1960s, E. L. Trist and his colleagues, also at Tavistock, proposed one of the major theories or models of organizational functioning. Known as the sociotechnical systems approach, it represented an attempt to take both the technological and social aspects of organizations into account. The work of the institute has been interdisciplinary in orientation and often psychodynamic in approach.

Among the important contemporary figures in occupational psychology in the United Kingdom are John Annett, presently holding the chair in psychology at Warwick University, who has carried out work on training with special reference to skill acquisition and the role of feedback; Peter Warr, whose main interests lie in psychological well-being and worker effectiveness; and Toby Wall, who is involved in job design and new technology. J. Child of Aston University has had an impact on the broader theoretical level in organizational psychology, and the MRC/ESRC research unit at Sheffield University has also made contributions.

Publications which consider occupational psychology from a British perspective include Warr (1978), Warr & Wall (1975), Pugh, et al. (1971), Shipley (1982), Stewart (1982), and Blackler (1982).

Environmental and Architectural Psychology

Environmental psychology came into being in Britain in the mid–1960s, although isolated studies predate this period (for example, Lee, 1954). The field emerged when psychologists became members of multidisciplinary teams carrying out research on the design and use of buildings. The first of these research groups was the Pilkington Research Unit based in Liverpool University, set up by a manufacturer of window glass. The unit had the task of studying, first, office and, then, primary-school environments. A subsequent unit was established at Strathclyde University in Glasgow. Known as the Building Performance Research Unit (BPRU), the psychologist associated with the group was David Canter. The charge was to develop standard assessment procedures for evaluating buildings. In 1974, Canter published *Psychology for architects*, one of the first books in the field. In 1972, the BPRU published *Building performance*, which is still an important reference work. In a 1976 review of psychology in the United Kingdom, B. M. Foss identified environmental psychology as an emerging field which was making contributions to architecture.

The only master's and doctoral programs in environmental psychology in Britain were instituted in 1972 at the University of Surrey under the directorship of Canter. A number of other universities and polytechnics offer undergraduate options in environmental psychology. Doctoral programs emphasizing office design also exist at the University of Aston in Birmingham, in keeping with the major interests of the applied psychology department there.

Research has been carried out by C. Spencer and his colleagues at the University of Sheffield into children's perceptions of their environments. Environmental investigations are also conducted in the geography department at the University of Sheffield and at schools of architecture.

Since there are only a few environmental psychologists in the United Kingdom, those who are academics also serve as consultants. The demands placed on researchers in this area to solve applied problems have prevented the discipline in Britain from becoming an artificial, laboratory-based field. Because environmental psychology is primarily an applied specialty, multidimensional scaling and other multivariate statistics are widely used.

Environmental psychologists serve a wide variety of clients including the government. Practitioners have, for example, contributed to government policy formulation regarding fires and human behavior, in addition to making such "on-the-spot" diagnoses of problems in buildings as the relationship between air conditioning and office workers' health. A recent publication describes the areas of work in which an environmental psychologist in practice may be employed (Canter, 1982); another details the origins and current trends of environmental psychology in the United Kingdom (Canter & Donald, 1987).

FUTURE DIRECTIONS

There is virtually no possibility that the trend established by the current Conservative government to remove as much of the educational, health, and welfare services as possible from the public sector will be reversed in the near future. This has consequences for all professional groups and academic disciplines, but for psychologists it will result in a reduction of positions in traditional applied areas and in the universities. The cutbacks in government funding of the discipline will also restrict the basic academic research which can be done.

Those wishing to be gainfully employed professional psychologists will have to argue the case for additional resources more vigorously. An increasing number of psychologists will also have to obtain support from the private sector because, while the biologically oriented subfields of the discipline and those associated with information technology are in relatively good standing within the universities, those concerned with social factors are less well supported. Again this is a reflection of the present government's views toward the social sciences.

The reduction of university positions in psychology creates many problems, especially in an economy that is relatively stagnant, particularly since British industry is notorious for its unwillingness to employ outside consultants and researchers. But there may also be advantages to this state of affairs, because many of the major and innovative contributions of British psychologists to their discipline and society have been forthcoming without much institutional support. In any case, British psychologists, even those in academic settings, will most likely be involved in some applied work related to socially relevant issues. Moreover, there are clear signs that the links to continental Europe will enhance this trend. One of the most probable consequences for the discipline is that traditional research methodologies appropriate for laboratory studies will be seen by more and more psychologists as having little relevance for the work most psychologists actually do.

One of the major socioeconomic changes occurring within most advanced industrial nations has to do with the structure and nature of work. The Warwick Institute of Employment Research, for example, estimates that unemployment in the United Kingdom will continue to exceed 3 million until the 1990s and perhaps beyond. It is not surprising, therefore, that there is already a marked interest in the study of unemployment and its psychological consequences. As Wallis (1984) notes, little is known about the role of attitudes toward unemployment. Evidence suggests that models developed in the 1960s may not be appropriate for the present and future. High levels of unemployment, for instance, have implications for the nature of education, and more research needs to be done to determine whether it is preferable to offer recreational training or a general education focused on generic skills.

It will also be necessary to understand the consequences of midlife career changes, which are becoming more common, and to determine ways to retrain effectively those individuals involved. In addition, there is an increasing demand for technologically skilled workers. Both of these developments will challenge the organizational psychologists of the future.

Quite likely, work hours will be reduced, perhaps to a three-day work week. Clearly individuals will need to find additional things to do in their free time. More research on leisure will undoubtedly be done by psychologists. One of the most serious problems may concern the attitudes of workers toward the unemployed, some of whom will be engaged in leisure-time activities on a full-time basis. Research has tended to focus on unemployment; a shift to the study of leisure may be necessary. Finally, there is the problem of civil unrest resulting from high levels of unemployment. The riots of the 1980s demonstrated that there is an urgent need to better understand the psychological aspects of such events.

Other developments in Britain which will surely impact on psychology are an increasing drug (particularly heroin) problem, the psychological implications of energy conservation measures, and an aging population.

Since psychology in the United Kingdom is becoming essentially an applied field, changes in the education and training of psychology students will be required. It also seems inevitable that monies for research will increasingly come from the private sector. As a result, it is possible that some psychology departments will become independent research institutes operating on a commercial basis. To survive in such a context, they will need to be flexible in terms of the research they undertake. Perhaps "generic" researchers capable of conducting studies in all applied areas will be trained. Such a development would, of necessity, foster a more interdisciplinary approach to both training and research. New technologies, particularly the computer, will continue to affect the training and work of psychologists.

In the country which produced Charles Darwin it should come as no surprise that British psychology is adapting to a changing sociopolitical environment for the sake of survival. Nor should the extent to which psychologists are striving to modify that environment, in order to make Britain a more confortable place to live and work, be underestimated. A conscious effort by psychologists is now under way to gain better coverage in the mass media, to organize a parliamentary lobby, to place psychologists in senior positions in civil service departments, to become more actively involved in community affairs, and to argue for the benefits of psychology on other than scholastic grounds. What British psychology will be like by the end of the twentieth century is impossible to predict. It will, however, be very different from what it is today.

REFERENCES

Argyle, M. (1979). Social behaviour as a function of situations. In G. P. Ginsburg (Ed.), *Emerging strategies in social psychological research*. Chichester: Wiley.

Baddeley, A. (1979). Is the British Ph.D. system obsolete? *Bulletin of the British Psychological Society*, *32*, 129–131.

Baddeley A. (1983). The Working Party on postgraduate education. *Bulletin of the British Psychological Society*, *36*, 9–12.

Ball, B., & Bourner, T. (1984). The employment of psychology graduates. *Bulletin of the British Psychological Society*, *37*, 39–40.

Bannister, D. (1981). Personal Construct Theory and research method. In P. Reason & J. Rowan (Eds.), *Human inquiry: A source book of new paradigm research*. Chichester: Wiley.

Bannister, D., & Agnew, J. (1977). The child's construing of self. In A. Landfield (Ed.), *Nebraska symposium on motivation. 1976*. Lincoln: Nebraska University Press.

Barden, V. E. (1979). Basic data for manpower planning in clinical psychology. *Bulletin of the British Psychological Society, 32*, 12–16.

Bartlett, F. C. (1932). *Remembering: A study in experimental and social psychology*. Cambridge: Cambridge University Press.

Bartlett, F. C. (1958). *Thinking: An experimental and social study*. London: Allen & Unwin.

Billig, M. (1982). *Ideology and social psychology*. Oxford: Blackwell.

Blackler, F. (1982). Organisational psychology. In S. Canter & D. Canter (Eds.), *Psychology in practice: Perspectives on professional psychology*. Chichester: Wiley.

Boring, E. G. (1950). *A history of experimental psychology* (2nd ed.). New York: Appleton-Century-Crofts.

British Psychological Society. (1978). Report of the Working Party on abuses of psychology for political purposes. *Bulletin of the British Psychological Society, 31*, 95.

Broadbent, D. (1980). Donald E. Broadbent. In G. Lindzey (Ed.), *A history of psychology in autobiography* (Vol. 7). San Francisco: Freeman.

Building Performance Research Unit. (1972). *Building performance*. London: Applied Science.

Burt, C. (1940). *The factors of the mind*. London: London University Press.

Butler, D. E. & Rose, R. (1960). *The British general election of 1959*. London: Macmillan.

Canter, D. (1974). *Psychology for architects*. London: Applied Science.

Canter, D. (1982). Psychology and environmental design. In S. Canter & D. Canter (Eds.), *Psychology in practice: Perspectives on professional psychology*. Chichester: Wiley.

Canter, D. (Ed.). (1985). *Facet theory: Approaches to social research*. New York: Springer-Verlag.

Canter, D., & Donald I. J. (1987). Environmental psychology in the United Kingdom. In D. Stokols & I. Altman (Eds.), *Handbook of environmental psychology*. New York: Wiley.

Canter, S., & Canter, D. (Eds.), (1982). *Psychology in practice: Perspectives on professional psychology*. Chichester: Wiley.

Canter, S., & Canter, D. (1983). Professional growth and psychology education. *Bulletin of the British Psychology Society, 36*, 283–287.

Clarke, A. D. B. (1979). Editorial: Seventy-five years of the *British Journal of Psychology*, 1904–1978. *Bulletin of the British Psychological Society, 32*, 161–165.

Coxon, A. P. M. (1982). *The user's guide to multidimensional scaling*. London: Heinemann.

Darwin, C. (1871). *The descent of man*. London: J. Murray.

Davis, A. Y. (1982). *Women, race and class*. London: Women's Press.

Drever, J. (1921). *The psychology of everyday life*. London: Methuen.

Eysenck, H. J. (1947). *Dimensions of personality*. London: Routledge and Kegan Paul.

Eysenck, H. J. (1980). Hans Jurgen Eysenck. In G. Lindzey (Ed.), *A history of psychology in autobiography* (Vol. 7). San Francisco: Freeman.

Farr, R. M. (Ed.). (1983). History of social psychology. *British Journal of Social Psychology, 22*, 273–373. (a)

Farr, R. M. (1983). Wilhelm Wundt (1832–1920) and the origins of psychology as an experimental and social science. *British Journal of Social Psychology*, *22*, 289–301. (b)

Fineman, S. (1981). Funding research: Practice and politics. In P. Reason & J. Rowan (Eds.), *Human inquiry: A sourcebook of new paradigm research*. Chichester: Wiley.

Flugel, J. C. (1933). *One hundred years of psychology: 1833–1933* (1st ed.). London: Gerald Duckworth.

Flugel, J. C., & West, D. J. (1964). *A hundred years of psychology: 1833–1933* (3rd ed.). London: Gerald Duckworth.

Foss, B. M. (1969). Psychology in Great Britain. *Supplement to the* Bulletin of the British Psychological Society. London: British Psychological Society.

Foss, B. M. (1976). United Kingdom. In V. Sexton & H. Misiak (Eds.), *Psychology around the world* (pp. 428–443). Monterey, CA: Brooks/Cole.

Foss, B. M. (Ed.). (1978). Psychology survey 1. Leicester: British Psychological Society.

Frost, A., & Canter, D. (1982). Consumer psychology. In S. Canter & D. Canter (Eds.), *Psychology in practice: Perspectives on professional psychology*. Chichester: Wiley.

Furnell, P. J. (1986). Lesbian and gay psychology: A neglected area of British research. *Bulletin of the British Psychological Society*, *39*, 41–47.

Galton, F. (1886). Regression towards mediocrity in hereditary stature. *Journal of the Anthropological Institute*, *15*, 246–263.

Galton, F. (1888). Co-relations and their measurement. *Proceedings of the Royal Society*, *45*, 135–145.

Gilmour, R., & Duck, S. (Eds.). (1980). *The development of social psychology*. London: Academic Press.

Haggard, M. P., & Shackel, B. (1978). Monitoring financial support for psychological research. *Bulletin of the British Psychological Society*, *31*, 3–8.

Harré, R. (1979). *Social being: A theory for social psychology*. Oxford: Blackwell.

Harré, R., & Secord, P. F. (1972). *The explanation of social behaviour*. Oxford: Blackwell.

Hearnshaw, L. S. (1964). *A short history of British psychology: 1840–1940*. London: Methuen.

Hearnshaw, L. S. (1979). The influence of Wundt on British psychology. *Bulletin of the British Psychological Society*, *32*, 446–451.

Hetherington, R. (1981). The changing role of the clinical psychologist. *Bulletin of the British Psychological Society*, *34*, 12–14.

Israel, J., & Tajfel, H. (Eds.). (1972). *The context of social psychology*. London: Academic Press.

Kelly, G. A. (1955). *The psychology of personal constructs* (Vol. 1). New York: Norton.

Lee, T. R. (1954). *A study of neighbourhood*. Unpublished doctoral dissertation, University of Cambridge, Cambridge.

Lowe, G., Bachler, L., Donaldson, J., Drewicz, J., Gill, A., & Morrissey, M. (1977). Topic areas in psychology as represented in British university examinations. *Bulletin of the British Psychological Society*, *30*, 218–219.

McDougall, W. (1908). *An introduction to social psychology*. London: Methuen.

McDougall, W. (1931). *World chaos: The responsibility of science*. London: Kegan Paul, Trench, Trubner.

Misiak, H., & Sexton, V. S. (1966). *History of psychology: An overview*. New York: Grune & Stratton.

Morris, P. E. (1984). What is the psychology PhD for? *Bulletin of the British Psychological Society, 37,* 228–229.

Over, R. (1984). Career prospects within British universities. *Bulletin of the British Psychological Association, 37,* 150–152.

Pearson, L., & Howarth, I. (1982). Training professional psychologists. *Bulletin of the British Psychological Society, 35,* 375–377.

Pope, M. L., & Keen, T. R. (1981). *Personal construct psychology and education.* London: Academic Press.

Profit-making psychiatric hospital open. (1985). *The Guardian* (October).

Pugh, D. S., Hickson, D. J., & Hinings, C. R. (1971). *Writers on organizations* (2nd ed.). Harmondsworth: Penguin.

Raven, J. (1977). Government policy and social psychologists. *Bulletin of the British Psychological Society, 30,* 33–39.

Reason, P., & Rowan, J. (Eds.). (1981). *Human inquiry: A sourcebook of new paradigm research.* Chichester: Wiley.

Reavley, W. (1982). Clinical psychology in practice. In S. Canter & D. Canter (Eds.), *Psychology in practice: Perspectives on professional psychology.* Chichester: Wiley.

Riley, S., & Palmer, J. (1976). Of attitudes and latitudes: A Repertory Grid study of perceptions of seaside resorts. In P. Slater (Ed.), *The measurement of interpersonal space by grid technique* (Vol. 1). London: Wiley.

Rodger, A., & Guest, D. (1969). Occupational psychology. In B. M. Foss (Ed.), *Psychology in Great Britain, supplement to the* Bulletin of the British Psychological Society *on the occasion of the International Congress of Psychology.* London: British Psychological Society.

Romanes, G. J. (1883). *Animal intelligence.* New York: Appleton.

Shepherd, M., Oppenheim, B., & Mitchell, S. (1971). *Childhood behaviour and mental health.* London: University of London Press.

Shipley, P. (1982). Psychology and work: The growth of a discipline. In S. Canter & D. Canter (Eds.), *Psychology in practice: Perspectives on professional psychology.* Chichester: Wiley.

Spearman, C. (1904). General intelligence objectively determined and measured. *American Journal of Psychology, 15,* 201–293.

Stewart, A. (1982). The occupational psychologist. In S. Canter & D. Canter (Eds.), *Psychology in practice: Perspectives on professional psychology.* Chichester: Wiley.

Stringer, P. (1974). Individual differences in the construing of shopping centre redevelopment proposals. In D. Canter & T. Lee (Eds.), *Psychology and the built environment.* London: Architectural Press.

Sully, J. (1895). *Studies of childhood.* New York: Appleton.

Tajfel, H. (1978). Interindividual and intergroup behaviour. In H. Tajfel (Ed.), *Differentiation between social groups.* London: Academic Press.

Tajfel, H., & Fraser, C. (Eds.). (1978). *Introducing social psychology.* Harmondsworth: Penguin.

Thomson, G. H. (1939). *The factorial analysis of human ability.* London: London University Press.

Thomson, R. (1968). *The Pelican history of psychology.* Harmondsworth: Penguin.

Topping, K. J. C. (1982). Psychology at work in education. In S. Canter & D. Canter (Eds.), *Psychology in practice: Perspectives on professional psychology.* Chichester: Wiley.

Vine, I. (1977). What we teach—and don't teach—to psychology students. *Bulletin of the British Psychological Society, 30,* 376–377.

Wallis, D. (1984). Occupational guidance and unemployment. In A. Gale & A. Chapman (Eds.), *Psychology and social problems: An introduction to applied psychology.* Chichester: Wiley.

Warr, P. B. (1978). *Psychology at work* (2nd ed.). Harmondsworth: Penguin.

Warr, P. B. & Wall, T. (1975). *Work and well-being.* Harmondsworth, Penguin.

Wolfendale, S. (1980). The educational psychologist's contribution to in-service education of teachers: A survey of trends. *Journal of the Association of Education Psychologists, 5,* 45–53.

Wright, H. J., & Payne, T. A. N. (1979). *An evaluation of a school psychological service.* Winchester: Hampshire County Council.

SUGGESTED READINGS

The most comprehensive account of British psychology until 1940 is provided by Hearnshaw (1964). Foss (1969) gives a more concise and up-to-date account. Most books presenting analyses of the history of psychology internationally make reference to major developments in the United Kingdom. Those by British authors, naturally, give fuller accounts; for instance, Flugel (1933), Flugel & West (1964), and Thomson (1968).

For reviews of social psychology, Gilmour & Duck (1980) and Farr (1983) are useful. Canter & Donald (1987) provide an overview of environmental psychology. For an insight into professional psychology as it is practiced in the United Kingdom, the reader should consult Canter & Canter (1982). Finally, a paper summarizing the articles published in the *British Journal of Psychology* since 1904 by Clarke (1979) is also of interest.

United States

Albert R. Gilgen

In the United States, the psychological enterprise broadly conceived includes the discipline of psychology with its academic-research and applied dimensions; psychiatry, a branch of medicine; psychoanalysis, practiced largely but not entirely by psychiatrists trained in various psychoanalytic institutes; a wide array of counseling fields staffed by individuals with master's or doctoral degrees in specialities extending from vocational or marital and sexual counseling; psychiatric nursing; and social work. While research is done by individuals in all of these professions, the great majority of psychiatrists, psychoanalysts, counselors, psychiatric nurses, and social workers are mainly concerned with providing help for people with problems, whereas about 40 percent of psychologists with doctoral degrees are engaged primarily in research and teaching. Because psychologists receive strong training in research methodologies, they not only do most of the experimental studies concerning things psychological but they are also in a good position to evaluate the claims and findings of others. Clinical psychologists, in particular, have become the overseers of the research done in the helping professions. Psychiatrists, on the other hand, retain the positions of leadership in mental health clinics and mental hospitals. This is because only those with a medical degree are permitted to prescribe drugs and because, to date, major insurance companies generally pay only for psychological services provided in settings employing at least one psychiatrist.

AMERICAN PSYCHOLOGY PRIOR TO WORLD WAR II

Since our primary concern is recent developments in psychology, only a brief sketch of events prior to World War II will be provided. From colonial times through the 1930s, the pivotal development was the emergence of psychology as a separate discipline of study in the United States during the 1880s. Along with a greater share of remarks concerning early twentieth-century psychology is included a short overview of the pre–1880s period, a period which has been ignored by most historians of American psychology (Roback, 1952; Evans, 1983).

1630s–1870s

Medieval scholasticism was imported formally into the American colonies with the founding of Harvard College in 1636 by the Puritans, a group of dissenters from the Anglican church who had come to Massachusetts in 1630. Established primarily to assure an educated clergy for the colonists and modeled after Emmanuel College, Cambridge, Harvard's curriculum emphasized logic; the ancient languages of Greek, Hebrew, Aramaic, and Syriac; rhetoric; and religion. Some training in arithmetic, geometry, physics, botany, astronomy, and history was also offered. Students read classical texts, recited what they learned, and debated standard philosophical issues. Psychological matters were usually considered within the context of physics or religion and centered on questions having to do with the mind or soul relative to the body or the relationships between and among sensation, emotion, the intellect, and the will.

The same basic curriculum was put in place at the College of William and Mary, founded by Anglicans in 1693, and at the College of Connecticut established in 1701 by Congregationalists and renamed Yale College in 1718. Books by Francis Bacon, Isaac Newton, John Locke, and other Enlightenment thinkers reached the colonies in 1714, however, and soon had an impact on what was being taught. Many students and some faculty found appealing the contentions that learning should be based on observation and induction rather than dogma and deduction, that the universe is governed by natural laws rather than a personal God, and that mind and consciousness are constructed in an orderly way from experience. Countering the new ideas which challenged established beliefs concerning religion, the nature of man, and the existing curriculum was the commonsense philosophy of Presbyterian Scots such as Thomas Reid (1710–1796) which proclaimed the priority of everyday human experiences and long-standing values over abstract scientific laws. In 1746 the College of New Jersey (later Princeton College and eventually Princeton University) was founded by Presbyterians to offer young men an alternative to the other colleges which were seen as being increasingly influenced by rationalism, deism, and naturalism. During the late eighteenth century and first half of the nineteenth century, Scottish commonsense philosophy was to have a powerful influence on higher education in the United States. With its emphasis on the practical aspects of life as opposed to abstract theory, this philosophy was a forerunner of the pragmatic and functional perspectives which have since the late nineteenth century characterized psychological thought in this country.

The thirteen colonies became an independent nation following the American revolution. From the 1780s until psychology emerged as a separate discipline of study in the 1880s, the population of the country increased from about 3.5

to just over 50 million people. By 1896, the thirteen original states had expanded to forty-eight, spanning the continent from the Atlantic Ocean to the Pacific.

Population growth and territorial expansion were accompanied by a tremendous growth of higher education. By 1890 there existed almost 1,000 institutions of higher learning including medical and dental schools. Most of these schools were four-year, church-founded liberal arts colleges, strongly bound to English and Scottish traditions. During the late eighteenth century, however, until the French Revolution, the influence of French educational perspectives was significant. Throughout most of the nineteenth century until 1914 when World War I broke out, American higher education was much influenced by developments in Germany. The success of the research-oriented German universities generated pressure within the United States to establish secular universities offering graduate programs in all areas of study. Furthermore, the establishment of Wilhelm Wundt's laboratory in Leipzig in 1879 demonstrated the viability of separate departments of scientific psychology. By the 1880s it was possible for American students to enter doctoral programs in psychology without traveling to Germany.

1880s–1930s

Between the 1880s and 1920, academic psychology became firmly established in the United States as a separate discipline of study. By 1918, doctorates in psychology could be earned at about twenty-five institutions. The American Psychological Association (APA), founded in 1892, had a membership of approximately 390 in 1920. A section of the APA for psychologists engaged in clinical work was established in 1917 indicating that a significant applied field was developing. Educational psychology inspired by the thinking and work of William James, G. S. Hall, Edward Thorndike, and John Dewey was also in the formative stage. In the earliest years of the new century, a department of educational psychology, apparently the first, was created at the University of Nebraska, and in 1910 the *Journal of Educational Psychology* was founded.

Although the nineteenth-century German university served as a prototype for the departmentally organized, research-oriented institutions of higher learning which were established in the United States starting in the 1870s and Wundt's psychological laboratory was the training ground for men who would create an independent discipline of psychology in this country, American psychologists almost immediately turned their attention to the study and measurement of mental functioning and individual differences rather than investigations of the structure of the human mind. It was the British tradition and the perspectives of Darwin, Galton, and applied statisticians such as Karl Pearson and R. S. Fisher, not German structuralism, which gave direction to the pragmatically oriented American psychologists.

This functional and practical orientation brought with it an interest not only in testing and statistics but also in abnormal psychology, applied psychology in general, and the study of learning processes and educational techniques. By World War I, a strongly behavioral outlook emerged which rejected mind and consciousness as the concerns of psychology and introspection as the method of gathering information. Psychology, according to John Watson, who had been influenced by Pavlov and Bekhterev and who is considered the "Father of Behaviorism," was to be the scientific study of animal and human behavior.

The United States entered World War I in 1917 and was therefore directly involved in the conflict for less than two years. During that time, however, psychologists were recruited by the government to develop and administer group intelligence tests, a task they accomplished with considerable success. This was significant because it gave additional credibility to the young discipline.

Despite much controversy during the 1920s among functionalists, behaviorists, a few structuralists, and eventually Gestaltists concerning the nature of scientific psychology, this decade was dominated by the radical behavioral perspectives of John Watson. Almost from the beginning, however, there were behaviorists who disagreed with many of Watson's ideas, and by the 1930s neobehaviorism emerged. Foremost among the neobehaviorists were Edwin Guthrie, Edward Tolman, B. F. Skinner, and Clark Hull. Influenced by logical positivism, psychologists likewise sought to develop a science based only on concepts linked to observable operations. Mainstream psychology was experimental, behavioral, functional, elementistic, associationistic, and positivistic. Gestalt and psychoanalytic perspectives had only a minor impact on the discipline before World War II.

While research on conditioning and learning predominated, significant work was also being done in such areas as sensation and perception, psychometrics, child psychology, and various applied fields. Noteworthy, too, was the initiation of several long-range longitudinal studies which are still in progress.

Although prominent European intellectuals left their homelands to escape from oppressive regimes in the 1920s, the greatest migration took place during the 1930s and early 1940s when the Nazis came to power in Germany and Austria. Many of these highly educated individuals came to the United States. Included in their numbers were virtually all of the European psychoanalysts, most of whom settled in the large urban centers of this country. Among the psychologists who fled to the United States were Wolfgang Köhler, Max Wertheimer, Kurt Lewin, Karl Duncker, Egon Brunswik, Else Frenkel-Brunswik, Karl and Charlotte Bühler, Rudolph Arnheim, Marie Jahoda, and David Rapaport. Social scientists Theodor Adorno and Paul Lazarsfeld, neurologist Kurt Goldstein, and physicist John von Neumann (a pioneer in the development of high-speed electronic computers), all of whom influenced American psychology, also came. Without question this migration accelerated the impact on psychology in the United States of psychoanalytic, Gestalt, and European social-psychological orientations (see Fleming & Bailyn, 1969; Fermi, 1971).

OVERVIEW OF THE POST–WORLD WAR II PERIOD

Since World War II, psychology in the United States has grown dramatically, diversified, and become more applied. Expansion in the areas of clinical, counseling, educational, and school psychology was particularly pronounced (American Psychological Association, 1985). The discipline has been influenced in turn by the war; psychoanalytic thinking, especially as it was manifested in neo-Freudianism and ego psychology; humanism, existentialism, and phenomenology starting in the 1950s with the client-centered approach of Carl Rogers; the ethological studies of Tinbergen and Lorenz; the linguistic perspective of Noam Chomsky; and the theory of cognitive development worked out by Swiss psychologist Jean Piaget. The impact of both technological innovations and progress in the neurosciences was significant throughout the period. The stimulus-response theories of conditioning and learning prevalent during the 1950s were gradually replaced by more cognitive conceptions. Clark Hull at Yale University was the most influential psychologist during the 1940s and 1950s and B. F. Skinner at Harvard University during the 1960s and early 1970s. Since the late 1970s a number of cognitively oriented psychologists, including Albert Bandura and Walter Mischel, both at Stanford University, have come into the limelight. The so-called cognitive revolution occurred. Methodologically, psychologists in the United States remain committed to experimental studies of human and animal behavior. Group studies involving the F-test (analysis of variance) are favored though correlational research also abounds. Contemporary psychology is probably best described as functional and behavioral in orientation, tempered by humanism and increasingly by cognitive perspectives and interests, and is very much attuned to developments in neurophysiology.

Throughout the period since 1945 there has been continuing discussion of the relative strengths and weaknesses of various research methodologies. Although the limitations of experimental investigations are well recognized by many U.S. psychologists, the controlled study, whether done in the laboratory or a more applied setting, is still the procedure of choice of most psychological researchers. There is a strong feeling that, while observations in the clinic or the real world are, of course, important, when we really want to know something, it is an experiment that will give us the answer. Professional incentives further encourage experimental investigations. Judged competency, for example, is usually based on the number of well-designed studies an individual can produce. Since experimental investigations generally take less time than clinical or field studies, there is distinct pressure for faculty, particularly junior staff members, to conduct short-run, narrowly focused experiments. Even when psychologists venture to undertake a book, the project of choice is a textbook or edited volume. Few attempt to organize the mountains of information and data which are being produced by increasing numbers of psychologists. Consequently, the discipline remains fragmented and unsystematic. This is probably the most serious problem besetting contemporary U.S. psychology (Gilgen, in press; Staats, 1983).

GROWTH OF THE DISCIPLINE

In 1946, the American Psychological Association (APA), the major organization of psychologists in the United States, was made up of nineteen divisions, published seven journals, and had a membership of about 4,500. Between 30 percent and 40 percent were in applied fields; the rest taught and did research. In terms of sheer numbers, most U.S. psychologists lived and worked in New York, California, Illinois, Pennsylvania, Ohio, Massachusetts, and Michigan, all states with large populations and major urban centers. On a per capita basis, the highest concentration of psychologists was in Washington, D.C., with most employed by the federal government. Eighty-four individuals earned doctorates in psychology in 1946; twenty-eight were women and fifty-six were men. The universities awarding the most psychology doctorates during the 1940–1944 period were Columbia University, the University of Iowa, the University of Minnesota, Ohio State University, Harvard University, Purdue University, Catholic University, Fordham University, the University of Michigan, and Northwestern University. Of the doctorates awarded in all disciplines, just over 4 percent were in psychology. *Psychological Abstracts*, a publication which provides a brief summary of articles and books published each year, listed 3,600 entries.

By 1965, APA consisted of twenty-three divisions and published thirteen journals. Membership had increased more than fivefold from around 4,500 in 1946 to over 23,500. Because of the especially vigorous growth of clinical psychology and to a lesser extent other applied fields, academic-research psychologists were by 1962 replaced by applied psychologists as the majority insofar as the membership of APA was concerned (Tryon, 1963). Most psychologists continued to work in large cities. While the greatest regional concentration was still in the industrialized Midwest and Northeast extending from Michigan to New York, it was clear that as more and more Americans moved to California, Texas, Florida, Colorado, and other sunny or scenic parts of the country, opportunities for increasing numbers of psychologists resulted. Almost 1,000 people were awarded doctorates in psychology in 1965; of these 80 percent were men. While the percentage of women awarded doctorates declined irregularly from a high of over 30 percent in the 1920s to about 12 percent in the late 1940s and early 1950s, more and more women relative to men were again entering the field at the doctoral level by the 1960s (Harmon, 1964). The universities offering the most doctorates in psychology in 1960 were New York University, the University of Michigan, Columbia University, Ohio State University, the University of Minnesota, Purdue University, the University of Chicago, the University of Texas, Harvard University, and the University of Iowa. It is noteworthy that while the University of Texas ranked only thirty-third in terms of the doctorates granted during the 1940–1944 period, by 1960 it ranked eighth. Of the doctorates awarded in all disciplines in 1962, over 7 percent were in psychology, a substantial increase over the 4.32 percent awarded in 1946. Entries in *Psychological Abstracts* exceeded 16,500.

By 1983, APA had expanded to forty divisions and had a membership of 56,400. Sixty-eight percent of the members were men and 32 percent were women. Of the master's-level members, 45 percent were women. Since the mid–

1960s increasing efforts have been made to provide opportunities for minorities and, according to Russo and colleagues (1981), by 1978 about 3 percent of APA members belonged to minority groups (1.2 percent Blacks, 1.0 percent Asians, 0.7 percent Hispanics, and 0.2 percent American Indians). Equal opportunities for women have also been a central issue, but regardless of employment setting, rank, or experience women in the field still have lower incomes on the average than men. Insofar as geographical distribution is concerned, most psychologists continue to live in the industrial Midwest and Northeast. The exodus to the South and West persists, however, and by the 1980s California had surpassed New York as the state with the most APA members. As the "Old South" urbanized and attracted both traditional and "new tech" businesses, more academics including psychologists joined the staffs of southern universities, particularly in North Carolina, Georgia, and Tennessee. Opportunities for applied psychologists in the cities of the South also followed. A similar, if somewhat less spectacular, trend occurred in the Pacific Northwest, especially in the state of Washington. Entries in the *Psychological Abstracts* burgeoned to almost 33,000.

Why did psychology in the United States grow so dramatically during the forty years since World War II? Obviously, both broad societal events as well as factors unique to the discipline were involved. Among the societal developments were a population growth of about 50 percent from 140 million in the mid–1940s to over 230 million in the early 1980s; a generally strong economy; increasing government support (both federal and state) of social and educational programs; an immense expansion of higher education generated not only by population growth and government support but by a lowering of admissions standards and the proliferation of two-year colleges and technical schools; and the availability of such technological innovations as copying machines, automatic test-scoring systems, television, and computers which among other things made it possible to teach and test large numbers of students. The exodus of European intellectuals to the United States during the 1930s and early 1940s in combination with the destruction of many urban centers in Europe and Japan also transformed the United States into the scientific and cultural center of the world for much of the period since World War II.

All academic disciplines and professions were affected by these national and international developments, but not all were affected as significantly as psychology. Among the special factors stimulating the growth of psychology as a whole was the upsurge of clinical psychology because university departments of psychology had to increase their staffs and facilities in order to train the clinicians. As a result of the APA's adoption, at the Boulder Conference in 1950, of a scientist-practitioner model for clinical psychology, which requires graduate students to take courses in the traditional scientific areas of the field including statistics and research methods, new faculty positions in all areas of psychological inquiry were created. This, in turn, attracted additional graduate students to the field. Acceptance of the scientist-practitioner model for clinical psychology, and actually for all applied areas of the field at the Ph.D. level, also facilitated growth in another way. Since experimental research tends to be emphasized in the dissertation studies of even applied graduate students, and since most experimental investigations take less time to design and conduct than do field or clinical projects, the time to earn the Ph.D. degree in all areas of psychology has usually been kept to five years of post-B.A. training. Moreover, in most instances it is less time consuming for a faculty member to oversee an experimental study than one involving extensive theoretical issues or research in more natural settings, thus allowing each instructor to supervise more students.

Psychology further benefited from being considered both a science and a helping profession. The fact that academic-research and applied psychologists belong to the same organization, namely APA, has clearly contributed to the field's being perceived in this dual way. This perception, however, probably has helped foster the confusion that surrounds the precise nature of the discipline. In any case, psychology's classification as a science has made psychologists eligible for funding from the National Science Foundation and the research branches of the military, while the discipline's classification as a helping profession has provided training and research funds from the National Institutes of Health (now part of the Department of Health and Human Services). Some psychological investigations have even been supported by agencies interested mostly in funding scholars in the humanities (for example, philosophy, history, literature).

Finally, psychology grew because there has been a perceived need in the United States for more psychological services in clinics, mental hospitals, schools, prisons, industries, and in the form of individual consulting, counseling, or psychotherapy and because psychology is to many an intrinsically very interesting subject. In most universities and colleges, for example, introductory courses in psychology are among the most popular of all offerings. In many institutions of higher learning psychology courses are included within general education programs, that is, programs consisting of courses every student must take to graduate. While, in many instances, some choice of courses is permitted within general education programs, sections of introductory psychology are regularly well attended. Large enrollments in lower-level courses make it economically feasible for departments to offer small sections of advanced courses.

DIVERSIFICATION WITHIN, AND FRAGMENTATION OF, THE DISCIPLINE

Comparison of the chapter headings of introductory textbooks published in the United States in the 1950s with more contemporary texts indicates that the basic concerns of the discipline have changed very little during the last forty years. Different studies and concepts have been highlighted, and the models and theories emphasized have changed; but throughout the post–World War II era there has been a strong consensus that psychology concerns sensation, perception, affects, learning and conditioning, memory, thinking and problem solving, language development, intelligence, psychological development in general, personality, individual differences and testing, abnormal behavior, social psychological processes (particularly those associated with small groups), techniques for changing human and animal behavior, and the nature of psychological research. A short overview of statistical techniques useful to psychologists is typically included, generally in an appendix. The most significant changes in U.S. psychology in recent years as reflected in introductory texts have probably been the reintroduction of consciousness and states of consciousness as serious concerns and elaboration of cognitive and linguistic processes, sex and gender as psychological variables, and the psychological changes associated with aging (gerontological psychology).

While the overall organization of psychological knowledge presented in U.S. textbooks has remained relatively stable, the discipline has in fact experienced significant diversification and persistent fragmentation. The number of APA divisions has increased enormously, dozens of new journals have appeared, new organizations are founded almost every year, and the *Annual Review of Psychology* frequently adds new research areas to its list of work which needs to be reviewed.

APA, which was reorganized in 1945 into a divisional structure to represent the interests of applied as well as academic-research psychologists, consisted of nineteen divisions in 1950. These divisions had to do with general psychology, the teaching of psychology, theoretical-experimental psychology, psychometrics, evaluation and measurement, physiological and comparative psychology, childhood and adolescence, personality and social psychology, social issues, aesthetics, abnormal psychology and psychotherapy, clinical psychology, consulting psychology, industrial and business psychology, educational psychology, school psychology, personnel and guidance, psychology in the public service, and military psychology.

In 1950, Division 4, concerned with psychometrics, was dropped because it was redundant with the focus of Division 5 on evaluation and measurement. Since then divisions serving the needs of psychologists in the following areas have been added: adult development and aging; engineering psychology; rehabilitation psychology; consumer psychology; theoretical and philosophical psychology; the experimental analysis of behavior (mostly inspired by the increasing influence of Skinnerian behaviorism by the late 1950s); history of psychology; community psychology; psychopharmacology; psychotherapy; hypnosis; humanistic psychology; mental retardation; population and environmental psychology; psychology of women; psychological aspects of religion; child, youth, and family services; health psychology; psychoanalysis; clinical neuropsychology; and psychology and law. A division concerned with the interests of state psychological associations was also organized in the early 1970s, and more recently a division representing psychologists in private practice was created.

Although most of the divisions which came into being since the 1940s are manifestations of the discipline's strong growth in the various applied areas, it is also important to note that one of the new divisions has to do with the history of psychology and another concerns philosophical matters. Membership in both organizations is small, but the existence of these organizations indicates that, though most psychologists in the United States are primarily concerned with experimental research or applied work, there are some who recognize the importance of placing psychological inquiry within historical and philosophical perspectives. The creation of a division for psychologists active in state psychological associations reflects the fact that the licensing of professionals in the United States is done by the states rather than the federal government, a situation facilitating active state organizations. There are also significant differences of opinion between the leadership of the APA and the memberships of certain state organizations on the matter of how much training is necessary for a person to be considered a qualified professional psychologist. The APA contends that the Ph.D. is the qualifying degree while some state organizations argue that a master's degree is generally sufficient.

Another index of the increasing diversification of U.S. psychology, as mentioned before, is the number of new journals. According to the *Author's guide to journals in psychology, psychiatry & social work* (Markle & Rinn, 1977), there were by the late 1970s over 450 regularly published, English-language journals in these three fields. Most of them are published in the United States and came into being during the last forty years. Markle and Rinn point out that worldwide several thousand journals (including newsletters and incidental publications) are apparently published in psychology, psychiatry, and social work.

Looking at the types of new journals which commenced publication during the post–World War II period, we find important behavioral journals such as the *Journal of the Experimental Analysis of Behavior* and the *Journal of Applied Behavior Analysis*, the former founded in 1958 and the latter in 1968. Both reflected the increasing influence of Skinnerian behaviorism starting in the late 1950s. In addition, however, we find journals concerned with existential, humanistic, phenomenological, Jungian, Adlerian, Rankian, transpersonal, cross-cultural, international, mathematical, cognitive, and thanatological psychology. There were also new publications having to do with the history of psychology, community psychology, school psychology, counseling psychology, family dynamics and therapies, the teaching of psychology, Black psychology, population psychology, as well as others concerning sex, homosexuality, autistic children, motor behavior, personal growth, altered states of consciousness and aggression. *Psychology Today*, targeted for an audience broader than psychologists and founded in 1967, was purchased in 1983 by APA. (This transaction has stirred controversy because the journal includes advertising for cigarettes and alcoholic beverages.)

The diversification of U.S. psychology is a function of several factors. First, considerable diversity is assured by the existence of separate departments of psychology and educational psychology at most universities and by the differences in requirements and emphases within departments of psychology relative to their experimental and applied programs. Second, growth and diversity are reciprocally related; the expansion of the discipline allowed for the flowering of more research areas and applied specialities, and the flourishing of new interests stimulated growth. Third, since there is some perception that psychologists are able to play a role in improving society, federal funds are usually made available for research relevant to social problems vieiwed as most pressing at any particular time. This serves as an incentive for psychologists to become interested in projects only peripherally related to their areas of expertise. Even without funds from the federal government, of course, emerging and continuing social problems generate work for psychologists both as researchers and helping professionals. Recently, for example, gerontological psychology has been stimulated by problems associated with the growth of the elderly segment of society. Lastly, diversity is fostered by the fact that psychology as an area of study and body of knowledge is fragmented and disorganized. New work tends to generate concepts, ideas, and data not systematically related to other relevant information. This process is perpetuated by the creation of new journals and organizations, compounded by the fact that incentives for doing theoretical research are minimal.

There is probably no way to tell, at this time, whether or not the diversity characteristic of U.S. psychology will in the long run lead to significant advances in psychological understanding. In my opinion, diversity generated by the growth of the discipline and inspired by progress in other disciplines, technological advances, and the needs of society should be encouraged. Fragmentation which is a function of psychological research devoid of essential contexts and relevant conceptual frameworks, however, impedes the process of psychological inquiry. Arthur Staats' book *Psychology's crisis of disunity* (1983) presents an insightful analysis of some of the problems associated with an unsystematic psychology.

THE FUNDING OF PSYCHOLOGY

Prior to the 1920s most of the support for psychology came from private universities. The first doctorate in psychology was conferred upon G. Stanley Hall by Harvard University in 1873. The next doctorate was not awarded until John Dewey received his degree from Johns Hopkins University in 1884. During the 1880s only Johns Hopkins awarded doctorates in psychology. In the 1890s and first decade of the twentieth century, most of the doctorates in psychology were granted by Clark University. By 1920 almost thirty institutions were offering advanced graduate training in psychology. The largest programs were at Clark University, the University of Chicago, Columbia University, Harvard University, and Cornell University, all private institutions.

During the 1920s, 1930s, and early 1940s doctoral programs in psychology were established at many state universities. By 1948 sixty-three universities and three exclusive women's colleges had each conferred at least one doctorate in psychology (Harper, 1949). Between 1884 and 1948, the universities awarding the most doctorates were Columbia University, the University of Iowa, the

University of Chicago, Ohio State University, Harvard University, Clark University, the University of Minnesota, Yale University, Cornell University, and the University of Pennsylvania.

It is clear that prior to World War II the principal financial support for psychology came from universities, first from private institutions but increasingly from large state universities. The only external funding for research was provided by a few private foundations, most notably the Laura Spelman Rockefeller Memorial, the Rockefeller Foundation, the Carnegie Corporation, and the Russell Sage Foundation (Smith, 1953). During 1917 and 1918, the years that the United States was involved in World War I, psychologists were employed by the army to develop and administer group intelligence tests. This was the first time the federal government provided notable support for professional psychologists.

Significant funding of psychology by the federal government started during World War II, particularly from 1941 to 1945 when the United States was formally involved in the conflict. Federal support of psychology following the war increased substantially for a number of interrelated reasons. First, science and technology were held in high regard because of the contributions, including the atomic bomb, made to the war effort by scientists and engineers. Second, faith in the capability of the federal government to design, finance, and administer programs to bring about prosperity and an improved society was augmented by victory in the war. Third, the depression of the 1930s had inhibited the birth rate so that in the late 1940s and 1950s a relatively small pool of young adults threatened to leave the country with a shortage of professional people. The federal government, therefore, provided funds to make it possible for a higher percentage of talented students than before to complete college and graduate education. Fourth, the expansion of higher education meant that more academicians would have to be trained so funds for assistantships and fellowships were maintained at a high level until the late 1960s. And, finally, because more helping professionals were needed quickly, the federal government stepped in to support the training of clinical psychologists.

As has already been discussed, among the most important developments in psychology in the United States during the post–World War II period has been the dramatic growth of the discipline, which was, in turn, a function of population growth, the monumental expansion of higher education, a generally robust economy, and an increasing need for psychological services. There are at present over 1,900 universities and four-year colleges in the country all of which, to my knowledge, offer at least an undergraduate program in psychology. In addition, psychology courses are offered at two-year institutions and many high schools. Most of the financial support for the psychological enterprise, consequently, still comes from the budgets of the individual states and private colleges and universities. What has changed since World War II, however, is the support that the discipline has received from the federal government both in terms of funds to train psychologists and in terms of research grants and contracts. While less significant, private funding has also been on the upswing. The Ford Foundation, for example, started providing monies for research in the behavioral sciences in 1951.

Developments which led to greater federal support of psychology include the Veterans Administration approval of a four-year training program for clinical psychologists (1946); the National Institute of Mental Health providing funds to train clinical psychologists, the National Science Foundation funding psychological research (the early 1950s); the National Institute of Mental Health extending support for research and training in areas of psychology other than clinical (1953); the increase in federal funding to train scientists and conduct scientific research following the successful launching by the Soviet Union of the first space vehicle (Sputnik) in 1957; the National Science Foundation creating an Office of Social Sciences (1959), which was given divisional status in 1960 (it was not until 1968 that legislation amended the National Science Foundation Act formally to sanction this division); and President Kennedy proposing a comprehensive community-based plan for helping the mentally ill and mentally retarded with Congress approving increased funding for the plan in 1963. In the late 1960s, Congress became skeptical of the benefits of large federal support of science; since then funds for research and training have been more difficult to obtain, especially for social scientists. During the early 1980s, economic problems and the Reagan administration's high priority on basic research in the natural sciences and engineering have continued to restrict federal support for psychology.

A recent study of research activities in psychology by APA's Human Resources Office (Nelson & Stapp, 1983) indicates that in 1982 almost 40 percent of all research projects were funded by the federal government. About 30 percent were supported by universities, colleges, and state and local governments; 22 percent by private foundations and businesses; and approximately 8 percent by unidentified sources. The federal agency funding the most projects was found to be the Alcohol, Drug Abuse, and Mental Health Administration, followed by the National Institutes of Health, the Department of Education, the Department of Defense, the National Science Foundation, and the Veterans Administration.

The subfields of psychology wherein the highest percentages of psychologists were funded (Lowman & Stapp, 1981) include engineering psychology (92.6 percent), psychopharmocology (86.7 percent), cognitive (82.1 percent), physiological (68.7 percent), quantitative (65.4 percent), psycholinguistics (60.0 percent), social (59.5 percent), experimental (58.9 percent), developmental (54.0 percent), comparative (52.2 percent), and psychometrics (51.8 percent). Specialities with the lowest percentages of researchers being funded were counseling, school, and clinical.

According to Lowman and Stapp, the overall funding of psychological research for fiscal year 1979 was about $530 million. The federal government provided about 79 percent of the money but only 54 percent of the awards. The rest of the funds came from other sources. Interestingly, while educational institutions and private foundations provide a large number of research awards, most are in the form of small grants or stipends.

Total federal funding for research and development in 1981 across all disciplines, and including that for defense, was approximately $35 billion. Of that, psychology received about 1.5 percent. In 1984 the federal government spent $46.7 billion dollars on research and development, much of the increase involving military projects (Keyworth, 1984). Currently no more than 1.0 percent of the federal research monies are apparently allocated for psychological research.

A study of the grants awarded by the National Institute of Mental Health during the 1948–1980 period (Gilgen, 1981a) shows that insofar as large grants are concerned the majority go to relatively few universities. Receiving most of the awards totaling $1 million or more over the years have been psychologists at Harvard University, the University of California (Los Angeles), Yale University, New York University, Columbia University, Stanford University, and Johns Hopkins University. The nonuniversity institutions awarded the most large awards were the Downstate Medical Center in New York, the Wright Institute in Ohio, and the Oregon Research Center.

A similar study of the major recipients of research funds from the National Science Foundation during the 1952–1978 period (Gilgen & Tolvstad, 1981) indicates that the psychologists receiving the most support were at Harvard University, the University of Michigan, the University of California (Berkeley), the University of Colorado, Indiana University, and Yale University. The three areas of research most often provided large grants were social, cognition and language, and conditioning and learning.

Few would argue that federal agencies should cease allocating funds for psychological research; nonetheless, there is some concern about increasing governmental intrusion into psychology. The intrusion is manifested in several ways. First, the direction of research is influenced by offering support for particular kinds of studies but not others. Second, grant getting can become an end in itself. Third, short-term studies are reinforced because many grants, though potentially renewable, provide support for only one year; and, finally, government guidelines for conducting both animal and human research have become increasingly stringent.

Readers who are interested in detailed funding studies of the discipline should write to the Human Resources Office of the American Psychological Association.

MAJOR PEOPLE, DEVELOPMENTS, AND INFLUENCES

While it is not possible to determine which post–World War II research findings, theories, applications of psychological knowledge, and new methodologies will in the long run turn out to be truly significant, we can identify those people, developments, and influences which predominated in American psychology during the period. One can, for example, specify the psychologists elected to the National Academy of Sciences (Over, 1981), those receiving various awards (see *American Psychologist*), those whose work is most highly cited (Endler, Rushton, & Roediger, 1978; various analyses by E. Garfield in *Current Con-*

tents), those whose studies are included in reprint or offprint series, those whose works are selected for the *Harvard List of Books*, those who have received the most research support (Gilgen, 1981a; Gilgen & Tolvstad, 1981), those most referenced in the *Annual Review of Psychology* (Gilgen & Hultman, 1979), and those whose work is discussed in introductory textbooks and books on history and systems. One can also identify important developments and issues by reading the analyses and demographic studies which regularly appear in the *American Psychologist* and the *APA Monitor* as well as the articles published by the *Journal of the History of the Behavioral Sciences*; it is also possible to do surveys of the perceived importance of people and events (Gilgen 1980, 1981b). A seven-year study which I conducted, based to some degree on all of these sources, resulted in a book entitled *American psychology since World War II: A profile of the discipline* (1982).

Using an organization which deviates slightly from that which structures the information in my 1982 book, let us briefly consider, in turn, the impact on American psychology of World War II, transformations of behaviorism, the Freudian influence, the resurgence of interest in psychological processes, the maturing of development psychology, and the challenge to psychiatry of clinical psychology.

World War II and American Psychology

The membership of APA was about 2,600 at the beginning of the war in 1939 and somewhat over 4,000 at the war's end in 1945. About one-third of the members worked full-time on projects related to the conflict and many more were employed by the government part-time. Mostly they constructed and administered tests, interviewed and classified personnel, provided clinical counseling and consultation, developed educational materials for the military, were involved in designing and implementing training programs, and conducted research related to military and war-induced societal problems. Some did sensory and perceptual investigations and human engineering research; a small number participated in psychological warfare studies.

The war decimated much of urban Europe and Asia leaving the United States unscathed and industrially strong. As a consequence this country emerged in the late 1940s as the world's educational and cultural center (the intellectual migration from Europe discussed earlier contributed to this situation). With the exception of Switzerland, where Piaget's work continued, the United States was clearly the place to be to study psychology and engage in psychological research, at least until relatively recently. Now there are active research programs and facilities in many countries.

With respect to American psychology, the war

had some bearing on each of the following events or developments: a) the accelerated growth of the discipline; b) the expansion of professional (particularly clinical) psychology; c) the spread of the psychoanalytic influence; d) the formulation of guidelines for research using human subjects; e) studies on anti-Semitism, prejudice, and rumor; f) analyses of concentration-camp experiences; g) research on peace, war, aggression, stress, and frustration; h) psychological projects solicited by the United Nations; i) increased interest in conducting interdisciplinary research; j) investigations suggested or made possible by technological developments; k) test development and validation; l) small-group research and the growth of social psychology; and m) talent searches and work on creativity. (Gilgen, 1982, p. 45)

Transformations of Behaviorism

Even though it is usually claimed that American behaviorism as a distinct school had ceased to exist by the 1950s, the behavioral orientation in American psychology has, I believe, gone through the following overlapping stages: classical behaviorism (1900–1925), the time of Edward Thorndike and John Watson (strongly influenced by Pavlov and Bekhterev); neobehaviorism (1920s–1940s), a period of great controversy when Clark Hull, Edward Tolman, Edwin Guthrie, and B. F. Skinner vied for preeminence and in the process brought to light the complexities associated with conditioning and learning processes; Hullian behaviorism (1940s–1950s), when Hull's complex hypothetico-deductive theory of behavior appeared most promising, particularly in terms of generating interesting testable hypotheses; Skinnerian behaviorism (1960s–1975), when operant conditioning techniques found application in most research and applied areas; and cognitive behaviorism (1975–present) during which time the limits of Skinnerianism became more apparent and cognitive perspectives, especially social learning theories, gained adherents.

The behavioral orientation has remained central to post–World War II American psychology for a variety of reasons, including interest on the part of psychologists, educators, and helping professionals of all types in ways to change human behavior (influence learning and performance); faith in laboratory research, observable phenomena, experimental methodologies, and animal studies; considerable success at devising techniques of value in almost all areas of research and applied subfields; a conservative approach to theory building; and a belief that, in general, the activities of people and other higher life forms are molded more by the environment than genes.

While the behavioral orientation has contributed to psychology by emphasizing accountability and semantic as well as procedural clarity and by providing extremely useful methodologies, the limitations of radical and simple stimulus-response approaches are evidenced by the fact that no single theory of human behavior has been forthcoming. Furthermore, cognitive, and therefore more complex, variables have since the early 1970s been increasingly seen as necessary by most American psychologists to account for behavior and behavior change.

The Freudian Influence

The impact of Freudian thought on American culture extends back to the pre–World War I years; by the 1920s, sociology, social work, the mental health profession, the child welfare movement, and psychiatry had all been significantly influenced by psychoanalytic views toward personality structure and development and psychopathology. Interestingly, psychology was not much affected by this complex orientation until about the mid–1930s, primarily because the mainstream of the discipline during the 1920s and 1930s was concerned with physiological processes, experiments using nonverbal methods, animal studies, testing, and statistical research (Bruner & Allport, 1940). The period between the two world wars was also the era of competing schools and neobehaviorism.

Other factors that delayed the influence of psychoanalysis on mainstream American psychology were "the lack of accurate English translations of most of Freud's major works, the fact that many of Freud's writings were problem-oriented rather than systematic, and the continuing development of Freud's ideas" (Gilgen, 1982, p. 72).

The Freudian sway accelerated during the late 1930s and 1940s because of the growth of clinical psychology, which required that psychologists become concerned with personality development, psychopathology, and psychotherapy, combined with the fact that most of the European psychoanalysts had moved to New York, Boston, and other American cities by the 1940s. The psychoanalytic impact on mainstream psychology in this country was most pronounced during the 1940s and 1950s; during that period prominent experimentalists, in particular the Yale Group (Hull, N. Miller, R. Sears, O. H. Mowrer, and others), took a careful look at Freud's ideas, and the training of clinical psychologists included a heavy dose of psychoanalytic theory. Neo-Freudianism and ego psychology, which placed more emphasis than did classical Freudian formulations on cultural and environmental factors, also made the psychoanalytic perspective more compatible with the American milieu.

Psychoanalysis influenced psychology in the United States by enriching personality theory; inspiring more interest in abnormal psychology; making talking therapies credible; encouraging research on infants and children; fostering dynamic (motivational) studies; providing a theoretical foundation for projective testing; helping bring about the "new look" in psychology which emphasized the interrelationships among perception, motivation, values, and past experience; and making the concept of anxiety more important insofar as theories of personality, psychopathology, therapy, and psychiatric classification systems of psychological problems are concerned (Gilgen, 1982). More recently, the psychoanalytic orientation has led to a minor resurgence of psychohistorical analyses. There is still a lively interest among American psychologists in psychoanalytic perspectives, as evidenced by an APA division that is concerned with psychoanalysis.

Progress in Developmental Psychology

Throughout the late 1940s and 1950s developmental psychology moved toward becoming an experimental discipline inspired most of all by the work of Eckhard

Hess, Donald Hebb, and Harry Harlow but also by the studies of Austin Riesen, Frank Beach, and some Hullians. The primary influences included the studies and perspectives of Austrian ethologists K. Lorenz, N. Tinbergen, and K. von Frisch; G. Coghill's research; and the theoretical formulations of Freud, Hull, Lewin, and Werner. Also of importance during this period was the work on perceptual learning conducted by James and Eleanor Gibson, Leo Postman, and others. The nature-nurture debate continued, centering around Coghill's theory based on animal research and Gesell's work with infants and children; both placed considerable emphasis on the role of genetic factors in psychological development.

During the 1960s, the main developments included the increasing influence of Piaget; the declining importance of classical Freudianism accompanied by the increasing significance of the ideas of the neo-Freudians, in particular Erik Erikson; the gradual replacement of Hullian by Skinnerian behaviorism; the importation of linguist Noam Chomsky's assumptions into the field; cross-cultural research on childrearing by Urie Bronfenbrenner, Jerome Kagan, and Milford Spiro, among others; the social learning theory of Albert Bandura; and studies of childhood autism and schizophrenia by Bruno Bettelheim and O. I. Lovaas. Perhaps that decade's most important development was the emergence of infant experimental psychology pioneered by Robert Fantz, Eleanor Gibson, Richard Walk, T. G. R. Bower, Lois Murphy, and Lewis P. Lipsitt, because their work bore directly on the nature-nurture issue. Also of consequence was the research on death and dying done by Herman Feifel, Edwin Shneidman, Norman Farberow, and Robert Litman.

Since the 1970s, significant advances in developmental psychology include continuing vigorous research on perceptual and cognitive processes, not only in the young but in the elderly as well; the surfacing of gerontological psychology; and the recognition that a life-span perspective is a requisite for a mature developmental psychology. This last development brought with it an interest in studying the middle-age period of human life. Throughout the postwar era, methodologies have become more sophisticated and interactional views of development adopted. Yet as Scholnick has recently pointed out, the field still seems in crisis (1985). But then, according to some, psychology and its various areas of study are always in turmoil and conflict (see most of the reviews in the *Annual Review of Psychology*).

Research on Mental and Affective Processes and States

While Hull was the predominant figure in American psychology during the 1940s and 1950s with the war and psychoanalysis the most important influences, and Skinnerian behaviorism predominated during the 1960s and 1970s, important research on sensory, perceptual, cognitive, and affective states and processes continued throughout the period. By the mid–1960s, the so-called cognitive revolution was taking place, and by the 1970s, the concepts of mind and consciousness, which most behaviorists had tried to expunge from the discipline, had regained much of their previous scientific legitimacy.

Developments during the 1940s, 1950s, and early 1960s which set the stage for the move toward a more cognitive psychology by the late 1960s included the persistence of Gestalt psychology; the "new look" movement; the research by Jerome Bruner, James and Eleanor Gibson, Harry Helson, Donald Hebb, Adelbert Ames, and Egon Brunswik on cognitive and perceptual processes, much of it concerned with the influence of past experience; the sensory-tonic theory of Heinz Werner and Seymour Wapner; research on sensory deprivation; renewed interest in the attentional processes inspired by wartime vigilance research, refined equipment, the studies of British psychologist Donald Broadbent, findings concerning the functioning of the reticular formation, the work of Soviet physiologist E. N. Sokolov on the orienting response, and looking-time studies inspired primarily by the work of Robert Fantz; investigations of sleeping and dreaming stimulated by the REM research done by E. Aserinsky and N. Kleitman; the advent of modern psychophysics based on detection and decision theory; the importation of information theory into psychology; Charles Osgood's development of the Semantic Differential technique for measuring the connotative meaning of concepts; a renewed interest in psycholinguistics catalyzed by the debate featuring Skinner's and Chomsky's views concerning language acquisition; advances in experimental cognitive social psychology where the central figures included Kurt Lewin, Fritz Heider, Jerome Bruner, and Leon Festinger; research on attitudes, opinions, and values; cognitive-style research deriving from psychoanalysis via ego psychologists Heinz Hartmann, George Klein, and Philip Holtzman; cognitively oriented personality theories such as George Kelly's theory of personal constructs; the publication of *Plans and the structure of behavior* in 1960 by N. Miller, E. Galanter, and K. H. Pribram, a book which represented the first systematic effort to investigate the relevance of cybernetic ideas for psychology; the influence of existentialism, phenomenology, and Eastern thought, which was significant by the mid–1960s; the increasing interest in altered states of consciousness brought about by the drug culture; and, of course, the profound impact of Piaget's work since the late 1960s.

The emergence of a more cognitive psychology, symbolized by the publication in 1967 of Ulric Neisser's *Cognitive psychology*, was really a quiet, gradual process, not a revolution, because all through the post–World War II period prominent American psychologists had been doing important research on mental and affective processes. At the same time, the increasing interest in cognition, linguistic processes, and eventually mind and consciousness was given a special boost by progress in the neurosciences and computer technology. It became clear that new findings concerning neurotransmitters, psychoactive drugs, hormones, brain lateralization, arousal centers, motivational subsystems, and the peripheral nervous system could not be ignored by psychologists. Likewise, the design of hardware and software to receive, store, process, and use information led naturally to the study of artificial intelligence.

Just a few words are in order concerning research on affects. While there has been strong interest in the study of anxiety and fear (negative states), there has been less systematic study of positive feelings such as love and contentment. Exceptions include Harlow's work on love in monkeys; Silvan Tompkins's analyses of positive affects; the work of Magda Arnold, Robert Plutchik, Joel Davitz, Stanley Schachter, and Robert Zajonc; and the perspectives of personality theorists, in particular, Eric Fromm, Abraham Maslow, Carl Rogers, and Rollo May.

Clinical Psychology Challenges Psychiatry

Prior to World War II, American clinical psychologists were primarily psychodiagnosticians administering and interpreting personality and intelligence tests. During the war they demonstrated that they were well trained to do psychotherapy as well as diagnostic work, and federal funds for training more clinicians were provided universities following the conflict. As a consequence, the field grew dramatically particularly during the 1950s, 1960s, and early 1970s, presenting an increasing challenge to psychiatry.

The psychoanalytic orientation predominated during the late 1940s and 1950s, but gradually client-centered (Carl Rogers), behavioral (Eysenck, Wolpe, Skinner), existential-phenomenological (May, Binswanger, Laing), social learning (Bandura), and other perspectives offered significant alternatives. Group and short-term therapies also burgeoned. The principal training model throughout the period was that of scientist-practitioner (the Boulder Conference Model) though, during the 1970s, the Vail Conference (1973) signaled a growing interest in more experientially oriented training. Accompanying this development was the advent of professional schools of clinical psychology, which now graduate more clinicians than do unversity doctoral programs.

Circumstances, in addition to increased funding, which profoundly influenced the clinical field include the emptying of the mental hospitals starting in the late 1950s due to the development of a variety of psychotherapeutic drugs, the fact that in most states the major insurance companies will not pay for the services offered by clinical psychologists in private practice, and within the last decade or so a strengthening of the view that serious psychological problems are diseases which need to be treated medically rather than psychotherapeutically. This contention is, of course, most forcefully expressed by the psychiatric community.

CONCLUSION

U.S. psychology has during the last four decades had a profound influence on psychology worldwide because of its sheer size and scope. At a time when the discipline had to rebuild in Europe, the Soviet Union, and Japan, psychology in the United States was well financed and growing vigorously. Because this country is characterized by a vast information production and dissemination capability (publications, libraries, computerized data bases, conferences, exchange programs, and so forth), and because the world's primary scholarly and scientific language is English, the discipline's impact internationally was assured. The negative aspects of countries importing psychology from the United States or other countries have already been discussed in the Introduction.

What, though, have been the contributions of U.S. psychologists which would seem relevant regardless of country or culture? Perhaps most important is the emphasis placed on accountability in both research and applied fields. A conservative approach to theory building on a grand scale has also had important payoffs, although it has at the same time contributed to producing a conceptually fragmented field. The American Psychological Association, which encompasses both academic/research and applied psychology (though now experiencing serious tensions), provides a good organizational model for the discipline because it enhances the sense of professional identity and the advocacy power of the field. While there is still room for improvement, impressive progress has been made in bringing about laws, credentialing procedures, and ethical guidelines which both define the discipline and protect the public.

In the area of research, one of the most consequential developments has been the coming into being of a truly experimental infant psychology. We now know much more about the sensory and perceptual capabilities of neonates and infants than we did twenty years ago. Skinner and the Skinnerians did the most to develop and refine techniques useful in essentially all research areas as well as the major applied fields.

In evaluating theoretical contributions, Hull's hypothetico-deductive approach failed to produce a general theory of behavior but was exceedingly productive in terms of generating fruitful hypotheses and research problems. However, the most creative U.S. psychological theorist, in my opinion, was James J. Gibson.

Relative to counseling and psychotherapy, perhaps the most important contribution was not any particular approach but recognition of the fact that human psychological and emotional problems are complex and can be explained and treated in a variety of ways. Much U.S. research has also demonstrated the limitations of tests.

Finally, I believe we have learned that psychology, no matter how well established in a country, is not a tool that can be used to change societies or fix societal problems quickly; it is, rather, a field of study and application which makes its contributions primarily by helping to create a more enlightened citizenry.

REFERENCES

American Psychological Association. (1985, December). *The changing face of American psychology*. (Report of the Committee on Employment and Human Resources). Washington, DC: Author.

Bruner, J. S., & Allport, G. W. (1940). Fifty years of change in American psychology. *Psychological Bulletin, 37*, 757–776.

Endler, N. S., Rushton, J. P., & Roediger, H. L. III. (1978). Productivity and scholarly impact (citations) of British, Canadian, and U.S. departments of psychology (1975). *American Psychologist, 33*, 1064–1082.

Evans, R. B. (1983). The origins of American academic psychology. In J. Brozek (Ed.), *Explorations in the history of psychology in the United States* (pp. 17–60). Lewisburg, PA: Bucknell University Press.

Fermi, L. (1971). *Illustrious immigrants: The intellectual migration from Europe, 1930–41*. Chicago: University of Chicago Press.

Fleming, D., & Bailyn, B.(Eds.). (1969). *The intellectual migration: Europe and America, 1930–1960*. Cambridge, MA: Harvard University Press.

Gilgen, A. R. (1980). Important events and influences in post–World War II American psychology: A survey study. *JSAS Catalog of Selected Documents in Psychology, 10*, Ms. 2144.

Gilgen, A. R. (1981). Major recipients of National Institute of Mental Health funds: The million dollar club. *JSAS Catalog of Selected Documents in Psychology, 11*, Ms. 2170.(a)

Gilgen, A. R. (1981). Important people in post–world War II American psychology: A survey study. *JSAS Catalog of Selected Documents in Psychology, 11*, Ms. 2171.(b)

Gilgen, A. R. (1982). *American psychology since World War II: A profile of the discipline*. Westport, CT: Greenwood Press.

Gilgen, A. R. (in press). The psychological level of organization in nature and the interdependencies among major psychological concepts. In A. Staats & L. P. Mos (Eds.), *Annals of theoretical psychology* (Vol. 5). New York: Plenum.

Gilgen, A. R., & Hultman, S. K. (1979). Authorities and subject-matter areas emphasized in *Annual Review of Psychology*, 1950–1974. *Psychological Reports, 44*, 1255–1262.

Gilgen, A. R., & Tolvstad, K. (1981). Major recipients of National Science Foundation funds for psychological research. *JSAS Catalog of Selected Documents in Psychology, 11*, Ms. 2278.

Harmon, L. R. (1964). Production of psychology doctorates. *American Psychologist, 19*, 629–633.

Harper, R. S. (1949). Tables of American doctorates in psychology. *American Journal of Psychology, 62*, 579–587.

Keyworth, G. A. (1984). Four years of Reagan science policy: Notable shifts in priorities. *Science, 224*, 9–13.

Lowman, R. P., & Stapp, J. (1981). Research activities in psychology: Funding and human resources. *American Psychologist, 36*, 1364–1394.

Markle, A., & Rinn, R. C. (1977). *Author's guide to journals in psychology, psychiatry & social work*. New York: Haworth Press.

Miller, G. A., Galanter, E., & Pribram, K. H. (1960). *Plans and the structure of behavior*. New York: Holt, Rinehart & Winston.

Neisser, U. (1967). *Cognitive psychology*. New York: Appleton-Century-Crofts.

Nelson, S. D., & Stapp, J. (1983). Research activities in psychology: An update. *American Psychologist, 38*, 1321–1329.

Over, R. (1981). Affiliations of psychologists elected to the National Academy of Sciences. *American Psychologist, 36*, 744–752.

Roback, A. A. (1952). *A history of American psychology*. New York: Collier.

Russo, N. F., Olmedo, E. L., Stapp, J., & Fulcher, R. (1981). Women and minorities in psychology. *American Psychologist, 36*, 1315–1363.

Scholnick, E. K. (1985). [Review of *Developmental psychology: Historical and philosophical perspectives*]. *Contemporary Psychology, 30*, 314–316.

Smith, M. B. (1953). The SSRC and psychology. *American Psychologist, 8*, 484–488.

Staats, A. W. (1983). *Psychology's crisis of disunity: Philosophy and method for a unified science*. New York: Praeger.

Tryon, R. C. (1963). Psychology in flux: The academic-professional bipolarity. *American Psychologist, 18*, 134–143.

Venezuela

José Miguel Salazar and Ligia M. Sánchez

NATURE AND SCOPE OF THE DISCIPLINE

Definition of Psychology/Psychological

In Venezuela the state confers upon universities degree-granting powers, and the degrees awarded are required for professional practice. Control of the practice of each discipline is left to professional associations (colegios or federations) via specific laws of professional practice.

The Law of Psychological Practice was passed by the National Congress in 1978. In it is included the official definition of psychology and psychological practice:

Article 2. Psychological Practice is understood as the use of knowledge acquired through the scientific study of human and animal behavior, for research and teaching in psychology, as well as for providing professional services, with or without payment, to individuals or to public or private institutions. This knowledge enables psychologists to make contributions in areas concerning human and animal behavior, through the exploration, description, explanation, prediction, guidance and modification of situations, in the context of pure research as well as within the framework of applied research, teaching, and private or institutional professional practice.

This knowledge also enables psychologists to contribute to the prevention of difficulties in the normal psychological development of individuals; the preparation of programs encouraging personal, educational and social development; and the solution of behavioral problems through the use of psychological techniques and procedures.

Organizational Structure

Also defined in the Law of Psychological Practice is the official organizational structure of psychology in Venezuela. The major organization is La Federación de Psicólogos de Venezuela [Venezuelan Psychological Federation] which integrates the Colegios de Psicólogos corresponding to the different geopolitical divisions (states) of the country. These organizations are nonprofit corporations with professional, legal, and economic functions and exist in the capitals of states where ten or more practicing psychologists reside. If there are fewer than ten psychologists in a state, they constitute a delegation and are associated with the nearest colegio. Membership in these associations is mandatory for the legal practice of psychology; registration in the social security department of the federation, Instituto de Prevision del Psicólogo (INPREPSI), is further required. Both the federation and the colegios have a senate, an executive board, and a disciplinary tribunal, elected every two years by the secret and direct balloting of all members who are in good financial standing.

These bodies are basically professional organizations serving to promote the dignity of the profession and the recognition of its social role, protect the economic and corporate interests of the profession as a whole and of its members individually, and encourage solidarity and mutual assistance among the memberships. By February 1984, La Federación de Psicólogos de Venezuela consisted of twelve colegios and seven delegations which represent nineteen of the twenty-three geopolitical entities that make up the country. The president of the executive board of the federation is Erik Becker, who first took office in 1975. The address of the organization is: Federación de Psicólogos de Venezuela, Apartado 62558, Caracas 1060-A, Venezuela. The headquarters of the Federación are located at Avenida Naiguatá, Macaracuay, Caracas 1070. Communication with any of the colegios may be accomplished by contacting the federation.

Venezuelan psychologists are also organized into scientific societies. Even though these societies are autonomous and do not share all the objectives of the federation, they receive its support. The federation fosters the organization of new societies by offering its premises for meetings and scientific events and, sometimes, giving economic support. The existing scientific societies are:

Asociación Venezolana de Psicología Social [Venezuelan Association of Social Psychology], Apartado 47101, Caracas 1041-A.

Asociación Venezolana de Psicología Vial [Venezuelan Association of Roads and Traffic Psychology], Apartado 62558, Caracas 1060-A.

Sociedad Venezolana de Psicología Adleriana [Venezuelan Society for Adlerian Psychology], Apartado 68340, Caracas 1062-A.

Sociedad Venezolana de Psicología del Deporte [Venezuelan Society for Sports Psychology], Apartado 62558, Caracas 1060-A.

Sociedad Venezolana de Psicología Escolar [Venezuelan Society of Educational Psychology], Apartado 47901, Caracas 1041-A.

Sociedad Venezolana de Rorschach [Venezuelan Rorschach Society], Apartado 68182, Caracas 1062-A.

Major Programs and Laboratories

Undergraduate Programs

There are three universities, two in Caracas and one in Maracaibo, which have undergraduate programs in psychology. All offer five-year programs (which include a thesis) for obtaining the degree of *licenciado en psicología*, which is the official credential for professional practice. The addresses of the three schools of psychology are:

Escuela de Psicología, Facultad de Humanidades y Educación, Universidad Central de Venezuela, Ciudad Universitaria, Caracas 1051.

Escuela de Psicología, Facultad de Humanidades y Educación, Universidad Católica Andrés Bello, Mantalbán, Caracas 1021.

Escuela de Psicología, Facultad de Ciencias Políticas, Administrativas y Sociales, Universidad Rafael Urdaneta, Apartado 614, Maracaibo, Edo. Zulia.

Graduate Programs

There are four universities offering graduate degrees in psychology. These degrees are *specialist* (requiring at least one year and no thesis), *magister* (usually requiring two years and a thesis), and *doctor* (requiring at least three years and a thesis).

The Universidad Central de Venezuela offers the following degrees: specialist in group dynamics, magister in experimental analysis of behavior, magister in social psychology, magister in instructional psychology, doctor in experimental analysis of behavior (now being organized), and doctor in social psychology (also being organized at this time). (Address: Comisión de Estudios para Graduados, Facultad de Humanidades y Educación, Universidad Central de Venezuela, Centro Comercial Los Chaguaramos Piso 5, Calle Edison, Los Chaguaramos, Caracas.)

The Universidad Simón Bolívar offers programs leading to the magister in psychology with specializations in individual, group, and culture; behavior technology and modification; and counseling and human development. The specialist degree is also offered in the last two areas. (Address: Decanato de Estudios de Postgrado, Universidad Simón Bolívar, Sartenejas, Baruta.)

The Universidad Católica Andrés Bello awards the degree of magister in industrial relations with emphases in human resources and labor relations. Specialist and magister degree programs in organizational development are also being developed. (Address: Dirección General de Estudios de Postgrado, Universidad Católica Andrés Bello, Montalbán, La Vega, Caracas 1021.)

The only graduate program available at the Universidad Rafael Urdaneta is the magister in communication processes in mental retardation. (Address: Vice-Rectorado de Investigación y Postgrado, Sector La Retirada, Universidad Rafael Urdaneta, Maracaibo, Edo. Zulia.)

There are also programs in clinical psychology associated with the following three mental hospitals:

Hospital Central de las Fuerzas Armadas, which offers a postgraduate course in psychiatry and clinical psychology involving two years of training. (Address: Hospital Central de las Fuerzas Armadas, Comisión de Postgrado, Ave. José Angel Lamas, San Martín, Caracas 1020.)

Centro de Salud Mental del Este [Health Ministry], providing a three-year postgraduate course in psychodynamic psychiatry and clinical psychology. (Address: Centro de Salud Mental del Este, El Peñón, Baruta 1080.)

Hospital Psiquiátrico, with a three-year postgraduate course in psychiatry and clinical psychology. (Address: Hospital Psiquiátrico, Ave. Principal, Lídice, Caracas 1010.)

Finally, the Instituto Universitario Pedagógico Caracas offers a magister degree in guidance. This institution is the leading teacher-training college in the country and the graduate program is open to both educators and psychologists. (Address: Instituto Universitario Pedagógico Caracas, Ave. El Ejército, El Paraíso, Caracas 1021.)

Laboratories

Instituto de Psicología, Universidad Central de Venezuela. The oldest and most important center for psychological research consists of two departments: the Department of Applied Research, which has sections on child development and family and on environmental psychology and nationalism; and the Department of Fundamental Research, which includes the Laboratory for the Experimental Analysis of Behavior. (Address: Instituto de Psicología, Facultad de Humanidades y Educación, Universidad Central de Venezuela, Apartado 47563 Caracas 1041-A.)

Servicio de Psicología, Escuela de Psicología, Universidad Central de Venezuela. This facility, whose main functions are training and public assistance, also offers research opportunities for students majoring in clinical psychology. Additionally, it provides refresher courses in clinical psychology to graduates. The theoretical orientation is behavioral. (Address: Servicio de Psicología, Ave. La Colina, Quinta Mitaqueri, Las Acacias, Caracas 1050.)

Unidad Multidisciplinaria Para El Estudio del Comportamiento [Multidisciplinary Unit for the Study of Behavior]. This unit has facilities for electroencephalography, the study of visceral processes, biofeedback, and psychological investigations. (Address: UMEC, Ave. La Colina, Quinta Mitaqueri, Las Acacias, Caracas 1050.)

Laboratorio de Psicología, Universidad de Los Andes. This is a research center attached to the Faculty of Medicine which carries out research principally related to academic achievement. (Address: Laboratorio de Psicología, Universidad de Los Andes, Apartado 411, Mérida, Edo. Mérida.)

Centro de Investigacion Para El Retardo Mental [Research Center for Mental Retardation]. This center is funded by the Rafael Urdaneta University and AZU-

PANE (a regional association of parents of mentally retarded children). (Address: Vice-Rectorado de Investigacion y Postgrado, Sector La Retirada, Universidad Rafael Urdaneta, Maracaibo, Edo. Zulia.)

Primary Function of Psychologists

Psychology in Venezuela is a well-recognized profession. There are psychologists in planning, decision making, consultative, and administrative positions. Furthermore, even though the first group of psychologists with Venezuelan degrees in psychology graduated only twenty-four years ago, a psychologist became a member of the National Cabinet as minister during the 1978–1984 constitutional period. In the new cabinet (1984–1988), another psychologist has been appointed minister.

In a recent unpublished study by Ligia M. Sánchez, based on a random sample of 450 of the 2,064 psychologists living in Venezuela in 1978, the broad scope of psychological practice was apparent. The results showed 26 percent of psychologists working for private institutions, 64 percent in the public sector, and only 5.3 percent in private practice.

Among psychologists employed by private institutions, most worked in the industrial and educational area. Many private primary schools employ psychologists for psychological assessment, the treatment of learning disabilities, teacher training, and curriculum design and evaluation. Psychologists in the industrial area are primarily involved in personnel recruitment and selection, industrial relations, and personnel evaluation and training.

It was found that psychologists associated with public institutions were mostly engaged in teaching in secondary schools, colleges, and universities; administrative activities at various levels (heads of departments or sections); coordinating activities in educational institutions, health services, social services, and the like; and specific psychological activities in applied fields. Those doing applied work, for example, did counseling in secondary schools and as part of student services at universities; clinical evaluations, within therapeutic teams, and some psychotherapeutic work, mainly with groups; personnel administration, job analysis, and implementing training programs; and work with communities and within the penal system.

Funding of the Discipline

At the undergraduate level, students at the state universities pay only a modest fee; most of the costs are paid for by the government. Master's-level students, however, assume approximately 70 percent of the costs. Students attending private universities, of course, pay a higher percentage of their expenses.

For research, the main sources of funding are the Consejo Nacional de Investigaciones Científicas y Technológicas (CONICIT) [National Council for Scientific and Technological Research] and the Consejo de Desarrollo Científico y

Tecnológico (CDCH) [Councils for Scientific and Humanistic Development] within each of the universities. The CDCH are supposed to earmark 10 percent of the university budget for research. There are no fixed amounts assigned to psychology; allocations are determined by evaluations of the projects proposed.

Other sources of financing are governmental entities such as the Corporations for Regional Development and private foundations. But none of these have large budgets. There is also the Fundación Gran Mariscal de Ayacucho (FUNDAY-ACUCHO), an official fund with a large scholarship program and monies to finance foreign lecturers and provide postdoctoral grants for university faculty.

Curriculum Models

Undergraduate Programs

There are undergraduate programs in psychology at Central University, Catholic University, and Rafael Urdaneta University, each program taking five years to complete and requiring a thesis. The courses of study differ in terms of the degree of specialization available.

Central University introduced what are called "pre-specializations" in 1970, which means that each student has to concentrate on one area during his or her last four semesters. These are: clinical (behaviorally oriented), counseling, educational, industrial, social, or general (psychoanalytic). Catholic University maintains a curriculum designed to train generalists in psychology. While there are a certain number of optional courses, students must take courses in the clinical, guidance, educational, industrial, and social areas during their last two years of study. Rafael Urdaneta University requires that all students take the same basic courses during the first six semesters. The last four semesters of the program they have to take at least one course in each of the following areas: educational, guidance, clinical, industrial, and group dynamics. In addition, they take optional courses and do their on-the-job training in clinical psychology, industrial-social psychology, or guidance-school psychology. It should be pointed out that all undergraduate programs include on-the-job training (*pasantías*) and are designed to produce professionals capable of working independently.

Graduate Programs

Central University offers a program leading to the specialist degree in group dynamics usually taking three semesters to complete. Over 40 percent of the required courses are on theoretical subjects, 12 percent on methodological procedures, and 45 percent are experiential activities. The Centro de Salud Mental del Este and the Hospital Psiquiátrico offer combined theoretical and on-the-job training that takes three years. The Hospital de las Fuerzas Amadas offers a similar two-year program.

The master's program at Simón Bolívar University is the oldest in Venezuela and very flexible. Students have to complete forty credits, including a thesis, but are free to choose among a wide range of elective subjects organized around three different options: individual, group, and culture (which is really social psychology); technology and the modification of behavior; and the counseling of human resources. Students also have the option of graduating as specialists in the same areas without doing a thesis.

Central University offers three master's programs. The program in the experimental analysis of behavior takes four semesters. About 40 percent of the curriculum consists of theoretical courses; the rest of the time involves research including a thesis. The program in social psychology involves about the same proportion of theoretical and methodological training. The master's degree in instructional psychology involves courses about equally divided among theoretical, methodological, and applied work. The master's program for communication processes in mental retardation at the Rafael Urdaneta University emphasizes on-the-job training with only about half the time spent on theoretical and methodological matters.

Currently no doctoral-level programs in psychology are available in Venezuela, although formal regulations for their implementation have recently been approved at Central University. These are to be research-oriented. Students will have the choice of specializing in either the experimental analysis of behavior or social psychology.

Major Journals

The three Venezuelan psychological journals are *Niños*, *Psicología*, and *Boletín de Avepso*. *Niños* [Journal of Child Neuropsychiatry and Related Sciences] was first published in 1967 and is now edited by INAPSI, Ave. Las Acacias No. 65, La Florida, Caracas 1050. *Psicología* first appeared in 1974. It is edited by Carlos Muñoz, Escuela de Psicología, Facultad de Humanidades y Educación, Universidad Central de Venezuela. (For some time monographic issues under the general title *Psicología-Temas* were published.) *Boletín de Avepso* [Bulletin of the Venezuelan Association of Social Psychology], published since 1978, is, at present, edited by Miriam Castillo, Asociación Venezolana de Psicología Social (AVEPSO), Apartado 47101, Caracas 1041-A.

The Laboratory of Psychology of the University of the Andes also quite regularly publishes research reports and monographs under the general title *Monografías*, edited by Oswaldo Romero García, Laboratorio de Psicología, Universidad de los Andes, Apartado 411, Mérida, Edo. Mérida, Venezuela. In addition, the Federation of Psychologists publishes a *Directorio* triannually. The current editor is Erik Becker, Federación de Psicólogos de Venezuela, Apartado 62558, Caracas 1060-A, Venezuela.

The Most Widely Used Introductory Textbooks

It is not customary even in introductory courses to use a particular textbook, although lecturers sometimes prepare materials that serve as the basic readings foundation for their courses. Among the most widely used texts included in the bibliographies of first-year courses are:

Buck, R. W. *Human motivation and emotion*. New York: Wiley, 1976.
Chaplin, J. P., & Krawiec, T. *Psicología: Sistemas y teorías* [Systems and theories of psychology]. México: Interamericana, 1978.
Cofer, C. N., & Appley, M. H. *Psicología de la motivación* [Psychology of motivation]. México: Trillas, 1971.
Forgus, R. *Percepción* [Perception]. México: Trillas, 1972.
Garrett, H. *Estadísticas en psicología y educación* [Statistics for psychology and education]. Buenos Aires: Paidós, 1966.
Glass, G. V., & Stanley, J. C. *Métodos estadísticos aplicados a las ciencias sociales* [Applied statistical methods for the social sciences].
Hilgard, E., & Bower, G. H. *Teorías del aprendizaje* [Theories of learning]. México: Trillas, 1973.
Salazar, J. M., Montero, M., Muñoz, C., Sánchez, E., Santoro, E., and Villegas, J. *Psicología sociale* [Social psychology]. México: Trillas, 1976.

Availability of *Psychological Abstracts* and Citation Indexes

All the universities with psychological programs receive *Psychological Abstracts*. In the library of the School of Psychology of Central University the collection goes back to 1944. The CONICIT (equivalent to the National Science Foundation in the United States) makes available, through NOTIS, all the most important computerized data bases in psychology. This agency also publishes catalogues of publications available in Venezuela. The *Social Science Citation Index* and the *Science Citation Index* are only available in the National Library.

Major Needs

The three major needs in present-day Venezuelan psychology are (1) more funds for research to adapt and create sociopsychological technologies useful to society; (2) more journals and books so that psychologists can more readily publish their findings and ideas (much work is never formally reported); and (3) strengthening professional organizations in order to ensure that the legal, economic, and social rights of psychologists are protected.

Relationships with Other Disciplines

There has been some disagreement as to the proper place of psychology within the framework of the academic fields. Both at Central University and at Catholic University the discipline is part of the Faculty of Humanities and Education, but at Rafael Urdaneta University it belongs to the Faculty of Political, Administrative, and Social Sciences. And at Simón Bolívar University it is housed within the Division of Humanities and Social Sciences.

Psychology has achieved the status of a recognized field within professional practice. At present, psychologists have good relations with psychiatrists, medical doctors, neurophysiologists, social workers, and other health professionals. There is, however, still some conflict with people in guidance who have their primary training in education. There is also some uneasiness relative to psychopedagogues working on learning disabilities, because in this area there are no clearly defined professional frontiers. Psychologists, lawyers, and sociologists have collaborated effectively on projects concerning social planning and research involving modifications in the law.

MAJOR TRENDS AND INFLUENCES SINCE WORLD WAR II

Demographic and Organizational Development

Organizations

The first organization of psychologists was the Asociación Venezolana de Psicólogos organized in 1957 by twenty-one psychologists who had been trained abroad. The organization was superseded by the Colegio de Psicólogos de Venezuela in 1961, after the first group of psychologists trained in Venezuela obtained their degrees. The Colegio de Psicólogos had its seat in Caracas. As the number of psychologists increased, many taking up residence in different cities in the country, sectional subdivisions of the colegio were established. In 1978, when the Law of Professional Practice was enacted, a federation came into being, in which the sectional units in the different states and in the federal district became colegios. This is the existing professional structure, as described earlier.

The first psychological scientific society was the Sociedad de Psicología Clínica that existed from 1969 to 1979. Also founded in 1969 were societies for industrial, guidance, and school psychologists, but these had short lifespans. In 1975, the Asociación Venezolana de Psicología Social [Social Psychology] was founded. In 1978, the Sociedad Venezolana de Psicología Escolar [School Psychology], the Sociedad Venezolana de Psicología del Deporte [Sports Psychology], and the Sociedad Venezolana de Psicología Humanista [Humanistic Psychology] were established. In 1983, three additional societies were created for psychologists concerned respectively with Adlerian psychology, the Rorschach test, and traffic psychology.

Membership Trends

In 1957, twenty-one psychologists founded the original organization of psychologists; by 1961, the Colegio de Psicólogos de Venezuela had 101 members, seventy-six trained in Venezuelan universities. By 1978, when the Law of Professional Practice was enacted, there were 2,275 psychologists in the country trained in national universities and 101 with foreign degrees. Presently there are about 3,500 psychologists in Venezuela.

Publication Trends

The first psychological periodical was *Cuadernos de Psicología* [Psychological Notes], which appeared in November 1958 only a few months after the School of Psychology was created at Central University; however, only three issues were published. During the 1960s and 1970s, several single-issue journals were published: *Revista Venezolana de Psicología* [Venezuelan Journal of Psychology], *Revista de Psicología* [Journal of Psychology], *Aprendizaje y Comportamiento* [Learning and Behavior]. More consistent has been the publication of *Psicología* [Psychology], under the auspices of Central University, which started publication in 1974, and the *Boletín de Avepso* [Bulletin of the Venezuelan Association of Social Psychology], of somewhat more recent vintage, sponsored by the Venezuelan Association of Social Psychology.

The Institute of Psychology of Central University published two annuals during the 1960s and founded a similar publication recently entitled *Contribuciones Recientes a la Psicología en Venezuela* [Recent Contributions of Psychology in Venezuela].

Conferences, Meetings, and Seminars

The First Psychological Seminar in Venuezuela took place at Central University in November 1959. A second seminar was held a few years later. Since then Venezuelan psychologists have frequently participated in the Annual Meeting of the Asociación Venezolana para el Avance de la Ciencia (ASOVAC) [Venezuelan Association for the Advancement of Science]; the regular meetings of the Instituto Nacional de Psiquiatría (INAPSI) [National Institute of Psychiatry]; the Venezuelan meetings of Mental Health; and the conferences of Asociacíon Venezolana de Padres de Niños Excepionales (AVEPANE) and Asociación Nacional de la Paralisis Cerebral (ANAPACE) (Associations for Handicapped Children).

Scientific gatherings have also been sponsored by various Venezuelan psychological societies. Specifically, the Venezuelan Association of Social Psychology has held four biennial national meetings of social psychologists, starting in 1977, and there have been two national meetings of educational psychologists. Other events include the First Meeting of Humanistic Psychology (1981), the First Meeting of Humanistic Psychology (1981), the First Meeting of Sports Psychology (1981), and the First National Symposium of Road Traffic Psychology (1983).

International meetings have also been held in Venezuela; for example, the first Latin American Seminar of Social Psychology (1975); the Fifth and Eighth International Symposia of Behavior Modification (1974 and 1978); the Encounter of Latin American Psychology (1981); and a biennial Meeting of the Board of the International Union of Psychological Science (1982). The XX Interamerican Congress of Psychology took place in Caracas in July 1985.

Major Trends in Funding

Funding for the discipline has been channeled mostly through the universities. Starting in 1979, however, with the creation of the Ministry for the Development of Intelligence, the government has allocated funds for research projects that are clearly psychological in nature.

The government-sponsored scholarship program FUNDAYACUCHO started considering psychology a priority area in 1980. As a result, many students traveled to the United States and Europe for graduate training in psychology.

Societal Developments That Influenced the Discipline

Psychology in Venezuela was sigificantly strengthened by the development of a democratic regime. Although there had been some psychology, and even an Institute of Psychology during the period of the dictatorship the national uprising of 1958, which marks the beginning of modern democracy in Venezuela, gave psychology a boost, and the study of psychology was formalized by the establishment of two schools of psychology. Soon thereafter jobs were created for psychologists in the education, public health and welfare departments. During the last twenty-five years, psychology as a profession has enjoyed a high status with many psychologists assuming responsible positions in society.

While it is still too early to say, it seems that the recent economic crisis may, paradoxically, have a positive effect on the development of Venezuelan psychology and other disciplines as well by strengthening graduate training in the country as students find it increasingly difficult to go abroad. Of course, it may also lead to unwanted professional isolationism.

Research and Theory

Major Orientations and Assumptions

The discipline, which was originally influenced by psychometrics, psychoanalysis, Piaget, and philosophy, eventually became more behavioral in orientation. Both radical (Skinnerian) behaviorism and cognitive-social behaviorism have had a significant impact. The Skinnerian experimental analysis of behavior assumed particular importance in the Department of Clinical Psychology and the Laboratory of the Institute of Psychology of Central University, in the Department of Behavioral Technology at Simón Bolívar University, and, temporarily, in the program at Catholic University. Social psychology, as a field of study and a theoretical orientation with a cognitive emphasis, has been a significant area since the 1960s, especially in Central University but also at Simón Bolívar University and the University of the Andes. Psychoanalysis, after an early period of influence, was deemphasized in the universities but has made a comeback in some academic circles during the 1980s; there also has been considerable interest in the Lacanian orientation. The most influential group relative to governmental policies pertaining to psychology is composed of the developmental psychologists who assumed significant positions in the Ministry for the Development of Intelligence during the 1979–1984 period. They are strongly Piagetian in orientation.

An analysis of the psychological literature published in Venezuela during the 1970–1980 period (Salazar & Rodriguez, 1984) indicated that 40 percent was behaviorial, 56 percent was cognitive, and 4 percent was psychoanalytic in orientation. Nevertheless, when trends are examined, it is clear that during the late 1970s there was overall an increase in interest in behavioral research.

It is important, however, to keep in mind that psychology in Venezuela has developed mostly in an applied direction. In the Salazar & Rodriguez survey, only 5 percent of the papers concerned basic research and 22 percent were theoretical discussions, many of which had to do with applied issues.

Questions of Most Concern

The central questions investigated by Venezuelan psychologists have to do with child development, teaching methods, work, attitudes and social communication, and psychological disorders. Child development is of particular concern to Venezuelan psychologists. The research efforts of a team of psychologists at the Institute of Psychology, which have extended over a number of years, have been systematic and produced several important publications. Project Venezuela, a broad national diagnostic investigation of the characteristics of the Venezuelan population, includes determining the norms related to the psychological development of children in different areas of the country. The various programs sponsored by the Ministry for the Development of Intelligence are, of course, also focused on child development. All this has been complemented by work done by teams, under the direction of the Ministry for the Inclusion of Women in Societal Development, designed to modify laws and regulations having to do with adoption, family relationships, and so forth.

Some behaviorally oriented psychologists are concerned with basic research in laboratory settings, using mostly rats and pigeons. Those with a social orientation, on the other hand, investigate attitudes frequently related to political issues and attitude changes, particularly those associated with the mass media. More recently there has been increasing interest in community development.

Major Contributions

The most significant contributions of Venezuelan psychologists include the following:

1. Theoretical and empirical work to demonstrate commonalities between operant and classical conditioning (R. Ruiz, M. Dembo, J. Penfold).

2. Empirical studies to demonstrate the importance of stimulation in child development and the negative effects of ecological deficits (I. Recagno, M. R. Frias de Orantes).

3. Empirical studies to demonstrate the negative effects of mass media, particularly television, relative to the formation of stereotypes in children (E. Santoro), and investigations of TV serials as instruments of socialization (M. Pulido and her team at the Ministry for the Inclusion of Women in Societal Development).

4. Identification of a widespread "ideology of dependence" expressed in a negative national "autostereotype" (J. M. Salazar), the demonstration of its historical roots, and attempts to explain the psychological meaning of the phenomenon (M. Montero).

5. Establishment of the relationship between locus of control and academic achievement, and the development of courses, taking this relationship into account, to improve academic achievement (O. Romero and his team at the psychology laboratory at the University of the Andes).

6. Development of social- and sexual-awareness courses within the context of education for motherhood in lower-class public maternity hospitals (E. Jimenez and her team at the National Institute for the Welfare of Minors).

7. Development of literacy using the principles of applied behavioral analysis (H. Casalta).

8. Empirical and theoretical establishment of instructional psychology as an autonomous concern (A. Orantes).

9. Development of environmental psychology in underdeveloped societies (E. Sánchez and E. Wiesenfeld).

10. Development of a nationwide project for child stimulation using mass media and face-to-face training (B. Manrique and her team in the family project).

11. Empirical studies, within a Piagetian orientation, to describe and understand the cognitive development of Venezuelan children and youths in different areas (C. Noguera, E. Escalona, J. M. Cadenas, M. R. Frias de Orantes).

12. Development of the Special Education Division in the Ministry of Education and creation of centers in all major cities (A. Lampe).

13. Development of a national vocational system (V. Constanzo) and national secondary-school guidance centers (A. Curcho, G. Naranjo, S. Essenfeld, J. Machado).

14. A human resource optimization model and its application in SIDOR, Venezuela's largest official industry (C. Pitaluga).

15. Empirical studies on Type-A behavior in isquematic heart diseases (A. Miñarro).

16. Empirical studies on family integration in Latin American societies (M. Bustamante).

17. Empirical studies on the economic value of domestic work in Venezuela (M. Pulido and her team).

Prominent Venezuelan Psychologists

Psychologists in Venezuela who have made the most significant contributions include: Erik Becker (organizer and first president of the Federation of Psychologists; legal aspects of psychology); María J. Bustamante (social psychology); José M. Cadenas (developmental/social psychology); Henry Casalta (experimental analysis of behavior); Edmundo Chirinos (organizer and first president of the Colegio de Psicólogos de Venezuela; neurophysiology); Vincent Constanzo (guidance psychology); Max Contasti (methodology); Aída Curcho (organizer of the Nationwide Guidance of Secondary-School Services); Francisco Del Olmo (organizer of the Asociación Venezolana de Psicología; pioneering work in testing and personnel selection); Miriam Dembo (psychometrics and experimental analysis of behavior); Yolanda De Venanzi (social psychology); Senta Essenfeld (guidance psychology); Nusia Feldman (educational psychology); Alba Fernández (children's recreation); Josefina Fierro de Ascanio (organizer of studies in developmental and educational psychology); Elena Granell (organizer of advanced studies; experimental analysis of behavior); Elisa Jiménez (applied social psychology); Aline Lampe (educational psychology and organizer of the Open University); Beatriz Manrique (developmental psychology); Gustavo Mendez (research on electoral behavior); Andres Miñarro (reorganizer of psychological studies at Catholic University; research on electoral behavior); Maritza Montero (social psychology); Juan B. Moretti (organizer of the Asociación Venezolana de Psicología); Carlos Muñoz (psychological journal editor); Carlos Noguera (developmental psychology); Alfonso Orantes (instructional psychology); Guillermo Perez Enciso (organizer of psychological studies in Central University); Carlos Pitaluga (industrial psychology; research on electoral behavior); Mercedes Pulido (social psychology and legal family protection); Alberto Ramírez (organizer of undergraduate and graduate studies in Rafael Urdaneta University); Ileana Recagno (developmental/social psychology); Oswaldo Romero García (educational/social psychology); Roberto Ruiz (experimental analysis of behavior); José Miguel Salazar (organizer of studies in experimental and social psychology); Euclides Sánchez (social/environmental psychology); Ligia Sánchez (organizer of graduate studies in Central University; legal aspects of psychology); and Eduardo Santoro (general/social psychology).

Major Controversies

There have been two main areas of controversy in Venezuelan psychology: one related to professional training, the other to theoretical orientations.

Since the late 1960s there has been widespread disagreement as to whether the training of "licenciates" should produce applied specialists or general psychologists. Traditionally, licenciate training takes five years after finishing high school. In 1970, Central University, however, opted for a two-year specialization program while Catholic University retained its generalist training program. The newest university, Rafael Urdaneta, offered a compromise. With the recent development of master's programs and increasing competition for jobs, there has been some rethinking of the licenciate program even at Central University.

The major theoretical confrontation has been between behaviorists (Skinnerians) and psychoanalysts particularly in the clinical field. Although, during the early phase of Venezuelan psychology, psychoanalytically oriented psychologists wielded some influence, since the mid–1960s the behaviorists have predominated. Recently, however, as was mentioned before, psychoanalysts have made a moderate comeback in some academic circles. Cognitive psychologists have, in general, assumed a sort of middle ground in the controversy.

Applied Areas

The first applications of psychology in Venezuela centered around the use of tests in school settings and personnel selection in oil companies. Later, psychologists worked in the clinical field, usually as part of mental health teams under the direction of psychiatrists.

After the 1970s, with the implementation of prespecializations at the undergraduate level and changes in the emphases given various aspects of psychological training, there was an increasing diversification of applied work. In the industrial field, attention has been given to organizational analysis; social psychologists have started to participate in community work, delinquency control, environmental psychology, electoral behavior, and marketing; school psychologists have gotten involved in the training of children with learning problems; guidance psychologists are working with groups; and clinical psychologists have increasingly applied behavior modification techniques to a variety of behavioral problems.

The emphasis on application has led to some original contributions. Most of these have involved the development of intervention techniques based on theoretical principles to solve specific problems. For example, E. Sánchez has used sociopsychological principles to increase social participation in marginal areas, and O. Romero Garcia has worked to increase internal locus of control among peasants and workers.

Contributions to Other Disciplines and Society

Perhaps the greatest influence of psychology on other disciplines in Venezuela has been in the educational field. Most schools have added psychologists to their staffs, and all teacher-training colleges and schools of education have very strong psychology departments. The fields of personnel administration, advertising, and political science have also been influenced by psychology.

In addition, psychologists have played an important role in the establishment of new universities, particularly the National Open University (Escotet, Lampe) and have held very important administrative positions within several universities.

Psychology as a profession has a high status in the country; much is expected of the discipline. Psychologists are included in most programs having to do with social development. Nevertheless, expectancies have in most instances not been transformed into reality. If, however, programs of the Ministry for the Development of Intelligence are successful, psychology will have made a great contribution to society.

Foreign Psychologists with the Most Influence on Venezuelan Psychology During the 1945–1982 Period

In the developmental and educational areas, the earliest influence was that of Jean Piaget. More recently the work of V. Micklebust, J. Bruner, and U. Bronfenbrenner has stimulated this area. Skinner has had a strong following, particularly among many psychologists who were originally under the influence of H. Eysenck. Among this same group of people, a very direct influence has been exerted by W. Schoenfeld, who traveled to Venezuela several times and is the supervisor of one of the research laboratories. At Catholic University, J. Wolpe has been influential. In social psychology, D. Campbell has provided important methodological guidance. The ideas and research of A. Bandura, M. Rokeach, and, more recently, M. Fishbein, with his theory of reasoned action, have also affected Venezuelan psychology. In guidance and in clinical psychology the major foreign figures have been Carl Rogers and Frederick Perls. As mentioned before, J. Lacan is very influential among those with a psychoanalytic orientation. Finally, F. Herzberg, D. Katz, and R. L. Kahn have had a considerable impact on industrial psychology.

PERSPECTIVES ON PSYCHOLOGY IN OTHER COUNTRIES

The way Venezuelan psychologists view psychology in other countries is influenced by their particular interests and their ideological positions. Even though a great number respect North American psychology, others are extremely critical and either look to developments in other countries—that is, France, England, and the Soviet Union—or work to create an indigenous orientation. Psychologists who emphasize the experimental analysis of behavior tend to laud the virtues of North American psychology; those who look to Europe (particularly the Piagetian school) are those in the developmental field; and interest in creating a Latin American psychology is most frequently found among social psychologists. Although there was great interest in Soviet psychology during the 1960s, when contacts were first established with Soviet psychologists, this interest has waned considerably.

FUTURE DIRECTIONS

The future of psychology in Venezuela will be closely connected with the economic future of the country and whether or not psychologists achieve what society expects of them. Graduate training will, we think, be strengthened and undergraduate training become more flexible so that graduates will have a better chance of fitting into the job market. Applied areas will continue to be emphasized and this will stimulate applied studies. These investigations, it is hoped, will lead to more basic research, but it will be focused on problems that derive from the needs of Venezuelan society.

PSYCHOLOGISTS WITH A STRONG INTEREST IN THE HISTORY OF PSYCHOLOGY

Becker, Erik. Apartado 61432—Chacao—Caracas, Venezuela.

Feldman, Nusia. Ave. Cota Mil No. 1—San Bernardino—Caracas, Venezuela.

Salazar, José M. Apartado 47018. Caracas 1041-A, Venezuela.

Sánchez, Euclides. Apartado 47018. Caracas 1041-A, Venezuela.

Sánchez, Ligia. Apartado 47563. Caracas 1041-A, Venezuela.

REFERENCES

República de Venezuela. (1978). Ley de Ejercicio de la Psicología [The Law of Psychological Practice]. Caracas: Editorial La Torre.

Salazar, J. M., & Rodríguez, P. (1984). 10 años de Investigación Psicológica en Venezuela in Instituto de Psicología [Ten years of psychological investigations in Venezuela in the Institute of Psychology]. *Contribuciones Recientes a la psicología en Venezuela* (Vol. II). Caracas: Universidad Central de Venezuela.

SUGGESTED READINGS

Del Olmo, F., & Salazar, J. M. (1981). 30 años del Instituto de Psicología [Thirty years of the Institute of Psychology]. *Contribuciones Recientes a la Psicología en Venezuela*. Caracas: Universidad Central de Venezuela.

Escuela de Psicología. Universidad Católica Andrés Bello. (1984). *Catálogo de Investigaciones*. Caracas: UCAB.

Escuela de Psicología. Universidad Central de Venezuela. *Psicología*.

Sánchez, E. (1983). Psychology in Venezuela. *Spanish Language Psychology, 3*, 57–62.

Sánchez, E., Weisenfeld, E., & Cronick, K. (1983). Environmental psychology in Venezuela. *Journal of Environmental Psychology, 3*, 161–172.

Yugoslavia

Vid Pečjak

DEMOGRAPHIC, SOCIOCULTURAL, AND HISTORICAL CONTEXTS

In order to understand contemporary Yugoslav psychology, some knowledge of its demographic, sociocultural, and historical aspects is necessary. Yugoslavia is a small European country with 22 million inhabitants. It became an independent state after World War I ended in 1918. Before that it was divided into several parts, some belonging to neighboring states and others, such as Serbia, which were independent. As a consequence, the economic development of the country was quite uneven, a situation which still exists today.

After World War II, the country became the Socialist Federal Republic of Yugoslavia, consisting of six federal units or republics. These are: Bosnia and Herzegovina, Croatia, Macedonia, Montenegro, Serbia, and Slovenia. Yugoslavia is a Socialist country. Its national and ethnic structure is very heterogeneous; it encompasses five different national groups, which speak three languages and use two alphabets, as well as many national minorities. Following the war, Yugoslavia underwent rapid industrial development and a marked rise in the educational level of its population.

For the above reasons, the development of psychology in Yugoslavia was not harmonious. In some sections of the country development closely followed the main trends of Central Europe, while elsewhere it only gained some measure of scientific and professional maturity a few decades ago.

In Croatia and Slovenia the beginnings of psychology can be found in the Renaissance. During the fifteenth and sixteenth centuries, some ten books on psychology from a philosophical point of view were written in Latin. These include: Jurij Dalmatinac, *De animae potentiis* [About mental abilities]; Jurij Dragašić, *De animae regni principe* [About the ruler mind]; and David Verbec, *Disputatio de temperamentis* [A debate about temperament]. However, the most important psychological book of this period was written by Marko Marulić from Split: *Psychologia de ratione animae humanae* [Psychology of the human soul].

In this book, the word "psychology" was used for the first time. The book itself has been lost, but we know of it from references by the author's contemporary Franjo Božičević-Natalis. The book was probably written in 1517 (Brožek, 1973).

The first psychological books written in Yugoslav languages appeared in the second part of the nineteenth century: H. Ristić, *Psihologija empirična* [Empirical psychology], 1895, in Serbocroatian; S. Besariček, *Iskustveno dušeslovje* [Experiential psychology], 1877, in Serbocroatian; and F. Gabršek, *Izkustveno dušeslovje*, [Experiential psychology], 1889, in Slovenian. Before Yugoslavia was established, some twenty psychological books (not counting manuscripts from the Renaissance) were published. Courses in psychology were taught at some high schools. But despite some attempts to build an empirically based psychology, a metaphysical and philosophical orientation prevailed.

At the beginning of the twentieth century, many Yugoslav scholars studied with famous European psychologists: Ljubomir Nedić, Branko Petronijević, and Mihajlo Rostohar with Wilhelm Wundt; Pavle Radosavljević and Vičentije Rakić with Meumann; Jelisaveta Branković with Wolfgang Köhler; Ramiro Bujas, Franc Veber, and Mihajlo Rostohar with Alexius Meinong; Zoran Bujas with Henri Piéron; and Borislav Stevanović with Aveling. Many of them became the pioneers of Yugoslav empirical psychology.

Psychology gained autonomy and started to become an empirical science in the period between 1918 and 1940. At the University of Zagreb, a psychological laboratory was established in 1920 as a part of a physiological institute belonging to the medical faculty. Its first chairman was Ramiro Bujas. Somewhat later two departments of psychology were founded. One was situated at the University of Belgrade (1928), with Borislav Stevanović as the head of the department; the other was at the University of Zagreb, directed by Ramiro Bujas. Since 1932 the Psychological Institute of Zagreb has been publishing the journal *Acta Psychologica Universitatis Zagrabiensis*. During this period some twenty original psychological books were published as well as many translations.

The development of academic psychology was accompanied by the development of applied psychology. Centers for professional training were founded in Belgrade (1930), Zagreb (1931), and Ljubljana (1938). Several tests for measuring abilities were constructed or adapted (for example, Binet's Intelligence Scale).

In the years between the two wars, psychology in Yugoslavia became autonomous and empirically based and gained some institutional status, yet its beginnings were quite modest. There were only some thirty people who were actively engaged in the field. After World War II, however, there was rapid growth and diversification.

NATURE AND SCOPE OF THE DISCIPLINE

Yugoslav psychology is quite heterogeneous with regard to its subject matter and its orientation; therefore, no general statement concerning the discipline's nature and scope can be given. It has been influenced by all psychological schools including those emphasizing psychoanalysis, behaviorism, humanism, and Marxism. To a considerable extent it can also be described as eclectic. Different orientations prevail in different centers, although they are all empirically based, and most concern applied matters.

The primary centers of teaching and research are university departments of psychology. Such departments can be found at eight Yugoslav universities, which are situated in Belgrade, Zagreb, Ljubljana (since 1950), Niš (since 1971), Skopje (since 1975), Rijeka (since 1978), Zadar (since 1979), and Novi Sad (since 1982). At the University of Sarajevo there is a Department of Education and Psychology (since 1977).

Every department of psychology offers all the main courses in theoretical and applied psychology. The following courses are mandatory at all universities: psychology of cognitive processes, personality, developmental psychology, social psychology, psychometrics, statistics, psychophysiology, history of psychology, psychopathology, industrial psychology, educational psychology, and clinical psychology. The courses may be labeled differently in some places, such as child psychology instead of developmental psychology. The scope of some courses, however, varies considerably from university to university. A two-term course at one university may be extended to four terms at another. There are certain courses such as traffic psychology and ecological psychology which are taught only at some universities.

After four years of study candidates may apply for a diploma. It makes them eligible to work as professional psychologists and to become members of psychological associations. To obtain a diploma students must pass a final exam where integrated knowledge of psychology is demanded. They must also submit a written paper of some length concerning their own, usually empirical, work. Some 15 percent of students continue graduate study for two more years to earn a master's degree. During these two years they must take a few courses, but the emphasis is on their master's thesis, which is usually quite involved and requires considerable experimental work. About 5 percent of the students eventually apply to do a doctoral dissertation. The dissertation represents a comprehensive research project which requires resourcefulness and independence of thought. In order to apply for a Ph.D., a candidate must have a master's degree or must have published a number of scientific papers of recognized merit.

Psychological inquiry is not limited to departments of psychology. Psychological institutes are also important centers of research. There are two such institutes: one is located at the University of Zagreb (since 1929), the other at the University of Belgrade (since 1961). Moreover, institutes of sociology and institutes of education employ many psychologists to do studies in social psychology and education.

Research programs are regulated by five-year plans which are designed specifically for each republic. There is, however, little coordination of investigatory activities among the republics. There are also a number of studies that are financed by specific institutions.

About three-quarters of all research is done in applied psychology, especially in the three classical disciplines: industrial psychology, clinical psychology, and educational psychology. Other applied fields, such as forensic psychology, military psychology, and sports psychology, are reasonably well represented. Except for space psychology, all branches of applied psychology are represented in Yugoslavia to some extent.

Most research done by academic psychologists is in the fields of personality, symbolic processes, psycholinguistics, cognitive development, psychophysiology, psychophysics, creativity, and signal detection. There are, in addition, many studies on human abilities.

Psychological research is financed by two sources. Some funding comes directly from enterprises such as factories, but most is provided by special self-management committees in each republic. Psychology used to get considerable support for its research; however, during the last ten years resources have been cut back because of economic problems.

Educational activities at universities and departments of psychology are financed by similar foundations. There are no private universities in Yugoslavia. Funds are scarce, not only for research but also for university libraries, equipment, and other educational needs.

Four psychological journals are published in Yugoslavia. *Acta Instituti Psychologici Universitatis Zagrabiensis* is published by the Psychological Institute at the University of Zagreb. Its content is limited to empirical reports written in English or French, and it is issued sporadically, at times only once a year. *Revija za psihologiju* [Psychological Journal] (since 1970) is published by the Association of Yugoslav Psychological Societies with its editorial center at the Department of Psychology, University of Zagreb. This journal includes all sorts of papers and is published twice a year. *Psihologija* [Psychology] (since 1967), published by the Psychological Society of Serbia, has its editorial office at the Department of Psychology, University of Belgrade. It includes a variety of articles and appears quarterly. *Primenjena psihologija* [Applied Psychology] (since 1980), a quarterly published by the Psychological Society of Croatia, has its editorial center at the Faculty of Letters, University of Zagreb, and features mostly papers on applied psychology.

There is another journal, *Anthropos* (since 1968), which is being published by several professional societies, including the Psychological Society of Slovenia. It accepts all types of papers and publishes four to six issues a year. Special bulletins featuring news and information about psychology in Yugoslavia and abroad are sporadically published by the Psychological Societies of Slovenia, Croatia, and Serbia. Yearly professional meetings are also organized by these societies and the papers presented are published in special books.

The psychology departments in Yugoslavia have not adopted the same basic textbooks. The majority of those used, however, are written by Yugoslav authors (for example, S. Radonjić, N. Rot, V. Smiljanić, P. Ognjenović, Z. Bujas, A. Fulgosi, M. Zvonarević, V. Pečjak, and J. Musek); among the few translated texts (mostly American) in use are books by J. Guilford, R. Woodworth, and C. Osgood.

Bibliographies of psychological literature published in Yugoslavia have been assembled twice by the Psychological Society of Croatia. They include basic bibliographic data (without summaries). The first edition is entitled *Bibliografija publiciranih radova iz psihologije člana Društava psihologa u Jugoslaviji do 1970 godine* [Bibliography of Psychological Literature by members of Psychological Societies of Yugoslavia, published until 1970] (1973). The second edition, a follow-up to the first, is entitled *Bibliograpfija publiciranih radova iz psihologije članova društava psihologa u Jugoslaviji 1971 i 1972 godine* [Bibliography of Psychological Literature by members of Psychological Societies of Yugoslavia, published in 1971 and 1972] (1975).

Some of the psychological societies in Yugoslavia irregularly publish membership directories providing personal data and information about fields of work and interests. However, no such book listing all the psychologists in Yugoslavia exists.

In their educational, research, and professional activities psychologists often cooperate with members of other disciplines such as educators, psychiatrists, and sociologists. But quite often their work together involves some disagreement. Nevertheless, quite a few books have been written and research projects completed as a result of interdisciplinary collaboration. All departments of psychology employ professors from other disciplines to teach subjects such as psychopathology and physiology as a part of the required curriculum for psychologists. Collaboration with other professionals is closest in those places where the nature of the work demands joint efforts. Psychologists employed by hospitals, factories, and schools, for example, are usually members of interdisciplinary teams.

The Psychological Association of Yugoslavia was established in 1950, together with the Psychological Societies of Serbia, Croatia, and Slovenia. Today psychological societies exist in Macedonia, Montenegro, and Bosnia and Herzegovina as well. The Psychological Association of Yugoslavia has, as a consequence, changed its name to the Association of Psychological Societies of Yugoslavia. Each society is quite autonomous relative to organizing its meetings and publishing psychological literature. The association is supervised by a board which plays a coordinative role. Every three or four years this board moves its office to another republic. Congresses of Yugoslav psychologists also take place every three or four years and are organized by different psychological societies, according to a predetermined order. Some psychological societies have their own ethical codes, but no general set of guidelines exists for Yugoslavia as a whole.

MAJOR TRENDS AND INFLUENCES SINCE WORLD WAR II

The development of Yugoslav psychology has followed a positively accelerating curve: at first growth was slow, then slightly faster, and finally very rapid. The most marked rise occurred after World War II. Different indicators can be used as criteria of progress; for instance, numbers of psychologists, books and articles, conferences and congresses, and departments of psychology. The curves reflecting all these indicators have approximately the same shape. In the past five years, a gradual and slight decline in growth has been evident, possibly signaling that we are approaching a plateau.

Right after the war there were only two departments of psychology at Yugoslav universities, one in Zagreb and the other in Belgrade. A few years later, a third opened in Ljubljana (its first chairman was M. Rostohar). Between 1970 and 1982, six new departments were established.

The Psychological Association of Yugoslavia had only fifty members when it was founded in 1950. Twenty years thereafter the membership of all psychological societies numbered more than 1,000 and reached almost 3,000 by 1980. In the last few years, membership has been increasing more slowly. Departments of psychology also report a significant decline in the number of candidates. This stagnation or decline is probably due to fewer employment opportunities for psychologists. In some Yugoslav cities, psychologists are threatened with increasing unemployment.

Six psychological congresses have been organized by Yugoslav psychologists: in 1960 at Bled, 1964 in Zagreb, 1967 in Belgrade, 1971 at Bled, 1974 in Skopje, 1977 in Sarajevo, 1980 in Zagreb, and 1984 in Herceg Novi. The Fifteenth International Congress of Applied Psychology was held in 1964 in Ljubljana. The number of papers presented at congresses has grown rapidly (see Figure 1). Figure 2 represents the papers given in various areas at the first through the fourth congresses. The greatest increase took place in industrial psychology followed by general (including the psychology of personality), clinical, educational, child, and social psychology, respectively.

Similar developmental trends appear when psychological literature published until 1972 is compared (see Table 1). In the fields of industrial and professional psychology 971 books and papers were published; 739 were published in general psychology, 352 in educational psychology, 420 in clinical psychology, 417 in social psychology, 217 in developmental psychology, 167 in methodology, and 47 in physiological psychology. Some disciplines are barely represented. There were, for example, only two papers on animal psychology.

In the postwar period, books by such well-known foreign authors as Woodworth, Osgood, Guilford, Fromm, Murphy, Allport, and Piaget were translated along with classics by Freud, Adler, and Jung. Shortly after the war, Soviet authors such as Kornilov, Smirnov, and Teplov prevailed; since then, works by Vygotsky and Luria have also been translated.

Figure 1
Papers Delivered at Congresses

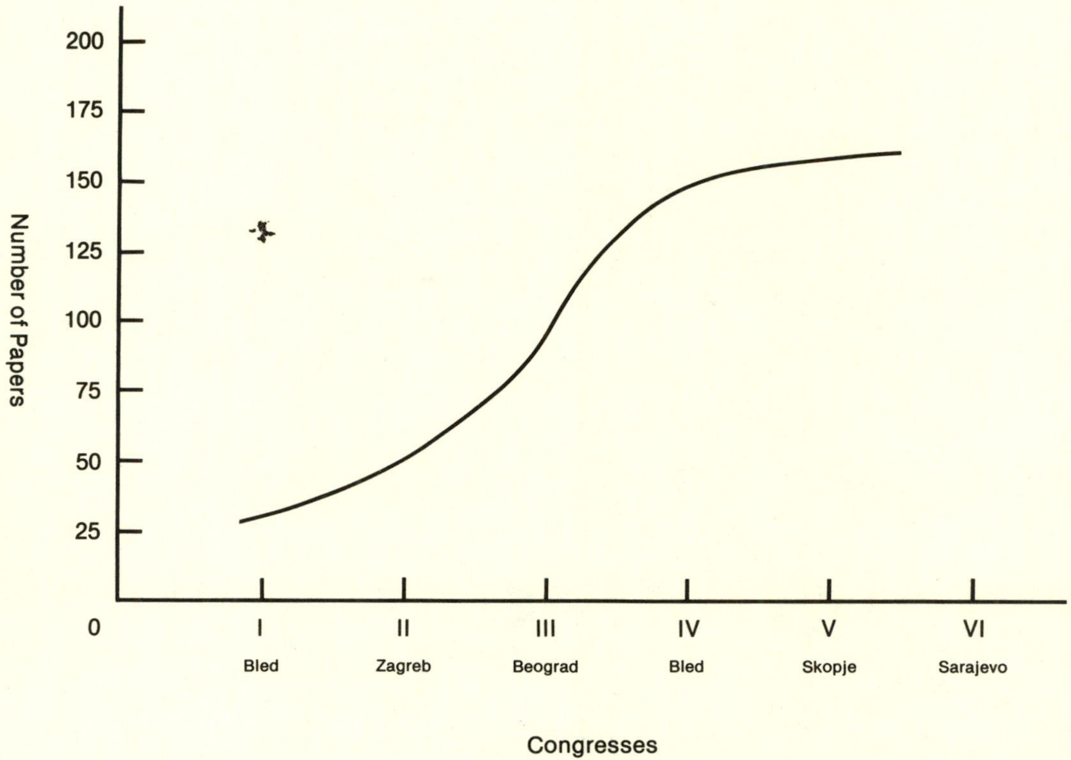

Number of Papers

200 175 150 125 100 75 50 25 0

I Bled   II Zagreb   III Beograd   IV Bled   V Skopje   VI Sarajevo

Congresses

Figure 2
Congress Papers by Major Area

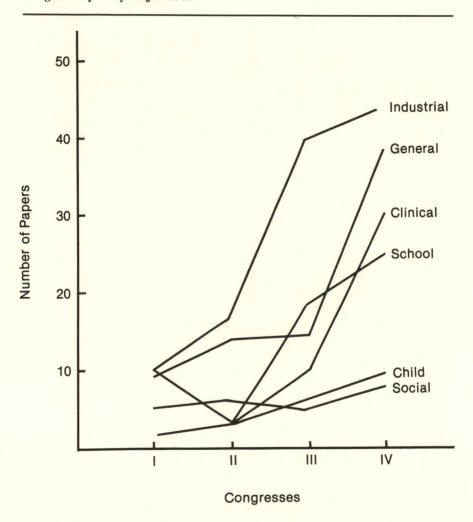

Table 1
Psychological Publications

Period	Number of Books and Papers
1921–1940 (20 years)	136
1941–1950 (war and immediate postwar period)	10
1951–1955	148
1956–1960	396
1961–1965	880
1966–1970	1330
1971–1972 (only two years)	546

Source: Based on Stary, 1975.

The growth of Yugoslav psychology was not just a matter of more psychologists, departments, congresses, books, journals, and papers; it also involved increasing diversification. Yugoslav psychologists have contributed to all important academic fields. The following areas, however, are most developed and emphasized: physiological psychology (Z. Bujas); sensory processes (Z. Bujas, A. Krković, B. Sremac, P. Ognjenović) with an emphasis on psychophysics (Z. Bujas, S. Szabo, P. Ognjenović, K. Brenk) and signal detection (I. Štajnberger, B. Šverko); abilities and their measurement (Z. Bujas, O. Ostojčić, I. Toličič, V. Smiljanić, D. Vinski, K. Momirović, R. Kvaščev); psycholinguistics (S. Savić, A. Fulgosi, G. Opačić, V. Pečjak, E. Bahovec, O. Glamuš, P. Ognjenović, I. Ivić, J. Musek); personality (A. Trstenjak, B. Popović, A. Fulgosi, J. Musek); mathematical psychology (A. Fulgosi, K. Momirović); learning (S. Radonjić, A. Fulgosi); and creativity (R. Kvaščev, I. Dizdarović, D. Žagar, A. Fulgosi, V. Pečjak).

Much of Yugoslav developmental psychology is related to educational topics and cognitive development (I. Ivič, J. Jovičić, R. Rosandič, L. Horvat). Yugoslav social psychology primarily investigates problems related to societal concerns such as political attitudes (I. Šiber, J. Obradović, R. Bojanović) and self-management by workers (N. Rot, M. Zvonarević, N. Havelka, J. Obradović, M. Šetinc, B. Kuzmanović). The history of psychology is being studied by V. Pečjak, S. Stary, M. Rotar, Ž. Korač, and K. Krstić, and psychological theory by S. Radonjić and V. Pečjak. The psychology of women is being investigated by V. Smiljanić and family psychology by N. Kapor-Stanulović and G. Čačinović. Yugoslav psychologists have also examined and written about many more specific issues and processes including emotions and the sources of aggression (T. Lamovec), the encoding of sensory information (A. Fulgosi, P. Ognjenović, S. Kostić), taste sensibility (Z. Bujas, L. Szabo), and lateral dominance (V. Smiljanić). Finally, research on tests of ability has been extensively conducted by V. Smiljanić, I. Toličić (prediction of school success), I. Štajnberger (standardization), M. Bogdanović, K. Momirović, A. Fulgosi (factor analysis), Z. Bujas (intelligence tests), R. Kvaščev (creativity tests), and B. Šali (projective tests).

Among special contributions of some importance, two deserve to be mentioned: first, the discovery by Z. Bujas that absolute sensory thresholds depend on the changes in the periphery of the analyzer and on the differential activation of neurons in the cortex; and, second, the discovery made by A. Trstenjak concerning reaction times for colors, which were found to depend on the wavelengths of light.

Many Yugoslav pyschologists have been serving as members of international research teams engaged in psychological research. A. Fulgosi worked with J. Guilford (University of Southern California); I. Toličić and L. Zorman collaborated with R. Peck (University of Texas); G. Opačić, T. Tomeković, and V. Pečjak with C. Osgood (University of Illinois); and L. Šebek and E. Konrad with Ošanin (Institute of Psychology in Moscow). An international research project concerning human symbolization was organized and led by V. Pečjak. Many Yugoslav psychologists have been teaching and doing research at foreign universities as visiting professors or recipients of grants; for instance, Z. Bujas (Rockefeller University), N. Rot (University of California at Berkeley), V. Pečjak (University of Illinois, University of Hawaii, Monash University), A. Fulgosi (University of Southern California), M. Jezernik (University of Hawaii, Constanza University), and J. Obradović (New York University). Some Yugoslav psychologists have remained at foreign universities on a permanent basis; L. Stankov (University of Sydney), S. Slak (University of Toledo), and V. Ahtik (University of Montreal) are a few examples.

During the entire period following World War II, Yugoslav psychology has been oriented more toward applied than academic psychology. Only about 200 psychologists out of 3,000 work in academic areas of psychology, while approximately 2,000 are practicing psychologists. In the immediate postwar period, the largest number of psychologists were employed in industrial psychology, especially as professional counselors, while later educational and then clinical psychologists became predominant.

Industrial psychology is one of the most diversified subfields of applied psychology. Psychologists are employed in industrial enterprises where they are involved in professional orientation, job analysis, professional education, advertising, and so forth. There are also special institutions having to do with vocational guidance, marketing, and employment. Industrial psychology is a part of the curriculum of all Yugoslav departments of psychology. Professors teaching in this area include B. Petz, B. Šverko, L. Šebek, E. Konrad, I. Štajnberger, R. Bojanović, and M. Guzina. Research in industrial psychology is largely done at universities, institutes, and work settings where industrial psychologists are employed. The following problems have received much attention: fatigue (Z. Bujas, B. Petz, V. Kolesarić), work accidents (B. Petz, D. Stary), job analysis (B. Šverko), and professional orientation (R. Popović, J. Golčić, Z. Ivezić). In stride with the extensive industrialization of the country after the war, the growth of industrial psychology was very rapid. The economic recession during the last five years, however, has been accompanied by a decline in the field and fewer job opportunities.

Educational and school psychologists naturally work in educational settings. In Slovenia, Serbia, and Croatia, some 20 to 30 percent of elementary schools employ psychologists, while in other republics the percentage is much smaller. About 30 percent of all Yugoslav psychologists work in the field of education. Educational psychology is also a part of the curriculum at all departments of psychology. Among professors in this field are L. Vučić, L. Zorman, B. Marentič-Požarnik, A. Ostojčić-Bujas, B. Bartolović, and I. Dizdarević. Most research has centered on readiness for school (I. Toličič, V. Smiljanič), social determinants of school success (I. Toličič, L. Zorman, I. Furlan), creativity training (R. Kvaščev), the psychology of gifted children (J. Makarović, I. Ferbežar, I. Dizdarević, Z. Ivezič), programmed learning (L. Vučić. V. Andrilović, I. Furlan), social relations in the classroom (D. Džordžević), and school grades (Z. Bujas, A. Ostojčić-Bujas, I. Car, I. Toličič).

Clinical psychology, which originally developed rather slowly, is now a prominent and diversified branch of applied psychology in Yugoslavia. Clinical psychologists work in hospitals (especially psychiatric facilities), counseling centers, centers for social work, medical rehabilitation centers, reform schools, prisons, and so forth. They are engaged in diagnostic as well as psychotherapeutic work. Psychotherapy in Yugoslavia makes use of different techniques deriving from various orientations including psychoanalysis, behavior therapy, client-centered therapy, Gestalt therapy, and transactional analysis. Leading specialists in this field are J. Berger (transactional analysis), K. Defilipis, L. Bregant (analytic therapy), H. Požarnik (treatment of sexual disturbances), M. Kramar, N. Čutarić (child psychotherapy), S. Bras (hypnotherapy, psychosomatics), and B. Šali (reading disabilities, psychosomatics). Clinical psychology is also a part of the curriculum at all departments of psychology in Yugoslavia; professors include B. Šali, O. Petrovič, J. Berger, and M. Krizmanič. Clinical psychologists are predominantly engaged in practical work; therefore their research activities are limited. Some of their work, however, has been quite significant, for example, B. Šali's studies on reading problems.

In addition to these classical areas of psychology, other applied subfields are quite well-developed, especially traffic psychology (S. Milosević, D. Sučević, M. Polič, B. Petz, B. Sremec, M. Miš), sports psychology (M. Čuk, K. Momirović, K. Golčić, M. Mejovšek), forensic psychology (M. Zvonarević, B. Dekleva, V. Skalar, V. Kovačević, S. Kljajić), military psychology, ecological psychology (M. Polić, A. Trstenjak), and economic psychology (A. Trstenjak, M. Kline).

Although there are eight departments of psychology and several institutions throughout the country where psychologists are employed, most psychological work is done in three main centers: Zagreb, Belgrade, and Ljubljana. At other facilities the development of psychology has been slower based on criteria such as the membership of psychological societies and the number of papers published. There are no clearly defined psychological schools or orientations in Yugoslavia, yet the differences in emphasis among the three main centers are considerable. In Zagreb, academic psychology prevails. It is "hard," experimental, and physiologically oriented. Social psychology is also a strong area there. In Belgrade, clinical and educational psychology are most prominent along with developmental and social. Psychology in Belgrade is relatively "soft" and heterogeneous. Most diverse of all is academic psychology in Ljubljana, where certain theoretical subjects, such as personality and the history of psychology, are well developed and most practical work is done in the fields of clinical and educational psychology.

Throughout Yugoslavia unemployment among psychologists in on the rise and only a few new positions are being created. The number of research projects and papers published is being reduced. The crisis is due to the rapid and extensive growth of psychology in the past combined with the present economic recession.

Stagnation is likely to continue. There is little hope that new departments of psychology will be created or that significantly more books will be published. Nor is significant growth of the psychological societies likely to resume. What can be done is to improve the quality of work done by Yugoslav psychologists, especially in teaching and in the fields of applied psychology, which are less affected by the economic recession. New growth may have to wait for the twenty-first century.

REFERENCES

Brožek, J. (1973). Marcus Marulus (1540–1524), author of *Psychologia*: Early references and the dating. *Proceedings of the 81st Annual Convention of the American Psychological Association, 8*, 21–22.

Stary, D. (1975). Publicirani radovi jugoslovenskih psihologa [Published works of Yugoslav psychologists]. *Revija za psihologiju, 5*, 129–135.

SUGGESTED READINGS

Brožek, J. (1972). Quantitative explorations in the history of psychology in Yugoslavia: Translations. *Psychological Reports, 31*, 397–398.

Pečjak, V. (1984). *Nastajanje psihologije* [Psychology in the making]. Sarajevo: Univerzum.

Zvonarević, M. (1964). A review of the development of psychology in Yugoslavia. *Bulletin de l'Association Internationale de Psychologie Appliquée, 13* (1), 3–8.

Name Index

Aarø, L. E., 349
Abe, J., 294
Aberastury, A., 91
Abma, R., 333
Adler, A., 67, 485, 558, 565, 579
Adorno, T., 218, 537
Agrell, J., 462
Aguilar, J., 311
Ahtik, V., 584
Ajuriaguerra, J. de, 189
Akhilananda, S., 253–54
Akishige, Y., 289
Albuquerque, T. L. de, 93
Alcaraz, V. M., 309
Alin, L., 472
Allen, H., 362
Allport, G. W., 4, 219, 414, 579
Allwood, C.-M., 473
Alm, H., 472
Almeida, E., 314
Alrutz, S., 462, 463, 464, 476
Alvarez, Fr. B., 297
Alvarez, G., 313
Ames, A., 552
Ananiev, B. G., 234, 423, 426, 428
Anastasi, A., 45, 86
Anderberg, R., 461, 462, 463, 465
Anderson, H., 472
Andersson, A., 470
Andersson, B., 479
Andrade-Palos, P., 315

Andrilović, V., 585
Angarita, B. V. de, 132
Angelini, A., 92
Angermaier, W. F., 72
Annett, J., 526
Anokhin, P. K., 426, 428, 431–32
Anshütz, G., 489
Antipoff, H., 79, 92
Anzieu, D., 189, 190
Appley, M. H., 564
Aragón, E. O., 298–99
Ardila, R., 5, 7, 8, 125–36
Argyle, M., 414, 502, 507, 525
Armelius, B.-Å., 472
Armelius, K., 472
Arnheim, R., 537
Arnold, M., 553
Arnold, W., 73
Aronson, E. 4
Ås, A., 365
Åsberg, M., 475
Aserinsky, E., 552
Ashour, A. M., 183
Astrup, C., 353, 362
Atatürk (Mustafa Kemal), 487
Atkinson, J. W., 92
Atkinson, R. A., 357, 403
Atkinson, R. C., 45, 357, 403
Atkinson, R. L., 45
Atrens, D. M., 45
Augustyn, J. C. D., 411
Auzias, M., 189

Aveling, F., 575
Averasturi, G., 138
Averroës (Ibn-Rushd), 495–96
Avicenna (Ibn-Sina), 487, 495
Ayala, H., 309, 311
Azaim, G. A., 183
Azuma, H., 7, 293

Baade, E., 349, 364
Bacher, F., 196
Bacher, J., 194
Bachmann, W., 234
Bachs, J., 446
Bäckström, L., 465
Bacon, F., 503, 535
Badeley, A. D., 526
Bahnsen, P., 167
Bahovec, E., 583
Bain, A., 503, 523
Baldwin, M. J., 2, 299
Baltes, P., 235
Bandura, A., 91, 204, 294, 314, 362,
  538, 551, 553, 572
Bannister, D., 521
Barbado, M., 441
Barendregt, J. T., 332, 335
Bartlett, F. C., 2, 26, 239, 506–7,
  520
Bartolache, J. I., 298
Bastien, C., 196
Battro, A., 91
Beach, F., 551
Beaudichen, J., 196
Beaunis, H., 185
Beauvois, M. F., 194
Becerra, F. C. de, 132
Becker, E., 558, 563, 569, 573
Bedolla, P., 315
Bee, H., 86
Begnum, O. H. Z., 355
Beizman, C., 190
Bejerot, N., 364
Bekhterev, V. M., 2, 420–23, 427, 537,
  549
Belanger, D., 104
Belinsky, V. G., 419
Benedict, R., 26
Benkö, A., 81, 92

Bent, D. H., 45, 51
Berger, J., 585
Bergès, J., 189
Berglund, B., 466, 468
Berglund, U., 466
Bergman, H., 476
Bergman, L., 471
Bergström, S. S., 466
Berkowitz, L., 474
Berliner, D. C., 72
Bernard, C. A., 496
Bernheim, H., 184–85
Bernstein, N. A., 426
Berryman, R., 91, 92
Bertrand, I., 184
Besariček, S., 575
Bettelheim, B., 551
Bezembinder, G. G., 333
Biaggio, A. M. B., 79–96
Bideaud, J., 196
Biescheuvel, S., 413–14
Bijou, S., 311
Binet, A., 2, 80, 172, 185, 462,
  486
Binswanger, L., 553
Biro, C., 313
Bjerke, T., 362
Bjørgen, I., 354, 365
Bjørgen, T., 362
Björkman, M., 461, 469, 471, 472
Blachowski, S., 2
Bladergroen, W. J., 331
Blakar, R. M., 352, 363
Blanc-Garin, J., 194
Blancheteau, M., 194
Blignaut, F. W., 413
Blix, A. S., 361–62
Blix, M., 463
Bloch, H., 195
Block, J., 359
Blonsky, P. P., 422
Blöschl, L., 72
Bø, O. O., 354
Boaz, G. D., 245
Bobrowska-Nowak, W., 385–86
Bodalvev, A. A., 430
Boekaerts, M., 336
Boerner, K., 72

Bogdanović, M., 583
Bogoslovsky, A. I., 423
Boiko, E. I., 425
Boizou, M.-F., 190
Bojanović, R., 583
Bokander, I., 467
Boltzmann, L., 68
Bonarius, J. C. J., 332
Bonaventura, E., 266
Bonis, M. de, 191, 194
Bonnet, C., 193
Borg, G., 469
Bori, C. M., 92
Boring, E. G., 3, 503
Böjesson, E., 466
Boroš, J., 158
Borzym, I., 383
Bose, G., 244
Boudilova, E. A., 426
Boulanger-Balleyguier, G., 189
Bouma, H., 330
Bousas, A., 308
Bovet, P., 194
Bower, G. H., 72, 564
Bower, T. G. R., 551
Bowlby, J., 3, 331, 502
Boysson-Bardies, B. de, 193, 195
Božičević-Natalis, F., 575
Braaten, L. J., 351, 354
Braatøy, T., 360
Branković, J., 575
Bras, S., 585
Bratfish, O., 469
Brattemo, C.-E., 475
Bregant, L., 585
Brehmer, B., 471, 472
Brelet, F., 190
Brenk, K., 583
Brenner, C., 72
Brenner, S.-O., 474
Bresson, F., 195
Brislin, R., 5, 7
Broadbent, D., 502, 506–7, 526, 552
Broadhurst, P. L., 502
Bronfenbrenner, U., 235, 551, 572
Brouchon, M., 193
Brown, L. B., 7

Brown, W., 506
Brozek, J., 4
Brugmans, H. J. F. W., 325
Bruner, C., 309
Bruner, J., 234, 352, 552, 572
Brunia, C. H. M., 330
Brunswik, E., 352, 472, 537, 552
Brust, H., 312
Bruun-Gulbrandsen, S., 364
Brzezinski, J., 385
Buck, R. W., 564
Budohaska, H., 380–81
Bühler, C., 67, 537
Bühler, K., 2, 67, 76, 537
Bujas, R., 575
Bujas, Z., 575, 578, 583
Bundesen, C., 170
Burt, C., 173, 239, 505, 520, 523
Bustamante, M., 569
Buytendijk, F. J. J., 326

Cabanis, P., 184
Cabrer, F., 309
Čačinovič, G., 583
Cadenas, J. M., 569
Cajal, R. y, 441, 451
Calleja, B. N., 316
Camarero, C., 445
Cameron, V. L., 26
Campbell, D. T., 5, 572
Campos, M., 315
Campos, N., 92
Cang, X. L., 293
Cannon, W., 478
Canter, D., 502–33, 527
Cantú, F., 307
Cao, Z. Q., 118
Caparrós, A., 451
Capello, H. M., 308, 316
Caplan, G., 265
Car, I., 585
Carnap, R., 68
Caron, J., 194
Carpintero, H., 446, 451
Carraher, T., 91
Carroy, J., 185–86
Casalta, H., 569
Cattell, J. McK., 2, 76

Cauzinille-Marmeche, E., 203–5
Cedeño Aguirre, M. L., 311
Chabert, C., 190
Chaplin, J. P., 564
Charcot, J. M., 1, 184–85
Chauchard, P., 293
Chavez, E., 298–99
Chelpanov, G. I., 421
Chen, D., 110
Chen, L., 110
Chen, Y. M., 118
Chen, Z. G., 119
Cherns, A., 7
Chernyshevsky, N. G., 419
Chiarottino, Z., 91
Child, J., 526
Chin, A. S., 5
Chin, R., 5
Ching, C. C. (Jing, Qicheng), 6, 7
Chirinos, E., 570
Chiva, M., 189
Chomsky, N., 18, 378, 538, 551, 552
Chorus, A. M. J., 325
Choynowski, M., 315
Christiansen, B., 350–51, 359, 360, 365
Cicero, M., 307, 308
Claparéde, E., 1, 2, 79–80
Clark, H., 234
Clarke, A. D. B., 502
Clarke, A. M., 502
Clausen, J., 360
Clauss, G., 72, 228, 232
Codol, J. P., 196
Coetzee, J. C., 404
Cofer, C. N., 564
Coghill, G., 551
Cohen, R., 472
Cole, M., 7
Colotla, V., 307, 309, 313
Comenius (Komenský, J. A.), 145
Condillac, E., 184
Confucius, 109
Conger, J. J., 73, 86
Constanzo, V., 569, 570
Contasti, Max, 570
Coover, G. D., 349

Cordero, J. N., 298
Corman, L., 190
Corres, P., 313
Corsí-Cabrera, M., 312
Corsini, R. J., 7
Covarrubias, A., 314
Coxon, A., 521
Craik, K., 506, 526
Crutchfield, R. S., 72, 212, 357
Cueli, J., 313
Čuk, M., 585
Cuny, X., 201
Curcho, A., 569, 570
Cureau, A. L., 26
Curthoys, I. S., 45
Čutarić, N., 585

Dabrowski, K., 384
Dalland, T., 349, 361
Dalmatinac, J., 574
D'Amorim, M. A. M., 92
Danielsson, A., 470
Darwin, C., 503–4, 529, 536, 419
Daumenlang, K., 73
David, H. P., 4
Davidson, P., 104
Dávila, G., 300, 307
Davison, G. C., 45, 72
Davitz, J., 553
Dawson, John, 5
Day, R. H., 59
Debray, R., 189, 190
Decroly, O. J., 80
Defilipis, K., 585
De Groot, A., 327, 330, 333, 336
De Jager, L. C., 411
Dekleva, B., 585
De Lange, S., 339
Delgado, R., 451
Dembo, M., 568, 570
Denis, M., 194
De Sanctis, S., 2
Descartes, R., 184, 496
Dewey, J., 80, 414, 536, 544
De Wolff, C. J., 324–46, 335
Diatkine, R., 189
Diaz-Fuentes, M., 307

Diaz-Guerrero, R., 7, 308, 313, 314, 315
Diaz-Loving, R., 297–323, 307, 315
Diekstra, R. F. W., 335
Dimbeg, U., 477
Dizdarović, I., 583, 584
Dobroliubov, A., 419
Doise, W., 8
Dominguez, B., 309, 311, 314
Donald, I. J., 502–33
Donders, F. C., 324
Dorna, A., 197–200
Dornic, S., 471–74
Douglas, V., 104
Draff, E., 307
Dragašić, J., 574
Dreier, O., 170
Drenth, P. J. D., 331, 335, 339
Drever, J., 4, 239, 508
Drever, J., Jr., 508
Druker-Colin, R., 312
Duijker, H. C. J., 3, 332
Dumas, G., 185
Duncker, K., 537
Dunér, A., 471
Dureman, I., 475, 477
Ďurič, L., 158
Durojaiye, M. O. A., 7, 24–36
Durup, H., 194
Dyregrov, A., 350
Džordževic, D., 585

Ebbinghaus, H., 228, 233, 491
Ebner, H., 72, 228
Eckardt, G., 228, 233
Eckblad, G., 354
Edgeworth, F. Y., 505
Ehrlich, M. F., 193
Ehrlich, S., 195
Eide, R., 350
Eikeland, H. M., 351
Eisenga, L. K. A., 333
Eisler, H., 468–69
Eitinger, M., 267
Ekehammar, B., 471
Ekeland, T. L., 363
Ekman, G., 461, 462, 464, 466, 467–69, 470, 473, 478

El Bahie, F., 175
El Gharib, R., 175
El Kabbani, I., 182
El Kaddah, H., 183
Elkin, D. G., 423
El Kousi, A. A., 173, 175
Ellertsen, B., 350
Elmgren, J., 461, 462, 463, 472
El Nahhas, K., 182
El Rakhawi, Y., 183
El Sayed, K., 175
Elshout, J. J., 330
Emmelkamp, P. M. G., 335
Enciso, G. P., 570
Eng, H., 363
Erikson, E., 414, 551
Eriksson, S., 466
Erisman, T., 68
Escalona, E., 569
Esperet, E., 193
Espmark, Y., 362
Esquirol, J. E. D., 184
Essenfeld, S., 569, 570
Euler, U. von, 477
Evrim, S., 490
Eysenck, H., 17, 315, 441, 502, 516, 522, 553, 572

Fabre, J. M.,. 194
Fagundes, L., 91
Falade, S., 26
Falcón-Guerrero, M., 307
Faleide, A., 354
Faller, A., 72
Fang, Z., 118
Fantz, R., 551, 552
Farag, S. E., 172–83, 175, 177, 182
Farberow, N., 551
Farrand, L., 2
Favez-Boutonnier, J., 186
Fayol, M., 193
Feather, N. T., 59
Fechner, G. T., 233, 440, 464
Feifel, H., 551
Feigl, H., 68
Fein, L. G., 5
Feldman, N., 570, 573

Feng, Z. L., 115
Ferbežar, I., 584
Fernández, A., 570
Fernández, G., 309
Fernández-Guardiola, A., 312
Ferreira, M. C. A., 92
Festinger, L., 219, 552
Fhaner, S., 473–74
Fichter, M. M., 8
Fierro de Ascanio, J., 570
Filho Lourenço, M. B., 92
Fischer, G., 72, 75
Fishbein, M., 572
Fisher, R. A., 502, 536
Florés, C., 196
Florés, M. M., 314
Florés d'Arcais, G. B., 293, 330
Forgas, J. P., 45
Forgus, R., 564
Forster, D. H., 415
Fortmann, H. M. M., 332
Foucault, M., 86, 91, 485
Fraczek, A., 382, 387
Fraisse, P., 191, 446
Frances, R., 194
Franke, E., 26
Frankenhaeuser, M., 468, 469, 478
Frankl, V., 67, 414
Fransella, F., 521
Franzen, O., 469
Fredrickson, M., 477
French, J., 359
Frenkel-Brunswik, E., 53, 359
Freud, S., 86, 190, 219, 244, 267, 314, 359–60, 463, 485, 506, 549, 551, 579
Frias de Orantes, M. R., 569
Friedrich, W., 228, 233
Frijda, N., 4, 330, 332
Frisch, K. von, 551
Frodi, A., 474
From, F., 167–68
Fromm, E., 300, 485, 553, 579
Fukuzawa, Y., 274–75
Fulgosi, A., 578, 583
Fulton, J., 361

Funatsu, T., 294
Furlan, I., 584

Gabrielsson, A., 466
Gabršek, F., 575
Gage, N. L., 72
Gaiarsa, A., 93
Galanter, E., 552
Gallegos, X., 313
Galperin, P., 234
Galton, F., 56, 504–5, 520, 536
Gao, J.-F., 110, 121
Garćia, B., 315
Garćia, O. R., 563, 570, 571
Garćia, S., 307
Garćia, V., 309
Gardell, B., 478
Gardner, G., 45
Garfield, E., 16
Garling, T., 467
Garrett, H., 564
Gasset, O. y, 441, 451
Gautrat, M., 191
Gaw'wad, L. A., 177
Geissler, H. G., 232
Gendlin, E. T., 293
Georges, C., 196
Gerhardt, R., 364
Germain, J., 441, 445, 446, 448
Gesell, A., 551
Geuter, U., 220
Gibello, B., 190
Gibello, M.-L., 190
Gibson, E., 551, 552
Gibson, J. J., 466, 551, 552, 554
Gilgen, A. R., 1–23, 534–56
Gilgen, C. K., 1–23
Gilly, M., 196
Giner de los Ríos, F., 440
Gjerde, P., 363
Gjesme, T., 354
Gjessing, H.-J., 351
Glamuš, O., 583
Glass, G. V., 564
Gliszczynska, X., 373, 385
Golčić, J., 584
Golčić, K., 585
Goldstein, K., 537

Golgi, C., 361
Gomes Penna, A., 92
Gomez, G., 315
Gonzalez, F., 139
Goodow, J., 40, 59
Gøtestam, K.-G., 353, 354, 362, 364, 463, 464, 476
Goude, G., 466, 468, 469
Grahnstedt, S., 350
Granell, E., 570
Graumann, C. F., 73, 208–21, 220
Greco, P., 195
Greene, J., 502
Gregory, R. L., 502
Grenness, C. E., 351, 365
Griesel, R. D., 400
Grosclaude, M., 191
Grundlach, H., 220
Grzelak, J., 381
Grzesiuk, L., 368–91, 384
Guan, L. C., 119
Guilford, J. P., 467, 578, 579, 583
Guillaumé, P., 80
Gulbrandsen, H., 359
Guo, R. J., 118
Guryka, A., 370, 373, 382–83
Guthrie, E., 537, 549
Gutjahr, W., 233
Gutke, J., 233
Guttman, L., 521
Guttmann, G., 67–78

Haavind, H., 352
Habermas, J., 218
Hacker, W., 228, 232, 234
Hagafors, R., 472
Hagekull, B., 477
Haggard, E., 359
Hagino, G., 294
Hagtvet, K., 351
Hahn, H., 68
Hall, C. S., 86
Hall, G. S., 275, 536, 544
Halpern, E., 258–73
Hammer, B., 461
Hammerborg, D., 350
Hansen, S., 479

Hansson, G., 466
Harlow, H., 551, 553
Harré, R., 525
Hartman, E. 352
Hartmann, H., 552
Hathaway, S. R., 313
Hatwell, Y., 191–97
Haug, J., 354
Havelka, N., 583
Haven, H., 274
Haven, J., 109
Havik, O., 350
Hay, L., 195
Hebb, D. O., 103, 447, 551, 552
Heckhausen, H., 73
Hefni, K., 177, 182
Hegge, T. G., 2
Heggelund, P., 354
Heider, F., 552
Heimer, L., 479
Hellström, Å., 469
Helm, J., 228, 233
Helmholtz, H., 228, 440
Helmreich, R. L., 315
Helson, H., 552
Helstrup, T., 349
Henriksson, B., 475
Herkner, W., 72
Hermans, H. J. M., 332
Hernández-Holtzman, E., 315
Hernándes-Peón, 300, 312
Herrlin, A., 461, 463, 472
Herskovits, M., 4, 5
Herzberg, F., 91, 414, 572
Herzen, A. I., 419
Hess, E., 551
Heszen-Klemens, I., 385
Hettema, P. J., 332
Heymans, G., 324–25, 345
Hiebsch, H., 228, 232–34
Hilgard, E. R., 45, 72, 86, 357, 403, 447, 564
Hillix, W. A., 4
Hjelmquist, E., 472, 474
Hobhouse, L. T., 504
Hofer, M., 73
Høffding, H., 163

Hoffman, J., 232
Hofstätter, P. R., 72
Hofstee, W. K. B., 331–32, 333
Hofsten, C. von, 466
Hogan, T. P., 98–108
Hogan, T. V., 97–108
Holdstock, T. L., 404
Hole, K., 350, 353
Holter, H., 352, 359
Holt-Hansen, K., 168
Holtzman, P., 552
Holtzman, W. H., 7
Holzkamp, K., 216, 235
Horkheimer, M., 218
Horvat, L., 583
Hu, C. Q., 120
Hudson, W., 412–13
Huerta, J., 311
Hugdahl, K., 461–83
Hull, C. H., 45, 51, 463, 471, 537, 538, 549, 550, 551–52, 554
Humble, K., 476
Hume, D., 503
Humphrey, G., 507
Hunter, W. S., 2
Hurtig, M., 203–5
Husen, T., 462
Husserl, E., 167, 465
Hutte, H. A., 332
Hviid, J., 169
Hygge, S., 477
Hyman, H., 359

İbn-Khaldun, 487, 495
İbn-Rushd (Averroës), 495–96
İbn-Sina (Avicenna), 487, 495
Ibor, J. L., 449
Ibsen, H., 359
Imada, H., 294
Imberty, M., 194
Indow, T., 290
Inglis, J., 104
Ingvar, D., 477
Innerhofer, P., 72
Innes, J. M., 45
Iskander, N., 177
Ismail, E. E., 178
Ito Sugiyama, M. E., 315

Ivey, A. E., 45
Ivezić, Z., 584
Ivić, I., 583
Iwahara, S., 4

Jacobson, E., 3
Jaederholm, G. A., 461, 462, 463
Jaeger, S., 220
Jahoda, G., 4, 5, 26, 525
Jahoda, M., 537
Jakobi, J.-M., 197–200
James, W., 298, 491, 504, 508, 536
Janet, P., 185
Janis, I. L., 359
Jankowski, K., 384
Jansson, G., 466
Järbe, T., 475
Jarl, V. C., 364
Jaspars, J. M. F., 332
Jenkins, J. C., 45, 51
Jezernik, M., 584
Jiao, S. L., 117
Jiménez, E., 569, 570
Jiménez-Cadena, A., 132
Jing, Q. (C. C. Ching), 112, 116, 121
Johansen, M., 168
Johansson, B., 472
Johansson, Gunn, 478
Johansson, Gunnar, 465–66
Johnson, T. B., 351
Johnson, C.-O., 473, 476
Jordaan, J. J., 411
Jordaan, W. J., 411
Jørgensen, J., 163
Jørgensen, P. S., 169
Jouffroy, T., 184
Jovičić, J., 583
Jung, C., 91, 242, 244, 292, 485, 579

Kaada, B., 349, 353, 361
Kader, M. A., 177
Kadzielawa, D., 385
Kaes, R., 190
Kafafi, R., 177
Kagan, J., 73, 86, 551

Kagitgibasi, C., 7
Kahn, R. L., 572
Kail, M., 195
Kakar, S., 254
Kalverboer, A. F., 335
Kaneko, T., 274–96
Kant, I., 233
Kapor-Stanulović, N., 583
Kasielke, E., 233
Katz, D., 359, 461, 463, 464, 467, 572
Kaufman, V. J., 423
Kebbon, L., 475
Keller, F., 86, 91, 92, 311
Kelly, G., 32, 331, 523
Kemal, M. (Atatürk), 487
Kempen, G. A. M., 330
Kennedy, S., 7
Kessen, W., 5
Khaldun, I., 495
Khalek, A. A., 175, 176, 177
Khol, J., 158
Kile, S., 351
Kimura, D., 104
Kintsch, W., 234
Klein, G., 552
Klein, M., 17, 91
Kleitman, N., 552
Kleiven, J., 355, 363
Kline, M., 585
Klineberg, O., 3, 5, 7, 8
Klix, F., 228, 232
Kljajić, S., 585
Kløve, H., 350, 353
Knudsen, F., 169
Koch, S., 11
Kodama, H., 292
Kodama, S., 294
Kodým, M., 145–60, 158
Koekebakker, J., 332
Kohler, C., 353, 361
Kohler, I., 76
Köler, W., 230, 537, 575
Kolck, O. L. van, 87
Kolesarić, V., 584
Komenský, J. A. (Comenius), 145
Kondáš, O., 158
Konorski, J., 380–81

Konrad, E., 583
Køppe, S., 161–71
Korač, Ž., 583
Kornilov, K. N., 422, 579
Koscielska, M., 383
Kossakowski, A., 228 , 229, 232, 234
Kostyuk, G. S., 425
Kotzé, J. C., 404
Kouzmin, E. S., 426, 427
Kovach, J. K., 5
Kovalev, A. G., 427
Kozelsky, I. P., 418
Kozielecki, J., 377–78, 387
Kozulin, A., 7
Kraft, V., 68
Kragh, U., 349, 364, 469–70
Kramar, M., 585
Krause, B., 229
Kravkov, S. V., 423
Krawiec, T. 564
Krech, D., 72, 212, 357, 359
Kreitler, H., 266
Krejčí, F., 145
Krekling, S., 352
Kringlen, E., 353, 354
Krishnan, B., 245
Krković, A., 583
Krstić, K., 583
Kruger, D., 404
Kuang, P. Z., 118
Kugelmass, S., 266
Külpe, O., 330
Kúnnapas, T., 466, 469
Kuo, Z. Y., 2
Kurcz, I., 378, 387
Kuzmanović, B., 583
Kvaščev, R., 583
Kveim, K. B., 352
Kyng, B., 169

Lacan, J., 86, 91, 568, 572
Ladygina-Kots, N. D., 423
Lafarga, J., 307, 308, 313
Lagache, D., 186
Lagmay, A., 7
La Grange, A. J., 413
Laing, R. D., 502, 553

Lambert, W., 104
Lambo, T. A., 26
La Mettrie, J. de, 184
Lamovec, T., 583
Lampe, A., 569, 570
Landauer, T. K., 130
Landquist, J., 463
Lange, N. N., 420
Langeveld, M. J., 326
Langfeld, H. S., 3
Langkjaer, A., 169
Lara-Tapia, H., 313
Larsen, A., 170
Larsson, K., 479
Lartique, T., 313
Lauterbach, W., 7
Lazarsfeld, P., 537
Lazarus, A., 413
Lazarus, R. S., 294
Lazursky, A. F., 422
Leavitt, H. H., 414
Lebovici, S., 189
Lecocq, P., 194
Leconte, P., 194
Lecoutre, B., 196
Lee, S. Y., 7
Lefèvre, A., 189
Lehman, A., 161, 167
Leite, D. M., 92
Lenin, N., 422, 439
Lennep, D. J. van, 326
Lennerlöf, L., 478–79
Le Ny, J. F., 193
Leontiev, A. N., 154, 234, 422,
    428
Lépine, D., 196
Leplat, J., 194, 196, 200–203
Levander, S., 475
Levelt, W. J. M., 330
Levi, L., 478
Levine, S., 349
Levinson, D., 8
Lévy-Leboyer, C., 201
Levy-Schoen, A., 193
Lewicki, A., 372, 376, 377, 383
Lewin, K., 219, 230, 537, 551,
    552
Lézine, I., 189

Li, C., 112
Li, J. Z., 118
Li, X. T., 119–20
Lidberg, L., 475
Lie, I., 351–52
Liébeault, A. A., 184
Lienert, G., 76
Lin, C. D., 115
Lin, W. J., 119
Lindberg, L., 472
Lindsay, P. H., 72, 447
Lindzey, G., 4, 86
Linhart, J., 145–60, 157, 158
Linschoten, J., 326
Lippmann, H. L., 81
Lipsitt, L. P., 551
Litman, R., 551
Liu, F., 114
Liu, J. H., 114
Liu, S. X., 118
Livson, N., 212, 357
Llull, R., 440
Løberg, T., 350
Locke, J., 503, 535
Loewe, H., 229
Lomonosov, M. V., 419
Lomov, B. F., 7, 154, 418–39
Lompscher, J., 232, 234
Longeot, F., 189, 196
Lonner, W. J., 5
López, F., 308, 311
López-Rodriguez, F., 309
Lorenz, K., 76, 516, 538, 551
Lourenço Filho, M. B., 79
Loutre, N., 189
Louw, D. A., 403
Louw, S. J., 415
Lovaas, O. I., 551
Lovell, H. T., 55
Lovibond, S. H., 59
Løvlie, A.-L., 354
Lu, Z. H., 115
Lu, Z.-W., 110
Lück, H. E., 220
Lukaszewski, W., 380
Lund, T., 351, 354
Lundberg, I., 473
Lundberg, U., 469, 478

Luria, A. R., 94, 422, 425, 426, 428, 579
Lysgaard, S., 359

Ma, M. C., 118
McCleary, R., 349, 361
McClelland, D., 92
Maccoby, M., 300
MacCrone, I. D., 413, 414
McDougall, W., 506, 507, 508, 516, 524–25
Macedo, L. de, 91
Mach, E., 68
Machado, J., 569
Madariaga, C., 441
Madsen, K. B., 168, 170
Magnussen, S., 352
Magnusson, D., 332, 466–67, 469, 470–71
Mahmoud, A. H., 182
Makarenko, A. S., 426
Makarović, J., 584
Malewski, A., 386
Malherbe, E. G., 404, 413, 414
Mallart, J., 441
Malone, M. J., 8
Malpass, R., 5
Mammen, J., 169
Mann, L., 59
Manrique, B., 569, 570
Mao Tse-tung, 110, 111
Marañón, G., 451
Marcondes, D., 93
Marek, J., 349
Marín, G., 137–44
Marmolin, H., 466
Marques, J., 92
Marton, F. 472
Marulić, M., 574
Maruszewski, M., 385
Marx, K. See Marxism and Marxism-Leninism (Subject Index)
Marx, M. H., 4
Mashour, M., 466
Maslow, A., 91, 553
Matalon, B., 197–200
Mathieu, J., 194
Matsumoto, M., 2, 275

Matysiak, J., 380
May, R., 553
Mead, G. H., 504
Meara, J. O., 415
Mecheryakov, A. I., 424
Medina-Liberty, A., 297–316, 311, 313
Medina-Mora, M. E., 313
Mehler, J., 195
Mehryar, A. H., 7
Meili, R., 72
Meinong, A., 68, 575
Meischner, W., 233
Meister, A., 234
Mejovšek, M., 585
Melikian, L. H., 7
Melin, L., 463, 476
Meljac, C., 189, 190
Mellenbergh, G. J., 333
Mencius, 109
Mendelsohn, P., 191–97
Mendez, G., 570
Métraux, A., 208–21, 220
Mettell, T., 92
Metzger, W., 293
Metzler, P., 228
Meumann, E., 575
Meyer, H., 167
Meyersson, B., 479–80
Meza y Gutierrez, J., 298–99
Michon, J. A., 330
Michotte, A., 2, 441
Micklebust, V., 572
Mika, S., 372, 381
Milika, L. K., 175, 176, 178
Mill, J. S., 184, 503
Millán, A., 300
Miller, N., 550, 552
Milner, B., 104
Milosević, S., 585
Miñarro, A., 569, 570
Minkovska, F., 190
Mintz, A., 4
Mira, E., 441
Mira y Lopez, E., 80, 92
Miš, M., 585
Mischel, W., 538
Misès, R., 189

Misiak, H., 6
Misumi, J., 290
Mittenecker, E., 72
Molenaar, W., 333
Molina, J., 309, 313
Momirović, K., 583, 585
Mönks, F. J., 339
Monroy Nase, Z., 313
Montero, M., 564, 569, 570
Montgomery, H., 473
Morales, M. L., 314
Morel, B., 184
Moretti, J. B., 570
Morgan, C. L., 504
Morgan, C. T., 130, 447, 491
Moscovici, S., 8
Motokawa, K., 289, 292
Motora, Y., 275, 293
Mourad, J., 173, 176
Mouret, E., 313
Moustgaard, I. K., 169
Mowrer, O. H., 361, 550
Mulder, M., 332
Müller, G. E., 463, 464
Müller, H., 228
Munn, N. L., 59
Munnichs, J. M. A., 331
Muñoz, C., 564, 570
Munsterberg, H., 239, 325
Murchison, C., 2
Murison, R. C. C., 349, 361
Murphy, G., 5, 250–51, 360,
   579
Murphy, L., 551
Musek, J., 578, 583
Mussen, P. H., 73, 86
Myasischev, V. N., 422
Myers, C. R., 7, 104
Myers, C. S., 241, 506
Myhre, G., 362

Nadelsticher, A., 314
Naesgaard, S., 167, 168
Nafstad, H. E., 352
Nandy, A., 246, 251, 255
Nansen, F., 361
Naranjo, S., 569
Neale, J. M., 45, 72

Nebylitsin, V. D., 425, 428
Necki, Z., 382
Nedić, L., 575
Neisser, U., 447, 552
Nell, V., 415
Neumann, J. von, 537
Neurath, O., 68
Newton, I., 535
Newton, J. W., 45
Nguyen-Xuan, A., 195
Nie, N. H., 45, 51
Nielsen, Geir, 363
Nielsen, Gerhard, 169
Nielsen, H. H., 169
Nielsen, T. I., 169
Nilsson, A., 470
Nilsson, L.-G., 471, 472–73
Nishi, A., 274
Nixon, M. C., 10, 37–66, 40
Noguera, C., 570
Nordland, E., 354
Nordlund, O., 476
Norman, D. A., 72, 447
Nørwig, A. M., 167
Nosal, C., 377
Novaes, M. H., 87, 92
Nuñez, R., 307, 313
Nyborg, H., 169
Nygård, R., 354
Nystedt, L., 466–67, 471, 474

Obonai, T., 289
Obradović, J., 583
Obuchowski, K., 379, 387
O'Driscoll, M., 45
Ognjenović, P., 578, 583
Öhman, A., 350, 353, 461–83, 475,
   477
Öhrwall, H., 463
Oleron, P., 193
Oliveira Lima, L. de, 91
Olmo, F. D., 570
Olsen, A. M., 355
Olweus, D., 350, 353
Ombredane, A., 26
Ommundsen, R., 363
O'Neil, W. M., 55, 59
Opačić, G., 583

Orantes, A., 569, 570
Orlebeke, J. F., 330
Ošanin, D., 583
Orsini-Bouichou, F., 195
Osgood, C. E., 4, 447, 552, 578, 579, 583
Öst, L.-G., 463, 467
Östberg, O., 474
Østergaard, L., 169
Ostojčić, O., 583
Ostojčić-Bujas, A., 585
Ostrosky, F., 312
Oswald, W. D., 73
Over, R. F., 59
Oyama, T., 294

Pacheco, J. R., 298
Paetzold, P., 229
Pailhous, J., 193, 195
Paivio, A., 104
Palmés, F. M., 441
Palos, P. A., 307
Parafita Bessa, P., 92
Paranjpe, A. C., 254
Pardel, T., 158
Parducci, A., 212
Pareek, U., 255
Parra, P., 298
Parygin, B. D., 427
Patiño-Muñoz, G., 297
Pauli, R., 73
Pavlov, I., 145, 234, 375, 377, 420–21, 425, 439, 537, 549
Pawlik, K., 73
Pear, T. H., 507
Pearce, P. L., 45
Pearson, K., 462, 505, 536
Pécheux, M. G., 195
Pečjak, V., 574–86, 578, 583
Peck, R., 583
Pedersen, R. H., 168
Peeters, H. F. M., 333
Pelechano, V., 446
Penna, A. G., 92
Penfold, J., 568
Peng, D. L., 117
Peng, R. X., 117
Peral, I., 445

Peralta, J., 307
Pérez-Cota, F., 313
Perls, F., 572
Perron, M., 189
Perron, R., 189, 190
Perruchet, P., 194
Perse, J., 190
Perski, A., 477
Peter the Great, 419
Peters, M., 72
Peters, W., 489
Petersen, E., 169
Petronijević, B., 575
Petrovsky, A. V., 426
Pettigrew, T. F., 414
Petz, B., 584, 585
Petzold, P., 232
Pfromm Netto, S., 79, 92, 93
Piaget, J., 12, 14, 18, 80, 86, 91, 94, 142, 189, 191, 193, 203, 217, 219, 234, 274, 289, 311, 331, 352, 365, 422, 435, 446, 450, 474, 485, 493, 538, 548, 551, 552, 567, 572, 579
Pichot, P., 190
Pick S., 307
Pick de Weiss, S., 314
Pierault-Le Bonniec, G., 195
Piéron, H., 1, 2, 80, 575
Pinillos, J. L., 441, 446
Pisarev, D. I., 419
Pitaluga, C., 569, 570
Plekhanov, G. V., 427, 439
Pleszewski, Z., 384
Plutchik, R., 553
Poitou, J. P., 194
Poitrenaud, J., 191
Polić, M., 585
Popović, B., 583
Popović, R., 584
Popper, K., 68, 218, 333
Popplestone, J., 5
Postman, L., 551
Potebnya, A. A., 439
Poulsen, H., 169
Požarnik, H., 585
Pozo, F. R. del, 313
Prabhu, P. H., 254

Praetorius, N., 169
Preyer, W., 233
Pribram, K. H., 552
Procházka, J., 145
Przetacznikowa, M., 372, 382,
    387
Pulido, M., 569, 570
Purkinje (Purkyně), J. E., 145
Pushkin, A., 419
Puységur, M. de, 184
Pynte, J., 193

Raab, E., 72
Raaheim, Kjell, 349
Rabbie, J. M., 332
Rabbitt, P., 474
Radonjić, S., 578, 583
Radosavljević, P., 575
Railo, W. S., 355
Raimbault, G., 191
Rajeh, E., 175
Rakić, V., 575
Ramakrishna Rao, K., 245
Ramírez, A., 570
Ramírez, S., 313, 314
Ramzi, N., 177
Rand, P., 354
Rapaport, D., 537
Rapoport, D., 189
Rasborg, F., 169
Rasmussen, E. T., 167
Rasmussen, W., 361
Ratajczak, Z., 385
Rattleff, A., 167, 168
Raubenheimer, I. van W., 392–417, 404,
    411, 416
Raundalen, M., 350
Rautenbach, C. H., 414
Rayek, E., 309, 312
Razi, Z., 495
Razran, G., 4
Recagno, I., 569, 570
Reich, W., 91, 360, 485
Reid, T., 503, 535
Reinert, G., 6
Reuchlin, M., 192, 194, 201,
    447
Reuning, H. F. E., 412

Revault D'Allonnes, C., 190
Révèsz, G., 325, 464
Rewentlow, I., 169
Reyes-Lagunes, L., 316
Reykowski, J., 370, 375–76, 379–80,
    384, 387
Ribes, E., 308–9, 311, 313
Ribot, T., 1, 184, 185, 491, 503,
    508
Richard, J. F., 194, 196
Richardson, A., 59
Richet, C., 184
Riesen, A., 551
Rifbjerg, S., 167
Riis, E., 364
Rijsman, J. B., 332
Ríos, F. de los, 445
Risberg, J., 477
Ristić, H., 575
Rivera, S., 314
Rivers, W. H., 505, 506, 508
Robles, O., 307, 313
Rodrigo, M., 126, 441
Rodrigues, A., 87, 92, 93
Rodríguez de Arizmendi, G.,
    315
Rodríguez-Valderrama, J., 132
Roe, R. A., 335
Roels, F. J. M. A., 325
Roesler, H.-D, 233
Rogers, A., 7
Rogers, C., 86, 219, 235, 292, 313, 341,
    354, 414, 538, 553, 572, 585
Rohracher, H., 67, 72, 73, 74,
    76
Rojas, J. A., 312
Rokeach, M., 386, 572
Romanes, G. J., 504
Romero, O., 569
Rommetveit, R., 352, 353, 359
Rong Hung, 109
Rönnberg, S., 463, 476
Rønnestad, H. M., 363
Rorschach, H., 558
Rosamilha, N., 92
Rosandič, R., 583
Rosenzweig, M. R., 8
Roskam, E. C. J., 333

Ross, S., 169
Rossi, J. P., 193
Rostohar, M., 575, 579
Rot, N., 578, 583
Rotar, M., 583
Roth, E., 73
Rothe, W., 169
Rotter, J. B., 315
Rouanet, H., 196
Rubin, E., 167–68
Rubinowitz, S., 479
Rubinstein, S. L., 154, 234, 422, 428
Ruch, F., 130
Rudolfer, N. da S., 79, 92
Ruffiot, A., 190
Ruiz, R., 568, 570
Ruiz Primo, A., 311
Rumar, K., 466
Runesson, S., 466
Rusalov, V. M., 426
Russell, R. W., 3, 4, 7, 59
Rutten, F. J. T., 325
Rutter, M., 502
Ryden, O., 470

Sagberg, F., 352
Sagvolden, T., 352, 361, 362
Sahagún, Fr. B. de, 297
Salam, M. A., 178
Salazar, J. M., 7, 557–73, 564, 569, 570, 573
Sälde, H., 475
Saleh, N., 177
Salhani, L., 197–200
Šali, B., 583, 585
Sánchez, E., 564, 569, 570, 571, 572
Sánchez, J. A., 132
Sánchez, L. M., 557–73, 570, 573
Sánchez, R. L., 313
Sand, R., 363
Sanders, A. F., 330
Sanders, C., 333
Sandström, C.-I., 464, 465
Sanford, N., 4
Sanguineti, Y., 314

San Juan, Huarte de, 440
San Román, A., 307
Santoro, E., 564, 569, 570
Santoyo, C., 309, 311
Santucci, H., 190
Sarhan, A. A., 183
Sato, K., 293
Saugstad, P., 352, 365
Savić, S., 583
Schaarschmidt, U., 237
Schachter, S., 553
Schalling, D., 475–76
Scheerer, E., 220
Scheirer, J., 7
Schindler, R., 234
Schioldborg, P., 348, 352
Schjelderup, H., 358, 360
Schlick, M., 68
Schliemann, A., 91
Schmidt, H.-D., 7, 222–38, 228, 229, 232–33
Schniermann, A. L., 2
Schoenfeld, W., 86, 572
Scholander, T., 475
Schonen, S. de, 195
Schönpflug, U., 212
Schönpflug, W., 212
Schroeder, H., 233
Schuster-Tyroller, G., 220
Schwendler, W., 7
Scott, W. A., 59
Sears, R., 550
Šebek, L., 583
Sechenov, I. M., 145, 420, 422, 423
Seeber, A., 234
Segall, M., 5
Segui, J., 193
Sek, H., 384
Selim III, 496
Selosse, J., 191
Selz, O., 330
Seminerio, F., 92
Sengupta, N. N., 239
Serpell, R., 7
Serrano, R., 298
Šetinc, M., 583
Settergren, G., 476

Severtsov, N. A., 439
Sexton, V. S., 6
Shao, J., 119
Shao, R. Z., 114
Shapiro, A., 360
Shapiro, D., 502
Shawran, P. R., 413
Sheehan, P. W., 59
Shemyakin, F. N., 423
Shen, E., 2
Shentoub, V., 190
Sherif, M., 497–98
Shebarev, P. A., 423
Shneidman, E., 551
Shugar, W. G., 378
Shuh, P., 110, 112, 121
Shvyrkov, V. B., 426
Šiber, I., 583
Siegman, A., 266
Siegwald, H., 461, 462
Sigsgaard, T., 167
Siguán, M., 441, 446
Silverman, R. E., 403
Simarro, L., 441
Simek-Downing, L., 45
Simon, B., 4
Simon, H. A., 117
Simon, T., 80, 486
Singh, R. B., 254
Sinha, D., 7, 239–57
Sinha, J. B. P., 7, 253
Sjöberg, L., 469, 471, 473
Sjöden, P. O., 476, 480
Skalar, V., 585
Skard, Å. G., 358, 363
Skarzynska, K., 381
Skawran, P. R., 408
Skinner, B. F., 17, 86, 91, 219, 293,
    300, 308, 314, 450, 537, 538, 543,
    549, 551, 552, 553, 554, 567, 570,
    572
Skorokhodova, O., 424
Slak, S., 584
Slangen, J. L., 330
Smedslund, J., 352, 353, 362
Smiljanić, V., 578, 583, 584
Smirnov, A. A., 423, 579
Smith, D. G., 508

Smith, G., 469–70
Smith, L., 351, 352
Smørvik, D., 352
Snijders, J. T., 331
Södersten, P., 479
Sokolov, E. N., 425, 552
Sokolowska, A., 385
Sokolyansky, I. A., 424
Solano-Flores, G., 311
Souief, M., 175, 177
Souza, D. de, 93
Spearman, C., 173, 239, 241,
    505
Speller, P., 311
Spelling, K., 169
Spence, J. T., 315
Spencer, C., 527
Spencer, H., 184, 504
Spérandio, J. C., 201
Spionek, H., 383
Spiro, M., 551
Sprung, H., 229
Sprung, L., 229, 233
Sremac, B., 583, 585
Staats, A., 11
Stabell, B., 352, 353
Stabell, U., 352, 353
Staeuble, I., 220
Štajnberger, I., 583
Stamback, M., 189, 190
Stankov, L., 584
Stanley, J. C., 564
Stary, S., 583
Stattin, H., 471
Steen, J. B., 361
Steen, T., 349
Steinbrenner, K., 45, 51
Stenild, M., 169
Stern, W., 230
Stevanocić, B., 575
Stevens, S. S., 468
Stevenson, H. W., 5, 7
Stigler, J., 7
Stout, G. F., 508
Stoyva, J., 350
Strelau, J., 376, 380, 387
Strotzka, H., 73, 74
Strumpfer, D. J. W., 404

Stumpf, C., 2, 228
Suárez, F., 440
Suvević, D., 585
Sudakov, K. V., 426
Sugiyama, S., 292
Sully J., 2, 505, 508, 523
Sultan, E. E., 177
Sun, G. D., 119
Sun, K.-L., 110
Sun, L. H., 119
Sundberg, H., 361, 364
Sundet, M., 354
Svebak, S., 350, 361
Svendsen, D., 349
Svensson, E., 473
Svensson, O., 471, 474
Šverko, B., 583
Sydow, H., 228, 229, 233
Szabo, S., 583
Szuman, S., 382

Tabouret-Keller, A., 193
Taine, H., 184
Tajfel, H., 525
Takahashi, M., 294
Takens, R. J., 324–46
Takuma, T., 294
Talancón, H. P., 307
Tanaka, K.-I., 292
Tanaka, Y., 4, 5, 293
Tang, C. M., 119
Tang, Y., 110
Tap, P., 190
Tart, C. T., 254
Taylor, F., 526
Taylor, J. G., 412
Teigen, K. H., 349, 365
Tembrock, G., 229
Ten Berge, J. M. F., 333
Teplov, B. M., 423, 424, 425, 426, 428, 579
Ter Meulen, R., 333
Thierry, H., 335
Thomae, H., 293
Thomas, W. I., 422
Thomson, G. H., 239, 505, 523
Thorndike, E., 80, 536, 549

Thouless, R. H., 414
Thulesius, L. K., 354
Thunberg, T., 463
Thurstone, L. L., 441, 468, 505
Tiberghien, G., 194
Tiller, P. O., 354, 359
Timpe, K.-P., 234
Tinbergen, N., 538, 551
Titchener, E., 239, 298
Todorov, J. C., 92, 308
Toličić, I., 583
Tolman, E., 537, 549
Toman, W., 76
Tomaszewski, T., 368, 372, 375–76, 377, 385
Tomatis, A., 414
Tomé, H., 190, 191
Tomeković, T., 583
Tomkins, S., 553
Tordrup, H., 167
Tordrup, S. A., 169
Törestad, B., 471
Torgersen, S., 352–53, 363
Torney-Purta, J., 7
Traubenberg, N. R de., 190
Traxel, W., 220
Trespalacios, J. L. F., 446
Triandis, H., 4, 5, 6, 8
Trist, E. L., 526
Trognon, A., 184–207
Trstenjak, A., 583, 585
Trzebinski, J., 378
Tschudi, F., 354
Tuke, D. H., 184
Tulving, E., 104
Tunç, S., 489, 490–91, 497–98
Turhan, M., 490
Turró, R., 441
Tyszka, T., 378
Tyszkowa, M., 383

Ubeda, M., 441
Uchida, Z., 292
Uhktomsky, A. A., 421
Ulvund, S. E., 354
Unamuno, M. de, 441
Ungerstedt, U., 479

Urdaneta, O., 132
Ursin, H., 347–67, 349, 353, 361, 364, 365
Ursin, R., 350, 353
Ushakova, T. N., 425
Ushinsky, K. D., 439
Usman, M. O., 494
Uznadze, D. N., 422, 437

Vaernes, R., 349
Valderrama, P., 313
Valencia, M., 312
Valentine, C., 523
Van de Geer, J. P., 333
Van den Berg, J. H., 414
Van der Leeuw, J., 414
Vaněk, M., 158
Van Hoorn, W., 333
Van Lieshout, C. F. M., 336
Van Parreren, C. F., 330, 336
Van Rappard, J. F. H., 333
Van Strien, P. J., 324–46, 333
Vasileysky, S. M., 423–24
Vassaf, G. Y. H., 484–501
Veber, F., 575
Veil, C., 191
Veláquez, D. N., 312
Velasco, M. G., 313
Velez, J., 313
Velloso, E., 80, 93
Venanzi, Y. de, 570
Veracruz, Fr. A. de la, 297
Verbec, D., 574
Vergnaud, G., 194, 196
Verwoerd, H. F., 413, 414
Villanger, R., 169
Villegas, J., 564
Villerbu, L., 191
Vinski, D., 583
Vives, L., 440
Vlek, C. A. J., 333
Vold, J. M., 359
Vollmer, F., 350
Vorweg, M., 228, 232–33, 234
Vossen, J. M. H., 330
Vroon, P., 333
Vučić, L., 585

Vurpillot, E., 195
Vygotsky, L., 94, 234, 422, 579

Waern, Y, 471, 474
Waft, H. J., 508
Wagenaar, W. A., 330
Waligora, B., 385
Walk, R., 551
Wall, T., 526
Wallon, H., 80, 203–4
Wan, R. Q., 118
Wang, S., 118
Wang Chong, 109
Wapner, S., 552
Warr, P., 526
Warren, H. C., 2
Warerink, J., 325, 414
Watson, J. B., 463, 537, 549
Weber, M., 464, 494
Webster, E., 104
Weil, P., 92
Weil-Barais, A., 203–5
Weinert, F. E., 73
Welford, A. T., 59
Werner, H., 230, 551, 552
Wertheimer, M., 294, 537
Westerlundh, B., 470
Whiting, J., 4
Whittaker, J. O., 130, 447
Wiesenfeld, E., 569
Wilcocks, R. W., 413, 414
Wilke, H. A. M., 332
Willems, P. J., 335
Willoughby, R. R., 2
Wilson, W. A., Jr., 212
Wittchen, H.-U., 8
Wittgenstein, L., 68
Witzlack, G., 229, 234
Wlodarski, Z., 378
Wolf, W., 307
Wolff, C. von, 419
Wolman, B., 447
Woloszynowa, L., 373, 375
Wolpe, J., 17, 413, 553, 572
Wolters, A. W. P., 507
Woodworth, R., 578, 579
Wosinski, W., 383
Wright, M. M., 7, 104

Wu, Q. E., 119
Wundt, W., 1, 161, 184, 231, 233, 239,
    274, 289, 294, 299, 363, 440, 503,
    504, 508, 536, 575

Xiao, X. S., 118
Xu, L. C., 112, 120
Xu, S. L., 119
Xue, Z. H., 119
Xun Kuang, 109

Yan, K. L., 119
Yang, J. B., 117
Yaroshevsky, M. G., 426
Yates, A. J., 59
Yela, M., 440–60, 441, 445, 449
Yerkes, R. M., 505
Yoichi, U., 275
Yong-jing, Y., 109
Yoshida, M., 294
Yu, B. L., 117

Zaborowski, Z., 381–82
Žagar, A., 583

Zajonc, R., 553
Zander, A., 294
Zaragueta, J., 441, 449
Zazzo, R., 189, 190
Zebrowska, M., 372, 382
Zeng, X. C., 117
Zewar, M., 173
Zhang, B. Y., 119
Zhang, H. C., 109–24, 112, 116
Zhang, J. T., 118
Zhang, S. F., 118
Zhang, W. T., 118
Zhang, Y. X., 109
Zhou, X. G., 110
Zhu, Z. X., 114–15
Zimbardo, P. G., 73, 130, 212
Znaniecki, F., 422
Zorman, L., 583
Zotov, A. J., 423
Zuo, M.L., 118
Zvonarević, M., 578, 583
Zwaardemaker, H., 324

Subject Index

Accreditation and/or licensing of psychologists. *See individual chapters*

Action theory, 232–33, 235, 376–87

Activity (Marxist-Leninist conception), 137, 147-58, 222, 375–76, 429–30, 432–35

Africa, psychology in, 14–15

African (Black) psychology, 24–36; achievements, 31; "African personality," 28; application of psychology in Africa, 30–31; association conferences and the need for a network, 3–34; child study, 24–25; course offerings, 28–29; early research, 26; magic, witchcraft, and traditional beliefs, 25–26, 28, 33; professional standards and ethics, 32–33; prospects, 35; publications, 29–30; research areas and trends, 29–30, 34–35; stigma against, 32–33; training opportunities, 27–28

Afrikaans psychology, 409–10

American influence. *See* United States psychology, influence of

American Psychological Association, Committee on International Relations, 2

American psychology. *See* United States psychology

Annual Review of Psychology, 3

Applied psychology, vigorous expansion of, 16–17. *See also individual chapters*

Asia Minor, early developments, 487, 494–96

Asian psychology, 15–16

Attribution theory, 331–32

Australian Army Psychology Corps, 55

Australian Psychological Society, 39–40

Australian psychologists visit the People's Republic of China, 6

Australian psychology, 37–66; abstracts and indices, 45–46; academic degrees, 41–42; academies, 62–63; curriculum models, 40–42; defitions of psychology, 37–38; employment of psychologists, 46–47; European and Asian immigrants, 58; funding, 53–55; influence on, 51–53; learned societies, 63; legal profession, 46; major needs, 59–60; notable psychologists, 58–59; organizational structures, 39–40; organizations, 51–53; programs, 63–66; publications, 53, 66; registration of psychologists, 58; relationships with other disciplines, 46–47; research, 47, 50; societal influences on, 55, 58; textbooks, 42–45; theoretical orientations and assumptions, 47–51; training psychologists, 40–42; women psychologists, 40

Austria, a neutral zone between East and West, 77

Austrian psychology, 67–78; curriculum models, 71; entrance requirements to programs, 75; functions of psychologists, 70; funding, 70–71, 75; future

directions, 76–77; influence worldwide, 76; journals, 71; nature and
scope of the discipline, 67–74; needs,
73–74; post-World War II trends and
influences, 74–77; programs and laboratories, 68–70; psychoanalysis, 67;
Psychological Abstracts and citation
indexes, 73; relationships with other
disciplines, 74; research and theory,
75; textbooks, 71–73
Aztecs, 297

Behaviorism (behavioral approaches, behavior modification, behavior therapy),
17–18, 91, 153, 163, 191–92, 218,
274, 292, 300, 308–9, 311, 313, 341,
392, 411, 421, 430–31, 450, 463, 476,
530, 536–37, 543, 549, 550, 553, 562,
563, 570, 576, 585
Berlin School, 170
Blacks in South Africa, 393, 398, 400,
404–7, 412, 413
Boulder Conference, 540, 553
Brazilian psychology, 76–96; abstracts,
87; applied areas, 93; behaviorism,
91; clinical psychology, over emphasis
of, 80, 86–87; contributions, 91–94;
curriculum, 81, 85–86; definition
of psychology/psychological, 81; demographic and organization indices of,
88–89; functions of psychologists, 84;
funding, 85; future directions, 94; historical overview, 79–81; historical research, 92–93; influences on, 79–80;
journals, 86; Melanie Klein, influence
of, 91; nature and scope of the discipline, 81–88; needs, 87–88; organizational structure, 81–83; perspectives on
psychology in other countries, 94; Portuguese influence on, 80; psychoanalytic influence, 80, 89, 91; relationships
with other disciplines, 88; research and
theory, 87, 89–93; research questions
of most concern, 91; textbooks, 86–87;
training programs, 83–84; since World
War II, 88–94
British empiricism and associationism,
274, 503

British influence on psychology, 365, 405
British psychology, 502–33; applied psychology, growth of, 528–29; applied
psychology and the Cambridge School,
505–7; British empiricism, 503; British
Psychological Society, 508–10; clinical
psychology, 522–23; Conservative
government, 527–28; curricula, 512–
15; early history, 502–8; educational
psychology, 523–24; employment of
psychologists, 517–19; environmental
and architectural psychology, 526–27;
eugenics, 504, 516; European influence
on, 521; evolutionary theory, 503–4,
525; funding, 510–11; funding cuts under the Conservative administration,
511; future directions, 527–29; Galton
and the London School, 504–5; homo-
sexual psychologists, 518; humanism,
523, 526; multi-dimensional scaling,
521; "new paradigm" research, 521;
occupational psychology, 525–26;
phenomenology, 521; politics, 515–17;
psychoanalysis, 506; psychologists as
expert witnesses, 515–16; psychometrics, 504–5, 522; registration of psychologists, 509; relevance of academic
programs, 519–20; research methodologies, 520–22; research orientation,
520–21; Scottish universities, 507–8;
Social Darwinism, 525; social psychology, 524–25; statistics, 521; training
programs, 512–15; unique character of,
503; women under-represented, 517–
18; World War I, 506; work, changing
nature of, 528
Buddhism, 274

Canadian psychology, 97–108; Canadian
Psychological Association, 98; curricula, 100; early developments, 97–98;
functions of applied psychologists, 99–
100; graduate programs, 100–103;
journals, 104–5; organizational structure, 98–99; population distribution of
Canada, 105–6; psychologists, demographics of, 100, 103; research and
theory, 103–4; research funding, 106–

7; trends and influences, 105–7; two founding nations, 105–6
Capitalism, 494
Cheiron Society, 5, 339
China. *See* People's Republic of China
Chinese psychology, 4–7, 15–16. *See also* People's Republic of China
Client-centered therapy, 313, 538, 585. *See also* Carl Rogers (Name Index)
Cognitive revolution, 549, 552
Cognitive styles, 552
Colombian psychology, 125–36; curriculum models, 129; definition of psychology, 125–26; five-year (1970–75) plan, 133; functions of psychologists, 127–28; funding, 129; journals, 129–30; nature and scope of the discipline, 125–31; needs, 131; organizational structure, 126–27; psychoanalysis, 131; *Psychological Abstracts*, 131; relationships with other disciplines, 131; roots, 125–26; societal influences on, 133; textbooks, 130; training programs, 127–28; training requirements, 133; women in psychology, 132–33; since World War II, 131–35
Common sense psychology, 352, 362
Communication, Soviet principle of, 433–34
Communism. *See* Marxism-Leninism, Socialist societies
Computerized data banks, 8. *See also* Information retrieval
Consciousness, 147–58, 167–68, 222, 422–25, 427, 432–35, 552
Contextualism, 192, 219–20
Critical Psychology, 216, 235
Cross-cultural psychology, 4, 5, 28–29, 398, 408, 551
Cuban psychology, 137–44; in clinical settings, 139–40; definition of psychology and psychological activities, 137–38; developments, 142–43; in educational settings, 139; functions of psychologists, 139–41; health psychology, 138, 140; history of, 137; journals, 142; Marxism, 137; organizational structure, 138–39; psychometrics, 140;

relationships with other disciplines, 143; research, 143; social psychology, 140; sports psychology, 140; training and curriculum models, 141–42; in work settings, 140
Current Contents: Social and Behavioral Sciences, 5
Curricula. *See individual chapters*
Curricular studies from an intercultural perspective, 6–7
Cybernetics, 234, 552
Czechoslovakian psychology, 145–60; behaviorism, 153; definition of psychology, 147; early history, 145–46; future developments, 158–59; Marxism-Leninism, 147–58; organization of research, 146–54; organizational structure of Czech psychology, 147–51; organizational structure of Slovak psychology, 151–53; post-World War II period, 146–47; regulation theory, 149, 155; research, 153–58; socialism, 146–58; textbooks, 158; theoretical and methodological foundations, 154–55

Danish psychology, 161–71; behaviorism, 163; developments prior to 1960, 166–68; developments since 1960, 168–69; dialectical materialism, 169, 170; diversification of, 168; employment of Danish psychologists, 164–66; Gestalt orientation, 167; hermeneutical approach, 169; journals and other publications, 164; phenomenological orientation, 166–68; professional associations, 164; psychoanalysis, 164; *Psychological Abstracts*, 170; research centers, 164; sources of information, 169–70; training programs, 161–63
Decision theory, 552
Defense mechanisms, 469–70
Definitions of psychology. *See individual countries*
Detection theory, 552
Determinism, Soviet principle of, 430–31
Developing countries. *See* Third World countries
Development, Soviet principle of, 432–33

Dialectical materialism, 137, 149–58,
    169–70, 226, 232, 235, 372, 376–77,
    422, 424–25, 428, 431, 434–35
Dutch psychology, 324–46; Anglo-Amer-
    ican empirical influence on, 327; ap-
    plied psychology, 334–36;
    behaviorism, 341; consolidating the
    profession, 326; developmental psy-
    chology, 331; empiricism, 326–27;
    employment opportunities, 342–45;
    European influence on, 339; experi-
    mental psychology, 330–31; French
    existential influence on, 326; funding,
    336–38; German and Swiss character-
    ology, 326, 327, 331; Health Service
    System, 341–42; history, 324–27; in-
    dustrial psychology emphasized, 334;
    international contacts, 338–39; neofas-
    cism, 332; Netherlands Institute for
    Psychologists, 339–40; personality re-
    search, 331–32; phenomenological-
    existential psychology, 326; psy-
    choanalysis, 326, 341; psychologists,
    number of, 327, 339; publication
    trends, 338; registration procedures,
    340–41; religious denominations, 325;
    research organization of, 336–39; so-
    cial psychology, 332–33; South Afri-
    can psychology, influence on, 15;
    Soviet influence on, 330; theory, meth-
    odology and history, 333; training pro-
    grams, 327–28, 330; unemployment of
    psychologists, 342–43; United States
    influence on, 327, 332, 338–39; uni-
    versity departments and curricula, 328–
    30
Dyslexia, 473

Ecological validity, 219, 223, 472
Ego psychology, 550
Egyptian psychology, 172–83; Cairo as a
    publishing center, 175–76; curricula
    and programs, 174–75; definition of
    psychology, 172; high paying jobs in
    the Gulf-oil countries, 174; historical
    background, 172–74; legal regulations,
    180–81; organizations, 181–82; period-
    icals and publications, 176–77; psycho-

analysis, 173–74; recent status of,
    174–75; references and textbooks,
    175–76; research, 177–78; research
    funding, 178; roles of psychologists,
    179–81; tests, 178–79
English, international language of sci-
    ence, 554
Eugenics, 56, 504, 516
European immigrants to Australia,
    58
European psychologists, cooperation
    among, 219, 339, 364–65
Evolution, 419, 425, 503–4
Existentialism, 326, 451, 538, 552,
    553

Facet theory, 521
Federal Republic of Germany. See Ger-
    man (FRG) psychology
Female psychologists. See Women in
    psychology
Fragmentation of psychology, 19,
    411
Frankfurt School, 218
French psychology, 184–207; back-
    ground, 184–86; behaviorism, 191,
    192; child psychology, 203–5; clinical
    psychology, 186–91; cognitive psy-
    chology, resurgence of, 192; computer
    technology, 192; developmental psy-
    chology, 192–96; experimental psy-
    chology, 191–97; Marxism, 199;
    projective techniques, 190; psychoanal-
    ysis, 186, 190, 204; psychometrics,
    190; social psychology, 197–200;
    women in psychology, 202; work psy-
    chology, 200–203
Fulbright-Hays Program, 3, 359, 488,
    492
Functionalism, 536
Funding. See individual countries

German and Swiss characterology,
    331
German Democratic Republic. See Ger-
    man (GDR) psychology
German (FRG) psychology, 208–21; be-
    haviorism, 218; clinical psychology,

growth of, 216–17; contextualism, 219–20; continuity with pre-World War II psychology, 215; controversies, 217–19; critical psychology, 216; curriculum, 211; definitions of psychology, 208; Europeanization of, 219; Frankfurt School, 218; functions of psychologists, 210; funding, 210–11, 214–15; future directions, 219–20; Gestalt psychology, 217; holistic psychology, 217; journals, 212; methods controversy, 218; nature and scope of the discipline, 208–13; Nazi regime, 215–16, 218; needs, 213; operationalism, 217; organizational structure, 208–9; orientation and assumptions, 217; perspectives on psychology in other countries, 219; positivist dispute, 218; programs and laboratories, 209–10; "psychoboom," 216; *Psychological Abstracts*, 212–13; psychologists world-wide perceived as most important, 219; publication trends, 214; relationships with other disciplines, 213; research and theory, 217–19; research institutes, 210; societal influence on, 215–17; student movement, 215–16; textbooks, 212; trends and influences since World War II, 214–19; United States influence on, 217, 219

German (GDR) psychology, 222–38; action and regulation theory, 232, 235; applied research, 233–34; cognitive research, 232–33; critical psychology, 235; curricula, 226–28; definition of psychology, 222–23; developing a socialist society, 225–26, 230–31; dialectical materialism, 226, 232, 235; ecological validity paramount, 223; functions of psychologists, 225–26; future directions, 235–37; growth of, 231; historical studies, 233; influences on, 234–35; interdisciplinary research, 229–30; international influence of, 235; journals, textbooks, and other publications, 228–29; nature and scope of the discipline, 222–30; Nazi regime, 230; organization and institutions, 223–25;

personality research, 232–33; Piaget's influence, 235; post-World War II period, 230–35; private practice prohibited, 226; relationships with other disciplines, 229–30; research and theory, 232–33; research planning, 223–24; Soviet influence on, 234; stimulus-response conceptions rejected, 223, 234; theoretical assumptions, 232–33; United States influence on, 234–35; Western psychology, perspectives on, 226–27

German research university, 536
Gerontological psychology, 551
Gestalt psychology, 167, 217, 233, 274, 289, 435, 465, 537, 552
Gestalt therapy, 585

Handbook of Cross-Cultural Psychology, 6
Hermeneutical psychology, 169
Hinduism, 253–54
History, facts-and-figures approach, 484–86
Holistic psychology, 217–18
Humanistic orientation, 376, 392, 411, 450–51, 523, 526, 538, 565, 576

Idealism, 419, 421
Importance of psychology, 13–14, 486–94
Indian psychology, 239–57; applied psychology and developments outside academia, 241–44; curricular changes needed, 247; developments since independence, 240–41; dissatisfaction with the discipline, 243–44; employment settings, 241; funding, 247–48; Hinduism, 253–54; historical background, 239–40; "Indian Psychology," 253; indigenization of the field, 247, 251–52, 255; journals are low quality, 244–46; "nurturant task-leader" concept, 253; organizational turmoil, 244–45; parapsychology, 245–46; professional associations and publications, 244–48; psychoanalysis, 240, 244, 254; psychologists, number of, 240–41; psy-

chologists tend to be generalists, 249–
50; religious and philosophical influence on, 253–55; research areas, 247;
research on poverty, 252; research
trends, 248–53; rural psychology, 252;
society, impact on, 242–44; tests borrowed from the West, 250; textbooks,
246–47; training programs, 240, 243–
44; trends since independence, 248–53;
United States influence on, 239; Western influence on, 246–47, 250–54
Indigenization of psychology, 247, 410,
572
Infant experimental psychology,
554
Information retrieval, 8, 19, 170
Information theory, 234, 552
Integration, Soviet principle of,
435
Integration of psychology, 411
Intellectual migration of the 1930s,
537
Interamerican Society of Psychology, 3,
14, 307
International Association of Applied Psy-
chology, founding of, 1
International Association of Cross-Cul-
tural Psychology, 5
International congresses and meetings,
early, 1–2
International Council of Psychologists
(ICP), 3, 5
International Council of Women Psychol-
ogists, 2–3
International Directory of Psychologists,
2, 3, 6
International exchanges, 8
International perspective on psychology,
a historical overview, 1–8
International Union of Psychological Science (IUPsyS), 3, 34, 58, 112, 138,
209, 231, 258, 293, 374, 394, 485,
566–67
Islam modernization, 494
Israeli psychology, 258–73; academic
ranks, 261; accreditation of psychologists, 259; curricula, 259–63; definition
of psychology, 258; employment set-

tings, 258–59; establishing departments, 265–66; financial support for
students, 263–64; funding of, 263–64;
heterogeneous population, 265–66; European and North American influences,
261, 266; Kibbutz socialist perspectives, 267; nature and scope of the discipline, 258–64; needs, 263–64; North
American influence on, 268; programs,
266; psychoanalysis, 267; psychologists, a high concentration of, 258; research, unique opportunities, 268;
research facilities, 261; societal influences on, 266–68; Soviet influence on,
266; training programs, 259–63; trends
and influences since World War II,
265–68

Japanese psychology, 274–96; applied
fields, 290–93; behaviorism, 274, 292;
Buddhism, 274; clinical psychology,
292; curricula, 281–83; definitions of
psychology, 274; development and
present status, 274–85; educational
psychology, 289; functions of psychologists, 279; Gestalt orientation, 274,
289; historical research on, 294; human
engineering and ergonomics, 292; international influence of, 293–94; journals, research reports, bibliographies,
283–84; laboratories and research institutes, 277–79; language barriers, 290;
mathematical psychology, 290; memory research, 289; organizations, 274–
77; phenomenology, 289; phonetic and
ideographic characters, research on,
289; psychoanalysis, 277, 292; research and theory, 285–90; research
funding, 279–81; sensory and perceptual research, 285, 289; social psychology, 290–91; Soviet influence on, 274;
stimulus-response approaches, 289;
since World War II, 285–93; textbooks, 284–85; Western influence on,
274, 293

Kibbutzim as natural laboratories,
268

Language barriers, 290, 403. *See also* English
Latin America, psychology in, 14
Life-span developmental psychology, 551
Locus of control research, 315, 569
Logical positivism, 68, 537

Magic and witchcraft in Africa, 25–26, 28
Marxism (Marxism-Leninism), 12–13, 110–11, 120–21, 137, 146–58, 199, 314, 376–77, 422, 427, 430–36, 451, 576
Materialism, 419, 431. *See also* Dialectical materialism
Medieval scholasticism, 440, 535
Mental illness, views toward during Ottoman Empire, 495–97
Mexican psychology, 297–316; academic exchange, 299–300; behaviorism, 300, 308–9, 311, 313; client-centered approach, 313; clinical psychology, 313; educational psychology, 311–12; experimental analysis of behavior, 308–9; foundations, 297–98; general experimental psychology, 309; historical overview, 297–300; history and philosophy of psychology, 313; journals, 301, 307; Marxism, 314; mental hospital, first on American continent, 297; professional associations, 307–8; programs and degrees, 300–301; psychoanalysis, 300, 313; psychophysiology, 312; research and applied psychology, 308–16; social and personality psychology, 314–16; United States influence on, 299–300; women studies, 314–15
Mind, return of the concept to psychology in the United States, 552
Mind-body issue, 419, 426, 440
Modernizationist view of Third-World countries, 483–86, 493–94
Motion, biological, 466

Nazi regime, 56, 215–16, 218, 230, 424, 488, 537

Neo-behaviorism. *See* Behaviorism
Neo-Freudianism, 550, 551. *See also* Psychoanalysis
Netherlands, The. *See* Dutch psychology
"New Look" movement, 552
Norwegian psychology, 347–67; applied areas, 362–64; arctic studies, 361–62; biological psychology, 361; British influence on, 365; common sense psychology, 352, 362; curricula, 356–57; deep sea diving studies, 349; demographics and organization, 358; drug addiction studies, 363–64; ethology, 361–62; functions of psychologists, 355; funding, 355; future, 365; health care aspect emphasized, 357–58; historical studies, 365; Institute for Social Research (Oslo), 359; journals, 357; nature and scope of the discipline, 347–58; needs, 357; organizations, 347–48; other disciplines, 357–58; perceptual research, 351–52; perspectives on psychology in other countries, 364; physiological research, 349; programs and laboratories, 348–55; psychoanalysis, 359–60; psychologists, number of, 358; Schjelderup-Edde pecking order research, 361; skeletomuscular psychophysiology, 360–61; social psychology, 352; somatic psychology, 350; textbooks, 357; Third World countries, 365; United States influence on, 364–65; women, research on, 352; women pioneers, 362–63; since World War II, 358–64

Operant conditioning. *See* B. F. Skinner (Name Index)
Operationism (operationalism), 217
Orienting response, 477, 552
Ottoman Empire, 487, 494–97

Parapsychology, 245–46
People's Republic of China, psychology in, 109–24; Chinese Psychological Society, 109–13; Cultural Revolution, 111–12; definition of psychology, 120–21; educational psychology, 114–16;

epilogue, 121; general and experimental psychology, 116–18; history of, 109–12; physiological and medical psychology, 118–20; pictographic language research, 115, 117, 118; Psychoanalytic Society founded, 110; research, advances in, 112–21; Soviet influence on, 110–11; training programs, 112

Personal Construct Theory, 523, 552

Personality, Soviet principle of, 434–35

Pestalozzi Society of Brazil, 79–80

Phenomenology, 166–68, 289, 326, 392, 411, 451, 521, 538, 552, 553

Phrenology, 298

Piagetian influence. See Jean Piaget (Name Index)

Polish psychology, 368–91; action theory, 375–86; applied psychology, 386–87; cognitive orientation, 376; curriculum model, 371; definitions of psychology, 368, 375–76; dialectical materialism, 372, 376–77; functions of psychologists, 370; funding, 370; future directions, 387–88; journals, 371; Marxism, 376–77; nature and scope of the discipline, 368–74; organizational structure, 368–69, 374–75; positive disintegration theory, 384; professional activities, 369; programs and laboratories, 370; *Psychological Abstracts*, 373; psychologists known internationally, 387; publication trends, 375–76; regulation theory, 375–86; research and theory, 368–69, 377–86; societal influences on, 376–77; Soviet influence on, 376–77; stimulus-response conceptions, 377; textbooks, 372; training programs, 369; since World War II, 374–87

Positive disintegration theory, 384

Positivism, 145, 151, 218

Pragmatism, 535

Private practice prohibited in the GDR, 226

Probabilistic functionalism, 472

Psychoanalysis, 17, 67, 80, 81, 89, 91, 110, 131, 164, 173–74, 186, 190, 204, 240, 244, 254, 267, 277, 292, 300, 313, 326, 341, 359–60, 392, 421, 451, 463–64, 469–70, 476, 506, 537, 538, 550, 553, 567, 570–71, 576, 585

Psychological Abstracts, 1, 73, 131, 170, 212–13, 373, 564

Psychological Index, 2

Psychological Register, 1

Psychology, conceptual fragmentation of, 19, 411; developments world-wide, 10–18; expansion of applied fields, 16–17; factors bearing on national psychologies, 9–10; importation of by Third World countries, 13–14, 486–94; integrative conceptions of, 411, 428; perspectives on how the discipline can contribute to society, 16; politico-economic changes influencing, 8–9; reaffirmation of the complexity of, 18; recognized as an international science, 8; revitalization of Europe, the Soviet Union and Asia, 11–12

Psychology around the World (Sexton & Misiak), 6

Psychometrics, genesis of, 505

Publishing, Cairo as a publishing center, 174–75

Racism, 516

Reflection, Marxist-Leninist conception of, 147–58, 222, 232, 420, 422–23, 429, 431–32

Reflection, Sechenov's theory of, 420

Reflexology, Bekhterev's theory of, 420

Regulation theory, 149, 155, 222, 232, 375–86

Rural psychology, 252, 498

Russian Academy of Sciences, establishment of, 418–19

Scholasticism, 440, 535

Scientist-practitioner model, 540, 553

Scottish common sense philosophy, 535

Scottish universities, growth of psychology in, 507–8
Semantic Differential technique, 552
Sensory deprivation, 552
Set, concept of, 422, 437
Social Darwinism, 525
Social interaction (communication), Soviet principle of, 433–34
Social learning theory, 549, 551, 553
Social psychology, controversial nature of in the Soviet Union, 426–27
Social Sciences Citation Index, 5
Socialist societies and psychology, 146–58, 225–26, 230–31
South African psychology, 392–417; African studies, 398; applied psychology, 414; associations, 393–94; background, 392; behaviorism, 392, 411; Blacks, 412; Blacks, education of, 393, 405; Blacks, research on, 398, 400, 413; Blacks in psychology, 404, 406–7, 410; British influence on, 405, 410; contributions, 412–23, 414; cross-cultural research, 399, 408; curricula, 401–2; definitions of psychology, 392–93; Dutch influence on, 15, 410; eclecticism, 413; English-speaking and Afrikaans-speaking institutions, 403, 409–10; fragmentation, 411; functions of psychologists, 400; funding, 400–401, 408–9; future directions, 415; German influence on, 411; historical studies, 415–16; humanism, 392, 411; Human Sciences Research Council, 396–97; industrial psychology emphasized, 393, 399, 401–2, 406; influential foreign psychologists, 414; intergration of, 411; interdisciplinary research, 404; journals, 402; membership trends, 406–7; nature and scope of the discipline, 392–405; needs, 403–4; neighboring countries, 415; organizational structure, 393–99; orientation and assumptions, 410–12; other disciplines, 404–5; perspectives on foreign psychologies, 415; phenomenology, 392,

411; programs and laboratories, 399–400, 405–6; psychoanalysis, 392; psychologists, most creative, 413; publication trends, 407–8; registration procedures, 394, 396; research and theory, 410–13; research institutes, 396–99; research on African society, 415; societal influences, 409–10; South Africa as a laboratory of human behavior, 409; South African Plan for Research in the Human Sciences (SAPRHS), 397; statutory recognition, 407; test development, 396, 398, 410, 414; textbooks, 402–3; training psychologists, 393, 399, 401–2; United States influence on, 411; since World War II, 405–15
Soviet psychology, 418–39; activity, concept of, 425, 429–35; behaviorism, 421, 430–31; child psychology, 425; communication and social interaction, principle of, 433–34; communication research important, 430, 433–34; consciousness, concept of, 422–25, 427, 432–35; curricula, 437–38; determinism, principle of, 430–31; development, principle of, 424–25, 432–33; dialectical materialism, 422, 424–25, 428, 431, 434–35; education of psychologists, 437–38; educational psychology most highly developed subfield, 425; engineering psychology emerges, 426; evolutionary theory, 419, 425; Gestalt psychology, 435; history, 418–30; idealism, 419, 421; influence on national psychologies, 234, 266, 274, 330, 376–77, 450, 572; integrative principles, 435–36; Marxism, 422, 427, 430–36; materialism, 419, 422, 424–25, 428, 431, 434–35; Nazi Germany, 424; October Revolution, 421–24; personality, principle of, 434–35; principles, major, 430–36; psychoanalysis, 421; reflection, principle of, 420, 422–23, 429, 431–32; reflexology, 420; research, planning for, 436–37; research centers and facilities, 436–37; set, concept of, 422, 437; so-

cial psychology reappears, 426–27; unity of activity and consciousness, 433; USSR Society of Psychologists, 438; during World War II, 424; since World War II, 424–30

Spanish psychology, 440–60; behaviorism, 450; curricula, 443–44; definitions, 442; demographic and organizational aspects, 448–50; existentialism, 451; functions of psychologists, 447; funding, 448; growth of, 450; historians of psychology, 451–52; historical overview, 440–42; humanism, 450–51; journals, 446; Marxism, 451; nature and scope of, 442–48; needs, 448; organizations, 444–46; orientations, 450–51; other disciplines, 448; phenomenology, 451; psychoanalysis, 451; psychologists, number of, 449; research and theory, 450–51; scholasticism, 440; Soviet influence on, 450; textbooks, abstracts, and indices, 446–47; university programs, 442–44; since World War II, 448–51

Sports psychology, 140

Stimulus-response conceptions, 223, 234, 289, 377, 430–31, 538, 549

Stockholm-Harvard connection, 468

Stress, 478

Structuralism, 536–37

Student movement of the 1960s, 186, 215–16

Swedish psychology, 461–83; behaviorism, 463, 476; clinical psychology, 474–76; cognitive psychology, 471–74; differential psychology, 462; experimental orientation, 463–64; Gestalt psychology, 465; history (1910–1950), 461–64; history (1950-present), 464–74; journals, 464; percept-genesis, experimental psychoanalysis, 469–70; perception, research on, 464–70; personality research, 470–71; phenomenology, 465; physiological psychology, 462–63; psychoanalysis, 463–64, 469–70, 476; psychobiology, 476–80; psy-

chophysics and scaling, 467–69; Stockholm-Harvard connection, 468; stress, research on, 478

Systems approaches, 234, 428

Tests, delay in standardization of in Egypt, 179; misuse of in Turkey, 486–87, 490, 492–93

Third-World countries, importation of psychology, 13–14, 486–94; modernization, histories of, 484–85, 493–94; Norwegian psyhologists, 365; psychology in, 7, 13–16, 498. See also chapters on relevant countries

Transactional analysis, 585

Turkish psychology, 15, 484–501; demographics, 485–86, 488–91; dependency on Western psychology, 488–94; export-import model, 486–94; French influence on, 489; German influence on, 489; historical approaches to, 484–86; modernization, 488–94; Ottoman-Islamic heritage, 494–97; rural psychology, need for, 498; societal influences on, 486–88; tests, misuse of, 486–87, 490, 492–93; toward a new psychology, 497–99; turmoil within, 492–93; United States influence on, 485–86, 488–91

United Kingdom. See British psychology

United Nations, 3

United States psychology, 534–56; affects, research on, 522–53; American Psychological Association, divisions, 542–43; behaviorism, 530, 536–37, 543, 549, 550, 553; Boulder Model, 540, 553; British influence, 536; client-centered approach, 538; clinical psychology, 553; cognitive revoultion, 538, 549, 552; conceptual structure of, 541–42; conclusion, 553–54; contributions world-wide, 554; demographics of, (1946) 538–39, (1965) 539, (1983) 539–40; developmental psychology, 551; developments, 547–53; diversification, 541–44; Eastern thought, influence of, 552; existentialism, 538, 552,

553; fragmentation, 541–44; French influence, 536; Freudian influence, 550; functionalism, 536; funding, 541, 544–47; funding, institutions receiving the most, 547; geographical location of psychologists, 539–40; German influence, 536; gerontological psychology, 551; Gestalt psychology, 537, 552; governmental intrusion, 547; graduate programs, early, 544–45; growth, 538–41; growth, factors underlying, 540–41; growth especially of applied fields, 539; history (prior to World War II), 534–37; history (since World War II), 537–38; humanism, 538; indices of importance, 547–48; infant research, 554; influence of, 11, 45, 217, 219, 234–35, 299–300, 327, 332, 338–39, 359, 364–65, 485–86, 488–91; influences on, 538, 547–53; intellectual migration, 537; journals, 543; "mind" and "consciousness" return, 552; minority psychologists, 539–40; "New Look" movement, 552; organizations, state, 543; orientations, 538; phenomenology, 538, 552, 553; pragmatism, 535; problem, most serious, 538; professional schools, 553; psychoanalysis, 537, 538, 550, 553; psychologists, major, 547–53; research on mental and affective processes and states, 551–53; scientist-practitioner model, 540; Scottish common sense philosophy, 535; social learning theory, 549, 551, 553; societal problems, 554; women psychologists, 538–40; during World War I, 537; World War II, 548–49; worldwide influence, 554

USSR. *See* Soviet psychology

Vail Conference, 553
Venezuelan psychology, 557–73; Adlerian emphasis, 565; applied areas, 571; behavioral approaches, 562, 563, 566, 567, 570; child psychology emphasized, 568; conferences, 566–67; contributions, 568–69, 571; controversies, 570–71; curricula, 562–63; definition of psychology, 557; employment settings of psychologists, 561; European influence on, 572; foreign psychologists who influenced, 572; functions of psychologists, 561; funding, 561–62, 567; future directions, 572–73; historians of psychology, 573; humanistic emphasis, 565; journals, 563; Lacanian emphasis, 568; Law of Psychological Practice, 557; locus of control research, 569; membership trends, 565–66; nature and scope of discipline, 557–65; needs, 564; negative national "autostereotype," 569; organizational structure, 557–58; organizations, 565; orientations and assumptions, 567–68; other disciplines, 564–65; perspectives on psychology in other countries, 572; Piagetian emphasis, 567, 568; programs and laboratories, 558–61; psychoanalysis, 567, 570–71; *Psychological Abstracts*, 564; psychologists, number of, 565–66; psychologists, prominent, 569–70; publication trends, 566; research and theory, 567–71; societal influences on, 567; Soviet influence on, 572; textbooks, 563–64; training programs, 562–63; United States influence on, 572; since World War II, 565–572
Vienna Circle, 68, 218
Vigilance research, 552

Western countries, anxiety in, 226–27
Western influence on psychology, 484–99. *See also United States influence and chapters on Third World countries*
Women, research on, 314–15, 352, 569, 583
Women in psychology, 2–3, 14, 40, 132–33, 202, 362–63, 517–18, 538–40
Work, changing nature of, 528
World War II and psychology in the United States, 548–49

Yugoslavian psychology, 574–86; applied areas, 584–85; behavioral approaches,

576, 585; client-centered therapy, 585; clinical psychology, 585; curricula, 576; demographics, 574–75; employment, 586; funding, 577; Gestalt therapy, 585; growth, 579; heterogeneous, 575–76; humanism, 576; industrial psychology, 584; interdisciplinary studies, 578; journals, 578; Marxism, 576; nature and scope of, 575–78; psychoanalysis, 576, 585; Psychological Association of Yugoslavia, 578; psychologists, numbers of, 579; publications, 582; research, 576–77, 579, 580, 581, 583–85; research orientations, 585; socio-cultural and historical contexts, 574–75; Soviet influence on, 579–80; stagnation, 586; textbooks, 577–78; training programs, 576; transactional analysis, 585; since World War II, 578–86

Contributors

Ruben Ardila obtained his Ph.D. from the University of Nebraska in 1970. He was president of the Colombian Federation of Psychology (1970–1974); president of the Interamerican Society of Psychology (1974–1976); chairman of the Department of Psychology, National University of Colombia (1970–1972); chairman and founder of the psychology department at the University of the Andes (1972–1976); and has since 1967 been director and founder of the psychology graduate program at the University of St. Thomas. He has written extensively on Latin American and international psychology. His address is: Apartado 88754, Bogotá, Colombia.

Angela M. B. Biaggio obtained her Ph.D. in educational psychology from the University of Wisconsin in 1967. She has been a senior researcher at the Brazilian National Research Council and a member of the board of directors of the Interamerican Society of Psychology. She has published extensively in national and international journals and has been involved in university teaching for many years. Her address is: Universidade Federal do Rio Grande do Sul, Pos-Graduação em Educação, 90 000 Porto Alegre, RS, Brazil.

David Canter is a professor of applied psychology at the University of Surrey where he also directs the graduate program in environmental psychology. He obtained his bachelor's degree and doctorate at the University of Liverpool. He is a fellow of the British Psychological Society and the managing editor of the *Journal of Environmental Psychology*. He is also a nonexecutive, part-time director of Compsoft, Ltd., and has published widely on a variety of topics in applied social psychology, research methodology, and environmental psychology. His major recent publications include *Facet Theory* and *The Research Interview: Uses and Approaches*. His forthcoming book reviewing developments in environmental psychology will be published soon.

Jacqueline Carroy, *Agrégée de Philosophie*, received a doctorate in psychology from the University of Paris VII in 1981. She has written a book on hysteria and possession and published articles on the history of hypnosis, psychiatry, and psychology in France in *Bulletin de Psychologie, Psychanalyse à l'Université,* and *Connexions*. She is currently a faculty member and director of psychological conferences at the University of Nancy II.

Evelyne Cauzinille-Marmeche received her doctorate (3d cycle) from the University of Paris VIII in 1973. She specializes in research in cognitive and child psychology, artificial intelligence, and didactics, and is presently associated with the Laboratoire de Psychologie du Développement et de L'Éducation de L'Enfant, University of Paris V, 46 rue Saint Jacques, 75005, Paris, France.

Marie-Ange Chabert (*Diplômè d'Etude Supérieure de Psychologie*, Sorbonne, 1965) is a clinical psychologist at the Henri Rouselle Hospital (1 rue Cabanis, 75014 Paris) and president of the clinical psychology section.

Matty Chiva received a *Docteur ès Lettres* from the University of Paris X–Nanterre in 1979. He conducts research on food habits and culture in a developmental context; the evolution of the expression of emotions, taste, and olfaction; and nonverbal communication. He is both a professor in and head of the Department of Child Psychology and the director of the Center of Child Psychology at the University of Paris X–Nanterre, 200 Avenue de la République, 92001 Nanterre Cédex, France.

Charles J. de Wolff received his doctorate from the Free University, Amsterdam, in 1963. He is a full professor of work psychology at the University of Nijmegen, and one of his interests is the development of psychology as a profession. Professor de Wolff is also secretary-general (treasurer) of the International Association of Applied Psychology.

Rolando Diaz-Loving received his Ph.D. in social psychology from the University of Texas at Austin in 1982. Since then he has been a professor in the graduate social psychology department, Faculty of Psychology, at the National University of Mexico. In 1985 he became head of that department. Dr. Diaz-Loving has published numerous articles on various social-psychological topics and is writing a textbook on the construction of personality and attitude measures for the Mexican culture. He is coeditor of the *Revista de Psicología Social y Personalidad* and president-elect of the Mexican Society of Social Psychologists.

Ian J. Donald obtained a B. A. in applied social science from Coventry Polytechnic in 1980. Since earning an M.sc. in environmental psychology from the University of Surrey, he has carried out doctoral research at the University of Aston in Birmingham, where he is codirector of the applied psychology division's organization and environment research group. He has done research in a variety of areas, most recently personnel selection, MDS analysis of therapeutic outcomes, and office evaluation. He has published articles on environmental evaluation, facet theory, and architectural design research. His first book, a general textbook of environmental psychology, is in press.

Alexandre Dorna earned a doctorate (3d cycle) from the University of Paris VIII in 1978. He does research on political psychology, communication, and organizational psychology, and has coauthored two books: *Ideologia y conductismo* (Ideology and behavior) and *Significations du comportementalisme* (Significance of behaviorism). He is currently associated with the Department of Psychology, University of Paris VIII, 2 rue de la Liberte, 93526 St. Denis Cédex, France.

M. O. A. Durojaiye earned his Ph.D. at the University of Manchester in 1968. He was professor of psychology at Makerere University, Kampala, Uganda, from 1971 to 1975. Before going to Makerere he was lecturer, then senior lecturer in psychology, at the Adult Education Department, University of Ibadan, Nigeria (1968–1970). He has also taught in England, and from 1964 until 1968 practiced in English child-guidance clinics. His research interests include the growth patterns of African children, intelligence tests, and occupational choice. He has been professor of educational psychology at the University of Lagos, Nigeria, since 1975.

Safwat Ernest Farag obtained his Ph.D. in psychology from Cairo University in 1975 and served as chairman of the board of directors of the Egyptian Psychologists Association in 1983 and as a member of the board of directors of the Egyptian Association of Psychological Studies in 1982. He has written books and articles on psychometrics, statistics, and creativity. From 1973 until 1984 he was associated with the psychology department of Cairo University. Since then he has been on the staff of the Department of Psychology, College of Education, King Saud University, Riyadh, Saudi Arabia.

Albert R. Gilgen obtained his Ph.D. from Michigan State University in 1965. His primary research interests concern the conceptual structure and fragmentation of psychology and the recent history of American psychology. He has edited one book and written another on the latter topic. Dr. Gilgen was a Fulbright-Hays exchange lecturer at the University College Galway in Ireland (1971–1972) and has since 1973 been head of the Department of Psychology at the University of Northern Iowa. He is a fellow of the American Psychological Association (Division I).

Carol K. Gilgen obtained a B. A. (1954) from Bryn Mawr College in Russian, an M. A. in political science (1964) from Kent State University, and has been a certified public accountant since 1980. She has done extensive editorial work in connection with her husband's two books on American psychology.

Carl F. Graumann obtained his Dr.phil. degree in 1952 from the University of Cologne and became privatdozent at the University of Bonn in 1959. Since 1963, he has been a professor at the University of Heidelberg. He has written books and articles on social-environmental psychology, phenomenological psychology, and the history of psychology. His address is: Psychologisches Institut, Universität Heidelberg, Hauptstrasse 47–51, D–6900 Heidelberg, Federal Republic of Germany.

Lidia Grzesiuk obtained her Ph.D in 1972 and the degree of habilitated doctor in 1978, both from the University of Warsaw. At the University of Warsaw, she has been head of the Division of Personality and Its Disturbances (1975–1976), head of the Division of Clinical Psychology (1976–1984), and vice-dean of the Department of Psychology (1984-present). Her many publications and research articles concern communication processes both in normal and mentally disturbed people, the relationships between psychological stress and physiological reactions, and the effects of psychotherapy. Her address is: Department of Psychology, Warsaw University, ul. Stawki 5/7, 00–183 Warsaw, Poland.

Giselher Guttmann earned the degree of Dr.phil. in psychology, zoology, and philosophy from the University of Vienna where he achieved the rank of habilitated doctor and associate professor of experimental and applied psychology in 1968 and full professor in 1972. He has been associated with the University of Vienna since 1959. In 1975–1976 he was dean of the "grund-und integrativwissenschaftliche Fakultät." At present he is head of the Institute of Psychology, University of Vienna Liebiggasse 5, A–1010, Vienna. He has written extensively on brain research, learning, and psychodiagnostics.

Esther Halpern did her undergraduate and master's work at McGill University and obtained her Ph.D in clinical psychology from Boston University in 1962. Her research interests include cognitive and linguistic development and anxiety and stress. She has served on the board of directors of the Corporation of Psychologists of the Province of Quebec, is a fellow of the American-Orthopsychiatric Association, and was recently president of the International Council of Psychologists. She has been on the faculty of Tel-Aviv University since immigrating to Israel in 1970.

Yvette Hatwell earned a *Doctorat de Lettres et Sciences Humaines* from the Université René-Descartes, Paris, in 1981, and does research on perception and cognition, visuo-motor coordination in infants and children, and visual deficiencies. She is the author of two books, one on Piagetian reasoning and the blind, the other on the tactile perception of space. She is currently professor of psychology at the University of Grenoble II and director of the Grenoble Laboratory of Experimental Psychology, Boite Postale 47 X, 38040 Grenoble Cédex, France.

Terrence P. Hogan received his Ph.D. from Catholic University in 1963. He is associate vice-president (academic) and professor of psychology at the University of Manitoba in Winnipeg, Canada. A clinical psychologist, he has served as chief of psychology service and assistant hospital director at a Veterans Administration hospital in Iowa (1963–1965), taught at Bradley University (1965–1967), and was in private practice at the Marshfield Clinic in Wisconsin from 1967 to 1969. Since 1969 he has been at the University of Manitoba in Canada. Dr. Hogan was president of the Canadian Psychological Association in 1982–1983 and is currently a member of the Social Sciences and Humanities Research Council of Canada.

Timothy V. Hogan obtained his Ph.D. from the University of Ottawa in 1966. His interests include child and developmental psychology, assessment, counseling, and psychopathology. He has worked with children and their families for twenty-five years, was director of a regional psychiatric facility, has been a school psychologist for over two decades, and served as a consultant to the Children's Aid Society and various aspects of the criminal justice system. He is a fellow of the Canadian Psychological Association and currently executive director of the Canadian Psychological Association.

Kenneth Hugdahl achieved both his Ph.D. (1977) and docent status (1981) in psychology at Uppsala University in Sweden where he was a lecturer from 1979 until 1984. Since 1984 he has held the position of full professor of psychology at the Institute of Somatic Psychology, University of Bergen, in Norway. He was editor of the *Scandinavian Journal of Behavior Therapy* (1980–1984), and his research interests include brain asymmetry and lateralization; the psychophysiology of emotions, conditioning, and learning; and phobias.

Michel Hurtig earned a doctorate in psychology (3d cycle) from Sorbonne University in 1966, and presently conducts research on measures of child development and differential psychology. Dr. Hurtig is presently associated with the department of psychology at the University of Provence, 621 Aix-en-Provence, France, and is chairman of the Section of Child Psychology of the French Society of Psychology.

Jacques-Marie Jakobi received his doctorate in social psychology (3d cycle) from the University of Paris in 1969. His research interests include paralinguistics in system and contract communication. His address is: G. R. P. "Jeune équipe

CNRS,'' U. E. R. de Psychologie, Université de Paris VIII, 2 rue de la Liberté, 93526 Saint-Denis Cédex.

Takayoshi Kaneko received his master's degree from the University of Missouri (1954) and his Ph.D. from the Tokyo University of Education (1963). Strongly influenced by the late Torao Obonai, his primary area of research is vision. He is on the editorial board of the journals *Japanese Psychological Research* and the *Japanese Journal of Psychology*. A professor at the University of Tsukuba, Tsukuba Science City, Dr. Kaneko is presently on the executive committee of the Japanese Psychological Association and is a voting representative of Japan for the International Union of Psychological Science.

Miloslav Kodým obtained his Ph.D. in 1967 from the Faculty of Philosophy, Charles University (Prague), and was awarded a C.sc. (a scientific degree) in 1971 by the Scientific Advisory Board of Pedagogics and Psychology (Prague). He achieved the ranks of associate professor (1972) and professor (1983) while associated with the Ministry of Education. Dr. Kodým's accomplishments include a professorship at the Department of Psychology, Faculty of Pedagogics, Charles University; chairman of the Scientific Advisory Board of Pedagogics and Psychology; and chief of the editorial board of the journal *Československá psychologie*. He is currently director of the Institute of Psychology of the Czechoslovak Academy of Sciences (Husova 4, 110 00 Prague 1).

Simo Køppe received his Mag.art. degree in 1977 from the University of Copenhagen. His research has focused on historical analyses of Freud's work and studies of scientific developments in Danish psychology. He is presently associated with the Psychological Laboratory at the University of Copenhagen (Njalsgade 94, DK–2300 Kbh. S., Denmark).

Jacques Leplat received his doctorate in letters and humane sciences from the University of Paris V in 1974. He is the director of the Laboratory of Industrial Psychology at the Ecole Pratique des Hautes Etudes (3d Section), and an associate at C. N. R. S. His principal research interests include cognitive psychology of work, human reliability, and work psychology. His address is: Laboratoire de Psychologie du Travail de l'E. P. H. E. 41 rue Gay-Lussac 75005 Paris.

Josef Linhart obtained his Dr.sc. degree in 1960 from Charles University in Prague where he was made university professor the same year. He became a corresponding member of the Czechoslovak Academy of Science in 1972. His many publications include four books: two on human learning, one on behavior and cognition, and a general introductory textbook. His address is: Czechoslovak Academy of Sciences, Institute of Psychology, Husova 4, 110 00 Prague 1, Czechoslovakia.

Boris F. Lomov received his Dr.sc. degree from Leningrad University in 1965. He became a corresponding member of the USSR Academy of Pedagogical Sciences in 1965 and a corresponding member of the USSR Academy of Sciences in 1976. In 1959 he organized and became head of the Laboratory of Engineering Psychology at Leningrad University where he was appointed dean of the Department of Psychology in 1966. In 1971, he was named director of the Institute of Psychology of the USSR Academy of Sciences. From 1968 until 1983 Dr. Lomov was president of the Society of Psychologists of the USSR, and elected vice-president of the International Union of Psychological Science in 1984. He has authored over 200 publications, many of them theoretical and historical analyses.

Gerardo Marín received his Ph.D. in social psychology in 1979 from De Paul University in Chicago. He is currently an associate professor of psychology at the University of San Francisco, California. He has received special awards from Colombian and Spanish psychological associations and is an honorary member of the Cuban Psychological Association. He has published widely in cross-cultural social psychology (five books, over thirty-five articles) and is currently developing a smoking-cessation program for U.S. Hispanics. He has served as an officer of psychological associations in Colombia, the Interamerican Society of Psychology, and the Latin American Social Psychology Association.

Benjamin Matalon earned his *Doctorat d'Etat* from the University of Provence in 1981, and has specialized in research in urban sociology. His current interests include the sociology of science and the research of methodologies of the social sciences. He is a professor of social psychology at the University of Paris VIII and director of the Laboratory of Social Psychology (C. N. R. S), 18 rue de la Sorbonne, 75005 Paris, France.

Adrian Medina-Liberty received his *licenciatura* from the National University of Mexico in 1977 and is currently working on his master's thesis at the same university. He has also been a professor at the Licentura (University of Mexico) since 1978, was coordinator of student practice from 1980 to 1984, and is now director of a seminar on the history of philosophy of psychology. Mr. Medina-Liberty has published articles on methodological, philosophical, and historical aspects of psychology. He is currently editing a book on experimental psychology.

Patrick Mendelsohn received a doctor of psychology degree from the University of Grenoble in 1981. He is an assistant researcher at C. N. R. S., Laboratory of Experimental Psychology (B. P. 47 XF–38040 Grenoble Cédex). His research interests include cognitive psychology of development, learning processes, the study of computer-programming activities by children, and the art of teaching computer-programming concepts at school.

Alexandre Métraux obtained his Dr.phil. degree in 1973 from the University of Basel in Switzerland. He has published books and articles on the theory and history of science, theoretical psychology, and general philosophical issues. He is presently associated with the Psychological Institute, University of Heidelberg (Hauptstrasse 47–51, D–6900 Heidelberg, Federal Republic of Germany).

Mary Creighton Nixon was awarded her Ph.D in 1968 by the University of Melbourne in Australia. She is a fellow of the Australian Psychological Society, past president of the Australian Psychological Society, and a former member of the Victorian Psychological Council. Her primary areas of interest include developmental psychology, professional ethics in psychological practice, and the history of Australian psychology. She coedited *Psychology in Australia: Achievements and Prospects* (1977) with R. Taft and is senior lecturer in psychology, Faculty of Education, at Monash University in Clayton (Victoria, Australia).

Arne Öhman obtained his Ph.D. at the University of Uppsala, Sweden, in 1971. He has published extensively, particularly on fear and emotion, and is past president of the Society for Psychophysiological Research and a fellow of the Society of Behavioral Medicine. He is currently professor at the Department of Clinical Psychology, Uppsala University (Box 1225, S–751 42, Uppsala, Sweden).

Vid Pečjak obtained his Ph.D. in 1965 at the University of Ljubljana in Yugoslavia. His interests include psycholinguistics and cognition, the history of psychology, and theoretical issues in psychology. In 1976 he received the award from the Yugoslav Scientific Foundation Boris Kidric for scientific work in psychology, was vice-president in 1974 of the Yugoslav Psychological Association, and is now a member of the board of directors of the European Association of Personality Psychology. He is currently professor of psychology at the University E. Kardelj of Ljubljana (Askerceva 12, 61000 Ljubljana, Yugoslavia). Dr. Pečjak is frequently a visiting professor at the University of Hawaii.

I. van W. Raubenheimer received his Ph.D. from Purdue University in 1968 and was appointed head of the then newly established Department of Industrial Psychology at the University of South Africa (Pretoria) in 1969. He was a member of the Department of Industrial Psychology at the University of Stellenbosch from 1974 until 1979 when he was invited to form and become chairman of the Department of Industrial Psychology at the Rand Afrikaans University. Professor Raubenheimer was president of the Institute of the RSA (1978–1982), the first chairman of the Council of the South African Psychological Association (1982–1984), and editor of the *Journal of Industrial Psychology*. He has published more than fifty scientific articles. His address is: Chairman, Department of Psychology, Rand Afrikaans University, Auckland Park Johannesburg, P. O. Box 524, Johannesburg, 2000.

José Miguel Salazar earned his B. A. degree at the University of Michigan and his Ph.D. (1957) at the University of London. He has been at the Universidad Central de Venezuela since 1958 where he established chairs in experimental and social psychology and became head of the School of Psychology (1969–1970), the Institute of Psychological Research (1978–1984), and the social psychology graduate program (1976–). He has done extensive research in social psychology and has worked to promote national and international professional psychological organizations. His address is: Universidad Central de Venezuela, Apartado 47018, Caracas 1041-A, Venezuela.

Liliane Salhani is an assistant lecturer at the University of Paris VII. She is in the process of completing her *these d'etat* at the Laboratory of Social Psychology of the University of Paris VII. Her research interests include diffusion of messages and their psychosocial conditions, control of expression, and thymic and aesthetic reactions.

Ligia M. Sánchez holds degrees in both psychology and philosophy from the Universidad Central de Venezuela and a master's in criminology from Cambridge University. She has been associated with Universidad Central since 1965 and its Institute of Psychological Research since 1975. She has directed one of the departments at the institute and conducted research on psychology as a discipline and profession in Venezuela. She has also been active in the Venezuelan professional organization of psychologists.

Hans-Dieter Schmidt obtained his Dr.sc.nat. degree from Humboldt University in 1966. His research interests lie primarily in the areas of comparative psychology, developmental psychology, decision making, and personality. Dr. Schmidt is associated with Sektion Psychologie de Humboldt-Universität (1020 Berlin, Oraníenburger Strasse 18, German Democratic Republic).

Durganand Sinha obtained an M. A. degree from Patna University in India in 1945 and an M.sc degree from Cambridge University in 1949. He was a national fellow (1973–1975), president of the International Association of Cross-Cultural Psychology (1980–1982), and was recently elected national fellow of the Indian Council of Social Science Research. His research areas are industrial psychology and social psychology. He has been particularly interested in the social psychology of development and change in Third World countries. Professor Sinha was director of the ANS Institute of Social Studies in Patna and is now associated with the Centre for the Advanced Study in Psychology, Allahabad University, Allahabad, India.

Roelf J. Takens earned his doctorate in 1973 at the University of Groningen. A clinical psychologist and psychotherapist, he is a senior staff member at the

Department of Psychology, Free University, Amsterdam. He is also a managing officer of the Netherlands Institute of Psychologists.

Alain Trognon received his doctorate in letters and humane sciences from the University of Paris X in 1981. He is a professor at the University of Nancy II, and has been secretary-general of the French Psychological Society since 1985. His research interests include the pragmatics of conversation, interlocution in small groups, decision making, and natural logic. His address is: Department of Social Psychology, Université de Nancy II, B. P. 33–97, 54015 Nancy Cédex.

Holger Ursin obtained an M. D. degree (1958) and a Dr.med. degree (1965) from the University of Oslo. Since 1974 he has been a professor at the Department of Physiological Psychology, University of Bergen (Årstadveien 21, 5000 Bergen, Norway). He is a prolific researcher and has numerous publications. Among his major interests are limbic structures and emotions, biological and psychological bases of psychosomatic disease, and the relationships between the ability to cope and health.

Pieter J. van Strien obtained his Dr.soc.sc. degree in 1964 at the University of Groningen in the Netherlands. His research interests include the methodology of applied social sciences, professional organizations and ethics, industrial democracy, and organizational change. He has been a full professor at the University of Groningen concerned until 1980 with the psychology of work and organizations and more recently with the foundations and history of psychology.

Gündüz Y. H. Vassaf received his B. A. degree from George Washington University (1968) and M. A. (1974) and Ph.D. (1977) degrees from Hacettepe University in Turkey. He has been on the board of directors of the International Council of Psychologists; a member of the Committee on Psychological Assessment of the International Association of Applied Psychology; a regional coordinator for Europe and the Middle East for the Division of Community Psychology, American Psychological Association; a member of the Committee on Psychologists for Peace and Against Nuclear War of the International Union of Psychological Science; and a founding member and vice-president of the Psychologists' Association of Turkey. Dr. Vassaf, along with more than 1,400 other academicians, resigned his position at Bogazici University in protest of the Turkish University law abrogating all academic freedom and autonomy. He is presently guest lecturer at Marburg University in West Germany. His permanent address is: Calikusu 11, 1. Levent, Istanbul, Turkey.

Annick Weil-Barais is a lecturer on the cognitive psychology of children and educational psychology. Her research interests include intellectual development, reasoning, and acquisition of scientific knowledge. Her address is: Department de Psychologie, Université de Paris VIII, 2 rue de la Liberté, 93526 Saint-Denis Cédex 02.

Mariano Yela obtained his Ph.D. from the University of Madrid in 1952. He studied with Thurstone and Neff (Chicago), Burt (London), and Michotte (Louvain). He is a member of the Spanish Academy of Sciences, served as president of the Spanish Psychological Association, and has been awarded several national and international prizes. Dr. Yela has published nine books, over 250 scientific papers, and more than 100 psychological tests. He is professor and head of the Department of Experimental Psychology at the University of Madrid (Facultad de Psicología, Universidad Complutense de Madrid, Campus de Somosaguas, Madrid 11, Spain).

Zhang Hou-can obtained her B.ed. degree in 1948 from Fu-jen University in Beijing (after 1949 no academic degrees were offered in China). She has been associated with Beijing Normal University since 1952 and in 1984 became chairperson of the Department of Psychology. Her research areas are experimental psychology, psychological statistics, and psychometrics. She is senior author of two books, one on statistics (1981), the other on experimental psychology (1983), and is an associate editor of *Acta Psychologica Sinica*. In December 1984 she was elected to be one of the two vice-presidents of the Chinese Psychological Society.

LIBRARY
DOES NOT

LIBRARY USE ONLY
DOES NOT CIRCULATE